Y0-DWM-047
OCÉANO ATLÁNTICO
San Agustín
Miami
TRÓPICO DE CÁNCER
La Habana
Matanzas
Cienfuegos
Camagüey
CUBA
Isla de Pinos
Guantánamo
Santiago de Cuba
REPÚBLICA DOMINICANA
Santiago
HAITÍ
Puerto Príncipe
Santo Domingo
JAMAICA
Kingston
Antillas Mayores
Islas Vírgenes
San Juan
Ponce
PUERTO RICO
Antigua
Guadalupe
Antillas Menores
Dominica
Martinica
Santa Lucía
Barbados
San Vincente
Granada
MAR DEL CARIBE
HONDURAS
NICARAGUA
Aruba
Curaçao
Bonaire
Margarita
Puerto de España
TOBAGO
TRINIDAD
Barranquilla
Cartagena
El Canal de Panamá
San José
Puerto Limón
Portobello
Colón
Panamá
Maracaibo
Caracas
COSTA RICA
PANAMÁ
Golfo de Panamá
Mérida
VENEZUELA
Medellín
COLOMBIA
GUYANA
BRASIL

¡Ya comprendo!

¡Ya comprendo!

A Communicative Course in Spanish

Matilde Olivella de Castells

California State University, Los Angeles

Prentice Hall
Englewood Cliffs, New Jersey 07632

Library of Congress Cataloging-in-Publication Data
Castells, Matilde Olivella de.
¡Ya comprendo!: a communicative course in Spanish/Matilde Olivella de Castells.
p. cm.
Includes index.
ISBN 0-13-976424-0
1.Spanish language--Textbooks for foreign speakers--English.
I.Title.
PC4128.C37 1990
468.2'421--dc20 89-2601
CIP

Editor: Karen Davy
Production Supervisor: Lisa G. M. Chuck
Production Manager: Nick Sklitsis
Text Designer: Pat Smythe
Cover Designer: Brian Sheridan
Photo Researcher: Rona Tuccillo
Illustrations: Jerry McDaniel
Endpaper maps: Vantage Art, Inc.
Illustration acknowledgments appear on pages 514-515, which constitute an extension of the copyright page.

Printed in the United States of America

10 9 8 7 6 5 4 3 2 1

ISBN 0-13-976424-0

Prentice Hall International (UK) Limited, *London*
Prentice-Hall of Australia Pty. Limited, *Sydney*
Prentice-Hall Canada Inc., *Toronto*
Prentice-Hall Hispanoamericana, S.A., *Mexico*
Prentice-Hall of India Private Limited, *New Delhi*
Prentice-Hall of Japan, Inc., *Tokyo*
Simon & Schuster Asia Pte. Ltd., *Singapore*
Editora Prentice-Hall do Brasil, Ltda., *Rio de Janeiro*

Preface

¡Ya comprendo! is a new program for beginning college Spanish. It introduces the culture of the Hispanic world; helps students learn Spanish vocabulary and structure; and suggests a sequence of activities designed to lead students to develop the complete spectrum of language skills and a readiness to use Spanish for personally meaningful communication. It emphasizes interaction among students and identifies the purposes of using language in order to help students achieve the proficiency that most instructors have always hoped to see by the end of the first-year course.

Characteristics of the Program

With the publication of its ACTFL Proficiency Guidelines in 1982, the American Council on the Teaching of Foreign Languages focused the attention of the language-teaching profession on a reorientation of objectives that had been gradually gaining support. Higher priority is now given to helping students develop communicative competence and language proficiency, that is, the ability to use language creatively and in culturally appropriate ways for authentic tasks in real-world settings. This orientation, discussed in conferences, articles, and books, represents a fundamental change in the way many universities and schools conduct language classes. It uses new sequences for presenting material so that it can be learned more efficiently. It reschedules the introduction of a few grammar structures, more important to written than to everyday spoken language, and supports them with appropriate activities, making room at the initial stages of instruction for more work with basic language functions.

The ACTFL Proficiency Guidelines significantly influenced the creation of this book, but so did the years of teaching experience of the author and her associates at California State University, Los Angeles. In addition, the author and one of her associates, Professor Hildebrando Villarreal, worked on the California Foreign Language Competency Project developing guidelines and materials for testing important skills at different levels of competency. A long-standing focus on teaching for communicative competence led the author team to devise numerous activities in which students practice communication in a variety of settings. Although the materials generally follow the sequences advocated in the Guidelines, they deviate slightly on occasion, reflecting classroom experience. While the number of grammatical structures presented for active oral mastery has been reduced, the textbook includes all the major structures traditionally taught. The emphasis of the program is on working with fewer structures and mastering those, rather than on tackling more and mastering fewer.

The dialogs and texts used in the book to present new language material are authentic but not overwhelming for students. Without compromising the authenticity of the material, the author team created or selected dialogs and texts in which new vocabulary and the number of new structures were controlled. These materials were written by native speakers or extracted from Spanish language sources such as magazines and newspapers. Native speakers from Argentina, Colombia, Mexico, Venezuela, and Spain have reviewed all of them for authenticity; particular selections were reviewed by speakers from other countries. The underlying goal of these texts, as of the other parts of the program, is to begin to familiarize students with the reality beyond the classroom, and to prepare them to use and comprehend Spanish as it is used by native speakers in a variety of situations.

¡Ya comprendo! does not attempt to present a systematic survey of the culture of the entire Hispanic world. It introduces selected material with the objective of acquainting students with various aspects of Hispanic behavior and attitudes and with important facts about the many different Hispanic countries. The text presents cultural material in limited quantities and at a pace intended to maintain interest in the Hispanic world, but not to distract from the program's primary focus on language acquisition.

In recent years language professionals have been refining their understanding of the role of listening in the acquisition of language. Listening is thought to play a major role in the communicative process. For many students, it is the primary way to internalize grammar and vocabulary. Accordingly, activities designed to promote the skills of listening comprehension now have a more prominent place in beginning language courses. This program specifies comprehension activities in the textbook itself and many more in the audio recordings and associated workbook/laboratory manual.

TPR, the total physical response technique, is one of the many ways to develop listening comprehension: The instructor gives commands in Spanish, and the students respond, not with words, but by carrying out the physical actions specified. The technique is based on the belief that understanding the spoken language should precede speaking and that physical movements in response to commands increase student comprehension and retention. *¡Ya comprendo!* begins with an optional section, **Actividades preliminares,** which relates TPR activities to classroom situations. Instructors may use the activities or not, adapt them to other settings, or use them in connection with vocabulary and structures presented elsewhere in the book. The Instructor's Manual that accompanies this program contains additional suggestions for implementing TPR activities.

Reading is another skill that receives special attention in *¡Ya comprendo!* Both the textbook and the workbook include comprehension activities that encourage students to practice skimming, scanning, extensive and intensive reading, and other strategies. The activities vary with the type of text and the purpose for reading it. After lesson 13, the reading selections, many taken from authentic Spanish language publications, serve to introduce and use certain tenses less frequent in the spoken language.

College students learning Spanish in a predominantly English-speaking country do not learn it the way children learn their first language, primarily because they are not immersed in Hispanic culture and do not dedicate sixteen hours a day to mastering the language of the community on which they depend for their every need. In addition, individuals of college age have developed a variety of personal learning styles. Some students are visually oriented, some hearing oriented, some need to order linguistic reality in terms of explicit grammatical concepts, some may work most efficiently with a computer, others may like to work as a team with a classmate. *¡Ya comprendo!* includes a wide range of options permitting students to adapt the materials to their individuality.

Starting with the textbook's **Actividades preliminares** and continuing with the varied activities and practical explanations in subsequent lessons, students can begin their acquisition of Spanish in a manner consistent with the ACTFL Proficiency Guidelines. As students progress, instructors can follow the text, supplement it with activities from the Instructor's Manual, or modify the program as required by the needs of each particular school. The program is suitable for instructors who want to teach a limited number of structures for greater mastery and proficiency, but at the same time it affords instructors who wish to teach additional structures ample opportunity to do so. Options within the program will help instructors to adapt the materials to a wide range of course designs.

Textbook

¡Ya comprendo! has several components: student textbook, laboratory recordings, workbook/laboratory manual, videocassette, self-instructional (CAI) software, instructor's annotated edition of the textbook, instructor's manual, printed tapescript, testing program, and transparency masters.

The textbook begins with optional **Actividades preliminares** devoted to TPR activities. Four short **Pasos** follow which serve as an introduction to other aspects of the course. The **Pasos** help students familiarize themselves with the sound system of Spanish, listen to more examples of the language in context, and start communicating in situations they will encounter in everyday life in a Hispanic community or country. Language production for the students in this initial stage consists of one-word answers or short phrases that can be easily mastered. Students also start developing an awareness and appreciation for Hispanic culture. The **Pasos** introduce greetings, expressions of courtesy, and saying good-bye; introductions; cognates; numbers; time; days of the week; classroom objects and expressions useful in the classroom; the alphabet; and some Spanish sounds.

The seventeen **Lecciones** are different from the **Pasos** in many ways. They are longer and each revolves around a general semantic theme—for example, school activities, family, food, sports, shopping, traveling. Lessons start by presenting key vocabulary related to the lesson theme and useful for communicating in real-life situations. A variety of activities encourage students to become familiar with the vocabulary and to use it in meaningful ways. A cultural section then focuses on the same theme and draws attention to characteristics of the Hispanic world—for example, educational systems, family ties, typical foods. This section, together with the authentic materials from various countries distributed throughout the text, will help students understand and appreciate Hispanic culture.

Three sections of language practice and grammar, called **En contexto,** follow the vocabulary and cultural material. Each begins with a short text—a dialog, ad, postcard, comic strip, article—that introduces grammatical structures along with additional vocabulary related to the theme of the lesson. English translations of these texts appear at the bottom of the page in early lessons; later on, only selected words are glossed in the margin. Short activities give students additional opportunities to use the new vocabulary. Grammar explanations are short and concern themselves with structures needed for everyday communication. Exercises following the grammar presentations encourage students to use the words presented at the beginning of the lesson plus some of the new words from the introductory text; they also continuously recycle words from previous lessons. The exercises progress from skill-getting to skill-using activities. They are contextualized and personalized as appropriate to sustain student interest and motivation and to aid comprehension. The goal of each sequence of activities is to encourage communication in situations that emulate as closely as possible real-life situations encountered in the Hispanic world. The activities offer students ample opportunities to create with the language and to express personal interests and preferences.

Reading selections on the lesson theme and comprehension and discussion exercises follow the last skill-using activities. New words are either glossed in the margins or given before the passage to facilitate comprehension. Verb tenses intended for recognition and understanding (see "Scope and Sequence," next page) are presented in pre-reading sections beginning with lesson 13. Instructors who wish to actively practice these verb tenses will find additional exercises and activities in the Instructor's Manual and in the *Cuaderno de práctica,* the workbook/laboratory manual.

After the reading, a section of **Situaciones** invites students to participate in situations that involve two or more people communicating with each other in role playing, problem solving, information getting, and other activities. These situations help students practice genuine communication in circumstances similar to what they may encounter outside the classroom.

Each lesson ends with a vocabulary list that divides the active words introduced in the lesson into semantic fields. The textbook itself concludes with verb tables, a Spanish-English and an English-Spanish vocabulary, and a grammar index.

Scope and Sequence

Since the 1950s, textbooks for beginning Spanish presented grammar structures—especially the verb tenses—in a certain order: the present indicative, then the preterit, leading on through to the present, imperfect, and compound subjunctives near the end of the book. Each new tense was supported in turn by a standard array of skill-getting drills. Since few classes completed all the textbook chapters in a single year, however, authors typically pared away more and more exercise material in successive editions, especially exercises supporting the tenses coming late in the sequence. This evolutionary shortening of textbooks meant that even in classes that did "cover the entire book," students would typically not achieve active control of most of the tenses studied. (The present subjunctive, sometimes held for teaching near the end of the book because it was complicated and potentially discouraging if presented for quick mastery, began to move forward in the sequence in response to the profession's recognition that it is critically important in Spanish and needs to be supported by an undiminished program of exercises.)

Not everyone was satisfied with the overall results achieved by the traditional grammar curriculum. Studies by government commissions and others concluded that language instruction in America was failing to produce widespread language competency of the sort required to ensure the country's success in international business and scientific competition. Criticism of this kind was one of the motivating factors leading to the publication of the ACTFL Proficiency Guidelines, intended as a contribution to the search for improved teaching results.

Universities throughout the world are eager to train students to speak on a more cultivated level, and Spanish departments naturally share in this aim. But beginning Spanish courses need to begin at the beginning, with the tenses most often used in real-life conversation.

The sequence of verb structures presented in *¡Ya comprendo!* begins with the present indicative, the present progressive, the commands and the present subjunctive, since talking about daily activities and plans for the future, as well as expressing wishes, needs, and desires are high-frequency items in everyday language. The past tenses, preterit and imperfect, and more uses of the subjunctive follow. Present and past perfect indicative and additional uses of the subjunctive complete the structures presented for active use. Having the subjunctive throughout several chapters in the book gives the students ample opportunity for using it in meaningful situations over several months. The remaining tenses are presented in pre-reading sections in the latter part of the book.

In *¡Ya comprendo!,* ample, but not excessive, amounts of exercise material support structures presented for active mastery, so that students do not feel overwhelmed or worry that they have missed some important activities. These exercises are organized in terms of language functions. Grammar explains the use of forms. Functions organize into broad general categories (like "asking permission") the purposes for which speakers use forms, that is, the behavioral applications of language to life. Losing sight of the possible uses of structures is probably an important reason so few of us can achieve active command of a second language in a short period of time. To master a structure, one needs to weave it extensively into a pattern of personally meaningful potential applications. By taking the time necessary to link classroom activities to a balanced array of language functions, *¡Ya comprendo!* aims to help learners apply what they learn in the classroom to the infinite variety of situations arising in real life.

The ACTFL Proficiency Guidelines reflect a realization that not everything can be learned at once, that is, in the first year. If anything is to be learned well, it must be practiced extensively, in a wide variety of formats and contexts. Time for this practice is gained by postponing some matters to more advanced levels of instruction. In *¡Ya comprendo!,* the future, imperfect subjunctive, conditional, and conditional perfect are presented for recognition. Some of these structures (for example, **me gustaría**) appear in *¡Ya comprendo!* as vocabulary in authentic dialogs and texts early in the book, but they are not formally treated until lesson 13 or later, where they are examined in connection with readings. They also appear in the verb tables at the back of the book, which show all verb tenses.

Few students emerging from traditional first-year Spanish courses are able to use in real-life conversations the structures presented for recognition in *¡Ya comprendo!* However, each language department has its own priorities. For classes that wish to teach some or all of these structures for active use, the Instructor's Manual and the *Cuaderno de práctica* include a wide array of skill-getting exercises. Students can reinforce classwork with these structures by regularly utilizing the *¡Ya comprendo!* CAI software supplement.

Ancillary Components

A program of cassette recordings is available on loan for copying by institutions that adopt the textbook. A site license authorizes the adopting institution to produce cassette copies for student use at home. The recordings include listening comprehension passages and activities, sound discrimination and pronunciation exercises, and structured and open-ended production activities. Students have many opportunities to hear short interviews, weather reports, newscasts, descriptions, and other materials.

The *Cuaderno de práctica,* a workbook/laboratory manual, parallels the textbook. Part of each lesson is for use in conjunction with the laboratory recordings. Materials for the use of students at home help develop their writing skills; as the lessons progress, writing activities involve more and more real-life writing tasks. Activities and puzzles test their grasp of vocabulary. Another section is based on the cultural materials of the textbook chapter. New reading selections and authentic materials supplement those in the textbook.

As a complement to the listening comprehension activities of the textbook and audio recordings and as an extension of the cultural aspects of *¡Ya comprendo!,* a videocassette is available without charge to institutions that have adopted the textbook. The cassette includes authentic cultural materials from the TV systems of Spain, Hispanic America, and the Hispanic networks of the United States.

The self-instructional CAI software accompanying *¡Ya comprendo!* includes drill-and-practice exercises in several formats, guided cloze reading exercises, and gamelike rapid recognition exercises. Simple menus guide the user through the activities; messages acknowledge correct responses and comment on incorrect ones; hints and help are always a keystroke away. Scores are automatically recorded for the instructor. Like the audio and video components, the software is available without charge to institutions that adopt the textbook, and a license permits the institution to duplicate the disks for student use at home.

¡Ya comprendo! includes a variety of materials meant to assist instructors. An instructor's annotated edition of the textbook, prepared by Professor Carmen Salazar of Los Angeles Valley College, adds to the student text many marginal notes suggesting ways that the materials may be presented, used, or expanded upon. A separate instructor's manual prepared by Professors Ronald M. Harmon and María R. Montaño-Harmon of California State University, Fullerton, contains additional suggestions for implementing and expanding activities found in the textbook, a model syllabus, and sample lesson plans. A complete testing program, prepared by Professor Salazar and Nancy Anderson reflecting their extensive background in foreign language test administration and design, is also available to adopting schools.

Acknowledgments

The author wishes to give special thanks to Professor Hildebrando Villarreal of California State University, Los Angeles, co-author of the *Cuaderno de práctica,* for his contribution to the preparation of activities, grammar explanations, and cultural notes in the textbook, as well as for having tested the material in pilot courses.

I also would like to express my gratitude to my colleague Professor Hugh

Kennedy for his contribution to the first lessons of the manuscript and to Mr. Roger Dorrell, Director of the Foreign Language Laboratory at California State University, Los Angeles, for his help in the preparation of the tapes for the pilot courses.

My thanks also to my former students and now colleagues, Ms. Mercedes Limón and Amanda Jiménez, for their refreshing ideas for activities in the various lessons, and to my son Ricardo Castells for his help in the preparation of the cultural sections, activities for the workbook, and classroom testing of some of the materials at Duke University.

I would like to acknowledge the following reviewers of the manuscript, whose comments and suggestions were extremely helpful in the preparation of the textbook: Margaret E. Beeson, Kansas State University; Brian Castronovo, California State University; Mary Lee Cozad, Northern Illinois University; Michelle A. Fuerch, Ripon College; Lynn Carbón Gorell, Pennsylvania State University; Carrie Grady, University of the District of Columbia; Barbara A. Johnson, Washington State University; John R. Kelly, North Carolina State University; Frederic W. Murray, Northern Illinois University; Michael Reider, West Virginia University; Renate Robinson, Northwestern University; Susan Schaffer, University of California, Los Angeles; Judith Strozer, University of Washington; Lourdes Torres, State University of New York, Stony Brook; Claudia María Vargas, University of Southern California.

My deepest appreciation to Professor Carmen Salazar, from Los Angeles Valley College, for the preparation of the Instructor's Annotated Edition of *¡Ya comprendo!* and the development of the testing program. Her experience in the classroom and her expertise in testing proved invaluable in both areas.

As a final note, I am deeply indebted to the students whose interest and participation made this project a memorable experience.

M.O.C.

Contents

Functions

Discuss daily activities
Ask for and provide information
Express needs
Ask about and express location

Lección 4 La familia 102

Functions

Identify and describe family members
Describe physical and emotional states
Provide information about a person's age and abilities
Ask about and express ownership
Express preferences and desires

Lección 13 Telegramas, tarjetas postales y cartas 312

Functions

Interpret and compose telegraphic messages
Communicate by phone, postcard, and letter
Report past events
Describe actions

Actividades preliminares

Optional total physical response (TPR) activities

The following drawings show activities that normally occur in the classroom. Your instructor may want to go over these **actividades** before beginning with the preliminary lessons, or **pasos.** Listening to these commands, observing your instructor and/or classmates acting them out, and performing them yourself will give you an excellent opportunity to hear and understand Spanish. Try to get the general meaning and react accordingly. Your instructor may want to combine several of these activities to see how much you can understand.

The more Spanish you hear in situations in which you understand most of what is being said, the sooner you will begin to communicate in Spanish.

Vaya a la puerta.

Vaya a su asiento.

Vaya a la pizarra.

Escriba su nombre.

Borre la pizarra.

Abra el libro.

Cierre la ventana.

Miren el reloj.

Escuche.

Salgan.

Entre.

Siéntese.

Levántese.

Levante la mano.

Tome la tiza.

Déme el lápiz.

PRIMER PASO*

In the Primer paso you will
a. greet people in formal and informal situations.
b. use appropriate expressions to say good-bye.
c. thank people and respond appropriately when thanked.
d. request permission and excuse yourself.
e. express regret.
f. ask for and give names.
g. introduce yourself.

MINIDIÁLOGOS[1]

Saludos

Señor Gómez Buenos días, señorita Mena.
Señorita Mena Buenos días. ¿Cómo está usted, señor Gómez?
Señor Gómez Bien, gracias. ¿Y usted?
Señorita Mena Muy bien, gracias.

Ana ¡Hola, Inés! ¿Qué tal? ¿Cómo estás?
Inés Regular, ¿y tú?
Ana Bastante bien, gracias.

Señora Yanes Buenas tardes, Felipe. ¿Cómo estás?
Felipe Bien, gracias. Y usted, ¿cómo está, señora?
Señora Yanes Mal, Felipe, mal.
Felipe Lo siento.

---

* *First step*
[1] The English version of the dialogs is at the bottom of the page.

Greetings
MR. GÓMEZ: Good morning, Miss Mena. MISS MENA: Good morning. How are you, Mr. Gómez? MR. GÓMEZ: Fine, thanks. And you? MISS MENA: Very well, thank you.

ANA: Hi, Inés. How's it going? How are you? INÉS: So-so. And you? ANA: Pretty well, thanks.

MRS. YANES: Good afternoon, Felipe. How are you? FELIPE: Fine, thanks. And how are you, ma'am? MRS. YANES: Not well, Felipe, not well. FELIPE: I'm sorry.

Dos estudiantes se dan la mano en la Universidad de Panamá.

1. Spanish has more than one word meaning *you.* Use **usted** when you talk to someone you address respectfully as **señor, señora, señorita, doctor,** and so on. Use **tú** when you talk to someone on a first-name basis (close friend, relative, child). The verb form **está** goes with **usted,** and **estás** goes with **tú.**
2. **¿Qué tal?** is a more informal greeting. It is normally used with **tú,** but it may also be used with **usted.**
3. Use **buenas tardes** from noon until nightfall. After nightfall, use **buenas noches** *good evening, good night.* In the summer, especially in places where dinner is served rather late (after 9:00 P.M.), you may use **buenas tardes** even at 8:00 in the evening.

despedidas	*saying good-bye*
adiós	*good-bye*
hasta luego	*see you later*
hasta mañana	*see you tomorrow*

Adiós is generally used when you do not expect to see the other person for a while. It is also used meaning *hello* when people pass each other but have no time to stop and talk.

expresiones de cortesía	*polite expressions*
por favor	*please*
gracias	*thanks, thank you*
de nada/por nada	*you're welcome*
con permiso	*pardon me, excuse me*
perdón	*pardon me, excuse me*

Con permiso and **perdón** may be used before the fact, as when asking a person to allow you to go by or when asking for a person's attention. Only **perdón** is used after the fact, as when you have stepped on someone's foot.

ACTIVIDADES

A You work at a hotel and have to greet people at different times of day. What greeting (**buenos días, buenas tardes, buenas noches**) would you use according to the following times?

9:00 A.M. 11:00 P.M. 4:00 P.M. 3:00 A.M. 10:00 A.M. 8:00 P.M.

B What expression (**perdón, con permiso**) will you use in the following situations?

1. You accidentally bump into someone.
2. You are trying to pass through a group of people.
3. You step on someone's foot at a store.
4. You stop someone to ask for directions.
5. You are at the movies and have to pass in front of someone to reach your seat.

C What expression (**gracias, de nada, por favor, adiós, hasta luego, lo siento**) will you use in the following situations?

1. Someone thanks you.
2. You are leaving a friend whom you are going to see later that evening.
3. You are asking a classmate for his notes.
4. You hear that your friend is sick.
5. You receive a present from a friend.
6. Your friend is going on a vacation to Spain.

D You meet the following people on the street. Greet them, ask how they are, and then say good-bye. One of your classmates will play the other role.

a classmate your friend's little brother an older lady
your history professor your doctor one of your cousins

Unas chicas se saludan en España.

MINIDIÁLOGOS

Presentaciones

Antonio Me llamo Antonio Mendoza. Y tú, ¿cómo te llamas?
Benito Benito Sánchez. Mucho gusto.
Antonio Igualmente.

Profesor ¿Cómo se llama usted?
Isabel Me llamo Isabel Mendoza.
Profesor Mucho gusto.
Isabel Encantada.

Profesora Su nombre, por favor.
José José Sánchez.

Mucho gusto is used by both men and women when meeting someone for the first time. A man may also say **encantado** and a woman **encantada.** When responding to **mucho gusto,** both **encantado/a** and **igualmente** may be used.

ACTIVIDADES

A You are an usher at a fund-raising banquet. Greet the guests formally and ask for their names. Your classmates will play the part of the guests.

B You meet some young people for the first time at commencement exercises. Introduce yourself and find out the other persons' names. Two of your classmates will play the other roles.

PRONUNCIACIÓN

Las vocales*

Spanish has five simple vowel sounds, represented in writing by the letters **a, e, i, o,** and **u.** These vowels are tense and short, and for all practical purposes, constant in length when pronounced in

---

Self-Introductions
ANTONIO: I'm Antonio Mendoza. And what's your name? BENITO: Benito Sánchez. Nice to meet you. ANTONIO: Likewise.
PROFESSOR: What's your name? ISABEL: My name is Isabel Mendoza. PROFESSOR: Pleased to meet you. ISABEL: Delighted.
PROFESSOR: Your name, please. JOSÉ: José Sánchez.

* *The vowels*

both stressed and unstressed syllables. In order to avoid the glide sound of English stressed vowels (e.g., *no, same*), do not move your tongue, lips, or jaw. Avoid also the *uh* sound of English unstressed vowels (e.g., *opera, about*).

1. **a** is similar to the *a* in *father,* but shorter and tenser.

   llama mañana banana Panamá encantada

2. **e** is similar to the *e* in *they,* but without the glide sound.

   sé nene este Sánchez bastante

3. **i** is similar to the *i* in *machine,* but without the glide sound.

   sí ni Mimí Inés Felipe

4. **o** is similar to the *o* in *no,* but without the glide sound.

   no con Mónica noches profesor

5. **u** is similar to the *u* in *tuna,* but without the glide sound.

   su tú mucho uno usted

EL ALFABETO

a	a	**j**	jota	**r**	ere
b	be	**k**	ka	**rr**	erre
c	ce	**l**	ele	**s**	ese
ch	che	**ll**	elle	**t**	te
d	de	**m**	eme	**u**	u
e	e	**n**	ene	**v**	ve o uve
f	efe	**ñ**	eñe	**w**	doble ve, doble uve
g	ge	**o**	o	**x**	equis
h	hache	**p**	pe	**y**	i griega
i	i	**q**	cu	**z**	zeta

The Spanish alphabet has more letters than the English alphabet. **Ch** and **ll** are considered single letters and are listed separately in most Spanish dictionaries and vocabularies. The letter **ñ** does not exist in English. Some Spanish grammars do not include **rr** in the alphabet, and words containing **rr** are alphabetized as in English.

Another name for **w** is **uve doble.** The letters **k** and **w** appear mainly in words of foreign origin.

Dos amigos se abrazan en México. El abrazo es muy común cuando los hombres se saludan.

ACTIVIDADES

A Spell aloud the following names of cities in Mexico.

Puebla Veracruz Acapulco Morelia Guadalajara

B You will be asked your name. Give your name and then spell it to be sure it is understood.

Modelo Su nombre, por favor.
David Montoya. D-a-v-i-d M-o-n-t-o-y-a.

EXPRESIONES ÚTILES EN LA CLASE *useful expressions in the classroom*

Escuche(n).	*Listen.*
Conteste(n).	*Answer.*
Pregunte(n).	*Ask.*
Pregúntele a su compañero/a.	*Ask your classmate.*
Repita(n).	*Repeat.*
Abra(n) el libro.	*Open the book.*
Cierre(n) el libro.	*Close the book.*
Voy a pasar (la) lista.	*I'm going to call (the) roll.*

When addressing just one person, Spanish uses a command form without **-n: escuche.** When addressing two or more people, the command form ends in **-n: escuchen.**

Although you may not have to use these expressions, you should recognize them and act accordingly. The following **Pasos** will present more **Expresiones útiles.**

Cultura

General awareness, titles, and some social customs

When you learn another language, you also learn about another culture—how people live, their family structure, their institutions, their social customs and attitudes, and so on. Gaining an understanding and appreciation for another culture enriches your own life, allowing an insight into your own language and culture.

Every lesson of this book will expose you to Hispanic culture through dialogs, readings, situations, and explanations. Cultural insights are further developed in the sections titled **Cultura.** In the **Primer paso** you have already learned about greetings, when to use them, and how to address people. In this corresponding cultural section, you will learn more about titles of respect and the ways in which people greet and address one another.

Other titles of respect besides **señor, señora,** and **señorita** are **don** and **doña.** Although the use of these titles may vary slightly from country to country, they all indicate formal relationships. The abbreviations for **señor, señora,** and **señorita** are **Sr., Sra.,** and **Srta.** They may be used with the first name, the last name, or both (**señora Mercedes, señor Martínez, señorita Berta Martínez**). There is no standard Spanish equivalent for *Ms.*; either **señora** or **señorita** is used. The abbreviations for **don** and **doña** are **D.** and **Da.** They are used with the first name (**don Felipe, doña Marta**) and with the first and last name together (**don Felipe Sánchez, doña Marta Jiménez**).

When saying hello or good-bye and when being introduced, Hispanic men and women almost always shake hands. When greeting each other, young girls and women often place their cheeks together, kissing not each other's cheek but the air. This is also the custom for men and women who are close friends; sometimes the man kisses the women's cheek. In Spain this kissing is done on both cheeks. Men who are close friends normally embrace and pat each other on the back.

Children and young people stand up and greet adults individually. Girls usually kiss men and women, while boys may kiss them or shake hands. Adults generally address children and young people as **tú,** but children and young people address adults as **usted.** Nevertheless, in some countries, especially in cities, children and young people may address adults who are close friends of the family as **tú.** Parents and children usually address each other as **tú,** but in some areas children may use **usted** when speaking to their parents.

VOCABULARIO

The vocabulary list that appears at the end of each **paso** and **lección** includes all the active words introduced in that chapter.

despedidas	*saying good-bye*
adiós	*good-bye*
hasta luego	*see you later*
hasta mañana	*see you tomorrow*
expresiones de cortesía	*polite expressions*
con permiso	*excuse me*
de nada/por nada	*you're welcome*
gracias	*thanks, thank you*
lo siento	*I'm sorry*
perdón	*excuse me*
por favor	*please*
presentaciones	*introductions*
¿cómo se llama usted?	*what's your name? (formal)*
¿cómo te llamas?	*what's your name? (familiar)*
encantado/a	*delighted*
igualmente	*likewise*
me llamo. . .	*my name is. . .*
mucho gusto	*pleased/nice to meet you*
su nombre	*your name*
saludos y contestaciones	*greetings and answers*
bien	*well*
bastante bien	*pretty well, rather well*
muy bien	*very well*
buenas noches	*good evening, night*
buenas tardes	*good afternoon*
buenos días	*good morning*
¿cómo está usted?	*how are you? (formal)*
¿cómo estás?	*how are you? (familiar)*
hola	*hello, hi*
mal	*not well, ill*
¿qué tal?	*how's it going?*
regular	*so-so*
personas	*people*
el profesor/la profesora	*professor, teacher*
señor (Sr.)	*Mr.*
señora (Sra.)	*Mrs.*
señorita (Srta).	*Miss*
tú	*you (familiar)*
usted	*you (formal)*
palabras útiles	*useful words*
y	*and*
palabras interrogativas	*question words*
cómo	*how*

SEGUNDO PASO*

In the Segundo paso you will
a. introduce people.
b. identify people.
c. describe yourself and others.

MINIDIÁLOGOS

Más presentaciones

Carlos	María, mi amigo José.
José	Mucho gusto.
María	Encantada.

Sr. Gómez	Doña Mirta, le presento a don José Flores.
Don José	Mucho gusto.
Doña Mirta	Igualmente.

Ana	Carlos, te presento a Marta.
Carlos	Mucho gusto.
Marta	Igualmente.

In an introduction, use **le presento** if you address the person as **usted;** use **te presento** if you address the person as **tú.** A simpler form is to use only the names of the persons you are introducing (**Carlos Ríos, Marta Díaz**).

---

* *Second step*

More introductions
CARLOS: María, my friend José. JOSÉ: Glad to meet you. MARÍA: Likewise.

MR. GÓMEZ: Doña Mirta, I'd like to introduce don José Flores to you. DON JOSÉ: Glad to meet you. DOÑA MIRTA: Likewise.

ANA: Carlos, I'd like to introduce Marta to you. CARLOS: Glad to meet you. MARTA: Likewise.

ACTIVIDAD

Decide whether to use the **le** (formal) or **te** (familiar) to introduce persons in the following situations. Two of your classmates will assume the roles of the other persons.

1. Introduce two classmates.
2. You run into two of your professors in the Administration building.
3. You and a friend are downtown and you run into a former boss.
4. You are at the cafeteria having a snack with a friend when another friend comes over.

COGNADOS

Cognates are words in English and Spanish that have the same origin and are similar in form and meaning. Since English shares so many words with Spanish, you will discover that you already know many words in Spanish. Here are some that are used to describe people.

The first group of cognates has only one form to describe a man or a woman.

competente	inteligente	paciente	realista
eficiente	interesante	parcial	rebelde
elegante	liberal	persistente	sentimental
idealista	materialista	pesimista	terrible
importante	optimista	puntual	valiente

The second group of cognates has two forms. The **o** form is used when describing a man and the **a** form when describing a woman.

activo/a	extrovertido/a	introvertido/a	romántico/a
agresivo/a	fantástico/a	lógico/a	serio/a
ambicioso/a	generoso/a	moderno/a	sincero/a
creativo/a	impulsivo/a	pasivo/a	tímido/a
discreto/a	indiscreto/a	religioso/a	tranquilo/a

You should be aware that there are some words that look like cognates, but do not have the same meaning in both languages. You will find some examples in future lessons.

Unos amigos conversan en una calle de Santiago de Chile.

IDENTIFICACIÓN Y DESCRIPCIÓN DE PERSONAS

—¿Quién es ese chico?
—Es Julio.
—¿Cómo es Julio?
—Es romántico y sentimental.

—¿Quién es esa chica?
—Es Carmen.
—¿Cómo es Carmen?
—Es activa y muy seria.

Point out: verb forms change according to the subject and that subject pronouns are often omitted.

Note: plural forms will be given later.

ser	*to be*
yo soy	*I am*
tú eres	*you are*
usted es	*you are*
él, ella es	*he/she is*

ACTIVIDADES

A Using positive characteristics, describe a student in your class.

Modelo **David es inteligente y sincero.**

B Think of an important person and then describe him/her.

Modelo **Woody Allen es liberal. Él no es elegante.**

Who's that boy?
It's Julio.
What's Julio like?
He's romantic and sentimental.

Who's that girl?
It's Carmen.
What's Carmen like?
She's active and very serious.

C Describe yourself to a classmate.

Modelo **Yo soy optimista. No soy rebelde.**

D Find out if the person next to you has the following personality traits.

Modelo **—¿Eres pesimista?**
—No, no soy pesimista o **—Sí, soy pesimista.**

optimista persistente sincero/a impulsivo/a

E **Entrevista** *Interview.* Get a student's attention and greet him/her; then find out who the person next to that student is, and what he/she is like.

F After hearing several students describe themselves, try to describe two of them from what you remember.

PRONUNCIACIÓN

Las consonantes

Some consonants are pronounced the same way in Spanish and English (e.g., **f, m**). Other consonants differ only slightly, while still others are completely different. In this section you will learn to pronounce some Spanish consonants that are slightly different from their English counterparts.

1. p

Spanish **p** is pronounced like English *p,* but it is never accompanied by a puff of air as the English *p* often is. Note the difference between these two words that your instructor will pronounce: **papá,** *papa.*

Pepe pino pan peso poco popular

2. t

Spanish **t** is pronounced by placing the tip of the tongue against the back of the upper front teeth, and it is never accompanied by a puff of air. English *t,* in contrast, is pronounced by placing the tip of the tongue against the gum ridge and it is often accompanied by a puff of air.

te tú tomate tono está optimista

3. c, q, s, z

Spanish **c** before a consonant or **a, o,** or **u** is pronounced like an English *c,* but without a puff of air. The Spanish letter combination **qu** before **e** or **i** is pronounced like an English *k,* but without a puff of air.

como café cuna típico qué quién

Spanish **c** before **e** or **i** is pronounced like English *c* before *e* or *i*.

cena cita cesto once gracias cinco

Spanish **s** and **z** are pronounced like the English *s* in *some*. They are never pronounced like an English *z* when placed between vowels.

señora está ese casa zeta tiza

EXPRESIONES ÚTILES EN LA CLASE

Escriba(n).	*Write.*
Lea(n).	*Read.*
Siga(n).	*Continue.*
Vaya(n) a la pizarra.	*Go to the chalkboard.*
Siénte(n)se.	*Sit down.*
Levánte(n)se.	*Stand up.*
La tarea, por favor.	*The homework, please.*

Dos jóvenes españoles pasean por las calles de Madrid.

Cultura

Social customs when greeting and body language

People in the United States generally maintain a certain physical distance when speaking with each other. If someone should cross that invisible boundary and get too close, an American will start to back away. Hispanics, however, are more comfortable if they are close to the people with whom they are talking. Among friends and acquaintances, Hispanics tend to be more touch-oriented as well. It is not uncommon to see a young man with his hand or arm on a friend's shoulder at several points during a conversation. Young girls and women are often seen strolling arm in arm.

Hispanics also tend to be rather animated in conversation, frequently employing hand movements and gestures that are commonly understood. The following drawings illustrate some of these gestures:

no

un momentito *a moment*
un poquito *a little bit*

tacaño *stingy*

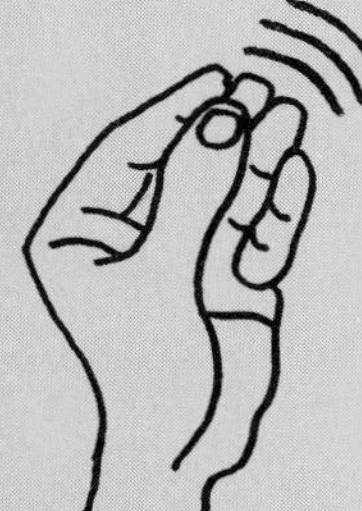

Está lleno.
It's full. (referring to a place)

después *later/after*

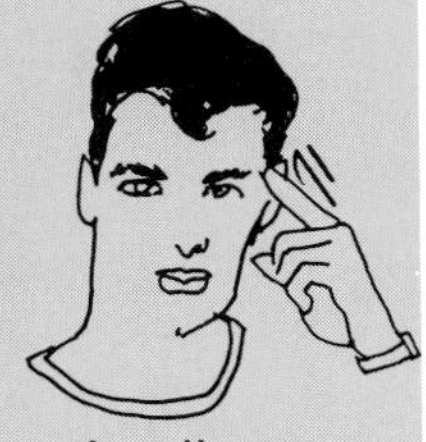

inteligente

VOCABULARIO

personas

el amigo/la amiga	*friend*
la chica	*girl*
el chico	*boy*
don	*title of respect for men*
doña	*title of respect for women*
él	*he*
ella	*she*
yo	*I*

descripción	*description*
activo	*active*
romántico	*romantic*
sentimental	*sentimental*
serio	*serious*

presentaciones	*introductions*
le presento a...	*I'd like you to meet . . . (formal)*
te presento a...	*I'd like you to meet . . . (fam.)*

verbos	*verbs*
eres	*you are (fam.)*
es	*he/she is, you are (formal)*
soy	*I am*

palabras útiles

ese/a	*that*
más	*more*
mi	*my*
no	*no*
sí	*yes*

palabras interrogativas

quién	*who*

Unos estudiantes hablan sobre sus clases en la Universidad de la República, en Montevideo, Uruguay.

TERCER PASO*

In the Tercer paso you will
a. identify objects.
b. ask and answer questions about the location of people and objects.
c. describe objects.

UN SALÓN DE CLASE[1]

—¿Qué es esto?
—Es un bolígrafo.

—¿Qué es esto?
—Es una tiza.

Use **¿Qué es esto?** when asking for the identification of an object.

* *Third step*

[1] *A classroom*

Unos estudiantes escuchan atentamente la explicación de su profesora en España.

ACTIVIDADES

A Your instructor will mention the names of different objects in the classroom. Point or walk to where they are.

B Your instructor will point to some of the objects in the classroom and ask you to identify them by asking **¿Qué es esto?**

C Enumerate the things you need for this class.

D Identify the items on the table to the right.

¿DÓNDE ESTÁ?[2]

enfrente de *in front of*
detrás de *behind*

sobre *on*
debajo de *underneath*

al lado de *beside*
entre *between*

¿Dónde está la profesora?
Está en la clase.

To ask for the location of a person or an object, use **dónde** + **está.**

---

[2] *Where is it?*

ACTIVIDADES

A Complete the following sentences according to the relative position of people or objects in the drawing.

1. La pizarra está ____ la profesora.
2. El diccionario está ____ la mesa.
3. Juan está ____ la profesora.
4. Mercedes está ____ Juan y María.
5. La mesa está ____ la ventana.
6. María está ____ Mercedes.

B Identify where your classmates are in relation to each other.

Modelo **Profesor/a** **¿Quién está al lado de Juan?**
Estudiante **María (está al lado de Juan).**

C Your instructor will select several items from your classroom and ask you where they are. Answer by giving their location in relation to a person or another object.

Modelo **—¿Dónde está el libro?**
—Está sobre el escritorio.

D Look at the seating chart below. The X marks your location.

1. Tell where Juan, Ángeles, Cristina, and Pedro are.
2. With a partner, ask questions about the location of other students.

María	Juan	Ester	Susana	Pedro
Carlos	Cristina	Ángeles	Alberto	Anita
Mercedes	Andrés	Roberto	Rocío	Pablo

X

E Ask some of your classmates about the location of various students and objects in the classroom.

Una profesora escucha las preguntas de una estudiante en la UNAM (Universidad Nacional Autónoma de México), la universidad más importante de ese país.

¿CÓMO ES[3]?

El reloj es redondo.

La ventana es cuadrada.

La pizarra es rectangular.

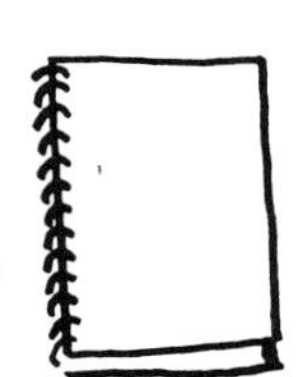

—¿Cómo es el diccionario?
—Es grande.
—¿Y el cuaderno?
—Es pequeño.

—¿Cómo es la regla?
—Es larga.
—¿Y la tiza?
—Es corta.

---

[3] What is it like?
The clock is round. The window is square. The chalkboard is rectangular.

What's the dictionary like? It's big. And the notebook? It's small.

What's the ruler like? It's long. And the chalk? It's short.

ACTIVIDADES

A **¿Verdadero o falso?** *True or false?* Tell whether each statement is true or false as your teacher or a classmate points to the item.

1. La puerta es cuadrada.
2. El escritorio es rectangular.
3. El salón de clase es pequeño.
4. La pizarra es redonda.
5. La ventana es rectangular.
6. El borrador es muy grande.
7. La tiza es pequeña.
8. El lápiz es largo.

B Describe the following objects in your classroom and tell where they are located in relation to a classmate.

la ventana	el cuaderno	el bolígrafo	la puerta	el escritorio
el pupitre	el reloj	el lápiz	la tiza	

C **Adivinanzas** *Guessing game.* By giving a series of clues, have your classmates identify the object you have in mind. Your classmates will have to ask questions to find out what the object is.

Modelo

Usted **Es redondo.**
Estudiante **¿Dónde está?**
Usted **Está en la pared.**
Estudiante **Es el reloj.**
Usted **Sí.**

PRONUNCIACIÓN

1. b, v

In Spanish, the letters **b** and **v** are pronounced the same. At the beginning of an utterance or after an **m** or **n**, Spanish **b** and **v** sound like English *b*. In all other positions, Spanish **b** and **v** are pronounced by allowing the breath to pass between the lips, which are almost closed. This sound does not exist in English.

bien	buenos	bonito	un vino	combate	vaca
sabe	Cuba	cabeza	uva	pavo	aviso
bebe	bebida	vive	bobo	babero	víbora

2. d

Spanish **d,** like **t,** is pronounced by placing the tip of the tongue against the back of the upper teeth. It is pronounced in two ways, depending upon its position in a word or sentence. At the beginning of a sentence or after **l** or **n,** the air flow is interrupted until the tongue moves back. In all other positions, **d** is similar to the pronunciation of the English *th* in the word *father.*

don	dónde	doña	doctor	día	dinero
adiós	comida	saludos	usted	médico	lado

EXPRESIONES ÚTILES EN LA CLASE

¿Comprende(n)?	*Do you understand?*
¿Tiene(n) alguna pregunta?	*Do you have any questions?*
Levante(n) la mano.	*Raise your hand.*

Other expressions that you may use in the classroom are:

No comprendo.	*I don't understand.*
No sé.	*I don't know.*
Tengo una pregunta.	*I have a question.*
Más despacio, por favor.	*More slowly, please.*
¿En qué página?	*On what page?*
¿Cómo se dice... en español?	*How do you say . . . in Spanish?*
¿Cómo se escribe... ?	*How do you spell . . . ?*
presente	*here (present)*
ausente	*absent*

Cultura

The Spanish language

Spanish, with some 300 million native speakers, is the fourth most widely used language. It is the official language of Spain and, in the New World, of Mexico, Cuba, Puerto Rico, the Dominican Republic, Guatemala, El Salvador, Honduras, Nicaragua, Costa Rica, Panama, Venezuela, Colombia, Ecuador, Peru, Bolivia, Paraguay, Uruguay, Chile, and Argentina.

Spanish is derived from Latin, the language spoken in the areas of Europe that were part of the Roman Empire. When Latin came in contact with the languages spoken in the various regions of the Iberian Peninsula, several dialects evolved. **Castilla** became the most important region in Spain (**España**), and eventually its language (**el castellano**) became the official language of Spain. When referring to the Spanish language, both **español** and **castellano** may be used.

The Arabs invaded Spain in 711 A.D. and remained there until 1492. During that time, many words of Arabic origin such as **álgebra, alcohol, cero** (*zero*), and **aceite** (*oil*) became part of the Spanish language.

When the Spaniards came to the New World, the languages spoken by the Indians contributed to the development of Spanish. Words such as **chocolate, tomate, coyote, maíz** (*corn*), and **aguacate** (*avocado*) are of Indian origin.

In the United States, especially in the West and Southwest, the influence of Spanish is evident in the names of cities (San Francisco, Las Vegas, San Agustin), states (Nevada, Montana), rivers (Colorado, Sacramento) and mountains (Sierra Nevada).

Una clase de computación en la ciudad de México. Para referirse a la capital y no al país, generalmente se escriben las letras D.F. (Distrito Federal) después de la palabra México.

VOCABULARIO

en el salón de clase — *in the classroom*

el bolígrafo	*ballpoint pen*
el borrador	*eraser*
el cesto	*wastepaper basket*
el cuaderno	*notebook*
el diccionario	*dictionary*
el escritorio	*desk*
el lápiz	*pencil*
el libro	*book*
la mesa	*table*
la pared	*wall*
la pizarra	*chalkboard*
la puerta	*door*
el pupitre	*student's desk*
la regla	*ruler*
el reloj	*clock, watch*
la silla	*chair*
la tiza	*chalk*
la ventana	*window*

personas

el/la estudiante	*student*

formas — *shapes*

cuadrado	*square*
rectangular	*rectangular*
redondo	*round*

tamaño — *size*

corto	*short*
grande	*big*
largo	*long*
pequeño	*small*

lugar — *location*

al lado (de)	*next to*
debajo (de)	*under*
detrás (de)	*behind*
enfrente (de)	*in front of*
entre	*between*
sobre	*on, above*

verbos

está	*he/she is, you are (formal)*

palabras útiles

el/la	*the*
en	*in*
esto	*this*
un/una	*a, an*

palabras interrogativas

dónde	*where*
qué	*what*

CUARTO PASO*

In the Cuarto paso **you will**
a. **use numbers from 0 to 99.**
b. **solve simple problems using those numbers.**
c. **tell time.**
d. **tell when an event takes place.**

MINIDIÁLOGO

Las preguntas de Lupe

Lupe Mamá, ¿cuántos días hay en una semana?
Mamá Pues, hija, hay siete.
Lupe ¿Y cuántas horas hay en un día?
Mamá Hay veinticuatro.
Lupe ¿Y cuántos días hay en un mes?
Mamá Hay veintiocho, veintinueve, treinta o treinta y un días. Depende.

ACTIVIDAD

Complete the sentences with the appropriate expression.

1. En una semana hay ___ días.
2. En un día hay ___ horas.
3. En un mes hay ___, ___, ___ o ___ días.

NÚMEROS 0–99

0	cero	5	cinco	10	diez
1	uno	6	seis	11	once
2	dos	7	siete	12	doce
3	tres	8	ocho	13	trece
4	cuatro	9	nueve	14	catorce

---

* *Fourth step*

Lupe's questions
LUPE: Mom, how many days are there in a week? MOTHER: Well, dear (*literally, daughter*), there are seven. LUPE: And how many hours are there in a day? MOTHER: There are twenty-four. LUPE: And how many days are there in a month? MOTHER: There are twenty-eight, twenty-nine, thirty or thirty-one. It depends.

15	quince
16	diez y seis (dieciséis)
17	diez y siete (diecisiete)
18	diez y ocho (dieciocho)
19	diez y nueve (diecinueve)
20	veinte
21	veinte y uno (veintiuno)
22	veinte y dos (veintidós)
23	veinte y tres (veintitrés)
24	veinte y cuatro (veinticuatro)
25	veinte y cinco (veinticinco)
26	veinte y seis (veintiséis)
27	veinte y siete (veintisiete)
28	veinte y ocho (veintiocho)
29	veinte y nueve (veintinueve)
30	treinta
31	treinta y uno
40	cuarenta
50	cincuenta
60	sesenta
70	setenta
80	ochenta
90	noventa

1. Numbers from 16 through 19 and 21 through 29 may be written as one word or as three words. Note the spelling changes and the written accent mark on some combined forms:

diez y ocho	dieciocho
veinte y dos	veintidós
veinte y tres	veintitrés

2. Beginning with 31, numbers are written as three words.

31	treinta y uno
45	cuarenta y cinco
58	cincuenta y ocho

3. The number *one* has three forms in Spanish: **uno, un,** and **una.** Use **uno** when counting: **uno, dos, tres.** Use **un** or **una** before nouns: **un borrador, una tiza; veintiún libros, veintiuna tizas.**[1]

4. Use **hay** for both *there is* and *there are.*

Hay un libro sobre la mesa.	*There is a book on the table.*
Hay dos libros sobre la mesa.	*There are two books on the table.*

ACTIVIDADES

A Su profesor/a va a leer (*is going to read*) un número de cada (*each*) grupo. Indique cuál (*which one*) es el número.

8	4	3	5	54	38	76	95
12	9	16	6	83	62	72	49
37	59	41	26	47	14	91	56

[1] Gender of nouns is presented in **Lección 1.** For now, use **un** (meaning *one*) with nouns that take **el,** and **una** with nouns that take **la.**

B Lea los siguientes (*following*) números.

6	16	26	39	46	56
2	14	75	83	54	97

C Lea los números y las palabras.

1 cesto	1 mesa	1 lápiz	1 silla
21 ventanas	41 libros	51 señores	81 chicas

D Conteste las siguientes preguntas.

1. ¿Cuántos estudiantes hay en la clase? 2. ¿Cuántos profesores o cuántas profesoras hay? 3. ¿Cuántos borradores? 4. ¿Cuántas sillas hay? 5. ¿Cuántas puertas hay en la clase? 6. ¿Cuántas ventanas hay?

E Lea los siguientes problemas y dé (*give*) la solución. Use **y** (+), **menos** (−) y **son** (=).

Modelo 2 + 4 = 6 **dos y cuatro son seis**

11 + 4 =	20 − 6 =	50 − 25 =
8 + 2 =	39 + 50 =	26 + 40 =
13 + 3 =	80 − 1 =	

F **¿Cuánto cuesta. . . ?** *how much is. . . ?* How much do you suppose the following items cost? Ask one of your classmates. ($$ = **dólares;** cents = **centavos**)

Modelo una regla

Usted **¿Cuánto cuesta una regla?**
Compañero/a **Cuesta un dólar.**

1. el libro de español
2. un lápiz
3. un bolígrafo
4. un diccionario
5. un cuaderno
6. un boleto (*ticket*) para un concierto

G **Números de teléfono y direcciones** *Addresses.* Lea la siguiente información:

Cafetería La Costa General Páez 40 4-23-48-37
Compañía La Nación Avenida Cuarta 7. 9-56-17-09
Museo Colón Calle Vigo 54 3-98-68-51
Hotel Orfila Chamberí 3 6-15-73-59

H **Adivinanzas.** You are "it"; choose a number from 0 to 99. Your classmates, in turn, try to guess your number. Tell them **más** if it is higher, **menos** if it is lower.

DÍAS DE LA SEMANA

lunes	*Monday*
martes	*Tuesday*
miércoles	*Wednesday*
jueves	*Thursday*
viernes	*Friday*
sábado	*Saturday*
domingo	*Sunday*

Septiembre

LUNES	MARTES	MIÉRCOLES	JUEVES	VIERNES	SÁBADO	DOMINGO
1	2	3	4	5	6	7
8	9	10	11	12	13	14
15	16	17	18	19	20	21
22 / 29	23 / 30	24	25	26	27	28

¿Qué día es hoy?	*What day is today?*
Hoy es...	*Today is . . .*

1. Hispanic calendars generally begin the week with **lunes.** Days of the week are not capitalized in Spanish.

2. Express *on* + a day of the week as follows:

el lunes	*on Monday*	los lunes	*on Mondays*
el domingo	*on Sunday*	los domingos	*on Sundays*

ACTIVIDADES

A **¿Qué día de la semana?** Según (*According to*) el calendario de septiembre, ¿qué día de la semana es el 2? ¿el 5? ¿el 30? ¿el 12? ¿el 23? ¿el 9?

B **Preguntas.** Conteste las siguientes preguntas.

1. ¿Qué día es hoy?
2. Si hoy es martes, ¿qué día es mañana (*tomorrow*)?
3. ¿Hay clase de español los domingos? ¿y los sábados?
4. ¿Qué días hay clase de español?

LA HORA

1. Use **¿Qué hora es?** to inquire about the hour. To tell time, use **es la** from one o'clock to one thirty and **son las** with all other hours.

Es la una.

Son las tres.

2. To express the quarter hour, use **cuarto** or **quince.** To express the half hour use **media** or **treinta.**

Son las dos y cuarto.
Son las dos y quince.

Es la una y media.
Es la una y treinta.

3. For time after the half hour (3:50, for example) say the following hour (4:00) and use **menos** to express the minutes.

   Son las cuatro menos diez.

   There are several alternate ways to tell time in Spanish. For now, follow the model above.

Una familia en el Parque de Chapultepec de la ciudad de México. Los sábados y los domingos este parque es el lugar de reunión de muchas familias mexicanas.

4. Add **en punto** for the exact time, **más o menos** for the approximate time.

Es la una en punto.
Son las cinco menos cuarto más o menos.

5. For A.M. and P.M., use the following:

de la mañana	(from 1:00 A.M. to 11:59 A.M.)
de la tarde	(from noon to approximately 7:00 P.M.)
de la noche	(from about 7:00 P.M. to midnight)

6. Use **¿A qué hora es?** to ask the hour at which something happens.

—¿A qué hora es la clase? —Es a las nueve y media.

ACTIVIDADES

A **¿Qué hora es en. . . ?** Diga (*Say*) qué hora es en las siguientes ciudades (*cities*).

B Add 15 minutes to each of the clock dials in Actividad A and reread. Give either exact or approximate time.

C **El horario de María** *María's Schedule.* Pregúntele a un/a compañero/a la hora de las clases y las actividades de María.

Modelo **—¿A qué hora es la clase de español?** **—Es a las nueve.**

lunes

9:00	clase de español
10:15	receso
10:30	clase de matemáticas
11:45	laboratorio
1:00	almuerzo°
2:00	clase de física
5:00	partido de tenis°

almuerzo: lunch
partido de tenis: tennis game

D ¿En qué página del libro está(n). . . ?

el calendario	los relojes	los días de la semana
el salón de clase	el alfabeto	

Una pizarra con las salidas de los vuelos en el Aeropuerto de Barajas de Madrid, la capital de España.

Una de las estaciones de ferrocarril de la ciudad de Madrid.

PRONUNCIACIÓN

1. g, j

At the beginning of an utterance or after **n,** Spanish **g** followed by **l, r, a, o,** or **u** is pronounced like English *g* in *garden.* In all other positions, Spanish **g** followed by **l, r, a, o,** or **u** is pronounced with no interruption to the air flow, similar to the rapid and relaxed pronunciation of English *g* in *sugar.* Note the difference in the pronunciation of **g** in these words that your instructor will say: **gata, la gata.**

gata	gusto	goma	gracias	grande	Domingo
amigo	lugar	regular	lechuga	agua	la gata

In the syllables **gue** and **gui,** the letter **g** is pronounced as above, but the **u** is not pronounced.

guerra guitarra guía Miguel seguir llegue

In Spanish, the pronunciation of the letter **g** in the syllables **ge** and **gi** and of the letter **j** is very similar to the pronunciation of English *h* in the word *heel.*

general ligero gigante viaje jugo jueves

2. r, rr

In Spanish, whenever the letter **r** occurs between vowels or after a consonant, its pronunciation is similar to English *d, dd, t,* or *tt* in words such as *matter, water* or *ladder,* pronounced rapidly by an American.

pero señora dinero pared tres otro

Spanish **r** at the beginning of a word, after **n** or **l,** and **rr** is pronounced by placing the tip of the tongue on the upper gum ridge and tapping it several times. This sound does not exist in English.

perro carro rico Roberto Enrique regalo alrededor

EXPRESIONES ÚTILES EN LA CLASE

cuente(n)	*count*
diga(n)	*say*
Abran el libro en la página...	*Open the book on page . . .*
Más alto, por favor.	*Louder, please.*
otra vez	*again*

Cultura

Attitudes concerning time in the Hispanic world

In Hispanic countries, events such as concerts, bullfights, and religious services begin on time. Normally, business meetings and medical appointments are also kept at the scheduled hour. However, informal social functions such as parties and private gatherings do not usually begin at a precise hour. In fact, guests are not expected to arrive until from one half to one full hour after the time indicated on an invitation. When in doubt, you may ask **¿hora americana?** or **¿hora inglesa?** (*precise time?*) to find out if you should be punctual.

Many countries use military time or the 24-hour clock, for train, bus, and plane schedules, as well as for television and radio programs.

Below is the bus schedule to the Ezeiza Airport, which is about one hour's drive from Buenos Aires, Argentina. If you were leaving on a flight at 8:00 P.M. on Tuesday, which bus would you take?

HORARIO DE SALIDAS DE LOS OMNIBUS

DESDE CARLOS PELLEGRINI 509, CAPITAL A AEROPUERTO EZEIZA

Lunes	Martes	Miercoles	Jueves	Viernes	Sabado	Domingo
05.30	05.30	05.30	05.30	05.30	05.30	06.30
06.30	06.30	06.30	06.30	06.30	06.30	07.30
07.30	07.30	07.30	07.30	07.30	07.30	09.00
09.00	09.00	09.00	09.00	09.00	09.00	10.00
10.00	10.00	10.00	10.00	10.00	10.00	11.00
11.00	11.00	11.00	11.00	11.00	11.00	12.30
12.30	12.30	12.30	12.30	12.30	12.30	13.30
13.30	13.30	13.30	13.30	13.30	13.30	15.00
15.00	15.00	15.00	15.00	15.00	15.00	16.00
16.00	16.00	16.00	16.00	16.00	16.00	17.00
17.00	17.00	17.00	17.00	17.00	17.00	18.30
18.30	18.30	18.00	18.30	18.00	18.00	19.30
19.30	20.30	19.00	20.30	19.00	19.30	20.30
		20.30		20.30	20.30	

VOCABULARIO[2]

tiempo — *time*
el día — *day*
la hora — *hour*
la mañana — *morning*
el mes — *month*
la semana — *week*
cuarto — *quarter*
en punto — *sharp*
hoy — *today*
media — *half*
menos — *minus, to* (in telling time)

personas
la hija — *daughter, dear*
la mamá — *mother*

verbos
depende — *it depends*
hay — *there is, there are*

palabras interrogativas
cuántos, cuántas — *how many*

palabras útiles
a — *at, to*
la pregunta — *question*
pues — *well*

expresiones útiles
¿A qué hora es...? — *At what time is ...?*
¿Qué hora es? — *What time is it?*
Es la... /Son las... — *It's ...*
más o menos — *more or less*

palabras adicionales[3]

verbos
dé — *give*
indique — *indicate*
va a... — *you are* / *he/she is* going to ...

otras palabras
cada — *each*
cuál — *which one*
según — *according to*
siguiente — *following*

---

[2] See pages 26–27 and 29 for the numbers and the days of the week.
[3] These words appear in the directions of the **Actividades.** You should recognize them since they will appear in future lessons. Cognates and words that were presented in **Expresiones útiles en la clase** have not been included in this list.

In Lección 1 **you will**

a. **discuss daily activities.**
b. **ask for and provide information.**
c. **express needs.**
d. **ask about and express location.**

Los estudios

Lección 1
La universidad

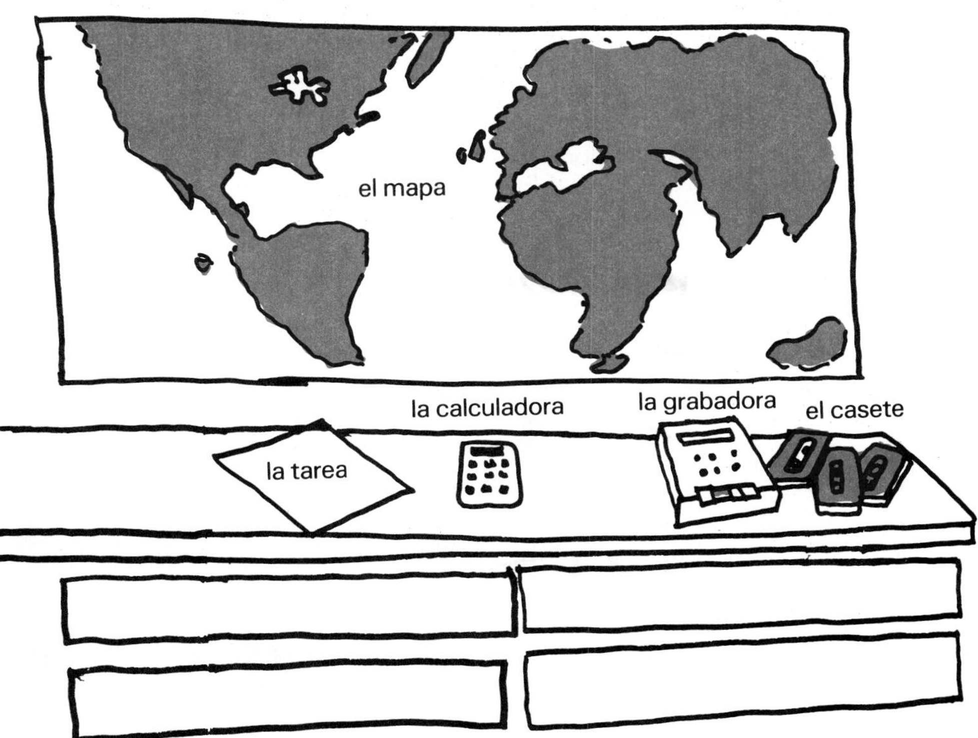

Juana estudia matemáticas.

Alfredo estudia español.

otras materias *other subjects*
economía
biología
historia
geografía
física
química
(p)sicología
contabilidad *accounting*

otras lenguas *other languages*
inglés
francés
chino
portugués
ruso
japonés
italiano
alemán *German*

Una clase en una escuela primaria de Isla Mujeres, México.

ACTIVIDADES

A Complete las siguientes oraciones (*sentences*) de acuerdo con el dibujo (*drawing*)[1] de las páginas 36–37.

1. El chico está enfrente de la ____.
2. La computadora está entre el ____ y la ____.
3. La tarea está entre la ____ y la ____.
4. El ____ está en la pared.
5. El casete está al lado de la ____.

B Pregúntele a uno/a de sus (*your*) compañeros/as dónde está cada objeto en ese dibujo. Él/Ella debe contestar diciendo (*should answer saying*) dónde está en relación con otro objeto.

C Asocie las palabras de la columna de la izquierda (*left*) con las materias de la columna de la derecha (*right*).

1. diccionario	a. química
2. números	b. biología
3. oxígeno	c. español
4. animales	d. historia
5. Freud	e. economía
6. dólares	f. geografía
7. Napoleón	g. contabilidad
8. mapa	h. sicología

D Asocie las ciudades (*cities*) de la columna de la izquierda con las lenguas de la columna de la derecha.

1. París	a. portugués
2. Panamá	b. ruso
3. Moscú	c. italiano
4. Shanghai	d. inglés
5. Río de Janeiro	e. japonés
6. Roma	f. español
7. Tokio	g. alemán
8. Frankfurt	h. chino
9. Londres	i. francés

E Dígale a uno de sus compañeros qué materias estudia usted. Después (*Then*) pregúntele qué estudia él/ella.

Modelo Usted **Yo estudio español, inglés y matemáticas. ¿Y tú?**
Compañero/a **Yo estudio física, contabilidad y español.**

---

[1] From here on, directions for the **Actividades** will be given in Spanish. In cases where the directions involve new vocabulary, English equivalents will appear in parentheses.

Cultura

Education in the Hispanic World

Educational systems in the Hispanic countries are highly centralized and often controlled by the Ministry of Education.

All students begin their instruction in elementary school (**la escuela primaria**). At the secondary school level (**la escuela secundaria**), some students enter a technical or vocational school; others attend a **colegio, instituto,** or **liceo** to complete the program (**bachillerato**), which prepares them for university study. In some countries there is a requirement of a year or two of additional work (**la preparatoria**). And in most Hispanic countries, students must pass rigorous entrance examinations before acceptance by a university.

The majority of middle-class students attend private schools, most of which are Catholic. Some young people, especially those who already have a job, take courses such as languages or accounting in private institutions.

Those students who attend a university immediately begin a specialized program. In general, the course of study is quite rigid, with only limited electives. Since very few Spanish-American or Spanish universities have dormitories, students usually live in private homes or guest houses (**pensiones/casas de huéspedes**).

EN CONTEXTO

En la universidad

David, un estudiante norteamericano, habla con Olga, una estudiante española, en la Universidad de Málaga.

Olga ¿Qué estudias este semestre, David?
David Estudio historia del arte, literatura, antropología y gramática española. ¿Y tú?
Olga Estudio informática. Además, trabajo con mi padre por las tardes.
David Por eso estás tan ocupada siempre.
Olga Un poco. Y tú, David, ya hablas español muy bien.
David ¡Qué va! Escucho las cintas en el laboratorio, hablo con los alumnos, pero necesito practicar más.

David, an American student, chats with Olga, a Spanish student, at the University of Málaga.
OLGA: What are you studying this semester, David? DAVID: I am studying art history, literature, anthropology, and Spanish grammar. And you? OLGA: I'm studying computer science. Besides, I work with my father in the afternoons. DAVID: That's why you are always so busy. OLGA: A little. And David, you already speak Spanish very well. DAVID: Oh, no! I listen to the tapes in the lab, I talk with students, but I need to practice more.

Para completar

Complete las oraciones con la información que se da (*is given*) en el diálogo.

1. Este semestre David estudia...
2. Olga estudia...
3. Olga trabaja por las...
4. Olga está siempre muy...
5. David escucha las cintas en el...
6. David necesita...

ACTIVIDADES

A Complete las siguientes oraciones sobre sus actividades en la universidad.

1. Este semestre estudio... 2. Mi clase favorita es... 3. El profesor/La profesora se llama...

B Complete el siguiente diálogo con su compañero/a.

Usted ¿Qué estudias este semestre/trimestre?
Compañero/a ...
Usted ¿A qué hora es la clase de ____?
Compañero/a ...
Usted ¿Quién es el profesor/la profesora?
Compañero/a ...

Unos alumnos conversan frente a la Facultad de Derecho en la Universidad de la República, en Montevideo.

GRAMÁTICA

Subject pronouns

	SINGULAR	PLURAL	
yo	*I*	nosotros, nosotras	*we*
tú	*you (familiar)*	vosotros, vosotras	*you (familiar)*
usted	*you (formal)*	ustedes	*you (formal)*
él	*he*	ellos	*they*
ella	*she*	ellas	

1. Spanish has many different equivalents for *you*: singular, plural, familiar, and formal. There are even regional variations. Your problem as a learner is to identify and select the right form from the various possibilities.

   Here are the forms used in Spain:

tú	vosotros/as
usted	ustedes

   These are the forms used in Hispanic America:

tú	ustedes
usted	

   In both Spain and Hispanic America, **tú** and **usted** are not interchangeable. As explained in **Primer paso, tú** is used with close friends, relatives, and children, while **usted** is used when addressing someone as **señor, señora, doctor,** and so on. When you are in doubt whether to use **tú** or **usted,** use **usted.**

   In Spain, the plural of **tú** is **vosotros** or **vosotras.** In other Spanish-speaking countries, the plural of both **tú** and **usted** is **ustedes.**

   Usted and **ustedes** are abbreviated in writing as **Ud.** or **Vd.,** and **Uds.** or **Vds.,** respectively.

2. There is no Spanish equivalent for the English subject pronoun *it.*

   Es redondo. — *It's round.*

3. Except for **ustedes,** the plural pronouns have masculine and feminine endings (**nosotros, nosotras, vosotros, vosotras, ellos, ellas**). Use the **-as** ending for a group composed only of females; use the **-os** ending for a mixed group or one composed only of males.

ACTIVIDAD

¿Qué pronombre (*pronoun*) usa usted?

1. Usted habla de (*about*) las siguientes personas:

   Sr. Martínez Alicia y Susana usted (*yourself*) Sra. Gómez
   Alfredo y Juana Ana y usted

2. Usted habla con las siguientes personas:

   su profesor de historia una azafata (*stewardess*) su íntimo amigo
   dos compañeros dos doctores un niño (*child*)

GRAMÁTICA

Present tense of regular *-ar* verbs

hablar *to speak*			
yo	habl**o**	nosotros/as	habl**amos**
tú	habl**as**	vosotros/as	habl**áis**
él/ella, usted	habl**a**	ellos/as, ustedes	habl**an**

1. The endings of Spanish **-ar** verbs (**-o, -as, -a, -amos, -áis, -an**) indicate the subject (who or what does the action). Therefore, subject pronouns are generally omitted, except for

emphasis	**Yo estudio** español.	*I study Spanish.*
clarification	**Él practica** mucho. (*not* **ella** *or* **usted**)	*He practices a lot.*
contrast	**Ella habla** francés; **nosotros hablamos** español.	*She speaks French; we speak Spanish.*

2. When you have two verbs in sequence, conjugate the first verb; the second verb is generally an infinitive (the form that ends in **-ar, -er,** or **-ir**).

   Ella **desea enseñar** aquí. *She wants to teach here.*

3. The Spanish present tense has various English equivalents.

   Yo **trabajo** en la oficina.
   I work in the office.
   I'm working in the office.
   I do work in the office.
   I'll work in the office.

4. Some common **-ar** verbs are: desear, enseñar, escuchar, estudiar, hablar, necesitar, practicar, trabajar.

The negative

1. Make sentences negative by placing the word **no** before the verb.

Ellos trabajan con mi padre. ⟶ Ellos **no** trabajan con mi padre.

2. When answering a question with a negative statement, say **no** twice.

—¿Enseñas francés?	*"Do you teach French?"*
—**No,** (yo) **no** enseño francés.	*"No, I don't teach French."*

ACTIVIDADES

A **En la clase de español.** Los estudiantes de la columna de la izquierda trabajan mucho en la clase. Los estudiantes de la columna de la derecha trabajan muy poco. Use la forma correcta de los siguientes verbos para expresar lo que hacen (*what they do*): **estudiar, trabajar, practicar, hablar, escuchar.**

	mucho	**poco**
Modelos	María	Alfredo
	María trabaja mucho.	**Alfredo trabaja poco.**
	Isabel	Pedro
	Alicia y yo	tú
	yo	Josefina y Marta

B **Un estudiante muy bueno.** David es un estudiante muy bueno. Dígale a su compañero/a lo que David hace (*does*) para sacar buenas notas (*to get good grades*). Después dígale lo que usted hace.

C **Un estudiante muy malo.** Dígale a su compañero/a lo que ese estudiante no hace.

D **Las clases de unos estudiantes.** Mire (*Look at*) la lista y dígale a un/a compañero/a lo que cada persona estudia. Después pregúntele a su compañero/a qué estudia él/ella.

1. Ana: inglés, matemáticas, contabilidad
2. Manuel: español, historia, química
3. José: antropología, geografía, economía
4. yo: . . .

E Mire el anuncio (*ad*) de la escuela Idiomas Serrano (*Serrano Language School*). Conteste las siguientes preguntas.

1. ¿Qué enseñan en Idiomas Serrano?
2. ¿Dónde está Idiomas Serrano?
3. ¿Cuál es el teléfono?

F En el salón de clase. Diga lo que hace cada persona en la clase.

EN CONTEXTO

En la librería°

bookstore

Pablo	Por favor, necesito comprar un diccionario de español.	
Dependiente	¿Un diccionario pequeño?	
Pablo	No, es para mi clase de español. Yo busco° un diccionario grande.	*I'm looking for*
Dependiente	Este diccionario es excelente. Es muy popular entre los estudiantes.	
Pablo	¿Y cuánto cuesta°?	*¿y. . . And how much is it?*
Dependiente	Ochenta pesos. El precio° es muy bueno.	*price*

Para completar

Complete las oraciones con la información que se da en el diálogo.

1. Pablo está en la. . .
2. Él necesita comprar un. . .
3. Él habla con. . .
4. El diccionario grande es popular entre los. . .
5. El diccionario cuesta. . .

Unos clientes examinan unos libros en una librería de Montevideo, Uruguay.

ACTIVIDADES

A ¿Qué necesita usted en estas clases? Asocie las materias de la columna de la izquierda con los objetos de las dos columnas de la derecha.

1. matemáticas	a. un mapa	d. una grabadora
2. geografía	b. una calculadora	e. un casete
3. español	c. un diccionario	f. una regla

B Usted necesita comprar un cuaderno para sus clases y va a la librería. Complete el siguiente diálogo con su compañero/a.

Usted Por favor, necesito...
Dependiente/a ¿Grande o pequeño?
Usted ... ¿Cuánto cuesta?
Dependiente/a ... ¿Necesita algo más (*anything else*)?
Usted ...

GRAMÁTICA

Noun gender

Nouns are words that name a person, place, or thing. In English all nouns use the same definite article, *the,* and the indefinite articles *a* and *an.* In Spanish, however, nouns are divided into two types: those that use **un** or **el** and those that use **una** or **la.**

Traditionally, nouns that require **un** or **el** are called *masculine* while those requiring **una** or **la** are called *feminine.* These terms are used in a grammatical sense and have nothing to do with biological gender. Spanish speakers do not perceive objects as having biological gender. Only when nouns refer to males (masculine) and females (feminine) are the terms meaningful in a biological sense.

Articles (singular)

	MASCULINE	FEMININE
DEFINITE ARTICLES	el	la
INDEFINITE ARTICLES	un	una

1. Usually nouns that end in **o** require **el** and those that end in **a** require **la.**

el libr**o** **el** cuadern**o** **el** diccionari**o** **la** mes**a** **la** sill**a** **la** ventan**a**

2. Other nouns that are generally used with **un** or **el** end in the following letters: **e, l, n, r,** and **s.**

el/un pupitre el/un papel el/un salón el/un borrador el/un mes

3. Other nouns that require **una** or **la** end in the following letters: **-d, -ción, -sión.**

   la/una actividad   la/una lección   la/una misión

4. Exceptions to these rules are few. Some common ones are

   el/un día   la/una clase   la/una noche   el/un mapa   la/una tarde

   Memorize the exceptions along with their article. You will come across others as you learn more Spanish.

5. With nouns referring to animate beings, biological gender determines whether to use **el/un** or **la/una.** Note that nouns ending in **o** change the **o** to **a** for the feminine, and that nouns that end in a consonant add **a** for the feminine.

   el/un amigo   la/una amiga   el/un profesor   la/una profesora

   Nouns ending in **-e** may remain the same (**el/la estudiante**) or have a feminine form ending in **-a** (**el dependiente, la dependienta**).

La Universidad de Sevilla en España. Sevilla es la capital de Andalucía, la región del sur de España.

ACTIVIDADES

A Dé el artículo indefinido; después el definido.

mesa	tarea	lección	profesor	chica	libro	pupitre	actividad
museo	pared	acción	señora	lápiz	librería	amigo	

B Complete este pequeño párrafo con artículos definidos.

María está en ___ clase de ___ profesora Sánchez. Ella trabaja en ___ laboratorio por ___ tarde. Por ___ noche ella estudia mucho.

C Complete estas oraciones con artículos indefinidos.

Susana necesita comprar ___ bolígrafo, ___ diccionario, ___ regla y ___ calculadora. Su amiga necesita ___ cuaderno y ___ casete. Ellas hablan con ___ dependiente.

D Pregúntele a su compañero/a cuánto cuesta cada uno de los siguientes objetos.

Modelo **Usted** ¿Cuánto cuesta la calculadora?
Compañero/a Cuesta diez dólares.

GRAMÁTICA

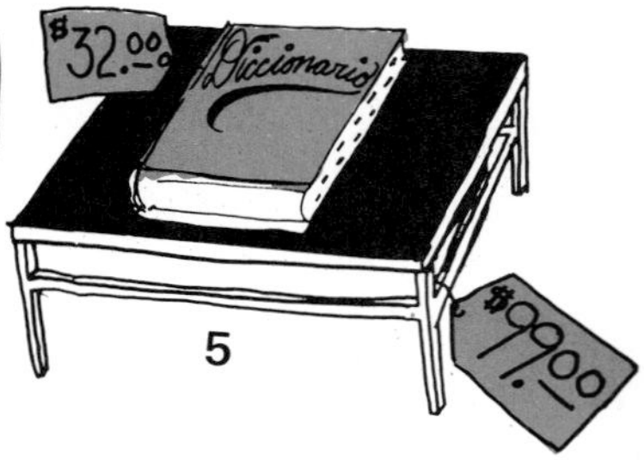

Noun plurals

1. Add **-s** to form the plural of nouns ending in a vowel (**silla/sillas**). Add **-es** to nouns ending in a consonant (**pared/paredes; señor/señores**). If a noun ends in **z,** change the **z** to **c** and add **-es** (**lápiz/lápices**).
2. Masculine plural forms (e.g., **amigos, profesores**) are used to refer to men and also to groups that include both men and women.

Articles (plural)

Definite and indefinite articles also have plural forms. The indefinite articles **unos/unas** have the meaning *some* in English.

		SINGULAR	PLURAL
DEFINITE	MASCULINE	el libro	los libros
	FEMININE	la chica	las chicas
INDEFINITE	MASCULINE	un libro	unos libros
	FEMININE	una chica	unas chicas

Use of definite articles

Spanish and English often use definite articles with nouns in similar ways, but in certain contexts the two languages differ. Use the definite article

1. before a title of respect (except **don** and **doña**) when you are talking *about* the person.

¿Cómo está **el** señor Romero? — *How is Mr. Romero?*
La Srta. Ortiz estudia economía. — *Miss Ortiz studies economics.*

Do not use the definite article when you are talking directly *to* the person.

¿Cómo está usted, señor Romero? — *How are you, Mr. Romero?*

2. to express *on* with the days of the week.

Hablo con Arturo **el** lunes. — *I'll talk to Arturo on Monday.*
Estudiamos **los** jueves. — *We study on Thursdays.*

3. with names of languages except when they immediately follow **de, en, hablar,** and **estudiar.**

El español no es difícil. — *Spanish isn't difficult.*
Estudio español. — *I study Spanish.*

ACTIVIDADES

A ¿Qué hay en la librería?
Su compañero/a y usted deben hacer una lista de los objetos y personas que generalmente hay en una librería. Después comparen su lista con la de otros estudiantes.

Modelo **Hay una mesa.**

B ¿Sabe (*Do you know*) **el plural?**

el precio	una clase	la tarea	el professor	una mesa	el reloj
el borrador	un papel	un estudiante	la pizarra	una tiza	la chica

C Complete este párrafo con artículos definidos. En algunos (*some*) casos no se necesita un artículo.

Nosotros estudiamos ____ español en ____ universidad. ____ clases son ____ lunes, miércoles y viernes. ____ español es muy interesante. Yo hablo ____ español con ____ profesor y con ____ estudiantes.

D Saludos. Haga las preguntas necesarias (*Ask the necessary questions*) para completar el siguiente diálogo. Salude al Sr. Chávez y pregúntele por (*about*) la Sra. Chávez. Su compañero debe hacer el papel (*should play the part*) del Sr. Chávez.

Usted ¿Cómo ____, Sr. Chávez?
Sr. Chávez Muy bien, gracias. ¿Y tú?
Usted ____. ¿Cómo ____ Sra. Chávez?
Sr. Chávez Está bien, gracias.

EN CONTEXTO

¿Dónde están los edificios (*buildings*)?

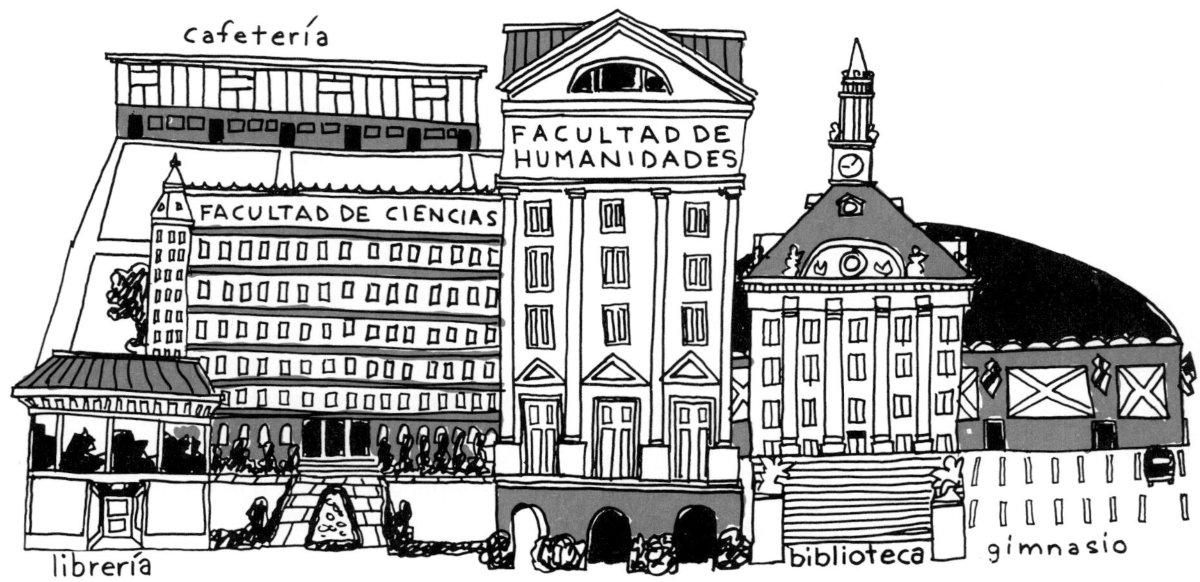

ACTIVIDADES

A Pregúntele a su compañero/a dónde están los diferentes (*various*) edificios de la universidad en el dibujo.

B Complete las siguientes oraciones con la palabra adecuada.

1. Compramos los libros en ___.
2. Escuchamos las cintas en ___.
3. Practicamos gimnasia en ___.
4. Estudiamos y consultamos libros en ___.
5. Hablamos con los compañeros en ___.

GRAMÁTICA

Present tense of the verb *estar*

estar *to be*	
yo estoy	*I am*
tú estás	*you are*
él, ella, usted está	*he/she is, you are*
nosotros/as estamos	*we are*
vosotros/as estáis	*you are*
ellos, ellas, ustedes están	*they are, you are*

1. Use **estar** to express the location of persons or objects.

—¿Dónde está el gimnasio? —Está al lado de la cafetería.
—¿Dónde está Pedro? —Está en la biblioteca.

2. Use **estar** to talk about states of health.

—¿Cómo estás? —Estoy muy mal.

ACTIVIDADES

A Pregúntele a su compañero/a dónde están los diferentes edificios de su universidad. Su compañero/a debe ser (*should be*) muy específico/a en su respuesta (*answer*).

B **Hora y lugares** *places.* Pregúntele a su compañero/a dónde está él/ella a las siguientes horas.

Modelo 8:00 A.M. Usted **¿Dónde estás a las ocho de la mañana?**
Compañero/a **Estoy en la clase de física.**

9:00 A.M. 1:00 P.M. 4:00 P.M. 11:00 A.M. 3:00 P.M. 10:00 P.M.

C Pregúnteles a dos de sus compañeros/as dónde están a) por la mañana, b) por la tarde, c) por la noche.

Modelo	Usted	**¿Dónde están ustedes por la tarde?**
	Compañeros/as	**Estamos en la biblioteca.**

D Mire los siguientes dibujos. Pregúntele a su compañero/a dónde están las personas y cómo están.

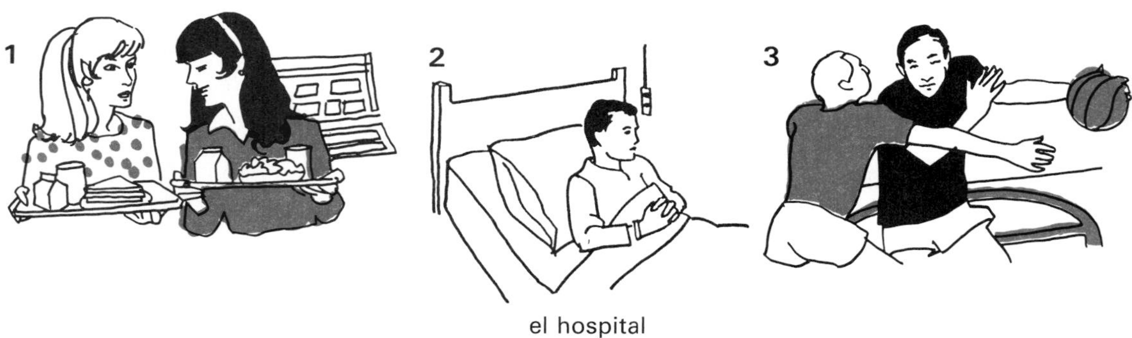

PRONUNCIACIÓN

Linking

One of the characteristics of spoken Spanish is that words are linked together, while in spoken English they are generally separated by a slight pause.

If a Spanish word ends in a consonant and the next word begins with a vowel sound, the consonant forms a syllable with the following vowel.

Nosotros hablamos español.

If a word ends in **a, e,** or **o** and the next word begins with another of these vowels, but not the same one, the resulting combination is linked.

Ana es   Paco está   no habla

If a word ends in a vowel and the next word begins with the same vowel sound, the two vowels are linked in careful speech. In rapid speech, the two vowels are pronounced as one.

una amiga ⟶ un**a**miga   ocho horas ⟶ och**o**ras

When two words are linked by any combination of **a, e,** or **o** with **i** or **u,** the vowels form a diphthong which is pronounced as one syllable.

mi amigo ⟶ m**ia**migo   la universidad ⟶ l**au**niversidad

la historia ⟶ l**ahi**storia   habla inglés ⟶ habl**ai**nglés

LECTURA*

Reading skills

Reading skills are as important as the ability to converse, especially as you begin and advance in the study of a language.

In real life we read for two reasons: for pleasure and to get information. There is such a great variety in the written information we read that a competent reader has to use different techniques to extract meaning from a text. The following are some important ideas, especially for persons beginning to read a second language.

Reading depends on more than just knowing words. Your previous experiences and knowledge of the world are assets you bring to the text that will help you comprehend many concepts. Many students feel they must understand every single word in order to understand the text. This is not so. Sometimes understanding key words—nouns and verbs—is all you really need in order to get the gist of what you are reading. Remember to read the title and subtitles, and to pay close attention to visual clues, such as pictures, charts, or print size. Use these aids to make educated guesses about the meaning of a text. Guessing the meaning of unknown words by using the context is an effective reading technique. You will be surprised how often your guesses are correct.

Once you have determined the general meaning of a text, you may want to go back and look for specific details. Remember that these techniques are not mutually exclusive and that we use several at the same time when we read.

Look at the following ad and read it, trying to get the general meaning. The size of the word **inglés** at the beginning, the use of cognates such as **programa, cursos, profesores, teléfono, nativos,** and the numbers will help you get the gist of the ad.

You knew that the ad referred to a language school before you read the last line, which is in English. Now read it a second time looking for specific details (e.g., the word **empresas** *businesses*). This second reading will give you additional information.

The **lecturas** *readings* at the end of each lesson have glosses on the side. Try to read the following **lectura** to get the gist of it, making educated guesses without looking at the glosses. Then read it a second time looking for specific details and consulting the glosses when necessary.

INGLÉS

- Programas de inglés en Empresas.
- Cursos en grupos de 3 a 6 alumnos en nuestros centros.
- Horario ininterrumpido de 8 de la mañana a 21.30.
- Profesores Universitarios nativos.

Caracas, 10. Teléfono 410 40 63 y 419 16 16

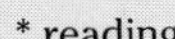

* reading

La informática

Éste es el programa oficial de la Facultad de Informática de la Universidad de Málaga para los alumnos de primer año. A la izquierda está el código o números que identifican cada materia y a la derecha está el nombre de las materias.

FACULTAD DE INFORMATICA

CÓD.	PRIMER CURSO
001	-Cálculo Infinitesimal
002	-Algebra
003	-Física
004	-Tecnología de los Computadores
005	-Laboratorio de Tecnología de Computadores
006	-Elementos de Programación
007	-Laboratorio de Programación I

Las materias son difíciles° y los alumnos deben estudiar mucho para poder aprobar°. Sin embargo°, la informática es una carrera muy popular y hay muchos alumnos en las clases por la importancia de las computadoras en el mundo° actual y en el futuro. Además los estudiantes saben° que hay muchas posibilidades de obtener trabajo después° de la graduación.

son... are difficult
pass / Sin... *Nevertheless*
world
know
after

PREGUNTAS

A La idea central de esta lectura es

a. los estudios de informática en la Universidad de Málaga.
b. los precios de las computadoras.
c. las actividades de los estudiantes de informática.

B Diga si las siguientes oraciones son verdaderas o falsas, de acuerdo con la lectura.

1. Hay cuatro materias en el programa de primer año.
2. Los alumnos de informática estudian muy poco.
3. Muchos alumnos estudian informática en la universidad.
4. Es difícil obtener trabajo después de la graduación.

Una estudiante de informática

Olga Marchena es una chica costarricense que estudia el primer año de informática en la Universidad de Costa Rica. Ella siempre está muy ocupada. Por las mañanas, de lunes a viernes, va a la universidad. Su primera clase empieza° a las nueve de la mañana. A las once más o menos Olga se reúne° con algunos compañeros en un café que está muy cerca° de la facultad. Allí° conversan y comen algo antes° de la siguiente clase.

Las clases terminan° a la una y media y Olga va a su casa° para almorzar° con su familia.

Por la tarde Olga ayuda° a su padre en la oficina donde trabaja con la computadora. Esta práctica es excelente para ella. Por las noches estudia, mira televisión o sale° con sus amigos.

begins
se... *gets together*
near / *There* / comen... *they eat something before*
end / *home*
para... *to have lunch*
helps
goes out

Preguntas

A La idea central de esta lectura es

a. las actividades de Olga.
b. la familia de Olga.
c. los estudiantes de informática.

B Diga si las siguientes oraciones son verdaderas o falsas, de acuerdo con la lectura.

1. Olga es una estudiante norteamericana.
2. Ella va a la universidad por las tardes.
3. Sus clases empiezan a las once.
4. Ella va a un café para almorzar con sus compañeros.
5. Olga trabaja en la oficina de su padre.
6. Olga siempre estudia por las noches.

C Complete el siguiente diálogo con su compañero/a.

Usted ¿A qué hora llegas a la universidad?
Compañero/a ...
Usted ¿A qué hora es tu primera clase?
Compañero/a ...
Usted ¿A qué hora es tu última (*last*) clase?
Compañero/a ...
Usted ¿Cuál es tu clase favorita?
Compañero/a ...

SITUACIONES

Read the information for each of the situations and role-play them with a partner.

1. You are talking about your job. Tell your partner (a) where you work, (b) the days of the week and the hours you work. Try to get the same information from him/her.
2. You need to buy some things (e.g., a book, some pencils, a calculator) for one of your classes; (a) tell your partner what you need, (b) ask where the bookstore is, (c) thank him/her, and (d) say good-bye.
3. You are at the bookstore: (a) ask the clerk for the location of what you want to buy, (b) ask how much it is, (c) pay the clerk, (d) count your change (**cambio**), and (e) thank him/her.
4. **Una entrevista.** Try to ask as many questions as possible of your partner (e.g., his/her name, what he/she studies). Share the information with your classmates.
5. Draw a university campus, locating the buildings and places given below. Your partner will ask you for the location of these buildings and places, and will draw his/her own version of where they are, according to the information you give. When you finish, compare the two drawings.

   cafetería, librería, gimnasio
   biblioteca, Facultad de Ciencias, Facultad de Humanidades

VOCABULARIO

en la clase

la calculadora — *calculator*
el casete — *cassette*
la cinta — *tape*
la computadora — *computer*
la grabadora — *tape recorder*
el mapa — *map*
el papel — *paper*
la tarea — *homework*

en la universidad — *at the university*

la biblioteca — *library*
la cafetería — *cafeteria*
el edificio — *building*
la facultad — *college, school*
el gimnasio — *gymnasium*
el laboratorio — *laboratory*
la librería — *bookstore*

lenguas — *languages*

el alemán — *German*
el chino — *Chinese*
el español — *Spanish*
el francés — *French*
el inglés — *English*
el italiano — *Italian*
el japonés — *Japanese*
el portugués — *Portuguese*
el ruso — *Russian*

materias — *subjects*

la antropología — *anthropology*
la biología — *biology*
las ciencias — *sciences*
la contabilidad — *accounting*
la economía — *economics*
la física — *physics*

la geografía	*geography*
la gramática	*grammar*
la historia	*history*
historia del arte	*art history*
las humanidades	*humanities*
la informática	*computer science*
la literatura	*literature*
las matemáticas	*mathematics*
la (p)sicología	*psychology*
la química	*chemistry*

personas

el alumno/la alumna	*student*
el dependiente/la dependienta	*clerk*
el padre	*father*
nosotros/nosotras	*we*
ellos/ellas	*they*
ustedes	*you (plural)*

tiempo	*time*
el semestre	*semester*
siempre	*always*

descripciones

excelente	*excellent*
ocupado	*busy*
popular	*popular*

nacionalidad

español/a	*Spanish*
norteamericano/a	*American*

verbos

buscar	*to look for*
comprar	*to buy*
desear	*to wish, to want*
enseñar	*to teach*
escuchar	*to listen to*
estar	*to be*
estudiar	*to study*
hablar	*to speak*
necesitar	*to need*
practicar	*to practice*
trabajar	*to work*

de compras	*shopping*
¿cuánto cuesta?	*how much is it?*
el dólar	*dollar*
el peso	*peso*
el precio	*price*

palabras útiles

además	*besides*
con	*with*
entre	*among*
este	*this*
los/las	*the*
otro(s)/otra(s)	*other*
para	*for, to*
pero	*but*
tan	*so*
unos/unas	*some*
ya	*already*

expresiones útiles

un poco	*a little*
por eso	*that's why*
¡qué va!	*of course not! no way!*

palabras adicionales

verbos

asocie	*match*
complete	*complete, fill in*

otras palabras

la derecha	*right*
el dibujo	*drawing*
la izquierda	*left*
la oración	*sentence*
el párrafo	*paragraph*
falso	*false*
verdadero	*true*

In Lección 2 **you will ask and answer questions concerning**
a. where people are from.
b. where and when events take place.
c. possessions.
d. descriptions of places, persons, and things.

Me llamo Luis López.
Soy de México. Soy bajo
y delgado, pero fuerte.
Yo estudio mucho
y saco buenas notas.

Me llamo Marta Chávez.
Soy española. Soy rubia.
Tengo el pelo corto. Soy
joven y alegre. Soy
soltera y muy trabajadora.

LUIS: My name is Luis López.
I'm from Mexico. I'm short and thin,
but strong. I study a lot and
get good grades.

MARTA: My name is Marta Chávez.
I'm Spanish. I'm blond. I have
short hair. I'm young and cheerful.
I'm single and a very hard worker.

Lección 2

Los compañeros de clase

¿Quién es?

Me llamo Arturo Mejía. Soy boliviano. Soy muy hablador, pero simpático. También soy alto. Tengo bigote, ojos verdes y pelo castaño.

Me llamo Lupe Villegas. Soy de Perú. No soy alta ni baja. Tengo el pelo largo. Soy callada, pero inteligente.

ARTURO: My name is Arturo Mejía. I'm Bolivian. I'm talkative but nice. I'm also tall. I have a moustache, green eyes, and brown hair.

LUPE: My name is Lupe Villegas. I'm from Perú. I'm neither tall nor short. I have long hair. I'm quiet, but intelligent.

ACTIVIDADES

A Asocie las siguientes características con la persona apropiada.

1. Tiene (*has*) el pelo largo.
2. Saca buenas notas.
3. Es de España.
4. Es fuerte.
5. Tiene bigote.
6. Es inteligente.
7. Es alegre.
8. Tiene ojos verdes.

a. Luis López
b. Marta Chávez
c. Arturo Mejía
d. Lupe Villegas

B Complete las siguientes oraciones de acuerdo con los dibujos y las descripciones.

1. Lupe es de...
2. Marta es...
3. Arturo tiene...
4. Luis es..., pero...
5. Marta es de...
6. Lupe tiene...

Descripción de personas

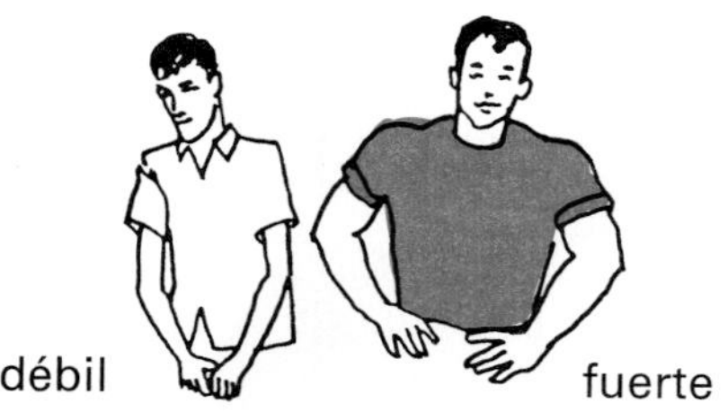

listo

tonto

alegre

triste

simpático

antipático

gordo

delgado

rubia

morena

trabajador

perezoso

rica

pobre

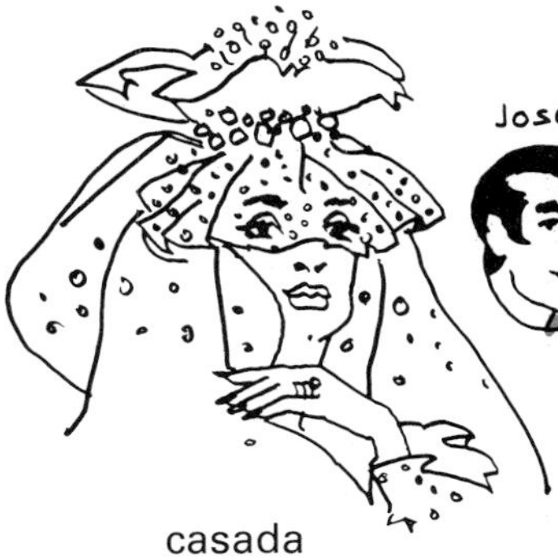

casada

soltera

ACTIVIDADES

A Complete las siguientes oraciones con opuestos (*opposites*).

Modelo Yo no soy vieja, soy **joven.**

1. Yo no soy malo/a, soy...
2. No soy perezoso/a, soy...
3. No soy antipático/a, soy...
4. Él no es tonto, es...
5. Ella no es pobre, es..
6. Él no es guapo, es...

B Complete las siguientes oraciones para describir a sus compañeros de clase.

1. ___ es alto.
2. ___ es hablador.
3. ___ es delgada y simpática.
4. ___ es alto y moreno.
5. ___ soltera y rubia.
6. ___ es trabajadora y lista.

C **Autodescripción**

1. Me llamo...
2. Soy... y...
3. No soy...
4. Trabajo en...
5. Deseo...

Dos estudiantes cerca de la Facultad de Derecho de la Universidad de Buenos Aires.

Cultura

The Hispanics

Even though the Hispanic nations share the same language, a common historical background, and similar traditions, customs, and values, they differ in many ways. Some of these differences are based on geography and on their economies, while others stem from the influence of ethnic subgroups unevenly distributed among them.

The Hispanic countries are located in Europe (Spain), North America (Mexico), and Central and South America. This vast territory includes nearly every imaginable type of geography and climate: cold, windswept lands; high mountains; deserts; fertile valleys and plains; jungles and tropical forests. Such differences affect the economy and culture of each country.

Most nations and races in the world have contributed to the present-day makeup of the populations of the Spanish-speaking countries. In Mexico and many parts of Central and South America, **mestizos** (people of mixed Indian and white ancestry) constitute a high percentage of the inhabitants. In the Caribbean, the original Indian population has practically disappeared, but the influence of blacks and mulattos (people of mixed black and white ancestry) is strong. Still other countries are conglomerates of immigrants from many sources, much like the United States. In Argentina, for example, waves of English, German, and especially Italian immigrants mixed with the Hispanic settlers who had arrived earlier.

Hispanics from various countries have profoundly influenced the development of the United States. Spaniards discovered and settled Louisiana and Florida, where in 1565 they founded Saint Augustine, the oldest city in this country. Spaniards and Mexicans conquered and settled the Southwest. They founded the first city west of the Mississippi, Santa Fe de Nuevo México, in 1609, eleven years before the Pilgrims landed on Plymouth Rock. With the Catholic missions in the states of Arizona, Texas, and California, Hispanic culture spread through the Southwest.

According to official government figures, there are some 19.4 million Hispanics in the United States. Unofficial figures put the number closer to 25 million, taking into account many undocumented workers who come to this country for economic or political reasons. Some experts believe that by the year 2000, Hispanics will total 30 to 35 million, which would make them the largest minority in this country.

Juan Ponce de León (¿1460?–1521), el primer gobernador de Puerto Rico y el descubridor de la Florida.

EN CONTEXTO

Un auto nuevo

Lucía Rafael tiene un auto nuevo.
Amparo ¿Y qué auto es?
Lucía No estoy segura. Sólo sé que es pequeño, pero muy cómodo.
Amparo ¿De qué color es?
Lucía Es amarillo y los asientos son negros. Es muy bonito. Mira, allí está Rafael.

Preguntas

Conteste las siguientes preguntas sobre el diálogo.

1. ¿Quién tiene un auto nuevo?
2. ¿Es grande el auto?
3. ¿De qué color es el auto?
4. ¿De qué color son los asientos?
5. ¿De qué marca (*brand*) es el auto?

más colores

anaranjado	*orange*	rojo	*red*
azul	*blue*	rosado	*pink*
blanco	*white*	café	*brown*
gris	*gray*	claro	*light*
morado	*purple*	oscuro	*dark*

ACTIVIDADES

A Asociaciones. ¿Qué colores asocia usted con estas palabras?

1. la noche
2. un dólar
3. Estados Unidos
4. Superman
5. un limón
6. las plantas
7. Drácula
8. las rosas
9. un elefante
10. una cebra
11. el autobús
12. un tigre

B Dígale a su compañero/a cuál es su auto favorito. Después escoja (*choose*) entre las características que aparecen más abajo (*appear below*) o use otras para describirlo (*to describe it*).

1. Marca
2. Color exterior; asientos
3. Características: bonito grande pequeño cómodo rápido económico

---

LUCÍA: Rafael has a new car. AMPARO: And what kind of car is it? LUCÍA: I'm not sure. I only know that it's small, but very comfortable. AMPARO: What color is it? LUCÍA: It's yellow and the seats are black. It's very pretty. Look, there's Rafael.

GRAMÁTICA

Adjectives

Adjectives are words that describe people, places, and things. Like articles (**el, la, un, una**) and nouns (**chico, chica**), they generally have more than one form. In Spanish an adjective must agree in gender (masculine or feminine) and in number (singular or plural) with the noun or pronoun it describes.

1. Some adjectives end in **-o** when used with masculine words and in **-a** when used with feminine words (**alto/alta**). To form the plural, these adjectives add **-s** (**altos/altas**).

SINGULAR	chic**o** alt**o**	chic**a** alt**a**
PLURAL	chic**os** alt**os**	chic**as** alt**as**

2. Other adjectives have only two forms, singular and plural. These end in **-e** or a consonant and agree only in number with the noun they describe. To form the plural, these adjectives add **-s** and **-es** respectively.

SINGULAR	amig**o** interesante chic**o** popular	amig**a** interesante chic**a** popular
PLURAL	amig**os** interesante**s** chic**os** popular**es**	amig**as** interesante**s** chic**as** popular**es**

3. Some adjectives that end in a consonant have four forms, however.

SINGULAR	alumn**o** español alumn**o** trabajador	alumn**a** español**a** alumn**a** trabajador**a**
PLURAL	alumn**os** español**es** alumn**os** trabajador**es**	alumn**as** español**as** alumn**as** trabajador**as**

Position of adjectives

Adjectives that describe a characteristic of a noun usually follow the noun.

Necesito un papel roj**o**. Es un hombre mal**o**.

Bueno, malo, and **grande** may precede nouns. When **bueno** and **malo** precede masculine singular nouns, they are shortened to **buen** and **mal.**

Es un **buen** libro. Es un **mal** hombre.

Grande is shortened to **gran** when it precedes any singular noun. Note, however, that **grande** means *large* when it follows a noun, but *great* or *wonderful* when it precedes.

Es una chica **grande.** *She's a big girl.*
Es una **gran** chica. *She's a great girl.*

ACTIVIDADES

A Descripciones. Usted administra una escuela y necesita unos empleados. Dígale a la agencia de empleos qué clase de persona necesita. Escoja entre las palabras que aparecen más abajo.

1. Busco una secretaria. . .

atractiva perezosa tonta trabajadora delgada
reservada vieja simpática alta habladora

2. Necesito un consejero (*advisor*). . .

independiente pasivo competente activo persistente
generoso callado interesante

3. Deseo emplear una profesora. . .

simpática imparcial romántica sincera rebelde
emocional paciente inteligente tonta importante

B ¿De qué color es (son). . . ?

1. Pregúntele a un/a compañero/a el color de los siguientes objetos.

Modelo ¿De qué color es tu bolígrafo?
Es azul.

tu auto tu lápiz tu diccionario tus ojos tu casa (*house*) tu libro de español

2. En el salón de clase. Pregúntele a un/a compañero/a el color de los siguientes objetos de la clase.

la pizarra el escritorio la puerta las ventanas el reloj las paredes

C Descripciones.

1. Usted es el supervisor/la supervisora de una fábrica (*factory*). El dueño/La dueña (*owner*) le hace las siguientes preguntas sobre un empleado. Trabaje con otro/a estudiante y conteste las preguntas.

Dueño/a ¿Cómo se llama ese señor?
Usted ...
Dueño/a ¿Cómo es?
Usted ...
Dueño/a ¿Es un buen trabajador?
Usted ...
Dueño/a Muchas gracias.
Usted ...

2. Usted es el/la gerente (*manager*) de una compañía. Usted desea tener (*to have*) más información sobre una empleada y habla con el supervisor/la supervisora.

Usted ¿Cómo se llama esa señora?
Supervisor/a ...
Usted ¿De dónde es?
Supervisor/a ...
Usted ¿Cómo es ella?
Supervisor/a ...
Usted Gracias.
Supervisor/a ...

D

¿Cómo es usted? Use dos adjectivos para explicar cómo es usted con las siguientes personas o en las siguientes situaciones.

Modelo con su amiga
Con mi amiga soy simpático/a y alegre.

1. con el profesor/la profesora
2. en el trabajo
3. en público
4. en la clase
5. con sus compañeros
6. con sus padres (*parents*)

E

Las diferencias. Mirta y Ángel son hermanos (*brother and sister*), pero son muy diferentes. Describa a Mirta y a Ángel.

Mirta es..., pero Ángel es...

Mirta tiene..., pero Ángel tiene...

EN CONTEXTO

El mundo hispano

ACTIVIDAD

¿De dónde es?

Lupe Villegas	Diana Samper	César Gómez	Carlos Arias
Arturo Mejía	Sara Rivero		

GRAMÁTICA

Present tense of the verb *ser*; uses of *ser*

	ser	*to be*	
yo	soy	nosotros/as	somos
tú	eres	vosotros/as	sois
él, ella, usted	es	ellos/as, ustedes	son

1. **Ser** is used with adjectives to describe persons, places, or things. For example, we can express our first impression of someone or something with **ser** and an adjective.

—¿Cómo es?
—Ella es bonita. La casa es grande. El auto es viejo.

2. **Ser** is used to express the nationality of a person; **ser** + **de** is used to express the origin of a person.

Nationality	*Origin*
Luis es chileno.	Luis es de Chile.
Ana es boliviana.	Ana es de Bolivia.

Indígenas con sus llamas en Cuzco, Perú. La ciudad del Cuzco era la antigua capital del Imperio de los Incas.

3. **Ser** + **de** is also used to express possession.

La casa es de Marta.	*The house is Marta's.*
Los libros son de José.	*The books are José's.*

De + **el** contracts to **del. De** + **la(s)** or **los** does not contract.

el auto **del** estudiante

el auto **de** { **la** señora / **las** señoras / **los** señores }

4. **Ser** is used to express the location and time of an event.

Location	
El baile es en la universidad.	*The dance is at the university.*
El examen es en el gimnasio.	*The exam is at the gymnasium.*
Time	
La fiesta es a las 9:00 de la noche.	*The party is at 9:00 P.M.*
El examen es a las 3:00.	*The exam is at 3:00 P.M.*

Ser and *estar* with adjectives

Ser and **estar** can be used with many of the same adjectives. However, the choice of verb determines the meaning of the sentence. They are not interchangeable. The use of **ser** or **estar** is determined by the person's perception of the situation.

1. **Ser** + adjective expresses what is considered to be the norm for a person or a thing.

Manolo es delgado.	*Manolo is thin.*	(He is a thin boy.)
Mirta es morena.	*Mirta is a brunette.*	(She has dark skin, hair, and eyes.)
La casa es pequeña.	*The house is small.*	(It's a small house.)

2. **Estar** + adjective expresses a change from the norm and/or a person's feelings.

Manolo está gordo.	*Manolo is fat.*	(He's gained weight recently.)
Mirta está rubia.	*Mirta is blond.*	(She dyed her hair.)
La casa está pequeña.	*The house is small.*	(The family has grown; the house has become small for them.)

3. More adjectives that can be used with **ser** or **estar** with the meanings described in sections 1 and 2 are

alegre nervioso/a tranquilo/a triste feliz (*happy*)

4. The adjective **contento/a** *happy, glad* is always used with **estar.**

Ella está muy contenta hoy.

5. Some adjectives have two meanings; one with **ser** and another with **estar.**

Ese señor es malo.	*That man is bad.* (evil)
Ese señor está malo.	*That man is sick.* (not well)
El chico es listo.	*The boy is clever.*
El chico está listo.	*The boy is ready.*
La manzana es verde.	*The apple is green.* (color)
La manzana está verde.	*The apple isn't ripe.*

Jóvenes puertorriqueños en el desfile del Día de Puerto Rico en Nueva York. En esta ciudad viven cerca de un millón de puertorriqueños.

ACTIVIDADES

A **Contexto.** Use la forma apropiada de **ser** o **estar** para describir una norma (*norm*) o un cambio (*change*).

1. Fernando is a good boy. *He is nice.* ___ simpático.
2. In New Mexico it rains very little in summer and the grass is always brown. This year it rained a lot. *The grass is green.* La hierba ___ verde.
3. You have seen coal before. *It is black.* ___ negro.
4. The sky over Los Angeles is usually brownish-gray. Today the wind is blowing and *it is blue.* ___ azul.
5. Everybody agrees about the color of snow. *It is white.* ___ blanca.
6. Marta is always in a good mood. *Marta is happy.* Marta ___ feliz.
7. Today Marta received a D and she is not herself. *Marta is sad.* Marta ___ triste.
8. Martín is an awful child. He always misbehaves. *He is terrible.* ___ terrible.

B Salude a su compañero/a. Dígale de dónde es usted y pregúntele de dónde es él/ella. Después salude a varios compañeros. Dígales de dónde es usted y pregúnteles de dónde son ellos.

C Dígale a su compañero/a cómo usted se siente (*you feel*) en las siguientes situaciones y pregúntele como se siente él/ella.

Modelo en la clase — Usted: **Estoy contento/a ¿Y tú?**
Compañero/a: **Yo estoy contento/a también** o **Yo estoy triste.**

1. en la carretera (*highway*)
2. en la clase de inglés
3. antes de un examen
4. en la universidad
5. en el trabajo
6. con muchas personas
7. en una fiesta
8. los lunes

D **Otros.** ¿Cómo describen otros a su...?

mamá   hermana (*sister*)   profesor/a   amigo/a   jefe/a (*boss*)
compañero/a de cuarto (*roommate*)

E **Primera impresión.** Usted ve (*see*) a estas personas por primera vez (*time*). ¿Cuál es su impresión?

1

2

F Otra persona ve lo siguiente por primera vez. ¿Cuál es la reacción de esta persona?

1. su casa — Es. . . y. . .
2. su auto (o motocicleta) — Es. . . y. . .
3. su salón de clase — Es. . . y. . .
4. su universidad — Es. . . y. . .

G **En la oficina del departamento de lenguas extranjeras** (*foreign languages*). Dígale a un estudiante nuevo quiénes son las siguientes personas y describa a estas personas.

Modelo Olga / morena / Bolivia
Es Olga. Es morena y es boliviana.

1. Renée / alta / Francia
2. Helmut / rubio / Alemania
3. Ian / simpático / Inglaterra
4. Orieta / delgada / Italia
5. Keiko / elegante / Japón
6. Alicia / inteligente / Colombia
7. Fernando / simpático / Puerto Rico
8. Yo / . . . / . . .

H **Posesiones.** Señale y además identifique algunos de los objetos de la clase. Su compañero/a debe decir (*should say*) de quién es.

Modelo
Usted **Es un lápiz.**
Compañero/a **Es de Marcia.**

I **Eventos.** Usted está a cargo (*in charge*) de la caseta (*booth*) de información en su universidad. Dígales a los visitantes dónde tienen lugar (*take place*) los siguientes eventos.

Modelo
Visitante **¿Dónde es el examen de español?**
Usted **Es en la biblioteca.**

la fiesta la conferencia (*lecture*) el concierto la manifestación (*demonstration*)
el banquete el concurso (*contest*)

Ahora dígales a los visitantes dónde están los siguientes lugares y edificios.

la biblioteca el salón de clase el gimnasio la librería el teatro
la oficina el estadio la cafetería

EN CONTEXTO

Preguntas y respuestas

¿Quién es?
¿Cuándo es el examen?

Viviana Domínguez

¿Qué hora es?
¿Quiénes están en la clase?

¿Cuántos estudiantes hay?
¿Dónde están?

¿Cuál es el libro de español?
¿De quién es el libro?

¿Cómo se llama? ¿Cómo es?
¿Cuánto papel hay?

ACTIVIDAD

Conteste las preguntas sobre cada uno de los dibujos anteriores.

GRAMÁTICA

Question words

cómo	*how/what*	**cuál/es**	*which*
dónde	*where*	**quién/es**	*who*
qué	*what*	**cuánto/a**	*how much*
cuándo	*when*	**cuántos/as**	*how many*

1. Question words ask for specific information about someone or something. Most question words have only one form (**cuándo, cómo**), some have two (**cuál, cuáles**), and one has four (**cuánto, cuánta, cuántos, cuántas**).

2. In an information question, question words generally come first, but in some cases another word may precede them.

¿**Qué** hora es?	¿**A qué** hora es la clase?
¿**Quién** es él?	¿**De quién** es el libro?

3. Use **por qué** to express *why.* The equivalent of *because* is **porque.**

—¿**Por qué** está Pepe en la biblioteca? —**Porque** necesita estudiar.

4. If the question can be answered affirmatively or negatively—with **sí** or **no**—do not use a question word. Subjects, if used, normally follow the verb, as in information questions.

—¿**Estudian ustedes** español? —Sí, estudiamos español.

5. Another way of asking a question is by placing an interrogative tag after a declarative statement.

Estudias español, ¿**verdad**?	*You study Spanish, don't you?*
Él es mexicano, ¿**no**?	*He's Mexican, isn't he?*

ACTIVIDADES

A Escoja entre las siguientes palabras para completar estas preguntas: **dónde, por qué, cuándo, cuál, quién, cuántos.**

1. —¿____ estudian ustedes? —En la Universidad Nacional.
2. —¿____ son tus clases? —Por la mañana.
3. —¿____ es tu profesor favorito? —El profesor Jiménez.
4. —¿____ es tu materia favorita? —El español.
5. —¿____ estudias español? —Porque es una lengua muy importante.
6. —¿____ alumnos hay en tu clase de español? —Veinticinco.

B **Entrevista.** Su amigo/a tiene muchas cosas (*things*). Usted desea saber (*to know*) cuántas cosas tiene. Use la forma correcta de **cuánto** en sus preguntas.

Modelo calculadoras **—¿Cuántas calculadoras tienes?**
—Tengo diez.

autos computadoras grabadoras relojes bolígrafos

C **Información.** Use las siguientes preguntas para entrevistar (*interview*) a su compañero/a. Comparta (*Share*) la información con la clase.

1. ¿Cómo te llamas?
2. ¿Cómo estás?
3. ¿Dónde trabajas?
4. ¿Cuántas clases tienes?
5. ¿Cuál es tu clase favorita? ¿Por qué?
6. ¿Cuándo estudias?
7. ¿Quién es tu mejor (*best*) amigo/a?
8. ¿Cómo es él/ella?

D **La publicidad** (*Advertising*). Lea el siguiente anuncio (*ad*) y hágales tres preguntas sobre el anuncio a sus compañeros.

E Haga preguntas sobre el siguiente dibujo a su compañero/a.

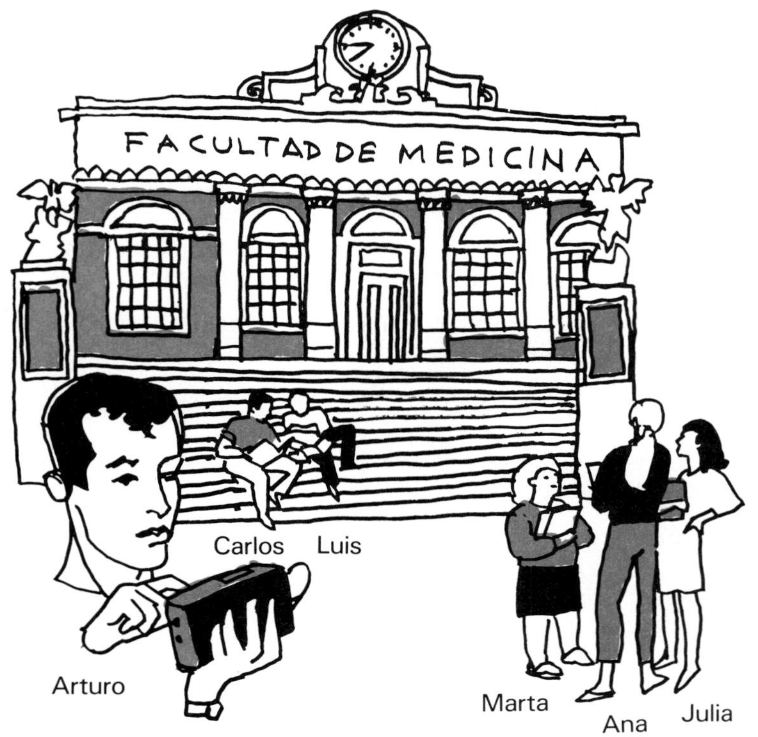

PRONUNCIACIÓN

1. l

At the beginning of a syllable, Spanish **l** and English *l* are pronounced alike. At the end of a syllable, Spanish **l** has, for all practical purposes, the same sound, but the pronunciation of English *l* changes. Compare the following words: **Lucas,** *Lucas;* **hotel,** *hotel.*

lápiz libro mal papel español alto

2. m, n

Spanish and English **m** are pronounced the same way.

mamá malo amable moreno mesa mexicano

At the beginning of a syllable, Spanish and English **n** are pronounced the same way. At the end of a syllable, Spanish **n** may vary according to the next consonant. Before **p, b,** and **v,** Spanish **n** is pronounced like an **m;** before **q, g, k, j, ca, co,** and **cu,** Spanish **n** is pronounced like **ng.**

japonés un bolígrafo un viejo inglés un casete

3. ñ

Spanish **ñ** is similar to the pronunciation of *ni* in the English word *onion* or *ny* in *canyon.*

español señora mañana pequeño tamaño

Un desfile hispano en Texas. La influencia hispana, especialmente mexicana, ha sido muy importante en el Suroeste de los Estados Unidos. En muchas zonas de esta región existen numerosas palabras y costumbres hispanas.

LECTURA

Los estereotipos

Escena 1

Es el primer día de clases y Michael Smith entra en la clase de español. La profesora es de Colombia y Michael espera ver° a una señora morena y baja, pero la señora que está en el salón es una señora alta, delgada y rubia.

espera... *expects to see*

Escena 2

Laura Villegas entra en su clase de inglés. El profesor es de Chicago y Laura espera ver a un señor alto, rubio y de ojos azules. El profesor es bajo, moreno y tiene ojos negros.

Estas dos escenas ocurren con frecuencia, pues los estereotipos son muy comunes cuando pensamos en° las personas de otras culturas. Para muchos norteamericanos, todos° los hispanos tienen ojos negros y son morenos y bajos. Para muchos hispanos, los norteamericanos tienen ojos azules y son altos y rubios. Estos estereotipos no representan la realidad. En los Estados Unidos, Hispanoamérica y España hay muchas personas morenas y bajas, y también hay muchas personas altas y rubias.

pensamos... *we think of*
all

También hay estereotipos relacionados con la comida°. Muchos piensan que todos los hispanos comen° tortillas, tacos y enchiladas, cuando en realidad ésa es sólo una parte de la comida típica de México y no es popular en España y otros países°. Algunos hispanos piensan que todos los norteamericanos comen hamburguesas° y perros calientes° con mucha salsa de tomate°.

food
eat
countries
hamburgers / perros... *hot d*
salsa... *catsup*

Los estereotipos sólo presentan una parte de la realidad. Cuando estudiamos una lengua podemos ir más allá de° estos estereotipos superficiales, ver la realidad total y apreciar y comprender mejor° otra cultura.

ir... *we can go beyond*
comprender... *better understand*

Preguntas

1. Complete los siguientes cuadros (*charts*) de acuerdo con la lectura.

Los hispanos según muchos norteamericanos

tamaño (*size*)	ojos	pelo	comida

Los norteamericanos según muchos hispanos

tamaño	ojos	pelo	comida

2. ¿Cómo son en realidad los hispanos y los norteamericanos?
3. ¿En qué país son populares las tortillas, los tacos y las enchiladas?
4. Según algunos hispanos, ¿qué comen los norteamericanos?
5. ¿Qué pasa (*happens*) cuando estudiamos una lengua?

SITUACIONES

1. You are interviewing applicants for a job in your company. You want to get the following information: name, where they are from, what they are studying, a self-description, and where they work now.

2. Think of a famous person or place. Your partner must ask you up to ten questions to determine who or what it is. You will answer **sí** or **no** until your partner guesses correctly.

3. Describe your room (**cuarto**) to a friend. Tell (a) what color it is, (b) if it is small or big, (c) what you need for it, and (d) what you have in it. Have your friend give you the same information about his/her room. You may need some additional vocabulary: **cama** (*bed*), **mesa de noche** (*nightstand*), **televisor** (*television set*), **radio.**

4. Talk to a classmate about your hometown. Greet him/her by telling your name and where you are from. Then tell as much as you can about the town (size, location, etc.). Your classmate should give you the same type of information about his/her home town.

5. A new student has just joined your class. Ask the student next to you who the new student is. Your classmate should give you as much information as possible about him/her.

6. Go around the room and ask your classmates the following questions. For each question, be sure to get a signature on a separate sheet of paper from all students who answer affirmatively. Create your own question for *f.*

   a. ¿Trabajas en la biblioteca?
   b. ¿Estudias química?
   c. ¿Tienes cuatro clases?
   d. ¿Eres alto/a y amable?
   e. ¿Es Historia Moderna tu clase favorita?
   f. ¿____________________?

7. Tell your friend that there is a party on Saturday. Your friend should (a) find out where the party will take place and (b) the time it will begin.

VOCABULARIO

colores

amarillo *yellow*
anaranjado *orange*
azul *blue*
blanco *white*
café *brown*
castaño *brown*
gris *gray*
morado *purple*
negro *black*
rojo *red*
rosado *pink*
verde *green*

descripción

alegre *happy, glad*
alto *tall, high*
antipático *unpleasant*
bajo *short, low*
bonito *pretty*
buen *good*
callado *quiet*
casado *married*
claro *light*
cómodo *comfortable*
contento *happy, glad*
débil *weak*
delgado *thin*
feliz *happy*
feo *ugly*
fuerte *strong*
gordo *fat*
gran *great*
guapo *good-looking, handsome*
hablador *talkative*
inteligente *intelligent*
joven *young*
listo *smart, ready*
mal *bad*
malo *bad, evil, sick*
moreno *brunet*
nervioso *nervous*
nuevo *new*
oscuro *dark*
perezoso *lazy*
pobre *poor*
rico *rich, wealthy*
rubio *blond*
simpático *nice, charming*
soltero *single*
tonto *silly, foolish*
trabajador *hardworking*
tranquilo *calm, tranquil*
triste *sad*
viejo *old*

el cuerpo *body*

el bigote *moustache*
los ojos *eyes*
el pelo *hair*

en la clase

el compañero/la compañera *classmate*
la nota *grade*

hispanos

argentino *Argentinian*
boliviano *Bolivian*
colombiano *Colombian*
cubano *Cuban*
chileno *Chilean*
mexicano *Mexican*
panameño *Panamanian*
peruano *Peruvian*
puertorriqueño *Puerto Rican*
salvadoreño *Salvadorian*
venezolano *Venezuelan*

vehículos

el auto *car*
el asiento *seat*

verbos

mirar	*to look at*
sacar	*to get*
ser	*to be*
tengo	*I have*
tiene	*he/she has, you have (formal)*
sé	*I know*

palabras interrogativas

cuál/cuáles	*which (one/s)*
cuándo	*when*
cuánto/cuánta	*how much*
de quién/de quiénes	*whose*
por qué	*why*

palabras útiles

allí	*there*
de	*from*
del	(*contraction of* **de** + **el**) *of the*
no... ni	*neither . . . nor*
porque	*because*
que	*that*
seguro	*sure*
sólo	*only*
también	*also, too*

palabras adicionales

verbos

comparta	*share*
describa	*describe*
escoja	*choose*
explique	*explain*

otras palabras

abajo	*below*
arriba	*above*
apropiado	*appropriate*
opuesto	*opposite*
todos	*all*

Los diseños de estos malacates *(clay spindle weights)* precolombinos, encontrados en excavaciones arqueológicas en México, muestran gran imaginación y originalidad.

In Lección 3 **you will**

a. discuss and inquire about daily activities.
b. order food.
c. ask for and give addresses and telephone numbers.
d. count from 100 to 1,000.
e. solve simple problems using those numbers.
f. make suggestions and future plans.

Lugares y actividades

en el estadio

Amelia trota en el estadio de la universidad.
Alberto corre. Él practica para una competencia (*meet*).

Lección 3
Las actividades de los estudiantes

Marta busca un libro en el estante. Manolo saca unos libros para su clase.

en la biblioteca

en una fiesta

Rafael toca la guitarra. Elvira canta una canción (*song*) popular. Unos muchachos y muchachas bailan y otros hablan.

ACTIVIDADES

A **¿Cuántos/as. . . hay en la biblioteca?** Hágales preguntas a sus compañeros/as usando (*using*) las siguientes palabras.

estudiantes computadoras diccionarios libros estantes

B **En la biblioteca.** Usted está en la biblioteca de su universidad. Dígales a sus compañeros/as lo que usted hace en la biblioteca y las cosas que hay allí.

Modelo **Yo saco unos libros de historia. Hay veinte alumnos y dos computadoras.**

C Complete las siguientes oraciones con las palabras a la derecha.

1. Amelia trota en el. . . de la universidad.	entrenador
2. Alberto practica para una. . .	estadio
3. El. . . toma el tiempo con el. . .	competencia
4. Alberto desea ser el. . . nacional.	cronómetro
	campeón

D Usted es un/a corredor/a (*sprinter*). Diga quién es usted y hábleles de su entrenamiento (*training*) a sus compañeros, completando el siguiente párrafo.

Me llamo ____. Practico ____. Mi entrenador/a es muy bueno/a. Se llama ____. Yo ____ todos los días en el ____ de la universidad. Cuando yo practico, mi entrenador/a toma el ____ con el ____. Yo deseo ganar (*win*) la ____ para ser el campeón/la campeona.

E Complete las siguientes oraciones con las palabras a la derecha.

1. Teresa toca la. . .	discos
2. Elvira canta una. . .	guitarra
3. Él. . . está al lado de Elvira.	música moderna
4. Elvira prefiere (*prefers*) la. . .	estéreo
5. Hay tres. . . sobre el estéreo.	canción

F Háblele sobre usted a su compañero/a escogiendo (*choosing*) las palabras apropiadas. Después su compañero/a debe hacer lo mismo (*the same*).

1. Yo (no) toco la guitarra. (el piano, el violín, el saxofón)
2. Yo (no) canto muy bien. (canto mal, canto regular)
3. Yo (no) escucho música moderna. (música clásica, rock)
4. En mi dormitorio (no) hay un estéreo y unos discos. (un radio, una grabadora)
5. En las fiestas yo (no) bailo. (canto, escucho música, hablo mucho)

Cultura

Student life in the Hispanic countries

Although there are similarities between student life in the Hispanic countries and in the United States, there are also differences. Some of the principal ones are in study programs, living arrangements, and social life.

Since very few universities have dormitories, students whose families reside near the university live at home while attending classes. Those who come from other cities or towns normally live in guest houses. Fraternities and sororities are not a part of Hispanic universities. Sports programs, which usually play an important role on campuses in the United States, are not generally included in Hispanic universities. Students who participate in sports do so at clubs and neighborhood parks.

Because there is less emphasis on campus life, students tend to maintain close contact with former friends. And although friendships do develop at the university, the ties to family and old friends remain strong.

In general, students are politically very aware and active, following both national and international events. When students disagree with the conditions at the university or in the country, they organize demonstrations and even strikes.

Cafés are very popular meeting places for people of all ages in Hispanic countries, and those that are close to schools or universities are often filled with students before and after classes. Students may have **café** (strong black coffee similar to *café espresso*), **café con leche** (strong coffee with hot milk), beer, soda, or sandwiches while they sit at a table and socialize with their friends, sometimes for hours on end.

Hispanic students have a great interest in North American culture. Modern American music is very popular, especially at parties and dance clubs. American films and television programs, while also popular, tend to give students a somewhat distorted idea of life in the United States.

Unas estudiantes conversan en una de las zonas verdes de la UNAM en México. El intercambio de ideas con sus compañeros y amigos es un aspecto muy importante en la vida de los estudiantes hispanos.

EN CONTEXTO

En un café

Las chicas están en un café. Nancy lee el menú y Lola y Olga miran a las personas que caminan por la acera. El camarero llega para tomar la orden.

Camarero Buenas tardes, señoritas. ¿Qué desean?
Nancy Para mí, un sándwich de jamón y queso.
Camarero ¿Y para beber?
Nancy Un té, por favor.
Camarero ¿Frío o caliente?
Nancy Frío.
Lola ¿Qué pasteles hay?
Camarero De pollo, de jamón y de manzana.
Lola Un pastel de pollo.
Nancy ¿Y qué tomas?
Lola Un refresco de limón.
Camarero (Escribe la orden.) ¿Y usted, señorita?
Olga Sólo un jugo de naranja.
Lola ¿Sólo un jugo? ¿Por qué no comes algo?
Olga No debo comer. Estoy a dieta.

Para completar

Complete las oraciones con la información que se da en el diálogo.

1. Las chicas están en...
2. Nancy desea un sándwich de jamón y queso y un...
3. En el café hay pasteles de...
4. Lola desea un pastel de...
5. Olga bebe sólo un...
6. Olga no debe comer porque está a...

The girls are at a café. Nancy reads the menu and Lola and Olga are looking at the people walking on the sidewalk. The waiter arrives to take the order.
WAITER: Good morning, ladies. What would you like? NANCY: For me, a ham and cheese sandwich. WAITER: Anything to drink? NANCY: Tea, please. WAITER: Hot or iced tea? NANCY: Iced tea. LOLA: What kind of pies do you have? WAITER: Chicken, ham, and apple. LOLA: Chicken pie. NANCY: And what are you going to drink? LOLA: Lemon soda. WAITER: (Writes the order) And you, Miss? OLGA: Just orange juice. LOLA: Just juice? Why don't you eat something? OLGA: I shouldn't eat. I'm on a diet.

Más comidas y bebidas

ACTIVIDADES

A **¿Qué platos desea?** Escoja un plato de cada grupo y dígale a su compañero/a cuáles son. Después él/ella debe decirle qué platos desea.

1. sopa de tomate, sopa de vegetales, sopa de pollo
2. espaguetis, pollo frito, pescado
3. vegetales, ensalada, pizza
4. helado de chocolate, banana, pastel de manzana

B Usted es el dueño/la dueña de un café. Prepare un menú. Compare su menú con el menú de su compañero/a.

C Usted tiene un amigo/una amiga en su casa. Pregúntele qué desea desayunar.

Modelo **—¿Qué deseas desayunar?** o **—¿Qué deseas para el desayuno?**
—Jugo de naranja, cereal y leche.

D **En el restaurante.**

1. Es la hora del almuerzo. Usted es el camarero/la camarera en un restaurante. Pregúnteles a dos clientes qué desean.
2. Es la hora de la cena. Su compañero/a es el camarero/la camarera y le pregunta qué desea cenar.

Jóvenes mexicanos disfrutando de la música en una discoteca de la ciudad de México. La música moderna es muy popular entre los jóvenes hispanos.

GRAMÁTICA

Present tense of regular *-er* and *-ir* verbs

comer		**vivir** *to live*	
yo	com**o**	yo	viv**o**
tú	com**es**	tú	viv**es**
él, ella, usted	com**e**	él, ella, usted	viv**e**
nosotros/as	com**emos**	nosotros/as	viv**imos**
vosotros/as	com**éis**	vosotros/as	viv**ís**
ellos/as, ustedes	com**en**	ellos/as, ustedes	viv**en**

1. The endings for **-er** and **-ir** verbs are the same, except for the **nosotros** and **vosotros** forms.
2. Some common **-er** and **-ir** verbs are **leer, deber, beber, correr, vender** (*to sell*), **escribir, abrir** (*to open*).
3. The verb **ver** (*to see*) has an irregular **yo** form.

   ver: **veo,** ves, ve, vemos, veis, ven

ACTIVIDADES

A ¿Qué no debe hacer (*do*) usted en los siguientes lugares?

1. En un café: hablar / correr / beber un refresco
2. En un gimnasio: trotar / tomar ron / practicar con el entrenador
3. En una discoteca: ver televisión / bailar / escuchar música
4. En una fiesta: tocar la guitarra / cantar / escribir
5. En la biblioteca: comer / buscar un libro / estudiar

B **Lugares y actividades.** ¿Qué hace usted en estos lugares? ¿Y otras personas?

en el dormitorio   en un restaurante   en el estadio   en el laboratorio
en la clase   en la librería

C Cambie (*Change*) el sujeto (*subject*) de cada párrafo por el sujeto entre paréntesis. Haga los cambios necesarios.

1. (**Yo**) María es una chica muy activa. Ella corre por la mañana. Después bebe un jugo, come cereal y toma una taza (*cup*) de café.
2. (**Ellos**) Ernesto es un chico liberado. Según Ernesto, los hombres deben trabajar en la casa. Por eso él limpia (*cleans*) la casa también.
3. (**Nosotros**) Marisel trabaja en un salón de belleza (*beauty parlor*). Ella vende cosméticos. Los viernes ella está en el salón a las ocho y media porque ese día hay muchos clientes.
4. (**Miriam**) Por la noche yo estudio, hablo por teléfono y veo televisión. A las diez y media, más o menos, bebo un vaso (*glass*) de leche con unas galletitas (*cookies*). Después leo un buen libro o escucho las noticias (*news*).

D Su compañero/a está a dieta. Dígale lo que debe y no debe comer o beber.

Modelo **Debes comer ensaladas. No debes beber refrescos.**

E Usted es un alumno/una alumna nuevo/a en la universidad y le hace las siguientes preguntas a otro/a alumno/a.

1. ¿Vives en el dormitorio?
2. ¿Trotas en el gimnasio?
3. ¿A qué hora abren el gimnasio?
4. ¿Desayunas en la cafetería?
5. ¿A qué hora abren la cafetería?

F Hágale a su compañero/a las siguientes preguntas. Después comparta la información con la clase.

1. ¿Cuántos libros lees al mes?
2. ¿Cuántos libros debe leer una persona?
3. ¿Cuál es tu libro preferido?
4. ¿Lees revistas (*magazines*) o periódicos (*newspapers*)? ¿Cuáles?

EN CONTEXTO

En la Facultad de Ciencias

Sara	¿Cuál es la dirección° de Marta?	*address*
Dulce	Creo° que vive en la calle° Manzanares, número 425.	*I believe / street*
Sara	Debo ir° a su casa después a repasar° álgebra para el examen del jueves.	*go / review*
Miriam	Yo también necesito repasar.	
Dulce	Pues ven° con nosotras.	*come*
Miriam	Está bien, pero debemos llamar por teléfono antes de ir.	
Sara	Sí, yo llamo ahora°. ¿Cuál es su número de teléfono?	*now*
Dulce	Es el 544-3318.	

Para completar

Complete las siguientes oraciones con la información que se da en el diálogo.

1. La dirección de Marta es...
2. Sara debe ir a casa de Marta a...
3. El examen de álgebra es...
4. Antes de ir las chicas deben...
5. El número de teléfono de Marta es el...

GRAMÁTICA

Numbers 100 to 1,000

100	cien/ciento	400	cuatrocientos/as	800	ochocientos/as
101	ciento uno	500	quinientos/as	900	novecientos/as
200	doscientos/as	600	seiscientos/as	1.000	mil
300	trescientos/as	700	setecientos/as		

Una manifestación estudiantil en Madrid, España. Muchas veces los estudiantes protestan o expresan sus opiniones por medio de una manifestación.

1. Spanish uses **cien/ciento** to say 100.
2. Use **cien** when no other number follows 100.

100 chicos	cien chicos
100 chicas	cien chicas

3. Use **ciento** with numbers from 101 to 199.

105 profesores	ciento cinco profesores
120 profesoras	ciento veinte profesoras.

4. **Uno** becomes **un** before a masculine noun and **una** before a feminine noun.

131 entrenadores	ciento treinta y un entrenadores
131 entrenadoras	ciento treinta y una entrenadoras

5. The numbers 200 through 900 agree in gender with the noun they modify.

200 escritorios	doscientos escritorios
200 sillas	doscientas sillas

6. Spanish normally uses a period instead of a comma when writing one thousand (**1.000**) and numbers greater than one thousand.

ACTIVIDADES

A Su profesor/a va a leer un número de cada grupo. Indique cuál es el número.

114 360 850 524 — 667 777 984 534
213 330 919 490 — 215 550 260 620
818 414 723 514 — 490 650 770 1.000

B Lea los siguientes números.

181 347 238 673 879 591 435 221 115 913 1.000 799

C Lea los siguientes números y palabras.

939 discos	486 estantes	71 camareras
765 grabadoras	870 entrenadores	627 pollos
693 canciones	621 cronómetros	1.000 casas
379 guitarras	538 pasteles	789 refrescos

D Lea los problemas siguientes y dé el resultado.

437	731	893	237
+ 83	+ 72	+ 15	+863

E Pregúntele a un/a compañero/a su (a) dirección (b) número de teléfono. Comparta esta información con la clase.

F **¿Cuánto cuesta(n). . . ?** Pregúntele a su compañero/a cuánto cuestan los siguientes objetos.

G Ésta es una información que generalmente se pide (*is requested*) en una entrevista. Use el siguiente diálogo como modelo para entrevistar a su compañero/a.

Entrevistador/a Su nombre, por favor.
Compañero/a . . .
Entrevistador/a ¿Estado civil (*marital status*)?
Compañero/a . . .
Entrevistador/a ¿Cuál es su dirección?
Compañero/a . . .
Entrevistador/a ¿Cuál es su número de teléfono?
Compañero/a . . .

EN CONTEXTO

La agenda de Laura

lunes	martes	miércoles	jueves	viernes	sábado	domingo
6	7	8	9	10	11	12
biblioteca 8:30 A.M. examen 5:00 P.M.	llamar a María 9:00 A.M. trabajar librería 4:00 P.M	terminar° proyecto 10: A.M. programa televisión 7:00 P.M.	estudiar en casa de Teté A.M. película° T.V. 10:00 P.M.	ir al° laboratorio 8:00 A.M. fiesta de Pablo 9:00 P.M.	ir a la playa° 11:00 A.M.	iglesia° 11:00 A.M. café 1:00 P.M. cine° 5:00 P.M.

finish *movie* *go to the* *beach* *church* *movies*

ACTIVIDADES

A Complete las siguientes oraciones según la agenda de Laura.

Modelo El día 7 por la mañana Laura va a (*is going to*) **llamar a María.**

1. El día 7 por la tarde Laura va a. . .
2. El día 8 por la mañana Laura va a. . .
3. El día 9 por la mañana Laura va a. . .
4. El día 11 Laura va a. . .

B Conteste las siguientes preguntas sobre las actividades de Laura.

1. ¿Qué día va a ir Laura a la biblioteca? ¿A qué hora? ¿Qué tiene Laura por la tarde?
2. ¿Con quién va a estudiar Laura? ¿Qué día?
3. ¿Qué va a hacer Laura el día 10?
4. ¿Dónde va a estar Laura el sábado?
5. ¿Cuándo va a ir Laura a la iglesia? ¿A qué hora?
6. ¿Qué días va a mirar televisión?

GRAMÁTICA

Present tense of *ir*

ir *to go*

yo	voy	nosotros/as	vamos
tú	vas	vosotros/as	vais
él, ella, usted	va	ellos/as, ustedes	van

1. Use **a** to introduce a noun after the verb **ir.** Whenever **a** is followed by the article **el,** they contract to form **al.**

Voy **a la** fiesta de María. *I'm going to Maria's party.*
Vamos **al** gimnasio. *We're going to the gymnasium.*

2. Use **adónde** when asking a question with the verb **ir.**

¿**Adónde** vas? *Where are you going?*

Some ways to express the future: present; *ir* + *a* + infinitive

1. To express future time use the present tense of **ir** + **a** + infinitive.

Ellos van a correr después. *They're going to run later.*
¿Vas a ir a la fiesta? *Are you going to go to the party?*

Unos estudiantes conversan y toman unos refrescos en un café de la Plaza Mayor de Madrid. Los cafés constituyen un aspecto muy importante en la vida social de muchos hispanos.

2. You may also express future time by using the present tense of the verb, especially when referring to a not too distant future. The context shows whether you are referring to the future or to the present time.

Vamos mañana.	*We're going tomorrow.*
¿Estudiamos esta noche?	*Are we going to study tonight?*

3. Some additional expressions that denote future time are

pasado mañana	*the day after tomorrow*
la semana próxima	*next week*
el mes próximo	*next month*
el año próximo	*next year*
el próximo fin de semana	*next weekend*

ACTIVIDADES

A Diga que usted va a hacer lo siguiente.

Modelo ver televisión / esta noche
Voy a ver televisión esta noche.

1. ir al café / esta tarde
2. hablar con mis amigos / el fin de semana
3. terminar la tarea / después
4. comer pescado / mañana
5. estudiar / pasado mañana
6. bailar / esta noche

B Hay un examen de español mañana. Diga las cosas que van a hacer los estudiantes antes del examen.

C Su amigo y usted van a ir a su restaurante favorito esta noche. Diga qué van a comer y beber.

D Yolanda desea perder peso (*lose weight*). Diga qué va a hacer Yolanda.

E Los dibujos muestran lo que Maribel va a hacer el próximo sábado. Diga lo que ella va a hacer y después diga lo que usted va a hacer.

F **Entrevista.** Pregúntele a su compañero/a sobre sus próximas vacaciones. Use las siguientes preguntas.

1. ¿Adónde vas a ir? 2. ¿Con quién vas a ir? 3. ¿Cuántos días vas a estar allí? 4. ¿Cuándo vas a ir? 5. ¿Qué lugares vas a visitar? 6. ¿A quién vas a visitar? 7. ¿Qué vas a comer y beber?

PRONUNCIACIÓN

1. ll, y

In most parts of the Spanish-speaking world, **y** and **ll** are pronounced like English *y* in the word *yoke,* but with more friction. At the end of a word, **y** sounds very similar to **i,** but if the next word begins with a vowel, **y** is pronounced like English *y* in *yoke.*

yo   llamo   ella   estoy   muy bien   muy alto   voy allí

2. x

Before a consonant, **x** is pronounced in Spanish as **s** or **ks.**

experiencia   explicación   experimento   texto   extensión

Between vowels, **x** is pronounced like English *ks* or Spanish **gs.** It is never pronounced like English *x.*

examen   sexo   existir   exacto   éxito

LECTURA

These suggestions for a successful party were taken from *Coqueta*, a Mexican magazine for young people. You may need the following words to understand the chart better.

exitosa	*successful*	las verduras	*vegetables*	la limpieza	*cleaning*
elegir	*to choose*	colocar	*to put*		
la bandeja	*tray*	el vaso	*glass*		

¿Vas a dar una fiesta?

PLANIFICACION

El plan maestro: El secreto para planificar una fiesta exitosa es: ¡organización!

<table>
<tr><th></th><th>2 DIAS ANTES</th><th>1 DIA ANTES</th><th>EL DIA DE LA FIESTA</th><th>DESPUES DE LA FIESTA</th></tr>
<tr><td>VIVIAN</td><td rowspan="2">Comprar la comida.</td><td rowspan="2">Preparar la bandeja de verduras, pastas, tortas, etc.</td><td rowspan="2">Colocar la comida en la mesa y hacer el ponche.</td><td rowspan="4">LIMPIEZA</td></tr>
<tr><td>MELISSA</td></tr>
<tr><td>MARTA</td><td>Decorar la casa.</td><td rowspan="2">Preparar ensaladas de pollo o papas, la bandeja de quesos, etc.</td><td>Preparar los platos, vasos, etc.</td></tr>
<tr><td>NELSON</td><td>Elegir la música y buscar el estéreo.</td><td>Hacer de disc jockey (DJ)</td></tr>
</table>

¡Vámonos de fiesta!

Preguntas

1. ¿Qué deben hacer Vivian y Melissa dos días antes?
2. ¿Quién está a cargo del estéreo?
3. ¿Cuándo deben preparar las ensaladas?
4. ¿Quiénes están a cargo de las ensaladas?

5. ¿Qué clases de ensalada van a preparar?
6. ¿Qué van a hacer Vivian y Melissa un día antes de la fiesta?
7. ¿Cuándo van a hacer el ponche?
8. ¿Qué van a hacer todos después de la fiesta?

Los viajes° de estudio

trips

Una de las actividades más interesantes y populares entre los estudiantes de muchas universidades españolas es el viaje de estudio, que generalmente se organiza en el tercer año de la carrera.

Algunos de los estudiantes del curso son las personas que están a cargo de la organización del viaje. Estos estudiantes deben averiguar° los precios de los boletos°, excursiones, hoteles y hostales, el itinerario, etc. Además es necesario conseguir° precios bajos pues los jóvenes no pueden gastar° mucho.

Para cubrir los gastos° del viaje los alumnos venden durante todo el curso boletos para rifas°, bolígrafos, dulces° típicos, camisetas°, etc. a amigos y parientes°. También organizan fiestas y venden las entradas°. De esta forma cada alumno puede ahorrar° durante varios meses el dinero° que va a necesitar para el viaje.

Para los estudiantes, el viaje de estudio es una oportunidad excelente para estar con buenos amigos y divertirse°, y también para visitar otro país, aprender° cosas nuevas y estar en contacto con otra cultura.

find out
tickets
to get / no... *cannot spend*
Para... *To cover the expenses*
raffles / *sweets* / *T-shirts*
relatives / *tickets*
save / *money*
have a good time / *learn*

¿Verdadero o falso?

Diga si las siguientes oraciones son verdaderas o falsas de acuerdo con la lectura.

1. Los alumnos hacen el viaje de estudio en el primer año.
2. Los profesores organizan el viaje.
3. Los estudiantes venden diferentes artículos para conseguir dinero para el viaje.
4. Sólo van al viaje los alumnos que sacan buenas notas.
5. En el viaje de estudio los estudiantes aprenden y también se divierten.

Unos alumnos en un viaje de estudio en las Islas Canarias. Estas islas españolas, situadas muy cerca de la costa oeste del Africa, ofrecen una variedad extraordinaria de paisajes.

SITUACIONES

1. You are a waiter/waitress at a café. Two of your classmates will play the part of the customers. Greet your customers and ask what they would like to eat and drink. Be prepared to answer any questions they may have.
2. You have ordered soup at a restaurant, but it is cold. Call the waiter and explain that the soup is cold. The waiter should apologize.
3. One of your friends is asking for your advice. He/She wants to be in shape for a track meet. Tell him/her what to do.
4. Itemize your expenses for next week. You are going to do the following: go to the movies, spend the day at the beach, eat at a restaurant, and go dancing. Tell your partner how much you are going to spend (**gastar**) for each of the things you plan to do.
5. Your friend is planning to go to a concert. Find out where and when the concert is, who is going to sing, and who is going to play the guitar. Then tell your classmates what you found out.
6. Tell your partner about your plans for tonight. Tell him/her (a) where you are planning to go, (b) with whom, and (c) what you are planning to do. Inquire about his/her plans.
7. Think about the great weekend you are going to have. Tell your partner about it.

Una joven trota en un parque de Santiago de Chile para mantenerse en buenas condiciones físicas.

Un coro de estudiantes practica en la Universidad de Guadalajara en México.

VOCABULARIO[1]

comunicación

el teléfono *telephone*
la televisión *television*

deportes *sports*

la competencia *meet*
el cronómetro *stop watch*

direcciones *addresses*

la calle *street*
el número *number*

diversiones *entertainment*

la canción *song*
el disco *record*
el estéreo *stereo*
la fiesta *party*
la guitarra *guitar*
la película *film*
el programa *program*

lugares

la acera *sidewalk*
el café *café*
la casa *house*
el cine *movies*
el estadio *stadium*
la iglesia *church*
la playa *beach*

[1] See page 90 for numbers 100–1,000.

muebles | *furniture*
el estante | *bookshelf*

personas
el camarero/la camarera | *waiter/waitress*
el entrenador/la entrenadora | *trainer, coach*

en un café o restaurante
el almuerzo | *lunch*
el arroz | *rice*
el atún | *tuna*
el café | *coffee*
la cena | *dinner, supper*
el cereal | *cereal*
la comida | *dinner, supper, food*
el desayuno | *breakfast*
la ensalada | *salad*
la fruta | *fruit*
la hamburguesa | *hamburger*
el helado | *ice cream*
el huevo | *egg*
el jamón | *ham*
el jugo | *juice*
la leche | *milk*
la lechuga | *lettuce*
el limón | *lemon*
la manzana | *apple*
el menú | *menu*
la naranja | *orange*
la orden | *order*
el pan | *bread*
  el pan tostado | *toast*
la papa | *potato*
  las papas fritas | *French fries*
el pastel | *pie*
el pescado | *fish*
el pollo | *chicken*
el queso | *cheese*
el refresco | *soda*
el sándwich | *sandwich*
la sopa | *soup*
el té | *tea*
el tomate | *tomato*
la tostada | *toast*
el vegetal | *vegetable*

descripción
caliente | *hot*
frío | *cold*
frito | *fried*

las clases
la agenda | *agenda, calendar*
el álgebra | *algebra*
el examen | *examination*
el proyecto | *project*

verbos
abrir | *to open*
bailar | *to dance*
beber | *to drink*
caminar | *to walk*
cantar | *to sing*
comer | *to eat*
correr | *to run*
creer | *to believe, to think*
deber | *should, ought to*
escribir | *to write*
ir | *to go*
leer | *to read*
llamar | *to call*
llegar | *to arrive*
repasar | *to review*
sacar | *to check out, to take out*
terminar | *to finish*
tocar | *to play, to touch*
tomar | *to drink, to take*
trotar | *to jog*
vender | *to sell*
ver | *to see*
vivir | *to live*

tiempo

ahora — *now*
antes — *before*
el año próximo — *next year*
después — *after*
el fin de semana — *weekend*
mañana — *tomorrow*
pasado mañana — *the day after tomorrow*

palabras útiles

al — (*contraction of* **a** + **el**) *to the*

expresiones útiles

algo — *something*
estar a dieta — *to be on a diet*
ven — *come*

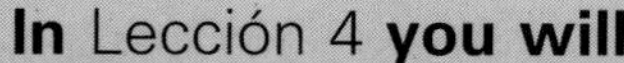

In Lección 4 **you will**

a. identify and describe family members.
b. describe physical and emotional states.
c. provide information about a person's age and abilities.
d. ask about and express ownership.
e. express preferences and desires.

Lección 4

La familia

La familia de Eduardo

Eduardo es el hijo de María y Jaime. Él es el nieto de don José y doña Olga, y es el sobrino de Jorge, Elena, Rita y Juan.

ACTIVIDADES

A Complete las siguientes oraciones de acuerdo con el árbol genealógico (*family tree*) de Eduardo.

1. La hermana de Eduardo se llama ___.
2. Don José y doña Olga son los ___ de Eduardo. Ellos tienen ___ hijas y ___ hijo.
3. Eduardo es el ___ de Jaime.
4. Jaime es el ___ de Eduardo, y María es la ___.
5. Juanito y Eduardo son ___.
6. Inés y Ana son ___.
7. Don José y doña Olga tienen ___ nietos y ___ nietas.
8. Eduardo es el ___ de Juan y Rita.
9. Inés es la ___ de Jorge y Elena.
10. María y Jaime son los ___ de Elenita.

B Escoja una persona de la familia de Eduardo. Su compañero/a debe decir cuál es su parentesco (*family relationship*) con Eduardo.

Modelo **—¿Quién es Ana?**
—Es la prima de Eduardo.

más parientes

el cuñado	*brother-in-law*
la cuñada	*sister-in-law*
el suegro	*father-in-law*
la suegra	*mother-in-law*
el yerno	*son-in-law*
la nuera	*daughter-in-law*

Un reunión familiar de varias generaciones en Bogotá, Colombia.

otras relaciones	*other relationships*
el esposo, el marido	*husband*
la esposa, la mujer	*wife*
el novio	*fiancé, boyfriend*
la novia	*fiancée, girlfriend*
el ahijado	*godson*
la ahijada	*goddaughter*
el padrino	*godfather*
la madrina	*godmother*

ACTIVIDADES

A Asocie los parientes de la columna de la izquierda con los de la columna de la derecha.

1. nieto	a. hijo
2. padrino	b. tío
3. madre	c. abuela
4. marido	d. ahijado
5. sobrina	e. suegro
6. nuera	f. esposa

B Complete las siguientes oraciones con la palabra apropiada.

1. La esposa de mi hijo es mi...
2. El hermano de mi esposo/a es mi...
3. La madre de mi esposo/a es mi...
4. Los hijos de mis hijos son mis...
5. Yo soy la madrina/el padrino de Roberto. Él es mi...

C **¿Quién es?** Describa a un miembro de su familia. Su compañero debe identificar a ese pariente.

Modelo **—No es muy vieja. Es la hermana de mi padre.**
—Es tu tía.

D **Entrevista.** Hágale las siguientes preguntas sobre su familia a su compañero/a. Él/ella le debe hacer las mismas preguntas a usted.

1. ¿Vives con tu familia?
2. ¿Cuántas personas hay en tu familia?
3. ¿Cuántos hermanos tienes? ¿Cómo se llaman?
4. ¿Cuántos tíos tienes? ¿Dónde viven?
5. ¿Tienes muchos primos?
6. ¿Cómo se llama tu primo/a favorito/a?

Cultura

Families in the Hispanic world

In the Hispanic world, the word **familia** generally refers not only to one's mother, father, and children but to other relatives as well. It is not unusual to have three generations living in the same house, and it is instilled in children at an early age that they should respect and help the elderly. Because Hispanic societies do not have the mobility that characterizes American society, most families tend to remain in the same city or town, maintaining close ties with one another.

However, industrialization and urbanization have had their effects on Hispanic societies, too. As they come of age, many young people leave small towns, hoping to find better-paying jobs in cities or in other countries. More women have entered the work force, and smaller families with one or two children are becoming common, especially in urban centers.

In Hispanic countries people use two last names (**apellidos**) following their given name. A person's first surname is the father's last name, and the second is the mother's maiden name. For example, if you see the name **Jorge Fernández Campos,** you know that **Fernández** is the first surname of Jorge's father and **Campos** is the first surname of Jorge's mother. Sometimes **y** is used between the two last names: **Jorge Fernández y Campos.** A married woman generally retains her maiden name followed by **de** and her husband's surname. Mrs. Fernández (Jorge's mother) would be known as **María Campos de Fernández** or **señora de Fernández.** Nevertheless, in legal documents, she would not use her husband's last name but her own.

Dos madres con sus hijos en el parque del Buen Retiro en Madrid. Este parque, conocido generalmente como el Retiro, es muy popular entre las familias madrileñas.

EN CONTEXTO

Las vacaciones de la familia Villegas

El Sr. Villegas quiere° visitar la ciudad de México donde tiene unos parientes. La Sra. de Villegas quiere visitar Guadalajara, pero los hijos prefieren ir a la playa. Joaquín quiere ir a Acapulco pues unos amigos van a pasar° sus vacaciones allí. Beatriz prefiere ir a Cancún. Ella lee muchos artículos sobre viajes en las revistas° y los periódicos°, y según estos artículos Cancún es un lugar maravilloso.

Además hay otro problema para este viaje: el perro y la gata de la familia. Según los padres, Sansón puede° ir a una guardería de perros° y Fifí a casa de la abuela. Joaquín prefiere dejar° el perro con su abuela. La Sra. Villegas piensa° que su madre está muy vieja para cuidar° dos animales y que Sansón va a estar muy bien en la guardería.

Las vacaciones de los Villegas empiezan° la semana próxima. ¿Adónde cree usted que van a ir? ¿Dónde van a dejar los animales?

wants
spend
magazines / newspapers
can / guardería... *kennel*
leave / thinks
take care of
begin

Para completar

Complete las siguientes oraciones sobre los Villegas.

1. El padre quiere ir a...
2. La madre prefiere ir a...
3. Acapulco es la ciudad que prefiere...
4. El hijo quiere visitar...
5. Fifí es...
6. Sansón es...

Una familia hispana en los Estados Unidos disfruta de una tarde al aire libre. Las familias hispanas tratan de mantener muchas de las costumbres y tradiciones de su país de origen.

GRAMÁTICA

Present tense of *e* ⟶ *ie* and *o* ⟶ *ue* stem-changing verbs

pensar *to think*		**volver** *to return*	
yo	**pie**nso	yo	**vue**lvo
tú	**pie**nsas	tú	**vue**lves
él, ella, usted	**pie**nsa	él, ella, usted	**vue**lve
nosotros/as	pensamos	nosotros/as	volvemos
vosotros/as	pensáis	vosotros/as	volvéis
ellos/as, ustedes	**pie**nsan	ellos/as, ustedes	**vue**lven

1. These verbs change the stem vowel **e** to **ie** and **o** to **ue** except in the **nosotros** and **vosotros** forms.
2. Other common verbs and their vowel changes are[1]

e ⟶ ie		**o ⟶ ue**	
empezar	*to begin*	almorzar	*to have lunch*
perder	*to lose*	contar	*to count*
preferir	*to prefer*	costar	*to cost*
querer	*to want, to love*	dormir	*to sleep*
		poder	*to be able to, can*

[1] Stem-changing verbs will be identified in vocabularies with **ie** or **ue** in parentheses: e.g., **pensar (ie); volver (ue).**

3. **Tener** (*to have*) and **venir** (*to come*), in addition to changing **e** ⟶ **ie,** have a completely irregular **yo** form.
   tener: ten**g**o, t**ie**nes, t**ie**ne, tenemos, tenéis, t**ie**nen
   venir: ven**g**o, v**ie**nes, v**ie**ne, venimos, venís, v**ie**nen
4. When the verb **pensar** is followed by an infinitive, it means *to plan to.*
   ¿Adónde **piensas ir** mañana? *Where are you planning to go tomorrow?*
5. The verb **jugar** (*to play—a game or a sport*) has the change **u** ⟶ **ue.**
   Mario j**ue**ga muy bien, pero nosotros jugamos regular.

ACTIVIDADES

A Diga a qué hora empiezan y a qué hora terminan las siguientes actividades.

Modelo las clases
Las clases empiezan a las ocho. Terminan a las cuatro.

1. la clase de español
2. la música en una discoteca
3. las noticias (*news*)
4. su programa favorito de televisión
5. los juegos de béisbol (*baseball games*)

B Las personas prefieren diferentes actividades. Diga lo que las siguientes personas prefieren hacer de acuerdo con el dibujo.

Modelo **María**
María prefiere correr.

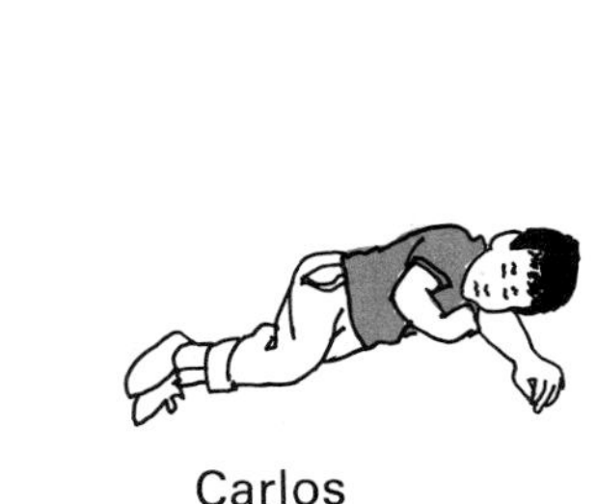

Carlos

el Sr. Pérez

Pablo Alberto

Marisa

nosotros

yo

C Usted es un hombre/una mujer de negocios (*businessman/woman*) que hace las siguientes transacciones. Diga si (*if*) usted gana (*make money*) o pierde.

Modelos Compro un estéreo por $100. Vendo el estéreo por $150.
Gano $50.
Compro un radio por $250. Vendo el radio por $220.
Pierdo $30.

1. Compro un teléfono por $60. Vendo el teléfono por $40.
2. Compro un diccionario por $30. Vendo el diccionario por $60.
3. Compro una computadora por $850. Vendo la computadora por $1000.
4. Compro 50 casetes por $200. Vendo los casetes por $160.

D ¿Qué cree usted que piensan hacer las siguientes personas?

Modelo María desea estar delgada.
María piensa correr mucho, o **estar a dieta,** o **comer poco.**

1. Alberto tiene un examen mañana.
2. Mi tía está muy enferma.
3. Mis primos están de vacaciones.
4. Nosotros queremos ver una película española.
5. Yo voy a ir a México.

E Hágale las siguientes preguntas a su compañero/a. Después comparta esta información con la clase.

1. ¿A qué hora almuerzas? ¿Con quién? ¿Dónde? 2. ¿Qué prefieres almorzar? 3. ¿Qué bebes a la hora del almuerzo? 4. ¿Duermes la siesta (*Do you take a nap*) después del almuerzo?

F Usted organiza una fiesta para celebrar el cumpleaños (*birthday*) de su hermano. Conteste las preguntas que él le hace sobre la fiesta.

1. ¿Cuántas personas vienen? 2. ¿A qué hora van a venir? 3. ¿Viene Arturo? ¿Y Ángeles y Rosa? 4. ¿Quién no puede venir? 5. ¿Qué discos tienes para la fiesta?

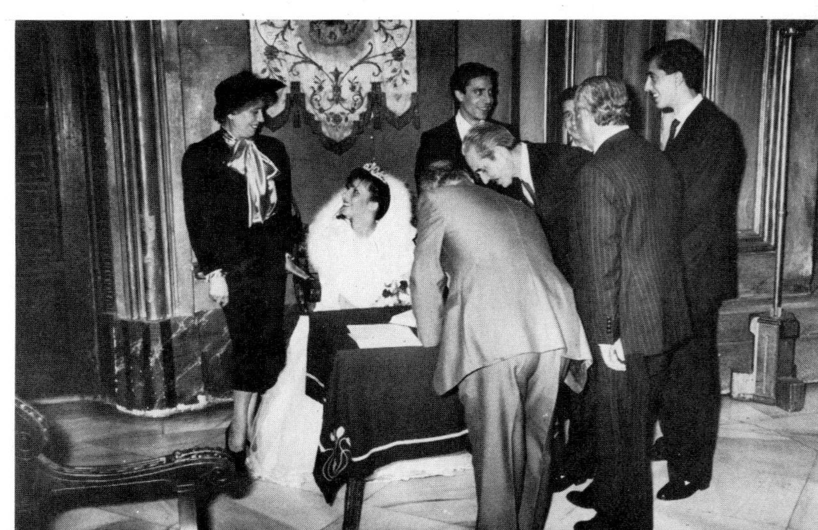

Una boda en Madrid. En los países hispanos es muy común que los amigos íntimos de las dos familias firmen como testigos (*sign as witnesses*) en la ceremonia.

EN CONTEXTO

¿Qué tienen estas personas?

Pablo tiene frío.

Carlos tiene hambre.

Pilar tiene calor.

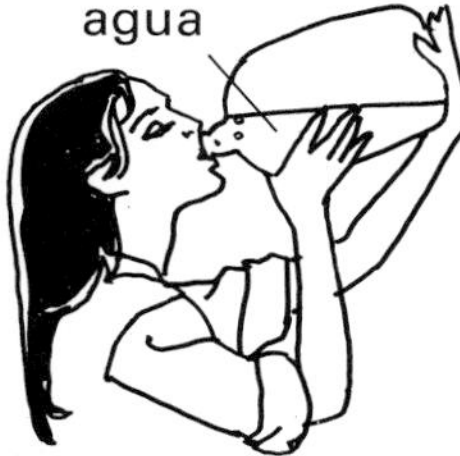

Susana tiene mucha sed.

El bebé tiene mucho sueño.

Eugenio tiene miedo.

GRAMÁTICA

Special expressions with tener

Spanish uses **tener** + noun in many cases where English uses *to be* + adjective. These expressions always refer to people or animals and never to things.

tener	*to be*
hambre	*hungry*
sed	*thirsty*
sueño	*sleepy*
miedo	*afraid*
calor	*hot*
frío	*cold*
suerte	*lucky*
razón	*right*
cuidado	*careful*
prisa	*in a hurry*

1. Use **mucho/mucha** for *very* with these expressions.

   Tengo **mucho** miedo. Tienen **mucha** hambre.

2. **Estar equivocado/a** means *to be wrong.*

   Juana **está equivocada.** Los Villegas no vuelven mañana. *Juana is wrong. The Villegas are not coming back tomorrow.*

3. Use **tener... años** *to be . . . years old* to express age.

   Jorge **tiene 21 años.** *Jorge is twenty-one years old.*

4. Use **tener ganas de** + infinitive to express that you feel like doing or are eager to do something.

   Tengo ganas de ir al cine. *I feel like going to the movies.*

5. Use **tener** + **que** + infinitive to express obligation.

   Tengo que repasar para el examen. *I have to review for the test.*

ACTIVIDADES

A Escoja la expresión correcta de acuerdo con la situación.

1. Mario va a comer mucho. Tiene sed. / Tiene miedo. / Tiene sueño. / Tiene hambre.
2. Asunción va a dormir 10 horas. Tiene calor. / Tiene cuidado. / Tiene prisa. / Tiene sueño.
3. Ellos van a tomar 6 refrescos. Tienen razón. / Tienen sed. / Tienen frío. / Tienen miedo.
4. Yo necesito llegar a la clase a las ocho. Tengo prisa. / Tengo suerte. / Tengo 20 años. / Tengo frío.

B Complete las siguientes oraciones con la expresión apropiada con **tener.**

1. Si no comemos bastante, después vamos a...
2. La película empieza a las 9:00 y son las 8:55. Por eso Juan...
3. En el desierto los turistas..., pero en el Polo Norte...
4. El león es muy valiente; nunca (*never*)...
5. Son las dos de la mañana y nosotros...
6. Necesito beber agua porque...
7. Cuando Luis juega a la lotería siempre gana; él...

C **Entrevista.** Use las siguientes preguntas para entrevistar a un/a compañero/a. Después comparta esta información con la clase.

1. ¿Cuántos años tienes? 2. ¿Tienes hermanos o hermanas? ¿Cuántos años tienen? 3. ¿Qué comes cuando tienes hambre? 4. ¿Qué prefieres tomar cuando tienes sed?

La abuela mira los trabajos que sus nietos hacen en la escuela. Las horas de las comidas les ofrecen a las familias la oportunidad de reunirse y conversar.

D La familia Menéndez quiere lograr (*achieve*) ciertas cosas. Diga lo que tienen que hacer.

Modelo Magdalena quiere hablar francés muy bien.
Ella tiene que estudiar mucho o **Tiene que practicar más** o **Tiene que vivir un año en Francia.**

1. El padre quiere estar más delgado.
2. La madre quiere ver la película *Carmen*.
3. Los primos necesitan unos libros.
4. El tío Paco quiere ser doctor en medicina.
5. Amparo quiere jugar (al) tenis muy bien.

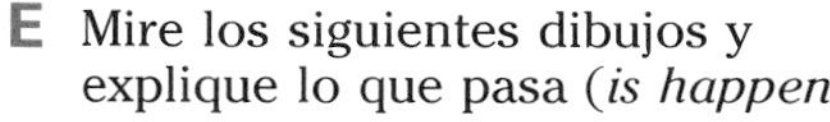

E Mire los siguientes dibujos y explique lo que pasa (*is happening*).

F **Entrevista.** Usted quiere saber lo que su compañero/a tiene que hacer esta noche (o mañana, o el próximo fin de semana) y lo que tiene ganas de hacer. Hágale las siguientes preguntas y comparta la información con la clase.

Usted ¿Qué tienes que hacer ____?
Compañero/a . . .
Usted ¿Y qué tienes ganas de hacer?
Compañero/a . . .

EN CONTEXTO

Una conversación entre dos niños

Para completar

Complete el siguiente cuadro según la conversación de los dos niños.

Opiniones diferentes

Según Lucila	Según Cuquito
su mamá es...	su mamá es...
su papá es...	su papá es...
sus hermanos son...	sus hermanos son...
su familia es...	su familia es...
Cuquito es...	

Mis opiniones

Lucila es una niña...
Cuquito es un niño...
Yo prefiero a... porque...

GRAMÁTICA

Possessive adjectives

mi, mis	*my*
tu, tus	*your*
su, sus	*his, her, its, your (formal), their*
nuestro(-s), nuestra(-s)	*our*
vuestro(-s), vuestra(-s)	*your (familiar plural)*

1. These possessive adjectives always precede the noun they modify.

mi mamá **tu** hermana

2. Possessive adjectives change number (and gender in the case of **nuestro** and **vuestro**) to agree with *the thing possessed,* not with the possessor.

mi casa, **mis** casas
nuestro padre, **nuestros** padres, **nuestra** familia, **nuestras** primas

3. **Su, sus** has multiple meanings. To ensure clarity, you can use **de** + the name of the possessor, or the appropriate pronoun, instead of the possessive adjective.

possible meanings

su madre {
la madre de ella (la madre de Elena)
la madre de él (la madre de Jorge)
la madre de usted
la madre de ustedes
la madre de ellos (la madre de Elena y Jorge)
la madre de ellas (la madre de Elena y Olga)

ACTIVIDADES

A Lea los siguientes párrafos usando los adjetivos posesivos correspondientes a las palabras subrayadas (*underlined*).

1. Roberto vive con ____ padres en la ciudad de México. De lunes a viernes él trabaja con ____ tío Miguel por las mañanas y por las tardes estudia en la universidad. Marisa, la novia de Roberto, vive en Cuernavaca y los fines de semana Roberto va a casa de ____ futuros suegros para visitar a ____ novia. Él piensa terminar ____ estudios el año próximo y buscar trabajo en Cuernavaca. El tío está muy contento con el trabajo de ____ sobrino y cree que ____ futuro está en la ciudad de México y no en Cuernavaca.

2. Diego y Alfredo viven en los Ángeles. ___ familia es mexicana y ellos hablan español con ___ padres, tíos y primos; pero Diego y Alfredo quieren vivir un tiempo en un país hispano. ___ abuelos viven en Mérida, la capital de Yucatán. Ellos van a hablar por teléfono con ___ abuelos para ver si pueden visitar Yucatán y estar en ___ casa durante dos meses.

3. Mi hermano y yo pensamos visitar Guadalajara el mes próximo. ___ compañero Félix Montaña va a estudiar este año allí y nosotros podemos estar en su apartamento. Nosotros queremos ir en auto, pero ___ auto es muy viejo. ___ amigos creen que no vamos a tener problemas pues en Guadalajara hay mecánicos excelentes.

B Su compañero/a le va a hacer preguntas sobre las cosas que usted tiene. Después usted le hace las preguntas a él/ella.

1. ¿Tienes auto? ¿Es pequeño tu auto? ¿De qué color es? 2. ¿Tienes perro? ¿Sacas a tu perro por la noche? ¿Dónde dejas tu perro cuando vas de viaje? ¿Cómo es tu perro? 3. ¿Tienes novio/a? ¿Cómo se llama? ¿Cuántos años tiene? ¿Cómo es?

C Usted le va a hacer preguntas a su compañero/a sobre sus hermanos. Comparta la información con la clase.

1. ¿Cuántos hermanos tienes? 2. ¿Viven en tu casa? 3. ¿Cómo se llama tu hermano mayor (*older*)? 4. ¿Y tu hermano menor (*younger*)? 5. ¿De qué color son los ojos de tu hermano mayor? ¿Y el pelo? 6. ¿De qué color son los ojos de tu hermano menor? 7. ¿Cuántos años tiene tu hermano menor? 8. ¿Son simpáticos tus hermanos?

PRONUNCIACIÓN

Stress and the written accent mark

Word stress is meaningful in both English and Spanish. Normally all words in both languages have one stressed syllable. If a person changes the stress to another syllable, the meaning of the word changes.

In English words like *permit* and *present* illustrate this very well. When the first syllable is stressed, these words are nouns; when the second syllable is stressed, they become verbs.

Nouns	*Verbs*
*per*mit	per*mit*
*pres*ent	pre*sent*

Differences in meaning due to stressing one syllable rather than another are more common in Spanish. One effect is to change the tense of a verb. Sometimes stress is indicated by a written accent mark.[2]

[2] In this lesson and in **Lecciones 5** and **6** you will learn the rules for accentuation.

Present	*Past*
hablo	ha**bló**
es**tu**dio	estu**dió**

If you know how to pronounce a word you can determine if it needs a written accent mark by applying a few simple rules. By the same token, if you see an unknown word, the presence or absence of a written accent mark will tell you where to place the stress.

Some rules for accentuation follow.

1. Interrogative and exclamatory words have a written accent mark on the vowel of the stressed syllable.

   ¿**Có**mo es tu primo? ¡**Qué** va!

2. Some one-syllable words have a written accent mark to distinguish them from words with the same spelling but different meaning.

el *the*	tu *your*	si *if*	te *(to) you*
él *he*	tú *you*	sí *yes*	té *tea*

3. All words stressed on the third from the last syllable have a written accent mark.

   física **sá**bado sim**pá**tico gra**má**tica mate**má**ticas

Jugadores de dominó en la Pequeña Habana, Miami. El dominó es un juego muy popular en muchos de los países hispanos.

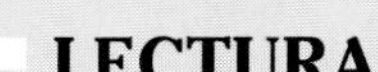

LECTURA

Las familias hispanas

Las familias hispanas, en general, son muy unidas y mientras° los hijos están solteros viven con sus padres. En muchos casos viven varias generaciones en la misma casa: los abuelos, los padres y los hijos. Los días de fiesta° o los fines de semana es común ver a dos o tres generaciones de la misma familia en un restaurante, en un café o en un parque.

while
días... *holidays*

En general, las relaciones con otros parientes son muy cordiales. Las personas mayores° (tíos, cuñados, primos) salen juntos o van a casa de uno de ellos para conversar o comer algo. Los primos jóvenes se reúnen con frecuencia, tienen amigos comunes, y van a fiestas, al cine o a un café.

personas... *adults*

Muchas familias hispanas que viven en los Estados Unidos mantienen° o quieren mantener estas costumbres° aquí. Esto causa a veces° conflictos en la familia. Hay jóvenes hispanos que prefieren la independencia que tienen los jóvenes norteamericanos y quieren vivir solos° o con algún amigo o amiga.

maintain/customs /
a... *sometimes*
by themselves

Los padres y los padrinos con el bebé el día del bautizo en Napa, California. Las relaciones entre los padrinos, los ahijados y sus padres son muy importantes en la cultura hispana.

Preguntas

1. En general, ¿dónde viven los hijos solteros de las familias hispanas?
2. ¿Salen juntas dos o tres generaciones de una familia en los países hispanos?
3. ¿Cómo son las relaciones con otros parientes?
4. ¿Adónde van los jóvenes de las familias hispanas?
5. ¿Por qué hay conflictos a veces en las familias hispanas que viven en los Estados Unidos?
6. ¿Vive usted solo/a o con su familia? ¿Qué prefiere usted?

La tercera edad°

Hoy en día°, especialmente en las ciudades, hay más mujeres que trabajan fuera°, y como los hijos estudian o trabajan, resulta difícil° cuidar a los ancianos° en la casa. Por este motivo existen residencias para la tercera edad que ofrecen servicios médicos y habitaciones° cómodas a los ancianos, pero el costo puede ser bastante alto para la familia.

Éste es un tipo de servicio relativamente nuevo en el mundo hispano, pues por tradición y costumbre los ancianos permanecen el la casa de sus familiares. A continuación pueden ver un anuncio de un periódico donde se explica lo que ofrece una residencia para la tercera edad.

tercera... *senior citizens* (literally, the third age)
Hoy... *Nowadays*
outside (the home) / difficult
elderly
rooms

¿Verdadero o falso?

Diga si las siguientes oraciones son verdaderas o falsas de acuerdo con la lectura y el anuncio.

1. Las residencias para la tercera edad son bastante nuevas en el mundo hispano.
2. Las residencias para la tercera edad cuestan muy poco.
3. En la residencia del anuncio no hay servicio médico de noche.
4. Los ancianos pueden ver televisión y vídeos.
5. Los ancianos deben comer en la habitación.
6. Si una persona desea recibir información debe llamar a las ocho.

SITUACIONES

1. You are doing some research regarding immigrants in this country. Diagram your partner's family tree as he/she describes it to you. Find out the country of origin of the various family members.
2. You are getting information for a census. Working with a partner, find out (a) how many members of his/her family live in the same house or apartment, (b) their ages, and (c) their marital status.
3. Find out (a) what city your partner wants to visit, (b) why, (c) when he/she is planning to go, and (d) with whom.
4. You are a very busy person. Tell your partner all you have to do on a typical day.
5. Find out your classmates' preferences. In a group of five or six classmates one of you will be in charge and act as secretary (**secretario/a**). Each person should rank the following kinds of movies according to preference. The student in charge will report the results to the class.

____ cómicas	____ de aventuras
____ dramáticas	____ de detectives
____ musicales	____ de misterio
____ románticas	____ de ciencia ficción
____ documentales	____ del oeste (*western*)

6. You are a law student (**estudiante de derecho**) who wants to quit school. Tell your mother/father that (a) you are not happy in school, (b) you want to quit school (**no quiero estudiar más**), (c) you don't have any friends, and (d) you prefer to work and have money. Your mother/father will try to persuade you not to quit.

VOCABULARIO[3]

animales

el gato — *cat*
la guardería de perros — *kennel*
el perro — *dog*

la familia — *family*

la abuela — *grandmother*
el abuelo — *grandfather*
la cuñada — *sister-in-law*
el cuñado — *brother-in-law*
la hermana — *sister*
el hermano — *brother*
la hija — *daughter*
el hijo — *son*
la nieta — *granddaughter*
el nieto — *grandson*
la nuera — *daughter-in-law*
los padres — *parents*
el papá — *dad*
el pariente/la parienta — *relative*
el primo/la prima — *cousin*

[3] See page 111 for expressions with **tener** + noun.

la sobrina	*niece*
el sobrino	*nephew*
la suegra	*mother-in-law*
el suegro	*father-in-law*
la tía	*aunt*
el tío	*uncle*
el yerno	*son-in-law*

otras relaciones

la ahijada	*goddaughter*
el ahijado	*godson*
la esposa/mujer	*wife*
el esposo/marido	*husband*
la madrina	*godmother*
la novia	*fiancée, girlfriend*
el novio	*fiancé, boyfriend*
el padrino	*godfather*

las vacaciones *vacation*

la ciudad	*city*
el dinero	*money*
el lugar	*place*
el problema	*problem*
el viaje	*trip*

personas

el bebé	*baby*
la estrella	*star*
el genio	*genius*
el millonario	*millionaire*
el niño/la niña	*child*

bebidas

el agua[4]	*water*

las publicaciones

el artículo	*article*
el periódico	*newspaper*
la revista	*magazine*

conceptos

la imaginación	*imagination*
la mentira	*lie*
la verdad	*truth*

descripciones

enorme	*enormous*
maravilloso	*marvelous*

verbos

almorzar (ue)	*to have lunch*
contar (ue)	*to count*
costar (ue)	*to cost*
cuidar	*to take care of*
dejar	*to leave*
dormir (ue)	*to sleep*
empezar (ie)	*to begin, start*
jugar (ue)	*to play (game, sport)*
pasar	*to spend*
pensar (ie)	*to think*
pensar + *inf.*	*to plan to + verb*
perder (ie)	*to lose*
poder (ue)	*to be able to, can*
preferir (ie)	*to prefer*
querer (ie)	*to want, to love*
tener (g, ie)	*to have*
venir (g, ie)	*to come*
visitar	*to visit*
volver (ue)	*to return*

expresiones

estar equivocado/a	*to be wrong*
tener... años	*to be . . . years old*
tener ganas de + *inf.*	*to feel like + pres. part.*
tener que + *inf.*	*to have to + verb*

posesión

mi, mis	*my*
tu, tus	*your*
su, sus	*his, her, your, its, their*
nuestro(s), nuestra(s)	*our*

palabras útiles

muchos	*many*
según	*according to*

---

[4] Although **agua** is feminine, it uses **el** and not **la** in the singular whenever the article is required. This happens when an article directly precedes a singular feminine noun beginning with stressed **a** or **ha: el agua, el hambre.**

In Lección 5 **you will**
a. ask about and describe living quarters.
b. discuss daily activities in the home.
c. ask about and discuss daily schedules.
d. express and describe activities related to grooming.

La casa de la familia Estévez

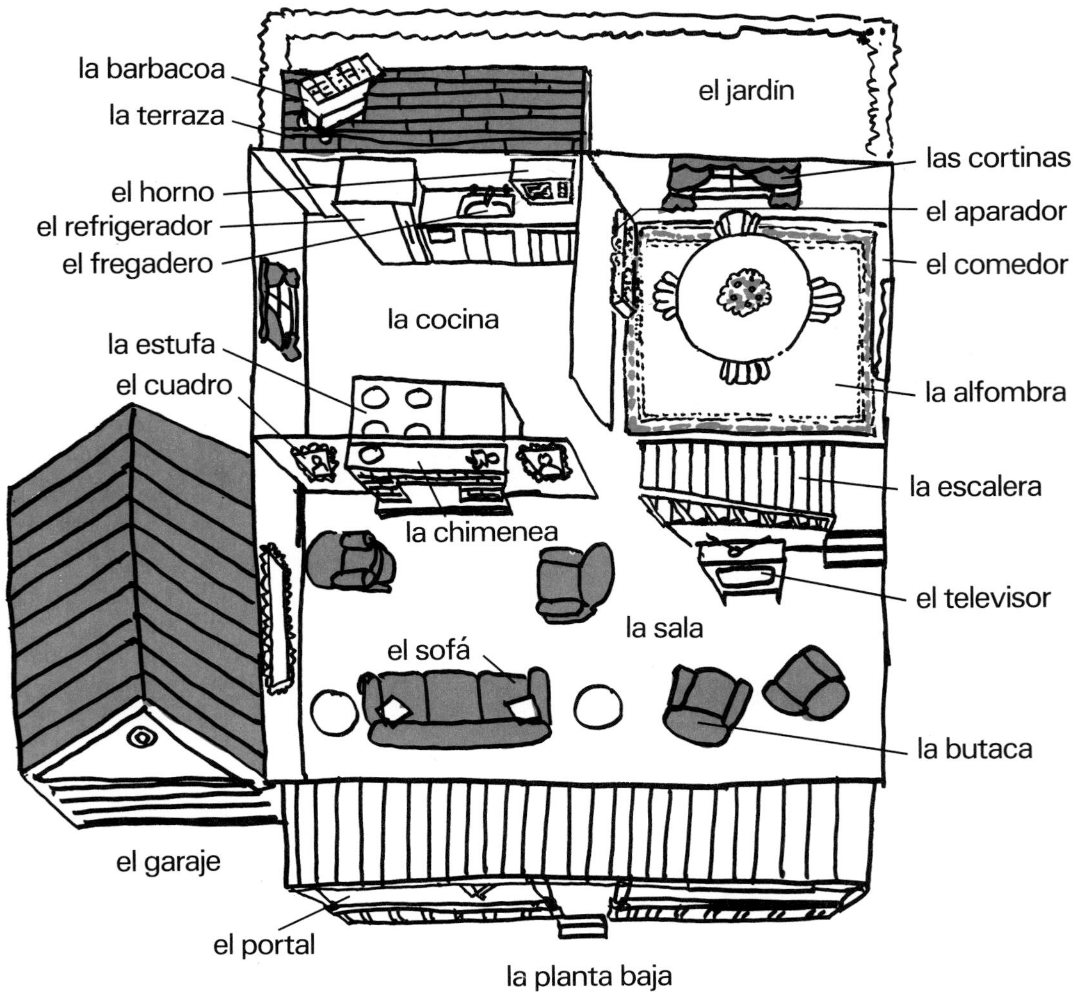

Lección 5

La casa y los muebles

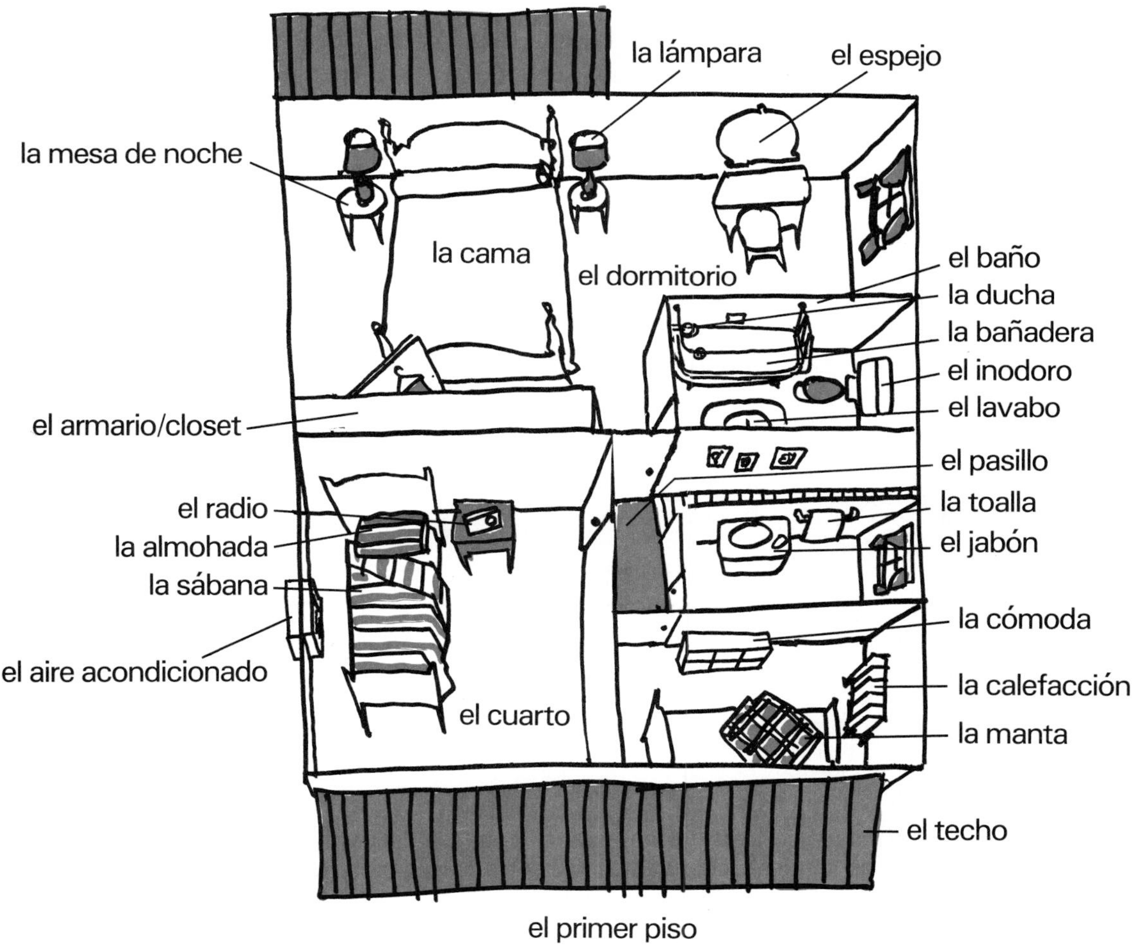

La casa de los Estévez está en las afueras° de la ciudad. Está lejos° del centro, pero cerca° de los padres de la Sra. de Estévez. Ellos no alquilan° la casa; la casa es de ellos.

outskirts / far
near / rent

electrodomésticos	*electrical appliances*
la batidora	*mixer*
la lavadora	*washing machine*
el lavaplatos	*dishwasher*
la licuadora	*blender*
el (horno) microondas	*microwave*
la plancha	*iron*
la secadora	*drier*

ACTIVIDADES

A **¿Dónde?** Asocie las siguientes actividades con las partes de la casa donde normalmente tienen lugar.

1. dormir	a. sala
2. ver televisión	b. comedor
3. dejar el auto	c. cocina
4. preparar la comida	d. garaje
5. correr y jugar	e. cuarto
6. almorzar	f. jardín

B ¿En qué parte de su casa están generalmente estos objetos y muebles?

1. la estufa	a. la cocina
2. la barbacoa	b. el baño
3. el sofá y las butacas	c. la sala
4. la licuadora	d. el dormitorio
5. la mesa de noche	e. el comedor
6. el jabón y las toallas	f. la terraza
7. el aparador	
8. la cómoda	
9. las almohadas y las sábanas	

C Usted es una persona muy curiosa y quiere saber cómo es la casa o apartamento de su compañero/a. Hágale las siguientes preguntas. Después él/ella va a hacerle las preguntas a usted.

1. ¿Vives en una casa, un apartamento o un condominio? 2. ¿Está cerca o lejos de la universidad? 3. ¿Es grande? 4. ¿Cuántos cuartos tiene? 5. ¿Tiene aire acondicionado y calefacción? 6. ¿Qué muebles tienes en la sala? 7. ¿Y en tu cuarto? 8. ¿Qué electrodomésticos hay en la cocina?

Cultura

Housing in the Hispanic world

Although the architectural style of houses varies somewhat from one Hispanic country to the next, houses are built to last a long time. Homes in urban areas are generally constructed of bricks or blocks; thus it is not unusual, especially in Spain, to find examples of those that have been inhabited for the last two or even three centuries.

A comparison of Hispanic and American homes shows that Hispanic homes tend to be smaller and closer together, but spacious homes can be found in affluent neighborhoods. A characteristic feature of middle-class homes and apartments, especially in Latin America, is the living quarters for domestic help. A fence or wall usually surrounds the property of the house, and wrought-iron grillwork covers the windows. Central air conditioning or heating is not common. Homes tend to lack many modern conveniences, but the current trend is to modernize the kitchen area by equipping it with electrical appliances.

The contrast in economic conditions between an average American family and a Hispanic one accounts for a lower percentage of home owners in the Hispanic world. The upper and middle classes in most Hispanic countries enjoy the privilege of owning a home. Because of the small proportion of upper and middle classes, however, much of the population does not have that privilege. Banks also present obstacles to the potential homeowner. They do not offer thirty-year mortgage loans as in the United States. Due to unstable economic conditions, the typical loan period is no more than ten years, resulting in very high monthly payments.

Since it is difficult for families or individuals to buy a house or apartment, most have to rent. Many people want housing that is close to the downtown area, where they can take advantage of public transportation, convenient shopping areas, and proximity to the workplace.

La casa Batló en Barcelona, España, es una de las construcciones más conocidas del gran arquitecto catalán Antonio Gaudí (1852–1926).

EN CONTEXTO

A la hora de la cena

Irma y Augusto son un matrimonio° joven. Los dos trabajan fuera y en la casa comparten las tareas domésticas°. — *(married) couple*; tareas. . . *house chores*

Augusto Ya son casi° las siete. ¿Pongo° la mesa? — *almost / Shall I set*
Irma Sí, por favor. Tengo que hacer° dos o tres cosas° en la cocina. — *do/ things*
Augusto Bueno, pero es temprano°. — *early*
Irma Sí, pero si comemos tarde° no salgo° de la cocina hasta las nueve. — *late / leave*
Augusto Irma, no salimos de la cocina, porque yo sí ayudo°. — *I do help*
Irma Es verdad. Por cierto°, ¿puedes sacar la basura°? — *By the way/ garbage*

Preguntas

1. ¿Trabaja Irma fuera de la casa?
2. ¿Ayuda Augusto en las tareas domésticas?
3. ¿Va a poner Irma la mesa?
4. ¿Dónde va a trabajar Irma?
5. ¿Es tarde o temprano?
6. ¿Por qué quiere comer temprano Irma?
7. ¿Quién va a sacar la basura?
8. Y usted, ¿trabaja mucho en su casa?

Los grandes edificios modernos de Caracas, la capital de Venezuela, contrastan con las casas de los barrios pobres de la ciudad.

Unas amigas conversan mientras lavan y secan los platos en un apartamento en Madrid.

otras tareas domésticas

barrer	*to sweep*
limpiar	*to clean*
pasar la aspiradora	*to vacuum*
sacudir	*to dust*
preparar la comida/cocinar	*to cook*
lavar/secar los platos	*to wash/to dry the dishes*
colgar(ue)/doblar la ropa	*to hang/to fold the clothes*
planchar	*to iron*
tender (ie)/hacer la cama	*to make the bed*

ACTIVIDADES

A Usted tiene que trabajar mucho en su casa hoy. ¿En qué orden va a hacer usted las siguientes tareas domésticas?

____ cocinar la cena
____ tender la cama
____ pasar la aspiradora
____ preparar el desayuno
____ planchar la ropa
____ lavar la ropa

B Pregúntele a su compañero/a qué tareas domésticas hacen las siguientes personas en su casa. Comparta esta información con el resto de la clase.

papá mamá hermano hermana tú

GRAMÁTICA

Present tense of *hacer, poner,* and *salir*

hacer:	**hago,** haces, hace, hacemos, hacéis, hacen
poner:	**pongo,** pones, pone, ponemos, ponéis, ponen
salir:	**salgo,** sales, sale, salimos, salís, salen

1. The **yo** form of these verbs is irregular; the other forms are regular.
2. **Poner** normally means *to put.* With electrical appliances, **poner** means *to turn on.*

   Ella va a **poner** los platos en el fregadero. — *She's going to put the plates in the sink.*
   Yo **pongo** la televisión por la tarde. — *I turn on the TV in the afternoon.*

3. **Salir** can be used with several different prepositions.

   a. To state that you are leaving a place, use **salir de.**

   Yo salgo de mi cuarto ahora. — *I'm leaving my room now.*

   b. To state your destination, use **salir para.**

   Salgo para tu casa. — *I'm leaving for your house.*

   c. To state with whom you go out or the person you date, use **salir con.**

   Ella **sale con** Mauricio. — *She goes out with Mauricio.*

ACTIVIDADES

A **¿Cuándo salen?** El curso termina el viernes. Sus compañeros y usted van a salir a horas diferentes. Diga a qué hora salen.

Modelo Juan / 8 A.M.
Juan sale a las ocho de la mañana.

1. Alicia / 9 A.M.
2. Pedro y Julio / 11:00 A.M.
3. mi amigo Luis / 3:00 P.M.
4. tú / 2:30 P.M.
5. yo / 1:00 P.M.
6. Mirta y Elda / 10:00 A.M.

B **¿Qué haces en la clase de español?** Su compañero/a le va a decir las cosas que su hermano hace en la clase de español. Conteste diciendo si usted hace esas cosas o no.

Modelo Mi hermano tiene la clase por la mañana. ¿Y tú?
Yo tengo la clase por la tarde o **Yo también tengo la clase por la mañana.**

1. Él hace la tarea por la noche. ¿Y tú?
2. Llega a la clase a las nueve. ¿Y tú?
3. Pone la tarea sobre el escritorio del profesor. ¿Y tú?
4. Habla español en la clase. ¿Y tú?
5. Sale de la clase a las diez. ¿Y tú?

C Diga dónde ponen las personas de la columna A las cosas de la columna B. Los lugares están en la columna C.

Modelo Compañero/a mi mamá / las toallas / el baño
Usted **Mi mamá pone las toallas en el baño.**

A	B	C
mi mamá	las sillas	la cocina
mi papá	la lámpara	el armario
mis hermanos	la batidora	el dormitorio
mi hermano y yo	el jabón	el pasillo
yo	el televisor	el garaje
	el gato y el perro	el comedor
	la barbacoa	la terraza
	el auto	el jardín
	la plancha	el baño
	los platos	la sala

D Complete el siguiente párrafo de acuerdo con el dibujo usando la forma correcta de **salir** + **de, para** o **con.**

1. Javier y Marcelo son hermanos. Ellos ____ ____ su casa. ____ ____ el cine. Javier siempre ____ ____ Marcelo los domingos por la tarde.

Ahora complete el siguiente párrafo de acuerdo con sus actividades.

2. Yo ____ ____ casa a las ____ de la mañana. ____ ____ la universidad. Llego a la universidad a las ____. Las clases terminan a las ____. A esa hora yo ____ ____ casa. Por las noches ____ ____ mi novio/a.

E **Entrevista.** Usted quiere saber qué hace su compañero/a en su tiempo libre. Hágale las siguientes preguntas.

1. ¿A qué hora sales de la universidad? 2. ¿Sales para tu casa o para el trabajo? 3. ¿Qué haces cuando llegas a tu casa? 4. ¿Pones la televisión por las noches? 5. ¿Qué programa prefieres? 6. ¿Cuándo limpias la casa? 7. ¿Con quién sales los fines de semana? 8. ¿Adónde van?

EN CONTEXTO

¿Qué hacen estas personas?

Juan lava **el auto.**
↓
Juan **lo** lava.

Alicia saca **la basura.**
↓
Alicia **la** saca.

Alfonso lava **los platos.**
↓
Alfonso **los** lava.

Ana tiende **las camas.**
↓
Ana **las** tiende.

Ella ayuda **al niño.**
↓
Ella **lo** ayuda.

Ramón ayuda **a las niñas.**
↓
Ramón **las** ayuda.

GRAMÁTICA

Direct object nouns and pronouns; the personal *a*

1. A direct object is a noun or pronoun that receives the action of the verb. In Spanish direct object nouns follow the verb. When direct object nouns refer to a specific person or group of

Vista de la Alhambra, residencia de los reyes árabes en Granada, España. Según muchos, la Alhambra es el palacio árabe más bello (*beautiful*) del mundo.

persons, or to a pet, the word **a** must precede them. This is called the personal **a** and has no equivalent in English.

Amanda seca **los platos.**	*Amanda dries the dishes.*
Amanda seca **a la niña.**	*Amanda dries the girl.*

2. Since the question word **quién(es)** refers to people, use the personal **a** when **quién(es)** is used as a direct object.

—¿**A quién** vas a ver? —Voy a ver a Pedro.

3. Direct object pronouns may refer to people, animals or things.

me	*me*	
te	*you*	*(familiar, singular)*
lo	*you*	*(formal, singular), him, it (masculine)*
la	*you*	*(formal, singular), her, it (feminine)*
nos	*us*	
os	*you*	*(familiar, plural)*
los	*you*	*(formal & familiar, plural), them (masculine)*
las	*you*	*(formal & familiar, plural), them (feminine)*

4. To avoid repetition use direct object pronouns when the direct object noun has already been mentioned. Place the direct object pronoun before the conjugated verb form and after the word **no** when it appears.

—¿Quieres mucho **a tu perro**? —Sí, **lo** quiero mucho.
—¿Magdalena prepara **la comida**? —No, **no la** prepara.

5. When there are both a conjugated verb form and an infinitive, a direct object pronoun can be placed before the conjugated verb form or be attached to the dependent infinitive.

—¿Vas a visitar a **Rafael**? —Sí, **lo** voy a visitar.
—Sí, voy a visitar**lo**.

ACTIVIDADES

A Conteste las siguientes preguntas sobre sus responsabilidades en la casa. Use pronombres en sus respuestas.

Modelo ¿Sacas la basura?
Sí, la saco o **No, no la saco.**

1. ¿Limpias tu cuarto? 2. ¿Limpias la cocina? ¿y el garaje? 3. ¿Lavas los platos? 4. ¿Secas los platos? 5. ¿Lavas la ropa? 6. ¿Cuelgas la ropa o secas la ropa en la secadora?

B Conteste las siguientes preguntas sobre las actividades de sus compañeros en la clase. Use pronombres en sus respuestas.

Modelo ¿Hablan español en la clase?
Sí, lo hablan.

1. ¿Contestan las preguntas? 2. ¿Leen revistas? 3. ¿Hacen la tarea? 4. ¿Escriben los diálogos? 5. ¿Estudian el vocabulario?

C Su hermanita le hace las siguientes preguntas. Conteste usando pronombres.

Modelo ¿Me ayudas ahora?
Sí, te ayudo ahora o **No, no te ayudo ahora.**

1. ¿Me quieres? 2. ¿Me vas a cuidar este fin de semana?
3. ¿Me extrañas (*miss me*) cuando no estoy aquí?

D Complete el siguiente diálogo con su compañero/a.

Usted ¿Dónde haces la tarea?
Compañero/a . . .
Usted ¿Cuándo la haces?
Compañero/a . . .
Usted ¿Quién te ayuda con la tarea?
Compañero/a . . .

E Dígale a su compañero/a lo que usted va a hacer en su cuarto esta tarde. Él/Ella debe decir si lo va a hacer también o no.

Modelo limpiar mi cuarto

Usted **Voy a limpiar mi cuarto.**

Compañero/a **Yo lo voy a limpiar (voy a limpiarlo) también** o **Yo no lo voy a limpiar (no voy a limpiarlo).**

sacudir los muebles — pasar la aspiradora — tender la cama — doblar la ropa — colgar la ropa

F **Entrevista.** Pregúntele a su compañero/a sobre sus relaciones con otras personas.

1. ¿Quién te comprende en tu casa?
2. ¿Quién te quiere?
3. ¿Quién te llama por teléfono?
4. ¿A quién ayudas tú?
5. ¿A quién saludas en la clase?
6. ¿A quién(es) quieres mucho?
7. ¿A quién(es) quieres un poco?

EN CONTEXTO

Las actividades de Rafael

Por la mañana

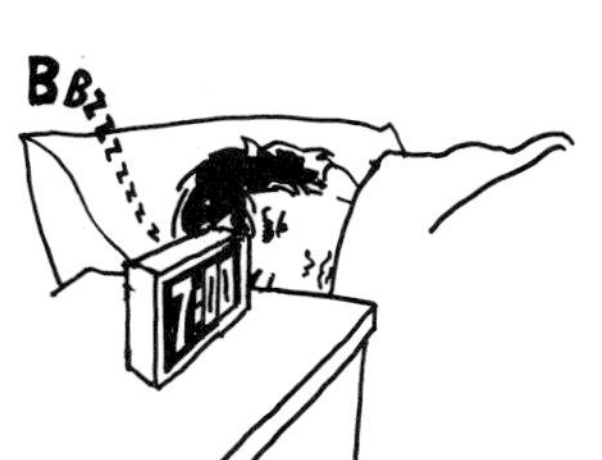

Rafael se despierta.

Se levanta.

Se lava los dientes.

Se afeita.

Se baña.

Se seca.

Se peina.

Por la noche

Rafael se sienta a ver la tele.

Se quita la ropa y los zapatos.

Se pone la piyama.

Se acuesta.

Se duerme.

Preguntas

1. ¿A qué hora se despierta Rafael?
2. ¿Dónde duerme Rafael?
3. ¿A qué hora se levanta?
4. ¿Dónde se afeita?
5. ¿Con qué se seca Rafael?
6. ¿Dónde se peina?
7. Por la noche, ¿se sienta a ver la tele en la cocina?
8. ¿Qué ropa se pone Rafael para dormir?
9. ¿Dónde se acuesta Rafael?
10. ¿A qué hora se duerme?

ACTIVIDADES

A ¿Cuál es la expresión opuesta?

1. se despierta	a. se pone la ropa
2. se levanta	b. se acuesta
3. se quita la ropa	c. se seca
4. se lava	d. se duerme

B Su profesor/a va a hablar sobre sus actividades, cuándo las hace, etc. Conteste diciendo lo que usted hace.

Modelo Yo me despierto a las siete.
Y yo (me despierto) a las ocho.

1. Yo me levanto a las siete y media. 2. Yo me lavo los dientes. 3. Yo me baño por la tarde. 4. Yo desayuno muy poco por las mañanas. 5. Yo llego a la universidad a las nueve. 6. Yo salgo a las cuatro. 7. Yo me acuesto a las once. 8. Yo me duermo a las doce más o menos.

GRAMÁTICA

Reflexive verbs and pronouns

yo	me lavo	*I wash myself*
tú	te lavas	*you wash yourself*
usted	se lava	*you wash yourself*
él	se lava	*he washes himself*
ella	se lava	*she washes herself*
nosotros/as	nos lavamos	*we wash ourselves*
vosotros/as	os laváis	*you wash yourselves*
ustedes	se lavan	*you wash yourselves*
ellos/ellas	se lavan	*they wash themselves*

1. Spanish uses reflexive pronouns and verbs to express what people do to or for themselves, that is, the subject does the action and the action is reflected back to the subject.

Non–reflexive
Margarita acuesta a su hijo. (Margarita is the doer; the son is the receiver.)

Reflexive
Margarita **se acuesta.** (Margarita is both the doer and the receiver.)

2. A reflexive pronoun refers to the same person as the subject. In English this is expressed by pronouns ending in *-self* or *-selves* (e.g., *myself, themselves*). Spanish uses reflexives in many cases where English does not (e.g., afeitarse, *to shave*).

3. Place reflexive pronouns before the conjugated verb and after the word **no** when it is used. Reflexive pronouns may precede the conjugated verb or be attached to the infinitive.

Yo (no) **me** voy a acostar a las diez.
Yo (no) voy a acostar**me** a las diez.

4. When referring to parts of the body and articles of clothing, use definite articles, and not possessives, with reflexive verbs.

Me lavo **los** dientes.   Me pongo **la** ropa.

5. The pronoun **se** attached to the end of an infinitive shows that the verb is reflexive.

lavar *to wash*   lavarse *to wash oneself*

6. Some verbs change meaning when used reflexively.

acostar	*to put to bed*	acostarse	*to go to bed, to lie down*
dormir	*to sleep*	dormirse	*to fall asleep*
ir	*to go*	irse	*to go away, to leave*
levantar	*to raise, to lift*	levantarse	*to get up*
llamar	*to call*	llamarse	*to be called*
quitar	*to take away*	quitarse	*to take off*

ACTIVIDADES

A Usted y su hermano tienen diferentes horarios. Diga las cosas que ustedes hacen y a qué hora las hacen.

Modelo despertarse mi hermano 8:00 yo 7:00
Mi hermano se despierta a las ocho.
Yo me despierto a las siete.

	mi hermano	yo
levantarse	8:15	7:05
afeitarse	8:20	7:10
bañarse	8:30	7:15
peinarse	8:45	7:20

B Describa las actividades de la familia Menéndez los lunes por la mañana.

Modelo la mamá / levantarse / 6:30
La mamá se levanta a las seis y media.

1. el papá / despertarse / 6:30
2. la mamá / peinarse
3. el papá / afeitarse / bañarse
4. el papá / despertar a los niños
5. los niños / lavarse los dientes
6. la mamá / preparar el desayuno
7. los niños / ponerse los zapatos
8. la familia / desayunar en el comedor

Una señora y su hija miran televisión en Bogotá, Colombia. La televisión, igual que en los Estados Unidos, es parte de la vida diaria en los países hispanos.

C Usted quiere saber cuánto tiempo necesita su compañero/a para hacer ciertas cosas. Hágale las siguientes preguntas. Después usted debe decir el tiempo que usted necesita.

Modelo Usted **¿Cuánto tiempo necesitas para lavarte?**
Compañero/a **Necesito diez minutos para lavarme.**
Usted **Y yo necesito quince minutos.**

1. ¿Cuánto tiempo necesitas para bañarte? 2. ¿Y para afeitarte (o maquillarte *to put on makeup*)? 3. ¿Y para peinarte?

D Usted y su mejor amigo/a están de vacaciones en Madrid. Diga las cosas que van a hacer mañana.

Modelo levantarse a las ocho
Nos vamos a levantar a las ocho o **Vamos a levantarnos a las ocho.**

bañarse ponerse zapatos cómodos desayunar en un café visitar el Museo del Prado almorzar en un restaurante típico ir al teatro cenar con unos amigos acostarse a la una

E Lea la siguiente selección sobre un día típico de Marcela Gracia. Después su compañero/a y usted van a hablar de las actividades de Marcela usando la tabla que sigue.

Modelo

nombre	Se llama Marcela Gracia.

Me llamo Marcela Gracia y vivo en Caracas. Soy locutora de televisión (*TV announcer*) y siempre estoy muy ocupada.

Me despierto a las 6:00 y hago ejercicio (*exercise*). A las 6:30 me baño, me peino, me maquillo (*put on makeup*) y luego desayuno. Me voy al trabajo a las 7:30.

Empiezo a trabajar a las 8:00. Tengo una reunión con mi jefe a las 9:30. Después hago muchas llamadas por teléfono entre 10:00 y 11:30. A veces tengo que salir para hablar con otras personas. Almuerzo a la 1:00 y vuelvo a los estudios a las 2:30. A esa hora me lavo los dientes, me peino y me maquillo otra vez. Mi programa empieza a las 3:30 y tengo que estar lista a las 3:15.

¿dónde vive?	
profesión	
6:00 a 6:30	
6:30 a 7:30	
8:00	
9:30	
10:00 a 11:30	
1:00 a 2:30	
2:30 a 3:15	
3:30	

F Dígale a su compañero/a todo lo que usted hace desde (*since*) que se despierta hasta que llega a la universidad. Después su compañero/a va a decirle a usted todo lo que hace los sábados por la mañana.

PRONUNCIACIÓN

Stress and the written accent mark (*continuation*)

1. Words that are stressed on the next to the last syllable

a. do not have a written accent mark if they end in **n, s,** or a vowel.

examen **ca**sas **pa**dre her**ma**na so**bri**no

b. have an accent mark if they end in any other letter.

lápiz **ú**til **dé**bil **már**tir **Fé**lix

2. Words that are stressed on the last syllable

a. have a written accent mark if they end in **n, s,** or a vowel.

es**tán** es**tás** es**tá** in**glés** ale**mán**

Those that end in **n** or **s** do not require an accent mark in the plural form since they then stress the next to the last syllable.

japo**nés** ⟶ **japone**ses ale**mán** ⟶ ale**ma**nes

b. do not have a written accent mark if they end in any other letter

ha**blar** ver**dad** espa**ñol** fe**liz** borra**dor**

Para una reunión en Bogotá, Colombia, unos amigos preparan parte de la comida mientras un niño los ayuda. Hoy en día los hombres hispanos están participando un poco más en las tareas domésticas.

A la hora del almuerzo en casa de una familia en Bogotá, Colombia.

LECTURA

Buscando apartamento

You are in Madrid looking for an apartment and you read the following ads in a newspaper. Choose one apartment telling why you prefer it. You may need the following words to better understand the ads.

lujo	*luxury*
vistas	*views*
Retiro	*a famous park in Madrid*
calidad	*quality*
entrega	*occupancy*
propio	*same*
c/	*abbreviation for* calle
desde	*from*
pts.	*abbreviation for* pesetas
piscina	*swimming pool*
entrada	*down payment*
obra	*construction (site)*
millón	*million*

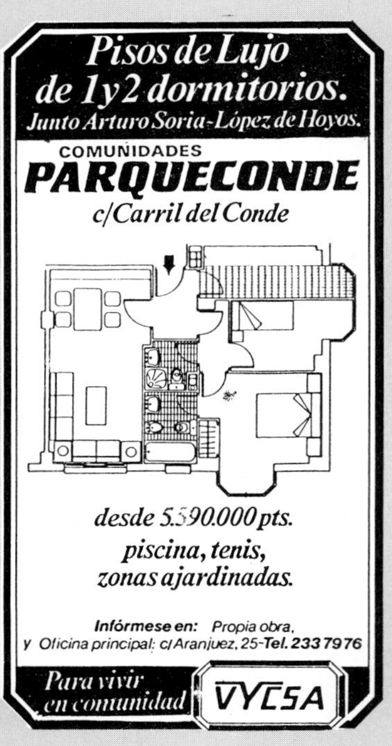

Bueno, bonito y barato°

inexpensive

El edificio de apartamentos donde viven Rafael Sotomayor y su mujer Juana es bastante nuevo, con un pequeño jardín y garaje para los autos de los inquilinos° (*tenants*). Está en Insurgentes Sur, una zona o colonia de la ciudad de México. El apartamento de los Sotomayor es cómodo y bonito, pero pequeño. El problema principal es que no está cerca del metro° y Rafael tiene que manejar° (*subway / to drive*) casi una hora todos los días para ir a su trabajo. Además, Juana va a empezar a trabajar en una oficina del centro el mes próximo y ellos prefieren alquilar un apartamento cerca de esta zona y así poder usar el metro para ir al trabajo.

Todos los días los Sotomayor leen el periódico para ver si encuentran° (*find*) un buen apartamento. Según Rafael, ellos buscan las tres «bes»: bueno, bonito y barato. Esto no es fácil° porque en las zonas que ellos prefieren los alquileres son bastante altos. *easy*

Hoy Juana va a ir a ver un apartamento en la colonia Irrigación, que está relativamente cerca del centro. Muchos de los edificios de esa colonia son más viejos que en otras zonas, pero los apartamentos son más grandes. Un problema es que generalmente no tienen garaje y en esa zona es difícil conseguir° uno. *get*

Preguntas

1. ¿Cómo es el edificio de apartamentos de los Sotomayor?
2. ¿Dónde está?
3. ¿Cómo es el apartamento donde viven?
4. ¿Por qué quieren mudarse?
5. ¿Dónde va a empezar a trabajar Juana?
6. ¿Dónde quieren vivir los Sotomayor?
7. ¿Cómo es el apartamento que ellos quieren?
8. ¿Adónde va a ir Juana hoy?
9. ¿Cómo son los apartamentos de esta colonia?
10. ¿Qué problema pueden tener los Sotomayor en esa zona?

La división del trabajo en la casa

The following selection was taken from *Telva,* a very popular Spanish magazine, showing with percentages the division of household chores among men and women in Spain. You may need the following vocabulary to better understand the selection.

		tiende	=	cuelga
coser	*to sew*	alimentos	=	comida
		fregar	=	lavar platos

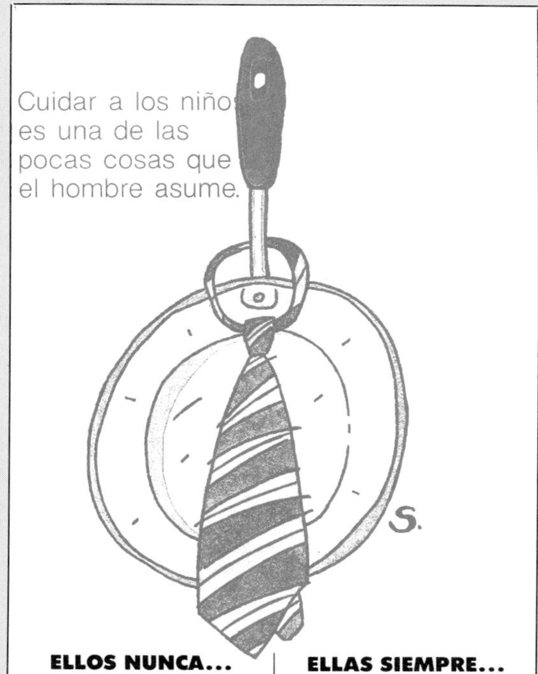

ELLOS NUNCA...

El 95 por ciento de los hombres **NUNCA** plancha ni cose un botón; el 85 por ciento **NUNCA** pone la lavadora ni tiende a secar la ropa; el 82 por ciento **NUNCA** pasa el aspirador; el 74 por ciento **NUNCA** se hace la cama y el 70 por ciento **NUNCA** cocina en casa y el 71 por ciento de ellos **NUNCA** se ocupa de comprar los alimentos.

ELLAS SIEMPRE...

El 81 por ciento de las mujeres españolas **SIEMPRE** prepara la comida; el 80 por ciento **SIEMPRE** cose toda la ropa de su casa; el 82 por ciento **SIEMPRE** plancha las prendas de su familia; el 75 por ciento **SIEMPRE** friega o pone el lavaplatos y el 70 por ciento de ellas **SIEMPRE** hacen la compra semanal o diaria.

Preguntas

1. ¿Quiénes trabajan más, los hombres o las mujeres?
2. ¿Qué porcentaje de mujeres cocina siempre?
3. ¿Qué porcentaje de hombres plancha o cose la ropa?
4. ¿Cree usted que estos porcentajes son más o menos como los porcentajes en los Estados Unidos?

Encuesta. ¿Qué porcentaje de las siguientes tareas domésticas cree usted que hace el hombre en este país: cocinar, lavar los platos, planchar, pasar la aspiradora, coser? Compare sus porcentajes con los de sus compañeros/as.

SITUACIONES

1. You want to sell your house/apartment. Explain to a real-estate agent what it is like.
2. You are talking to a prospective roommate. Tell him/her what he/she can and cannot do or have.
3. You are looking for an apartment to rent. You saw one that you like. Explain to a friend that the apartment (a) is near the university, (b) is on the ground floor, (c) has a big kitchen, (d) doesn't have a dining room, and (e) has a garage. He/She will ask you how much it is, and you will answer the question.
4. Ask your partner (a) what time he/she gets up on weekdays (**entre semana**), (b) what he/she has for breakfast, (c) what time he/she leaves for school, (d) what time he/she returns, and (e) what time he/she goes to bed.
5. You are at a furniture store. Your partner will play the part of the salesperson. Tell him/her that (a) you are looking for a desk and chair for your room, (b) the chair has to be big and comfortable, and (c) you don't want to spend (**gastar**) much money. The salesperson should tell you about the desks and chairs they have. Say that you want to see them.
6. You visited the home of a famous actor/actress. Tell your partner whose house it was and describe it.

VOCABULARIO[1]

en una casa

el aire acondicionado	*air conditioning*
el armario/closet	*closet*
el baño	*bathroom*
la calefacción	*heating*
la cocina	*kitchen*
el comedor	*dining room*
el cuarto/dormitorio	*bedroom*
la chimenea	*fireplace*
la escalera	*stairs*
el garaje	*garage*
el pasillo	*hall*
el piso	*floor*
la planta baja	*first floor*
el portal	*porch*
la sala	*living room*
el techo	*roof*
la terraza	*terrace*

muebles y accesorios	*furniture and accessories*
la alfombra	*carpet, rug*
el aparador	*china cabinet*
la butaca	*armchair*
la cama	*bed*
la cómoda	*dresser*
la cortina	*curtain*
el cuadro	*picture*
el espejo	*mirror*
la lámpara	*lamp*
la mesa de noche	*night stand*
el sofá	*sofa*

[1] See pages 130–132 and 135–136 for direct object and reflexive pronouns.

electrodomésticos — *electrical appliances*
la aspiradora — *vacuum cleaner*
la batidora — *mixer*
la lavadora — *washing machine*
el lavaplatos — *dishwasher*
la licuadora — *blender*
el (horno) microondas — *microwave oven*
la plancha — *iron*
el/la radio — *radio*
el refrigerador — *refrigerator*
la secadora — *drier*
el televisor — *TV set*

para la cama
la almohada — *pillow*
la manta — *blanket*
la sábana — *sheet*

en el baño
la bañadera — *tub*
la ducha — *shower*
el inodoro — *toilet*
el jabón — *soap*
el lavabo — *washbowl*
la toalla — *towel*

en la cocina
la estufa — *stove*
el fregadero — *sink*
el plato — *dish, plate*

en el jardín — *yard, garden*
la barbacoa — *barbecue*
la basura — *garbage*

personas
el matrimonio — *(married) couple*

el cuerpo — *body*
los dientes — *teeth*

la ropa — *clothes*
el/la piyama — *pajamas*
los zapatos — *shoes*

verbos
acostar (ue) — *to put to bed*
acostarse — *to go to bed, to lie down*
afeitar — *to shave*
alquilar — *to rent*
ayudar — *to help*
bañar — *to bathe*
barrer — *to sweep*
cocinar — *to cook*
colgar (ue) — *to hang*
compartir — *to share*
despertar (ie) — *to wake up*
doblar — *to fold*
dormirse (ue) — *to fall asleep*
hacer — *to do, to make*
irse — *to go away, to leave*
lavar — *to wash*
levantar — *to raise*
levantarse — *to get up*
limpiar — *to clean*
pasar la aspiradora — *to vacuum*
peinar — *to comb*
planchar — *to iron*
poner — *to put, to turn on*
preparar — *to prepare*
quitar — *to take away, to remove*
quitarse — *to take off*
sacudir — *to dust*
salir — *to go out, to leave*
secar — *to dry*
sentarse (ie) — *to sit down*
tender (ie) la cama — *to make the bed*

lugares
las afueras — *outskirts*
el centro — *downtown, center*
cerca (de) — *near*
fuera (de) — *outside*
lejos (de) — *far*

tiempo
tarde — *late*
temprano — *early*

palabras útiles
casi — *almost, hardly*
la cosa — *thing*

expresiones útiles
por cierto — *by the way*
las tareas domésticas — *house chores*

In Lección 6 **you will**

a. **ask and answer questions concerning weather conditions.**
b. **express/describe physical abilities.**
c. **express on-going actions.**
d. **use numbers from 1,000 to 2,000,000.**
e. **express sequence and order.**
f. **express dates.**

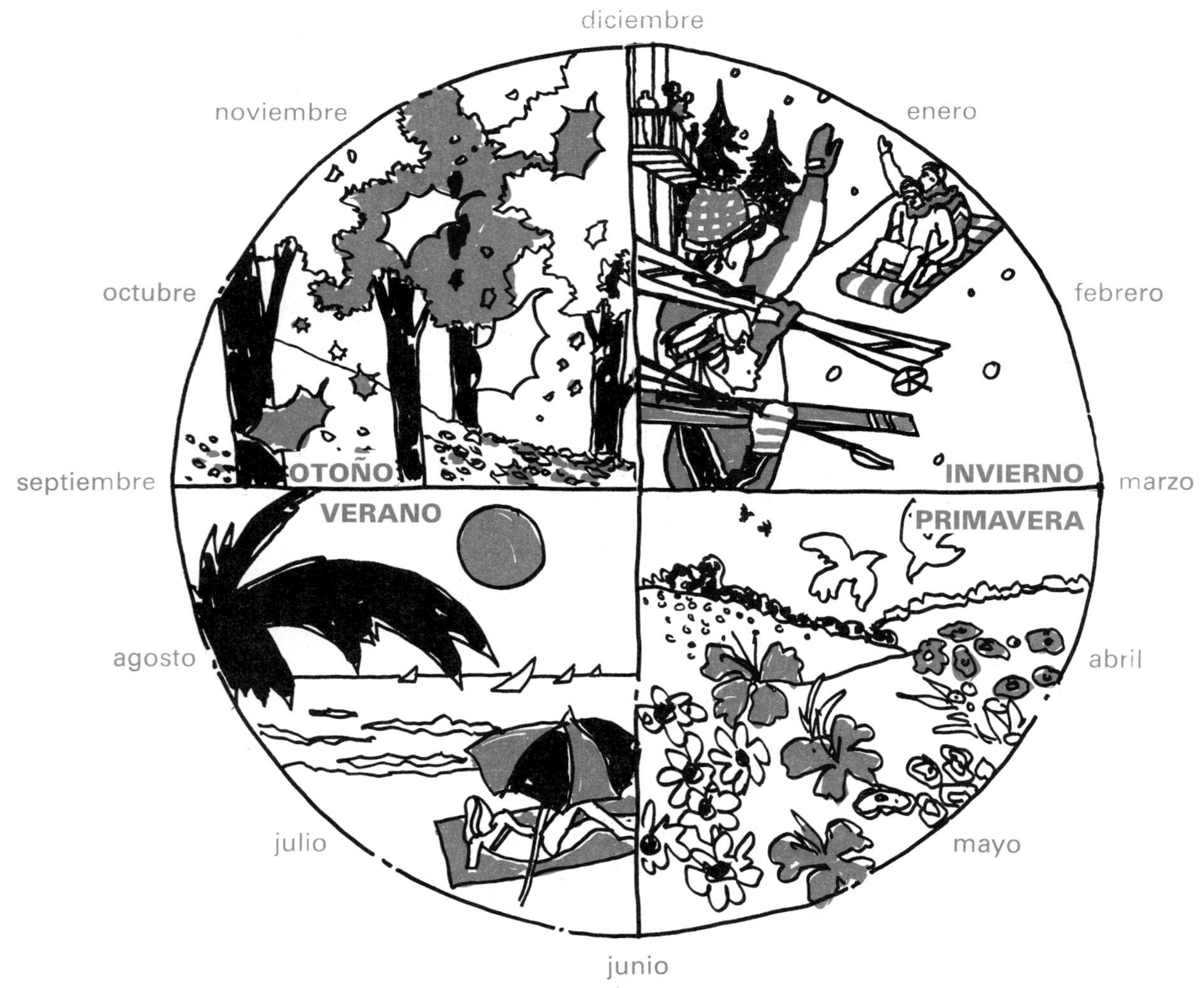

Lección 6

Los deportes

Las estaciones y los meses del año

Alicia esquía cuando hay mucha nieve.

Paco juega (al) fútbol con sus amigos.

Alicia monta (en) bicicleta y Paco patina.

Paco nada en la piscina.

Unas personas esperan el autobús en San Sebastián, un famoso lugar de veraneo en la costa norte de España. Esta zona del norte de España es un lugar de mucha lluvia.

el tiempo

¿Qué tiempo hace?	*How's the weather?*
Hace { buen / mal } tiempo.	*The weather is { fine. / bad.*
Hace (mucho) { frío. / calor. / fresco. / viento. / sol.	*It's (very) { cold. / hot. / cool. / windy. / sunny.*
Está (muy) { claro/despejado. / nublado/nuboso.	*It's (very) { clear. / cloudy.*
Nieva. / Está nevando.	*It's snowing.*
Llueve. / Esta lloviendo.	*It's raining.*

1. Use the verb **hacer** to ask about and to express weather conditions. With the adjectives **claro/ despejado** and **nublado/nuboso,** use **estar.**
2. To express *very,* use **mucho** with **hace** and **muy** with **está.**

   Hace **mucho** frío y está **muy** nublado.

3. Hispanic countries use the Centigrade system to measure temperature. The thermometer below shows both the Centigrade and Fahrenheit systems so you can compare them.

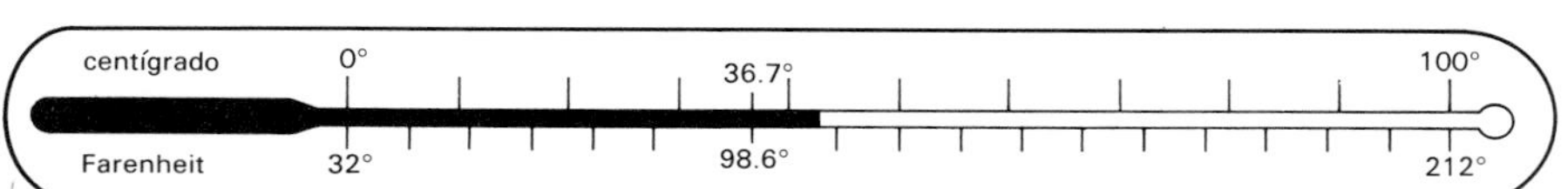

ACTIVIDADES

A Asocie las estaciones de la columna de la izquierda con los meses y las condiciones del tiempo de la columna de la derecha.

1. primavera
2. verano
3. otoño
4. invierno

a. hace frío
b. abril y mayo
c. octubre
d. hace mucho calor
e. hace fresco
f. los días son más cortos
g. hay muchas flores (*flowers*)
h. los días son más largos

B Diga en qué meses del año ocurren estas cosas.

1. Empiezan las clases en la universidad.
2. Nieva en Vermont.
3. Llueve aquí.
4. Es el Día de la Independencia.
5. Empieza el año.
6. Termina el año.

C Éstas son las temperaturas máximas y mínimas de diferentes ciudades de España. Escoja una ciudad y complete el siguiente diálogo con su compañero/a. Para convertir del sistema centígrado a Fahrenheit, debe multiplicar por (*multiply by*) 1.8 y añadir (*add*) 32. (e.g., 10°C × 1.8 = 18; 18 + 32 = 50°F)

España	M.	m.	España	M.	m.	España	M.	m.
Albacete	29	12	Huelva	35	18	Palma	29	12
Algeciras	23	17	Huesca	29	15	Pamplona	29	13
Alicante	25	17	Ibiza	23	16	Pontevedra	22	12
Almería	30	23	Jaén	30	15	Salamanca	28	13
Ávila	25	13	Jerez	30	19	S. Sebastián	18	15
Badajoz	35	17	La Coruña	17	13	Santander	18	14
Barcelona	22	17	Lanzarote	25	19	Santiago	18	11
Bilbao	17	14	Las Palmas	25	19	Segovia	26	12
Burgos	26	12	León	27	13	Sevilla	32	20
Cáceres	32	19	Lérida	28	14	Soria	25	10
Cádiz	26	14	Logroño	24	12	Tarragona	25	15
Castellón	29	16	Lugo	19	10	Tenerife	24	20
Ceuta	23	19	Mahón	24	16	Teruel	26	11
C. Real	32	15	Málaga	28	19	Toledo	29	18
Córdoba	35	18	Melilla	21	19	Valencia	26	17
Cuenca	28	13	Murcia	27	15	Valladolid	27	13
Gerona	27	14	Orense	23	13	Vitoria	14	12
Granada	32	16	Oviedo	16	13	Zamora	30	14
Guadalajara	30	14	Palencia	29	12	Zaragoza	30	16

ABREVIATURAS.–M.: Temperatura máxima.–m.: Temperatura mínima.–

Usted ¿Qué temperatura hace en ___?
Compañero/a Unos ___ grados más o menos.
Usted ¿Por el día o por la noche?
Compañero/a Por ___.
Usted ¿Cuánto es eso en Fahrenheit?
Compañero/a . . .

D Piense en el lugar donde usted quisiera (*would like*) pasar sus vacaciones. Su compañero/a le va a hacer las siguientes preguntas sobre el clima en ese lugar y sus actividades allí. Después usted le debe hacer las mismas preguntas a su compañero/a.

1. ¿Adónde quieres ir? 2. ¿Qué tiempo hace allí en el invierno? ¿y en el verano? 3. ¿Nieva allí? 4. ¿Cuándo llueve? 5. ¿Cuándo piensas ir? 6. ¿Qué vas a hacer allí?

E Usted está a cargo del pronóstico (*forecast*) del tiempo en un canal de televisión. Explique qué tiempo va a hacer mañana según los siguientes mapas.

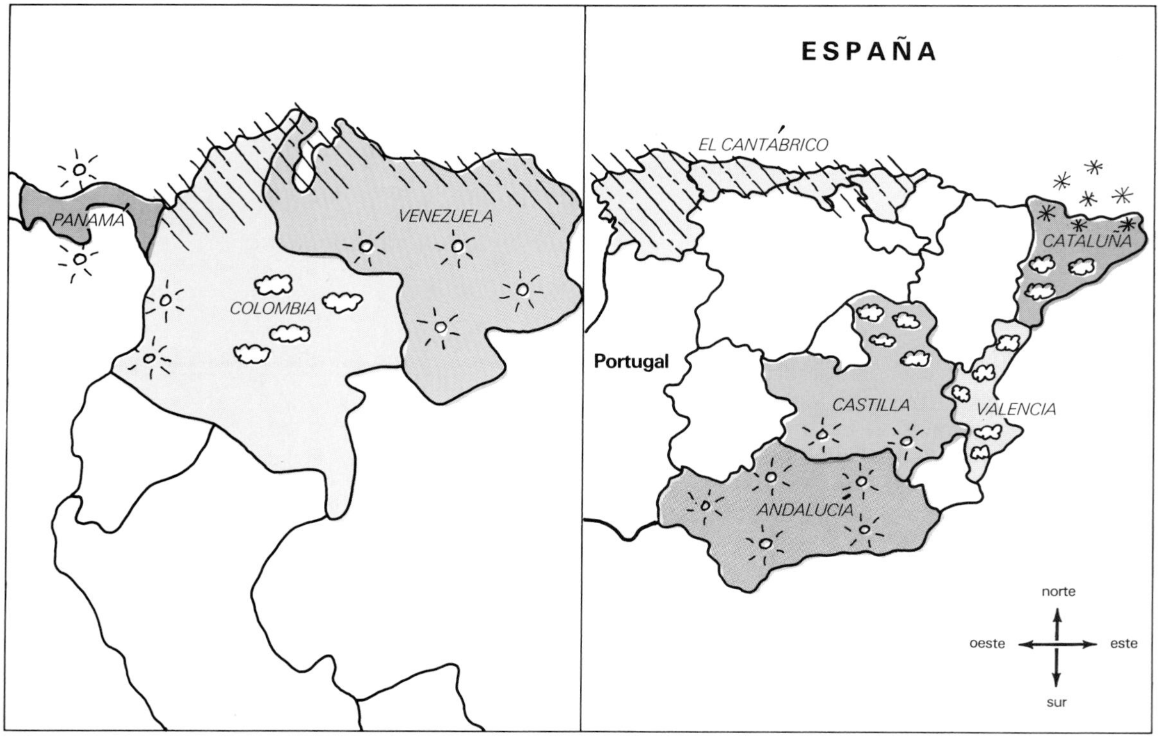

PANAMÁ
VENEZUELA
COLOMBIA

ESPAÑA
EL CANTÁBRICO
CATALUÑA
Portugal
CASTILLA
VALENCIA
ANDALUCÍA
norte
oeste
este
sur

Un partido de fútbol en las afueras de Bogotá, Colombia.

Cultura

Sports in the Hispanic world

Sports are important events for both participants and spectators in the Hispanic world, as they are in the United States. However, differences exist between Hispanic countries and the United States in the kinds of sports traditionally popular, in those newly popular, in the fans, and in sports heroes.

In the United States no one sport captures the heart and attention of the majority of the citizens; there are three major ones, baseball, basketball, and football. In Hispanic countries, soccer dominates; it is even the national sport of many of these nations. Most children grow up playing soccer and everyone has a favorite local team. In some countries a national team is selected from the best players of different teams around the country. This team then represents the country in annual international tournaments, and every fourth year plays for the World Cup (**la Copa del Mundo/la Copa Mundial**) which truly determines who is the world champion.

The predominance of one sport as local and national pastime helps to explain the fervor of the sports fan in Spanish-speaking countries. Virtually everyone has played and likes soccer. Teams and players have ardent supporters who are extremely loyal—or critical when their team does not play well. During international competitions fans see their team as an extension of their country. Thus, the national honor and pride are at stake when teams compete. For this reason and others, fans become very vocal and involved when their teams are playing.

Although soccer is easily the dominant sport, baseball also enjoys a large following, especially in the Caribbean and the Gulf of Mexico. The caliber of players from this area is such that many are drafted by the major leagues in the United States and go on to win top awards in baseball.

Boxing has also been popular for many years and numerous world champions have come from Argentina, Cuba, Mexico, Nicaragua, and Puerto Rico. Cuba, where athletes are not regarded as professional, continues to be a perennial powerhouse in amateur boxing.

There are a number of sports not traditionally associated with Hispanic countries that have attracted many followers. Basketball has been growing in appeal; Spain now has a professional basketball league with Spanish and American players and knowledgeable fans. In addition, students from the Dominican Republic, Venezuela, and Argentina are now playing for top college teams in the United States. Tennis, golf, Grand Prix racing, skiing, cycling, men's and women's volleyball, and weightlifting are other sports which have become popular.

Sports heroes in Hispanic countries take on different dimensions from those in the United States. Due to the diversity of sports interests of Americans, no one game or player dominates. However, in countries where there are only a handful of star athletes, they get tremendous national coverage and attention, which results in the creation of sports heroes. A recent article about Gabriela Sabatini, a young Argentine tennis star, states that she is already as famous and revered as the world-known writer Jorge Luis Borges and closing in on the liberator Simón Bolívar. It would be difficult for a U.S. sports star to achieve that kind of fame.

EN CONTEXTO

Un partido de béisbol

Nuestro equipo de béisbol es excelente. Los jugadores practican todos los días. En estos momentos ellos están jugando.

Si ganamos este partido, ganamos el campeonato. Los aficionados están muy emocionados y ahora están aplaudiendo.

Algunos aficionados no están de acuerdo con una decisión del árbitro. Uno de los jugadores y el árbitro están discutiendo.

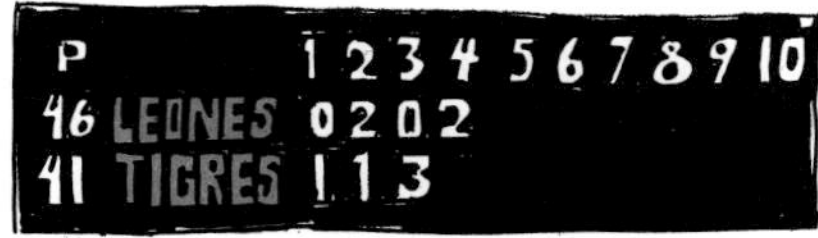

Es un partido muy reñido. El equipo contrario es también muy bueno, pero nuestro equipo está ganando.

Un partido de béisbol en el Estadio de Béisbol de Caracas, Venezuela. El béisbol es el deporte más popular en toda el área del Caribe.

Unos jóvenes juegan al vólibol, pasatiempo popular en las playas de Perú.

Para completar

Complete las siguientes oraciones de acuerdo con la información correcta.

1. Nuestro equipo de béisbol es
   a. bueno.
   b. regular.
   c. muy bueno.
2. En estos momentos los jugadores están
   a. aplaudiendo.
   b. jugando.
   c. practicando.
3. En el estadio hay
   a. pocas personas.
   b. mucho público.
   c. muchos árbitros.
4. El árbitro y uno de los jugadores están
   a. bailando.
   b. conversando.
   c. discutiendo.
5. El equipo contrario está
   a. ganando.
   b. corriendo.
   c. perdiendo.

otros deportes y actividades

el baloncesto/básquetbol	*basketball*
el boxeo	*boxing*
el esquí	*skiing*
el golf	*golf*
el judo/yudo	*judo*
la natación	*swimming*
el tenis	*tennis*
el vól(e)ibol	*volleyball*
bucear	*to skin/scuba-dive*
pescar	*to fish*

ACTIVIDADES

A En grupos de cuatro estudiantes haga la siguiente encuesta. Compare los resultados de su grupo con los de otro grupo.

1. deporte favorito
2. jugador/a favorito/a
3. asistencia (*attendance*) a los partidos
   a. todos
   b. casi todos
   c. algunos
   d. ninguno (*none*)
4. ver los partidos por televisión
   a. todos
   b. casi todos
   c. algunos
   d. ninguno

B Hágale las siguientes preguntas sobre deportes a su compañero/a. Después él/ella va a hacerle las mismas preguntas a usted. Comparta la información con la clase.

1. ¿Qué deporte practicas?
2. ¿Dónde lo practicas? ¿Con quién? ¿Cuándo?
3. ¿Ves los partidos de fútbol? ¿y los de béisbol?
4. ¿Cuál es tu jugador favorito?

GRAMÁTICA

Present progressive: *estar* + *-ndo*

	PRESENT **estar**	PRESENT PARTICIPLE **-ndo**
yo	estoy	
tú	estás	hablando
él, ella, usted	está	comiendo
nosotros/as	estamos	escribiendo
vosotros/as	estáis	
ellos/as, ustedes	están	

1. Form the present progressive with the present of **estar** and the present participle (**-ndo**).

2. To form the present participle, add **-ando** to the stem of **-ar** verbs and **-iendo** to the stem of **-er** and **-ir** verbs.

   hablar ⟶ hablando
   comer ⟶ comiendo
   escribir ⟶ escribiendo

3. When the verb stem of an **-er** or an **-ir** verb ends in a vowel, add **-yendo.**

   leer ⟶ leyendo
   creer ⟶ creyendo

4. The **-ir** verbs that change the stem vowel **o** to **ue** in the present (**dormir** ⟶ **duermo**), have the change **o** ⟶ **u** in the present participle.

   Ellos están d**u**rmiendo.

5. Place reflexive and direct object pronouns before the conjugated form of **estar** or attach them to the present participle. Notice that when the pronoun is attached to the present participle, an accent mark is needed on the stressed syllable.

   Pedro **se** está peinando. Pedro está pein**á**ndo**se**.
   Arturo **lo** está mirando. Arturo está mir**á**ndo**lo**.

6. Use the present progressive to emphasize an action in progress at the moment of speaking.

   Marcela estudia mucho. (normally)
   Marcela está estudiando. (at this moment)

7. Contrary to English, Spanish does not use the present progressive to refer to a time in the near future. The present is used instead.

   Salgo esta noche. *I'm leaving tonight.*

El esquí se practica en algunas zonas de los Andes como en el Club Andino Boliviano.

ACTIVIDADES

A Diga lo que las siguientes personas están haciendo de acuerdo con la situación.

1. Andrés tiene un examen esta tarde. Por eso, él
   a. está repasando con un compañero.
   b. está jugando tenis con su novia.
   c. está conversando con sus amigos en un café.
2. Mañana hay una competencia muy importante y los atletas
   a. están bailando en la fiesta.
   b. están practicando en el estadio.
   c. están sacudiendo los muebles.
3. Es la hora del desayuno y los niños
   a. están jugando en el parque.
   b. están montando bicicleta en la calle.
   c. están comiendo el cereal en el comedor.
4. Esta noche vienen unos amigos a cenar a casa de los Gorostiza. Por eso la señora
   a. está comprando un coche grande.
   b. está cocinando un plato especial.
   c. está nadando en la piscina.
5. Uno de los jugadores de béisbol no está de acuerdo con la decisión del árbitro. Ellos
   a. están conversando.
   b. están discutiendo.
   c. están pescando.

B **¿Qué están haciendo?** Estudie los dibujos y diga lo que están haciendo las personas.

1

2

3

4
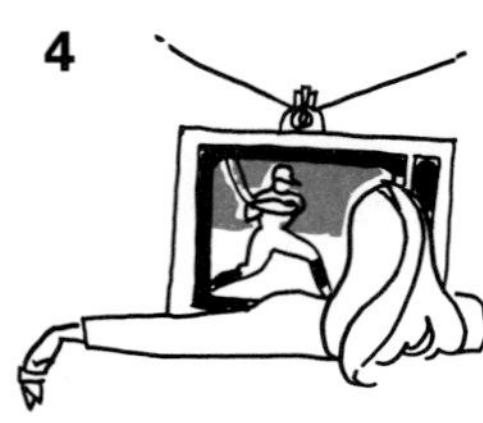

5

6

C **Lugares y actividades.** Usted está en los siguientes lugares. ¿Qué actividades observa?

la clase de español — su casa — la biblioteca — un estadio de béisbol — una discoteca — la playa

D **El parque.** Estudie el siguiente dibujo y determine lo que están haciendo las personas.

E **Pantomimas.** Piense en una actividad (leer, cantar, dormir, etc.). Usted debe imitar esa actividad y sus compañeros deben decir lo que está haciendo usted.

EN CONTEXTO

Escuelas de deportes

- Alumnos de 10 a 18 años.
- Internos o externos.
- Cursos semanales del 25 de Julio al 15 Agosto.
- En Castelldefels.

Desde: **50.000** ptas.

- Cursos semanales Julio y Agosto.
- Aprendizaje y práctica en circuitos de 4 campos por cursillo.

Desde: **67.200** ptas.

- Alumnos de 9 a 15 años. Internos y externos.

1.er turno: del 1 al 9 de Julio.
2.º turno: del 11 al 19 de Julio.
3.er turno: del 22 al 30 de Julio.

Desde: **37.500** ptas.

¿Verdadero o falso?

Diga si las siguientes oraciones son verdaderas o falsas de acuerdo con los anuncios de las escuelas de deportes.

1. Un chico de 19 años puede ir a la escuela de tenis.
2. Las clases en la escuela de tenis empiezan el 25 de julio.
3. Los cursos en la escuela de tenis cuestan 50.000 pesetas.
4. La escuela de tenis está en Marbella.
5. En la escuela de golf hay cursos en el invierno.
6. Los cursos de golf cuestan 67.200 pesetas.
7. Los alumnos de los cursos de básquetbol pueden tener de 9 a 15 años.
8. Los cursos en la escuela de básquetbol cuestan 20.000 pesetas.

GRAMÁTICA

Numbers 1,000 to 2,000,000

1.000	mil	10.000	diez mil
1.001	mil un(o)/una	100.000	cien mil
1.100	mil cien(to)	150.000	ciento cincuenta mil
2.000	dos mil	500.000	quinientos mil
		1.000.000	un millón (de)
		2.000.000	dos millones (de)

1. Use **mil** for *one thousand.*
2. Use **cien mil** for *one hundred thousand,* but use **ciento** with any number greater than 100,000 up to 199,000.

100.000	cien mil
101.000	ciento un mil
130.000	ciento treinta mil

3. Use **cientos/as** with numbers greater than two hundred thousand.

200.000 (libros)	doscient**os** mil libros
350.000 (niñas)	trescient**as** cincuenta mil niñas
500.000 (mesas)	quinient**as** mil mesas

4. Use **un millón** to say *one million.* Use **un millón de** when a noun follows.

1.000.000	un millón
1.000.000 (sillas)	un millón **de** sillas

ACTIVIDADES

A Su profesor/a va a leer un número de cada grupo. Indique cuál es el número.

4.000	6.000	7.500	10.200
15.000	20.300	32.000	40.100
100.000	400.000	600.000	900.000
340.000	460.000	880.000	750.000
670.000	275.000	296.000	1.000.000
530.000	315.000	775.000	995.000

B Lea los siguientes números y palabras.

1.000 clases	12.531 cuadernos	1.000.000 de autos	1.001 árbitros
60.000 aficionados	400.000 pesos	1.100 jugadores	101.000 casas
720.000 casetes	5.000 discos	170.000 personas	950.000 dólares

C **Entrevista.** Determine quién nació (*was born*) en los siguientes años. Consiga (*get*) su firma (*signature*) en una hoja de papel. Si algún (*any*) estudiante no nació en uno de estos años, debe decir cuándo nació.

Modelo 1940 ¿Naciste (*were you born*) en 1940?

Carlos Viramontes

1963 ________	1969 ________
1964 ________	1970 ________
1965 ________	1971 ________
1966 ________	1972 ________
1967 ________	1973 ________
1968 ________	1974 ________

D **Eventos futuros.** Diga en qué año van a ocurrir los siguientes hechos.

Modelo Brasil va a ir a la luna (*moon*)
En 1998.

1. Los Yankees van a participar en la Serie Mundial (*World Series*).
2. Un inglés va a ser el campeón mundial de boxeo.
3. Una mujer va a ser la presidenta de los Estados Unidos.
4. Vamos a tener paz (*peace*) en todo el mundo.
5. Los astrónomos van a descubrir otro planeta.
6. Van a descubrir una cura (*cure*) para el cáncer.
7. Vamos a tener una depresión mundial.
8. No vamos a tener más petróleo.
9. El inglés, el chino y el español van a ser las lenguas oficiales del mundo.
10. Van a descubrir vida (*life*) en otros planetas.

E Casas y precios. Describa estas casas y diga cuánto cuestan.

Modelo

Nueva Orleans, Luisiana
2 cuartos, 1 baño, sala, cocina moderna, jardín, garaje. Precio: $115.000

La casa está en Nueva Orleans. Tiene dos cuartos y sólo un baño. La sala es grande. No tiene comedor, pero la cocina es muy moderna. Tiene un jardín detrás y un garaje para un auto. Cuesta ciento quince mil dólares.

Pasadena, California
3 cuartos, cocina, sala, 2 baños, comedor, jardín, garaje. Precio: $247.000

Phoenix, Arizona
3 cuartos, sala, cocina, comedor, 2 baños, piscina, jardín grande, garaje para 2 autos. Precio: $455.000

Miami, Florida
4 cuartos, sala, cocina, 2½ baños, terraza, garaje. Precio: $150.000

Beverly Hills, California
5 cuartos, 5 baños, sala, biblioteca, comedor, cocina, piscina, jardín, garaje para 3 autos. Precio: $2.000.000

GRAMÁTICA

Ordinal numbers

primero/a	*first*	sexto/a	*sixth*
segundo/a	*second*	séptimo/a	*seventh*
tercero/a	*third*	octavo/a	*eighth*
cuarto/a	*fourth*	noveno/a	*ninth*
quinto/a	*fifth*	décimo/a	*tenth*

1. Ordinal numbers agree in gender and number with the nouns they modify.

segundo edificio cuarta casa

2. **Primero** and **tercero** drop the **-o** before masculine singular nouns.

primer partido **tercer** partido

ACTIVIDADES

A Conteste las preguntas de acuerdo con el siguiente cuadro.

Fila 3	Carlos	Carolina	Gabriela	Lorenzo	Jaime	Javier	Alma
Fila 2	Elena	Ester	Elías	Melisa	Lupe	Linda	Ana
Fila 1	Pedro	Ninfa	Lidia	Lucía	José	Clara	Paz
Asientos	1	2	3	4	5	6	7
				usted			

1. ¿Quién está en la primera fila, en el segundo asiento?
2. ¿Quién está en la tercera fila, en el sexto asiento?
3. ¿Quiénes están en la segunda fila?
4. ¿Quién está en la tercera fila, en el primer asiento?
5. ¿Dónde está Lupe? ¿Y Javier?
6. ¿Dónde están Gabriela y Linda? ¿Y usted?

B **Orden de los días.** Conteste las preguntas que su compañero/a le va a hacer sobre el orden de los días de la semana.

Modelo ¿Qué día de la semana es el lunes?
El lunes es el primer día de la semana.

GRAMÁTICA

Dates

1. To express the date in Spanish, use cardinal numbers (**dos, trece**), except for the first day of the month (**primero**).

—¿Cuál es la fecha?
—¿Qué fecha es hoy?
} —Es el 14 de febrero (de 1991).

2. Use **el** for *on* when referring to dates.

La fiesta es **el** cuatro de mayo. *The party is on May fourth.*

ACTIVIDADES

A Asocie los acontecimientos (*events*) de la columna de la izquierda con las fechas de la columna de la derecha.

1. Día de la Independencia	a. 12 de octubre de 1492
2. Descubrimiento de América	b. 4 de julio de 1776
3. John F. Kennedy muere	c. 21 de mayo de 1927
4. Lindbergh cruza el Atlántico	d. 22 de noviembre de 1963

B Complete las siguientes oraciones con la fecha del cumpleaños de las personas.

1. Mi cumpleaños es...
2. El cumpleaños de mi novio/a (o mejor amigo/a) es...
3. El cumpleaños de mi padre (o madre) es...
4. El cumpleaños de mi hermano/a es...

C Pregúnteles a cuatro de sus compañeros cuándo es su cumpleaños.

EN CONTEXTO

Un partido muy importante

1

Arturo quiere conseguir una entrada para el partido.

2

Arturo sigue la flecha para ir a la taquilla.

3

El empleado dice que no hay entradas.

4

José tiene dos entradas y lo invita para el partido.

5

Los amigos se ríen y Arturo pide dos cervezas.

6

El camarero sirve las cervezas mientras los amigos conversan.

Preguntas

1. ¿Qué quiere comprar Arturo?
2. ¿Adónde va para comprarla?
3. ¿Por qué está triste Arturo?
4. ¿Quién tiene entradas para el partido?
5. ¿Por qué está contento Arturo?
6. ¿Qué sirve el camarero?

ACTIVIDAD

Una invitación. Complete el siguiente diálogo con su compañero/a.

Usted	Tengo dos entradas para el partido del sábado. ¿Quieres ir?
Compañero/a	Sí, . . .
Usted	El partido es a las ____. Yo puedo estar en tu casa a las ____ más o menos. ¿Está bien?
Compañero/a	____. Y después yo te invito a cenar. ¿De acuerdo?
Usted	. . .

GRAMÁTICA

Present tense of *e* ⟶ *i* stem-changing verbs

pedir *to ask for, to order*

yo	**pi**do
tú	**pi**des
él, ella, usted	**pi**de
nosotros/as	pedimos
vosotros/as	pedís
ellos/as, ustedes	**pi**den

1. These verbs change the stem vowel **e** to **i** except in the **nosotros** and **vosotros** forms.
2. Other common **e** ⟶ **i** verbs are

conseguir	*to get*
decir	*to say*
reír(se)	*to laugh*
sonreír(se)	*to smile*
servir	*to serve*
seguir	*to continue, to follow*
vestir	*to dress*
vestirse	*to get dressed*

3. The verbs **seguir** and **conseguir** also have the orthographic change **gu** ⟶ **g** in the **yo** form to maintain the same **g** sound.

   seguir: si**g**o, sigues, sigue, seguimos, seguís, siguen

4. The verb **decir,** in addition to changing **e** ⟶ **i,** has an irregular **yo** form.

   decir: di**g**o, dices, dice, decimos, decís, dicen.

5. These stem-changing verbs also change the stem vowel **e** to **i** in the present participle.

   El camarero está s**i**rviendo el vino.

ACTIVIDADES

A ¿Qué comida sirven en los siguientes lugares?

Modelo en un restaurante chino
Sirven arroz frito y pollo con vegetales.

1. en un restaurante mexicano
2. en un restaurante francés
3. en un restaurante de servicio rápido
4. en un restaurante italiano
5. en la cafetería de la universidad

B ¿Qué piden las siguientes personas cuando van a un restaurante o a una cafetería?

Modelo **Piden sopa, sándwiches y leche.**

Olga y Pedro

1

Alicia

2

nosotros

3

tú

4

mis padres

C **¿Sí o no?** ¿Cómo contestan las siguientes personas estas preguntas?

Modelo (su padre) ¿Tiene una familia grande?
Él dice que sí. o **Él dice que no.**

1. (su profesor) ¿Tiene usted buenos estudiantes?
2. (usted) ¿Habla usted dos lenguas?
3. (sus amigos) ¿Estudian mucho?
4. (su madre) ¿Cocina usted todos los días?
5. (usted) ¿Tiende su cama y barre su cuarto?

D **¿Qué sigue?** Diga lo que sigue en las siguientes secuencias.

Modelo 1, 2, 3, . . . ¿Qué sigue?
Sigue el (número) 4.

1. 10, 20, 30, 40, 50, . . .
2. lunes, miércoles, . . .
3. alto, bajo; gordo, delgado; rubio, . . .
4. 3, 6, 9, . . .
5. bebé, niño, joven, . . .
6. ¿Cómo estás? . . .
7. 200, 400, 600, . . .
8. enero, febrero, marzo, . . .

E **¿Quién sigue a quién?** Explique lo que ocurre en los siguientes dibujos. Debe usar dos o tres oraciones para cada dibujo.

Entrevistas sobre ropa y programas de televisión. Usted le debe hacer una de las entrevistas a su compañero/a. Él/Ella le va a hacer la otra entrevista a usted.

1. ¿Cuánto tiempo necesitas para vestirte?
   ¿Cómo te vistes, con ropa moderna o clásica?
   ¿Te pones la misma ropa para la universidad y para una fiesta?
   ¿Crees que las personas gastan demasiado (*too much*) en la ropa?
2. ¿Cuáles son tus tres programas favoritos de televisión?
   ¿Con cuál programa te ríes más?
   ¿Puedes hablar sobre lo que pasa en uno de estos programas?

PRONUNCIACIÓN

Stress and the written accent mark (*continuation*)

1. The combination of unstressed **u** or **i** with another vowel forms a dipthong which is pronounced as one syllable.

   b**ai**le f**ie**sta b**ue**no beb**ie**ndo

2. When an accent mark is needed, place it over the **a, e,** or **o,** not over the **i** or **u.**

   Dios adi**ó**s bien tambi**é**n seis diecis**é**is

3. If the **i** or **u** is stressed, a diphthong is not formed: the vowels form two syllables. A written accent mark is required over the the **i** or **u.**

   cafeter**í**a pa**í**s fr**í**o Ra**ú**l

The combination of **i** and **u** forms a diphthong.

ciudad cuidado jesuita

DEPORTES PRACTICADOS	
	% práctica semanal
Fútbol	**18,8**
Carrera a pie	**13,0**
Baloncesto	**10,8**
Ciclismo	**10,4**
Tenis	**9,5**
Natación	**8,8**
Danza y gimnasia	**8,5**
Fútbol sala	**8,0**
Atletismo	**6,7**
Artes marciales	**4,1**
Pelota (frontón)	**3,6**
Tenis mesa	**3,4**
Voleivol	**3,2**
Tiro y caza	**3,1**
Balonmano	**1,9**
Montañismo	**1,3**

Fuente: ICEF, 1986

POR QUÉ HACE DEPORTE EL ESPAÑOL		
	1985	**1980**
Por hacer ejercicio fisico	**65**	**58**
Porque me gusta el deporte	**53**	**47**
Por diversión y pasar el tiempo	**52**	**51**
Por encontrarse con amigos	**28**	**25**
Por mantener la línea	**28**	**15**
Por evasión (escaparse de lo habitual)	**14**	**14**
Porque le gusta competir	**7**	**–**
Por hacer carrera deportiva	**2**	**2**
Otros motivos	**5**	**2**

LECTURA

Un deporte muy popular entre la juventud (*young people*)

The following selection was taken from *Blanco y negro,* a Sunday supplement of the prestigious Spanish newspaper *ABC.* From it you can see how popular professional American basketball is in Spain. You may need the following words to better understand the selection:

a partir de	*beginning at*	se conoce	*is known*
presenciar	*to see, to watch*	mitad	*half*
encuentros	*games*	subir	*to increase*
extranjera	*foreign*	campos	*fields*

LOS viernes, a partir de las once y media de la noche, entre un millón ochocientas mil y dos millones de personas conectan la Segunda Cadena de Televisión Española. Lo hacen para presenciar encuentros de baloncesto, que no es el primer deporte en España. Pero además son partidos de una competición extranjera, la profesional de los Estados Unidos, donde no actúa un solo jugador español y donde no se conoce «en vivo» a uno solo de sus participantes. La cosa tiene aún más importancia si se sabe que más de la mitad de los espectadores de estos encuentros de la NBA están entre los diez y los veinte años. Los periódicos dan ya información diaria de los resultados de esta competición y hay varias revistas especializadas que viven tanto de hablar del baloncesto norteamericano como del español. La audiencia tiene tendencia a subir en todos los campos. El director del programa televisivo «Cerca de las estrellas», Ramón Trecet, no se quiere apuntar ningún mérito en este fenómeno multitudinario:

—El baloncesto tiene ya implantación importante en España. Por otra parte, es muy televisivo y espectacular. En todo caso, está claro que es el deporte de la juventud.

¿Verdadero o falso?

Diga si las siguientes oraciones son verdaderas o falsas de acuerdo con la lectura.

1. Los aficionados al básquetbol pueden ver los partidos de la NBA en la televisión española.
2. El baloncesto es el deporte más popular en España.
3. Los espectadores ven los partidos por la tarde.
4. La mayor parte de los espectadores son muy jóvenes.
5. Hay publicaciones especializadas en el baloncesto.
6. Los periódicos dan los resultados de los partidos de la NBA.

7. Ramón Trecet es un jugador español de baloncesto.
8. «Cerca de las estrellas» es un programa de la televisión española.

The next reading selection explains two sports that originated in the Hispanic world.

Dos deportes de origen hispano

Entre los muchos deportes que se practican en los países hispanos hay dos que tienen su origen allí: el pato y el jai-alai o pelota vasca. El primero es de la Argentina y el segundo, de España.

Hoy en día° muy pocas personas juegan al pato. Es un deporte muy rudo° que tiene su origen en el campo° argentino. Hay cuatro jugadores en cada equipo y todos montan a caballo°. La pelota que usan tiene asas° y los jugadores tratan de agarrarla° por una de las asas. Después tienen que pasar la pelota por un aro° con una red°. Muchos dicen que es más o menos un juego de básquetbol a caballo, pero los jugadores de pato dicen que este deporte es mucho más difícil y violento.

nowadays / rough
countryside
horse / handles
grab it
ring / net

El pato es el deporte nacional de la Argentina. Los gauchos° argentinos son los primeros que juegan al pato. Al principio° no usaban° una pelota; usaban un pato vivo° dentro de una bolsa de cuero°. Por eso este deporte se llama pato.

Argentine cowboys
Al... *At the beginning /* no... *didn't use*
pato... *live duck /* bolsa... *leather bag*

El jai-alai es un deporte muy rápido y dinámico. Los jugadores o pelotaris usan un guante° que tiene una cesta° larga y curva. Allí reciben la pelota y la

glove / basket

Jugadores de jai-alai en Guernica, España. Este deporte vasco es muy popular en muchos países hispanos.

lanzan° contra una de las paredes de la cancha donde juegan. El jugador del otro equipo contesta y el juego continúa hasta que un jugador pierde. Este deporte es muy peligroso° porque la pelota es muy dura° y va a una velocidad muy grande. En estos partidos muchas personas del público apuestan° y es muy interesante ver cómo las apuestas cambian° durante el partido. En los Estados Unidos juegan al jai-alai en Las Vegas, en la Florida y en Bridgeport, Connecticut.

throw
dangerous / hard
bet
change

Preguntas

1. ¿Qué dos deportes tienen su origen en el mundo hispano?
2. ¿De qué países son estos deportes?
3. ¿Cómo es la pelota que usan hoy en día para jugar al pato?
4. ¿Quiénes juegan primero al pato?
5. ¿Qué usan estas personas al principio?
6. ¿Quiénes son los pelotaris?
7. ¿Qué usan para recibir la pelota?
8. ¿Cómo es la pelota que usan?
9. ¿Qué hacen muchas personas del público durante los partidos de jai-alai?
10. ¿Dónde juegan al jai-alai en los Estados Unidos?

SITUACIONES

1. You want to take a trip to New Mexico. Ask your friends (a) what the weather is like in the fall and the spring, (b) about the temperature, because you cannot be there if it is very hot, (c) about the rain, and (d) what people do when they visit New Mexico.
2. Find out where your partner is from. Then ask four questions about the weather in his/her hometown and state.
3. Introduce yourself to a student in class. Find out about his/her sports interests. You may want to know what sports he/she plays, where, with whom, if he/she plays well, and so on. Finish the conversation and thank the student.
4. You are living in a dormitory on campus. Your mother/father calls. Another student will play the part of your parent. He/She asks what you are studying, what you are doing right now, if you are eating well, if you are washing your clothes, if you are studying a lot, and other questions related to school and your social life.
5. You are being questioned about your activities on Saturdays. Tell step by step (e.g., **Primero**. . ., **Segundo**. . .) what you do on Saturdays. Be thorough in your narration.
6. You and your partner will play the roles of a newspaper reporter and a well-known athlete. Interview this athlete and try to find out as much as possible about his/her (a) family, (b) activities, (c) plans for the future, and so on. Share this information with the class.

VOCABULARIO[1]

deportes	*sports*
el baloncesto/básquetbol	*basketball*
el béisbol	*baseball*
la bicicleta	*bicycle*
el boxeo	*boxing*
el campeonato	*championship*
el equipo	*the team*
el esquí	*skiing*
el fútbol	*soccer*
el golf	*golf*
el judo/yudo	*judo*
la natación	*swimming*
el tenis	*tennis*
el vól(e)ibol	*volleyball*
en el estadio	
la decisión	*decision*
la entrada	*ticket*
la flecha	*arrow*
el partido	*game*
la taquilla	*ticket office*
estaciones	*seasons*
el invierno	*winter*
el otoño	*autumn*
la primavera	*spring*
el verano	*summer*
bebidas	*beverages*
la cerveza	*beer*
lugares	
la escuela	*school*
la piscina	*pool*
personas	
el aficionado	*fan*
el árbitro	*umpire, referee*
el empleado	*employee*
el jugador/la jugadora	*player*
tiempo	*weather*
la nieve	*snow*
el sol	*sun*
el viento	*wind*
claro/despejado	*clear*
fresco	*cool*
nublado/nuboso	*cloudy*
descripción	
contrario	*opposite, contrary*
emocionado	*excited*
importante	*important*
reñido	*close (game)*
verbos	
aplaudir	*to applaud*
bucear	*to skin/scuba-dive*
conseguir (i)	*to get*
conversar	*to converse, to talk*
decir (g, i)	*to say*
discutir	*to argue*
esquiar	*to ski*
ganar	*to win*
invitar	*to invite*
llover (ue)	*to rain*
montar	*to ride*
nadar	*to swim*
nevar (ie)	*to snow*
patinar	*to skate*
pedir (i)	*to ask for, to order*
pescar	*to fish*
reírse (i)	*to laugh*
seguir (i)	*to follow, to continue*
servir (i)	*to serve*
sonreírse (i)	*to smile*
vestir (i)	*to dress*
vestirse (i)	*to get dressed*

[1] See pages 144, 156, and 158 for the months of the year and the numbers.

palabras útiles

algunos	*some*
mientras	*while*
si	*if*

expresiones útiles

¿Cuál es la fecha?	*What's the date?*
en estos momentos	*right now, at this moment*
estar de acuerdo	*to agree*
¿Qué tiempo hace?	*What's the weather?*
todos los días	*everyday*

In Lección 7 **you will**

a. **talk about and describe clothing.**
b. **make and answer telephone calls.**
c. **ask for and tell prices.**
d. **express needs.**
e. **express likes and dislikes.**
f. **express satisfaction and dissatisfaction.**

El escaparate de una tienda

más ropa

el abrigo	*coat*
la blusa	*blouse*
la bufanda	*scarf*
los calcetines	*socks*
la camiseta	*T-shirt*
la chaqueta	*jacket*
el impermeable	*raincoat*
las medias	*stockings*
el sombrero	*hat*
el traje	*suit*
el traje de baño	*bathing suit*
los vaqueros/jeans	*blue jeans*
el vestido	*dress*

Lección 7

De compras

El escaparate de un almacén de Madrid. En los últimos años la moda española ha adquirido mucha importancia en los países europeos.

ACTIVIDADES

A **¿Cuánto cuesta(n)?** Usted quiere saber (*know*) el precio de la ropa que está en el escaparate. Pregúntele a su compañero/a.

Modelo **—¿Cuánto cuesta el suéter?**
—Cuesta $45,00.
—¿Cuánto cuestan los zapatos tenis?
—Cuestan $35,00.

B Usted quiere saber dónde compra la ropa su compañero/a y cuánto paga (*pays*).

Modelo **—¿Dónde compras las camisas?**
—Las compro en...
—¿Cuánto pagas por una camisa?
—Pago...

C Pregúntele a su compañero/a qué ropa lleva (*wears*) cuando

hace frío   hace calor   llueve   va a una fiesta   practica deportes
va a la playa   está en su casa

D **¿Quién es?** Describa la ropa que lleva un/a compañero/a sin decir su nombre. Sus compañeros deben tratar de adivinar (*guess*) quién es esa persona.

Modelo Usted: Lleva una falda roja, una blusa blanca y un suéter gris.
Compañero/a: Es Amelia.

Cultura

Shopping in the Hispanic world

See IM, **Lección 7, Cultura.**

Shopping in the Hispanic world offers many choices. Very popular among tourists as well as the local people are the markets (**mercados**), where one can find a wide range of items, from food supplies to beautiful handicrafts. In the **mercados,** a common practice is for buyers to bargain (**regatear**) for a better price. In many cases, the final price is substantially lower than the asking price.

Although department stores (**almacenes**) and shopping malls (**centros comerciales**) are not very common in the Hispanic world, there are some notable examples: **El Corte Inglés,** a chain department store in the principal cities of Spain; **Unicentro** shopping mall in Bogotá, Colombia; and the **Centro Ciudad Comercial Tamanaco, Plaza Las Américas,** and **Concresa** in Caracas, Venezuela. Small stores (**tiendas**) that specialize in certain merchandise are more common. In these places, prices are fixed and people do not bargain.

In some Hispanic cities, such as Buenos Aires, Santiago, and Madrid, one can find streets that are closed to traffic, allowing people to shop with ease. They are similar to the pedestrian malls in the United States.

Shopping hours vary among the different countries. In many cities, stores close at lunch time (which may be as late as one thirty) and reopen in the afternoon (usually between four and five). Stores also close on Saturday afternoon. However, these customs are slowly changing in order to accommodate shoppers.

A typical sight in Hispanic countries are street vendors. They sell all kinds of merchandise, including food, clothing, toys, and handicrafts. In some countries they perform varied services such as sharpening knives and scissors, repairing or cleaning cars right on the street, and fixing up buildings.

Una turista compra un poncho en un mercado de Oaxaca en México. La belleza (*beauty*) de los diseños y los colores brillantes son características de los chales, sarapes y otros artículos tejidos (*woven*).

EN CONTEXTO

Una conversación por teléfono

Josefina está en su casa. El teléfono suena y ella contesta.

Josefina ¡Aló!
Paula Josefina, te habla Paula. ¿Cómo estás?
Josefina Bien, ¿y tú?
Paula Muy bien. Mira, Josefina, te llamo porque hay unas rebajas° muy buenas en el Centro Comercial° Tamanaco. Yo pienso ir esta tarde. ¿Quieres venir?
Josefina Yo, encantada. El sábado es el cumpleaños de Pilar y quiero comprarle un regalo°.
Paula ¿Qué piensas regalarle°.
Josefina Todavía° no sé. Ella siempre lleva° ropa muy bonita. Quizás una pulsera°, un cinturón°...
Paula Allá seguramente encuentras algo. Entonces paso por ti° a las dos y media. ¿Te parece bien°?
Josefina Perfecto. Te espero° a las dos y media.
Paula Hasta la tarde.
Josefina Hasta entonces.

sales / Centro... *Shopping Center*
comprarle... *buy her a present*
to give her
still / *wears*
Quizás... *Perhaps a bracelet* / *belt*
paso... *I'll pick you up*
¿Te... *Is it OK with you?*
Te... *I'll wait for you*

Preguntas

1. ¿Quién llama a Josefina?
2. ¿Qué dice Josefina cuando contesta el teléfono?
3. ¿Adónde va a ir Paula esta tarde?
4. ¿Por qué va a ir allí?
5. ¿Qué quiere comprar Josefina?
6. ¿Cuándo es el cumpleaños de Pilar?
7. ¿Qué piensa regalarle Josefina?
8. ¿A qué hora van a ir a las tiendas?

ACTIVIDADES

A Hágale las siguientes preguntas a su compañero/a. Comparta la información con la clase.

1. ¿Hablas mucho por teléfono? ¿Con quién hablas más? 2. ¿Compras cosas por teléfono? ¿Qué compras? 3. ¿Usas el directorio telefónico? ¿Cuándo?

B Usted llama a un amigo/una amiga para ir a un centro comercial. Debe decirle a qué centro comercial va a ir, qué piensa hacer allá y a qué hora puede pasar por él/ella.

GRAMÁTICA

Indirect object nouns and pronouns

me	*(to), (for) me*	nos	*(to), (for) us*
te	*(to), (for) you (fam.)*	os	*(to), (for) you (fam.)*
le	*(to), (for) you (formal), him, her, it*	les	*(to), (for) you (formal), them*

1. Indirect object nouns and pronouns tell to or for whom an action is done.

   El profesor **me** explica la lección. — *The professor explains the lesson to me.*

2. Indirect object pronouns have the same form as direct object pronouns except in the third person: **le** and **les.** Place the indirect object pronoun before the conjugated verb form. It may be attached to an infinitive or to a present participle when these are together with a conjugated verb.

   Te voy a comprar un regalo.
Voy a comprar**te** un regalo. — *I'm going to buy you a present.*

   Juan **nos** está preparando la cena.
Juan está preparándo**nos** la cena. — *Juan is preparing dinner for us.*

3. When the indirect object is a noun, the corresponding indirect object pronoun is normally used as well.

   Yo **le** compro un regalo a **Victoria.** — *I'm buying Victoria a present.*

Unos jóvenes hablan por teléfono en Guadalajara, México.

4. Since **le** and **les** have several meanings, **le** is often clarified with the preposition **a** + **él, ella,** or **usted,** and **les** with **a** + **ellos, ellas,** or **ustedes.**

Le hablo a **usted.**	*I'm talking to you.* (not to him)
Siempre **les** compro algo a **ellos.**	*I always buy them something.*

5. For emphasis, use **a** + **mí, ti, nosotros/as,** and **vosotros/as** in addition to the indirect object pronouns **me, te, nos,** and **os** respectively.

Juan **me** escribe **a mí.**	*Juan writes to me.* (not to you)
Pedro **te** habla a **ti.**	*Pedro is talking to you.* (not to someone else)

The verb *dar* to give

dar: doy, das, da, damos dais, dan

This verb is almost always used with indirect object pronouns. Notice the difference between **dar** (*to give*) and **regalar** (*to give as a gift*).

Ella le **da** el casete a Pedro.	*She gives Pedro the cassette.*
Ella le regala el casete a Pedro.	*She gives Pedro the cassette.* (as a gift)

ACTIVIDADES

A Usted está cuidando a un niño en su casa. Diga las cosas que usted hace.

Modelo preparar la comida
Yo le preparo la comida.

dar la comida   poner la piyama   poner la televisión   lavar la cara
quitar los zapatos   leer un cuento (*story*)

B Usted quiere ir a esquiar a las montañas (*mountains*) este fin de semana. Su compañero/a de cuarto no quiere ir. Trate de convencerlo/la (*Try to convince him/her*) diciendo todo lo que usted va a hacer por él/ella la semana próxima.

Modelo lavar el auto
Si vas conmigo, te voy a lavar (voy a lavarte) el auto.

preparar el desayuno   planchar la ropa   servir el desayuno en la cama
pasar la aspiradora   hacer la tarea   regalar un/a...

C Diga todas las cosas que su profesor/a hace o no hace por ustedes.

Modelo hacer preguntas
Nos hace preguntas.
limpiar la casa
No nos limpia la casa.

hablar en español dar la tarea preparar el almuerzo explicar las lecciones
dar buenas notas regalar entradas

D Usted está en Venezuela de vacaciones. Diga quién(es) le escribe(n) a usted. Después, diga a quién(es) le(s) escribe usted.

Modelo **Mi hermano me escribe todas las semanas.**
Le escribo a mi profesor de español.

E Usted quiere vivir una vida sana (*healthy life*). Pregúntele a su compañero/a qué le recomienda. Su compañero/a puede usar algunas de las sugerencias (*suggestions*) que están más abajo o darle sus propias (*own*) sugerencias.

Modelo
Usted ¿Qué me recomiendas?
Compañero/a Te recomiendo hacer ejercicio.
Usted ¿Qué más me recomiendas?
Compañero/a Te recomiendo dormir ocho horas.

1. comer pescado
2. caminar
3. beber mucha agua
4. nadar en la piscina
5. comer frutas y vegetales
6. no tomar mucha cerveza
7. no comer papas fritas
8. ir al gimnasio

F Este mes es el cumpleaños de varias personas. Diga qué les va a regalar usted y qué les va a regalar su amigo Pedro.

Modelo María Cristina
Yo le voy a regalar (voy a regalarle) una bufanda.
Pedro le va a regalar un libro.

nuestro entrenador mi hermana Ricardo Silvia

G ¿Qué les dice usted a las diferentes personas en estas situaciones?

Modelo Es el cumpleaños de su prima y usted va a verla.
Le digo: «Feliz cumpleaños» («Felicidades»).

1. Sus padres le regalan un auto deportivo.
2. Usted tiene dos entradas para un concierto y llama a un/a amigo/a.
3. Usted está en un café y viene el camarero.
4. Su novio/a quiere ir a esquiar a las montañas, pero hace mal tiempo.
5. Un amigo lo/la invita para ir al cine, pero usted tiene un examen mañana.

Un moderno almacén de la ciudad de México.

EN CONTEXTO

En una tienda

Josefina	Paula, ¿qué te parece esa billetera°?	*wallet*
Paula	Es bonita. Y ésta es muy bonita también.	
Josefina	¿Cuánto cuesta ésa?	
Paula	Setecientos bolívares[1].	
Josefina	Está un poco cara°.	*expensive*
Paula	¡Ay, Josefina! No está cara.	
Josefina	Pues yo creo que sí. Mira, allá hay unos cinturones rebajados°.	cinturones. . . *marked down belts*
Paula	Vamos a verlos. (Las chicas miran los cinturones)	
Josefina	Este cinturón es precioso°. Y aquél también.	*beautiful*
Paula	Además están muy baratos°.	*inexpensive*
Josefina	Sí, y muy de moda. No pierdo más tiempo. Le compro este cinturón a Pilar.	
Paula	Entonces vamos a pagar° a la caja°.	*pay / cash register*

Preguntas

1. ¿Qué miran las chicas primero?
2. Según Josefina, ¿son baratas o caras? ¿y según Paula?
3. ¿Qué otras cosas ven las chicas?
4. ¿Cómo son los precios?
5. ¿Qué le va a comprar Josefina a Pilar?
6. ¿Por qué va a ir a la caja?

[1] Monetary unit in Venezuela. In 1989 a dollar was the equivalent of about 40 **bolívares.**

más accesorios

el anillo	*ring*
los aretes	*earrings*
la bolsa	*purse*
la cadena	*chain*
el collar	*necklace*
los guantes	*gloves*
el pañuelo	*handkerchief*

ACTIVIDADES

A A usted le van a regalar ciertas cosas. Dígale a su compañero/a lo que usted prefiere de cada grupo. Después su compañero/a le debe decir qué prefiere él/ella.

1. una pulsera, un anillo, una cadena
2. un suéter, una sudadera, una camisa
3. una billetera, un cinturón, un pañuelo
4. un abrigo de visón (*mink*), un impermeable, una chaqueta
5. una camiseta, un traje de baño, unos zapatos tenis

B Dígale a su compañero/a qué cosas tiene usted en su billetera o en su bolsa.

GRAMÁTICA

Demonstrative adjectives and pronouns

Demonstrative adjectives agree in gender and number with the noun they modify. Whereas English has two sets of demonstratives (*this, these* and *that, those*), Spanish has three.

this	este vestido esta blusa	*these*	estos vestidos estas blusas
that	ese abrigo esa bufanda	*those*	esos abrigos esas bufandas
that (*over there*)	aquel anillo aquella tienda	*those* (*over there*)	aquellos anillos aquellas tiendas

1. Use **este, esta, estos,** and **estas** when referring to people or things that are close to you in space or time.

   Este señor no está de acuerdo. — *This gentleman doesn't agree.*
   Esta tarde vamos de compras. — *We're going shopping this afternoon.*

2. Use **ese, esa, esos,** and **esas** when referring to people or things that are not close to you. Sometimes they are close to the person you are addressing.

   Esa blusa que llevas es muy bonita. — *The blouse you're wearing is very pretty.*

3. Use **aquel, aquella, aquellos** and **aquellas** when referring to people or things that are more distant.

   Aquella tienda es muy cara. — *That store (over there) is very expensive.*

4. Demonstratives can be used as pronouns. Add a written accent mark to the stressed vowel to distinguish demonstrative pronouns from demonstrative adjectives.

   Compran **esta** billetera y **ésa.** — *They buy this wallet and that one.*
   ¿Qué anillo prefieres, **éste** o **aquél**? — *What ring do you prefer, this one or that one?*

5. To refer to a general idea or concept and to ask for the identification of an object, use **esto, eso** or **aquello.**

   Ellos trabajan mucho y **eso** es muy bueno. — *They work a lot and that's very good.*
   ¿Qué es **esto**? Es un collar. — *What's this? It's a necklace.*
   ¿Qué es **aquello**? Es un cinturón. — *What's that (over there)? It's a belt.*

ACTIVIDADES

A Escoja el demostrativo correcto según cada situación.

este ese aquel

1. Yo tengo un libro a mi lado. Yo digo: «____ libro es muy interesante».
2. Mi hermana lleva un impermeable muy bonito. Yo le digo: «____ impermeable es muy elegante».
3. Mi amigo dice que el auto rojo que está allá es de Pepe. Yo le digo: «____ auto no es de Pepe».

estas esas aquellas

4. Yo le estoy hablando a mi amiga sobre dos chicas que están cerca. Yo le digo: «____ chicas salen con mis hermanos».
5. Tú estás hablando de las botas que llevas y dices: «____ botas son viejas».
6. Mi amigo está mirando unas casas que están un poco lejos. Él dice: «Ofelia vive en una de ____ casas».

B Complete el siguiente diálogo usando los demostrativos correctos de acuerdo con el dibujo.

Adela	___ blusa es bonita, pero ___ vestido está muy feo.
Carmen	Es verdad, y también ___ botas.
Adela	¿___ sombrero y ___ abrigo están rebajados?
Carmen	No, pero ___ cinturón sí está rebajado.

C Usted va a quitarles varios objetos a sus compañeros y los va a poner en diferentes lugares del salón de clase. Después llama a un compañero y él/ella debe decir de quién es cada objeto usando la forma correcta de **ese, este** o **aquel.**

Modelo **Este bolígrafo es de Alberto.**
Esos cuadernos son de David.

D Conteste las siguientes preguntas sobre diferentes personas y objetos de la clase usando la forma correcta de los pronombres **éste, ése** o **aquél,** de acuerdo con la distancia.

Modelo ¿Prefieres esta silla?
No, prefiero ésa (aquélla).

1. ¿Lees ese cuaderno?
2. ¿Escribes estas palabras?
3. ¿Estudias con ese estudiante?
4. ¿Necesitas este lápiz? ¿y ese bolígrafo?
5. ¿Abren ustedes aquella ventana?

E Complete cada situación de la columna de la izquierda con un comentario lógico de la columna de la derecha.

1. Los jugadores hacen ejercicio todos los días.
2. No hay comida en este café.
3. Piensan visitar el Amazonas.
4. Mi nombre no está en la lista de esta clase.

a. Esto es absurdo.
b. Aquello es muy interesante.
c. No entiendo esto.
d. Eso es muy bueno.

F **¿Qué es esto (eso, aquello)?** Señale (*Point to*) diferentes objetos de la clase y pídales a sus compañeros que los identifiquen. Use el pronombre correspondiente según la distancia.

EN CONTEXTO

En un almacén°

department store

Dependienta Buenas tardes. ¿En qué puedo servirles°? — ¿En... *May I help you?*

Josefina Me gusta° este vestido de rayas°, pero no encuentro mi talla°. — Me... *I like* / de... *striped* / *size*

Dependienta ¿Qué talla usa usted?

Josefina La treinta[2].

Dependienta Aquí hay uno. Los probadores° están allá, a la derecha. (Josefina se prueba° el vestido y sale.) — *fitting rooms* / se... *tries on*

Paula Te queda° muy bien. Además la tela° es preciosa. — Te... *It fits* / *material*

Josefina A mí me gusta, pero está un poco caro.

Paula ¡Otra vez!° Mira, yo te puedo prestar° dinero si lo necesitas. — ¡Otra... *again!* / *lend*

Josefina No, es que tú gastas° mucho y yo no, especialmente en un vestido. — *spend*

Dependienta Yo le puedo mostrar° otros que son muy bonitos y no son tan caros. — *show*

Preguntas

1. ¿Qué vestido le gusta a Josefina?
2. ¿Qué talla usa?
3. ¿Quién le consigue un vestido de su talla?
4. ¿Dónde están los probadores?
5. ¿Cómo le queda el vestido a Josefina?
6. ¿Por qué no lo quiere comprar?
7. ¿Qué le dice Paula a Josefina?
8. ¿Qué va a mostrarle la dependienta a Josefina?

---

[2] This chart shows the approximate equivalents of various sizes.

U.S.A.	8	10	12	14	16	18	20
Spain	38	40	42	44	46	48	50
Some other Hispanic countries	28	30	32	34	36	38	40

Un mercado cerca de la catedral en una calle de Barcelona, España. En muchas ciudades hispanas se levantan pequeños mercados al aire libre ciertos días de la semana.

expresiones útiles en las tiendas

Me queda grande.	*It's too big.*
Me queda ancho.	*It's too wide.*
Me queda estrecho.	*It's too narrow.*
Me gustaría cambiar esto.	*I'd like to exchange this.*
Combinan muy bien.	*They go together.*
de cuadros	*plaid, checked*
de color entero	*solid*

ACTIVIDADES

A Escoja la contestación adecuada para cada situación.

1. La blusa de rayas rojas y la falda azul son muy bonitas.
2. Este vestido es talla 32 y yo uso la talla 34.
3. Esta blusa es preciosa, pero muy cara.
4. Me gustaría probarme esta chaqueta.
5. Los zapatos son 38 y yo uso el número 37.

a. Sí, te queda muy estrecho.
b. Y combinan muy bien.
c. El probador está allí.
d. Aquí hay otras más baratas.
e. Te quedan grandes.

B Usted está de compras en un almacén. Su compañero/a es el/la dependiente/a. Usted le debe explicar qué ropa necesita. Su compañero/a debe hacerle preguntas y explicarle lo que tienen en el almacén.

C Usted es el/la dependiente/a de una tienda. Su compañero/a se está probando ropa, pero no le queda bien. Él/Ella debe explicarle por qué no le queda bien y usted debe tratar de solucionar el problema.

GRAMÁTICA

The verb *gustar*

1. Spanish uses the verb **gustar** to express likes and dislikes. However, **gustar** is not used the same way as the English verb *to like.* **Gustar** is more similar to the expression *to be pleasing (to someone).*

   Me gusta ese vestido. *I like that dress. (That dress is pleasing to me.)*

2. In this construction, the person or thing liked is the subject. The indirect object pronoun shows to whom something is pleasing.

Me	gusta el traje.	*I*	*like(s) the suit.*
Te		*You (fam.)*	
Le		*He, She, You (formal)*	
Nos		*We*	
Os		*You (fam.)*	
Les		*They, You (formal)*	

3. Generally, only two forms of **gustar** are used: **gusta, gustan.** If one person or thing is liked, use **gusta.** If two or more persons or things are liked, use **gustan.**

   Me **gusta** ese collar. — *I like that necklace.*
   No me **gustan** esos anillos. — *I don't like those rings.*

4. To express what people like or do not like to do, use an infinitive after **gustar.**

   Me gusta caminar por la mañana. — *I like to walk in the morning.*
   No me gusta correr. — *I don't like to run.*

5. To emphasize or clarify the indirect object pronoun, use **a** + noun or pronoun.

   A Marina le gusta el abrigo.
   A ella le gusta esa tienda.

6. Other Spanish verbs that follow the pattern of **gustar** are **encantar** (*to delight, to love*), **interesar** (*to interest*), **parecer** (*to seem*), and **quedar** (*to fit, to have something left*).

ACTIVIDADES

A Reacciones. Diga si a usted le gustan o no los siguientes lugares, personas o actividades. Trabaje con un compañero/a.

Modelo Compañero/a **California.**
Usted **Me gusta (No me gusta) California.**
Compañero/a **las fiestas**
Usted **Me gustan (No me gustan) las fiestas.**

lugares	personas	actividades
esta universidad las tiendas las cafeterías la playa	el presidente Julio Iglesias los niños Gloria Estefan	esquiar nadar estudiar los conciertos

B **Reportando reacciones.** ¿Qué le gusta o no le gusta a su mejor amigo/a?

Modelo los jugadores el entrenador
Le gustan los jugadores, pero no le gusta el entrenador.

esos almacenes
los deportes
dormir tarde
esa canción
la música popular
jugar al tenis
la comida china
bailar
las clases
los conciertos
nadar
ir de compras
la ropa moderna
beber Coca-Cola
los programas de radio

C Hable con tres compañeros/as y diga lo que le gusta de ellos/as (*what you like about them*).

Modelos **Me gusta tu blusa. Me gustan tus zapatos (de) tenis.**

D ¿Qué le(s) encanta a estas personas?

Modelo **A mi hermano le encantan los partidos de béisbol.**
A mis tíos les encanta ver televisión.

personas	actividades
a mis amigos/as a mi novio/a a mi entrenador a los estudiantes a los jugadores	leer novelas románticas bailar salsa ir al cine ver partidos de fútbol gastar dinero

E **¿Qué te gusta hacer?** Pregúntele a su compañero/a qué le gusta hacer. Debe averiguar (*find out*) por lo menos tres cosas y compartir la información con la clase.

Modelo
Usted **¿Qué te gusta hacer?**
Compañero/a **Me gusta esquiar.**
Usted **¿Y qué más te gusta hacer?**
Compañero/a **Me gusta bailar.**

F Preséntele estos problemas a su compañero/a. Él/Ella debe darle la respuesta correcta.

Modelo **Usted** Pilar tiene $50,00. Paga $20,00 por un suéter. ¿Cuánto dinero le queda?
Compañero/a Le quedan $30,00.

1. Ernesto tiene $75,00. Le presta $20,00 a su hermano. ¿Cuánto dinero le queda?
2. Erica tiene $20,00. Ella va al cine y a cenar con una amiga. El cine cuesta $5,00 y la cena $12,00. ¿Cuánto dinero le queda?
3. Yo tengo $40,00. Compro un suéter por $39,00. ¿Cuánto dinero me queda?

G **¿Es usted un/a comprador/a** (*buyer*) **compulsivo/a?** Este cuestionario va a darle la respuesta. Compare sus resultados con un compañero/a.

1.	Le doy mucha importancia a la ropa.	sí	no
2.	Me fijo° en la ropa que llevan las personas.	sí	no
3.	Les pido solicitud° de crédito a todas las tiendas.	sí	no
4.	Cuando voy a una tienda siempre compro algo.	sí	no
5.	Les recomiendo a mis amigos tiendas y almacenes nuevos.	sí	no
6.	Cuando tengo dinero siempre voy de compras.	sí	no
7.	Si no tengo dinero, uso las tarjetas° de crédito.	sí	no

Sí = 2 puntos
No = 0 puntos
De 8 a 14 puntos. Usted es un/a comprador/a compulsivo/a.
De 4 a 7 puntos. Usted es un/a comprador/a normal.
De 0 a 3 puntos. Usted es un poco tacaño/a. Le recomendamos renovar su ropa.

I notice
application
cards

Frente a El Corte Inglés, la cadena más importante de almacenes de España.

LECTURA

Unos regalos

Usted necesita comprar ciertas cosas. Lea los siguientes anuncios y diga a qué tienda iría usted (*would you go*) para comprarlas.

1. Es el cumpleaños de su sobrino de cinco años.
2. Usted necesita ropa informal.
3. Busca un regalo para el Día de las Madres.

La ropa

La ropa que se usa en las ciudades de los países hispanos y las ciudades de los Estados Unidos es muy similar. Sin embargo°, la ropa que llevan las personas mayores es, en general, más conservadora y formal que la que llevan las personas de su misma edad en los Estados Unidos. Por ejemplo, en una playa o en un club una señora puede llevar una camiseta y unos pantalones cortos o *shorts,* pero si esa misma señora tiene que ir a otro lugar, como el supermercado que está cerca de su casa, se pone un vestido, o una blusa con una falda o unos pantalones largos.

Nevertheless

En los lugares calurosos°, especialmente en el verano, los hombres usan mucho la guayabera en vez de° una camisa. Las guayaberas son muy frescas y prácticas, y además pueden ser muy elegantes y bonitas. En algunos países como México, las guayaberas pueden llevar bordados° al frente.

hot
en... *instead of*
embroidery

Entre los jóvenes, la moda norteamericana es muy popular. Antes, para ir a la universidad, los jóvenes llevaban° traje o una chaqueta. Hoy en día, llevan

used to wear

jeans con camisas o camisetas y zapatos tenis a casi todas partes. Sin embargo, en general, la ropa que llevan es un poco más conservadora que la que llevan los jóvenes norteamericanos.

Una de las cosas que más les gusta a los turistas que visitan los mercados de Hispanoamérica es la ropa típica que pueden comprar allí. Como es natural, esta ropa varía de un país a otro. Los dibujos, la combinación de colores y los bordados hechos a mano° son la admiración de los compradores. Los indígenas° que normalmente hacen estos bordados no han seguido° cursos de diseño o de combinación de colores, y sin embargo sus trabajos son, en la gran mayoría de los casos, verdaderas obras° de arte. Muchas veces las modas norteamericana y europea se inspiran en estos trajes típicos.

bordados... *hand-made embroidery* / *Indian*
no... *have not taken*
works

Para completar

Complete las siguientes oraciones con la respuesta correcta de acuerdo con la información que se da en la selección.

1. Si comparamos la ropa que llevan las personas mayores en los países hispanos y en los Estados Unidos, podemos decir que en los países hispanos la ropa es más
   a. informal.
   b. cómoda.
   c. tradicional.
2. En general, las señoras no van a las tiendas con
   a. pantalones cortos.
   b. vestidos.
   c. faldas.
3. La guayabera es una especie de
   a. camiseta
   b. corbata.
   c. camisa.
4. Hoy en día para ir a la universidad, los jóvenes llevan
   a. traje y corbata.
   b. vaqueros.
   c. trajes típicos.
5. En los mercados de Hispanoamérica los turistas compran
   a. vaqueros a buenos precios.
   b. ropa de diseño español.
   c. trajes con bordados a mano.

HASTA 24 MESES

SIN ENTRADA

COMPRE AHORA Y EMPIECE A PAGAR EN FEBRERO

Cocina a gas 4 fuegos. Modelo "SEARS". Encimera y laterales en acero inoxidable. Autolimpiable, quemadores esmaltados, tapa de cristal con cajón calientaplatos.

~~41.900~~ **32.900**

CANTIDADES LIMITADAS

SITUACIONES

1. You are in your favorite clothing store:
   (a) tell the clerk what you need (e.g., pants, shoes, and so on),
   (b) ask for the price of each item,
   (c) say if you like each one or not, and
   (d) decide if you will buy it/them.
2. You find the item to the right advertised in a newspaper. Tell a classmate
   (a) what it is,
   (b) what its features are,
   (c) what it costs, and
   (d) when you can start to pay.
3. You are going to take some friends to your favorite place (**una playa, una ciudad,** and so on). Tell them what you like about it and what you will show them. Your friends should ask some pertinent questions about this place.

   Modelo **Los voy a llevar a la universidad. A mí me gusta mucho la piscina. También me gusta la biblioteca. Yo les voy a mostrar la cafetería, el estadio y la piscina.**
4. You need to borrow money to buy a jacket. You are going skiing Saturday and you don't have a nice jacket. Explain the situation to a friend and ask him/her to lend you some money.
5. You are trying on some clothes; (a) tell the salesperson that they don't fit you, (b) ask for a bigger (or smaller) size, and (c) thank the salesperson.
6. You are a salesperson at a clothing store and a client has bought a sweater. You should (a) ask the client to go to the cash register, (b) tell him/her how much it is, and (c) ask if he/she is going to pay cash (**en efectivo**) or with a credit card.

VOCABULARIO[3]

los accesorios

el anillo	*ring*
los aretes	*earrings*
la billetera	*wallet*
la bolsa	*purse*
la cadena	*chain*
el cinturón	*belt*
el collar	*necklace*
los guantes	*gloves*
el pañuelo	*handkerchief*
la pulsera	*bracelet*

las compras	*shopping*
el almacén	*department store*
la caja	*cash register*
el centro comercial	*shopping center*
el dependiente, la dependienta	*store clerk*
el escaparate	*store window*
el probador	*fitting room*
las rebajas	*sales*
la talla	*size*
la tela	*material*
la tienda	*store*

el cumpleaños	*birthday*
el regalo	*present*

la ropa

el abrigo	*coat*
la blusa	*blouse*
las botas	*boots*
la bufanda	*scarf*
los calcetines	*socks*
la camisa	*shirt*
la camiseta	*T-shirt*
la corbata	*tie*
la chaqueta	*jacket*
la falda	*skirt*
el impermeable	*raincoat*
las medias	*stockings*
los pantalones	*pants*
el sombrero	*hat*
la sudadera	*jogging suit, sweat shirt*
el suéter	*sweater*
el traje	*suit*
el traje de baño	*bathing suit*
los vaqueros/jeans	*jeans*
el vestido	*dress*
los zapatos (de) tenis	*tennis shoes*
de color entero	*solid color*
de cuadros	*plaid*
de rayas	*striped*

descripción

ancho	*wide*
barato	*inexpensive, cheap*
caro	*expensive*
estrecho	*narrow, tight*
perfecto	*perfect*
precioso	*beautiful*
rebajado	*marked down*

verbos

cambiar	*to change, to exchange*
contestar	*to answer*
dar	*to give*
encantar	*to delight, to love*
encontrar (ue)	*to find*
esperar	*to wait for*
gastar	*to spend*
gustar	*to like, to be pleasing to*
interesar	*to interest*
llevar	*to wear*

---

[3] For indirect object pronouns and demonstratives, see pages 175–176 and 179 respectively.

mostrar (ue)	*to show*
pagar	*to pay*
parecer	*to seem*
pasar por	*to pick up*
prestar	*to lend*
probarse (ue)	*to try on*
quedar	*to fit, to have something left*
regalar	*to give (a present)*
sonar (ue)	*to ring*
usar	*to wear, to use*

palabras útiles

aló	*hello*
allá	*over there*
entonces	*then*
especialmente	*especially*
quizá(s)	*perhaps, maybe*
seguramente	*for sure*
todavía	*still*

expresiones útiles

a la derecha	*on the right*
Creo que sí.	*I think so.*
¿En qué puedo servirle(s)?	*May I help you?*
estar de moda	*to be fashionable*
perder (ie) el tiempo	*to waste time*

El mercado de Guanajuato en México, donde se pueden comprar artesanías y toda clase de vegetales frescos.

In Lección 8 **you will**

a. talk about the workplace and professions.
b. express opinions.
c. give orders.
d. give and follow directions.
e. express knowledge of facts.
f. express and ask for acquaintance of people.

Las profesiones y los oficios

En el hospital

el médico

En el bufete

la abogada

En la peluquería

la peluquera

Lección 8

El trabajo

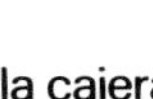

Un mecánico examina un auto en Jerez de la Frontera. En esta ciudad española se produce el vino de Jerez *(sherry)* y hay una Escuela de Arte Ecuestre donde se entrenan los famosos caballos andaluces *(Andalusian horses).*

otras profesiones, oficios y ocupaciones[1]

el actor	*actor*
la actriz	*actress*
el ama de casa[2]	*housewife, homemaker*
el arquitecto	*architect*
el/la astronauta	*astronaut*
el bombero	*fireman*
el/la dentista	*dentist*
el enfermero	*nurse*
el hombre/la mujer de negocios	*businessman/businesswoman*
el ingeniero	*engineer*
el obrero	*worker*
el/la piloto	*pilot*
el plomero	*plumber*
el policía/la (mujer) policía	*policeman/policewoman*
el/la recepcionista	*receptionist*
el secretario	*secretary*
el (p)sicólogo	*psychologist*
el/la (p)siquiatra	*psychiatrist*
el veterinario	*veterinary*

[1] The feminine form of masculine singular nouns ending in **-o** or a consonant follows the general rule (final **o**→**a**; final consonant + **a**), except in the cases indicated. In professions where women have been latecomers, some Spanish speakers may still use the masculine form, but this is changing. Example: **Ella es arquitecto/arquitecta.**

[2] Although **ama de casa** is feminine, it uses **el** and not **la** in the singular because it begins with a stressed **a**.

ACTIVIDADES

A Asocie una o más profesiones con los siguientes lugares de trabajo.

el hospital el aeropuerto la clase el bufete la cocina la peluquería
el taller el banco un estudio de Hollywood

B Dígale a su compañero/a cuál es la ocupación de cada miembro de su familia.

C Usted quiere saber cuál es la ocupación actual de su compañero/a y qué quiere ser en el futuro. Complete el siguiente diálogo y comparta la información con la clase.

Usted ¿Dónde trabajas?
Compañero/a ____. Soy ____.
Usted ¿Qué quieres ser en el futuro?
Compañero/a ____.

D Exprese su opinión sobre cómo deben ser estas personas para tener éxito (*to be successful*).

Modelo un piloto ¿inteligente? ¿joven? ¿perezoso? ¿ . . . ?
Debe ser inteligente y serio. No debe ser perezoso.

1. un/a (p)siquiatra — ¿valiente? ¿romántico/a? ¿irónico/a? ¿antipático/a? ¿inteligente? ¿ . . . ?
2. un actor/una actriz — ¿guapo/a? ¿atractivo/a? ¿simpático/a? ¿delgado/a? ¿alto/a? ¿ . . . ?
3. un hombre/una mujer de negocios — ¿autoritario/a? ¿serio/a? ¿perezoso/a? ¿viejo/a? ¿responsable? ¿ . . . ?

Ahora su compañero/a y usted van a decir cómo debe ser

un/a recepcionista un/a astronauta un ama de casa

Una arquitecta examina unos planos en México. Poco a poco las mujeres comienzan a ocupar puestos que antes estaban reservados para los hombres.

Cultura

Work and economic environment in the Hispanic countries

Unemployment **(desempleo, paro)** is a major problem in the Hispanic world. In May 1988, official figures placed unemployment at 19.85% in Spain; in other countries, such as Bolivia and Peru, it can run even higher. However, these figures do not give an accurate picture of the economic environment in each country because they do not take into account the "underground economy"—the often large numbers of people who buy and sell goods or offer services without paying taxes or following government regulations.

In countries with political instability, there is usually less investment activity, resulting in fewer opportunities for employment. Many workers therefore emigrate to the United States in hopes of finding jobs and better living conditions. The controversial Immigration Reform and Control Act of 1986 seeks to legalize the status of the many men and women who came to the United States without the necessary documentation before January 1, 1982, allowing them to emerge from a "phantom society." These workers have made significant contributions to the United States economy.

Another serious problem in the Hispanic countries is inflation (**inflación**). In Argentina, wartime inflation ran higher than 1,000% in 1982 after the Falkland Islands War (**Guerra de las Malvinas**), a conflict between Great Britain and Argentina over the sovereignty of the Falkland Islands. Inflation brings spiraling prices, and in order to keep up, many workers take on more than one job (**pluriempleo**). This extra income is seldom reported.

Technological advances have been introduced in the Hispanic world, but they are generally much less widespread than in the more industrialized countries. This factor, together with a poor job market, has brought many technicians and professionals to the United States to look for further opportunities to advance their careers. This "brain drain" (**fuga de cerebros**) is a serious problem for Hispanic countries, which are losing the human resources necessary for continued development.

Some of these countries face an additional serious problem in the lack of a middle class. It is indeed difficult for any country to form a strong economic base and sustain a period of progress without a sizable middle class. The tremendous difference between the very small elite and rich ruling class and the very large and poor lower socio-economic masses is painfully obvious.

Spain, which has a middle class, has shown what a country can do to improve itself and the future of its people. While restoring the monarchy in 1975, Spain also reestablished a democratic government just two years later. This strengthened political, legal, and economic institutions throughout the country, enabling Spain to join the European Common Market. As a result, unemployment is decreasing, and Spain has experienced marked improvement in the standard of living, increased productivity, and achieved lower rate of inflation.

Un trabajador hispano recoge uvas en el valle de Napa en California. La importante industria del vino en California depende en gran parte de estos hombres y mujeres que trabajan en el campo.

EN CONTEXTO

Anuncios[3]

1

SE NECESITA
DIRECTOR

- **Para hotel de 3 estrellas con más de 150 habitaciones.**
- **Situado en el sur de España.**

Enviar solicitudes con *curriculum vitae* y pretensiones económicas al apartado de Correos de Madrid número 46.283.

2

SE NECESITAN
VENDEDORES DE MUEBLES
CON EXPERIENCIA

Solicitar entrevista con el Sr. Alonso. Tel. 697 54 06.

Preguntas

1. ¿Qué se necesita en el primer anuncio?
2. ¿Cómo es el hotel?
3. ¿Dónde está?
4. ¿Adónde se deben enviar las solicitudes?
5. ¿Qué se necesita en el segundo anuncio?
6. ¿Deben tener experiencia?
7. ¿A quién deben llamar para una entrevista?
8. ¿Cuál es el número de teléfono?

---

[3] *Ads*

1. enviar *to send* la solicitud *application* pretensiones económicas *desired salary* apartado de Correos *P.O. Box*
2. vendedor *salesperson* solicitar *to apply (for a job)*

ACTIVIDADES

A Usted está buscando trabajo. Diga en qué orden ocurren las siguientes cosas.

Me llaman de la Compañía Rosell para una entrevista.
Leo los anuncios del periódico.
Voy a la compañía para la entrevista.
Envío mi curriculum a la Compañía Rosell.
Me ofrecen (*offer*) el puesto de vendedor/a.

B Hágale las siguientes preguntas a su compañero/a. El trabajo puede ser real o imaginario. Comparta la información con la clase.

Usted ¿Dónde trabajas?
Compañero/a . . .
Usted ¿A qué hora llegas al trabajo?
Compañero/a . . .
Usted ¿A qué hora sales del trabajo?
Compañero/a . . .
Usted ¿Cuántas personas trabajan allí?
Compañero/a . . .
Usted ¿Qué haces en tu trabajo?
Compañero/a . . .

Una joven puertorriqueña lee la sección de anuncios clasificados en busca de trabajo en Nueva York.

El Generalife, residencia de campo de los reyes árabes, en Granada.

La España árabe y cristiana

El Alcázar de Segovia.

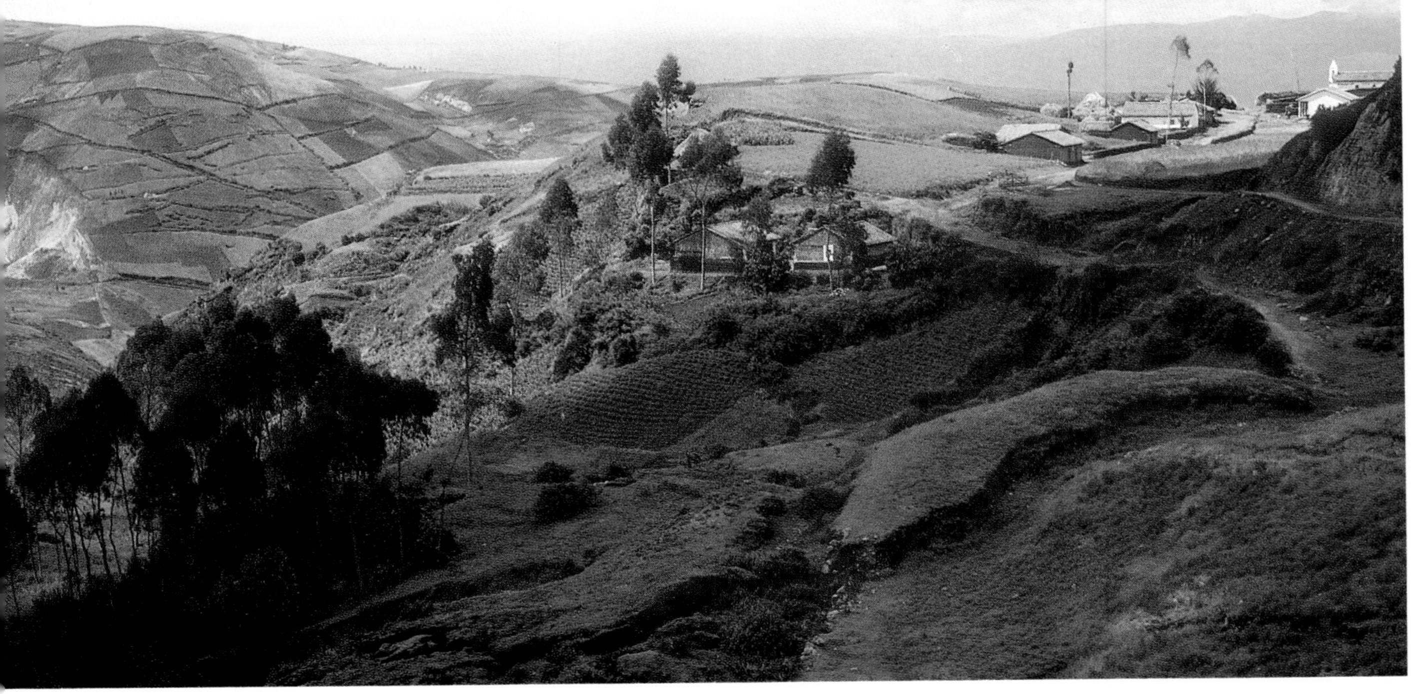

Un paisaje de la provincia de Carchi en Ecuador.

En las afueras de Tulum, ciudad maya de México.

Paisajes del mundo hispano

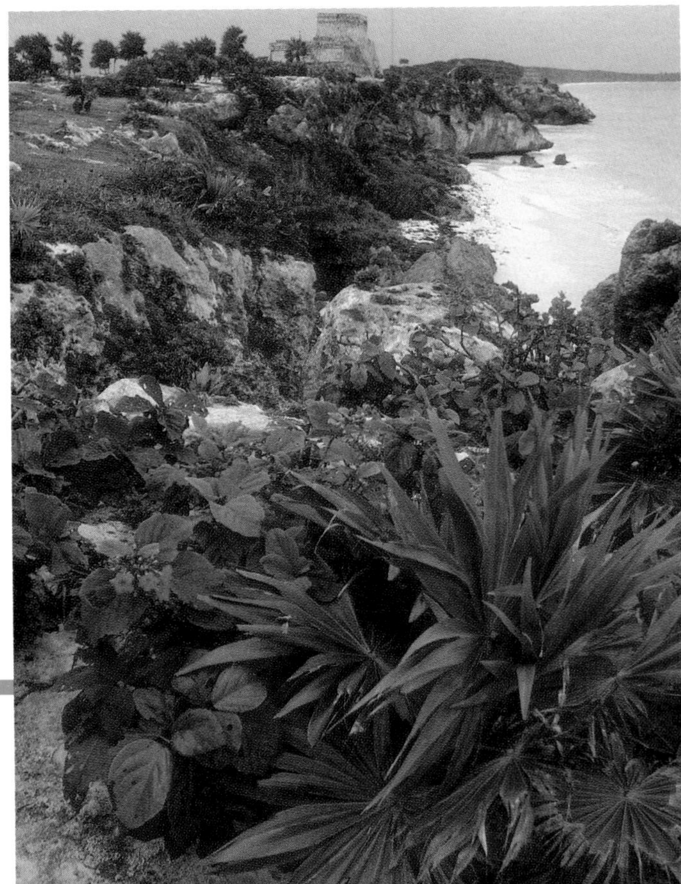

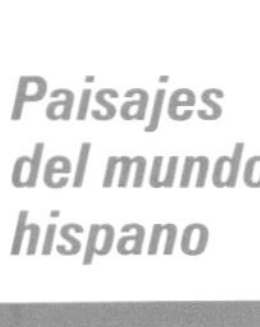

Bariloche en la Argentina.

El salto de Hacha en Canaima, Venezuela.

Vista de los Andes en el Perú.

La Plaza Mayor de Madrid, España.

Casas en Montevideo, Uruguay.

Un mercado al aire libre en Montevideo, Uruguay.

Pueblos y ciudades

La ciudad colonial
de Guanajuato en México.

Vista de la ciudad de México.

Semana Santa en Caracas, Venezuela.

Una corrida de toros en España.

La Iglesia de la Sagrada Familia en Barcelona, España.

La ciudad inca de Machu Picchu en Perú.

Las ruinas mayas de Tikal en Guatemala.

Fiestas tradicionales y joyas arquitectónicas

Edificios antiguos y modernos de la ciudad de Caracas.

El Nuevo Mundo

La Misión de San Juan Capistrano, una de las construcciones hispanas de California.

GRAMÁTICA

Se + verb

Se habla español.	*Spanish is spoken.*
Se necesitan enfermeros.	*Nurses (are) needed.*
Se vende (un) auto en buenas condiciones.	*Car in good condition for sale.*
Se venden libros aquí.	*Books (are) sold here.*

1. Spanish uses the **se** + verb construction when emphasis is on the action and not on the person(s) responsible for the action.
2. The subject usually follows the verb.
3. The verb is the **él, ella, usted** verb form or the **ellos, ellas, ustedes** verb form depending on the subject.
4. **Se** followed by the **él, ella, usted** verb form is also used to express English indefinite *one*.

Se come muy bien aquí. *One eats very well here.*

ACTIVIDADES

A Diga en qué orden se preparan unos espaguetis. Trabaje con un compañero/a.

Se pone salsa de tomate sobre los espaguetis.
Se hierve (*boil*) el agua con un poco de sal.
Se ponen los espaguetis en el agua que está hirviendo.
Se escurren (*drain*) los espaguetis.
Se pone queso rallado (*grated*) sobre los espaguetis y la salsa.
Se cocinan los espaguetis unos ocho minutos.

B Asocie las actividades de la columna de la izquierda con los lugares de la derecha.

actividades	**lugares**
1. Se baila y se canta.	a. un centro comercial
2. Se vende ropa.	b. un estadio
3. Se habla español.	c. una discoteca
4. Se juega fútbol.	d. mi auto
5. Se sirve vino.	e. una cama grande
6. Se duerme bien.	f. Nueva York
7. Se necesita mucho dinero.	g. mi dormitorio
8. Se bebe cerveza.	h. la América Latina
9. Se vive bien.	i. un restaurante italiano

C Usted es el/la director/a de un drama. Un empleado le pregunta dónde se ponen unos muebles en el escenario (*stage*). Trabaje con su compañero/a y contéstele de acuerdo con el siguiente dibujo.

Modelo ¿Dónde se pone la butaca?
Se pone al lado de la chimenea.

1. ¿Dónde se pone la mesa redonda?
2. ¿Dónde se pone el sofá?
3. ¿Dónde se ponen las mesas cuadradas?
4. ¿Dónde se pone la silla?
5. ¿Y la alfombra? ¿Y la mesa rectangular?

D **Anuncios locos.** Con un/a compañero/a, lea estos anuncios «locos» y diga cuáles les gustan más.

1. Se vende un loro (*parrot*) porque habla mucho.
2. Se busca un/una esposo/a leal (*loyal*).
3. Se necesita urgentemente un robot para hacer todas las tareas de español.
4. Se busca un/a compañero/a de cuarto que no ronque (*snore*).
5. Se compra un fantasma para aterrorizar a mi suegro/a. También se acepta un Drácula o un Frankenstein.
6. Se necesitan tres extraterrestres para organizar un club de baile.

Ahora prepare con un/a compañero/a dos anuncios locos para compartir con la clase.

EN CONTEXTO

En la oficina del señor Macía

Pedro Domínguez solicita trabajo en una compañía. Hoy tiene la entrevista y toca a la puerta de la oficina del gerente.

Preguntas

1. ¿A quién quiere ver Pedro?
2. ¿Qué le dice el gerente cuando toca a la puerta?
3. ¿Es Pedro el programador de computadoras?
4. ¿Qué puesto solicita Pedro?
5. ¿A quién van a despedir?

ACTIVIDADES

A ¿Qué haría usted (*would you do*) en las siguientes situaciones. Escoja la respuesta adecuada.

1. Usted toca a la puerta de una oficina y le dicen: «Pase».
   a. Digo adiós.
   b. Cierro la puerta.
   c. Entro en la oficina.
2. Su jefe (*boss*) lo llama y le dice que tienen que despedir a veinte empleados, que usted está entre ellos y que siente mucho darle la noticia (*news*). Usted le contesta:
   a. «¡Qué bueno!»
   b. «Estoy muy contento con la noticia».
   c. «Yo también lo siento».
3. Usted está trabajando en su oficina y un cliente viene a verlo. Usted le dice:
   a. «Siéntese, por favor».
   b. «Yo no quiero hablar con usted».
   c. «¿Quién es usted?»
4. Usted trabaja en la Compañía de Teléfonos. Un cliente se queja (*complains*) de un error en su cuenta (*bill*). Usted le contesta:
   a. «Estoy muy contento con esa información».
   b. «No se preocupe. Vamos a rectificar el error en la computadora».
   c. «Hoy no tengo ganas de trabajar».

B Usted va a entrevistar a una persona que solicita trabajo en su compañía. Complete el siguiente diálogo con su compañero/a.

Usted Su nombre, por favor.
Compañero/a . . .
Usted ¿Dónde trabaja usted y qué hace allí?
Compañero/a . . .
Usted ¿Por qué quiere trabajar en nuestra compañía?
Compañero/a . . .

La filmación de unas escenas para una película en una calle de Barcelona, España. Una de las zonas más interesantes de esta ciudad es la parte antigua, conocida como el Barrio Gótico por los numerosos edificios de este estilo.

GRAMÁTICA

Formal commands

1. Commands are the verb forms used to tell others to do something. Use formal commands with people you address as **usted** or **ustedes.** To form these commands, drop the final **-o** of the **yo** form of the present tense and add **e** for **-ar** verbs and **a** for **-er** and **-ir** verbs.

hablar:	hablo	⟶	habl**e** (usted)	habl**en** (ustedes)	*speak*
comer:	como	⟶	com**a** (usted)	com**an** (ustedes)	*eat*
escribir:	escribo	⟶	escrib**a** (usted)	escrib**an** (ustedes)	*write*

Verbs that are irregular in the **yo** form of the present tense will maintain the same irregularity in the command.

pensar:	pienso	⟶	piense (usted)	piensen (ustedes)	*think*
dormir:	duermo	⟶	duerma (usted)	duerman (ustedes)	*sleep*
poner:	pongo	⟶	ponga (usted)	pongan (ustedes)	*put*

2. The use of **usted** and **ustedes** is optional. When used, they normally follow the command.

   Pase. Pase usted. *Come in.*

3. To make a negative command, place **no** before the affirmative command.

   No salga ahora. *Don't leave now.*

4. Verbs ending in **-car, -gar, -zar,** and **-guir** have orthographic changes.

sacar:	saco	⟶	sa**que**, sa**quen**
jugar:	juego	⟶	jue**gue**, jue**guen**
almorzar:	almuerzo	⟶	almuer**ce** almuer**cen**
seguir:	sigo	⟶	si**ga**, si**gan**

5. Formal commands of the verb **estar** have written accent marks (**esté, estén**). The **usted** form of **dar** has a written accent mark (**dé**) to distinguish it from the preposition **de.**
6. Object and reflexive pronouns follow and are attached to an affirmative command. Note the written accent mark over the stressed syllable.

   C**ó**mprela. H**á**blele. Si**é**ntese.

7. Object and reflexive pronouns precede a negative command.

   No **la** compre. No **le** hable. No **se** siente.

8. The verbs **ir, ser,** and **saber** (*to know*) have irregular command forms.

   ir: ⟶ vaya, vayan **ser:** ⟶ sea, sean **saber:** ⟶ sepa, sepan

ACTIVIDADES

A Usted está hablando con su secretario/a y le dice las cosas que debe hacer en la oficina. Use mandatos formales.

Modelo llamar al Sr. Palma
Llame al Sr. Palma.

1. contestar esta carta (*letter*)
2. buscar la carta del Sr. Vega
3. llamar a la Sra. Narváez
4. pedir más información al banco
5. cerrar la puerta
6. terminar el proyecto

B Usted es el/la entrenador/a de un equipo de vólibol. Dígales a los jugadores las cosas que deben hacer. Use mandatos formales.

Modelo practicar todos los días
Practiquen todos los días.

1. comer bien
2. tomar mucha agua
3. acostarse temprano
4. dormir ocho horas
5. llegar temprano a la práctica
6. correr todas las mañanas

C Usted es el/la profesor/a. Uno de los estudiantes le va a preguntar si tiene que hacer ciertas cosas. Conteste usando mandatos formales y los pronombres correspondientes.

Modelo ¿Estudio esta lección?
Sí, estúdiela.

1. ¿Contesto estas preguntas?
2. ¿Escucho el casete?
3. ¿Escribo estas palabras?
4. ¿Leo la lección ocho?
5. ¿Hago la tarea?

D Ahora dígale lo que no debe hacer.

Modelo ¿Contesto las preguntas en inglés?
No, no las conteste en inglés.

1. ¿Escucho canciones americanas en la clase?
2. ¿Escribo los anuncios en inglés?
3. ¿Termino la tarea en la clase?
4. ¿Hablo francés con mis compañeros?
5. ¿Ayudo a mi compañero en el examen?

E Dígales a estas personas lo que deben hacer de acuerdo con las situaciones. Use mandatos formales.

Modelo El Sr. Álvarez no está contento en su trabajo.
Busque otro trabajo.

1. El Sr. Jiménez necesita un vendedor en su compañía.
2. Una persona está tocando a la puerta de su oficina.
3. Sus amigos quieren hablar con el profesor Gómez.
4. El Sr. Peña quiere saber qué película van a poner en la televisión esta noche.
5. La Sra. Hurtado no quiere vivir en una casa y está buscando un apartamento.
6. Su hermano quiere comprarle un regalo a su novia.

F Usted tiene mucho dinero y tiene varias personas que hacen todo el trabajo en su casa. Dígale a cada una de esas personas lo que deben hacer. Use mandatos formales.

Modelo **Lave el Rolls-Royce azul, por favor.**

EN CONTEXTO

Una reunión de ventas°

reunión... *sales meeting*

La Srta. Marta Vázquez trabaja en la Compañía Garzón en Córdoba, una importante ciudad argentina. Su sueldo° no es muy bueno, pero espera ganar° más muy pronto. Hoy la Srta. Vázquez está en Buenos Aires para asistir° a una reunión de ventas. Ella sabe que el edificio de la compañía está muy cerca de su hotel, pero como no conoce° bien la ciudad, le pregunta a un policía.

salary / earn
attend
no... *doesn't know*

Srta. Vázquez Perdón, ¿sabe usted dónde está la calle Posadas?
Policía Sí, cómo no. Está muy cerca, a unas cinco cuadras°. — *blocks*
Srta. Vázquez Por favor, me puede usted indicar...
Policía Con mucho gusto. Mire, siga derecho° por esta calle hasta la próxima esquina°. Allí doble° a la izquierda. Camine tres cuadras más y cruce° la plaza. Ésa es la calle Posadas.

siga... *go straight ahead*
corner/turn
cross

Preguntas

1. ¿Dónde trabaja la Srta. Vázquez?
2. ¿Gana mucho dinero en su trabajo?
3. ¿Por qué está en Buenos Aires?
4. ¿Qué calle busca la Srta. Vázquez?
5. ¿A quién le pregunta la Srta. Vázquez?
6. ¿Dónde tiene que doblar a la izquierda?
7. ¿Cuántas cuadras más tiene que caminar?
8. ¿Qué tiene que cruzar?

La Bolsa del Mercado *(stock market)* de Buenos Aires, Argentina.

ACTIVIDADES

A ¿Qué hace usted en estas situaciones?

1. Usted está montando bicicleta por la calle. A su derecha hay un perro enorme que empieza a ladrar (*bark*).
   a. Doblo a la derecha.
   b. Empiezo a cantar.
   c. Sigo derecho.
2. Usted está caminando en la playa y ve a su mejor amigo enfrente de usted.
   a. Doblo a la izquierda.
   b. Sigo derecho y no lo miro.
   c. Saludo a mi amigo.
3. Usted tiene una entrevista en una sucursal (*branch*) del Banco de Comercio y no sabe dónde está.
   a. Voy al cine.
   b. Busco la dirección en la Guía Telefónica.
   c. Miro un programa de entrevistas en la tele.
4. Esta tarde usted tiene una entrevista para un trabajo muy importante y tiene que decidir qué ropa se va a poner.
   a. Me pongo un buen traje.
   b. Llevo mi traje de baño.
   c. Me pongo zapatos tenis.

B Preséntele a su compañero/a las siguientes situaciones.

1. Quieres ir a esquiar, pero no tienes dinero. ¿Qué haces?
2. Quieres ver un programa de televisión y tu televisor no funciona (*works*). ¿Qué haces?
3. Necesitas buscar trabajo para el verano. ¿Qué haces?

C Usted está caminando en la ciudad de Alcalá de Henares en España. Varios turistas le preguntan dónde están algunos lugares. De acuerdo con el siguiente plano, dígales cómo llegar. Trabaje con su compañero/a y cambien de papel (*change roles*).

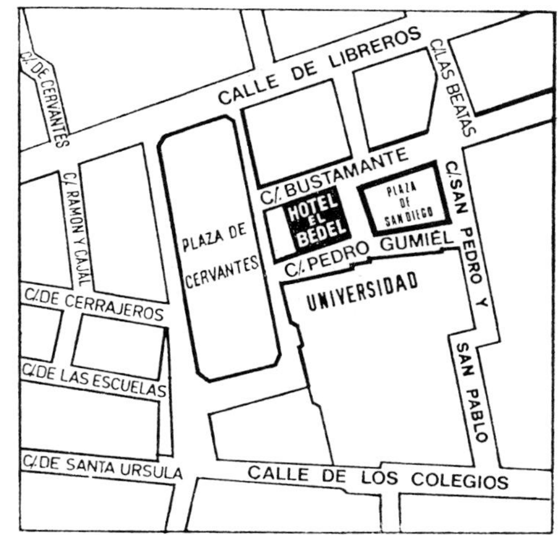

1. Usted está en
   a. la calle Libreros esquina a la calle Las Beatas
   b. la calle Cervantes
   c. la calle Las Escuelas
2. Instrucciones para llegar
   a. a la Plaza de Cervantes
   b. a la Universidad de Alcalá
   c. al Hotel El Bedel

GRAMÁTICA

Saber and *conocer*

	saber	**conocer**
yo	sé	conozco
tú	sabes	conoces
él, ella, usted	sabe	conoce
nosotros/as	sabemos	conocemos
vosotros/as	sabéis	conocéis
ellos/as, ustedes	saben	conocen

1. Both **saber** and **conocer** mean *to know,* but they are not used interchangeably. The **yo** form of these verbs is irregular; the other forms are regular.
2. Use **saber** to express knowledge of facts or pieces of information.

Él sabe dónde está el banco. — *He knows where the bank is.*

3. Use **saber** + infinitive to express that you know how to do something.

Yo sé cocinar.	*I know how to cook.*

4. Use **conocer** to express that you are acquainted with someone or something. **Conocer** also means *to meet*. Remember to use the personal **a** when referring to people.

Yo conozco a Pedro Rivas.	*I know Pedro Rivas.*
No conozco esa compañía.	*I don't know that company.*
Ella quiere conocer a Luis.	*She wants to meet Luis.*

ACTIVIDADES

A ¿Sabe usted quién es?

Modelo Es una chica muy pobre que va a un baile. Allí conoce a un príncipe, pero a las 12:00 de la noche ella debe volver a su casa.
Sí, sé quién es. Es Cenicienta (*Cinderella*).

1. Es un gorila gigante con sentimientos (*feelings*) humanos.
2. Es un hombre de otro planeta con una doble personalidad. Trabaja como empleado en una oficina, pero cuando lleva una ropa azul especial puede volar (*fly*).
3. Es un hombre joven, blanco, fuerte, educado por unos monos (*monkeys*) en la jungla.
4. Es un detective privado. Es inglés, alto y delgado. Su asistente es un médico.
5. Es un jugador de baloncesto muy famoso. Es negro, alto y lleva gafas (*glasses*).

B Preguntas

1. ¿Conoce usted a tres personas en esta clase? ¿Quiénes son?
2. ¿Conoce usted a otros profesores? ¿Cómo se llaman?
3. ¿Conoce usted a un actor o una actriz de Hollywood? ¿Quién es?
4. ¿Conoce a alguna persona famosa?
5. ¿Desea usted conocer a alguna persona famosa? ¿A quién? ¿Por qué desea conocerla?

C ¿Qué sabes hacer?

¿Qué sabes hacer? Pregúntele a su compañero/a si sabe hacer las siguientes cosas. Después pregúntele qué otras cosas sabe hacer. Comparta esta información con la clase.

Modelo bailar música rock
—¿Sabes bailar música rock?
—Sí, sé bailar música rock o **No, no sé bailar música rock.**

tocar guitarra — planchar bien — jugar tenis — trabajar con computadoras
nadar — usar el microondas — hacer tacos — (otras cosas)

D Complete este pequeño diálogo con un/a compañero/a. Use las formas correctas de **saber** o **conocer.**

Usted ¿____ a esa chica?
Compañero/a ¡Sí, cómo no! Yo ____ a todas las chicas aquí.
Usted Entonces ____ dónde vive.
Compañero/a No, no lo ____.
Usted Pero ____ su número de teléfono, ¿verdad?
Compañero/a No, tampoco lo ____.
Usted Y ¿____ cómo se llama?
Compañero/a Pues, la verdad es que no lo ____.
Usted ¿Cómo dices que la ____? Tú no ____ dónde vive, tú no ____ su nombre.
Compañero/a Es que yo tengo muy mala memoria.

GRAMÁTICA

Pronouns after prepositions

1. After a preposition (e.g., **a, de, para, sin** *without*), Spanish uses the subject pronouns except for **mí** and **ti.** In **Lección 7,** you used **a** + pronoun to clarify or emphasize the indirect object pronoun.

Juan **me** habla **a mí,** no **te** habla **a ti.**
Le va a prestar el auto a **ella.**
A nosotros nos gusta esquiar.

2. Do not use **mí** and **ti** after the following prepositions:

a. after **con**, use **conmigo** and **contigo.**

—¿Vas **conmigo**? —Sí, voy **contigo.**

b. after **entre**, use **yo** and **tú.**

Entre tú y **yo** terminamos el trabajo.

ACTIVIDADES

A La familia Rivas está en un restaurante. ¿Qué le piden al camarero?

Modelo El Sr. Rivas quiere pescado. ¿Qué dice?
Para mí, pescado y papas fritas.

1. Las dos chicas quieren pollo frito y vegetales. ¿Qué dicen?
2. La Sra. Rivas quiere espaguetis y ensalada. ¿Qué dice?
3. El niño pequeño quiere sopa. ¿Qué dice la Sra. Rivas?
4. La niña pequeña quiere pizza. ¿Qué dice el Sr. Rivas?

B Usted está organizando una excursión a la playa. De acuerdo con la siguiente lista, diga con quién va a ir cada una de las personas.

Modelo nosotros: Pedro, Magdalena
Pedro y Magdalena van a ir con nosotros.

1. yo: Alicia, Marta, Consuelo
2. tú: Carmen, Alberto, Carlos
3. él: Jorge, Javier, Arturo
4. ellos: Mónica, Rafael

C Usted va a ir a un concierto con unos amigos. Complete el siguiente diálogo con su compañero/a usando pronombres.

Usted ¿Vas conmigo?
Compañero/a No, no voy ___.
Usted ¿Con quién vas a ir?
Compañero/a Voy a ir con ___.
Usted ¿Dónde te vas a sentar?
Compañero/a Entre ___ y ___.

Una oficina de empleo en Madrid. El paro o desempleo ha disminuido en España, pero todavía hay muchas personas sin trabajo.

LECTURA

Buscando trabajo

Las siguientes personas están buscando trabajo y leen en el periódico los anuncios que aparecen más abajo. ¿Cuál de los anuncios debe contestar cada una de las personas y por qué?

Personas

1. Pedro Heredia Solís, 35 años
   graduado universitario
   experiencia como cajero y administrador de un supermercado
   habla español y francés
2. Adela Sánchez Toraño, 28 años
   graduada universitaria
   experiencia de cuatro años en el bufete de un abogado
   habla español, inglés y algo de francés
3. Juan Gómez Machado, 20 años
   dos años de estudios universitarios
   experiencia como camarero en un café.

Anuncios

Lea ahora los anuncios para captar (*to get*) la idea general y poder asociar el anuncio con la persona apropiada.

FABRICANTE DE ALIMENTOS PARA ANIMALES DE COMPAÑIA
PRECISA
JEFE DE VENTAS
Imprescindible experiencia sector alimentación. Preferible con estudios Comerciales y Marketing. Residencia en Madrid
Apartado Correos n.° 14.724
28080 MADRID. Referencia 196

Perteneciente a la cadena Internacional de restaurantes de lujo **SUNTORY,** busca personal con motivo de su próxima inauguración:

COCINEROS

con o sin experiencia
hasta 25 años de edad
Enviar historial detallado con datos personales y fotografía reciente a:
c/ Ayala, 20 - 3.° E. 28001 MADRID
RESTAURANTE SUNTORY

JOVEN LICENCIADO/A EN DERECHO

Con buen conocimiento de inglés necesita empresa de servicios para interesante trabajo jurídico administrativo, jornada completa. Se valorará positivamente conocimiento de alemán o francés
Enviar oferta detallada manuscrita al **número 190688, Apartado de Correos 40, 28080 Madrid**

Lea ahora los anuncios con más cuidado para poder contestar las preguntas. Las siguientes palabras pueden ayudarlo/la a entender mejor los anuncios.

fabricante	*manufacturer*
precisa	*needs*
jefe de ventas	*sales manager*
imprescindible	*essential*
lujo	*first class, (luxury)*
licenciado en derecho	*lawyer*
jornada completa	*full-time*

Preguntas

1. ¿Qué necesitan en el anuncio número 1?
2. ¿Es necesario tener experiencia para contestar este anuncio?
3. ¿Qué clase de comida vende la compañía?
4. ¿Qué necesitan en el anuncio número 2?
5. ¿Puede contestar el anuncio una persona sin experiencia?
6. ¿Qué se debe enviar para contestar el anuncio número 2?
7. ¿Adónde se debe enviar?
8. ¿Qué buscan en el anuncio número 3?
9. ¿Puede solicitar la plaza una persona de 50 años?
10. ¿Qué otras lenguas es necesario saber para solicitar la plaza?

El empleado o empleada ideal

El siguiente perfil del empleado o empleada ideal es el resultado de una encuesta° realizada entre hombres y mujeres de negocios. *survey*

ASÍ DEBE SER EL/LA EMPLEADO/A IDEAL

1. trabajador/a
2. responsable
3. honrado/a° *honest*
4. inteligente
5. tener iniciativa
6. mostrar una actitud positiva

Todos los encuestados están de acuerdo en que el empleado que nadie° quiere en su empresa es el chismoso°. Según los encuestados, este tipo de persona sólo crea problemas y un mal ambiente° en la oficina o la fábrica°. «Es como un cáncer que crece° y acaba° con las buenas relaciones que deben existir en los lugares de trabajo», dijo° uno de los encuestados haciéndose eco de la opinión general.

no one / *gossiper* / *atmosphere/factory* / *grows/ends* / *said*

Después de expresar sus opiniones sobre los empleados, los encuestados debían decir las cualidades que debe tener el jefe o jefa ideal. Aquí hay más diferencias entre sus opiniones, pero todos coinciden en que debe ser trabajador, inteligente y justo.

¿Verdadero o falso?

Diga si las siguientes oraciones son verdaderas o falsas de acuerdo con la información que se da en el artículo.

1. Las personas que toman parte en esta encuesta tienen experiencia para contestar bien las preguntas.
2. Los encuestados creen que los empleados deben obedecer (*obey*) siempre al jefe o jefa.
3. El chismoso es una persona simpática que ayuda a los empleados a pasar mejor las horas de trabajo.
4. En esta encuesta sólo se expresan opiniones sobre el empleado o empleada ideal.

El trabajo

El trabajo es una parte muy importante de nuestra vida. No sólo nos proporciona° los medios económicos para mantenernos, sino que° también puede producir mucha satisfacción si podemos escoger el oficio o profesión que nos gusta. Esto resulta muy importante pues hay momentos en que tenemos que dedicarle muchas horas extras al trabajo y abandonar otras actividades que nos interesan. Si no nos gusta el trabajo que realizamos, estas horas extras de trabajo intenso nos pueden hacer muy infelices.

offers/sino... *but*

Según muchos psicólogos y expertos, el exceso de trabajo puede ser bueno cuando es temporal, pues nos ayuda a eliminar energía acumulada, quemar° calorías y hasta olvidar° algunos de los problemas que todos tenemos en la vida. Pero hay otros casos en que el exceso de trabajo es permanente debido a° necesidades económicas o psicológicas. A veces estas necesidades económicas (gastos por enfermedades o accidentes, deudas, etc.) son tan importantes que la situación nos obliga a trabajar para satisfacerlas y no tenemos otras opciones.

burn
forget
debido... *due to*

Cuando el exceso de trabajo se debe a necesidades psicológicas la situación es diferente pues existen otras opciones. Para estas personas «trabajomaníacas» el descanso° es como un pecado°, y el trabajo es una obsesión. Estas personas que tienen que estar ocupadas todo el día necesitan ayuda para poder establecer prioridades en su vida y comprender que también es muy importante disfrutar° de otras cosas como la compañía de los amigos, el teatro, la televisión, los deportes, etc.

rest / sin
enjoy

El siguiente dicho°, que es muy antiguo y popular en el mundo hispano, presenta una filosofía con respecto al trabajo que podría° ayudar mucho a las personas que no saben descansar: «Hay que trabajar para vivir, no vivir para trabajar».

saying
could

¿Verdadero o falso?

Diga si las siguientes oraciones son verdaderas o falsas de acuerdo con la lectura.

1. Una persona puede ser feliz cuando tiene un trabajo que le gusta.
2. Según los psicólogos, el trabajo intenso es siempre malo para las personas.
3. Un efecto del trabajo intenso temporal es que la persona no piensa en sus problemas personales.

4. A veces las personas trabajan mucho por problemas económicos o psicológicos.
5. Las personas que necesitan trabajar todo el tiempo no saben disfrutar de la vida.
6. La idea que expresa el dicho hispano de esta lectura es que tenemos que trabajar todos los días para ser felices.

Opiniones

Ponga en orden de importancia los siguientes aspectos de la vida. Diga cuál es el más importante para usted y por qué. Compare sus respuestas con las de otros estudiantes.

____ objetos materiales
____ dinero
____ casa
____ viajes
____ trabajo
____ familia
____ amigos
____ estudios
____ deportes
____ salud *(health)*

SITUACIONES

1. You are the president of an important company that is going to start a new advertising campaign (**campaña de publicidad**). Bring in two ads that you like and show them to the person in charge of advertising. He/She should ask you (a) why you like them and (b) where you want to place them.
2. You are going to take a trip to Chile for one month. A neighbor is housesitting for you during this time. Tell your neighbor what to do and what not to do while you are gone. You may use the following verbs in your instructions: **limpiar, lavar, barrer, llamar, preparar, cerrar, abrir, hablar, invitar, apagar** (*turn off*).
3. Tell a student who is new to this country how to write a check step by step. Explain the following: (a) where to put the date, (b) where to write the payee's name, (c) where to write the amount (**cantidad**) in numbers, (d) where to write the amount in words, and (e) where to sign (**firmar**) the check.

Banco Comercial

No. 775

Fecha ____________

Páguese a la orden de ______________________________ $ ________

la suma de ____

____

⑆021000021⑆ 025 1 132767⑈ 0285 ⑉0000001100⑉

4. You are standing in front of your house. A car stops and the driver asks for directions to go downtown. Give him/her the directions.
5. You are interviewing a prospective employee for your company. Ask him/her (a) where he is working, (b) why he/she wants to change jobs, (c) what salary he/she wants, and (d) why he/she wants to work for your company.

VOCABULARIO

profesiones y oficios

el abogado	*lawyer*
el actor	*actor*
la actriz	*actress*
el ama de casa	*housewife, homemaker*
el arquitecto	*architect*
el/la astronauta	*astronaut*
el bombero	*fireman*
el cajero	*cashier*
el cocinero	*cook*
el/la dentista	*dentist*
el director	*director, manager*
el/la electricista	*electrician*
el enfermero	*nurse*
el gerente	*manager*
el hombre/la mujer de negocios	*businessman/businesswoman*
el ingeniero	*engineer*
el mecánico	*mechanic*
el médico	*medical doctor*
el obrero	*worker*
el peluquero	*hairdresser*
el/la piloto	*pilot*
el plomero	*plumber*
el policía/la (mujer) policía	*policeman/policewoman*
el programador	*programmer*
el (p)sicólogo	*psychologist*
el/la (p)siquiatra	*psychiatrist*
el/la recepcionista	*receptionist*
el secretario	*secretary*
el vendedor	*salesman*
el veterinario	*veterinary*

lugares

el banco	*bank*
el bufete	*lawyer's office*
la compañía	*company*
la cuadra	*city block*
la esquina	*corner*
la habitación	*room*
el hospital	*hospital*
el hotel	*hotel*
la oficina	*office*
la peluquería	*beauty salon, barbershop*
el taller	*shop*

trabajo

el anuncio	*ad*
la entrevista	*interview*
la experiencia	*experience*
la plaza	*position*
el puesto	*position*
la reunión de ventas	*sales meeting*
la solicitud	*application*
el sueldo	*salary*

verbos

asistir	*to attend*
cerrar (ie)	*to close*
conocer (zc)	*to know, to meet*
cruzar (c)	*to cross*
despedir (i)	*to dismiss, to fire*
doblar	*to turn*
entender (ie)	*to understand*
entrar	*to enter, to come in*
enviar	*to send*
indicar (qu)	*to indicate*
ganar	*to earn*
pasar	*to come in*
preguntar	*to ask (a question)*
saber	*to know*
seguir derecho	*to go straight ahead*
tocar (qu) (a la puerta)	*to knock*

pronombres

conmigo	*with me*
contigo	*with you (fam.)*

palabras útiles

izquierda	*left*
pronto	*soon*
tampoco	*neither, not either*

expresiones útiles

cómo no	*of course*

In Lección 9 **you will**

a. talk about and describe body movements.
b. give orders informally.
c. give advice informally.
d. give and follow instructions.
e. express weight and measurements.
f. make comparisons.

Las partes del cuerpo

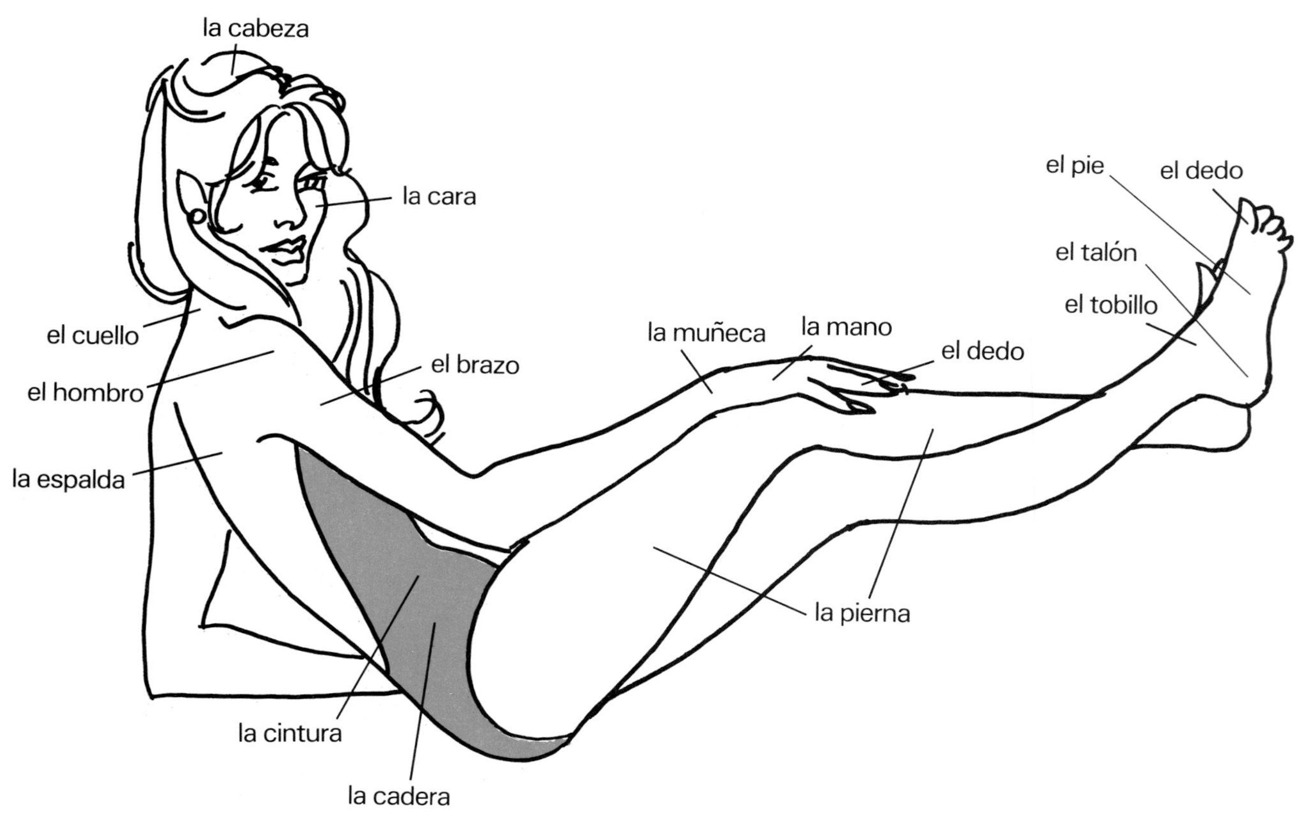

Lección 9

El cuerpo y los ejercicios

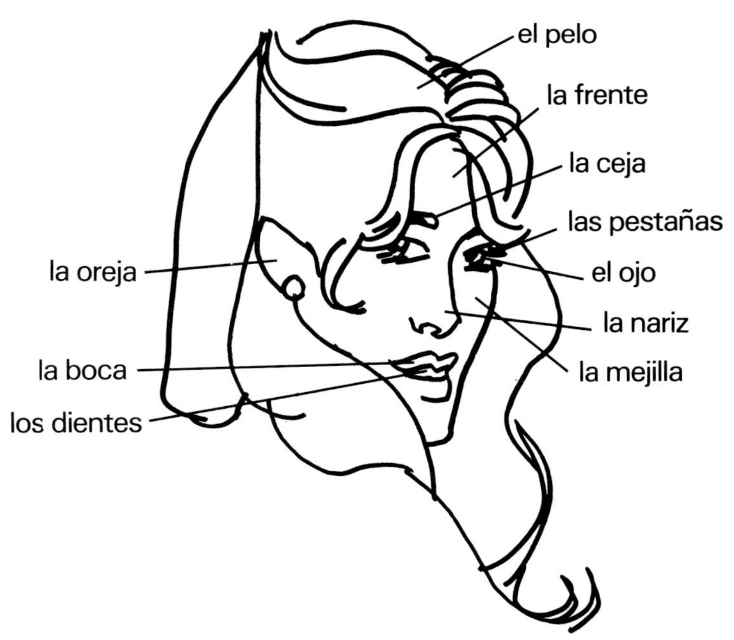

ACTIVIDADES

A Asocie las partes del cuerpo con las siguientes acciones.

las partes del cuerpo	**acciones**
1. la boca	a. tocar el piano
2. los ojos	b. comer algo
3. los dedos	c. pensar
4. el oído	d. caminar
5. la cabeza	e. tocar a la puerta
6. los pies	f. leer un libro
7. la mano	g. escuchar música

B Asocie la ropa y los accesorios con las partes del cuerpo.

la ropa	**las partes del cuerpo**
1. las calcetines	a. la muñeca
2. el anillo	b. el dedo
3. los guantes	c. el cuerpo
4. la blusa	d. las orejas
5. el collar	e. el cuello
6. los aretes	f. la cabeza
7. el reloj	g. los pies
8. el sombrero	h. las manos

C Señale diferentes partes del cuerpo preguntando **¿Qué es esto?** Sus compañeros/as deben identificar las partes del cuerpo.

Cultura

Physical fitness and exercise in the Hispanic world

See IM, **Lección 9, Cultura.**

Physical fitness and exercise have always been of interest in the Hispanic world. In recent years, as in the United States and Europe, this interest has grown, affecting many aspects of Hispanic life.

Nowadays, it is not unusual to see office workers, business people, senior citizens, students, and others setting aside time for some kind of physical activity. As a result, there are more and more places for people to meet and pursue their interest in exercise and fitness. Most large cities have **gimnasios** as well as public and private health clubs and spas. In cities like Buenos Aires, Bogotá, Mexico City, Madrid, and Barcelona, for example, you can find health clubs or spas with names such as **Gimnasio del Presidente, Club Gimnástico Bilbao,** and **Casa del Deporte.** And for those staying closer to home, television and radio programs focus on fitness and good nutrition. You can pick up the newspaper of almost any major Hispanic city and find such programs listed.

This interest in developing healthy bodies is also reflected in the number of advertisements and articles dealing with this topic in Hispanic publications. Popular magazines such as **Vanidades, Cambio 16, Gente** (*People*), and **Muy interesante** quite often have articles devoted to the subject. Specialized magazines like **Salud y belleza** (*Health and beauty*) and **Corredores** are published regularly. Bookstands have special sections filled with books on fitness and nutrition.

At the same time, health food stores are increasingly popular. They are known by several names, among them **almacén de salud, centro naturista,** or **herboristería.** All kinds of natural and exotic health foods can be purchased at these stores.

Many people who are interested in fitness and health are similarly concerned with maintaining proper body weight.

Unos jóvenes hacen unos ejercicios de calentamiento en un parque de Oaxaca, México.

They may consult charts such as the following one taken from the book **Salud y nutrición,** which indicates the ideal weight for men and women according to their height. Since the metric system is used throughout the Hispanic world, weight is measured in kilos instead of pounds (1.6 pounds per kilo), and height in meters instead of feet (3.3 feet per meter).

PESO IDEAL

HOMBRES

Estatura (con zapatos) metros	Talla pequeña kilogramos	Talla mediana kilogramos	Talla grande kilogramos
1,58	51-54	53-58	57-64
1,60	52-55	55-60	59-65
1,63	54-56	56-65	60-67
1,65	55-58	58-63	61-70
1,68	57-60	60-65	63-71
1,70	58-62	61-67	64-73
1,73	60-64	63-69	67-75
1,75	62-66	64-71	69-77
1,78	63-68	67-74	70-79
1,80	65-70	69-75	72-81
1,83	68-72	70-77	74-83
1,85	69-73	73-80	76-86
1,88	71-76	74-82	78-88
1,90	73-78	75-83	81-90
1,93	75-80	78-86	83-92

MUJERES

Estatura (con zapatos) metros	Talla pequeña kilogramos	Talla mediana kilogramos	Talla grande kilogramos
1,47	42-44	43-48	47-54
1,50	43-46	44-50	48-55
1,52	43-47	46-51	49-57
1,55	45-48	47-53	51-58
1,58	46-50	48-54	52-59
1,60	48-51	50-55	53-61
1,63	49-53	51-57	55-63
1,65	50-54	53-59	57-64
1,68	52-56	54-61	58-66
1,70	53-58	56-63	60-68
1,73	55-59	58-65	62-70
1,75	57-61	60-67	64-72
1,78	59-63	62-68	66-74
1,80	61-65	63-70	68-76
1,83	63-67	65-72	69-78

EN CONTEXTO

El calentamiento° y los ejercicios

Antes de correr, saltar°, levantar pesas° o hacer ejercicio es importante dedicar unos cinco o diez minutos para calentar los músculos y así evitar° accidentes. Los siguientes dibujos muestran algunos de los movimientos que puedes hacer antes de una sesión de ejercicios. Estos movimientos no son difíciles°, al contrario, son muy fáciles°. Debes hacer cada movimiento diez veces° por lo menos°.

warm-up
jump / levantar... *lift weigh*
avoid
difficult
easy / *times*
por... *at least*

1. Levanta los brazos.

2. Respira por la nariz. No respires por la boca.

3. Sube y baja los hombros.

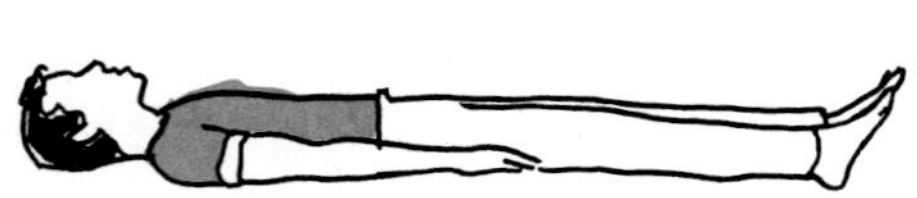
4. Acuéstate.

5. Mueve los dedos.

6. Dobla la rodilla derecha.

¿Verdadero o falso?

Diga si las siguientes oraciones son verdaderas o falsas de acuerdo con la selección anterior.

1. Se recomienda hacer movimientos de calentamiento antes de una sesión de actividad fuerte.
2. Es importante dedicar unos treinta minutos a los movimientos de calentamiento.
3. Los movimientos o ejercicios de calentamiento les evitan problemas a las personas.
4. Debes hacer estos movimientos por la mañana y por la noche.
5. Los movimientos de calentamiento son difíciles de hacer.

ACTIVIDADES

A Su profesor/a le va a pedir que haga ciertos movimientos. Siga sus instrucciones.

B Hágale las siguientes preguntas a su compañero/a. Comparta la información con la clase.

1. ¿Cuándo haces ejercicio? 2. ¿Dónde haces ejercicio? 3. ¿Cuánto tiempo dedicas a los ejercicios? 4. ¿Haces ejercicios de calentamiento? 5. ¿Prefieres hacer ejercicio solo/a (*alone*) o con otras personas? ¿Por qué?

GRAMÁTICA

Informal commands

1. Use informal commands with persons you address as **tú.** To form the affirmative **tú** command, use the present indicative **tú** form without the final **s.**

	PRESENT INDICATIVE		TÚ AFFIRMATIVE COMMAND
llamar:	(tú) llamas	⟶	llama (tú)
leer:	(tú) lees	⟶	lee (tú)
abrir:	(tú) abres	⟶	abre (tú)

El Parque Güell en Barcelona, diseñado por el famoso arquitecto Antonio Gaudí, donde se puede caminar al aire libre y descansar de las presiones de la vida en una gran ciudad.

2. To form the negative **tú** command, use the **usted** command + **s.**

	USTED COMMAND			**TÚ** NEGATIVE COMMAND
llamar:	llame	(usted)	⟶	no llames (tú)
leer:	lea	(usted)	⟶	no leas (tú)
abrir:	abra	(usted)	⟶	no abras (tú)

3. The use of **tú** is optional. When used, it normally follows the command.

4. Some **-er** and **-ir** verbs have shortened affirmative **tú** commands, but their negative command takes the long form like that of other verbs.

poner:	pon, no pongas	**hacer:**	haz, no hagas
salir:	sal, no salgas	**decir:**	di, no digas
tener:	ten, no tengas	**ir:**	ve, no vayas
venir:	ven, no vengas	**ser:**	sé, no seas

5. Placement of object and reflexive pronouns with **tú** commands is the same as with **usted** commands.

a. Affirmative	**b.** Negative
Cómprala.	No la compres.
Háblale.	No le hables.
Siéntate.	No te sientes.

6. The plural of **tú** commands in Spanish America is the **ustedes** command.[1]

Escribe (tú). Escriban (ustedes).

---

[1] The plural of **tú** in Spain is **vosotros.** To form the affirmative **vosotros** command, change the **r** of the infinitive to **d: hablar ⟶ hablad; comer ⟶ comed; escribir ⟶ escribid.**

To form the negative **vosotros** command, use the stem of the infinitive (except stem-changing **-ir** verbs) and add **-éis** for **-ar** verbs and **-áis** for **-er** and **-ir** verbs: **hablar ⟶ no habléis; comer ⟶ no comáis; escribir ⟶ no escribáis.**

Stem-changing **-ir** verbs change the **e** or **o** of the stem to **i** and **u** respectively: **preferir ⟶ no prefiráis; pedir ⟶ no pidáis; dormir ⟶ no durmáis.**

ACTIVIDADES

A Escoja el consejo (*advice*) adecuado que usted debe dar de acuerdo con la situación.

1. Su compañero saca notas muy bajas en la clase de química.
   a. Mira más programas de televisión.
   b. Practica en el laboratorio.
   c. Ve al cine con tu novia.
2. Su hermano quiere estar más delgado.
   a. No comas hamburguesas.
   b. No hagas ejercicio.
   c. No bebas té.
3. Su amiga quiere organizar una fiesta.
   a. Ve al cine por la noche.
   b. Repasa la lección.
   c. Invita a un grupo simpático.
4. A su amiga le gusta una sudadera que ve en una tienda.
   a. Cómprala.
   b. Préstala.
   c. Contéstala.
5. Su compañero quiere ir a un partido de fútbol muy importante.
   a. Saluda a tus amigos.
   b. Compra la entrada hoy.
   c. Practica con el entrenador.

Una madre besa a su hija en Oaxaca, México. El cuidado y el cariño que se les da a los niños es muy importante para que puedan ser adultos sanos física y mentalmente.

B Un estudiante extranjero quiere hacer unas compras en la tienda La Elegante del Centro Comercial Continente y no sabe dónde está. Déle las siguientes instrucciones para llegar allá.

Modelo salir de la Facultad de Ciencias
Sal de la Facultad de Ciencias.

1. doblar a la derecha
2. seguir derecho hasta la calle Príncipe
3. tomar el autobús 32
4. bajarse en la Plaza San Martín
5. cruzar la plaza
6. doblar a la izquierda en la calle Real
7. caminar tres cuadras y allí está el centro comercial

C Usted está cuidando a un niño de seis años. Dígale todas las cosas que debe hacer.

Modelo despertarse **Despiértate.**

1. levantarse
2. lavarse la cara y los dientes
3. vestirse
4. ponerse las medias y los zapatos
5. venir a desayunar
6. beber el jugo de naranja
7. comer el cereal
8. salir a jugar

D Usted está a cargo de una clase de ejercicios. Sus alumnos están haciendo mal algunos ejercicios. Dígales lo que deben hacer.

Modelo Magdalena respira por la boca.
Magdalena, no respires por la boca.

1. Juan dobla las rodillas.
2. Berta mueve las caderas.
3. Alfonso baja los brazos.
4. Irma sube los hombros.
5. Francisco salta.
6. Rafael levanta los pies.

E Su compañero/a tiene una entrevista esta tarde. Dígale qué debe hacer y qué no debe hacer para causar una buena impresión.

Modelo **Llega temprano. No hables demasiado.**

F Piense en alguna actividad y dígale a su compañero/a que la haga. Su compañero/a debe hacerla.

Modelo **Pon la mano derecha sobre el hombro izquierdo.**

EN CONTEXTO

El peso (*weight*)

Eduardo pesa 80 kilos.
Eduardo pesa menos que Álvaro.

Álvaro pesa 95 kilos.
Álvaro pesa más que Eduardo.

La estatura

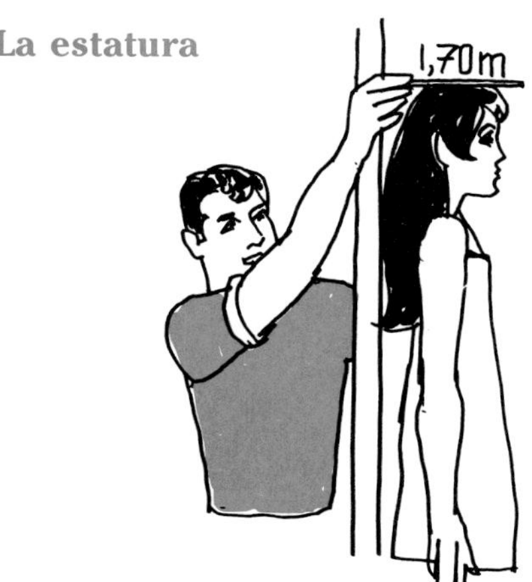

Juliana mide 1 metro 70.
Juliana es más alta que Adela.

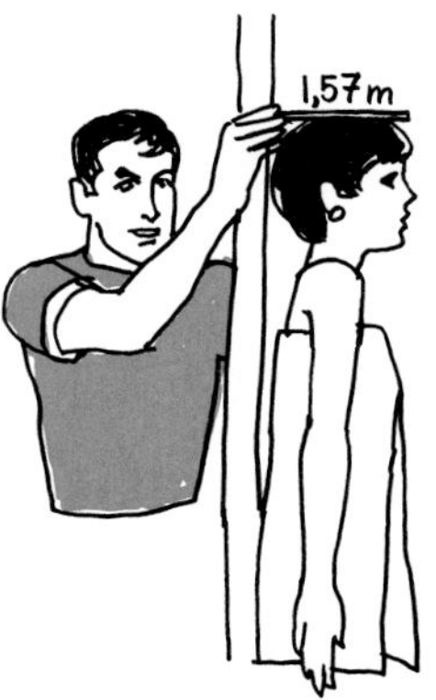

Adela mide 1 metro 57.
Adela es más baja que Juliana.

ACTIVIDADES

A Preguntas

1. ¿Cuánto mide la pizarra? ¿y el salón de clase? ¿y la puerta?
2. ¿Cuánto mide su habitación?
3. ¿Cuál es más grande, el salón de clase o su habitación?
4. ¿Cuál es más pequeño, el libro o el lápiz?

B Pregúntele a su compañero/a cuánto mide en metros y cuánto pesa en kilos. Después su compañero/a debe hacerle las mismas preguntas a usted (no es necesario decir la verdad). Use la siguiente tabla con las equivalencias aproximadas para las conversiones. Si su peso o su estatura no aparece en la tabla, dé un número aproximado basándose en los números de la tabla.

ESTATURA		PESO	
PIES	*METROS*	*LIBRAS*	*KILOS*
5	1,52	90	41
5,1	1,55	100	45,5
5,2	1.58	110	50
5,3	1,60	120	54,5
5,4	1,62	130	59
5,5	1.65	140	63,5
5,6	1,68	150	68
5,7	1,70	160	72,5
5,8	1,73	170	77
5,9	1,75	180	81,5
5,10	1,78	190	86
5,11	1,80	200	91
6	1,83	210	95
6,1	1,85	220	100
6,2	1,88	230	104,5

GRAMÁTICA

Comparisons of inequality

1. Use **más. . . que** or **menos. . . que** to express unequal comparisons.

Ella es { más / menos } activa que él.	*She is { more / less } active than he.*
El doctor tiene { más / menos } pacientes que el especialista.	*The doctor has { more / fewer } patients than the specialist.*

2. Use **de** instead of **que** before numbers.

Humberto tiene **más de** veinte años.
Jorge pesa **menos de** 80 kilos.

3. The following adjectives have regular and irregular comparative forms.

bueno	más bueno/mejor	*better*
malo	más malo/peor	*worse*
pequeño	más pequeño/menor	*smaller*
joven	más joven/menor	*younger*
grande	más grande/mayor	*bigger*
viejo	más viejo/mayor	*older*

Menor and **mayor** normally refer to a person's age.

La doctora es { mayor / menor } que la enfermera.

Este gimnasio es { mejor / peor } que aquél.

ACTIVIDADES

A Compare a estos dos estudiantes usando los adjetivos que aparecen más abajo.

Modelos **Felipe es más activo que Gloria.**
Gloria es menos activa que Felipe.

Gloria López Reyes

Edad: 19 años
Estatura: 1, 60 m.
Peso: 50 kilos
Promedio: A
Actividades: Club de Latín
Presidenta del Club de Ciencias
Honores: Beca (*scholarship*) de matemáticas
Intereses: lectura, arte, música clásica

Felipe Saura Torres

Edad: 20 años
Estatura: 1, 80 m.
Peso: 84 kilos
Promedio: B
Actividades: Club de Baile
Redactor (*editor*) del periódico
Honores: Premio (*prize*) por sus editoriales
Intereses: deportes, baile, música popular, guitarra

serio	simpático
delgado	trabajador
atlético	popular
inteligente	joven
alegre	interesante
fuerte	alto

B Compare estas dos clínicas.

Modelo **La Clínica Villalón tiene menos camas que la Clínica El Bosque.**

Clínica Villalón	**Clínica El Bosque**
18 camas	80 camas
8 doctores	30 doctores
10 enfermeras	50 enfermeras
12 cuartos	50 cuartos
farmacia y cafetería	farmacia y cafetería
salón de cirugía (*surgery*)	2 salones de cirugía
laboratorio	2 laboratorios
servicio de ambulancia	servicio de ambulancia
médico residente 24 horas	2 médicos residentes 24 horas

C Compare a las siguientes personas.

1. Woody Allen y Robert Redford
2. Madonna y Cher
3. Fernando Valenzuela y Don Mattingly
4. Julio Iglesias y Plácido Domingo

D Con un compañero/a compare los precios de las oficinas más caras del mundo.

Modelo **Las oficinas de Chicago son más caras que las de Madrid.**

LAS OFICINAS DE ALQUILER MAS CARAS DEL MUNDO

Tokio	16.690 ptas. m²
Londres	14.989 ptas. m²
New York	6.674 ptas. m²
París	6.633 ptas. m²
Hong Kong	6.493 ptas. m²
Chicago	4.207 ptas. m²
Los Angeles	4.177 ptas. m²
Madrid	3.734 ptas. m²
San Francisco	3.573 ptas. m²
Frankfurt	3.543 ptas. m²
São Paulo	2.848 ptas. m²
Barcelona	2.637 ptas. m²
Bruselas	2.335 ptas. m²
Amsterdam	1.912 ptas. m²

EN CONTEXTO

En una clase de ejercicios aeróbicos

Hay tantas chicas como chicos en la clase de ejercicios.
Felipe es tan fuerte como Arturo.
Ana es tan alta como Lucía.
Carlos pesa tanto como Arturo.

Preguntas

1. ¿Dónde están estas personas?
2. ¿Qué están haciendo?
3. ¿Cuántos hombres hay? ¿y mujeres?
4. ¿Quién pesa tanto como Carlos?
5. ¿Quién salta tanto como Marcia?
6. ¿Quién es más baja, Ana o Lucía?

ACTIVIDADES

A Diga qué cosas se hacen y no se hacen en un gimnasio.

Modelo ver televisión
No se ve televisión.

bailar	saltar	levantar los brazos	tocar el piano	dormir
hacer la tarea	cocinar	hablar	correr	

B Llame por teléfono a su amigo/a para ir al gimnasio. Complete el siguiente diálogo con su compañero/a.

Amigo/a ¡Aló!
Usted ___, te habla ___. ¿Cómo estás?
Amigo/a ___. ¿Y tú?
Usted ___. Te llamo porque ___. ¿Quieres venir?
Amigo/a ___.
Usted Paso por ti a ___.
Amigo/a Te espero ___.

GRAMÁTICA

Comparisons of equality

tan. . . como	*as . . . as*
tantos/as. . . como	*as many . . . as*
tanto/a. . . como	*as much . . . as*
tanto como	*as much as*

1. Use **tan. . . como** to express equal comparisons with adjectives.

Él es **tan** alto **como** ella. — *He is as tall as she.*

2. Use **tanto(s)/tanta(s). . . como** to express equal comparison with nouns.

Cristina tiene **tanto** trabajo **como** su amiga. — *Christina has as much work as her friend.*
Hay **tanta** leche **como** café. — *There is as much milk as coffee.*
Hay **tantos** chicos **como** chicas. — *There are as many boys as girls.*
Hay **tantas** enfermeras **como** técnicos. — *There are as many nurses as technicians.*

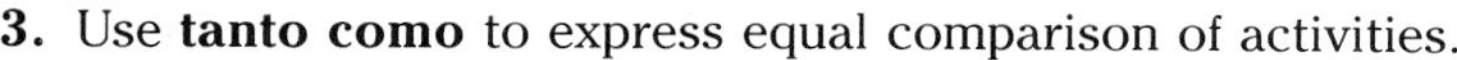

3. Use **tanto como** to express equal comparison of activities.

La enfermera trabaja **tanto como** el doctor. *The nurse works as much as the doctor.*

ACTIVIDADES

A Complete las siguientes oraciones. Trabaje con un/a estudiante.

1. Soy tan inteligente como...
2. Un tigre come tanto como...
3. Mi novio/a es tan guapo/a como...
4. En Nueva York hay tantos teatros como...
5. Los Ángeles es tan bonito como...
6. King Kong es tan feo como...

B Use las cinco características que aparecen en la tabla para comparar a los estudiantes.

Modelo **Vilma tiene tantos hermanos como Marta** o **Vilma tiene más hermanos que Ricardo.**

	Pedro	Vilma	Marta	Ricardo
clases	5	5	4	6
dinero	$15	$8	$15	$8
hermanos	3	4	4	3
discos	225	253	253	309
casetes	45	38	56	56

Unos jóvenes levantan pesas en un gimnasio de México.

C El Dr. López y la Dra. Garcés son unos cirujanos (*surgeons*) excelentes. Compárelos usando las siguientes palabras.

Modelos famoso **El Dr. López es tan famoso como la Dra. Garcés.**
ganar dinero **La Dra. Garcés gana tanto dinero como el Dr. López.**

bueno	tener pacientes	inteligente	enfermeras
trabajar	tener libros	viajar	saber

D **Opiniones.** Exprese su opinión comparando las siguientes personas o cosas. Puede usar las palabras que aparecen entre paréntesis o usar otras palabras.

Modelo comida china y comida italiana (buena)
La comida china es tan buena como la comida italiana o **La comida china es mejor/peor que la comida italiana.**

1. Tina Turner y Liza Minelli
(famosa / rica / simpática / alta)
2. autos norteamericanos y autos japoneses
(bueno / grande / caro / cómodo / fuerte)
3. dos ciudades (e.g., Nueva York y San Francisco)
(teatros / cines / restaurantes / habitantes / hoteles)
4. dos programas de televisión
(triste / largo / bueno / simpático / malo)

Unos estudiantes venezolanos hacen ejercicio y trotan en los terrenos de la Universidad de Caracas.

LECTURA

Esta selección sobre los ejercicios aparece en el libro *Salud y nutrición.* Las siguientes palabras pueden ayudarlo/la a entender mejor la selección y la tabla.

rato	*while*
aire libre	*open air*
desarrollar	*develop*
montañismo	*(mountain) trekking, hiking*
la respiración se entrecorta	*breathing becomes short*
con cuidado	*carefully*
parar	*to stop*
sin olvidar	*without forgetting*

¿Existe el deporte ideal?

Se dice que el mejor deporte es caminar un buen rato todos los días y, a ser posible, al aire libre lejos de la contaminación urbana. Este ejercicio, como todos aquellos que más se acercan a los movimientos naturales, que en su día practicaban los hombres primitivos, son los ideales para desarrollar armónicamente el cuerpo humano: la natación, el montañismo, la marcha, el salto...

La marcha, tan de moda hoy día, es un buen deporte, pero hay que realizarlo de manera progresiva y con cuidado. Lo mejor es adoptar un trote rítmico, respirando adecuadamente, de tal manera que te permita hablar con facilidad a la persona que está a tu lado. Si no es así, y la respiración se entrecorta en exceso, es mejor parar y proseguir al cabo de un rato.

El gráfico siguiente da una idea aproximada de las actividades que pueden influir en cada uno de los factores resistencia, flexibilidad y fuerza, sin olvidar la forma en que contribuyen a liberar la tensión y la ansiedad.

Actividad	Resistencia	Flexibilidad	Fuerza	Relajación
Atletismo	**	****	***	**
Baile	***	****	*	****
Ciclismo	****	**	***	****
Fútbol	***	***	***	*
Golf	*	**	*	****
Jogging	****	**	**	****
Marcha	**	*	*	****
Montaña	***	*	**	**
Natación	****	****	****	****
Squash	***	***	**	**
Subir escaleras	***	*	**	*
Tenis	**	***	**	**
Trabajos domésticos	*	**	*	*
Yoga	*	***	*	****

* *Muy poco útil*   *** *Bastante útil*
** *Util*   **** *Muy útil*

¿Verdadero o Falso?

Diga si las siguientes oraciones son verdaderas o falsas de acuerdo con la lectura.

1. El mejor deporte es trotar.
2. Es muy bueno hacer ejercicios de movimientos naturales.
3. Es mejor caminar en las ciudades.
4. Para caminar es una buena idea empezar poco a poco.
5. Los ejercicios ayudan a eliminar las tensiones.

Preguntas

Para contestar las siguientes preguntas consulte la tabla de actividades.

1. ¿Cuáles son los ejercicios que son muy útiles para la resistencia?
2. ¿Qué ejercicio es más útil para la flexibilidad, el tenis o la natación?
3. ¿Qué ejercicio le da más fuerza a la persona, subir escaleras o el ciclismo?
4. ¿Qué ejercicios ayudan menos a la relajación?
5. Según la tabla, ¿cuáles son los mejores ejercicios?

¿Cuál es? Escoja una de las actividades que aparecen en la tabla. No le diga a su compañero/a cuál es. Sólo le debe decir cuántos asteriscos tiene en una categoría. Su compañero/a debe tratar de adivinar cuál es.

Modelo

Usted	**Tres asteriscos en flexibilidad.**
Compañero/a	**El fútbol.**
Usted	**No. Dos asteriscos en relajación.**
Compañero/a	**El tenis.**
Usted	**Muy bien.**

Lea el siguiente anuncio sobre un lugar llamado Pardiñas 50 y conteste después las preguntas.

1. ¿Es grande o pequeño este lugar?
2. ¿Quiénes atienden al público?
3. ¿Qué pueden hacer las personas allí?
4. ¿Por qué se llama Pardiñas 50?
5. ¿Por qué dice el anuncio que este lugar es «algo más que un gimnasio»?
6. ¿Qué le interesa a usted más de este gimnasio? ¿Por qué?

SITUACIONES

1. You are expecting company for the weekend. Your friend has come to help you with the housework. Tell your friend to (a) open the windows, (b) vacuum the living room, (c) put towels in the bathroom, and (d) prepare a salad.
2. You are organizing a surprise party for a friend. Two of your classmates are going to help. Tell them (a) what they should do, (b) what they should bring, (c) whom they should call, and so on. Your classmates should give you some ideas about the party.
3. Compare your university with a rival school. You may use the following elements to compare them: (a) athletic teams (e.g., football, basketball), (b) size, (c) number of students, (d) tuition, (e) professors, (f) departments, (g) . . .
4. Imagine you are a foreign student. You want to go someplace on campus. Ask your partner where it is located. Your partner will give you directions to get there.
5. Your best friend tells you that he/she is feeling very depressed (**deprimido/a**). Tell him/her (a) to go out with friends, (b) to talk to other people, (c) to call you, and (d) to do some exercise. Add any other advice you may deem necessary.
6. Compare two sports with respect to activity, players, interest, and so on, telling why you prefer one over the other. Ask your partner about his/her favorite sport.
7. Select two cars you are familiar with and compare them with respect to size, speed, price, appearance, shape, prestige, weight, and any other characteristic you can think of.

8. You are "lucky" today. Everyone is asking you for directions. Look at the map below and tell each person how to get to his/her destination.

You are at	Person wants to go to
a. Clínica San Camilo	El Corte Inglés
b. Palacio de los Deportes	Plaza de toros
c. Plaza de M. Becerra	Torre España

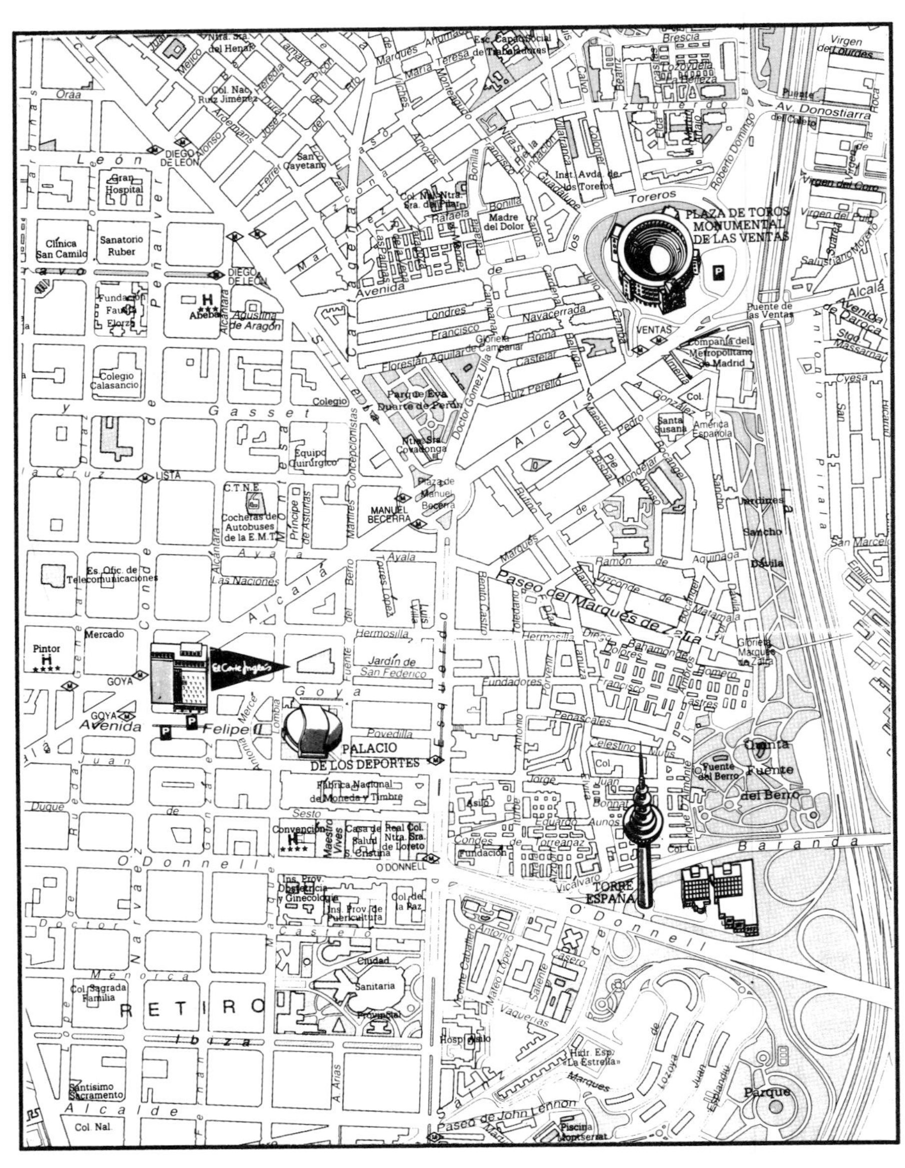

VOCABULARIO[2]

ejercicios

el accidente	*accident*
el calentamiento	*warm-up*
los ejercicios aeróbicos	*aerobics*
el movimiento	*movement*
el músculo	*muscle*
el peso	*weight*
la sesión	*session*

estatura	*height*
el metro	*meter*
el pie	*foot*

peso	*weight*
el kilo	*kilo*
la libra	*pound*

descripciones

difícil	*difficult*
fácil	*easy*
mayor	*bigger, older*
mejor	*better*
menor	*smaller, younger*
peor	*worse*

tiempo

el minuto	*minute*

verbos

bajar	*to lower, to bring down*
calentar (ie)	*to warm up*
dedicar (qu)	*to dedicate*
doblar	*to bend*
evitar	*to avoid*
medir (i)	*to measure*
mover (ue)	*to move*
pesar	*to weigh*
respirar	*to breathe*
saltar	*to jump*

palabras útiles

cada	*each*
el dibujo	*drawing*
siguiente	*following*
vez	*time*

expresiones útiles

al contrario	*on the contrary*
más... que	*more . . . than, adj. + est than*
menos... que	*less . . . than, fewer . . . than*
por lo menos	*at least*
tan... como	*as . . . as*
tanto/a... como	*as much . . . as*
tantos/as... como	*as many . . . as*

---

[2] For parts of the body, see pages 216–217.

In *Lección 10* **you will**

a. plan menus.

b. order food.

c. express wishes and hope.

d. make requests.

e. express opinions.

f. express doubt.

g. express fear and worry.

h. express joy and satisfaction.

Supermercado La Cubanita

zanahorias
0,48 kilo

vinagre
1,20 1/2 litro

espinacas
0,50 1/2 kilo

aceite
2,29 1/2 litro

salsa de tomate
0,23 lata

pimiento verde
1,00 kilo

azúcar
1,49 kilo

sal
1,00 1/2 kilo

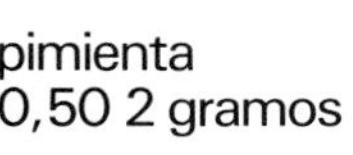

pimienta
0,50 2 gramos

mostaza
1,35

mayonesa
1,89

arroz
1,19 kilo

Lección 10

La comida

Su mercado latino

aguacates
0,50 cada uno

papas
1,00 2 kilos

limones
0,60 docena

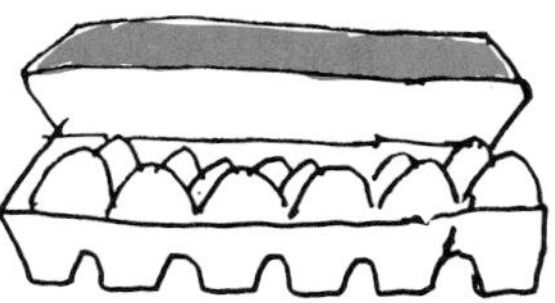
huevos
1,09 docena

pavo
1,99 1/2 kilo

lechuga
0,40

ajo
0,90 1/4 kilo

cebollas
0,50 kilo

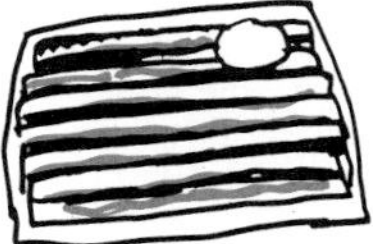
tocino
1,98 1/2 kilo

carne molida
2,79 1 kilo

ACTIVIDADES

A Pregúntele a su compañero/a el precio de algunos de los comestibles en el Supermercado La Cubanita.

Modelo Usted **¿Cuánto cuestan las zanahorias?**
Compañero/a **Cuestan 48 centavos el kilo.**

B Con un/a compañero/a haga una lista de la comida que tienen en el refrigerador y en la despensa (*pantry*). Después otros/as compañeros/as les van a preguntar qué tienen ustedes.

Refrigerador	Despensa
leche	cereal
tomates	azúcar
carne	salsa de tomate

Modelo Compañero/a **¿Qué tienen en el refrigerador?**
Usted **Tenemos leche, tomates y carne.**
Compañero/a **¿Qué tienen en la despensa?**
Usted **Tenemos cereal, azúcar y salsa de tomate.**

C La señora García está preparando su lista de compras para la semana. Prepare la lista según las comidas que quiere servir.

Quiere servir

fruta
vegetales
ensalada
2 clases de carne
comida para el desayuno
una cena italiana

Lista de compras

D En grupos de tres personas decidan lo que van a cenar. Preparen un menú y una lista de lo que tienen que comprar. Después las personas de otro grupo les van a hacer las siguientes preguntas.

1. ¿Cuál es el menú?
2. ¿Qué tienen que comprar?
3. ¿A cuántas personas van a invitar?
4. ¿Cuánto va a costar la cena?

Cultura

Food in the Hispanic world

When shopping for food in Hispanic countries, people generally go to specialty stores (**panadería,** bakery; **carnicería,** meat market; **heladería,** ice-cream shop; **dulcería,** or **pastelería,** pastry shop; **frutería,** fruit store; **pescadería,** fish market). However, many people who live in the cities find it more convenient and sometimes more economical to shop at supermarkets.

Hispanic cuisine varies not only from country to country but also from region to region. Some of the more popular dishes throughout the Hispanic countries are **la paella,** a Spanish dish made of rice, seafood, and chicken; **el arroz con pollo,** which may be cooked in water, chicken broth, white wine, or beer; and the Mexican **enchiladas** and **tacos,** made with **tortillas** (corn or wheat dough shaped like a very thin pancake) filled with meat or chicken. Many Hispanic dishes are becoming increasingly popular in the United States, especially in the Southwest and in cities like Miami, Chicago, and New York, where the necessary ingredients can be easily found in supermarkets and Latin stores.

Mealtimes in Hispanic countries differ from those in the United States. People typically eat breakfast (**el desayuno**) at around 7:00 or 8:00 A.M. Breakfast normally consists of **café con leche** or **chocolate caliente** with bread, a sweet roll, and sometimes juice or fruit. This is a light breakfast, so people sometimes have a snack in the late morning.

The main meal of the day is lunch (**el almuerzo** or **la comida**), eaten between 1:00 and 3:00 P.M., depending on the country. Normally the entire family can eat together, because children return from school around 1:00 and many businesses close at lunchtime. This is changing, however, especially in cities, due to the distances, traffic, and time involved. Lunch consists of soup or beans, rice and/or potatoes, salad, and a fish or meat dish. After the dessert, adults usually drink coffee.

Supper (**la cena** or **comida**) is served after 7:00 or 8:00 P.M., sometimes as late as 10:00 or 11:00 in Spain. Dinner is generally lighter than lunch. Because it is eaten rather late, many Hispanics have an afternoon snack (**la merienda**), which may consist of pastries or small sandwiches and tea, coffee, or a soft drink.

Dining etiquette differs somewhat from that in the United States. In Hispanic countries, it is a custom that people place both forearms on the table while eating. In Spain and other countries, people eat with the fork in the left hand and the knife in the right. Fruits are generally peeled and eaten with a knife and fork.

Una frutería de Buenos Aires.

EN CONTEXTO

Una invitación a cenar

La Sra. Ochoa tiene invitados esta noche y está muy ocupada. Tiene que sacar la vajilla° y las copas°, poner la mesa y preparar la cena. Ella está en la cocina hablando con su hija Petra. *china / glasses*

Sra. Ochoa	Necesito ir al supermercado. Esta noche los Morales vienen a cenar.	
Petra	¿Quieres que vaya? Yo no tengo clases hasta las once.	
Sra. Ochoa	Me alegro° que puedas ir. Tengo tanto que hacer.	Me... *I'm glad*
Petra	Tú te preocupas mucho, mamá. Los Morales son casi de la familia.	
Sra. Ochoa	Sí, pero a mí me gusta que todo quede° perfecto.	*to be*
Petra	Bueno, ¿qué necesitas?	
Sra. Ochoa	Necesito que traigas° medio kilo de mantequilla°, pan, dos kilos de camarones° y helado de vainilla.	*bring / butter* *shrimp*
Petra	¿Tienes verduras°?	*vegetables*
Sra. Ochoa	Espero que haya en el refrigerador. (Abre el refrigerador.) Sí, hay suficientes°.	*enough*
Petra	¿Algo más?	
Sra. Ochoa	No, eso es todo. Aquí tienes el dinero.	

Para completar

Complete las siguientes oraciones según el diálogo

1. Los invitados de esta noche son...
2. La mamá tiene que poner...
3. Para ayudar a su madre Petra va a ir...
4. Para la cena la mamá necesita...
5. En el refrigerador hay...
6. Para las compras, la mamá le da a Petra...

Un moderno supermercado en Caracas, Venezuela.

Vamos a poner la mesa

ACTIVIDADES

A Usted es el administrador/la administradora de un restaurante y está entrenando a un camarero. Dígale dónde debe poner cada cosa de acuerdo con el dibujo.

Modelo **Ponga el cuchillo a la derecha del plato.**

B Usted necesita comprar los ingredientes de su receta favorita. Dígale a su compañero/a cuáles son los ingredientes que necesita.

C Usted está muy ocupado/a porque tiene invitados esta noche. Dígale a su compañero/a todas las cosas que tiene que hacer.

GRAMÁTICA

Indicative versus subjunctive

In previous lessons you have used the present tense of the indicative mood (**Yo sé que Pepe estudia español.**). The indicative is used to state facts (what is happening, happens regularly, has happened), or is certain to happen. Thus, in the above sentence, I am stating the fact that I know something (**sé**) and also the fact that Pepe studies Spanish (**estudia**).

You have also learned commands (**usted** or **ustedes**), which are forms of the subjunctive. Spanish uses the subjunctive to express what we want to happen (**Quiero que vayas al supermercado.**), hope will happen (**Espero que vuelvas pronto.**), and in situations in which there is an emotional reaction (**Me alegro que vayas.**).

Present subjunctive

	hablar	comer	vivir
yo	hable	coma	viva
tú	hables	comas	vivas
él, ella, usted	hable	coma	viva
nosotros/as	hablemos	comamos	vivamos
vosotros/as	habléis	comáis	viváis
ellos/as, ustedes	hablen	coman	vivan

1. To form the present subjunctive use the **yo** form of the present indicative, drop the final **o**, and add the subjunctive endings. Notice that as with **usted/ustedes** commands, **-ar** verbs change the **a** to **e**, and **-er** and **-ir** verbs change the **e** and **i** to **a.**
2. The present subjunctive forms of verbs with irregular indicative **yo** forms are

conocer:	conozca, conozcas...	**tener:**	tenga, tengas...
decir:	diga, digas...	**traer:**	traiga, traigas...
hacer:	haga, hagas...	**venir:**	venga, vengas...
poner:	ponga, pongas...	**ver:**	vea, veas...
salir:	salga, salgas...		

Una antigua dulcería de la ciudad de México. En los pueblos y ciudades hispanas hay numerosas dulcerías donde se pueden comprar los dulces típicos de la región.

3. The following verbs have irregular forms:

   ir: vaya, vayas... **saber:** sepa, sepas... **ser:** sea, seas...

4. The verbs **dar** and **estar** require written accent marks.

   dar: dé, des, dé, demos deis, den
   estar: esté, estés, esté, estemos, estéis, estén

5. Stem changing **-ar** and **-er** verbs follow the same pattern as in the present indicative.

   pensar: p**ie**nse, p**ie**nses, p**ie**nse, pensemos, penséis, p**ie**nsen
   volver: v**ue**lva, v**ue**lvas, v**ue**lva, volvamos, volváis, v**ue**lvan

6. Stem-changing **-ir** verbs follow the pattern of the present indicative, but have an additional change in the **nosotros** and **vosotros** forms.

   preferir: pref**ie**ra, pref**ie**ras, pref**ie**ra, pref**i**ramos, pref**i**ráis, pref**ie**ran
   dormir: d**ue**rma, d**ue**rmas, d**ue**rma, d**u**rmamos, d**u**rmáis, d**ue**rman

The subjunctive used to express wishes and hope

1. When the verb of the main clause expresses wanting or hoping, use a subjunctive verb form in the dependent clause.

main clause	dependent clause	
La jefa quiere	que (él) **haga** el trabajo.	*The boss wants him to do the work.*
Yo espero	que **termine** temprano.	*I hope he'll finish early.*

   Notice that there is a different subject in each clause. If there is no change in subjects, use an infinitive instead of a clause with the subjunctive.

   Yo **espero terminar** temprano. — *I hope to finish early.*
   La jefa **quiere hacer** el trabajo. — *The boss wants to do the work.* (*herself*)

2. Common verbs that express wanting and hoping are **desear, esperar, necesitar, pedir, preferir, permitir** (*to permit*), **prohibir** (*to prohibit or forbid*), and **querer.** With the verbs **pedir, permitir,** and **prohibir,** Spanish may use an indirect object.

   Me prohíbe que (yo) entre. — *He forbids me to go in.*
   Les permite que salgan esta noche. — *He allows them to go out tonight.*

3. With the verb **decir,** use the subjunctive in the dependent clause when expressing a wish or an order. Use the indicative when reporting something.

   Dice que los niños **duermen.** — *She says (that) the children are sleeping.* (reporting)
   Dice que los niños **duerman.** — *She says (that) the children should sleep.* (an order)

The subjunctive used with verbs of emotion

1. When the verb of the main clause expresses emotion (fear, happiness, sorrow, and so on), use a subjunctive verb form in the dependent clause.

Sentimos que no **puedan** venir.	*We're sorry (that) they can't come.*
Me alegro de que **estés** aquí.	*I'm glad (that) you're here.*

2. Common verbs that express emotions are **alegrarse (de), sentir, gustar,** and **temer** (*to fear*).

ACTIVIDADES

A Usted está organizando una reunión del club de español. Dígales a sus compañeros lo que usted quiere que hagan para la reunión.

Modelo Marta / traer los vasos
Quiero que Marta traiga los vasos.

1. Alberto / invitar a los profesores
2. Julia y Ángeles / preparar la ensalada
3. Vilma / comprar los refrescos
4. Roberto / traer el estéreo
5. Juan y Berta / poner la mesa

B Ustedes piensan ir de excursión el sábado y reciben esta nota de su amigo David. ¿Qué dice David que ustedes deben hacer para la excursión?

Modelo preparen unos sándwiches
David dice que preparemos unos sándwiches.

Llamen a Federico.
Pasen por María.
Desayunen bien antes de salir.
Salgan temprano.
Traigan refrescos.

C Usted tiene invitados a cenar esta noche. Diga qué cosas quiere usted que pasen.

Modelo Deseo que... **Deseo que vengan temprano.**

1. Quiero que...
2. Espero que...
3. Prefiero que...
4. Necesito que...

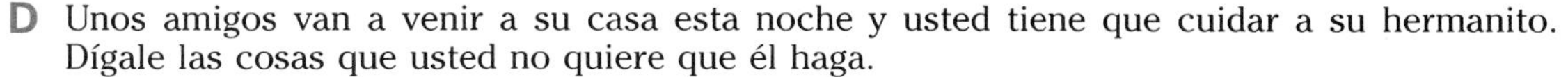

D Unos amigos van a venir a su casa esta noche y usted tiene que cuidar a su hermanito. Dígale las cosas que usted no quiere que él haga.

Modelo **No quiero que salgas a la calle.**

E Los amigos de Arturo quieren que él haga las siguientes cosas este sábado. Diga que él no quiere hacerlas o que él quiere hacer otras cosas.

Modelo Quieren que se levante temprano.
Pero él no quiere levantarse temprano o **Pero él quiere levantarse tarde.**

1. Quieren que vaya a la playa con ellos.
2. Quieren que juegue vólibol en la playa.
3. Quieren que invite a su hermana.
4. Quieren que vaya al cine después.
5. Quieren que cene en el centro con ellos.

F Usted va a tener una entrevista para un trabajo. Diga todas las cosas que usted espera o necesita hacer ese día.

Modelo **Necesito (Espero) salir temprano.**

G Usted va a visitar a un amigo que está en la clínica. ¿Qué le dice usted a su amigo?

1. Siento que...
2. Me alegro de que...
3. Espero que...
4. Deseo que...

H En grupos de tres estudiantes hagan una lista de las actividades que permiten o prohíben en una fábrica o en una oficina.

Modelo **Permiten que salgan temprano para ir al médico.**
Prohíben que beban cerveza en la cafetería.

Unos clientes esperan a que los atiendan en una charcutería de Madrid. Los jamones serranos que están colgados al fondo son típicos de España.

EN CONTEXTO

En un restaurante

Ana Celia y Margarita quieren perder peso. Están en un restaurante que sirve comida sana y con pocas calorías.

RESTAURANTE SU SALUD[1]
Comida sana a buenos precios

Menú

Sándwiches		Sopas	
Sándwich de aguacate y tomate	2,50	Sopa de tomate	2,50
Sándwich de pavo y lechuga	3,80	Sopa de cebolla	2,50
Sándwich de atún	3,80	Sopa de pollo	3,00
Sándwich de pollo	4,00	Sopa de papas	2,50
Sándwich de alfalfa y requesón	2,50	Sopa de zanahoria	2,50

Platos combinados

$6,50	$7,50
Pavo asado	Pescado al horno
Puré de papas	Papas hervidas
Ensalada de lechuga y tomate	Espinacas
Yogur de fresa	Sorbete de naranja

Postres		Bebidas	
Frutas de la estación	2,00	Leche descremada	1,50
Yogur	1,50	Jugo de naranja	2,00
Gelatina	1,50	Té	1,00
		Café descafeinado	1,00
		Agua mineral	1,00

Gracias por su visita y conserve su salud.
No se admiten propinas.

Ana Celia ¿Crees que a Gilberto le guste esta comida?

Margarita No, yo no creo que le guste. A él le encantan las salsas, la carne, los postres...

Ana Celia Bueno, ¿por qué no lo invitamos y así la prueba? Quizás le guste.

Margarita Si lo invitas a un restaurante francés o español, seguro que acepta. Pero aquí, dudo que acepte.

Preguntas

1. ¿Cómo se llama el restaurante?
2. ¿Qué tipo de comida sirven?
3. ¿Por qué van a ese restaurante Ana Celia y Margarita?
4. ¿A quién quiere invitar Ana Celia?
5. ¿Qué clase de comida prefiere Gilberto?
6. ¿Cree Ana Celia que él va a aceptar la invitación?

---

[1] requesón *cottage cheese* asado *roast* hervidas *boiled* descremada *nonfat* propina *tip*

ACTIVIDADES

A Usted y su compañero/a están en el restaurante Su Salud. Lean el menú y decidan qué van a pedir.

B Usted es vegetariano/a. Diga qué platos puede usted comer de cada grupo.

grupo 1	grupo 2	grupo 3
sopa de pollo y vegetales	sándwich de jamón y queso	carne asada, papas fritas y ensalada
sopa de zanahoria	sándwich de ensalada de pollo	espaguetis con salsa de tomate y ensalada de espinacas
sopa de cebolla	sándwich de tomate, alfalfa y aguacate	pescado frito, arroz y verduras

C Prepare con su compañero/a dos clases de menú: un menú normal y un menú vegetariano.

		No.	Precio	
	LECHON ASADO MOROS Y CRISTIANOS YUCA CON MOJO ENSALADA PAN Y MANTEQUILLA	1	2.85	ROAST PORK MIXED BL BEANS & RICE CASAVA SALAD BREAD & BUTTER
	APORREADO DE TASAJO MOROS Y CRISTIANOS PAPAS O PLATANOS ENSALADA PAN Y MANTEQUILLA	2	2.95	MASHED DRY MEAT MIXED BL BEANS & RICE POTATOES OR PLANTAINS SALAD BREAD & BUTTER
	BISTEC DE JAMON MOROS Y CRISTIANOS PLATANOS FRITOS ENSALADA PAN Y MANTEQUILLA	3	2.95	HAM STEAK MIXED BL BEANS & RICE FRIED PLANTAINS SALAD BREAD & BUTTER
	PICADILLO MOROS Y CRISTIANOS PAPAS FRITAS ENSALADA PAN Y MANTEQUILLA	4	2.95	GROUND BEEF MIXED BL BEANS & RICE FRENCH FRIES SALAD BREAD & BUTTER
	POLLO FRITO MOROS Y CRISTIANOS PAPAS FRITAS ENSALADA PAN Y MANTEQUILLA	5	2.95	FRIED CHICKEN MIXED BL BEANS & RICE FRENCH FRIES SALAD BREAD & BUTTER
	RUEDA DE SERRUCHO MOROS Y CRISTIANOS PAPAS FRITAS ENSALADA PAN Y MANTEQUILLA	6	2.95	KING FISH MIXED BL BEANS & RICE FRENCH FRIES SALAD BREAD & BUTTER
	BOLICHE ASADO MOROS Y CRISTIANOS PLATANOS FRITOS ENSALADA PAN Y MANTEQUILLA	7	2.95	CUBAN ROASTBEEF MIXED BL BEANS & RICE FRIED PLANTAINS SALAD BREAD & BUTTER
	2 CROQUETAS DE JAMON MOROS Y CRISTIANOS PAPAS FRITAS ENSALADA PAN Y MANTEQUILLA	8	1.75	2 HAM CROQUETTES MIXED BL BEANS & RICE FRENCH FRIES SALAD BREAD & BUTTER
	LECHON ASADO TAMAL EN HOJA YUCA CON MOJO ENSALADA PAN Y MANTEQUILLA	9	2.95	ROAST PORK CORN CUBAN TAMAL CASAVA SALAD BREAD & BUTTER
	MASAS DE PUERCO FRITAS MOROS Y CRISTIANOS PLATANOS FRITOS ENSALADA PAN Y MANTEQUILLA	10	3.25	FRIED PORK MIXED BL. BEANS & RICE FRIED PLANTAINS SALAD BREAD & BUTTER

ESPECIAL PARA LLEVAR LECHON ASADO, MOROS Y CRISTIANOS YUCA CON MOJO $2.50 (IMPUESTO Y ENVASE INCLUIDO)

ESTE MENU NO PUEDE SER VARIADO. THIS MENU CAN NOT BE CHANGED.

FUERA DE ESTE MENU USTED PUEDE PEDIR "A LA ORDEN" OUT OF THIS MENU YOU MAY ORDER "A LA CARTE"

El menú de un restaurante de Miami, donde la comida cubana es también muy popular entre muchos norteamericanos.

GRAMÁTICA

The subjunctive used with verbs and expressions of doubt

1. When the verb in the main clause expresses doubt or uncertainty, use a subjunctive verb form in the dependent clause.

Dudo que ella **conozca** a Amanda. — *I doubt that she knows Amanda.*

2. When doubt is implied with the verbs **creer** and **pensar** in questions or in the negative, use a subjunctive verb form in the dependent clause. If no doubt is implied, use the indicative.

¿Crees que { **lleguen** / **llegan** } hoy? — *Do you think they'll arrive today?*
No, no creo que **lleguen** hoy. — *No, I don't think they'll arrive today.*

3. Since the expressions **tal vez** (*perhaps*) and **quizá(s)** convey doubt, the subjunctive is normally used.

{ Tal vez / Quizá(s) } ella **pruebe** el postre. — *Perhaps she'll try the dessert.*

ACTIVIDADES

A **¿Qué cree usted?** Diga su opinión sobre las cosas que se afirman más abajo.

Modelo Hay vida en Marte.
Creo que hay vida en Marte o **Dudo/no creo que haya vida en Marte** o **Tal vez/Quizá(s) haya vida en Marte.**

1. Los Yankees tienen los mejores jugadores.
2. El yogur tiene muchas calorías.
3. Todos debemos beber mucha agua.
4. Los amigos son más importantes que el dinero.
5. Los médicos visitan a los enfermos en su casa.
6. El pescado es mejor que la carne para la salud.
7. Es importante hacer ejercicio regularmente.
8. La comida afecta nuestra personalidad.

B Su compañero/a dice muchas mentiras. Él/Ella va a decir las cosas que hace, las personas que conoce, etc. y usted le va a decir a otro/a compañero/a que usted lo duda.

Modelo **—Hablo todos los días con Eddie Murphy.**
—Dudo que él hable todos los días con Eddie Murphy.

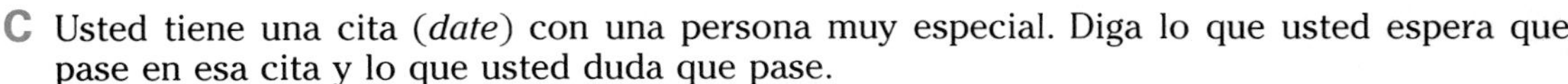

C Usted tiene una cita (*date*) con una persona muy especial. Diga lo que usted espera que pase en esa cita y lo que usted duda que pase.

Modelo **Espero que me invite a comer.**
Dudo que vayamos a un restaurante elegante.

D En grupos de cuatro estudiantes determine la opinión de sus compañeros/as sobre los siguientes temas.

Modelo las vacaciones

Usted **Creo que las vacaciones son importantes para todos. ¿Y tú qué crees?**

Compañero/a **Dudo que las vacaciones muy cortas sean buenas para todos.**

la lotería la televisión la música popular la universidad los doctores
la vida en los Estados Unidos

En un restaurante de Málaga, España, una pareja observa cómo les sirven paella, uno de los platos más populares en el mundo hispano. La paella se hace básicamente con arroz, carne, mariscos *(seafood)*, cebolla, ajo y azafrán *(saffron)*.

Unos jóvenes en uno de los muchos restaurantes y cafeterías que sirven comida cubana en Miami.

EN CONTEXTO

Miami

Miami es la ciudad más famosa de la Florida. Hay muchísimos hoteles grandes, especialmente en las playas. Tiene el mayor número de cubanos de cualquier° ciudad de los Estados Unidos, tal vez porque está cerca de Cuba y porque el clima es como el de Cuba. *any*

La Pequeña Habana es la zona más hispana de Miami. Mide unos seis kilómetros cuadrados y está cerca del centro comercial de Miami. Además es una de las zonas más antiguas° de la ciudad. *old*

La Calle Ocho está en la Pequeña Habana. En esta calle hay muchas tiendas y negocios y también están allí los mejores restaurantes de comida cubana. Los platos típicos como los frijoles° negros y el arroz, los plátanos fritos, el cerdo° asado, el picadillo (carne molida cocinada con cebolla, pimiento verde y ajo) y el café cubano se encuentran en todos los menús. Se habla español en todas partes y las personas que visitan estos lugares reciben la impresión de estar en un país hispano. *beans* *pork*

¿Verdadero o falso?

Diga si las siguientes oraciones son verdaderas o falsas, de acuerdo con la selección leída.

1. El clima de Miami es diferente del clima de Cuba.
2. Miami tiene más cubanos que otros lugares de los Estados Unidos.
3. La Pequeña Habana está lejos del centro de los negocios de Miami.
4. Los restaurantes cubanos están cerca de la Pequeña Habana.
5. El pavo asado es un plato típico cubano.
6. En la Calle Ocho se habla español en las tiendas y los restaurantes.

Preguntas

1. ¿Cuál es la ciudad más famosa de la Florida?
2. ¿Dónde hay muchos hoteles grandes?
3. ¿Qué platos típicos sirven en los restaurantes cubanos?
4. Describa la Pequeña Habana.

GRAMÁTICA

The superlative

1. To form the superlative use a definitive article + noun + **más/menos** + adjective. To express *in* or *at* with the superlative use **de.**

Es **el** traje {más / menos} caro (**de** la tienda). — *It is the {most / least} expensive suit (in the store).*

2. Do not use **más** or **menos** with **mejor, peor, mayor,** and **menor.**

Son **los mejores** alumnos de la clase. — *They're the best students in the class.*

3. You may leave out the noun when using the superlative.

Es el más caro de la tienda. — *It's the most expensive (one) in the store.*
Son los mejores de la clase. — *They're the best in the class.*

Superlative with *-ísimo*

1. To express the idea of *extremely* add the ending **-ísimo(-a, -os, -as)** to the adjective. If the adjective ends in a consonant, add **-ísimo** directly to the singular form. If it ends in a vowel, drop the vowel before adding **-ísimo.**

fácil	El examen es **facilísimo.**	*The exam is extremely easy.*
grande	La casa es **grandísima.**	*The house is extremely big.*
bueno	Los jugadores son **buenísimos.**	*The players are extremely good.*

2. The following orthographic changes occur when **-ísimo** is added.

c → q	poco → poquísimo
g → gu	largo → larguísimo
z → c	feliz → felicísimo

ACTIVIDADES

A La universidad. Complete la información con un compañero/a.

Modelo Compañero/a **el edificio más alto**
Usted ***La biblioteca* es el edificio más alto.**

1. el edificio más grande
2. la clase más interesante
3. el/la mejor profesor/a
4. el libro más caro
5. la peor comida de la cafetería
6. el/la estudiante menor (edad)
7. el deporte más popular
8. la materia menos difícil

B Preguntas personales. Hágale las siguientes preguntas a su compañero/a. Comparta la información con la clase.

1. ¿Quién es tu mejor amigo/a?
2. ¿Cuál es el peor día de la semana para ti?
3. ¿Cuál es la clase más fácil este semestre/trimestre?
4. ¿Quiénes son los mejores profesores?
5. ¿Dónde venden la mejor pizza? ¿y la mejor hamburguesa?
6. ¿Cuál es la mejor película de este año?
7. ¿Cuál es el peor programa de televisión este año?
8. ¿Cuál es el mejor equipo de béisbol este año? ¿y el peor?
9. ¿Cuáles son los mejores jugadores?
10. ¿Quién es el mejor entrenador?

C Opiniones. Usted y su compañero/a están en el teatro. Él/ella le da su opinión y usted está de acuerdo con todo lo que dice. Use el adjetivo terminado en la forma apropiada de **-ísimo.**

Modelo Compañero/a **Este drama es muy interesante.**
Usted **Sí, es interesantísimo.**

1. Las entradas son muy caras.
2. Los actores son buenos.
3. Los asientos son cómodos.
4. El programa es muy largo.
5. El actor principal es muy viejo.
6. La actriz principal es muy simpática.

D Haga oraciones sobre los diferentes estudiantes de la clase usando los siguientes adjetivos.

Modelo alto **Pedro es el estudiante más alto de la clase.**

simpático	inteligente	fuerte	serio	paciente
elegante	listo	trabajador	optimista	popular

E **Un concurso.** Usted está a cargo de anunciar (*announce*) los/las ganadores/as de un concurso de aficionados al arte. Escoja a los ganadores/as entre sus compañeros/as y anúnciele a la clase en qué categoría van a recibir el premio. Anuncie primero los premios principales y después los premios de consolación.

Modelo **La mejor diseñadora es la Srta. Asunción Benítez.**

Premios principales	**Premios de consolación**
mejor cantante (*singer*)	más creativo
mejor actor/actriz	más ingenioso
mejor bailarín/bailarina (*dancer*)	más rápido
mejor pianista/violinista	más sensitivo

Ahora piense en otras categorías posibles y anuncie a los ganadores/as.

Un puesto en una calle de Nueva York donde se pueden probar muchos platos típicos de la cocina hispana.

LECTURA

Un verdadero banquete

Los alumnos extranjeros están organizando una fiesta para celebrar el final del curso. Cada uno va a llevar° un plato típico de su país. Todos quieren que sus compañeros norteamericanos prueben diferentes platos. De esta forma pueden conocer mejor la cocina hispana.

José María es un estudiante español y él va a llevar una tortilla española. David, un estudiante norteamericano, le pregunta dónde va a comprar las tortillas de maíz para su plato. José María le explica que la tortilla española se prepara con huevos y patatas° y que es una *omelette.*

Guadalupe, una chica de México, dice que su mamá hace los mejores chiles rellenos° de México y que le va a pedir que prepare unos.

Mercedes, que es cubana, dice que ella va a llevar el arroz y los frijoles negros. Vivian, su compañera de cuarto, es puertorriqueña y dice que sin arroz con gandules° la comida no va a estar completa y que ella lo va a preparar.

Todos están seguros que esta fiesta va a ser un verdadero banquete.

llevar: *to take*
patatas: *potatoes (in Spain)*
chiles... *peppers filled with cheese*
gandules: *peas (in Puerto Rico)*

¿Verdadero o falso?

Diga si las siguientes oraciones son verdaderas o falsas de acuerdo con la lectura.

1. Los alumnos van a llevar platos típicos de los países hispanos.
2. La tortilla española se prepara con maíz.
3. Los chiles rellenos son típicos de México.
4. La madre de la estudiante mexicana hace unos chiles rellenos muy buenos.
5. El arroz con gandules es típico de Cuba.
6. La chica cubana va a llevar arroz y frijoles negros.

Preguntas

1. ¿Qué están organizando los estudiantes extranjeros?
2. ¿Qué va a llevar cada estudiante extranjero?
3. ¿De dónde es Ana María?
4. ¿Qué plato va a llevar?
5. ¿Qué se necesita para hacer una tortilla española?
6. ¿Quién va a preparar el plato mexicano?
7. ¿Qué plato típico cubano va a llevar Mercedes?
8. Según Vivian, ¿qué plato necesitan?

Una fruta excelente

La siguiente lectura está tomada de un anuncio donde se describe una fruta y sus características. Al leerla trate de determinar cuáles son estas características y quiénes deben comer esta fruta. Los siguientes palabras le pueden servir para entender mejor la selección.

alimenta	*nourishes*
no debe faltar	*should not be missing*
hierro	*iron*
aporta	*supplies*
crecimiento	*growth*

El plátano alimenta mucho

Generalmente, lo que les gusta a los niños no les alimenta. Y lo que les alimenta, no les gusta.

El plátano es una excepción. Alimenta mucho y les encanta.

Por su gran valor nutritivo, el plátano no debe faltar nunca en la dieta infantil. El plátano contiene más proteínas, calcio y hierro que ninguna otra fruta fresca. Por eso es tan bueno para los niños. Porque les aporta una buena cantidad de sustancias indispensables para el crecimiento, de la forma más sencilla.

¿A que nunca tiene problemas cuando le da un plátano a su hijo?

¿Verdadero o falso?

Diga si las siguientes oraciones son verdaderas o falsas de acuerdo con la lectura.

1. En general a los niños les gusta la comida que alimenta.
2. El plátano alimenta a los niños y además les gusta.
3. El plátano contiene muchas proteínas y minerales.
4. Los niños pueden ser más saludables si comen plátanos.

Preguntas

1. En general, ¿qué les gusta a los niños?
2. ¿Por qué es el plátano una excepción?
3. Explíquele a su compañero/a por qué debe comer plátano.

SITUACIONES

1. Ask a classmate which Hispanic foods he/she likes the best. Also ask him/her about other ethnic foods.
2. Find out about the food that your partner buys every week: (a) where he/she buys it, (b) how much it costs, and (c) who cooks the meals.
3. You and a friend are at a restaurant in a Spanish-speaking country. You will do the talking for the two of you. Another student will be the waiter/waitress. Tell the waiter/waitress (a) that you want to be far from the door, (b) that you want menus, (c) ask what the special for the day **(plato del día)** is, (d) say that you want two specials with wine for your friend and a large Coca-Cola for you, and (e) ask if you can pay with a credit card **(tarjeta de crédito).**
4. You are unable to go to the market this week because you were in an accident. Call a friend and ask him/her to go for you. Tell your friend over the phone what you want him/her to buy. You will need some items from the following categories: (a) **carne,** (b) **verduras,** (c) **frutas,** and (d) **para beber.**
5. Go to your local market and find the section where they have Hispanic foods. Write down the names of the foods you can find, the prices, and if possible, what they are used for. During the next class meeting, interview a classmate about what he/she discovered. Then he/she will interview you. Report your findings to the class.

VOCABULARIO

comida

el aceite — *oil*
el aguacate — *avocado*
el ajo — *garlic*
la alfalfa — *alfalfa*
el/la azúcar — *sugar*
el camarón — *shrimp*
la carne molida — *ground meat*
la cebolla — *onion*
el cerdo — *pork*
la espinaca — *spinach*
la fresa — *strawberry*
los frijoles — *beans*
la gelatina — *gelatin*
la mantequilla — *butter*
la mayonesa — *mayonnaise*
la mostaza — *mustard*
el pavo — *turkey*
la pimienta — *pepper*
el pimiento verde — *green pepper*
el puré de papas — *mashed potatoes*
el requesón — *cottage cheese*
la sal — *salt*
la salsa de tomate — *tomato sauce*
el sorbete — *sherbet*
el tocino — *bacon*
la vainilla — *vanilla*
la verdura — *vegetable*
el vinagre — *vinegar*
el yogur — *yogurt*
la zanahoria — *carrot*

en el restaurante

la botella de vino — *bottle of wine*
la copa — *(stemmed) glass*
la cuchara — *spoon*
la cucharita — *teaspoon*
el cuchillo — *knife*

el mantel	*tablecloth*
el plato	*plate, dish*
plato combinado	*combination plate*
el postre	*dessert*
la propina	*tip*
la servilleta	*napkin*
la taza	*cup*
el tenedor	*fork*
la vajilla	*china*
el vaso	*glass*

en el supermercado

la docena	*dozen*
el gramo	*gram*
la lata	*can*
el litro	*liter*

la salud	*health*
las calorías	*calories*
descafeinado	*decaffeinated*
descremado	*nonfat*
hervido	*boiled*
sano	*healthy*

lugares

el país	*country*
el supermercado	*supermarket*
la zona	*zone*

una cena

la invitación	*invitation*
el invitado	*guest*

descripciones

antiguo	*old*
asado	*roast*
famoso	*famous*
latino	*Latin*

verbos

aceptar	*to accept*
admitir	*to admit, to allow*
alegrarse	*to be glad*
conservar	*to conserve, to keep*
dudar	*to doubt*
esperar	*to hope, to expect*
permitir	*to permit, to allow*
preocuparse	*to worry*
prohibir	*to prohibit, to forbid*
quedar	*to be, to remain*
sentir (ie)	*to be sorry*
temer	*to fear*
traer	*to bring*

palabras útiles

cualquier	*any*
quizá(s)/tal vez	*maybe*
suficiente	*enough*

expresiones útiles

en todas partes	*everywhere*
eso es todo	*that's all*

In Lección 11, **you will**

a. **describe health conditions.**
b. **express opinions.**
c. **express attitudes.**
d. **express expectations and wishes.**

Lección 11

La salud y los médicos

El cuerpo humano por dentro

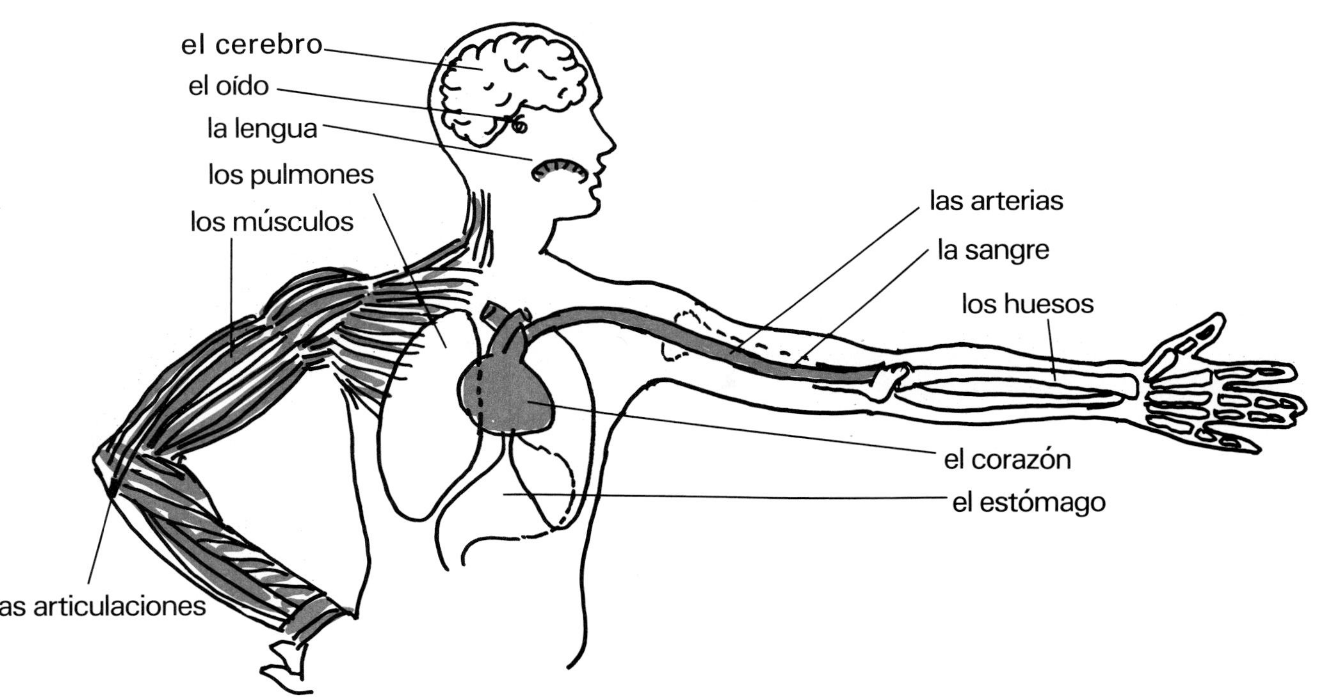

ACTIVIDADES

A Asocie las actividades de la izquierda con las partes del cuerpo de la derecha.

1. escuchar	a. el corazón
2. respirar	b. la lengua
3. mover la sangre	c. el estómago
4. hablar	d. el oído
5. pensar	e. el cerebro
6. digerir (*digest*) la comida	f. la sangre
7. circular por las arterias	g. los pulmones
8. permitir movimientos	h. las articulaciones

B **Entrevista.** Use las siguientes preguntas para entrevistar a un/a compañero/a. Comparta la información con la clase.

1. ¿Vas al médico con frecuencia? 2. ¿Cómo se llama tu médico? 3. ¿Dónde está su consultorio? 4. Si estás enfermo/a (*sick*), ¿va tu médico/a a tu casa? 5. ¿Cómo es tu médico/a?

Una farmacia de Miami. Muchas de las farmacias hispanas ofrecen el servicio de enviar medicinas a otros países.

Farmacias de guardia

De nueve y media de la mañana a diez de la noche: Puerta Nueva, 3 (esquina a Carretería). Gallito, 1 (junto ambulatorio Los Girasoles, sector Carretera Cádiz) frente a barriada La Paz. Avenida Juan Sebastián Elcano, 123 (Pedregalejo, junto cochera de autobuses). Capitán Huelin, 11 (Haza de Cuevas, detrás del Cine Cayri). Arroyo de los Angeles, Bl. Venus (frente Colegio Gibraljaire). Urbanización Parque del Sur, Bl. 16 (Ciudad Jardín). Alemania, 3-7 (junto antiguo mercado de mayoristas).

De diez de la noche a nueve y media de la mañana: Larios, 8, teléfono 211915. Serrato, s/n (barriada Santa Isabel), teléfono 333345.

TORREMOLINOS-BENALMADENA

De nueve y media de la mañana a diez de la noche: Arroyo de la Miel, Avda. de la Concepción, Bloque I (a 80 metros centro salud), Benalmádena. Montemar, calle Aladino, 19, Torremolinos.

De diez de la noche a nueve y media de la mañana: Arroyo de la Miel, Avda. de la Concepción, Bloque I (a 80 metros centro salud), Benalmádena

Cultura

Doctors, hospitals, and pharmacies in the Hispanic world

Although there have been many advances in medical care in Hispanic cities, the majority of doctors and hospitals cannot afford the latest technological equipment. Modern health care is even less available in rural areas. In general, there are no hospitals in small towns or farming areas. People depend on first-aid centers (**casas de socorro**), the town doctor, the midwife (**comadrona**), and even on healers (**curanderos**), who use herbs and objects, such as shells, believed to have healing powers.

In many Hispanic countries, medical-school graduates are often obliged to spend one year working in rural areas. This gives them experience in diagnosing and treating patients and in turn offers those patients much needed health care.

A distinction exists in the Hispanic world between a **clínica** and a **hospital.** A **clínica** is privately run and charges fees. A **hospital** is operated by the government or by a religious or charitable organization, and usually provides free medical care. In many cases, relatives may stay at the **hospital,** sometimes in the patient's room. Relatives can relieve some of the nurses' duties as well as contribute to the patient's well-being.

American medicines are available in Hispanic countries, though sometimes under a different name. Prescriptions are not necessary in many cases, and pharmacists have more freedom in advising patients than in the U.S. Pharmacists may also give injections and take the patient's blood pressure. Neighborhood pharmacies rotate night and holiday duty (**farmacias de turno/de guardia**), thereby providing 24-hour service. Local newspapers print lists showing pharmacy schedules, such as the one on page 262.

Una farmacia en Barcelona. El contacto personal que se establece con el farmacéutico es muy importante en la cultura hispana.

EN CONTEXTO

En el consultorio° de la doctora Suárez

office

La Sra. Muñoz está enferma. Tiene catarro° y un poco de fiebre. *cold*

Dra. Suárez ¿Cómo se siente, Sra. Muñoz?

Sra. Muñoz Me siento muy cansada°. Además, me duele la garganta° y también me duelen los oídos. *tired / me. . . I have a sore throat*

Dra. Suárez ¿Usted fuma°? *smoke*

Sra. Muñoz No, doctora.

Dra. Suárez Bueno, vamos a examinarle la garganta y los oídos. Abra la boca, por favor. Diga «Ah». (Examina a la Sra. Muñoz.) Tiene una infección en los oídos. No es muy seria, pero es necesario que se cuide. ¿Es usted alérgica a los antibióticos?

Sra. Muñoz No, doctora.

Dra. Suárez Entonces le voy a recetar° unos antibióticos. Es importante que tome las pastillas° cada° cuatro horas. Además, descanse° y beba mucho líquido. (Le da una receta a la Sra. Muñoz.) *prescribe / pills / every / rest*

Sra. Muñoz ¿Y para la fiebre, doctora?

Dra. Suárez Puede tomar aspirinas. Pero con los antibióticos es probable que la fiebre le baje muy pronto.

¿Verdadero o falso?

Diga si las siguientes oraciones son verdaderas o falsas de acuerdo con el diálogo.

1. A la Sra. Muñoz le duele la garganta.
2. La Dra. Suárez está muy cansada.
3. La Sra. Muñoz tiene una infección en los pulmones.
4. La Sra. Muñoz es alérgica a la aspirina.
5. Ella debe tomar los antibióticos cada cuatro horas.
6. Ella debe descansar y tomar líquidos.

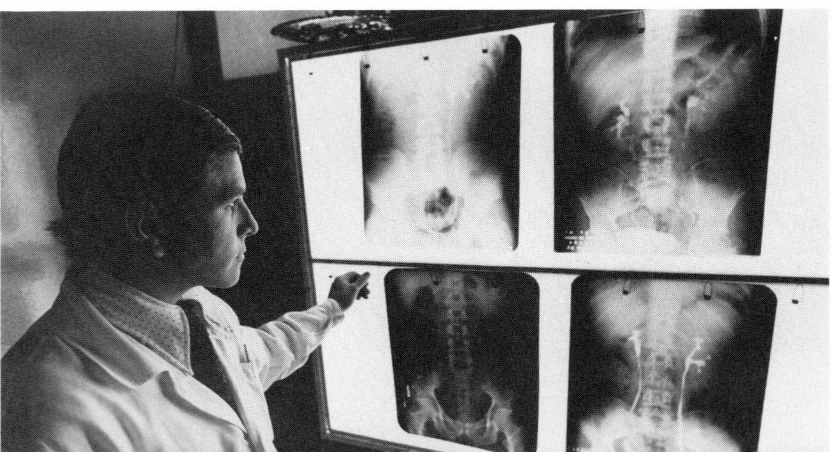

Un médico examina unas radiografías en Bogotá, Colombia.

expresiones útiles para hablar con los médicos

guardar cama	*to stay in bed*	el análisis	*analysis*
hacer gárgaras	*to gargle*	la inyección	*injection*
tener gripe	*to have the flu*	una fractura	*fracture*
tener dolor de...	*to have a(n) . . . ache*	la presión/la tensión	*pressure*
tener tos	*to have a cough*	la radiografía	*x-ray picture*
toser	*to cough*	los síntomas	*symptoms*

ACTIVIDADES

A Usted es el médico/la médica. ¿Qué recomienda usted en los siguientes casos?

1. Su paciente tiene una infección en los ojos.
   a Nadar en la piscina.
   b Tomar antibióticos.
   c Leer mucho.
2. A su paciente le duele mucho la espalda.
   a Ir a la playa.
   b Beber mucho líquido.
   c No hacer ejercicio.
3. Su paciente tiene fiebre y le duele el cuerpo.
   a Descansar y tomar aspirinas.
   b Comer mucho y caminar.
   c Ir a su trabajo y después al cine.
4. Estamos en primavera y su paciente es alérgico al polen de muchas plantas.
   a Ir al campo (*countryside*) para respirar el aire.
   b Dormir en una habitación con aire acondicionado.
   c Trabajar en el jardín.
5. A su paciente le duele la garganta y tiene tos.
   a Hacer gárgaras.
   b Ir a esquiar.
   c Salir y hablar con sus amigos.
6. Su paciente se siente muy mal. Usted no sabe lo que tiene.
   a Enviarlo a la casa.
   b Hacerle unos análisis.
   c Decirle que no se preocupe.
7. Su paciente tiene un pie fracturado.
   a Correr tres kilómetros todos los días.
   b Tomar clases de baile.
   c Hacer una radiografía.

B ¿A quién debo llamar? Explíquele a su compañero/a sus síntomas o lo que usted necesita. Su compañero/a le va a decir a quién debe llamar de acuerdo con los anuncios.

Modelo Usted **Necesito un examen médico para un nuevo trabajo.**
Compañero/a **Llama a la Dra. Corona López.**

1. Me da dolor de cabeza cuando leo o miro televisión.
2. Siempre me siento triste y deprimido/a y no puedo dormir.
3. Mi hermano pequeño está enfermo y tiene fiebre.
4. No puedo respirar bien y tengo la piel (*skin*) irritada.
5. Me duelen mucho los dientes cuando como.
6. Necesito una operación.

SEGUNDO PISO

Dr. Fco. Javier Amador Cumplido
CIRUGÍA Y ENFERMEDADES DE LOS OJOS
86-43-57
CONSULTORIO 204

Dr. Héctor Molina Oviedo
PSIQUIATRA
86-51-49
CONSULTORIO 102

Dra. Silvia Corona López
MEDICINA INTERNA
86-51-49
CONSULTORIO 102

Dr. Jaime A. Rodríguez Peláez
PEDIATRA NIÑOS Y ADOLESCENTES
86-17-15
CONSULTORIO 212

CLÍNICA DE ASMA Y ALERGIAS
Dr. Rubén Shturman

AMSTERDAN 219-A 2° PISO
294-3866 584-0153

Dra. Gabriela Jacobo de Alcaraz
CIRUJANO DENTISTA
86-48-44
CONSULTORIO 314

Dr. Raúl Elguezábal R.
MEDICINA FAMILIAR Y CIRUGÍA
86-34-73 EU. 428-4846
CONSULTORIO 309

C Complete el siguiente diálogo con otro/a estudiante. Usted debe ser el/la doctor/a.

Doctor/a ¿Cómo te sientes, ____?
Estudiante ...
Doctor/a Tienes un poco de fiebre. ¿Te duele la cabeza?
Estudiante ...
Doctor/a ¿Qué otros síntomas tienes?
Estudiante ...
Doctor/a ¿Eres alérgico/a a la penicilina?
Estudiante ...
Doctor/a Te voy a recetar ____. Si no te sientes bien mañana, me llamas.

GRAMÁTICA

Indicative and subjunctive after impersonal expressions

1. Use the indicative after impersonal expressions that denote certainty.

Es verdad que Ana fuma mucho. — *It's true that Ana smokes a lot.*

Other expressions that require the indicative are: **es cierto que, es evidente que, es obvio que,** and **es seguro que.**

2. In the negative, these expressions normally take the subjunctive.

No es cierto que fume tanto. — *It's not true that she smokes a lot.*

3. Use the subjunctive with expressions that denote possibility, probability, importance, or other value judgments.

Es probable que venga hoy. — *It's probable that he will come today.*

Other expressions that require the subjunctive are: **es posible que, es importante que, es bueno que, es mejor que** and **es lógico que.**

ACTIVIDADES

A Complete las siguientes oraciones con las formas correctas del verbo entre paréntesis.

1. Es cierto que Aurelio (trabajar) en esa oficina. Él llega todos los días a las nueve de la mañana, luego es probable que (estar) allí ahora.
2. Es evidente que las personas que (fumar) tienen más problemas del corazón. Según los médicos, es importante que las personas (saber) esto.

B Usted es un/a médico/a y le da instrucciones a un paciente que tiene gripe. Use las expresiones **es importante que** o **no es bueno que** con las siguientes frases para darle las instrucciones.

Modelo beber bastante líquido — **Es importante que beba bastante líquido.**
salir de la casa — **No es bueno que salga de la casa.**

dormir bastante
comer mucho
tomar la medicina
ir a la universidad
bañarse con agua fría
hacer ejercicio
trabajar mucho
mirar televisión
abrir la ventana

C ¿Qué les sugiere a sus amigos/as cuando no se sienten bien? Escoja el consejo y trabaje con varios/as estudiantes.

Modelo Amigo/a **Tengo dolor de estómago.**
Usted **Es necesario que descanses.**

amigos/as	**usted**
dolor de cabeza	hacer ejercicio
fiebre	acostarse
dolor de estómago	tomar bastante jugo
tos	descansar
ojos irritados	dormir bastante
una alergia	tomar té con limón
dolor de muelas (*toothache*)	tomar dos aspirinas
dolor de espalda	llamar al médico
dolor de garganta	ir al dentista
estar nervioso/a	hacer gárgaras

D **¿Por qué se sienten mal?** Usted es médico/a. Varios/as amigos/as vienen a su consultorio a decirle cómo se sienten. Usted les hace una pregunta y les dice lo que deben hacer.

Modelo dolerle la cabeza mirar televisión
Amigo/a **Me duele la cabeza.**
Usted **¿Miras mucha televisión?**
Amigo/a **Sí, tres o cuatro horas.**
Usted **Pues es importante que no mires televisión.**

sus amigos/as	**usted**
dolerle la garganta	hablar mucho
dolerle el estómago	comer a horas irregulares
dolerle los ojos	leer con poca luz (*light*)
dolerle los pies	caminar mucho
dolerle la espalda	trabajar en el jardín

E **Situaciones.** Complete las siguientes oraciones de acuerdo con la situación.

1. La Sra. Ortiz va al médico porque no se siente bien. Ella trabaja más de diez horas todos los días y no duerme bien. Además come muchos dulces y no toma vitaminas ni hace ejercicio. Usted es el médico/la médica. ¿Qué le dice usted a la Sra. Ortiz?

   Es obvio que... Es natural que... Es necesario que...

2. Julia estudia español en la universidad. Ella quiere trabajar en un país hispano después de su graduación. ¿Qué le dice usted a Julia?

   Es cierto que... Es importante que... Es mejor que...

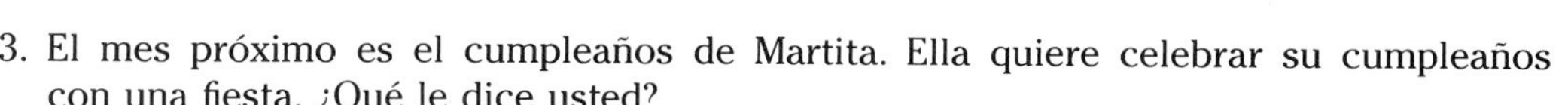

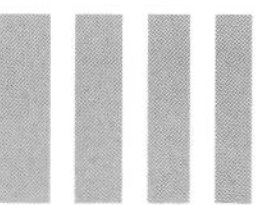

3. El mes próximo es el cumpleaños de Martita. Ella quiere celebrar su cumpleaños con una fiesta. ¿Qué le dice usted?

   Es posible que... Es verdad que... Es muy importante que...

EN CONTEXTO

En el hospital

Ojalá que te mejores pronto.

Ojalá que puedas jugar muy pronto.

Preguntas

1. ¿Dónde está la chica enferma?
2. ¿Qué tiene en la boca?
3. ¿Qué quiere su amiga?
4. ¿Por qué está el chico en cama?
5. ¿Qué quiere su amigo?

ACTIVIDADES

A Diga si usted se cansa (*get tired*) o no se cansa con las siguientes actividades.

Modelo ver televisión
Yo (no) me canso cuando veo televisión.

estudiar español	jugar fútbol	ir a la playa
hacer ejercicio	trabajar	escuchar música

B Pregúntele a su compañero/a si hace ejercicio, cuándo y dónde lo hace. Si su compañero/a no hace ejercicio explíquele por qué debe hacerlo.

GRAMÁTICA

The subjunctive after *ojalá*

The expression **ojalá (que),** which originally meant *may Allah grant that . . .,* is always followed by the subjunctive. Its equivalent in English is *I/we hope.* The word **que** is optional after **ojalá.**

Ojalá que ellos vengan temprano.	*I hope they'll come early.*
Ojalá (que) pueda ir al gimnasio.	*I hope I can go to the gym.*

ACTIVIDADES

A Su hijo/a va a estudiar en otra ciudad y usted está preocupado/a. Exprese lo que usted desea usando **Ojalá que. . .**

Modelo lavar la ropa todas las semanas
Ojalá que laves la ropa todas las semanas.

1. dormir ocho horas todos los días
2. estudiar mucho
3. comprar una buena calculadora
4. ser feliz allí
5. aprender mucho
6. no gastar mucho dinero
7. comer regularmente
8. llegar temprano a clase
9. estar contento
10. leer muchos libros
11. recibir buenas notas
12. escribir frecuentemente

ahora exprese lo que usted desea para usted el próximo semestre/trimestre.

B Su mejor amiga va a tener un bebé. ¿Cómo quiere usted que sea el bebé? Use **Ojalá que. . .** y los siguientes verbos en sus oraciones.

Modelo ser **Ojalá que sea saludable.**

tener estar pesar medir venir

C Usted tiene sus propias ideas de cómo debe ser su primer puesto. Use **Ojalá que. . .** para hablar de sus ideas.

Modelo **Ojalá que el sueldo sea bueno.**

D Usted tiene muchas ganas de ir a la fiesta más importante del año en su club. Su amigo/a le va a hacer unas preguntas acerca de la fiesta. Contéstelas usando **Ojalá que. . .**

Modelo Amigo/a **¿Qué van a servir en la fiesta?**
Usted **Ojalá que sirvan comida mexicana.**

1. ¿Con quién vas a ir? 2. ¿Qué vas a hacer en la fiesta? 3. ¿Quiénes van a estar allí? 4. ¿Qué tipo de música van a tocar? 5. ¿A qué hora va a terminar?

GRAMÁTICA

The equivalents of English *let's*

1. **Vamos** + **a** + infinitive is commonly used in Spanish to express English *let's* + verb.

Vamos a empezar ahora.	*Let's begin now.*

2. Use **vamos** by itself to mean *let's go*. The negative *let's not go* is **no vayamos.**

Vamos al gimnasio.	*Let's go to the gym.*
No vayamos al gimnasio.	*Let's not go to the gym.*

3. There is another equivalent for *let's* + verb in Spanish; it is the **nosotros** form of the present subjunctive.

Hablemos de la cena.	*Let's talk about supper.*
No hablemos de la cena.	*Let's not talk about supper.*
Corramos.	*Let's run.*
No corramos.	*Let's not run.*
Abramos esta botella.	*Let's open this bottle.*
No abramos esta botella.	*Let's not open this bottle.*

4. Remember that stem-changing **-ir** verbs change from **e→i** and **o→u** in the **nosotros** form of the present subjunctive.

Sirvamos el vino ahora.	*Let's serve the wine now.*
No durmamos en ese cuarto.	*Let's not sleep in that room.*

5. The final **-s** of reflexive affirmative commands is dropped when the pronoun **nos** is attached.

Levantemos	+	nos	⟶	Levantémonos.
Sirvamos	+	nos	⟶	Sirvámonos.

ACTIVIDADES

A Usted y su mejor amigo/a van a cambiar su vida totalmente porque quieren ser más saludables. Su amigo/a le dice lo que deben hacer y usted le contesta reafirmando lo que él/ella dice.

Modelo comer más verduras
Su amigo/a **Vamos a comer más verduras.**
Usted **Sí, comamos más verduras.**

1. comer menos comida frita
2. tomar leche descremada
3. ver menos televisión
4. levantarse a las 6:00

5. correr más
6. beber más jugo
7. dormir ocho horas
8. acostarse temprano
9. hacer ejercicio
10. comprar más fruta
11. nadar más
12. jugar golf

B Usted y unos/as amigos/as van a ir a San Francisco por una semana. Diga lo que usted quiere que todos/as hagan en la ciudad cada día.

Modelo comer en Fisherman's Wharf
Comamos en Fisherman's Wharf el domingo por la noche.

1. ir a la ópera
2. visitar el Hotel St. Francis
3. ir a Sausalito
4. descansar
5. montar en un tranvía (*streetcar*)
6. ver el puente Golden Gate
7. cenar en el Hyatt Regency
8. almorzar en el barrio chino
9. ver un partido de béisbol
10. caminar por el Parque Golden Gate

	lunes	martes	miércoles	jueves	viernes	sábado
mañana						
tarde						
noche						

Un anuncio en contra del uso del tabaco en el metro de Madrid.

C Usted y sus compañeros van a tener una fiesta fantástica y ahora mismo están haciendo los preparativos (*plans*). Con dos compañeros usen los siguientes verbos para determinar cómo va a ser la fiesta.

Modelo **Invitemos a Carlota, Lucía, Pablo y Marcos.**

invitar	servir	empezar	terminar	tomar	comprar	comer
preparar	decorar	tocar	bailar	hablar	traer	tener

EN CONTEXTO

El campo y la ciudad

La vida en el campo es muy diferente a la vida en las ciudades, pero todos los lugares, ya sean rurales o urbanos, tienen sus aspectos buenos y malos.

Las personas que viven en el campo tienen muchas ventajas°. El ritmo de la vida es más lento y tranquilo y se siente menos presión. El aire es más puro y hay poca contaminación porque no hay tantos vehículos ni tantas fábricas°. Por estas razones es muy sano vivir en el campo.

Pero la vida rural no es ideal, ni mucho menos. En el campo hay que° trabajar mucho para ganarse la vida°. No hay muchas actividades sociales en estas zonas para las personas que desean una vida activa. A veces no se tienen los mismos servicios públicos que en las áreas urbanas. Un problema perenne es el desempleo. Por eso muchas familias dejan el campo y se van a las ciudades.

Para las personas que viven en los pueblos°, la ciudad representa una manera de mejorar su vida. Allí esperan obtener una educación mejor o un buen trabajo y tener un nivel de vida° más alto. Hay servicios públicos, atención médica, buenas comunicaciones y toda clase de actividades sociales, culturales y deportivas.

Las personas que llegan a la ciudad muy pronto se dan cuenta de° que no todo es bueno allí. La vida urbana no es lenta y tranquila como en el campo; el individuo siente mucha más presión. El número de habitantes, autos y fábricas produce un alto índice de contaminación. La salud de la persona sufre en todos los aspectos.

El campo y la ciudad tienen ventajas y desventajas y el individuo tiene que escoger dónde quiere vivir.

advantages
factories
hay... *it's necessary*
ganarse... *earn a living*
towns
un nivel... *standard of living*
se... *realize*

Para completar

Complete las oraciones según la selección anterior.

1. Las ventajas de vivir en el campo son...
2. Las personas que viven en el campo...
3. Las ventajas de la ciudad son...
4. Un problema en la ciudad es...

ACTIVIDADES

A Use la expresión **hay que** + infinitivo para decir todas las cosas que se deben hacer para ser saludables.

Modelo **Hay que comer muchas verduras.**

B Con un/a compañero/a haga una lista de las ventajas y desventajas de vivir en un pueblo. Compartan su lista con la clase.

C Complete el siguiente diálogo con un/a compañero/a. Después su compañero/a debe hacerle las mismas preguntas a usted.

Usted ¿Dónde prefieres vivir?
Compañero/a . . .
Usted ¿Por qué?
Compañero/a . . .
Usted ¿Qué ventajas tiene vivir en ese lugar?
Compañero/a . . .

GRAMÁTICA

Relative pronouns

1. The relative pronouns **que** and **quien(es)** are used to combine two sentences into one. They refer to an antecedent (a noun or pronoun that has been previously mentioned) and introduce a subordinate clause.

Las personas son tranquilas.	*The persons are calm.*
Las personas viven en el campo.	*The persons live in the country.*

Las personas **que** viven en el campo son tranquilas.
(antecedent: personas; subordinate clause: que viven en el campo)

2. **Que** is the most commonly used relative pronoun. It may refer to persons or things.

Las vitaminas **que** yo tomo son excelentes.
Ése es el doctor **que** me receta las vitaminas.

3. **Quien(es)** only refers to persons; it may replace **que** in a clause set off by commas.

Los Márquez, { **quienes** / **que** } viven en la ciudad, prefieren el campo.	*The Márquezes, who live in the city, prefer the country.*

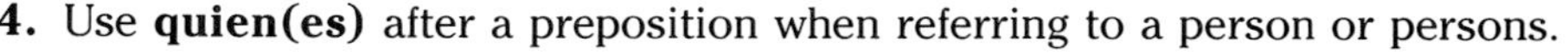

4. Use **quien(es)** after a preposition when referring to a person or persons.

Allí está la persona **a quien** le debes dar el dinero.	*There is the person to whom you should give the money.*

ACTIVIDADES

A Primero estudie los dibujos y después hable de la ciudad y el campo.

La ciudad y el campo

Modelos **La ciudad es un lugar que tiene muchos autos.**
El campo es un lugar que es muy limpio.

B **¿Cómo son?** Estudie los dibujos y después diga cómo es la persona de la ciudad y cómo es la del campo.

Modelos **Es una persona que trabaja en una oficina.**
Es una persona que trabaja al aire libre.

C **Mi ciudad o pueblo.** Dígale a la clase cómo es su ciudad/pueblo. Mencione por lo menos tres o cuatro características.

Modelos **Vivo en una ciudad que. . .**
Vivo en un pueblo que. . .

D Complete las siguientes selecciones con el pronombre relativo **que** o **quien** según convenga.

1. Una telenovela (*soap opera*)

Mi corazón es la telenovela ___ (1) tiene más público. El actor principal es Álvaro Montalvo. Él es el actor de ___ (2) todos hablan. La crítica cree que este año va a ganar el premio Talía ___ (3) es el equivalente del Oscar norteamericano. El 90 por ciento de las chicas dice que Álvaro es el actor con ___ (4) les gustaría salir. Silvina Bosque es la actriz principal. En la telenovela ella está enamorada de (*is in love with*) Álvaro, pero Álvaro no la quiere. Esmeralda del Valle es la chica a ___ (5) él quiere, pero Esmeralda no es buena. A ella sólo le interesa el dinero de Álvaro. La telenovela es muy melodramática y siempre hay problemas ___ (6) mantienen el interés del público.

2. Una conversación entre dos amigos

La fiesta es mañana y Jorge no tiene compañera. Él está en la cafetería con Evaristo, ___ (1) es su mejor amigo. En esos momentos entra una chica muy guapa.

Jorge Ésa es la chica a ___ (2) voy a invitar para la fiesta.
Evaristo ¿Conoces a Angélica?
Jorge No, no la conozco, pero no importa.
Evaristo ¡Por favor, Jorge! Angélica Domínguez es la chica a ___ (3) todos quieren invitar. Es simpática, inteligente y bonita. Además tiene novio.
Jorge No importa. Mi corazón me dice que ésa es la chica con ___ (4) voy a pasar el resto de mis días.
Evaristo Estás tan ridículo como las telenovelas. No te voy a presentar a Angélica. Te voy a presentar al siquiatra ___ (5) vive cerca de casa.

SÁBADO 8

PRIMERA CADENA

0.50.—Clásicos en blanco y negro. *Cadenas rotas.*
2.45.—La luna (repetición).
3.45.— ★ Documentos TV.
4.45.— ★ Corrupción en Miami.
5.35.—La buena música.
6.30.—★De película.
7.30.—Largometraje. *Los amantes crucificados.*
9.10.—La Rosa Amarilla.
10.00.—Cajón desastre.
13.15.—Lotería.
13.30.—Suplementos 4.
14.30.—Sábado revista.
15.00.—Telediario fin de semana.
15.30.—El tiempo.
15.35.—Ferdy.
16.05.—Primera sesión. *Los conquistadores de Atlantis.*
17.45.—Rockopop.
19.35.—McGyver.
20.30.—Telediario fin de semana.
21.05.—Informe semanal.
22.20.—Sábado cine. *¿Qué me pasa, doctor?*
0.10.—Rokambole.

SEGUNDA CADENA

13.30.—Objetivo 92.
15.00.—Estadio 2.
23.00.—Buscando el arco iris.
0.40.—Andalucía abierta.

LECTURA

¿Lleva usted una forma de vida sana?

El siguiente examen o test, tomado de la publicación semanal *Blanco y negro,* le puede ayudar a determinar si usted va a tener una vida larga y saludable. Las preguntas son fáciles y usted puede contestarlas rápidamente. Después de anotar sus respuestas en una hoja de papel, vea la solución para saber cómo vive usted. Las siguientes palabras le pueden ayudar a entender mejor las preguntas y la solución.

repercute	*reflects*
bienestar	*well–being*
descuidada	*careless*
excedido de peso	*overweight*
ingiere	*drinks*
promedio	*average*
ansiedad	*anxiety*
cotidianas	*daily*
conduce	*drive*
ligero	*slight*
avance	*improvement*
compromiso	*commitment*
riesgos	*dangers*

Test

¿Lleva usted una forma de vida sana?

Su salud y su longevidad dependen mucho de la forma de vida que usted lleva. Lo que usted hace día tras día es parte de su estilo de vida. Y éste repercute sobre su bienestar físico. La conducta descuidada en cualquier campo puede llevar a serios problemas de salud. Conteste cada pregunta en alguna de las variantes marcadas, y fíjese después en la solución.

1. ¿Con qué frecuencia hace usted ejercicios físicos?
   a) Cuatro o cinco veces por semana.
   b) Tres veces por semana.
   c) Una vez por semana.
   d) Rara vez.

2. ¿Con qué frecuencia prefiere usted subir escaleras, aunque haya ascensores o escaleras mecánicas?
   a) Casi siempre.
   b) Frecuentemente.
   c) Ocasionalmente.
   d) Rara vez.

3. ¿Cuántas horas diarias dedica a ver la televisión?
   a) Menos de una hora.
   b) Una o dos horas.
   c) Dos o cuatro horas.
   d) Cuatro o más horas.

4. ¿Está usted excedido de peso?
   a) No.
   b) Sí, un par de kilos.
   c) Sí, de tres a diez kilos.
   d) Sí, más de diez kilos.

5. ¿Cuántas copas de bebidas alcohólicas —cerveza, vino o licores— ingiere usted como promedio en la semana.
   a) Nada.
   b) Una a siete copas.
   c) Ocho a quince copas.
   d) Más de quince.

6. ¿Cuántos cigarrillos fuma por día?
   a) Ninguno.
   b) Menos de cinco.
   c) Entre cinco y diez.
   d) Más de diez.

7. ¿Fuma usted marihuana o usa alguna otra droga ilegal?
   a) No.
   b) Rara vez.
   c) Ocasionalmente.
   d) Con frecuencia.

8. ¿Ingiere bebidas alcohólicas en las seis horas siguientes a píldoras tranquilizantes, barbitúricos, antihistamínicos o alguna droga?
   a) No.
   b) Rara vez.
   c) Ocasionalmente.
   d) Frecuentemente.

9. ¿Utiliza usted drogas como el valium y similares?
   a) No.
   b) Rara vez.
   c) Ocasionalmente.
   d) Frecuentemente.

10. ¿Con qué frecuencia se siente deprimido?
    a) Casi nunca.
    b) Rara vez.
    c) Ocasionalmente.
    d) Frecuentemente.

11. ¿La ansiedad o la tensión interfieren con sus actividades cotidianas?
    a) Casi nunca.
    b) Rara vez.
    c) Ocasionalmente.
    d) Frecuentemente.

12. ¿Consigue usted dormir en forma satisfactoria?
    a) Siempre.
    b) Habitualmente.
    c) Ocasionalmente.
    d) Rara vez.

13. ¿Conduce usted su automóvil a mayor velocidad que los límites fijados?
    a) No.
    b) Sí, pero con un exceso de cinco kilómetros por hora.
    c) Sí, entre cinco a quince kilómetros por hora.
    d) Sí, a más de quince kilómetros de exceso.

14. ¿Usa usted el cinturón de seguridad en el automóvil?
    a) Siempre.
    b) Habitualmente.
    c) Rara vez.
    d) Nunca.

15. ¿Conduce usted alguna vez bajo la influencia del alcohol, las drogas o alguna medicación?
    a) Nunca.
    b) Rara vez.
    c) Ocasionalmente.
    d) Con frecuencia.

SOLUCIÓN

Marque un punto por cada respuesta en a), dos por cada b), tres por cada c), cuatro por cada d).

Entre 16 y 25 puntos: **Usted tiene un excelente estilo de vida, basado en costumbres sensatas y mostrándose alerta sobre su salud personal.**

Entre 26 y 35 puntos: **Posee usted un muy buen estilo de vida, y con un ligero avance llegará a la categoría de excelentes.**

Entre 35 y 45 puntos: **Usted tiene una buena comprensión de los principios generales de la salud, pero necesita un poco más de firmeza y de compromiso para alcanzar un estilo de vida más sano.**

Entre 46 y 55 puntos: **Usted está incurriendo en riesgos innecesarios con su salud y debería fijarse como objetivo el mejorar su estilo de vida.**

Más de 56 puntos: **Son la indicación de que usted ignora los hábitos de la buena salud o que ha resuelto ignorarlos. Está en la zona de peligro y debería comenzar hoy mismo a mejorar su estilo de vida.**

Preguntas

1. Después de determinar cuántos puntos usted tiene, diga cuál es su estilo de vida según la solución.
2. ¿Cómo puede mejorar su forma de vida?
3. ¿Cuál es su punto más débil?
4. ¿Cuál es su punto o cuáles son su puntos más fuertes?
5. Si su estilo de vida puede mejorar, ¿qué va a hacer usted para tener una forma de vida más sana?

¿Te quieres o no te quieres?

Éste es un anuncio del Ministerio de Sanidad y Consumo animando a las personas a que se cuiden. Después de leer el anuncio, conteste las siguientes preguntas.

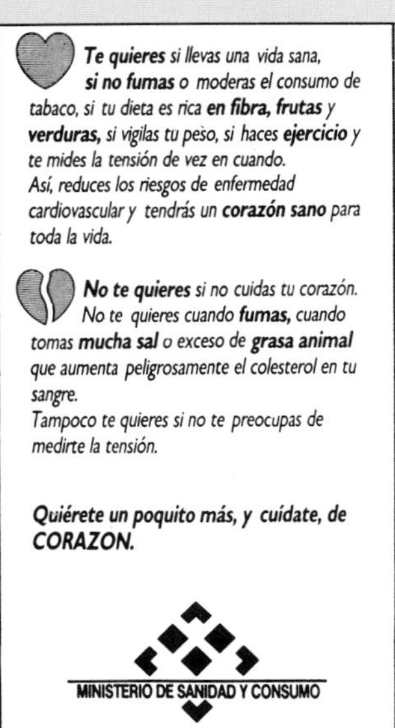

1. ¿Cuál es la idea principal de este anuncio?
2. Según el anuncio, ¿qué hace una persona que se quiere?
3. ¿Y qué hace una persona que no se quiere?

¿Me quiero o no me quiero?

Dígale a su compañero/a si usted está entre las personas que «se quieren» o entre las que «no se quieren» y explíquele qué hace usted para estar entre esas personas. Después su compañero/a le debe decir en qué grupo está él/ella y qué hace para estar en ese grupo.

SITUACIONES

1. Your friend is a heavy smoker: (a) ask your friend how many cigarettes (**cigarrillos**) he/she smokes a day, then (b) tell him/her to cut down (**fumar menos**), and (c) give some good advice such as going to the gym, walking, chewing gum (**masticar chicle**), and so on.
2. You are at the dentist's office. Tell the dentist (a) that you have a toothache, and (b) that you are afraid. The dentist will tell you (a) not to be afraid, (b) that it is not going to hurt, and (c) that he/she will give you some anesthesia (**ponerle anestesia**).
3. Play the part of a patient. One of your classmates will play the part of a doctor. Describe all your symptoms. The doctor should ask pertinent questions and prescribe some medication. You should also ask the doctor some questions.
4. You are visiting your friend at a hospital: (a) tell your friend that he/she looks fine, (b) ask when he/she is leaving the hospital, (c) tell him/her that you are giving a party for your birthday, and (d) that you hope he/she will be able to come.
5. You have the flu and you call your doctor. Tell him/her that you (a) feel very tired and (b) have a headache, a fever, and a sore throat. Your doctor should tell you what to do.
6. Read the following cartoon about an uncooperative patient. What do you think the doctor and the wife will ask the patient? You may need the word **adivinar** (*to guess*) to better understand the situation.

VOCABULARIO[1]

el cuerpo humano

la arteria	*artery*
la articulación	*joint*
el cerebro	*brain*
el corazón	*heart*
el estómago	*stomach*
la garganta	*throat*
el hueso	*bone*
la lengua	*tongue*
el músculo	*muscle*
el oído	*(inner) ear*
el pulmón	*lung*

la salud

el catarro	*cold*
la fiebre	*fever*
la fractura	*fracture*
la gripe	*flu*
la infección	*infection*
el síntoma	*symptom*
la tensión/la presión	*pressure*

tratamiento médico

el análisis	*analysis*
el antibiótico	*antibiotic*
la aspirina	*aspirin*
la inyección	*injection*
el líquido	*liquid*
la pastilla	*pill*
la radiografía	*X ray picture*
la receta	*prescription*

lugares

la fábrica	*factory*
el pueblo	*town*

la ciudad y el campo

la comunicación	*communication*
la contaminación	*air pollution*
el desempleo	*unemployment*
la desventaja	*disadvantage*
la educación	*education*
los servicios públicos	*public services*
la ventaja	*advantage*
la vida	*life, living*

personas

el habitante	*inhabitant*
el individuo	*individual*

descripciones

alérgica	*allergic*
cansado	*tired*
cultural	*cultural*
deportivo	*sport*
enfermo	*sick*
fracturado	*fractured, broken*
lento	*slow*
puro	*pure*
rural	*rural*
serio	*serious*
social	*social*
urbano	*urban*

verbos

descansar	*to rest*
doler (ue)	*to hurt*
escoger (j)	*to choose*
examinar	*to examine*
fumar	*to smoke*
guardar cama	*to stay in bed*
hacer gárgaras	*to gargle*
mejorar	*to improve*
obtener (ie)	*to obtain*
recetar	*to prescribe*
sentirse (ie)	*to feel*
sufrir	*to suffer*
toser	*to cough*

[1] See page 267 for words used in impersonal expressions.

palabras útiles

el aspecto	*aspect*
ojalá	*I (we) hope*

expresiones útiles

ganarse la vida	*earn a living*
hay que + *inf.*	*it's necessary to + verb*
nivel de vida	*standard of living*
tener dolor de. . .	*to have a(n) . . . ache*
tener tos	*to have a cough*

Una doctora española le toma la tensión a su paciente.

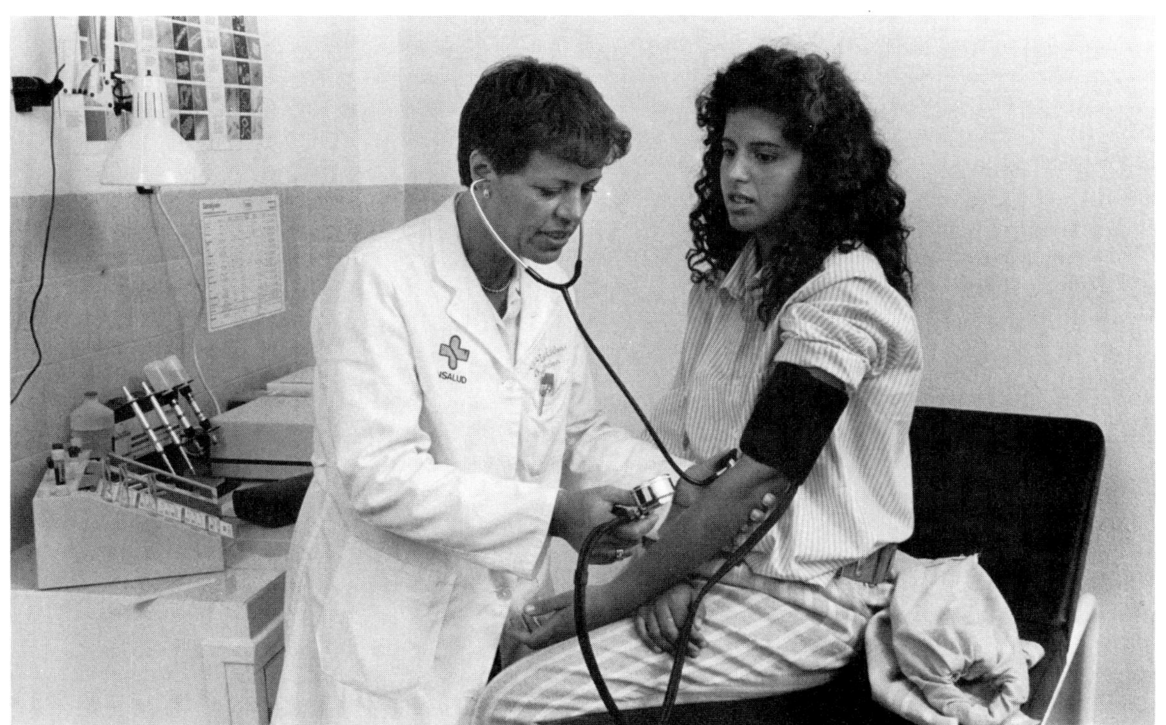

In Lección 12 **you will**

a. make travel arrangements.
b. ask about and discuss travel schedules.
c. report past events.
d. express denial.
e. express uncertainty.

En el aeropuerto

Los pasajeros hacen cola frente al mostrador de la aerolínea.

Lección 12

Los viajes

En la estación de ferrocarril

Ella va a viajar en tren porque no le gusta manejar.

En el puerto

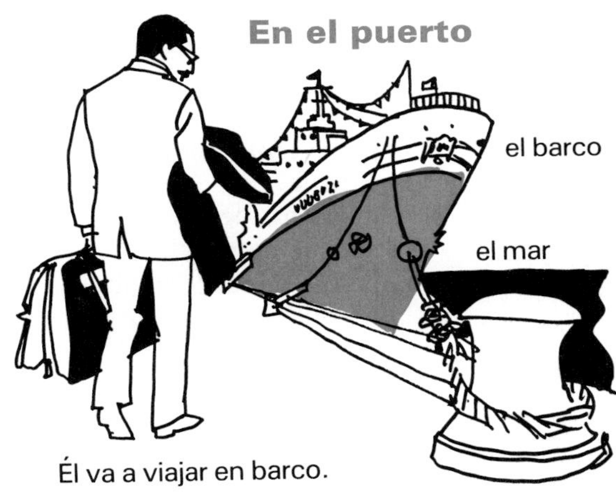

Él va a viajar en barco. Va a tomar un crucero.

la carretera

la gasolinera/ la estación de servicio

el autobús

el camión

la motocicleta

el coche/ carro deportivo

la gasolina

A otras personas les gusta manejar y prefieren viajar por carretera.

El aeropuerto de Cali en Colombia.

más vocabulario para viajeros

la aduana	*customs*
el inspector de aduana	*customs inspector*
el cheque de viajero	*traveler's check*
el pasaje de ida y vuelta	*round-trip ticket*
la tarjeta de embarque	*boarding pass*
la hora de llegada	*arrival time*
el pasaporte	*passport*
la visa/el visado	*visa*
el metro	*subway*
facturar/chequear el equipaje	*to check the luggage*
hacer la maleta/empacar	*to pack*
revisar el equipaje	*to inspect the luggage*

ACTIVIDADES

A **Entrevista.** Hágale las siguientes preguntas a su compañero/a. Después él/ella le debe hacer las mismas preguntas a usted. Comparta la información con la clase.

1. ¿Prefieres viajar en tren, en avión o en barco? ¿En autobús o en automóvil? ¿Por qué? 2. ¿Te gusta viajar de día o de noche? ¿Por qué? 3. ¿Qué aerolínea te gusta más? ¿Por qué?

B Su compañero/a y usted van a visitar Chile. Hagan una lista de cinco cosas que deben hacer antes del viaje. Comparen su lista con la lista de otros estudiantes.

C Diga cómo va a viajar cada persona.

el viaje

1. Julia va a tomar un crucero por el Mediterráneo. Va a visitar varios puertos y muchas ciudades interesantes.
2. Arturo va a ir de Málaga a Madrid. Va a viajar por tierra (*land*). Su medio de transporte tiene comedor, bar y camas.
3. Margarita quiere visitar a sus parientes en Buenos Aires. Su medio de transporte no tiene camas, pero es muy rápido y va por el aire.
4. Carmen quiere visitar las pirámides de Teotihuacan cerca de la ciudad de México. A ella no le gusta manejar, pero quiere ir por carretera.
5. Diego va a visitar a sus abuelos. Él no tiene que comprar un pasaje; sólo necesita comprar gasolina.

medio de transporte

a. Viaja en avión.
b. Viaja en barco.
c. Viaja en auto.
d. Viaja en autobús.
e. Viaja en tren.

D **¿Qué piden estas personas?** Asocie la situación con la respuesta correcta.

1. El Sr. Vargas tiene mucho dinero y le gusta estar muy cómodo en el viaje.
2. La Srta. Marcela Armenteros es alérgica a los cigarrillos.
3. Al Sr. Venegas le gusta mirar el paisaje (*landscape*).
4. Joaquín Torres tiene poco dinero y quiere gastar muy poco.
5. El Sr. Gabriel Méndez es vegetariano.
6. La Sra. Luz María López sale para Caracas hoy y vuelve el mes próximo.

a. un asiento de ventanilla
b. la sección de no fumar
c. una comida especial
d. un asiento en primera
e. un asiento en la clase turista
f. un pasaje de ida y vuelta

Cultura[1]

Los viajes en los países hispanos

Los países hispanos le ofrecen al viajero una gran variedad de escenarios y de culturas. En ellos se pueden encontrar restos de antiguas civilizaciones, ciudades cosmopolitas con todas las comodidades de la vida moderna, pueblos donde parece que el tiempo se ha detenido°, y playas, montañas, selvas° y paisajes de una belleza extraordinaria.

Para viajar entre ciudades importantes en España, hay personas que usan el avión, pero el tren y los autobuses se usan más. El sistema de ferrocarril se llama RENFE (Red° Nacional de Ferrocarriles Españoles). Los trenes son buenos, especialmente el Talgo que es el más rápido. Este tren hace muy pocas paradas° y le ofrece muchas comodidades al viajero. Otros trenes como los expresos y los rápidos viajan a menos velocidad que el Talgo y son menos cómodos. La mayor parte de los trenes en España tienen servicio de primera y de segunda clase; además, algunos tienen coches cama° y los viajeros pueden escoger entre departamentos privados, donde pueden dormir hasta cuatro personas, o departamentos de seis literas° donde uno comparte el departamento con otras personas a quienes probablemente no conoce.

Una parada de autobuses en Tegucigalpa, Honduras. El bus es el medio de comunicación que más se usa en la mayoría de las ciudades hispanas.

Las carreteras en España son buenas, pero la mayoría son de sólo dos vías°. Hay algunas autopistas° que son similares a las carreteras interestatales de los Estados Unidos, pero para viajar por ellas es necesario pagar peaje°. La mayor parte de los autobuses que comunican las ciudades importantes son muy cómodos, tienen baño y vídeo, y en algunos casos si el viaje es muy largo les sirven comida a los pasajeros.

En España el número de automóviles ha aumentado° mucho en los últimos años—alrededor° de dos millones de autos entre 1987 y 1988—a pesar de que° la gasolina es muy cara. La gente joven normalmente usa el transporte público o las motocicletas para trasladarse de un lugar a otro en las ciudades.

---

[1] Beginning with this lesson, the culture sections will be in Spanish. se ha detenido *has stopped* selvas *jungles* Red *Network* paradas *stops* coches cama *sleeping cars* literas *berths* dos vías *two lanes* autopistas *freeways or superhighways* peaje *toll* ha aumentado *has increased* alrededor *around* a pesar de que *in spite of*

El metro de Caracas. En algunas de las estaciones de este moderno metro se encuentran unos bellos vitrales *(stained glass)* de la artista venezolana Mercedes Pardo.

En Hispanoamérica las montañas, especialmente los Andes en la América del Sur, las selvas, los ríos y los desiertos hacen que la construcción de carreteras y de vías de ferrocarril sea muy cara y complicada. La estación de las lluvias en el trópico dificulta todavía más la construcción. A pesar de todos estos problemas, se construyó la Carretera Panamericana que comunica a Norteamérica con Centro y Suramérica. Esta carretera es un importante medio de comunicación y una extraordinaria obra de ingeniería.

La aviación fue° una solución para el transporte en Suramérica. Hoy en día hay muchos vuelos de carga y de pasajeros entre las diferentes ciudades, pero el costo resulta muy alto para la mayor parte de la población, y los autobuses y trenes son los medios de transporte que más se usan entre ciudades y pueblos. Hay autobuses modernos, pero también hay muchos que son viejos y hacen numerosas paradas.

En las ciudades del mundo hispano la población normalmente depende del transporte público. El metro ha ayudado° a mejorar la situación del tráfico al mismo tiempo que ofrece un medio de transporte económico en ciudades como Madrid y Barcelona en España, y Santiago, Buenos Aires, Caracas y la ciudad de México en Hispanoamérica.

fue *was* ha ayudado *has helped*

EN CONTEXTO

Un accidente

Arturo está caminando por la acera cuando ve a su amigo Juan. Juan tiene un tobillo vendado° y camina con muletas°. *bandaged / crutches*

Arturo	¿Qué te pasó°, Juan?	*happened*
Juan	Ayer° choqué° con un taxi. El chofer no frenó° porque no vio la luz° roja y le dio° a mi carro. Gracias a Dios° yo sólo me torcí° un tobillo.	*yesterday / I collided / didn't brake* *light / hit / Gracias. . . Thank God* *twisted*
Arturo	¿Te llevaron° al hospital?	*did they take*
Juan	Sí, me llevaron en ambulancia.	
Arturo	¿Y tu carro?	
Juan	Pues tengo que cambiarle una puerta y un guardabarros°, pero el seguro° del taxi cubre° todo.	*fender* *insurance / covers*

Para completar

Complete las siguientes oraciones de acuerdo con el diálogo.

1. Arturo ve a su amigo Juan en. . .
2. Juan no puede caminar bien porque. . .
3. El chofer del taxi no vio. . .
4. Juan fue al hospital en. . .
5. Quien paga todo es. . .

Partes de un coche

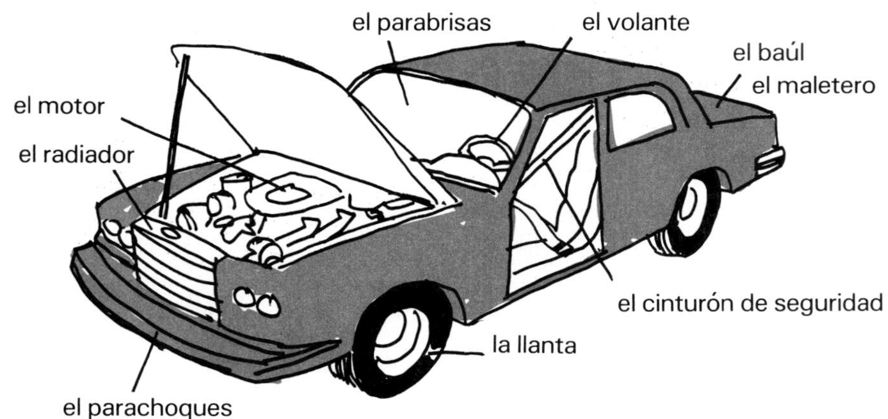

más palabras útiles

la licencia de manejar	*driver's license*
la multa	*fine*
el semáforo	*traffic light*
estacionar	*to park*
parar/hacer alto	*to stop*

ACTIVIDADES

A Asocie las descripciones de la columna de la izquierda con las palabras de la columna de la derecha.

1. Las personas que viajan en un auto deben usarlo como protección.
2. Lugar donde se pone el equipaje.
3. Lugar donde se pone agua para que no se caliente el motor.
4. Sirve para proteger (*protect*) el carro delante y detrás.
5. Está delante del chofer y sirve para doblar o ir derecho.
6. Documento necesario para manejar un coche.
7. Una señal de tráfico que tiene luz roja, verde y amarilla.
8. Pago que debe hacer una persona cuando no sigue las regulaciones de tránsito.

a. el maletero/el baúl
b. el volante
c. el cinturón de seguridad
d. el radiador
e. el parachoques
f. la multa
g. la licencia de manejar
h. el semáforo

B Complete el siguiente diálogo sobre un accidente con su compañero/a.

Usted ¿Qué te pasó, ___?
Compañero/a Choqué con ___.
Usted ¿Te llevaron al hospital?
Compañero/a . . .
Usted ¿Cómo te sientes ahora?
Compañero/a . . .
Usted ¿Y qué le pasó a tu carro?
Compañero/a Tengo que cambiarle ___.
Usted ¿Quién va a pagar los gastos?
Compañero/a . . .

C **Entrevista.** Hágale las siguientes preguntas a su compañero/a. Después él/ella le debe hacer las mismas preguntas a usted. Comparta la información con la clase.

1. ¿Te gusta manejar? 2. ¿Te gustan los autos grandes o pequeños? 3. ¿Qué autos prefieres, los americanos, los japoneses o los europeos? 4. ¿Cuál es tu auto favorito? ¿Y tu color favorito?

GRAMÁTICA

Preterit tense

Spanish has two simple tenses to express the past: the preterit and the imperfect (**el pretérito, el imperfecto**).[2] Use the preterit to express actions initiated or completed in the past.

	hablar	**comer**	**vivir**
yo	habl**é**	com**í**	viv**í**
tú	habl**aste**	com**iste**	viv**iste**
él, ella, usted	habl**ó**	com**ió**	viv**ió**
nosotros/as	habl**amos**	com**imos**	viv**imos**
vosotros/as	habl**asteis**	com**isteis**	viv**isteis**
ellos/as, ustedes	habl**aron**	com**ieron**	viv**ieron**

1. Note the accent mark in the **yo** and the **él, ella, usted** forms. These forms of the verb **ver** do not have accent marks because they have only one syllable: **vi, vio.**
2. The **nosotros** preterit form of **-ar** and **-ir** verbs is the same as the present. Context will indicate whether it is present or past.

   Llegamos temprano. } *We arrive early.* / *We arrived early.*

3. Stem-changing **-ar** and **-er** verbs do not change in the preterit.

pensar:	pensé, pensaste, pensó, pensamos, pensasteis, pensaron
volver:	volví, volviste, volvió, volvimos, volvisteis, volvieron

[2] The preterit is presented in **Lecciones 12, 13,** and **14;** the imperfect is presented in **Lección 15.**

4. Verbs ending in **-car, -gar,** and **-zar** have a spelling change in the **yo** form.

sacar:	sa**qué,** sacaste, sacó, sacamos, sacasteis, sacaron
llegar:	lle**gué,** llegaste, llegó, llegamos, llegasteis, llegaron
empezar:	empe**cé,** empezaste, empezó, empezamos, empezasteis, empezaron

5. The verb **dar** uses the endings of **-er** and **-ir** verbs.

dar: di, diste, dio, dimos, disteis, dieron

6. Some time expressions that you can use with the preterit to denote past time are

anoche	*last night*
anteayer	*the day before yesterday*
anteanoche/antenoche	*the night before last*
la semana pasada	*last week*
el mes pasado	*last month*

Las autopistas y los pasos a diferentes niveles hacen de Caracas una de las ciudades más modernas de Hispanoamérica.

ACTIVIDADES

A Ponga en orden las actividades de Manuel el lunes pasado.

Se despertó a las siete.
Estudió con un compañero por la tarde.
Asistió a sus clases por la mañana.
Salió con un amigo y cenaron en un café.
Se acostó a dormir.
Se levantó, se lavó los dientes y se bañó.
Su padre lo llevó a la universidad.
Volvió a la casa para almorzar.
Desayunó con sus padres.

B Su compañero/a le va a decir que las siguientes personas siempre llegan a tiempo al trabajo. Usted le va a contestar que hoy llegaron tarde.

Modelo Juan
Compañero/a **Juan siempre llega a tiempo.**
Usted **Pero hoy llegó tarde.**

Amanda los inspectores nosotros ellas yo tú

C Ayer usted manejó de su casa a la universidad. Diga las cosas que pasaron desde que salió de su casa hasta que almorzó en la cafetería.

Modelo salir de casa a las...
Salí de casa a las ocho.

1. manejar media hora
2. estacionar en la calle...
3. llegar a la biblioteca a las...
4. estudiar con... una hora
5. caminar a la Facultad de Humanidades
6. hablar con la profesora...
7. entrar en la clase de sicología a las...
8. salir de la clase a las...
9. comer una hamburguesa en la cafetería
10. beber un refresco

D Usted viajó en avión la semana pasada. Diga las cosas que pasaron en el vuelo cambiando los infinitivos al pretérito.

La azafata (saludar) a los pasajeros, les (explicar) el uso de los cinturones de seguridad y les (indicar) las salidas de emergencia. El avión (salir) a las once y poco después el piloto (hablar) sobre el vuelo. Después yo (tomar) una cerveza y mi hermano (tomar) un jugo de naranja. El señor de al lado (comer) mucho y (beber) tres copas de vino. Detrás de nosotros unos amigos (conversar) todo el tiempo. Después del almuerzo nosotros (ver) una película. El avión (llegar) a Miami a su hora.

E **Los trabajos de un ama de casa.** Lea el siguiente párrafo cambiando los verbos al pretérito.

La Sra. Campos se levanta temprano, toma el desayuno y empieza a trabajar. Primero limpia los baños y pasa la aspiradora en la sala y las habitaciones. Después lava la ropa y prepara el almuerzo. A la una come un sándwich y una ensalada y bebe una taza de café. Después de almuerzo habla por teléfono con una amiga y le escribe una carta a su hermana. Por la tarde plancha la ropa, se baña y prepara la comida para la familia. Sus hijos llegan a eso de las cinco y la ayudan a poner la mesa. Su marido llega a las seis y media, descansa un rato y se baña antes de la cena. A las ocho se sientan a la mesa para cenar. Después de la cena el Sr. Campos y sus hijos lavan y secan los platos. A eso de las nueve todos miran uno o dos programas de televisión y después se acuestan.

F Pregúntele a su compañero/a sobre sus actividades de ayer. Después él/ella le va a hacer las mismas preguntas a usted.

Modelo levantarse temprano
—¿Te levantaste temprano?
—Sí, me levanté temprano o **No, no me levanté temprano.**

1. desayunar en casa
2. tomar vitaminas
3. manejar a la universidad
4. estudiar en la biblioteca
5. asistir a la clase de español
6. comer en la cafetería
7. beber leche
8. correr por la tarde
9. bañarse después
10. ver televisión por la noche

G Usted va a entrevistar a dos actores famosos que trabajaron en la misma película y les hace las siguientes preguntas sobre sus experiencias durante la filmación. ¿Qué contestan ellos?

Modelo —¿Cuántos meses trabajaron en África?
—Trabajamos dos meses.

1. ¿En qué país trabajaron?
2. ¿Dónde vivieron durante esos dos meses?
3. ¿Se enfermaron (*Did you get sick*) durante la filmación?
4. ¿Cuándo terminaron la filmación en África?
5. ¿Qué otros países visitaron en África?
6. ¿Cuándo empezaron a filmar en España?
7. ¿Cuánto tiempo filmaron en España?
8. ¿Creen ustedes que la película va a ganar un Oscar?

H Dígale a su compañero/a las cosas que usted hizo (*did*) el domingo pasado. Después él/ella le va a decir lo que hizo.

EN CONTEXTO

En la agencia de viajes

Cliente Quisiera° hacer una reservación para ir a Guadalajara el día 15. — *I'd like*

Agente de viajes ¿Por la mañana o por la tarde?

Cliente Prefiero por la mañana.

Agente de viajes Un momento, por favor. Lo siento, señor. El vuelo que sale por la mañana está lleno°. No hay ningún asiento disponible°. Puedo ponerlo en la lista de espera. — *full* / ningún... *any seats available*

Cliente ¿Y el de la tarde?

Agente de viajes Déjeme ver°. Hay muchos asientos vacíos°, pero ese vuelo hace escala° en Mazatlán. Si a usted no le importa°... — Déjeme... *Let me see* / *empty* / hace... *makes a stopover* / Si... *If you don't mind*

Cliente A nadie° le gusta hacer escala, pero si no hay ningún otro vuelo... — *No one*

Agente de viajes ¿Por qué no reserva un asiento en este vuelo y lo pongo en la lista de espera para el otro? Siempre hay alguien° que cancela. — *someone*

Cliente Está bien.

Agente de viajes ¿Cómo va a pagar, en efectivo° o con tarjeta de crédito? — *cash*

Cliente Con tarjeta de crédito.

Para completar

Complete las siguientes oraciones de acuerdo con el diálogo.

1. El cliente quiere ir a...
2. Él prefiere ir por...
3. El vuelo de la mañana está...
4. En el vuelo que sale por la tarde hay...
5. El vuelo de la tarde hace...
6. El cliente va a reservar un asiento en...
7. Para el vuelo de la mañana él va a estar en...
8. El cliente va a pagar...

ACTIVIDADES

A Usted quiere saber qué planes tiene su amigo/a para sus vacaciones. Hágale las siguientes preguntas y comparta la información con la clase.

1. ¿Adónde vas a ir?
2. ¿Cómo vas a ir?
3. ¿Cuánto tiempo vas a estar allí?
4. ¿Qué vas a hacer allí?
5. ¿Vas a llevar tu cámara?
6. ¿Dónde vas a comprar los pasajes?
7. ¿Vas a pagar en efectivo o con tarjeta de crédito?

B Complete las siguientes oraciones usando las expresiones de la derecha según la situación.

1. El autobús tiene sesenta asientos y hay diez pasajeros. El autobús está...
2. El avión va directamente de Nueva York a Buenos Aires. Es un vuelo...
3. El avión tiene ciento veinte asientos y hay ciento veinte pasajeros. El vuelo está...
4. No hay asientos disponibles en el vuelo. El agente de viajes me pone en la...
5. Para comprar gasolina para mi carro tengo que ir a la...

lista de espera.
casi vacío.
estación de servicio.
lleno.
sin escalas.

C Usted tiene que ir a San Francisco para tomar un crucero a Acapulco. Asocie las actividades de la columna de la izquierda con los lugares de la columna de la derecha.

1. Compro el pasaje para el crucero en...
2. Hago las maletas en...
3. Tomo el tren para San Francisco en...
4. Llego a San Francisco y tomo un taxi en...
5. Después tomo el barco en...
6. Llego a Acapulco y revisan mi equipaje en...

la aduana.
la estación de ferrocarril.
el puerto.
mi casa.
la agencia de viajes.
la calle.

D Usted tomó un crucero por el Caribe. Dígale a su compañero/a cinco cosas que usted hizo o no hizo durante el viaje. Puede escoger entre las actividades que aparecen más abajo o hablar de otras si usted prefiere.

participar en juegos
bailar por la noche
visitar puertos interesantes
bañarse en playas muy bonitas
comer y beber mucho
estudiar español
conocer a otras personas
nadar en la piscina

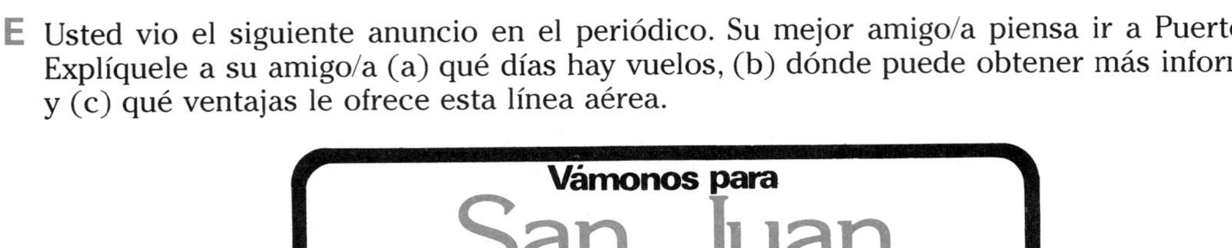

E Usted vio el siguiente anuncio en el periódico. Su mejor amigo/a piensa ir a Puerto Rico. Explíquele a su amigo/a (a) qué días hay vuelos, (b) dónde puede obtener más información y (c) qué ventajas le ofrece esta línea aérea.

GRAMÁTICA

Affirmative and negative expressions

affirmative		negative	
todo	*everything*	**nada**	*nothing*
algo	*something, anything*		
todos	*everybody, all*	**nadie**	*no one, nobody*
alguien	*someone, anyone, somebody*		
algún, alguno (-a, -os, -as)	*some, several, any, someone*	**ningún, ninguno (-a, -os, -as)**	*no, not any, none*
o. . . o	*either . . . or*	**ni. . . ni**	*neither . . . nor*
siempre	*always*	**nunca**	*never, (not) ever*
una vez	*once*		
alguna vez	*sometime, ever*		
algunas veces	*sometimes*		
a veces	*at times*		
también	*also, too*	**tampoco**	*neither, not either*

1. Negative words may precede or follow the verb. If they follow the verb, use the word **no** before the verb.

Nadie vive aquí. | **No** vive **nadie** aquí. } *No one/Nobody lives here.*

2. Spanish can use two or more negatives in the same sentence, while English normally uses only one.

No hay **nada** sobre la mesa.	*There isn't anything on the table. (Literally, There isn't nothing on the table.)*
No saluda **nunca** a **nadie.**	*He never greets anybody. (Literally, He doesn't never greet nobody.)*

3. **Alguno** and **ninguno** shorten to **algún** and **ningún** before a masculine singular noun.

¿Ves alguno? *but* ¿Ves **algún** coche? *Do you see any car?*
No veo ninguno. *but* **No** veo **ningún** coche. *I don't see any car.*

4. The plural form **ningunos/as** is seldom used in Spanish.

¿Hay algunos pasajeros allí?	*Are there any passengers there?*
No hay **ningún** pasajero.	*No, there aren't any passengers.*

5. Use the personal **a** when **alguno/a/os/as** and **ninguno/a** refer to a person and are the direct object of the verb. Use it also with **alguien** and **nadie** since they always refer to people.

¿Conoces **a** alguno de los chicos?	*Do you know any of the boys?*
No conozco **a** ninguno.	*I don't know any.*
¿Conoces alguno de los libros?	*Do you know any of the books?*
No, no conozco ninguno.	*No, I don't know any.*

ACTIVIDADES

A **¿Qué hace usted durante sus vacaciones?** Complete cada oración usando una de estas palabras: **siempre, a veces, nunca.** Trabaje con un/a compañero/a y comparta la información con la clase.

1. Durante las vacaciones yo ____ me acuesto muy tarde.
2. ____ me levanto temprano.
3. ____ voy a la playa.
4. ____ como en restaurantes muy elegantes.
5. ____ voy a los partidos de béisbol.
6. ____ voy a bailar a las discotecas.
7. ____ les escribo a mis amigos.
8. ____ alquilo películas y las veo en casa.

B Dígale a su compañero/a con qué frecuencia (**algunas veces, todas las semanas,** etc.) participa (o no participa) usted en las siguientes actividades. Después pregúntele si él/ella participa en esas actividades.

Modelo trotar
Usted **Yo troto tres veces a la semana. ¿Y tú?**
Compañero/a **Yo no troto nunca** o **Yo troto a veces.**

1. ver la televisión
2. viajar en tren
3. llamar a mis amigos
4. esquiar
5. ir de compras
6. manejar al campo
7. escuchar música clásica
8. tomar el metro
9. ir al cine
10. jugar al tenis (fútbol, béisbol, etc.)
11. caminar a la universidad
12. preparar la cena

C Usted quiere comer en un restaurante que acaban de abrir. Su amigo/a piensa que el restaurante es muy malo. Hágale las siguientes preguntas. Su amigo/a va a contestarle negativamente usando la forma correcta de **ningún.**

Modelo ¿Sirven platos típicos?
No, no sirven ningún plato típico.

1. ¿Preparan platos de dieta?
2. ¿Tienen buenas ensaladas?
3. ¿Sirven pescado fresco?
4. ¿Tienen vinos españoles?
5. ¿Hay camareras amables?

D Su amigo/a no tiene deseos de hacer nada. Hágale las siguientes preguntas y él/ella las va a contestar negativamente.

Modelo ¿Vas a llamar a alguien?
No, no voy a llamar a nadie.

1. ¿Vas a visitar a alguien? 2. ¿Vas a ver algún programa esta noche? 3. ¿Vas a estudiar o vas a escuchar música? 4. ¿Vas a escribirle a algún amigo? 5. ¿Vas a comer con tu novio/a? 6. ¿Vas a leer algún libro? 7. ¿Qué vas a hacer entonces?

E Usted y su compañero/a están planeando un viaje juntos. Dígale las cosas que usted quiere hacer o no quiere hacer. Su compañero/a debe contestar diciendo si quiere hacerlas o no.

Modelo comprar el pasaje dos semanas antes
Usted **Yo quiero comprar el pasaje dos semanas antes.**
Compañero/a **Yo también** o **Yo quiero comprar el pasaje una semana antes.**

no comprar el pasaje en el aeropuerto
Usted **Yo no quiero comprar el pasaje en el aeropuerto.**
Compañero/a **Yo tampoco** o **Yo quiero comprar el pasaje en la agencia de viajes.**

1. llegar temprano al aeropuerto
2. facturar el equipaje
3. dormir durante el vuelo
4. conocer a otros pasajeros
5. no llevar mucha ropa
6. pedir un asiento en el pasillo
7. no ver la película
8. no gastar mucho dinero

F Diga qué cosas le gustan o no le gustan de la lista que aparece más abajo. Su compañero/a debe decir si le gustan o no.

Modelo los postres de chocolate

Usted **A mí me gustan los postres de chocolate.**
Compañero/a **A mí también** o **A mí no.**

viajar en avión

Usted **A mí no me gusta viajar en avión.**
Compañero/a **A mí tampoco** o **A mí sí.**

1. tener un coche nuevo
2. levantarme temprano
3. hacer ejercicio
4. ir al médico
5. los coches deportivos
6. sacar malas notas
7. la ropa deportiva
8. sentirme mal

G Usted está en la aduana y el inspector le hace las siguientes preguntas. Trabaje con un/a compañero/a.

Inspector ¿Tiene algo que declarar?
Usted No,. . .
Inspector ¿Trae usted alguna planta?
Usted No,. . .
Inspector ¿Tiene usted más de $10.000?
Usted No,. . .
Inspector Por favor, abra el equipaje.
Usted . . .

H Usted y un amigo están en una fiesta en casa de Luisa. Ella viene adonde están ustedes y les hace estas preguntas. Trabajen en grupos de tres personas y completen el siguiente diálogo.

Luisa ¿Quieres comer algo?
Usted . . .
Luisa Y tú, ¿quieres que te sirva algo?
Su amigo . . .
Luisa ¿Quieren probar algunos postres?
Usted . . .
Su amigo . . .
Luisa ¿Desean beber algo?
Usted . . .
Su amigo . . .

EN CONTEXTO

La imaginación y la realidad

ACTIVIDADES

A Usted compró un carro (o una moto). Su compañero/a quiere saber cómo es y le va a hacer las siguientes preguntas. Después él/ella debe compartir la información con la clase.

1. ¿De qué color es? 2. ¿Es grande? 3. ¿Consume mucha gasolina? 4. ¿Cuánto costó? 5. ¿Dónde lo/la compraste? 6. ¿De qué marca es?

B Su compañero/a va a hacer un viaje en moto. Hágale preguntas para obtener la siguiente información: (a) adónde va a ir, (b) qué piensa hacer allí, (c) si va a ir solo o con un/a compañero/a, y (d) cuánto tiempo va a estar fuera.

GRAMÁTICA

Indicative and subjunctive in adjective clauses

1. An adjective clause is a dependent clause that is used as an adjective.

   Hay algunos estudiantes **trabajadores.** (adjective)

   Hay algunos estudiantes **que son trabajadores.** (adjective clause)

   The word that the adjective clause modifies (**estudiantes**) is the antecedent.

2. Use the indicative in an adjective clause that refers to a person, thing, or place (antecedent) that exists or is known or specific.

Hay alguien que **habla** 34 lenguas.	*There is someone who speaks 34 languages.*
Quiero viajar en el tren que **sale** por la mañana.	*I want to travel on the train that leaves in the morning. (you know there is such a train)*

3. Use the subjunctive in an adjective clause that refers to a person, thing, or place that does not exist or is not known or not specific.

No hay nadie que **hable** 34 lenguas.	*There isn't anyone who speaks 34 languages.*
Quiero viajar en un tren que **salga** por la mañana.	*I want to travel on a train that leaves in the morning. (any train as long as it leaves in the morning)*

4. When the antecedent is a specific person and functions as a direct object, use the personal **a** and the indicative. If the antecedent is not a specific person, use the subjunctive and no personal **a.**

Busco { **a** una / **a** la } estudiante que **trabaja** aquí.	*I'm looking for { a / the } student who works here.*
Busco una estudiante que **trabaje** aquí.	*I'm looking for a student who works here. (any student)*

5. In questions you may use the indicative or the subjunctive; nevertheless, if you are not sure about the existence of the antecedent use the subjunctive.

¿Hay alguien que { **entiende** / **entienda** } esto?	*Is there anyone who understands this?*

ACTIVIDADES

A Usted sabe que hay una agencia de viajes muy buena en Acapulco. Déle información sobre la Agencia Las Hamacas a su compañero/a de acuerdo con el siguiente anuncio.

Modelo **Hay una agencia que planea viajes al extranjero.**

TURISMO

∘ Las Hamacas ∘

SERVICIO DE VIAJES
LE PLANEAMOS SU VIAJE A CUALQUIER PARTE
DE MÉXICO Y DEL EXTRANJERO

BOLETOS DE AVIÓN, DE BARCO, RENTA DE AUTOS, VIAJES TODO PAGADO, RESERVACIONES A HOTELES, LOBBY HOTEL ACAPULCO IMPERIAL

521-24 **528-59**
5-22-79 LLAME LE ENVIAMOS SUS BOLETOS

COSTERA M. ALEMÁN N° 251, ACAPULCO, GRO.

B Diga que ninguna agencia ofrece los siguientes servicios.

Modelo regalar pasajes
No hay ninguna agencia que regale pasajes.

1. vender aviones
2. cambiar cheques
3. abrir el 25 de diciembre
4. servir comidas
5. vender pasajes a Marte
6. comprar autos

C Conteste las siguientes preguntas sobre los alumnos de la clase de español. Si la respuesta es afirmativa diga quién es.

Modelo ¿Hay alguien que lleve una sudadera blanca?
Sí, hay alguien que lleva una sudadera blanca. Marta.
¿Hay alguien que hable cuatro lenguas?
No, no hay nadie que hable cuatro lenguas.

1. ¿Hay alguien que sea alto y delgado?
2. ¿Hay alguien que mida ocho pies?
3. ¿Hay alguien que sea moreno y tenga el pelo corto?
4. ¿Hay alguien que sepa contar en español?
5. ¿Hay alguien que conozca al Presidente?
6. ¿Hay alguien que tenga un avión?
7. ¿Hay alguien que estudie para ser médico?
8. ¿Hay alguien que quiera vivir en Madrid durante un año?

D Usted quiere ir a Villa de Leiva, un pueblo colonial de Colombia. Usted le hace las siguientes preguntas a su agente de viajes. Trabaje con un/a compañero/a.

Usted ¿Hay algún vuelo que vaya a Villa de Leiva?
Agente No,. . .
Usted ¿Hay algún autobús que pueda tomar?
Agente Sí,. . .
Usted ¿Hay algún buen hotel allí?
Agente Sí,. . .

E Usted tiene que hacer un trabajo urgente y muy importante en su oficina y necesita unos empleados que lo ayuden. Dígale a su jefe/a qué clase de empleado necesita. Él/ella le va decir si hay o no hay un empleado así en la compañía.

Modelo Necesito a alguien que programe la computadora.
Sí, hay alguien que programa la computadora o
No, no hay nadie que programe la computadora.

1. Necesito a alguien que sepa usar mi computadora.
   Sí, hay. . .
2. Necesito un empleado que hable inglés, japonés y español.
   No, no hay. . .
3. Necesito un empleado que pueda trabajar esta noche.
   No, no. . .
4. Entonces, un empleado que pueda trabajar este fin de semana.
   Sí, hay. . .
5. Necesito un empleado que lleve estos documentos al banco ahora.
   Sí, hay. . .

F Usted quiere saber si su compañero/a conoce a ciertas personas. Hágale las siguientes preguntas. Si la respuesta es afirmativa, su compañero/a debe decir quién es esa persona y cómo es.

Modelo vivir en Panamá
Usted **¿Conoces a alguien que viva en Panamá?**
Compañero/a **Sí, conozco a alguien que vive en Panamá.**
Uno de mis primos. Es un chico muy simpático
o **No, no conozco a nadie que viva en Panamá.**

1. tener un Rolls Royce
2. hablar ruso
3. viajar a Europa este año
4. trabajar en el aeropuerto
5. saber canciones mexicanas

G Complete la oraciones de la columna de la izquierda con la información de la columna de la derecha.

Modelo Vamos a tomar un vuelo sale a las tres.
Vamos a tomar un vuelo que sale a las tres.

Me gustan los vuelos
Compramos unas blusas
Conozco varias ciudades
Alquilaron una casa
Conozco un hotel

es interesante.
no hacen escala.
tiene buenas comidas.
tienen buen clima.
son pequeños y bonitas.
tiene piscina.
es elegante.
salen y llegan a tiempo.
no cuestan mucho.

H Lea el siguiente anuncio y diga cómo es el Hotel Rubens.

Modelo **Es un hotel que está en Barcelona.**

SU HOTEL EN BARCELONA
*** HOTEL RUBENS ***
Zona residencial y tranquila, junto Plaza Lesseps. Todas las Habitaciones con TV color, vídeo, ambiente musical, calefacción. Parking, Restaurante, solárium, etc.

Individual	Doble	Cama Supl.
3.600	4.300	1.000

ESTANCIAS SUPERIORES A 1 SEMANA, GRANDES DESCUENTOS
Pº Ntra. Sra. del Coll, 10 (Barcelona 08023)
Reservas: Tel. 93 / 219 12 04. Tx. 98.718

I Usted y su compañero están hablando con un agente de viajes. Díganle cómo debe ser el hotel que ustedes desean en San Cristóbal, una pequeña ciudad de México. Cada uno debe decir por lo menos dos cosas que esperan encontrar en el hotel.

Modelo
Agente **¿Qué tipo de hotel desea?**
Usted **Queremos un hotel que sea tranquilo.**
Compañero/a **Queremos un hotel que esté cerca del centro.**

J Describa a las personas en la tabla y después describa a un/a amigo/a.

Modelo
Compañero/a **¿Cómo es Olivia?**
Usted **Es una muchacha que tiene 24 años.**

NOMBRE	EDAD	DIRECCIÓN	OJOS	PELO	NACIONALIDAD	PROFESIÓN
Olivia	24	Pío Pico 34	negros	negro	española	abogada
Danilo	28	San Luis 18	verdes	rubio	colombiano	contador
amigo/a						

K Usted es un idealista y siempre busca las cosas o las personas ideales. Describa cómo espera usted que sean estas personas o cosas.

Modelo la casa ideal
Busco una casa que esté frente al mar, que sea grande y que tenga cinco cuartos.

1. el amigo/la amiga ideal
2. el profesor/la profesora ideal
3. el novio/la novia ideal
4. la cocina ideal
5. el carro ideal
6. el viaje ideal

Un tranvía en una calle de Asunción, Paraguay. Los tranvías han desaparecido de la mayor parte de las ciudades hispanas.

La Estación del Norte de Madrid. Los trenes se usan mucho como medio de comunicación entre las ciudades españolas.

LECTURA

Evite accidentes

Este anuncio de la Secretaría de Comunicaciones y Transportes de México les da consejos (*advice*) muy importantes a las personas que manejan. El anuncio es fácil de leer, pues hay muchos cognados y usted sabe el resto de las palabras, excepto «ingerir» que quiere decir «beber».

Antes de salir a carretera revise su vehículo
No ingiera bebidas alcohólicas antes o durante su viaje
No maneje con exceso de velocidad
Use el cinturón de seguridad
Antes de cruzar la vía del tren... haga alto total

EVITE ACCIDENTES

Para completar

A Complete las siguientes oraciones con la información que se da en el anuncio anterior.

1. Antes de empezar el viaje usted debe...
2. Las personas que manejan no deben...
3. Todas las personas que van en el auto deben usar...
4. Los choferes deben parar...

B Usted y su compañero/a deben pensar en otros consejos para evitar accidentes. Comparta sus consejos con los otros estudiantes.

Puerto Rico

El anuncio de la siguiente página es de Iberia, la línea aérea española. La forma del cupón de la derecha imita una parte de El Morro, la fortaleza que está a la entrada de la bahía de San Juan. Esta parte de El Morro es un símbolo de Puerto Rico y se ve también abajo a la izquierda, entre el nombre de Iberia y el de Puerto Rico. El Morro es uno de los edificios coloniales más interesantes que hay en San Juan, la capital de Puerto Rico. La parte antigua de la ciudad es el Viejo San Juan. Allí no se puede construir ningún edificio moderno para mantener su aspecto colonial.

Las siguientes palabras le pueden ayudar a entender mejor el anuncio.

se mezcla	*combines*
sabor	*flavor*
disfrutar	*to enjoy*
rincones	*places, corners*
a pleno sol	*full sun*
D.P. (distrito postal)	*zip code*

Puerto Rico: 9 días desde 149.900 Pts.*

Al sol del Caribe. En invierno y en verano, así es Puerto Rico. Una isla donde las playas no acaban nunca. Donde la naturaleza más exótica se mezcla con el sabor de sus construcciones coloniales. Una isla donde la palabra clave es disfrutar. Con sus gentes, su folklore y los mil rincones que usted puede descubrir a pleno sol. Incluso en invierno. Iberia pone a su alcance el atractivo de Puerto Rico desde 149.900 Ptas.

Incluyendo viaje en vuelo regular ida y vuelta, 9 días de estancia en un magnífico hotel, traslados aeropuerto-hotel-aeropuerto, Tour por el viejo San Juan y visita a St. Thomas. También podrá disfrutar de la magia de tres espectáculos folklóricos y el regalo de ron del país.

Infórmese en Iberia, en su agencia de viajes o en la Oficina de Turismo del Estado Libre Asociado de Puerto Rico en Madrid.

ESTADO LIBRE ASOCIADO DE PUERTO RICO
OFICINA DE TURISMO

IBERIA
LINEAS AEREAS DE ESPAÑA

Para mayor información, envíe este cupón a la Oficina de Turismo de Puerto Rico. Pedro Texeira, 8, 4º 28020 Madrid.

Nombre ______
Dirección ______
Población ______ D.P. ______

BN

A Conteste las siguientes preguntas con la información que se da en el anuncio.

1. ¿Cuánto cuesta el viaje a Puerto Rico?
2. ¿Qué incluye ese precio?
3. ¿Qué tiempo hace en Puerto Rico en invierno y en verano?
4. ¿Dónde está la Oficina de Turismo de Puerto Rico en Madrid?
5. ¿En qué otros lugares le pueden dar información sobre este viaje?
6. ¿Qué puede decir usted sobre San Juan?

B Usted y su compañero/a están planeando un viaje a San Juan. Hagan una lista de las cosas que necesitan para el viaje y todo lo que piensan hacer allí.

Al Andalus Expreso

El siguiente anuncio es de un tren muy elegante, Al Andalus Expreso, que visita distintos lugares de Andalucía. Al Andalus fue el nombre que los árabes le dieron a la región que está al sur de España, lo que hoy en día conocemos como Andalucía. Los árabes permanecieron en España desde el año 711 d.C.[3] hasta el año 1492 y su influencia, especialmente en la arquitectura, se nota más en Andalucía que en otras regiones españolas. Granada, una de las provincias de Andalucía, fue el último reino (*kingdom*) árabe en España. El mapa en la siguiente página muestra las ciudades que están incluidas en este viaje.

En español, la palabra tren se usa en algunas expresiones que no tienen que ver con los trenes. En este anuncio se usan las expresiones **a todo tren** (*complete luxury*) y **tren de vida** (*way of life*). Otras palabras que le pueden ayudar a entender mejor el anuncio son

el placer	*pleasure*	*alcance*	*reach*
bello	*beautiful*	*escribir a máquina*	*to type*
mayúsculas	*capital letters*	*C.P. (código postal)*	*zip code*
inolvidable	*unforgettable*		

[3] En español **d.C.** es la abreviatura para «después de Cristo». Su equivalente en inglés es A.D.

A Conteste la siguientes preguntas sobre el anuncio.

1. ¿Qué ciudades visita el tren Al Andalus Expreso?
2. ¿Cuánto cuesta el pasaje?
3. ¿Qué clase de tren es Al Andalus Expreso?
4. ¿Qué recibe usted si envía el cupón?

B Usted y sus compañeros/as deben pensar en las ventajas de viajar en tren, avión, autobús o coche. Divídanse en grupos de cinco o seis personas. Cada grupo debe escoger un medio de transporte. Después deben tratar de convencer a los otros grupos de que su medio de transporte es el mejor.

SITUACIONES

1. You are at a train station in Madrid. Tell the employee (a) you need a round–trip ticket to Valencia, (b) the day of departure and return, (c) ask him/her how much it is, and (d) find out what time the train leaves.
2. You visited a friend over the weekend and had a great time. Tell your partner (a) whom you visited, (b) what you did on Saturday, and (c) when you returned.
3. You witnessed an accident. Your partner will be the policeman/woman and will ask you several questions about the accident: (a) when it happened, (b) where it happened, and (c) how many injured people (**heridos**) you saw.
4. You are the owner of a travel agency and you are looking for a young person to help you in the afternoon and on weekends. With a classmate write an ad including the following: (a) salary, (b) hours, and (c) any other pertinent information.
5. You are at a travel agency and you want to take a trip to Puerto Rico. Your partner will play the part of the travel agent. Find out the following information: (a) how much the ticket is, (b) when the plane leaves and arrives, (c) if you need a passport, (d) what hotel they can recommend, (e) how much the hotel is, and (f) if you can pay with a credit card.
6. You want to visit a Spanish-speaking country, but you haven't made up your mind which. A travel agent is going to help you plan your vacation. He/She is going to ask you several questions. Answer them so that he/she can recommend where to go.

Agente Buenos días. Bienvenido a Viajes Marina.
Usted . . .
Agente ¿En qué puedo servirle?
Usted . . .
Agente ¿Prefiere España, México, el Caribe, Centroamérica o Sudamérica?
Usted . . .
Agente ¿Entiende y habla español?
Usted . . .
Agente ¿Prefiere las playas o las ciudades?
Usted . . .
Agente ¿Prefiere un hotel de primera clase o un hotel más económico?
Usted . . .
Agente ¿Cómo le gusta viajar?
Usted . . .
Agente Bueno, creo que usted debe ir a ____ porque... ¿Qué le parece?
Usted . . .

7. You need to buy a car. Tell the salesperson (a) what kind of car you want, (b) ask what car he/she has. The salesperson will tell you the advantages of the cars they sell, such as price, gas consumption (**consumo**), and features.

VOCABULARIO[4]

el aeropuerto	
la aerolínea	*airline*
el mostrador	*counter*
la puerta	*gate*
la sala de espera	*waiting room*
el vuelo	*flight*
en un avión	
la sección de (no) fumar	*(no) smoking section*
la ventanilla	*window*
lugares	
la aduana	*customs*
la carretera	*highway*
la estación de ferrocarril	*railroad station*
la estación de gasolina/gasolinera	*service station*
el mar	*sea*
el puerto	*port*
medios de transporte	
el autobús	*bus*
el avión	*plane*
el barco	*ship*
el camión	*truck*
el carro/coche	*car*
el metro	*subway*
la moto(cicleta)	*motorcycle*
el taxi	*taxi*
el tren	*train*
personas	
el/la agente de viajes	*travel agent*
el cliente/la clienta	*client*
el/la chofer	*driver*
el inspector	*inspector*
el pasajero	*passenger*
viajes	
la agencia de viajes	*travel agency*
el boleto/pasaje	*ticket*
el boleto de ida y vuelta	*round–trip ticket*
el crucero	*cruise*
el cheque de viajero	*traveler's check*
el destino	*destination*
el equipaje	*luggage*
la gasolina	*gas*
la hora de llegada/salida	*arrival/departure time*
la licencia de manejar	*driver's license*
la lista de espera	*waiting list*
la maleta	*suitcase*
el maletín	*attaché case*
la mochila	*backpack*
el pasaje	*ticket*
el pasaporte	*passport*
la reservación	*reservation*
la tarjeta de crédito	*credit card*
la tarjeta de embarque	*boarding pass*
la visa/el visado	*visa*
partes de un coche	
el baúl/maletero	*trunk*
el cinturón de seguridad	*safety belt*
el guardabarros	*fender*
la llanta	*tire*
el motor	*motor*
el parabrisas	*windshield*
el parachoques	*bumper*
el radiador	*radiator*
el volante	*steering wheel*

[4] For affirmative and negative expressions, see page 296.

el accidente

la ambulancia — *ambulance*
la muleta — *crutch*
el seguro — *insurance*

el tráfico

la luz — *light*
la multa — *fine*
el semáforo — *traffic light*

descripción

deportivo — *sports*
disponible — *available*
lleno — *full*
vacío — *empty*
vendado — *bandaged*

verbos

cancelar — *to cancel*
cubrir — *to cover*
chequear/facturar — *check (luggage)*
chocar — *to collide*
dejar — *to let, to permit*
empacar/hacer la maleta — *to pack*
estacionar — *to park*
frenar — *to brake*
importar — *to mind, to matter*
manejar — *to drive*
parar/hacer alto — *to stop*
pasar — *to happen*
reservar — *to make a reservation*
revisar — *to examine, to inspect*
torcer (ue) — *to twist*
viajar — *to travel*
volar (ue) — *to fly*

tiempo

anoche — *last night*
anteanoche/antenoche — *the night before last*
anteayer — *the day before yesterday*
ayer — *yesterday*
pasado/a — *last*

expresiones útiles

en efectivo — *cash*
gracias a Dios — *thank God*
hacer cola — *to stand in line*
hacer escala — *to make a stopover*
quisiera — *I would like*

SEDECO, S.A. servicio al conductor y Ayuda en Carretera, se complace en comunicar las ventajas que disfrutan nuestros socios, y que a partir de hoy pueden ser de Vd.

1.° Servicio de grúa gratuito en todo el país, bien sea por avería o por accidente, las 24 h. del día incluso festivo y nocturno
2.° Servicio permanente de mecánicos
3.° Dos puestas a punto, mano de obra gratuita
4.° Cambios de aceite, mano de obra gratuita
5.° Mantenimiento y averías rápidas, mano de obra gratuita
6.° Revisión carburación, exceso de consumo, mano de obra gratuita

Oficinas y Talleres:
FERNANDO EL CATOLICO, 27
TELEFONO 26 23 12
MALAGA

In Lección 13 **you will**

a. interpret and compose telegraphic messages.
b. communicate by phone, postcard, and letter.
c. report past events.
d. describe actions.

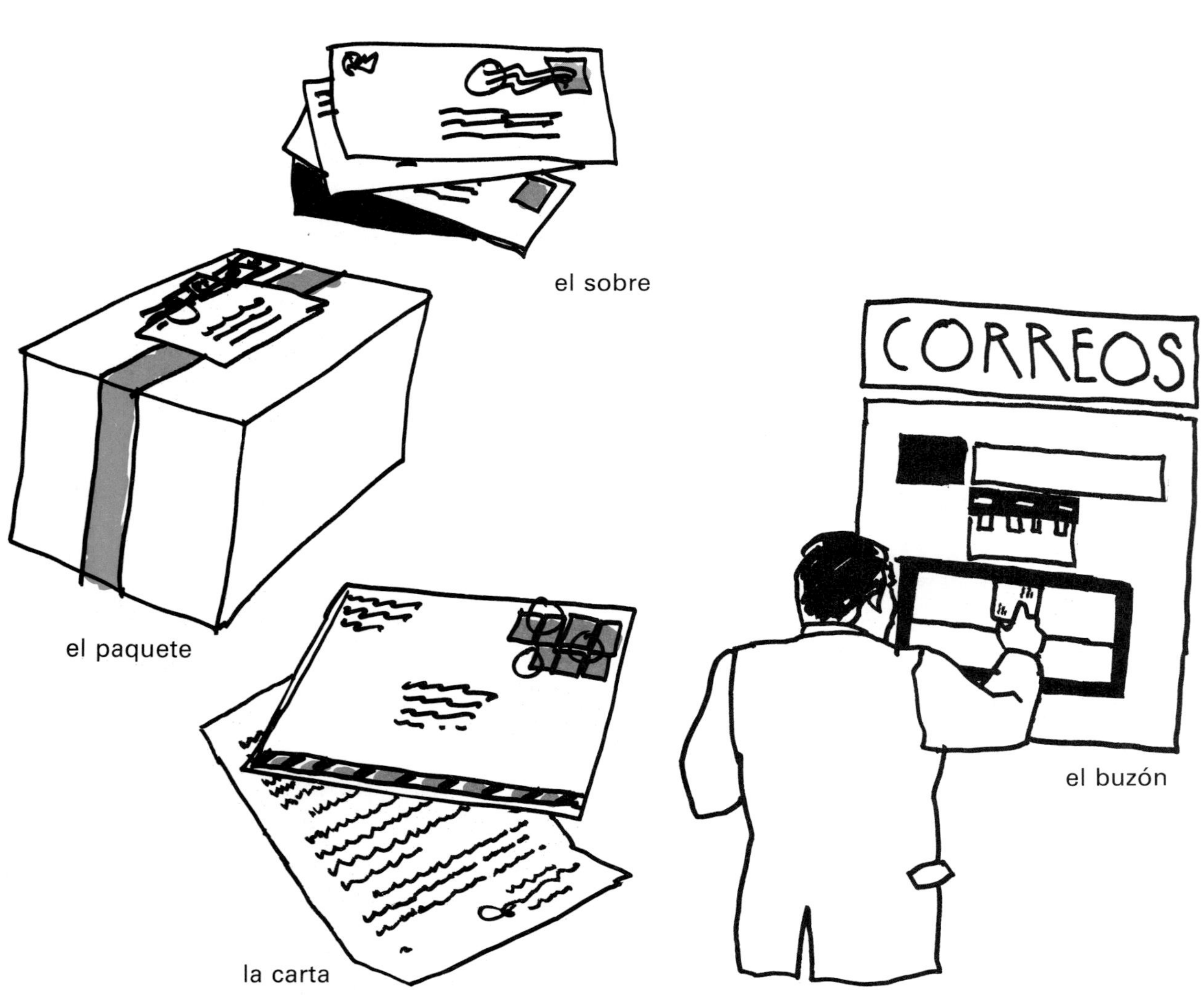

Lección 13
Telegramas, tarjetas postales y cartas

Un telegrama

FORMA DGTN-81

ESTADOS UNIDOS MEXICANOS

TELEGRAFOS NACIONALES

SECRETARIA DE COMUNICACIONES Y TRANSPORTES
DIRECCION GENERAL DE TELEGRAFOS NACIONALES

T. G. N.

TELEGRAMA PARA TRANSMITIR CON ABSOLUTA SUJECION AL REGLAMENTO EN VIGOR.

NUM.	PALABRAS	VALORES	H.D.

(ANOTE USTED AQUI CLASE DE SERVICIO QUE DESEE UTILIZAR) urgente

PROCEDENCIA Guadalajara EL 10 DE marzo 1990

SR. Aurelio Montalvo

DOMICILIO Calle 86 nº 96-11 TELEFONO NUM. 257-4698

DESTINO Bogotá, D.E. Colombia

Llego marzo 14 8:30 a.m. vuelo 418
Cariños
Emilia

Andrés Terán #1553
Colonia Chapultepec, Guadalajara

DOMICILIO DEL SIGNATARIO UNICAMENTE PARA CASOS DE ACLARACION

más palabras útiles

el sello/la estampilla	*stamp*
la oficina de correos/el correo	*post office*
el cartero	*mailman*
mandar	*to send*
recibir	*to receive*

ACTIVIDADES

A Complete las siguientes oraciones con la palabra adecuada.

1. El lugar donde las personas recogen la correspondencia y compran sellos es el . . .	cartero
2. Para mandar una carta la ponemos dentro de un. . .	sobre
3. La persona que reparte (*delivers*) cartas, tarjetas, etc. es el. . .	correo
4. El depósito que generalmente está en la acera para poner las cartas es el. . .	sello
5. No se puede mandar una carta sin escribir la dirección y ponerle un. . .	buzón

B Preguntas

1. ¿Cuándo manda usted un telegrama?
2. ¿Adónde se debe ir para mandar un telegrama?
3. ¿Se puede mandar un telegrama desde la casa?
4. ¿Qué es más caro, un telegrama, una carta o una llamada telefónica?

C Hágale las siguientes preguntas a su compañero/a. Después él/ella debe hacerle las mismas preguntas a usted.

1. ¿A quién le escribes?
2. ¿Cuándo le escribes?
3. ¿Cómo son tus cartas?
4. ¿Prefieres escribir o llamar por teléfono?

Cultura

El teléfono, las cartas y el servicio postal en los países hispanos

El sistema de comunicaciones en el mundo hispano es muy similar al de este país, aunque existen algunas diferencias. Como en los Estados Unidos, el teléfono es una parte esencial de la vida diaria en una ciudad; sin embargo, en algunas ciudades hispanas resulta muy difícil conseguir un teléfono en ciertas zonas, especialmente en las afueras. Siempre se puede encontrar un teléfono público para hacer una llamada, pero no hay tantos como en los Estados Unidos. En algunas ciudades como Buenos Aires es necesario tener una ficha° para poder usar un teléfono público. Generalmente se pueden conseguir estas fichas en una tienda o quiosco cerca del teléfono. A veces existen problemas en el servicio telefónico debido a diversos factores como la falta de capital para invertir en mejoras, el rápido crecimiento° de algunas ciudades y aun°, en algunas zonas, la lluvia.

La expresión que se usa para contestar el teléfono varía entre los países hispanos: **diga** o **dígame** en España, **hola** en la Argentina y el Perú, **oigo** o **qué hay** en Cuba. **Aló** también se usa mucho. Cuando una persona hace una llamada telefónica es común que le pidan que se identifique con una de estas preguntas: **¿Quién habla?, ¿Con quién hablo?** o **¿De parte de quién?** En Colombia también se acostumbra° preguntarle **¿Con quién hablo?** a la persona que contesta el teléfono. Esto generalmente no se hace en otros países.

En inglés, en una carta familiar o comercial se usa la palabra *dear* para dirigirse° a la persona a quien le escriben la carta. En español se usan palabras diferentes según el tipo de carta. La palabra **querido/a** tiene una connotación afectiva y sólo se usa entre familiares o personas muy amigas. La palabra **estimado/a** es más formal; se usa en las cartas comerciales o entre personas que no son tan amigas. En las cartas fami-

Unos jóvenes hablan por teléfono en Buenos Aires.

ficha *token* crecimiento *growth* aun *even* se acostumbra *it is customary* dirigirse *to address.*

liares en inglés se pone una coma después de la palabra *dear* y el nombre de la persona; en las cartas comerciales se usan dos puntos°. En español se usan dos puntos en las cartas familiares y en las comerciales.

Los sobres se dirigen de la misma forma en las dos lenguas, pero en español el número de la zona postal°, también conocido como código postal o distrito postal, generalmente se pone antes del nombre de la ciudad. El equivalente de *P.O. Box* es **apartado.**

Los sellos o estampillas se pueden comprar en correos, en quioscos o en algunas papelerías. Para escribir al extranjero, muchas personas usan un **aerograma** en vez de papel de carta y sobre. El aerograma es una hoja de papel que ya tiene un sello impreso y que cuando se dobla y se cierra se convierte en el sobre. No está permitido poner nada dentro de los aerogramas, pero se usan bastante porque son más económicos.

dos puntos *colon* zona postal *zip code*

Para que la carta llegue en el menor tiempo posible, debe enviarse **urgente** o **entrega especial.** Cualquier cosa de valor debe mandarse por correo certificado°. Los telegramas se pueden mandar desde un correo, pero en algunos países es necesario ir a una oficina de la compañía de teléfonos.

A continuación pueden ver una selección de un folleto° publicado por la Dirección de Correos y Telégrafos de España donde se explican algunos de sus servicios.

certificado *registered* folleto *brochure*

Dirección General de Correos y Telégrafos

Porque el Servicio de Telégrafos dispone de los medios más modernos y sofisticados, podemos afirmar que

LAS COMUNICACIONES TELEGRÁFICAS SON LAS COMUNICACIONES DEL FUTURO

SERVICIO DE TELEGRAMAS Y RADIOTELEGRAMAS

Los telegramas.

¿Dónde y cómo pueden depositarse?

Recuerde que Vd. puede poner *sus telegramas*

— *personalmente* en nuestra red de Oficinas

— *a través del teléfono* desde su domicilio, o

— *a través del télex*, desde su posición de abonado, si Vd. tiene condición de tal.

Los telegramas pueden ser:

NACIONALES, e

INTERNACIONALES, y éstos, a su vez,

— *Continentales* si van dirigidos a países europeos y a los asiáticos y africanos de la cuenca mediterránea, e

— *Intercontinentales*, los destinados al resto del mundo.

Todos estos telegramas pueden cursarse con carácter ORDINARIO y, también, con carácter URGENTE, previo abono de la tasa reglamentaria

Una de las oficinas de correos de la ciudad de México. En las oficinas de correos de los países hispanos siempre hay un continuo movimiento de público.

EN CONTEXTO

Una conversación por teléfono

Sirvienta ¡Aló!
Jorge ¿La casa de los señores Ávila?
Sirvienta Sí, señor. ¿Con quién desea hablar?
Jorge Con la Srta. Ávila, por favor.
Sirvienta ¿De parte de quién?
Jorge De Jorge Bermúdez.
Sirvienta Un momento, por favor. Señorita Emilia, la llaman por teléfono de parte de Jorge Bermúdez.
Emilia ¡Hola, Jorge! ¿Cómo estás?
Jorge Muy bien, ¿y tú?
Emilia Bien. Ayer fui a Monserrate con mis primos y lo pasamos muy bien.° — lo... *we had a great time*
Jorge Emilia, te oigo° muy mal. ¿Puedes hablar más alto°? — *hear* / más... *louder*
Emilia Es que hay mucho ruido°. Mi primito se cayó° y está llorando°. ¿Me oyes ahora? — *noise* / se... *fell*; *crying*
Jorge ¡Aló, aló! No te oigo nada. Creo que se cayó la comunicación°. — se... *we were cut off*
Emilia Yo sí te oigo, pero tenemos una conexión muy mala.
Jorge Cuelga°. Te vuelvo a llamar enseguida°. — *Hang up* / Te... *I'll call you right back*

¿Verdadero o falso?

Diga si las siguientes oraciones son verdaderas o falsas, de acuerdo con la conversación telefónica.

1. La sirvienta quiere saber quién llama.
2. Emilia no se siente muy bien hoy.
3. Emilia fue a casa de unos amigos ayer.
4. Emilia se cayó en casa de sus amigos.
5. Jorge le pide a Emilia que hable más bajo.
6. La comunicación telefónica es mala.
7. Emilia cuelga porque no quiere hablar con Jorge.
8. Jorge va a llamar a Emilia otra vez.

vocabulario útil para hablar por teléfono

el indicativo/el prefijo	*area code*
la operadora	*operator*
la guía telefónica/de teléfonos	*telephone directory*
llamada de cargo revertido/a cobrar	*collect call*
llamada de larga distancia	*long–distance call*
marcar/discar	*to dial*

ACTIVIDADES

A Usted está en Santiago de Chile y tiene que hablar con un amigo que está en otra ciudad de Chile. Diga en qué orden ocurren las siguientes cosas.

Marco el O.
Hablo con mi amigo.
Cuelgo el teléfono.
Le doy a la operadora el indicativo, el número y el nombre de la persona.
La operadora me comunica.

B Éste es un anuncio de la guía telefónica de Bogotá sobre los teléfonos públicos. Observe el anuncio con cuidado y conteste después las preguntas sobre el dibujo y el mensaje del anuncio. Las siguientes palabras le pueden ayudar a entenderlo mejor.

dañado	*out of order, damaged*	recordar	*to remember*
E.T.B.	Empresa de Teléfonos de Bogotá	avisar	*to notify*

1. ¿Qué hay detrás de los edificios?
2. Describa los edificios.
3. ¿Qué vehículos ve usted?
4. ¿Qué tiempo hace?
5. Describa a las personas.
6. ¿Cuáles son los puntos importantes que hay en el mensaje de este anuncio?

C Complete la siguiente conversación telefónica con su compañero/a.

Usted	¡Aló!
Compañero/a	____, te habla ____. ¿Cómo estás?
Usted	. . . ¿Y tú qué tal?
Compañero/a	. . . Te llamo porque esta noche hay una fiesta de sorpresa en casa de Carmen Ferrándiz. ¿Puedes ir?
Usted	Sí,. . . ¿A qué hora es?
Compañero/a	. . . Me alegro que puedas ir. Te veo esta noche.
Usted	. . .

GRAMÁTICA

Preterit of *ir* and *ser*

ir, ser	
fui	fuimos
fuiste	fuisteis
fue	fueron

Ir and **ser** have identical forms in the preterit.

Preterit tense of stem-changing *-ir* verbs (*e*→*i*) (*o*→*u*)

preferir		dormir	
preferí	preferimos	dormí	dormimos
preferiste	preferisteis	dormiste	dormisteis
pref**i**rió	pref**i**rieron	d**u**rmió	d**u**rmieron

1. The preterit endings of stem-changing **-ir** verbs are the same as those used for regular **-ir** verbs.
2. All **-ir** verbs whose stem vowel **e** changes to **ie** or **i** in the present tense change the same vowel to **i** in the **él, ella, usted** form and the **ellos, ellas, ustedes** form.
3. Other verbs which follow the **preferir** pattern are **pedir, despedir, seguir,** and **servir.**
4. **Dormir** and **morir** (*to die*), whose stem vowel **o** changes to **ue** in the present tense, change the same vowel to **u** in the **él, ella, usted** form and the **ellos, ellas, ustedes** form.

Preterit of *-er* and *-ir* verbs whose stem ends in a vowel

leer		oír[1]	
leí	leímos	oí	oímos
leíste	leísteis	oíste	oísteis
leyó	leyeron	oyó	oyeron

1. The preterit endings of verbs whose stem ends in a vowel are the same as those of regular **-er** and **-ir** verbs, except for the **él, ella, usted** form and the **ellos, ellas, ustedes** form which end in **-yó** and **-yeron** (**leyó, oyeron**).
2. Other verbs like **leer** and **oír** are **caer, creer,** and **construir** (*to build*).

ACTIVIDADES

See IM, **Lección 13,** for additional activities.

A **Encuesta.** Usted quiere saber cuántas personas hicieron ciertas cosas ayer. Hágales las siguientes preguntas a un grupo de sus compañeros/as y cuente las respuestas afirmativas. Después cada grupo debe compartir la información con los otros grupos.

1. ¿Quiénes leyeron el periódico ayer?
2. ¿Quiénes oyeron las noticias?
3. ¿Quiénes fueron al cine?
4. ¿Quiénes miraron televisión?
5. ¿Quiénes durmieron siete horas o más?
6. ¿Quiénes durmieron menos de seis horas?

B Estudie la siguiente tabla y pregúntele a un/a compañero/a qué hizo cada una de estas personas.

Modelo Usted **¿Qué hizo Raquel por la tarde?**
Compañero/a **Fue a un café.**

	Carlos	Raquel	Susana y Mirta
Por la mañana	leer el periódico	dormir hasta las diez	ir a la oficina de correos
Por la tarde	construir un avión de papel	ir a un café; pedir ensalada	leer un libro
Por la noche	oír un programa de música	preferir estar en casa con sus amigas	invitar a unos amigos a cenar; servir espaguetis

[1] The forms of the present tense of **oír** are: **oigo, oyes, oye, oímos, oís, oyen.**

C Ahora usted debe decirle a su compañero/a todo lo que usted hizo el sábado pasado. Después su compañero/a le debe decir lo que él/ella hizo.

D Entreviste a un/a compañero/a acerca de su vida en la escuela secundaria. Después comparta la información con la clase.

Modelo Usted ¿Dónde estudiaste la secundaria?
Compañero/a Estudié la secundaria en San Antonio.

1. ¿Practicaste muchos deportes en la secundaria? ¿Cuáles? 2. ¿Conociste a muchos/as muchachos/as? 3. ¿Te gustó la secundaria? ¿Por qué? 4. ¿Te dormiste en una clase alguna vez? ¿En cuál? 5. ¿Leíste muchos libros? ¿Cuáles?

E Usted fue a una oficina de correos. Dígale a un/a compañero/a que usted hizo lo siguiente.

Variation: **Dígale a la clase lo que su compañero/a hizo.**

1. ir a la oficina de correos a las 9:30
2. leer las noticias en el tablero (*notice board*)
3. ir a la ventanilla donde venden estampillas
4. pedir 20 estampillas de 25 centavos
5. pagar las estampillas
6. escribir la dirección en el sobre
7. depositar la carta en el buzón

F **Situaciones locas.** Lea estas situaciones locas con su compañero/a y diga cuál le parece más loca o más simpática.

1. Ayer recibí un telegrama de mil quinientas palabras.
2. Ayer mi gato le ganó una pelea (*fight*) al elefante de mi vecina.
3. Ayer empecé un programa de ejercicios aeróbicos y bajé quince kilos.
4. Ayer cené en un restaurante francés muy elegante y sólo pagué quince centavos.
5. Ayer choqué con un autobús. Mi moto está perfecta, pero el autobús está destruido.

Ahora trabaje con su compañero/a y prepare dos situaciones locas sobre lo que usted hizo o le pasó para compartir con la clase.

G **Personajes importantes.** Piense en un personaje importante. Sus compañeros le van a hacer preguntas para tratar de saber quién es el personaje. Abajo se ofrecen algunas posibilidades, pero pueden usar sus propios personajes y además deben hacer más preguntas.

Preguntas posibles	Personajes posibles
1. ¿Fue usted hombre o mujer?	Adán
2. ¿Cuándo murió usted? o ¿Está usted vivo? (*Are you alive?*)	Romeo o Julieta
	Albert Einstein
3. ¿Fue Ud. músico (científico, artista, político, etc.)?	Margaret Thatcher
	Shakespeare
4. ¿Dónde vivió usted?	Marilyn Monroe

EN CONTEXTO

Una tarjeta postal

Emilia le mandó la siguiente tarjeta a su amiga Ana Luisa Amescua, quien la recibió una semana después. Emilia está pasando unos días en casa de unos primos en Bogotá. Éste es su primer viaje a Bogotá y ella no está acostumbrada° a la altura de esa ciudad (unos 2.600 metros[2]). Aunque° Bogotá está relativamente cerca del ecuador°, debido a la altura la temperatura es más bien fresca y de noche puede hacer bastante frío. Sin embargo, en «tierra caliente», a una hora u[3] hora y media de Bogotá por carretera, la temperatura es mucho más alta.

no... *is not used*
Although
equator

BOGOTA. COLOMBIA.

Cerro de Monserrate, importante centro turistico que se encuentra localizado al oriente de Bogotá, altura 10.000 pies sobre el nivel del mar.
Monserrate Hill, an important tour center which is located at the East of Bogotá, with a 10.000 Feet height on the level of the sea.

F.180

17 de marzo

Querida Ana Luisa:
El martes llegué a Bogotá después de un vuelo muy bueno. El miércoles mis primos me llevaron a conocer la parte antigua de la ciudad. Es preciosa. Ayer hicimos una excursión a Ibagué, en tierra caliente. Hizo muchísimo calor. Vinieron varios amigos de mis primos y lo pasamos muy bien.
Muchos recuerdos a tu familia, y para ti un abrazo y un beso de
Emilia

Fotorama APARTADO AEREO NO. 20053 BOGOTA 2, D. E. COLOMBIA S. A. Tel.: 2457453

Srta. Ana Luisa Amescua
Calle Encanto N° 47
Colonia Florida
México, D.F.
México

Ejemplar de Colección

---

[2] 8.600 pies

[3] In Spanish, **o** changes to **u** before a word beginning with **o** or **ho: ocho o siete,** but **siete u ocho.** Also, **y** changes to **e** before a word beginning with **i** or **hi: Isabel y Alicia,** but **Alicia e Isabel.**

Una vista de Bogotá, la capital de Colombia, donde se observan los modernos edificios de la ciudad y la cordillera de los Andes al fondo.

Para completar

Complete las siguientes oraciones de acuerdo con la información que se da en la explicación sobre el viaje de Emilia y la tarjeta postal.

1. Ana Luisa recibió...
2. Emilia llegó a Bogotá...
3. El vuelo de Emilia fue...
4. El miércoles Emilia visitó...
5. Ayer Emilia fue a...

Preguntas

Ahora conteste las siguientes preguntas sobre Ibagué y Bogotá.

1. ¿Por qué hace frío en Bogotá?
2. ¿Dónde hace más frío, en Bogotá o en Ibagué?
3. ¿Cuánto tiempo tiene que manejar una persona para ir de Bogotá a tierra caliente?
4. ¿Cómo es el clima de Ibagué?

ACTIVIDADES

A Usted y su compañero/a están preparando un viaje a Colombia. Piensan visitar Bogotá y también otras ciudades como Ibagué. Hagan una lista de la ropa que necesitan para este viaje.

B Usted está en una oficina de correos de Colombia para enviar un paquete a unos amigos. Complete el siguiente diálogo con su compañero/a.

Usted ¿Cuánto pesa el paquete?
Empleado ...
Usted ¿Cuánto cuesta si lo mando por vía aérea?
Empleado ...
Usted ¿Y si lo mando por correo ordinario?
Empleado ...
Usted Bueno, lo voy a mandar por ____.

GRAMÁTICA

Irregular preterits

The following verbs have irregular preterit forms. All of them have an **i** in the stem and do not stress the last syllable in the **yo** and **él, ella, usted** forms.

INFINITIVE	NEW STEM	PRETERIT FORMS
hacer:	hic	h**i**ce, h**i**ciste, h**i**zo, h**i**cimos, h**i**cisteis, h**i**cieron
querer:	quis[4]	qu**i**se, qu**i**siste, qu**i**so, qu**i**simos, qu**i**sisteis, qu**i**sieron
venir:	vin	v**i**ne, v**i**niste, v**i**no, v**i**nimos, v**i**nisteis, v**i**nieron

The verbs **decir, traer,** and all verbs ending in **-ducir** (e.g., **traducir** *to translate*) have a **j** in the stem and use the ending **-eron** instead of **-ieron. Decir** also has an **i** in the stem.

INFINITIVE	NEW STEM	PRETERIT FORMS
decir:	dij	d**i**je, d**i**jiste, d**i**jo, d**i**jimos, d**i**jisteis, d**i**jeron
traer:	traj	traje, trajiste, trajo, trajimos, trajisteis, trajeron
traducir:	traduj	traduje, tradujiste, tradujo, tradujimos, tradujisteis, tradujeron

[4] The verb **querer** in the preterit normally means *to try,* in the sense of wanting but failing to do something.

ACTIVIDADES

A Diga lo que Emilia y sus primos hicieron durante el viaje de Emilia a Colombia.

Modelo ver la Plaza Bolívar
Vieron la Plaza Bolívar.

lunes	ir a una corrida de toros (*bullfight*)
	visitar el Museo Colonial
	traducir unos anuncios para unos turistas
martes	hacer un viaje a Ibagué
	comprar unas cosas en Ibagué
	traer regalos de Ibagué
miércoles	querer entrar en el Museo del Oro
	hacer cola para entrar en el museo
	venir a la casa con unos amigos
jueves	perder los cheques de viajero
	ir a la estación de policía
	decirle al policía el problema
viernes	buscar los cheques todo el día
	no encontrar los cheques
sábado	ir a la estación de autobuses
	volver a la parte antigua de la ciudad
	mandar un telegrama a los padres de Emilia

B **De vacaciones en Puerto Rico.** Usted y su amigo/a están de vacaciones en Puerto Rico por dos semanas. Dígale a un/a compañero/a qué trajeron y qué no trajeron ustedes.

Modelo sombrero
Traje un sombrero o **No traje sombrero.**
Mi amigo trajo un sombrero o **No trajo sombrero.**

calcetines	impermeable	licencia de manejar	ropa formal
zapatos tenis	cheques de viajero	piyama	vaqueros
traje de baño	cámara	aspirinas	ropa interior

C Las siguientes personas quisieron hacer ciertas cosas ayer pero fue imposible. Con un/a compañero/a determine qué quisieron hacer.

Modelo tu entrenador
Mi entrenador quiso cambiar la fecha del partido (pero fue imposible).

tu novio/a	tus compañeros/as	tu profesor/a
tu mejor amigo/a	tu perro	

D **La historia de una tarjeta postal.** Lea los siguientes párrafos cambiando los verbos al pretérito.

Dos de mis mejores amigos (ir) al Perú en agosto. Desde allí me (mandar) una tarjeta postal, pero ellos no (escribir) el número de la zona postal. (Volver) a los Estados Unidos en noviembre. Enseguida me (llamar) y (venir) a verme a mi apartamento. Ellos me (traer) un suéter precioso y me (decir) que el viaje (ser) magnífico. Los tres (hablar) mucho del Perú y yo les (hacer) muchas preguntas.

Después ellos me (preguntar) por la tarjeta postal. Yo les (contestar): «¿Qué tarjeta?» En ese momento el cartero (tocar) a la puerta con la tarjeta de mis amigos.

E **Mis actividades.** Conteste las siguientes preguntas sobre sus actividades. Trabaje con un/a compañero/a y después hágale las mismas preguntas a él/ella.

Modelo Compañero/a **¿Qué hiciste ayer?**
Usted **Vine a la universidad a estudiar.**

1. ¿Qué hiciste en la casa esta mañana?
2. ¿Qué hiciste ayer en la clase? ¿después de la clase?
3. ¿Qué hiciste el fin de semana? ¿anoche? ¿el jueves?

El Museo del Oro en Bogotá. En este museo existe la mejor colección de objetos precolombinos de oro del mundo.

EN CONTEXTO

¿Cómo escriben y hablan?

Sofía escribe a máquina rápidamente.

Pepito escribe lentamente.

La entienden fácilmente.

Lo entienden difícilmente.

ACTIVIDADES

A Diga qué cosas hace usted rápidamente y qué cosas hace usted lentamente.

Modelo subir las escaleras
Subo las escaleras lentamente (rápidamente).

hablar inglés   escribir a máquina   limpiar la casa   manejar   caminar   comer   leer

B Hay cosas que podemos hacer fácilmente (o con facilidad) y hay otras cosas que podemos hacer difícilmente (o con dificultad). Usted y su compañero/a deben completar las siguientes oraciones de acuerdo con su manera de ser (*the way you are*).

Modelo Yo entiendo los problemas...
Yo entiendo los problemas fácilmente (con facilidad, difícilmente, con dificultad).

1. Yo aprendo bailes nuevos...
2. Hablo con personas desconocidas...
3. Les presto cosas a mis amigos...
4. Les doy consejos a otras personas...
5. Escribo cartas...
6. Hablo en público...
7. Monto en bicicleta...
8. Devuelvo (*I return*) cosas en las tiendas...

GRAMÁTICA

Adverbs

You have used many common Spanish adverbs when expressing time (**ayer, mañana, anoche, siempre**), place (**aquí, allí, debajo**), degree (**más, menos, tanto como**), how things are done (**bien, mal, regular**), and so on. Spanish also uses adverbs ending in **-mente** to qualify how things are done.

1. To form these adverbs add **-mente** to the feminine form of the adjective (**rápida → rápidamente**), or to adjectives ending in a consonant (**difícil → difícilmente**), or the vowel **-e** (**alegre → alegremente**).

El carro pasó **rápidamente.**	*The car went by rapidly.*
Habló **fácilmente.**	*She spoke easily.*
Pagaron **amablemente.**	*They paid courteously.*

2. When two or more adverbs are together, the suffix **-mente** need only be attached to the last one.

Contestaste **clara** y **lentamente.**	*You answered clearly and slowly.*

3. Other commonly used adverbs ending in **-mente** are

generalmente	normalmente	frecuentemente
realmente	básicamente	simplemente
tranquilamente	regularmente	perfectamente
relativamente	tradicionalmente	lógicamente

4. Instead of an adverb Spanish may use some adjectives or **con** + noun to qualify how things are done.

Leyó { **rápidamente.** / **rápido.** }	Leyó **con rapidez.**
Habló **fácilmente.**	Habló **con facilidad.**

5. Place an adverb that modifies a verb as close as possible to the verb.

El Sr. Urrutia caminó lentamente por la acera.	*Mr. Urrutia walked slowly along the sidewalk.*
Ellos explicaron claramente el problema.	*They explained the problem clearly.*

When expressing what generally or normally happens with an adverb ending in **-mente,** the adverb is commonly placed at the beginning of the sentence.

Generalmente salimos los viernes.	*We generally go out on Fridays.*

Comparison of adverbs

1. Use the following structures to make comparisons with adverbs:

tan	*adverb*	como	(comparison of equality)
más / menos	*adverb*	que	(comparison of inequality)

Ofelia escribe **tan bien como** Andrés. — *Ofelia writes as well as Andrés.*
Un avión viaja **más rápidamente que** un autobús. — *An airplane travels faster than a bus.*

2. The following adverbs have irregular forms for comparisons of inequality

bien	→ mejor	Yo canto **mejor** que Héctor.
mal	→ peor	Héctor canta **peor** que yo.
mucho	→ más	El cartero camina **más** que usted.
poco	→ menos	Ese niño come **menos** que tu hijo.

3. To express the idea of *extremely* you may add the suffix **-ísimo** to an adverb. Adverbs ending in **-mente** do not normally add **-ísimo.**

Llegaron muy tarde. Llegaron **tardísimo.**

ACTIVIDADES

A ¿Cómo hace su compañero/a las siguientes actividades? Escoja verbos de las columnas de la izquierda para sus preguntas. Su compañero/a debe contestar con un adverbio apropiado de las dos columnas de la derecha.

Modelo caminar rápidamente

Usted **¿Cómo caminas?**
Compañero/a **Camino rápidamente.**

escribir a máquina	bailar salsa	lentamente	claramente
trabajar	manejar	tranquilamente	perfectamente
cantar	jugar béisbol	normalmente	fácilmente
hablar español	tocar el violín	alegremente	terriblemente

B Complete las oraciones de acuerdo con sus actividades.

Modelo Yo quiero... independientemente.
Yo quiero vivir en mi apartamento independientemente.

1. Me gusta... tranquilamente.
2. Prefiero... lentamente.
3. No viajo... diariamente.
4. Voy a... regularmente.
5. Puedo... perfectamente.

C Usted y su familia están de vacaciones en una playa y reciben una carta de un/a amigo/a que quiere saber cómo es el lugar y qué se puede hacer allí. ¿Cómo contestan ustedes las preguntas?

Modelo ¿Qué hacen normalmente por las tardes?
Normalmente vamos a la playa.

1. ¿Adónde salen regularmente?
2. ¿Adónde van por la noche generalmente?
3. ¿Pueden conversar tranquilamente en la playa?
4. ¿El lugar es relativamente tranquilo?
5. Básicamente, ¿qué les gusta más de ese lugar?

D Usted es un/a reportero/a para el periódico de su universidad y quiere saber más detalles (*details*) acerca de un campamento (*camp*) en las montañas. Hágale las siguientes preguntas a un/a compañero/a y después comparta la información con la clase.

Modelo Usted ¿Vienes regularmente a este lugar?
Compañero/a **Sí, vengo todos los veranos.**

1. Generalmente, ¿qué hacen por las mañanas?
2. Normalmente, ¿qué actividades tienen para las muchachas?
3. ¿Sirven las comidas puntualmente?
4. ¿Cuesta más el campamento este año?
5. Básicamente, ¿hay un ambiente sano?
6. Honestamente, ¿qué piensas de este lugar?

E Usted va a una fiesta con un/a estudiante nuevo/a que le hace muchas preguntas acerca de las personas que están allí. Su compañero/a va a hacer el papel del estudiante y usted va a contestar sus preguntas.

Modelo Compañero/a ¿Quién baila tan bien como ella?
Usted **Yo bailo tan bien como ella.**

1. ¿Quién canta mejor que él?
2. ¿Llegó alguien más tarde que nosotros?
3. ¿Quién es aquella muchacha que tocó la guitarra mejor que Eva?
4. ¿Quién salió más temprano que la muchacha del vestido azul?
5. ¿Alguien baila mejor que tú?

F **Opiniones.** Usted y su compañero/a deben decir si están de acuerdo o no con las siguientes ideas. Expliquen por qué.

1. Generalmente los programas de televisión tienen mucha violencia.
2. Básicamente los carros japoneses son mejores que los norteamericanos.
3. Realmente los alumnos de la escuela secundaria estudian poco.
4. Tradicionalmente los mejores jugadores de fútbol de los equipos de las universidades pasan a ser profesionales.

LECTURA

Antes de leer: the future tense

You have learned and used several verb tenses since you began to study Spanish. To express what is going on or happens normally you use the present indicative tense; to emphasize what is actually in progress you use the present progressive; to express your wishes, hopes, or doubts you use the present subjunctive; to report past events you use the preterit; and to express future plans you use the present tense or the construction **ir** + **a** + infinitive.

English uses two verb forms to express future time (*they are going to read; they will read*). In addition to the two ways mentioned in the previous paragraph, Spanish also has a future tense. You do not have to use this future tense in order to communicate in Spanish, but you should be able to recognize it when reading or listening.

The future tense is formed by the infinitive plus the future endings: **-é, -ás, -á, -emos, -éis, -án.** These endings are the same for **-ar, -er,** and **-ir** verbs.

	hablar	**comer**	**vivir**
yo	hablaré	comeré	viviré
tú	hablarás	comerás	vivirás
él, ella, usted	hablará	comerá	vivirá
nosotros/as	hablaremos	comeremos	viviremos
vosotros/as	hablaréis	comeréis	viviréis
ellos/as, ustedes	hablarán	comerán	vivirán

Few verbs are irregular in the future, and their irregularities are only found in the stem. An easy way to remember these irregular forms is to divide them into three groups. The first group (**-er** verbs) drops the **e** from the infinitive ending.

INFINITIVE	NEW STEM	FUTURE FORMS
haber:	habr	habré, habrás, habrá, habremos, habréis, habrán
poder:	podr	podré, podrás, podrá, podremos, podréis, podrán
querer:	querr	querré, querrás, querrá, querremos, querréis, querrán
saber:	sabr	sabré, sabrás, sabrá, sabremos, sabréis, sabrán

The second group (**-er** and **-ir** verbs) replaces the **e** or **i** of the infinitive ending with a **d.**

INFINITIVE	NEW STEM	FUTURE FORMS
poner:	pondr	pondré, pondrás, pondrá, pondremos, pondréis, pondrán
tener:	tendr	tendré, tendrás, tendrá, tendremos, tendréis, tendrán
salir:	saldr	saldré, saldrás, saldrá, saldremos, saldréis, saldrán
venir:	vendr	vendré, vendrás, vendrá, vendremos, vendréis, vendrán

The third group consists of two verbs (**decir, hacer**) that do not follow the previous patterns.

INFINITIVE	NEW STEM	FUTURE FORMS
decir:	dir	diré, dirás, dirá, diremos, diréis, dirán
hacer:	har	haré, harás, hará, haremos, haréis, harán

The use of the future in Spanish is similar to the use of the construction *will* (or *shall*) + verb in English. The only difference is that Spanish may also use the future tense to express probability in the present.

Mandaré la carta mañana. — *I'll send the letter tomorrow.*
Saldremos la semana próxima. — *We'll leave next week.*
Serán las tres de la tarde. — *It's probably three in the afternoon.*

COMPRENSIÓN E IDENTIFICACIÓN

Lea el siguiente párrafo sobre los planes de unos estudiantes para el próximo fin de semana.

Nosotros pensamos salir el viernes después del almuerzo para la casa que tienen los padres de Jacinto en el campo. Iremos en mi auto, y si no tenemos ningún problema, llegaremos a la casa a eso de las siete. Allí estaremos en contacto con la naturaleza y podremos descansar sin ruidos y sin teléfono.

También podremos leer y dormir bastante. Probablemente caminaremos por las mañanas y comeremos muchas frutas y vegetales que cultivan allí. No veremos televisión porque gracias a Dios no la tienen. Será un cambio fabuloso que nos vendrá muy bien después de esta semana de exámenes.

Diga si las siguientes oraciones son verdaderas o falsas de acuerdo con la información del párrafo.

1. Los estudiantes piensan salir a eso de las siete.
2. Van a ir en el carro de los padres de Jacinto.
3. Van a pasar unos días muy tranquilos en el campo.
4. Van a comer comida sana durante el fin de semana.
5. Trabajaron mucho y necesitan descansar.

Ahora lea el párrafo otra vez identificando las formas del futuro.

Una joven compra una revista en uno de los muchos quioscos que venden revistas y periódicos en Santiago de Chile.

Los horóscopos

Los horóscopos son muy populares en las revistas y los periódicos hispanos. El primer horóscopo que van a leer, tomado de la revista española *Blanco y negro,* es muy sencillo. Sólo presenta cuatro aspectos muy importantes de la vida: el amor (*love*), la salud, el trabajo y el dinero. Usted y su compañero/a deben buscar sus signos y compararlos. Después deben contestar las siguientes preguntas y compartir la información con la clase.

Horóscopo

Optimista Leo

Óptimo ★★★ Regular ★
Bueno ★★ Pésimo ●

Signos afortunados de la semana

LEO (23-7 al 23-8)
Amor ★★★ Trabajo ★★★
Salud ★★★ Dinero ★★★

ARIES (21-3 al 20-4)
Amor ★★★ Trabajo ★★★
Salud ★★★ Dinero ★★

Signos favorables de la semana

SAGITARIO (23-11 al 21-12)
Amor ★ Trabajo ★★
Salud ★★ Dinero ★★

LIBRA (24-9 al 23-10)
Amor ★★ Trabajo ★★
Salud ★ Dinero ★★

Signos indiferentes de la semana

CÁNCER (22-6 al 22-7)
Amor ★ Trabajo ★★
Salud ★ Dinero ★

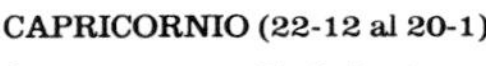

CAPRICORNIO (22-12 al 20-1)

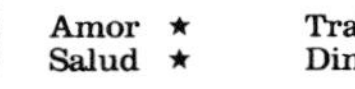

Amor ★ Trabajo ★
Salud ★ Dinero ★

Signos desfavorables de la semana

TAURO (21-4 al 20-5)
Amor ★ Trabajo ★
Salud ★ Dinero ●

ACUARIO (21-1 al 19-2)
Amor ★ Trabajo ★
Salud ★ Dinero ●

VIRGO (24-8 al 23-9)
Amor ● Trabajo ★
Salud ★ Dinero ●

GÉMINIS (21-5 al 21-6)
Amor ★ Trabajo ★
Salud ★ Dinero ★

PISCIS (20-2 al 20-3)
Amor ★ Trabajo ★
Salud ★ Dinero ★

Signo pésimo de la semana

ESCORPIO (24-10 al 22-11)
Amor ● Trabajo ●
Salud ★ Dinero ●

Por NIRAK ARYEVLIS

1. ¿Cuál es tu signo?
2. ¿Cómo es tu signo esta semana? (afortunado, favorable, etc.)
3. ¿Quién es más afortunado en el amor?
4. ¿Quién va a tener mejor salud esta semana?
5. ¿Cómo va a estar el trabajo esta semana para los dos? ¿y el dinero?

En la página siguiente está el horóscopo para todo el año publicado en *Vanidades*[5], una revista muy popular en Hispanoamérica y entre los hispanos que viven en los Estados Unidos. El tiempo futuro se usa mucho en los horóscopos, pero como pueden reconocerlo no tendrán dificultad en entender las predicciones para el año.

Primero busque su horóscopo de acuerdo con su signo. Después anote cuáles son las predicciones que usted considera más importantes. Su compañero/a le va a preguntar cuáles son. Después usted le debe preguntar lo mismo a su compañero/a.

Las siguientes palabras le podrán ayudar a entender mejor su horóscopo y el de su compañero/a.

Aries:	fijarse *to set*
Taurus:	asunto *matter;* pareja *partner*
Géminis:	nacidos *those born;* tener presente *to keep in mind;* aprovechar *to take advantage*
Cáncer:	alcanzar *to obtain*
Leo:	herir *to hurt*
Virgo:	apoyo *support;* jugar un papel *to play a part*
Libra:	contratiempo *disappointment;* aprovechar *to take advantage*
Escorpión:	alcanzar *to obtain;* atareado *busy*
Sagitario:	no ha logrado *you have not achieved;* alejado *far away*
Capricornio:	brillar *to shine;* nubarrones *dark clouds;* encarar *to face*
Acuario:	alcanzar *to obtain;* esfuerzo *effort;* empeño *persistence;* rechazar *to reject*
Piscis:	perseguir *to pursue;* desde hace *for;* herramienta *tool*

[5] Leonor Andrassy, "Horóscopo" © Editorial América, S.A., Vanidades Continental #1, 8 de enero de 1988.

horóscopo

Por Leonor Andrassy

ARIES

Marzo 21
- a -
Abril 19

Para Aries, los primeros días del año serán ideales para fijarse un plan a seguir. En el trabajo tendrá la oportunidad de mejorar si se lo propone. Nuevas ideas, nuevos métodos pueden ser especialmente valiosos. Si no es necesario, no viaje en estos días. El momento es muy favorable para tratar con personas influyentes. Evite las discusiones. Sea más prudente y diplomático . . .

CÁNCER

Junio 22
- a -
Julio 22

Los primeros días de este año son magníficos para entrevistas de todo tipo. Si fuera más discreto se evitaría problemas. Si se lo propone, los planes del año pasado, que no hizo realidad, pueden llegar a un final feliz. Viaje corto con algunas sorpresas. Las circunstancias se han combinado de tal manera que puede alcanzar triunfos en su trabajo, siempre que usted sea más positivo.

LIBRA

Septiembre 22
- a -
Octubre 22

Este año que comienza traerá a Libra un poco de todo: mucha felicidad y algunos contratiempos. Exceso de energía mental, en los primeros días, que debe aprovechar para llevar adelante todas las ideas que tiene acumuladas. El momento es bueno para los asuntos que requieren negociaciones. Si piensa entrevistarse con alguna persona importante, es conveniente que lo haga el 8.

CAPRICORNIO

Diciembre 22
- a -
Enero 19

Este año será, para los nacidos bajo este signo, en general bueno. El sol brillará, aunque a veces surgirán pequeños nubarrones. Gran habilidad en la forma de encarar la realidad. En el trabajo, algunos conflictos por haber mezclado la amistad con los negocios. Cierta confusión en materia económica. Emplee todo su encanto en reconquistar a la persona que es el centro de su vida.

TAURO

Abril 20
- a -
Mayo 20

A Tauro se le presenta un año muy movido con pequeños triunfos que traerán momentos de felicidad inmensa. Los primeros días del año se presentan con mucha actividad. Los intelectuales tendrán grandes sorpresas. Si tiene que resolver algún asunto de tipo personal debe hacerlo ahora. Pueden surgir diferencias de criterio con su pareja. Alguien llega a su vida inesperadamente . . .

LEO

Julio 23
- a -
Agosto 22

El año en general no tendrá grandes complicaciones para los hijos de Leo. Una cosa debe tener muy presente: controlar su carácter, a veces demasiado impetuoso, que puede herir a los que están cerca de usted, especialmente al hombre o mujer con quien comparte su vida. Su gran creatividad será reconocida. Para los más jóvenes, nuevos romances. Posibilidad de cambios en el trabajo.

ESCORPIÓN

Octubre 23
- a -
Noviembre 21

Lo que no ha logrado el año pasado podrá alcanzarlo este año, si se lo propone. Los primeros días de este período seguirán siendo extremadamente atareados, sobre todo en lo relacionado con los asuntos personales. Su energía y vitalidad serán muy altas, lo que será una ventaja, pero debe tener cuidado con los excesos. Domine su carácter, a veces un poco agresivo. Vida social activa.

ACUARIO

Enero 20
- a -
Febrero 19

Los acuarianos alcanzarán este año lo que se propongan, todo depende del esfuerzo y empeño que pongan en sus planes. Los primeros días serán especialmente útiles y agradables para enriquecer su círculo de amistades. Invitaciones a diferentes lugares que no debe rechazar, puede hacer muy buenos contactos en estas reuniones. ¡Sorpresas en la vida sentimental de Acuario!

GÉMINIS

Mayo 21
- a -
Junio 21

Los nacidos bajo este signo tendrán grandes oportunidades en este año, especialmente en los primeros días; tiene que tener muy presente que las oportunidades se presentan, pero usted tiene que saber aprovecharlas. Debe ponerse al día en los asuntos pendientes. ¿Por qué no hace un análisis de los fallos del año pasado? Es la mejor forma de no cometer los mismos errores en este año . . .

VIRGO

Agosto 23
-a -
Septiembre 21

Este año será muy positivo para Virgo. Personas influyentes continuarán ayudándolo. La habilidad artística que caracteriza a este signo le impulsará a mejorar su casa. Podrá contar con el apoyo de su familia. Preocupación por problemas de salud de personas que están cerca de usted. Los primeros días serán muy positivos para el amor. Los amigos jugarán un papel muy importante.

SAGITARIO

Noviembre 22
- a -
Diciembre 21

El año que comienza seguirá con el mismo ritmo del año pasado aunque con algunas sorpresas. . . Los primeros días de este período serán los más felices para los sagitarianos. Tendrá las mejores oportunidades para llevar adelante sus proyectos personales y conseguir lo que no ha logrado el año pasado. Personas alejadas adquieren importancia en sus proyectos. Dedíquele tiempo al amor. . .

PISCIS

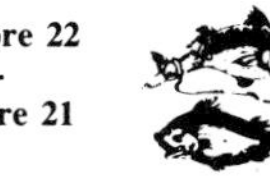

Febrero 20
- a -
Marzo 20

Para Piscis, las cosas mejorarán este año. Durante los primeros días, el ambicioso pisciano debe centrar su atención y esfuerzos en sus asuntos profesionales, ya que le será más fácil que nunca antes obtener lo que está persiguiendo desde hace tanto tiempo. Debe cuidarse de no humillar a las personas que están cerca de usted. Cuidado si tiene que trabajar con herramientas.

Bogotá, 20 de marzo

Querida Dulce:

Estoy pasando unos días maravillosos en Colombia. Mis tíos son un encanto y mis primos, ni hablar. Salimos todos los días y siempre tienen planes pues quieren que conozca todas las cosas interesantes que hay aquí.

Ayer me llevaron al Museo del Oro. Allí tienen más de 25.000 objetos precolombinos de oro. Es algo increíble. Hay una sala que sólo se abre a ciertas horas y que tiene todas las paredes cubiertas de objetos de oro. Por fuera uno no se da cuenta que hay una sala allí, pues sólo ve una pared, pero esa pared es la puerta. Antes de ir al museo mis primos me explicaron todo esto, pero así y todo me sorprendí cuando la pared se movió. Después que entramos en la sala oscura, la puerta se empezó a cerrar lentamente y de repente se encendieron las luces. Yo tuve que cerrar los ojos por todo el brillo del oro. Tú tienes que venir a cononcer esto. Como quieres estudiar un año fuera, ¿por qué no vienes a Bogotá? Aquí hay universidades muy buenas y además están mis primos que tienen muchas ganas de conocerte y que te pueden ayudar y presentar a sus amigos.

Este fin de semana vamos a ir a Cartagena. Dicen que es una ciudad preciosa. Además allí podremos disfrutar de la playa.

Dentro de dos semanas estaré de nuevo con ustedes y les contaré con más detalles. Recibe un abrazo y un beso de

Emilia

Una carta

A la izquierda está la carta que Emilia le mandó a su amiga Dulce contándole de sus vacaciones en casa de sus tíos en Bogotá. En esta carta ella le escribe sobre sus experiencias en el Museo del Oro° de Bogotá. Este museo pertenece al Banco de la República y tiene la colección de objetos precolombinos de oro más grande del mundo. Además tiene una colección extraordinaria de esmeraldas°. Colombia es el mayor productor de esmeraldas del mundo, con más del 80 por ciento de la producción mundial.

Museo... *Gold Museum*

emeralds

Emilia también le cuenta sus planes para ir a Cartagena, una de las ciudades más interesantes de la América del Sur. Está situada en la costa norte de Colombia, y es famosa por sus playas y su arquitectura colonial, especialmente las fortalezas° que defienden su bahía. La más conocida de éstas es el Castillo de San Felipe, que se considera la mejor obra de arquitectura militar que construyeron los españoles en América. El Castillo de San Felipe fue terminado en 1667 y está a un lado de la ciudad. Tiene galerías subterráneas que lo conectan con el centro. El sistema de ventilación y el de acústica son impresionantes obras de ingeniería.

fortresses

¿Verdadero o falso?

Diga si las siguientes oraciones son verdaderas o falsas de acuerdo con la introducción a la carta.

1. El Museo del Oro está en Bogotá.
2. Los objetos de oro del museo son muy modernos.
3. Cartagena es famosa por sus esmeraldas.
4. En Cartagena hay edificios muy interesantes de la época colonial.
5. Hay túneles que comunican una de las fortalezas de Cartagena con el centro de la ciudad.

Preguntas

Conteste las siguientes preguntas sobre la carta de Emilia.

1. ¿Qué fecha tiene la carta?
2. ¿Está contenta Emilia en Bogotá?
3. ¿Por qué se sorprendió Emilia en el Museo del Oro?
4. ¿Qué ventajas puede tener Dulce si va a estudiar a Bogotá?
5. ¿Cuándo se va a ir Emilia de Bogotá?

SITUACIONES

1. You need stamps to mail some letters and you go to the post office to buy them: (a) tell the employee that you want to send two letters air mail to the United States, (b) ask him/her to weigh them for you, and (c) ask him/her how much it is.
2. You want to mail a package to a friend. You take the package to the post office and ask the employee to (a) weigh it for you, (b) tell you how much it is to send it air mail or regular mail (**correo ordinario**). Then, (c) decide how you will send it and tell the employee.
3. Call a friend's house and ask to talk to him/her. The person who answers the phone says that your friend is not in. Ask the person to tell your friend (a) that you called, and (b) that you need to talk to him/her. Leave your telephone number, thank the person, and say good-by. Your partner will write down your message.
4. You call a friend and he/she answers the phone. Identify yourself and greet your friend. Then (a) say that you and some friends are going to the movies this afternoon, (b) give the name of the film, and (c) ask if he/she would like to go. If the answer is yes, give the time and place you are going to meet. If the answer is no, say that you are sorry he/she cannot come.
5. You are talking to your friend about your last trip. Tell (a) where and when you went, (b) how you went, (c) what you did there, and (d) if you liked it or not. Then try to find out the same information from your friend.
6. You are the director of a school play. Tell one of the actors that he/she should (a) walk slowly on the stage (**escenario**), (b) speak clearly, (c) look at the audience (**público**), and (d) leave rapidly.
7. You are in Bogotá and need to make a long-distance telephone call to your mother. Give the operator (a) your mother's full name, (b) the city and country, (c) the area code and telephone number, and (d) the number you are calling from.
8. You are helping a friend make a telephone call. Find out if (a) it is a local or a long-distance call, and (b) if it is a collect call. Make the call and tell your friend (a) that it is busy, and (b) to call later.

CONTESTADOR CASSETTE

Asociado al teléfono, facilita la contestación y recepción de las llamadas telefónicas.

Cuota de conexión ...... 6.000 pts.
Cuota de abono mensual . 1.381 pts.

VOCABULARIO[6]

el correo — *post office*
el buzón — *mail box*
la carta — *letter*
la estampilla/el sello — *stamp*
el paquete — *package*
el sobre — *envelope*
la tarjeta postal — *post card*
el telegrama — *telegram*

el teléfono
la conexión — *connection*
la guía telefónica/de teléfonos — *telephone directory*
el indicativo/el prefijo — *area code*
llamada de cargo revertido/a cobrar — *collect call*
llamada de larga distancia — *long–distance call*
el ruido — *noise*

geografía
la altura — *height, elevation*
el ecuador — *equator*
la temperatura — *temperature*
la tierra — *land*

las personas
el cartero — *mailman*
la operadora — *operator*
el sirviente/la sirvienta — *servant, maid*

expresiones de afecto
el abrazo — *embrace*
el beso — *kiss*
el cariño — *love, affection*
querido/a — *dear*
recuerdos — *regards*

verbos
caerse — *to fall*
colgar (ue) — *to hang up*
escribir a máquina — *to type*
llorar — *to cry*
mandar — *to send*
marcar/discar — *to dial*
oír — *to hear*
recibir — *to receive, to get*
traducir — *to translate*

palabras útiles
aunque — *although*
enseguida — *immediately*

expresiones útiles
¿de parte de quién? — *who's calling?*
debido a — *due to*
estar acostumbrado/a — *to be used to*
hablar más alto — *to speak louder*
pasarlo bien — *to have a good time*
se cayó la comunicación — *we were cut off*
volver a + infinitivo — *verb + again*

[6] For a list of commonly used adverbs ending in **-mente,** see page 328.

In Lección 14 **you will**

a. **explain needs.**
b. **describe and get hotel accommodations.**
c. **report past events.**
d. **express possession (emphatic).**

La ciudad y la playa

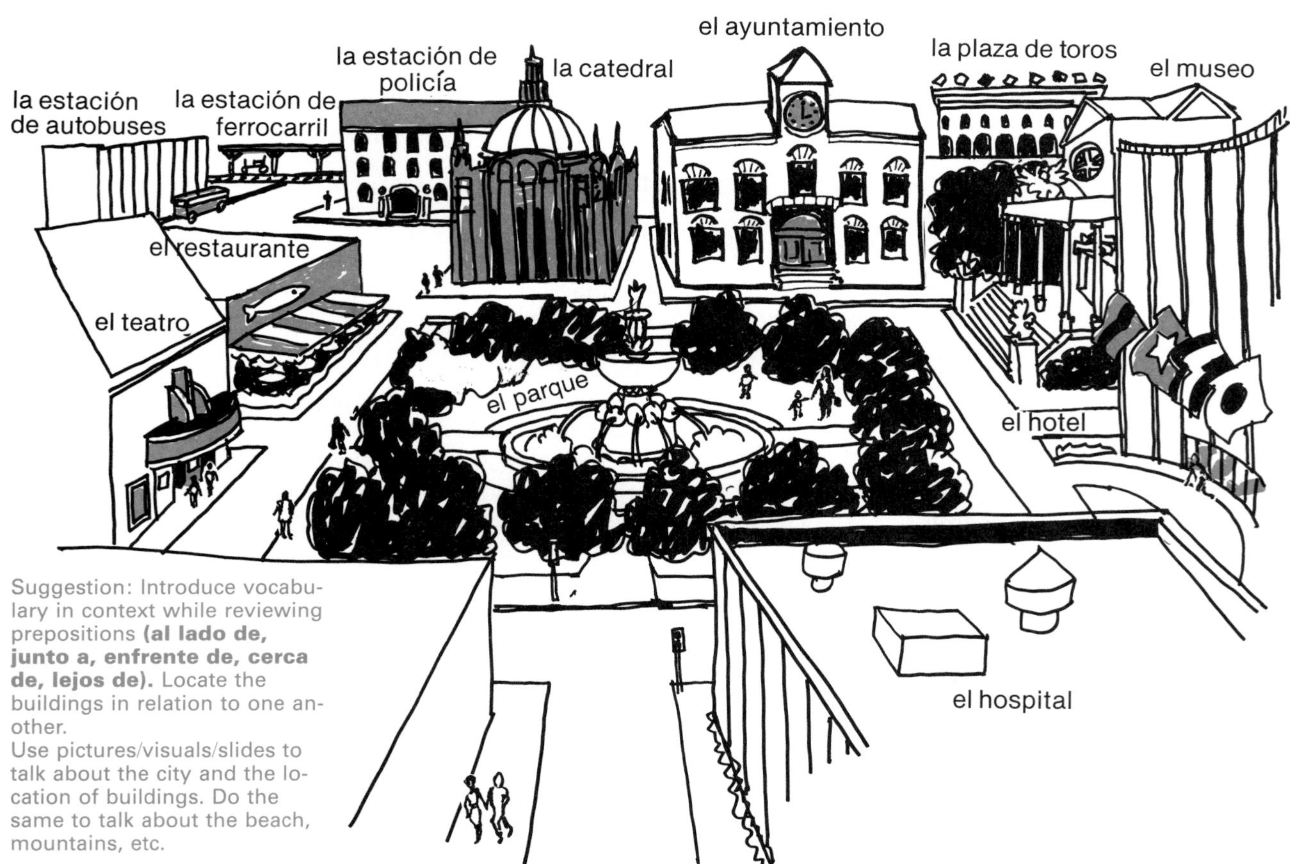

Suggestion: Introduce vocabulary in context while reviewing prepositions **(al lado de, junto a, enfrente de, cerca de, lejos de).** Locate the buildings in relation to one another.
Use pictures/visuals/slides to talk about the city and the location of buildings. Do the same to talk about the beach, mountains, etc.

Muchas personas prefieren pasar las vacaciones en una ciudad porque allí pueden ver muchas cosas interesantes.

Lección 14

De vacaciones

Otras personas prefieren pasar sus vacaciones en la playa donde pueden descansar y olvidar las presiones de la vida moderna.

La playa de Luquillo, una de las playas más famosas de Puerto Rico.

ACTIVIDADES

A Hágale las siguientes preguntas a su compañero/a. Comparta la información con la clase.

1. ¿Dónde pasas normalmente tus vacaciones? 2. ¿Con quién vas? 3. ¿Cuánto tiempo pasas allí? 4. ¿Adónde fuiste el año pasado? 5. ¿Te gustó el lugar? ¿Por qué?

B Escoja la ciudad, las montañas o el campo y dígale a su compañero/a por qué prefiere pasar sus vacaciones allí.

C Usted quiere que su amigo/a pase las vacaciones con usted en una playa. Dígale cinco cosas que pueden hacer allí para tratar de convencerlo/la.

Las ruinas de Palenque en México muestran los extraordinarios adelantos que había logrado la cultura maya antes de la llegada de los españoles.

D Éste es un anuncio de un periódico español sobre campamentos de verano. Trabaje con un/a compañero/a y (a) dígale qué actividades del anuncio le interesan a usted y (b) pregúntele cuáles le interesan a él/ella. Después comparen estas actividades con las que ofrecen los campamentos que ustedes conocen.

Tus Mejores Vacaciones

- Ajedrez • Atletismo
- Baloncesto • Balonmano
- Fútbol • Gimnasia Rítmica • Piragüismo
- Tenis de Mesa • Turismo Ecuestre • Vela
- Voleibol • Vuelo

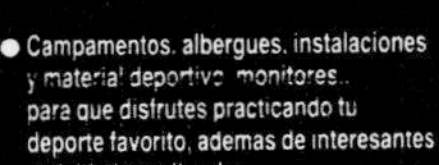

Cultura

El turismo en los países hispanos

Las atracciones turísticas de España están a la par con° las de cualquier país europeo, y su clima, playas, museos, castillos y monumentos atraen a visitantes de todo el mundo. Según la Secretaría General de Turismo, en 1987 llegaron a España, que tiene unos 38 millones de habitantes, más de 59 millones de turistas que le dejaron al país unos 15 mil millones de pesetas[1].

Madrid, la capital de España, les ofrece a los turistas tantas atracciones como cualquiera de las ciudades europeas más conocidas: museos, especialmente el Museo del Prado que tiene una de las mejores colecciones de pintura del mundo; el Palacio Real; conventos, parques y bibliotecas; conciertos, obras de teatro; excelentes restaurantes y pequeños cafés.

Como España tiene tanto que ofrecerles a los turistas, el gobierno ha tratado de facilitarles su estancia en el país. En 1926, siendo Comisario Regio de Turismo el Marqués de la Vega–Inclán, se inició en España el sistema de paradores. Éstos son hoteles que ofrecen todas las comodidades del mundo moderno en castillos antiguos, palacios y monasterios a través de° todo el país. Hoy en día los paradores son muy populares tanto entre los españoles como los extranjeros.

Además de los paradores, el gobierno ha creado hosterías, que son restaurantes que están decorados según el estilo de la región y que sirven platos típicos, y refugios, que son hoteles que están fuera de las ciudades en zonas donde se puede esquiar, cazar° o pescar.

Unos turistas caminan frente a la Plaza de España en Madrid. En esta plaza están las esculturas de Don Quijote y Sancho Panza, los inmortales personajes de la novela de Miguel de Cervantes.

México es otro país donde el turismo constituye una industria muy importante. En 1987, según la Secretaría General de Turismo, unos cinco millones y medio de turistas visitaron México y gastaron más de dos mil millones de dólares. Esto crea puestos de trabajo y ayuda a mejorar la situación de desempleo en ese país.

---

[1] **Mil millones** is the Spanish equivalent of an English billion. The Spanish **billón** is the equivalent of the English trillion. a la par con *equal to* a través de *throughout* cazar *hunt*

Los turistas se maravillan al visitar las ruinas de las ciudades mayas en Yucatán, Monte Albán en Oaxaca o las pirámides de Teotihuacan cerca de la ciudad de México y ver los adelantos° que existieron en esas culturas. El Museo Antropológico y los nuevos descubrimientos del Templo Mayor de los aztecas en la ciudad de México son pruebas del progreso y desarrollo° que alcanzaron las culturas indígenas antes de la llegada de los españoles.

México tiene playas famosas como Cancún en el Caribe y Acapulco en la costa del Pacífico, donde se puede descansar lejos de las tensiones de las ciudades. Hay muchos hoteles en todo el país, desde los más económicos hasta los más caros y lujosos, para satisfacer los gustos de cualquier viajero.

España y México son los países que atraen más turismo en el mundo hispano y es lógico que estén orgullosos° de su herencia° cultural y de su riqueza° artística. Sin embargo°, los otros países también tienen mucho que ofrecerles a los turistas. Para los que tienen interés en la arquitectura precolombina, una visita a las ruinas mayas de Copán en Honduras o a las fortalezas y ciudades incas del Perú es una experiencia inolvidable°. Aquellos que prefieren ver objetos precolombinos de oro pueden encontrar excelentes colecciones en Colombia, Perú y Costa Rica. Y los que prefieren la cerámica o la artesanía antigua o moderna pueden encontrarlas en todos los países hispanos.

La arquitectura colonial, con sus iglesias, edificios de gobierno, palacios y fortalezas, es uno de los aspectos más interesantes de las ciudades hispanoamericanas. El estilo de muchos de estos edificios es un buen ejemplo de la unión del arte español e indígena.

Unos turistas en la recepción de un hotel en Oaxaca, México. Cerca de esta ciudad están las maravillosas ruinas de Monte Albán, centro ceremonial de los zapotecas, otra de las grandes culturas precolombinas.

Argentina y Chile tienen excelentes zonas montañosas para esquiar. Como estos países están situados en el hemisferio sur, su invierno corresponde al verano en el hemisferio norte y algunos atletas europeos y norteamericanos viajan a estos países para practicar el esquí durante los meses de julio, agosto y septiembre.

adelantos *advances* desarrollo *development* orgullosos *proud* herencia *heritage* riqueza *wealth*
Sin embargo *However* inolvidable *unforgettable*

EN CONTEXTO

En la recepción del hotel

Empleado	Buenas tardes, señores.	
Sr. García Urrutia	Buenas tardes. Hicimos una reservación para una habitación doble para esta noche.	
Empleado	¿A nombre de quién?	
Sr. García Urrutia	A nombre de los Sres. García Urrutia.	
Empleado	Un momento, por favor. Lo siento, pero no la puedo encontrar.	
Sr. García Urrutia	Yo tengo la confirmación. Creo que la puse° en mi maletín.	*I put*
Empleado	No se moleste°, señor. Aquí está. La pusieron bajo el nombre de Urrutia. Perdone.	No... *Don't bother*
Sr. García Urrutia	No se preocupe. Nosotros estuvimos° en este hotel el año pasado y nos gustó mucho. Por eso quisimos regresar.	*were*
Empleado	Gracias. Es usted muy amable. Llene y firme° esta tarjeta, por favor. ¿Me puede dar su pasaporte?	*sign*
Sr. García Urrutia	Aquí lo tiene.	
Empleado	Gracias. Su habitación es la 612. El botones° los va a acompañar°.	*bellboy* / *accompany*

Para completar

Complete las siguientes oraciones según la información que se da en el diálogo.

1. Los Sres. García Urrutia están en...
2. Ellos tienen una reservación para...
3. El empleado no puede encontrar...
4. En el hotel pusieron la reservación bajo el nombre de...
5. Los Sres. García Urrutia estuvieron en ese hotel...
6. El Sr. García Urrutia le da su pasaporte al...
7. La habitación de los Sres. García Urrutia es...
8. La persona que los va a acompañar es el...

vocabulario útil en un hotel

el ascensor	*elevator*	la lavandería	*laundry*
el bar	*bar*	la llave	*key*
la cuenta	*bill*	el mensaje	*message*
el estacionamiento	*parking*	la tintorería	*cleaners*
la habitación sencilla	*single room*		

ACTIVIDADES

A Asocie las siguientes palabras.

1. la llave	a. el teléfono
2. la tintorería	b. la habitación
3. el botones	c. el equipaje
4. la cuenta	d. la ropa
5. el mensaje	e. el dinero

B Hágale las siguientes preguntas a su compañero/a. Después comparta la información con la clase.

1. ¿Vas a un motel o a un hotel cuando viajas?
2. ¿Qué hoteles conoces?
3. ¿Haces reservaciones antes de ir a un hotel o motel?
4. ¿Las haces por teléfono o escribes al hotel/motel?
5. ¿Por qué es importante hacer reservaciones?

GRAMÁTICA

More irregular preterits

The following irregular verbs have a **u** in the preterite stem. As in the group of verbs presented in **Lección 13,** the **yo** and **él, ella, usted** forms do not stress the last syllable.

INFINITIVE	NEW STEM	PRETERIT FORMS
estar:	estuv	estu**v**e, estu**v**iste, estu**v**o, estu**v**imos, estu**v**isteis, estu**v**ieron
tener:	tuv	**tuv**e, **tuv**iste, **tuv**o, **tuv**imos, **tuv**isteis, **tuv**ieron
poder:	pud	**pud**e, **pud**iste, **pud**o, **pud**imos, **pud**isteis, **pud**ieron
poner:	pus	**pus**e, **pus**iste, **pus**o, **pus**imos, **pus**isteis, **pus**ieron
saber[2]**:**	sup	**sup**e, **sup**iste, **sup**o, **sup**imos, **sup**isteis, **sup**ieron

[2] **Saber** in the preterit normally means *to learn* or *to find out.* Supe que llegaron anoche. *I learned that you arrived last night.*

ACTIVIDADES

A La semana pasada los estudiantes de su clase organizaron una excursión. Cada estudiante trajo algo y lo puso en una de las cestas. Dígale a su compañero/a qué pusieron las siguientes personas.

Modelo Alicia / las servilletas
Alicia puso las servilletas.

1. Julio / la ensalada
2. Alberto y Beatriz / los manteles
3. Margarita / los sándwiches
4. La profesora / el postre
5. Ustedes / los refrescos
6. Tú / . . .

B Las siguientes personas no pudieron hacer la tarea. Diga qué excusa dieron estas personas y después diga cuál es su excusa.

Modelo Irma. . . se sintió mal anoche.
Irma no pudo hacer la tarea porque se sintió mal anoche.

1. Esperanza. . . tuvo que ir al médico.
2. Norma y Elvira. . . tuvieron un examen ayer.
3. Fermín y Cecilia. . . estuvieron ausentes.
4. Tú. . . perdiste el libro.
5. Aurelio. . . no supo hacerla.
6. Yo. . .

C **Sus vacaciones el año pasado.** Pregúntele a su compañero/a dónde estuvo el año pasado. Él/ella debe usar uno de los anuncios para contestar sus preguntas. Después usted va a compartir la información con la clase.

AEROPERÚ
Visite Machu Picchu; dos días en Cuzco, cinco días en Lima en el Hotel El Inca. Todo de primera. Desayuno incluido
$1.259,00

AEROLÍNEAS ARGENTINAS
7 días en Buenos Aires, dos días en Bariloche, dos días en Iguazú. Hoteles de lujo. Servicio especial. Un viaje inolvidable
$1.987,00

IBERIA
Una semana en la Costa del Sol y otra en Madrid
Hoteles Meliá
$1.750,00

1. ¿Adónde fuiste en tus vacaciones?
2. ¿Cuánto costó el viaje?
3. ¿En qué aerolínea fuiste?
4. ¿En qué hotel te pusieron?
5. ¿Cuánto tiempo estuviste allí?
6. ¿Qué pudiste hacer allí?
7. ¿Pudiste hablar español con otras personas?
8. ¿Tuviste alguna experiencia inolvidable?

D **El robo del año.** Alguien entró anoche en el Banco Internacional y se llevó un millón de dólares. Hay varias personas investigando el robo. Todos están de acuerdo en que el ladrón (*thief*) es el gerente del banco y van a decir por qué lo supieron.

Modelo la secretaria... el gerente recibió una llamada misteriosa
La secretaria lo supo porque el gerente recibió una llamada misteriosa.

1. el detective... escuchó un mensaje en el contestador automático (*answering machine*)
2. los policías... llegó a su casa en un coche nuevo
3. su cuñado... lo oyó hablar con un banco suizo
4. los empleados... compró una casa de medio millón de dólares
5. tú... encontraste un maletín lleno de dinero en su oficina
6. yo...

E Sus amigos/as estuvieron de vacaciones la semana pasada. Usted quiere saber dónde estuvieron, qué hicieron, qué visitaron, y muchas cosas más. Hágales las preguntas necesarias a dos de sus compañeros/as para obtener la siguiente información.

Modelo dinero que gastaron
Usted **¿Cuánto dinero gastaron?**
Compañero/a **Gastamos $800.**

1. ciudad(es) donde estuvieron
2. medio de transporte que usaron
3. nombre del hotel donde estuvieron
4. tiempo que estuvieron
5. lugares y personas que conocieron
6. platos típicos que probaron
7. otras cosas que pudieron hacer

F Usted fue a una fiesta cuando estuvo de visita en casa de unos primos. Su compañero/a quiere saber más de la fiesta. Conteste sus preguntas.

Modelo Compañero/a **¿Cuántas personas fueron a la fiesta?**
Usted **Fueron unas 50 personas.**

1. ¿Conociste a alguien?
2. ¿Con quién fuiste?
3. ¿Pudiste bailar?
4. ¿Qué comiste?
5. ¿Qué bebiste?
6. ¿Qué te pusiste para la fiesta?

EN CONTEXTO

En la taquilla

Antonio llegó al teatro a las 8:20.
Varias personas están haciendo cola frente a la taquilla.

Antonio está en la cola hace 20 minutos.

Antonio llegó hace media hora.
La función empieza a las nueve.
¡Por fin compró los boletos!

ACTIVIDADES

A Encuesta. Usted quiere saber qué obras de teatro prefieren sus compañeros/as. En grupos de seis o siete, cada uno/a debe decir cuál prefiere. Determine el resultado y comparta la información con la clase.

cómicas clásicas musicales dramáticas infantiles de misterio

B Entrevista. Su compañero/a fue al teatro cuando estuvo en Nueva York. Hágale las siguientes preguntas para saber qué hizo ese día.

1. ¿Cuándo fuiste al teatro? 2. ¿Fuiste solo/a? 3 ¿Hiciste cola para comprar los boletos? 4. ¿Cuánto tiempo estuviste en la cola? 5. ¿Cuánto costaron los boletos? 6. ¿A qué hora empezó la obra? 7. ¿Qué obra viste? Háblame de la obra. 8. ¿Qué hiciste después de la función?

GRAMÁTICA

Hace with expressions of time

1. To state that an action began in the past and continues into the present, use **hace** + the length of time + **que** + the present tense of the verb.

Hace dos horas **que** trabajan. *They've been working for two hours.*

If you begin the sentence with the present tense of the verb, do not use **que.**

Trabajan **hace** dos horas.

2. To indicate the time that has passed since an action started or was completed, use **hace** + length of time + **que** + the preterit tense of the verb. **Hace** is the equivalent of *ago.*

Hace dos horas **que** llegaron. *They arrived two hours ago.*

If you begin the sentence with the preterit tense of the verb, do not use **que.**

Llegaron **hace** dos horas.

ACTIVIDADES

A Complete las siguientes oraciones de acuerdo con sus experiencias. Después su compañero/a debe completarlas. See IM, **Lección 14, Gramática.**

1. Estudio español hace... Hablé español por primera vez hace...
2. Tengo un auto (una moto, una bicicleta) hace...
   Mi auto (moto, bicicleta) es... Yo lo/la compré hace...
3. Conozco a mi novio/a (mejor amigo/a) hace... Él/ella es...
4. Mi programa favorito de televisión es... Yo veo ese programa hace...

B Éstas son las actividades de diferentes personas que están de vacaciones. Diga cuánto tiempo hace que estas personas están ocupadas.

Modelo Los turistas llegaron a la agencia de viajes a las diez. Son las once.
Hace una hora que están en la agencia.

1. El niño empezó a nadar a las once. Son las once y media.
2. El Sr. Matos empezó a mirar televisión a las nueve. Son las doce.
3. Las jóvenes entraron al museo a las cuatro. Son las seis.
4. Margarita llegó al aeropuerto a las doce de la noche. Son las tres de la mañana.
5. Usted está en Lima, Perú. Llegó a... y son las...

C Los Molina estuvieron de vacaciones la semana pasada. Diga cuánto tiempo hace que hicieron lo que aparece en los dibujos.

Modelo

Salieron (Tomaron el tren) hace. . . días.

D **Entrevista.** Hágale las siguientes preguntas a su compañero/a. Comparta la información con la clase.

1. ¿Dónde vives? ¿Cuánto tiempo hace que vives allí? 2. ¿Cuánto tiempo hace que estudias en esta universidad? ¿Y por qué estudias español? 3. ¿Practicas algún deporte? ¿Cuánto tiempo hace que lo practicas? ¿Juegas mucho mejor ahora?

E Usted hizo un viaje hace algún tiempo. Su compañero/a le va a hacer preguntas sobre ese viaje.

1. ¿Adónde fuiste? 2. ¿Cuánto tiempo pasaste allí? 3. ¿Qué hiciste? 4. ¿Te gustaría volver? ¿Por qué?

EN CONTEXTO

Un problema serio

Ernesto ¿Dónde están mis maletas?
Ángel ¿No las trajo el botones?
Ernesto No, mira, trajo las maletas tuyas pero no las mías.
Ángel Pero ésas no son las mías. Deben ser de otra persona.
Ernesto Pues enseguida llamo a la recepción. ¡Ojalá que las maletas nuestras estén allí! ¿Tienes tu cámara?
Ángel Sí, está en mi mochila. ¿Y la tuya?
Ernesto Está en mi maleta.
Ángel Bueno, pero tienes el dinero.
Ernesto Sí, aquí, en el bolsillo°. ¡Ay, pero no está! Ahora sí que tenemos un problema.

° *pocket*

¿Verdadero o falso?

Diga si las siguientes oraciones son verdaderas o falsas de acuerdo con el diálogo.

1. Ernesto busca sus maletas.
2. Ángel trajo las maletas.
3. El botones trajo las maletas de Ángel y Ernesto.
4. Los chicos van a llamar a la recepción.
5. Las cámaras de los chicos están en la habitación.
6. Ernesto tiene el dinero en el bolsillo.

Unas personas frente a la taquilla de un multicine en Sevilla, España.

ACTIVIDADES

A Hágale las siguientes preguntas a su compañero/a. Comparta la información con la clase.

1. ¿Sacas buenas fotos?
2. ¿Cuándo sacas fotos generalmente?
3. ¿Qué cámara tienes?
4. ¿Pones las fotos en un álbum?
5. ¿Les muestras las fotos a tus amigos?

B Lea los siguientes consejos para antes y después del revelado (*developing*). Dígale a su compañero/a qué consejos sigue o no sigue usted cuando toma fotos. Las siguientes palabras pueden ayudarle a entender mejor los consejos.

polvo	*dust*
archivador	*filing jacket*
colecciónelos	*keep them*

CONSEJOS IMPORTANTES PARA HACER BUENAS FOTOS Y CONSERVARLAS:

*** ANTES DEL REVELADO**
- Mantener limpia y cuidada la cámara.
- Evite el polvo, el calor y la humedad.
- No deje mucho tiempo el rollo en la cámara y envíelo rápidamente a revelar.

*** DESPUÉS DEL REVELADO**
- No saque los negativos del archivador.
- No corte los negativos.
- No toque los negativos con los dedos.
- Colecciónelos en una carpeta o álbum igual que las fotos.

Si sigue estas indicaciones, conseguirá mejores fotos y sus negativos estarán siempre dispuestos para hacer nuevas ampliaciones.

Ros FOTOCOLOR

GRAMÁTICA

Stressed possessive adjectives

mío	mía	míos	mías	*my, (of) mine*
tuyo	tuya	tuyos	tuyas	*your (fam.), (of) yours*
suyo	suya	suyos	suyas	*his, her, its, your (formal) their, (of) his, hers*
nuestro	nuestra	nuestros	nuestras	*our, (of) ours*
vuestro	vuestra	vuestros	vuestras	*your (fam.), (of) yours*

The stressed possessive adjectives follow the noun they modify and agree with it in gender and number. An article or demonstrative usually precedes the noun.

El cuarto **mío** es grandísimo.	*My room is very big.*
La maleta **mía** está en la recepción.	*My suitcase is at the front desk.*
Esos primos **míos** llegan mañana.	*Those cousins of mine arrive tomorrow.*
Las llaves **mías** están en la puerta.	*My keys are in the door.*

Possessive pronouns

SINGULAR				PLURAL			
MASCULINE		FEMININE		MASCULINE		FEMININE	
el	mío	la	mía	los	míos	las	mías
	tuyo		tuya		tuyos		tuyas
	suyo		suya		suyos		suyas
	nuestro		nuestra		nuestros		nuestras
	vuestro		vuestra		vuestros		vuestras

1. Possessive pronouns have the same form as stressed possessive adjectives.
2. The definite article precedes the possessive pronoun and they both agree in gender and number with the noun they refer to.

¿Tienes la mochila suya?	*Do you have his backpack?*
Sí, tengo **la suya.**	*Yes, I have his.*

3. After the verb **ser,** the article is usually omitted.

Esa ropa es mía.	*Those clothes are mine.*

4. To be more specific and clear, the following structures may be used to replace any corresponding form of **el suyo.**

la mochila suya ⟶ la suya {
la de él *his*
la de ella *hers*
la de usted *yours (sing.)*
la de ellos *theirs (masc.)*
la de ellas *theirs (fem.)*
la de ustedes *yours (pl.)*

ACTIVIDADES

A Usted y su compañero/a deben identificar los siguientes objetos y decir de quién son.

Modelo

La bicicleta es mía (tuya, suya, nuestra)

B Es el fin del año escolar y un/a amigo/a está ayudando a empacar las cosas de usted y de su compañero/a de cuarto. Conteste sus preguntas.

Modelo esta lámpara

Compañero/a **¿De quién es esta lámpara?**
Usted **Es suya** o **Es mía.**

esos casetes	los cuadernos	las revistas	el afiche (*poster*)
estos discos	el radio	esta toalla	este mapa

C Usted tiene exámenes la semana próxima y va a estudiar con un/a compañero/a. Hágale las siguientes preguntas. Él/ella debe contestar usando pronombres posesivos.

Modelo —¿Quieres ir en mi auto o en el tuyo?
—Quiero ir en el tuyo.

1. ¿Prefieres estudiar en mi casa o en la de Marta?
2. ¿Quieres mi cuaderno o el de Pedro?
3. ¿Hablaste con mi profesor o con el tuyo?
4. ¿Leíste mi proyecto o el de Arturo?
5. ¿Quieres mis apuntes (*notes*) o los de mis hermanos?

D Su compañero/a va a hablarle de sus cosas. Contéstele explicando cómo son las suyas.

Modelo **—Mi apartamento es pequeño y cómodo.**
—Y el mío es grande y viejo.

mi perro mis amigos mis compañeras mi bicicleta mi cuarto
mi novio/a

E Usted va a hablarle a su compañero/a sobre su casa y su familia usando la forma correcta de **nuestro.**

Modelo cocina
Nuestra cocina es muy moderna.

familia vecinos (*neighbors*) abuelos casa auto padres

LECTURA

Antes de leer: the past subjunctive

In **Lecciones 10, 11,** and **12,** you studied the forms and uses of the present subjunctive. In this lesson you are going to learn the past subjunctive, also called the imperfect subjunctive. The emphasis will be on knowing how the past subjunctive is formed and on recognizing it when reading or listening.

All past subjunctive verb forms, regular and irregular, are based on the **ellos/as, ustedes** form of the preterit. Drop the **-on** preterit ending, and substitute the past subjunctive endings. The following chart will help you see how the past subjunctive is formed.

INFINITIVE	ELLOS/AS, USTEDES PRETERIT FORM	PAST SUBJUNCTIVE
hablar:	hablar~~on~~	hablara, hablaras, hablara, habláramos, hablarais, hablaran
comer:	comier~~on~~	comiera...
vivir:	vivier~~on~~	viviera...
estar:	estuvier~~on~~	estuviera...
hacer:	hicier~~on~~	hiciera...
poder:	pudier~~on~~	pudiera...
poner:	pusier~~on~~	pusiera...
querer:	quisier~~on~~	quisiera...
saber:	supier~~on~~	supiera...
tener:	tuvier~~on~~	tuviera...

The same general rules that determine the use of the present subjunctive also apply to the past subjunctive, with a few exceptions. The present subjunctive is oriented to the present or future while the imperfect subjunctive focuses on the past.

Quiere que **preparemos** la comida para las ocho. (hoy → present subjunctive)
Quiso que **preparáramos** la comida para las ocho. (ayer → past subjunctive)

Unas vacaciones en Chile

Lea los siguientes párrafos sobre lo que Adriana hizo antes de sus vacaciones en Chile. Adriana es una esquiadora excelente y piensa salir la semana próxima para Portillo, uno de los centros de esquí más importantes de la América del Sur.

Antes de mis vacaciones en Portillo fui a ver al Dr. Sánchez Hurtado. Él me dijo que tuviera mucho cuidado al esquiar este año. Desde que me caí hace dos años siempre me dice lo mismo. Es verdad que el año pasado tuve algunos problemas con el tobillo derecho, pero ya me siento muy bien. Como yo quiero ir a las Olimpiadas de Invierno tengo que practicar mucho para poder clasificar entre los atletas mejores. El doctor me dijo además que siempre hiciera ejercicios de calentamiento antes de esquiar. Eso es tan elemental que casi me reí en su cara. El pobre doctor es muy amigo de mis padres y me conoce hace muchos años así que todavía me trata como una niña. Me pidió que llamara a un doctor amigo de él y que lo saludara de su parte. Además me pidió que le trajera de Chile alguna revista de medicina.

Después de la consulta fui a la agencia de viajes para buscar mi boleto. Según el agente mi asiento está en la sección de fumar. Yo le dije que el entrenador nos prohibió que estuviéramos entre los fumadores y le pedí que me cambiara de asiento. Me dijo que quizás pudiera reservar varios asientos. Yo le pedí que reservara uno para mí y dos para mis amigos. Así podremos hacer el viaje juntos y pasarlo mejor.

¿Verdadero o falso?

Diga si las siguientes oraciones son verdaderas o falsas de acuerdo con la selección anterior.

1. Adriana va a practicar su deporte favorito en Chile.
2. Ella tuvo un accidente este año.
3. El médico es un amigo de la familia.
4. El médico le dijo que no fumara.
5. El doctor no conoce a ningún médico en Chile.
6. Adriana quiere competir en las Olimpiadas.
7. Adriana cambió su asiento en la agencia de viajes.
8. Ella va a hacer el viaje sola.

Un hotel diferente

Este anuncio se refiere a un hotel diferente. Después de leerlo debe contestar las preguntas. El siguiente vocabulario le podrá ayudar a entender mejor la selección.

cuestión	*a matter*
hacer noche	*spend the night*
próximo	*near*
asearse	*to tidy oneself*

Para completar

Complete las oraciones de acuerdo con la información que se da sobre el hotel en la selección.

1. Este hotel es diferente porque...
2. Es para personas que...
3. Está...
4. En este hotel las personas...
5. Se hace una reserva...
6. La compañía... ofrece este servicio.

Programa comercial

Esta selección explica los beneficios que varios hoteles le ofrecen al hombre de negocios. Las siguientes palabras pueden ayudarle a entender mejor el anuncio.

lanzar	*start*
el alojamiento	*lodging*
la tarifa	*cost*
hospedarse	*to stay, lodge*
encaminado a lograr	*designed to provide*
agilizar	*to speed up*
la disposición	*availability*
el enjuague	*rinse*
rastrillo desechable	*disposable razor*

17 Grandes beneficios de hotel en una gran tarjeta

Programa Comercial

★ ★ ★ ★ ★

Hoteles Fiesta Americana, Fiesta Inn, Holiday Inn y Holiday Inn Crowne Plaza, tienen el gran placer de lanzar su "PROGRAMA COMERCIAL", el más rico en beneficios para los hombres de negocios, como usted.

1. Su reservación le garantiza una magnífica habitación sin necesidad de depósito ni límite para su hora de llegada.
2. En caso de llegar sin reservación y que el hotel esté lleno, nos encargaremos de todos los detalles, para conseguirle alojamiento en la mejor habitación de otro hotel.
3. Descuento mínimo garantizado del 25% en habitación sobre la tarifa al público.
4. Centro Ejecutivo: Todos los servicios de una oficina dentro del hotel.
5. Plan de Incentivos Vacacionales: Usted puede ganar cortesías y descuentos en nuestros hoteles (incluyendo los de playa) al ir acumulando las noches que se hospede con nosotros.
6. Salida Express agilizando ampliamente los trámites de pago y salida del hotel.
7. Disposición de efectivo hasta por $ 25,000 M.N. con cargo a su cuenta.
8. Llamada de despertador con café o jugo y periódico a su elección en su habitación.
9. Derecho a extender la hora de salida hasta por 4 horas sin cargo extra.
10. Cortesías en su baño: shampoo, enjuague, rastrillo desechable, jabón perfumado y gorra de baño.
11. Preregistro para ahorrarle tiempo en su llegada al hotel.
12. Preasignación de una magnífica habitación de acuerdo a sus gustos particulares.
13. Bebida Nacional de bienvenida a su elección.
14. Media botella de vino nacional de cortesía en comida o cena.
15. Dulce o chocolate y flor en habitación como cortesía nocturna diaria.
16. Facilidades de cortesía para aseo de calzado.
17. Promoción especial en renta de autos.

Entonces son diecisiete beneficios verdaderamente grandes, encaminados a lograr la total satisfacción de un hombre de negocios como usted...

AHORA SOLO FALTA SU SOLICITUD: Llame usted al (91-5) 570-81-22 extensiones 770, 771, 785 y recibirá en breve las formas necesarias para que, llenándolas, pueda usted gozar de las extraordinarias ventajas de nuestro PROGRAMA COMERCIAL. Por supuesto, en la recepción de cada uno de nuestros hoteles, que se muestran en la parte inferior, puede solicitar dichas formas.

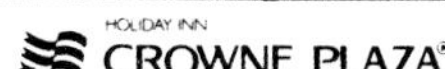

Conteste las siguientes preguntas de acuerdo con la selección.

1. ¿Qué beneficios tienen que ver con la habitación?
2. ¿Qué beneficios se relacionan con el aseo?
3. ¿Qué beneficios tienen como fin ahorrarle tiempo al hombre de negocios?
4. ¿Qué beneficios tienen que ver con algo para beber o comer?
5. En su opinión, ¿cuál es el mejor beneficio para un hombre de negocios?

SITUACIONES

1. You have to make a reservation for a hotel: (a) explain that you need a double room, (b) find out the price per night, (c) ask if it includes breakfast, and (d) check if they have transportation to and from the airport.
2. Tell a friend where you spent your vacation last year. Try to persuade him/her to go there. Tell him/her (a) where this place is, (b) what you can do there, (c) what it costs (a bargain), and (d) how long you stayed.
3. You are a clerk in a hotel. Help a family who wants to stay in your hotel. First greet the family and ask them if you can help them. Then find out if they have a reservation, and ask (a) how many rooms they need, (b) how many single or double rooms, (c) how long they need the rooms, and (d) how they want to pay (cash, traveler's checks, or credit card). Then ask them to fill out a form and thank them.
4. You are not completely satisfied with your room and you go talk with the clerk. Greet the clerk and tell him/her that (a) you don't have hot water or heat, (b) you need soap and towels. Then ask him if you can have another room, and say that you would like a room on the tenth floor.
5. You and two friends are going to spend your vacation in the mountains and already have your basic supplies. From the following list of extra items, choose three you are going to take and tell your friends why: **un periódico, un walkman, un televisor portátil, dos libros, un despertador** (*alarm clock*), **un traje de baño, una canoa, una linterna** (*flashlight*), **fósforos** (*matches*), **un radio.**
6. You and some friends are trying to decide what to do for a three-day weekend. Each one will choose one of the following places and explain why you should all go there. Use the following reasons to convince your friends.

   Lugares: la playa, el campo, una ciudad grande, las montañas

   Motivos: la comida, la tranquilidad, el aire puro, la música, las fiestas, el teatro, los bailes, los museos, el sol, las noches, la naturaleza, el silencio

7. You have had a busy week in Mexico doing many things. Tell your friend (a) what places you visited, (b) what you saw, (c) what you were able to do, (d) what you bought, and (e) what and where you ate. Your friend will ask you some pertinent questions.

VOCABULARIO[3]

lugares	
el ayuntamiento	*city hall*
la catedral	*cathedral*
la estación de policía	*police station*
el museo	*museum*
el parque	*park*
la plaza de toros	*bullring*
el teatro	*theater*
la naturaleza	*nature*
el árbol	*tree*
la arena	*sand*
la flor	*flower*
la montaña	*mountain*
la ola	*wave*
el hotel	
el ascensor	*elevator*
el bar	*bar*
el botones	*bellboy*
la confirmación	*confirmation*
la cuenta	*bill*
el estacionamiento	*parking*
la habitación doble/sencilla	*double/single room*
la lavandería	*laundry*
la llave	*key*
el mensaje	*message*
la recepción	*reception*
la tintorería	*cleaners*
el teatro	
la función	*show*
la cámara	*camera*
la ropa	
el bolsillo	*pocket*
descripciones	
amable	*nice*
verbos	
acompañar	*accompany*
firmar	*to sign*
llenar	*fill out*
molestar(se)	*to bother*
olvidar	*to forget*
regresar	*to come back*
sacar fotos	*take pictures*
expresiones útiles	
¿a nombre de quién?	*under whose name?*
bajo el nombre de...	*under . . .'s name*

Los toros de hoy

Nombre	Num.	Capa	Kilos
«Gacetrillo»	10	Negro	542
«Caracolillo»	21	Negro	531
«Carazul»	37	Negro	552
«Manzanito»	33	Negro	536
«Pintadito»	31	Negro	584
«Cañurino»	8	Negro	539

[3] See page 355 for possessive adjectives and pronouns.

In Lección 15 **you will**

a. talk about and describe holiday activities.
b. express ongoing actions in the past.
c. extend an invitation.
d. accept or decline an invitation.
e. express goals and purposes.
f. express intense reactions.
g. ask for and give a definition or an explanation.

Fechas importantes

el cuarto jueves de noviembre
el Día de Acción de Gracias

En los Estados Unidos las familias se reúnen para celebrar este día.

el 14 de febrero
el Día de los Enamorados o
el Día del Amor y la Amistad

Laura y Jorge están enamorados y van a salir esta noche.

Lección 15
Fiestas y tradiciones

el 4 de julio
el Día de la Independencia

Hay desfiles con bandas y muchas personas ponen banderas al frente de su casa.

el 31 de octubre
el Día de las Brujas

En los Estados Unidas los niños se disfrazan y se divierten mucho.

Unos niños junto a unos Reyes Magos en la ciudad de México. El Día de los Reyes Magos es una fiesta muy importante para los niños hispanos.

más días y fechas importantes	
la Nochevieja	*New Year's Eve*
el Año Nuevo	*New Year's Day*
la Nochebuena	*Christmas Eve*
la Navidad	*Christmas*
el Carnaval	*Mardi gras*
la Pascua	*Passover, Easter*
la Semana Santa	*Easter week*
el Día de los Muertos/Difuntos	*All Souls' Day*
el Día de la(s) Madre(s)	*Mother's Day*

ACTIVIDADES

A Asocie las descripciones de la izquierda con las fiestas de la derecha.

1. Empieza el año.
2. Los niños salen y piden dulces.
3. Les damos regalos a los amigos y parientes.
4. Las personas bailan en la calle y se divierten mucho.
5. Termina el año.

a. el Día de las Brujas
b. la Navidad
c. el Año Nuevo
d. la Nochevieja
e. el Carnaval

B **Entrevista.** Hágale a su compañero/a las siguientes preguntas. Después él/ella le debe hacer las mismas preguntas a usted.

1. ¿Qué fiestas celebra tu familia? 2. ¿Qué días son esas fiestas? 3. ¿Quiénes van a tu casa para celebrarlas? 4. ¿Qué hacen para celebrarlas?

C Complete las siguientes oraciones.

1. Mi fiesta favorita es... 2. Es mi fiesta favorita porque... 3. Para celebrar ese día yo...

Cultura

Días de fiesta y tradiciones en el mundo hispano

Muchos de los días de fiesta y fechas importantes que se celebran en los Estados Unidos también se celebran en los países hispanos, pero con ciertas diferencias. Por ejemplo, la Navidad es una fecha muy importante en ambas° culturas; en los Estados Unidos ése es el día que Santa Claus les lleva regalos a los niños, mientras que en algunos países hispanos es Papá Noel o el Niño Dios. En otros países hispanos los Reyes Magos° son quienes les llevan regalos a los niños el 6 de enero, conocido en el mundo hispano como el Día de los Reyes Magos.

El Día de Acción de Gracias no existe en los países hispanos, pero las familias generalmente se reúnen en Nochebuena y cenan juntos ese día. Los platos que se sirven en esa cena varían de un país a otro. Después de la cena muchas familias van a la misa de medianoche o **Misa del Gallo.**

Las fiestas religiosas son muy importantes en la cultura hispánica. Cada pueblo o ciudad tiene su santo patrón (o santa patrona) y observan su día con ceremonias religiosas, procesiones y, a veces, ferias. Muchos de los hispanos también celebran el día de su santo; por ejemplo, un chico que se llama José celebra su santo el día de San José, o sea° el 19 de marzo. Ese día sus familiares y amigos lo felicitan y algunos le regalan algo, tal como° se hace en los Estados Unidos por el cumpleaños. Algunos calendarios y periódicos muestran los nombres de los santos para cada día.

La Semana Santa es extremadamente importante en los países hispanos. En general las oficinas cierran los jueves al mediodía y no vuelven a abrir hasta el lunes por la mañana. En Andalucía, la región del sur de España, se celebra la Semana Santa de una manera impresionante, especialmente en las ciudades de Sevilla, Granada y Málaga. Durante toda la semana hay procesiones que comienzan por la tarde, casi siempre después de las seis. Algunas no termi-

Una de las procesiones durante la Semana Santa en Sevilla.

ambas *both* Reyes Magos *Wise Men* o sea *that is* como *as*

Estas carretas adornadas «hacen el camino» para llegar al Rocío, un pequeño pueblo de Huelva, donde está la ermita de la Virgen del Rocío. En este pueblo se reúnen cerca de un millón de personas para celebrar la fiesta de la Virgen del Rocío.

nan hasta la madrugada°. Las imágenes religiosas se colocan° en unas andas (plataformas decoradas con plata°, oro, bronce, etc.) que se llevan por las calles. Algunas de estas andas pesan más de tres toneladas y se necesitan más de doscientos hombres para cargarlas°. La combinación del fervor religioso, la música, los miles de velas° y los penitentes encapuchados°, hacen de estas procesiones un espectáculo inolvidable.

Otras ceremonias religiosas, como los bautizos y la primera comunión, son también eventos sociales y para celebrarlos se invita a los parientes y a los amigos más íntimos. Generalmente los invitados le llevan un regalo al niño o niña que bautizan o celebra su comunión.

Los cumpleaños son también importantes en el mundo hispano. En las fiestas de niños frecuentemente hay una piñata. La forma de ésta puede variar (una estrella, un toro°, un payaso°), pero todas tienen caramelos° o dulces y a veces frutas o pequeños regalos. La piñata se cuelga y cada niño trata de romperla con un palo°. Para hacerlo más difícil le cubren los ojos al niño y le dan vueltas° para que no sepa exactamente dónde está la piñata. A veces uno de los adultos mueve la cuerda° donde está colgada la piñata para que los niños no la puedan alcanzar. Cuando finalmente se rompe la piñata caen al suelo todos los caramelos y cada niño trata de conseguir tantos como pueda. En algunos países la piñata tiene un fondo de cartón° con cintas° de colores y cada niño tira° de una para que el fondo caiga.

Cuando una joven cumple los quince años generalmente se celebra esta fecha con **la fiesta de quince** o **quinceañera,** similar a los bailes de *Sweet Sixteen.* Muchas familias hispanas que viven en los Estados Unidos celebran los quince años con una fiesta muy elaborada y formal.

hasta la madrugada *until early morning* se colocan *are placed* plata *silver* cargarlas *carry them* velas *candles* encapuchados *hooded* toro *bull* payaso *clown* caramelos *candies* palo *stick* dan vueltas *spin around* cuerda *cord* carton *cardboard* cintas *ribbons* tira *pulls*

EN CONTEXTO

La abuela recuerda° otros tiempos

remembers

En mi época la vida de la gente° joven era° diferente. No teníamos° la libertad ni las comodidades° que tiene la juventud° hoy en día, pero tampoco teníamos el problema de las drogas y la inconformidad de hoy. Era una vida más tranquila y más sana. Nos reuníamos° en casa de amigos, escuchábamos música, organizábamos fiestas y excursiones, salíamos en grupo y nos divertíamos° mucho. Creo que éramos más felices.

people / was / No. . . We didn't have comforts / youth

Nos. . . *We used to get together*

nos. . . *we had a great time*

Entonces, como no existía la televisión, las familias tenían más tiempo para hablar y los niños no veían esos programas donde hay tanta violencia y sexo. Se respetaba a las personas mayores y había° más seguridad en las calles.

there was

Hasta la música era diferente. Tenía melodía y era más suave y romántica. Además, no tocaban tan alto como hoy en día, ni la gente se movía tanto para bailar. Definitivamente, eran otros tiempos.

¿Verdadero o falso?

Diga si las siguientes oraciones son verdaderas o falsas, según las ideas de la abuela.

1. Antes la gente joven lo pasaba muy bien.
2. Las muchachas no salían de excursión.
3. En esa época el problema de las drogas era serio.
4. Las familias veían buenos programas de televisión.
5. La gente era más conforme entonces.
6. La orquestas de antes tocaban muy alto.
7. Los jóvenes eran más felices.
8. La gente se sentía más segura.

Una familia en el cementerio el Día de los Muertos en la ciudad de México.

ACTIVIDADES

A Complete las siguientes oraciones para describir cómo eran ciertas cosas antes.

Modelo Los aviones eran más... y no tenían...
Los aviones eran más pequeños y no tenían tantos asientos.

1. Las ciudades eran... y tenían...
2. Las casas eran... y no tenían...
3. La gente joven era más... y...
4. Los automóviles eran... y no tenían...
5. La vida era...

B La vida moderna tiene muchas ventajas. Con su compañero/a haga una lista de cinco.

GRAMÁTICA

Preterit and imperfect

English has one past tense, but Spanish, as mentioned in **Lección 12,** has two: the preterit and the imperfect.

English	Spanish	
PAST TENSE	PRETERIT	IMPERFECT
I did	(yo) hice	(yo) hacía

The preterit and imperfect are not interchangeable. When talking about the beginning or end of an event, the Spanish speaker will use the preterit. To talk about (a) the middle or ongoing part of an event or (b) customary or habitual actions in the past, the speaker will use the imperfect.

In the preceding monolog, the grandmother used the imperfect because she was explaining what used to happen (ongoing or habitual actions) when she was young. If she had been talking about what she did yesterday (terminated action), she would have used the preterit.

Some time expressions that are normally used with the imperfect are **mientras, a veces, siempre, generalmente,** and **frecuentemente.**

Imperfect of regular and irregular verbs

	hablar	**comer**	**vivir**
yo	habl**aba**	com**ía**	viv**ía**
tú	habl**abas**	com**ías**	viv**ías**
él, ella, usted	habl**aba**	com**ía**	viv**ía**
nosotros/as	habl**ábamos**	com**íamos**	viv**íamos**
vosotros/as	habl**abais**	com**íais**	viv**íais**
ellos/as, ustedes	habl**aban**	com**ían**	viv**ían**

1. Note that the endings for **-er** and **-ir** verbs are the same and that every verb form has an accent mark over the **í** of the ending.
2. The Spanish imperfect has several English equivalents.

   Mis amigos estudiaban mucho. { *My friends studied a lot.* / *My friends were studying a lot.* / *My friends used to study a lot.* / *My friends would study a lot.* (implying a repeated action) }

3. Stem-changing verbs do not change in the imperfect.

   Ella no **duer**me bien ahora, pero antes **dormía** muy bien.

4. Only three verbs are irregular in the imperfect.

   ir: iba, ibas, iba, íbamos, ibais, iban
   ser: era, eras, era, éramos, erais, eran
   ver: veía, veías, veía, veíamos, veíais, veían

5. The imperfect form of **hay** is **había** (*there was, there were, there used to be*).

Uses of the imperfect

Use the imperfect to

1. express habitual or repeated actions in the past.

   Nosotros **íbamos** a la playa todos los días.

2. express an action that was in progress in the past.

   En esos momentos Agustín **hablaba** con su hermana.

   You may also use the imperfect of **estar** + present participle (imperfect progressive) to emphasize the on-going activity.

   En esos momentos Agustín **estaba hablando** con su hermana.

3. describe characteristics and conditions in the past.

   La casa **era** blanca, con techo rojo, y **tenía** dos dormitorios.

4. tell time in the past.

   Era la una, no **eran** las dos.

5. tell age in the past.

   Ella **tenía** dieciocho años entonces.

ACTIVIDADES

A Diga qué cosas hacía o no hacía usted cuando tenía cinco años.

Modelo vivía cerca de mis primos
Yo vivía (no vivía) cerca de mis primos.

1. vivía con mis padres
2. estudiaba español
3. montaba bicicleta
4. jugaba con mis amigos
5. miraba televisión
6. ayudaba a mi mamá
7. tenía un perro grande
8. iba al cine
9. me acostaba temprano

B **En la escuela secundaria.** Diga con qué frecuencia hacían usted y sus amigos estas cosas.

Modelo organizar excursiones
Frecuentemente (o nunca, o a veces) organizábamos excursiones.

siempre   frecuentemente   a veces   casi nunca   nunca

1. estudiar mucho
2. tener fiestas
3. nadar en la piscina
4. hacer la tarea
5. ir a los partidos de fútbol
6. salir con los amigos
7. almorzar juntos
8. hablar por teléfono

C Hoy en día hacemos muchas cosas que antes no se hacían o no hacemos cosas que antes se hacían. Lea cada oración y diga cómo era la vida antes.

Modelo Hoy en día se viaja mucho en avión.
Antes no se viajaba (mucho) en avión o **Se viajaba poco en avión,** o **Se viajaba en tren.**

1. Hoy en día muchas mujeres trabajan en oficinas.
2. Ahora las chicas salen solas.
3. Ahora se practican muchos deportes.
4. Hoy en día manejamos coches muy rápidos.
5. Ahora muchas personas compran comida congelada (*frozen*).
6. Ahora hay mujeres astronautas.
7. Hoy en día se venden muchos productos japoneses.
8. Hoy en día hay mucha violencia en las películas.

D Lea las siguientes oraciones y decida si debe usar el pretérito o el imperfecto.

1. (Fueron, Eran) las dos de la mañana cuando ellos (llegaron, llegaban) al hotel.
2. La fiesta de quince años que mis padres le (dieron, daban) a mi hermana (fue, era) algo muy especial.
3. Cada Navidad (fuimos, íbamos) a casa de mis abuelos y Papá Noel nos (trajo, traía) muchos regalos.

4. Recuerdo que un año mis padres no le (compraron, compraban) una piñata a mi hermano.
5. Mientras Ernesto (cantó, cantaba) los muchachos (escuchaban, escucharon) con mucha atención.
6. Durante el Carnaval todos (fueron, iban) a la plaza a ver los bailes.
7. El Día de las Madres (llevé, llevaba) a mi mamá a un concierto de rock.
8. Todos los años para la Nochevieja Ester y Martín (fueron, iban) a casa de los Solís y allí (bailaron, bailaban) hasta las dos o las tres de la mañana.

E Lea los siguientes párrafos y complételos con el pretérito o el imperfecto de los verbos entre paréntesis.

La semana pasada Enrique —(1)— una fiesta e —(2)— a todos sus amigos. —(3)— una fiesta sorpresa para celebrar el cumpleaños de su amiga Carmen que —(4)— con él en la universidad. Carmen —(5)— en su tercer año y —(6)— bastante porque las clases —(7)— difíciles.

Enrique —(8)— todos los arreglos (*planning*) desde la comida hasta la música. Cuando Carmen —(9)— a la casa de Enrique todo —(10)— oscuro, pero en el momento en que ella —(11)— a la puerta se —(12)— todas las luces y —(13)— la fiesta. —(14)— una verdadera sorpresa para Carmen.

1. (tener)
2. (invitar)
3. (ser)
4. (estudiar)
5. (estar)
6. (trabajar)
7. (ser)
8. (hacer)
9. (llegar)
10. (estar)
11. (tocar)
12. (encender)
13. (empezar)
14. (ser)

F **Entrevista.** Usted quiere saber cómo era la vida de su compañero/a cuando era pequeño/a. Hágale las siguientes preguntas y comparta la información con la clase.

1. ¿Dónde vivías? 2. ¿Estaba tu casa (apartamento) en el centro o en las afueras? 3. ¿Cómo era tu casa (apartamento)? 4. ¿Dormías solo/a o con algún miembro de tu familia? 5. ¿A qué escuela ibas? 6. ¿Cómo se llamaba tu profesor/a favorito/a? ¿Cómo era? 7. ¿Quién era tu mejor amigo/a? ¿Cómo era? 8. ¿Qué deportes practicabas? 9. ¿Qué programas de televisión veías? 10. ¿Qué te gustaba hacer los fines de semana?

G Piense en las vacaciones cuando usted era pequeño/a y dé la mayor información posible siguiendo el siguiente esquema.

Lugar: nombre, descripción
Personas que iban: número, parientes, amigos
Actividades: día, noche
Actividad favorita: descripción

EN CONTEXTO

El cumpleaños de Amparo

Salen para comprar el vestido.

Caminan por la calle para llegar a la tienda.

Amparo paga 10.000 pesos por el vestido.

Las amigas de Amparo vienen para felicitarla por su cumpleaños. Todos estos regalos son para Amparo.

Preguntas

1. ¿Qué quiere comprar Amparo?
2. ¿Para qué día lo necesita?
3. ¿Para dónde van las chicas?
4. ¿Cuánto paga Amparo por el vestido?
5. ¿Para qué van los amigos a casa de Amparo?
6. ¿Para quién son los regalos?

ACTIVIDADES

A Su compañero/a y usted están organizando una fiesta de sorpresa para celebrar el cumpleaños de una amiga. Hagan una lista de las cosas que tienen que hacer antes de la fiesta.

B Su compañero/a quiere saber las cosas que usted y sus amigos hacían en las fiestas cuando eran pequeños. Conteste las siguientes preguntas.

1. ¿Dónde eran las fiestas?
2. ¿Eran por la tarde o por la mañana?
3. ¿Qué hacían en las fiestas?
4. ¿Cuál era el juego más popular?
5. ¿Qué comían?
6. ¿Adónde iban después de las fiestas?

GRAMÁTICA

Por and *para*

Por and **para** are often translated as *for* or *by,* depending on the context, but they are not interchangeable. Choosing one or the other will affect the meaning of the sentence.

1. Use **por** to

a. indicate exchange or substitution.

Venden la casa **por** $50.000.	*They sell the house for $50,000.*
Cambió ese suéter **por** éste.	*He changed that sweater for this one.*
Andrés va a trabajar **por** mí.	*Andrés is going to work for (instead of) me.*

b. express unit or rate.

Yo camino 5 kilómetros **por** hora.	*I walk 5 kilometers per hour.*
El interés es diez **por** ciento.	*The interest is ten per cent.*
Se vende el pescado **por** kilo.	*Fish is sold by the kilo.*

c. express means of transportation.

Lo mandaron por avión.	*They sent it by plane.*

d. indicate general or imprecise location in space or time.

Está **por** allá.	*It's around there.*
Llegan **por** la noche.	*They'll arrive at (during the) night.*

2. Use **para** to express judgment.

Para nosotros, ésta es la mejor tienda.	*For us, this is the best store.*

Por and *para* contrasted

1. To express movement and destination

por	**para**
passing through or by a place	going toward a place
Caminan **por** la playa.	Caminan **para** la playa.
They walk along the beach.	*They walk towards the beach.*
Maneja por el túnel.	Maneja para el túnel.
He drives through the tunnel.	*He drives towards the tunnel.*

2. To express time

por	**para**
time during which an action takes place	deadline
Lo necesitamos **por** tres meses.	Lo necesitamos **para** el martes.
We need it for three months.	*We need it for Tuesday.*

3. With actions

por	**para**
a. cause or reason why something is done	a. for whom something is intended or done
Compró la casa **por** ella.	Compró la casa **para** ella.
He bought the house because of her.	*He bought the house for her.*
b. followed by a noun to express the object of an errand	b. followed by an infinitive to indicate intention or purpose
Fueron **por** gasolina.	Fueron **para** comprar gasolina.
They went for gas.	*They went to buy gas.*

ACTIVIDADES

A Usted necesita pintar su apartamento y le dice a su amigo cuándo van a estar listas las diferentes partes de la casa.

Modelo cocina / el lunes
La cocina va a estar lista para el lunes.

1. mi dormitorio / el martes
2. la sala / el sábado
3. el baño / el jueves
4. el pasillo / el domingo

B Mire los siguientes dibujos y diga hacia (*towards*) dónde va cada persona y por dónde pasa para llegar allí.

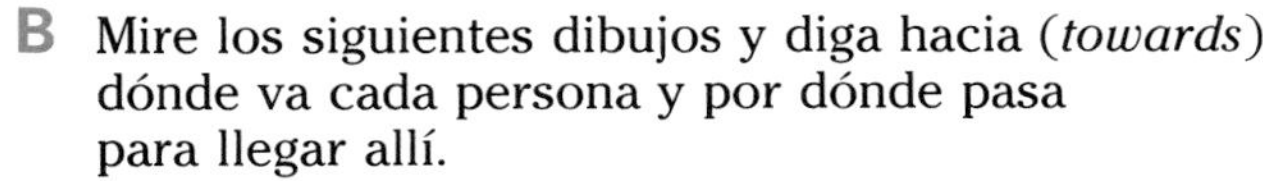

Modelo

El alumno camina por el pasillo.
Él va para su clase de español.

C Las siguientes personas van a diferentes lugares. Use su imaginación y diga para qué van a esos lugares.

Modelo El Sr. Martínez va a la estación de gasolina.
Va para comprar gasolina.

1. Juan va al cine.
2. Mónica y Laura van al gimnasio.
3. Adolfo va a la piscina.
4. Joaquín va al supermercado.
5. Magdalena va al Centro Comercial Los Arcos.
6. Alejandro va a la farmacia.

D Complete el párrafo con **por** o **para** según el contexto.

Pasado mañana es el 24 de septiembre y es el santo de Mercedes. Su madrina, la Sra. de Ortiz, compró un regalo muy bonito ____ Mercedes. La Sra. de Ortiz vive en otra ciudad y quiere que Mercedes reciba el regalo ____ el 24. Ella decide mandarlo ____ avión. ____ la mañana prepara el paquete y sale ____ el correo. Cuando llega al correo va ____ la ventanilla de los paquetes. El empleado lo pesa y le dice que tiene que pagar 500 pesos ____ el paquete.

E Complete cada oración de acuerdo con sus propias experiencias.

1. Para mí, el mejor programa de televisión es... porque...
2. El mes próximo salgo de vacaciones. Voy para... Pienso ir por... Voy a estar allá por...
3. Yo quiero comprarme... Voy a pagar... por...
4. Para el sábado yo tengo que... No sé si voy a hacerlo el viernes por la tarde o...
5. Yo (no) camino... kilómetros por hora. A mí (no) me gusta caminar porque...
6. Mañana es el santo de mi novio/a. Para comprarle un regalo voy a ir a... No quiero pagar más de... por el regalo.
7. Para las Navidades yo quiero que me regalen... Yo prefiero ese regalo porque...
8. Esta noche vamos a celebrar el aniversario de mis padres. Para tener todo listo, por la mañana voy a... y por la tarde voy a...

EN CONTEXTO

Una invitación para una fiesta

Alfonso ¡Qué bueno que las veo! Las iba a llamar esta noche. El sábado es el santo de Antonio, y Magdalena y yo estamos organizando una fiesta en casa.

Josefina ¿Este sábado?

Miriam ¿En qué mundo vives, Josefina? Por supuesto° que sí. Este sábado es 13 de junio. — Por... *Of course*

Josefina ¡Qué barbaridad°! El tiempo vuela. — *It's amazing!*

Alfonso Queríamos invitarlas. ¿Creen que puedan ir?

Josefina Yo, encantada. ¿Y tú, Miriam?

Miriam Lo siento mucho, Alfonso, pero este sábado quedé° en ir a la finca° con mis primos. De todas formas°, gracias por la invitación. — *I agreed* / *farm* / De... *Anyway*

Alfonso Por favor, no le digan nada a Antonio. Va a ser una sorpresa. ¿Te imaginas la cara que va a poner°? — la... *his face*

Miriam ¡Qué pena° no poder verlo! — Qué... *What a pity*

Preguntas

Conteste las siguientes preguntas con la información que se da en el diálogo.

1. ¿Por qué quería Alfonso hablar con las chicas?
2. ¿Para quién es la fiesta?
3. ¿Dónde va a ser?
4. ¿Por qué se organiza la fiesta?
5. ¿Quiénes organizan la fiesta?
6. ¿Puede ir Josefina? ¿y Miriam?
7. ¿Adónde va a ir Miriam este sábado?
8. ¿Por qué no pueden decirle nada a Antonio?

ACTIVIDADES

A ¿Qué dice usted en estas situaciones? Escoja la expresión correcta para cada situación.

1. Lo/La invitan a una fiesta y usted no puede ir.
2. El auto de su amigo no funciona. Él le pregunta si lo puede llevar a su casa y usted va a hacerlo.
3. Lo/la invitan a una fiesta y usted acepta la invitación.
4. Es el santo de una amiga y usted la saluda en una fiesta en su casa.

a. Por supuesto.
b. Lo siento.
c. Felicidades.
d. Encantado/a.

B Su compañero/a lo/la invitó a un concierto, pero usted tiene muy mala memoria y no recuerda la fecha, la hora y el lugar. Pregúntele a su compañero/a y comparta la información con la clase.

C Complete el siguiente diálogo con su compañero/a.

Compañero/a ¡Hola, ____! Te iba a llamar esta noche. Mañana nos vamos a reunir en casa de ____ después del partido de ____. ¿Puedes ir?
Usted No, ____. Quedé en ir a ____. Gracias por la invitación.

Una niña trata de romper una piñata en Matagalpa, Nicaragua.

GRAMÁTICA

Exclamatory *qué*

1. Use **qué** + noun as an equivalent of *what* + *a* + noun.

¡Qué fiesta! — *What a party!*

2. When the noun is modified by an adjective, add **tan** or **más.**

¡Qué fiesta { tan / más } buena! — *What a great party!*

3. Use **qué** + adjective as an equivalent of *how* + adjective.

¡Qué lindo! — *How pretty!*
¡Qué raro! — *How odd!*

Interrogative *qué* and *cuál(es)* with *ser*

1. Use **qué** + **ser** when you want to ask for a definition or an explanation.

—¿Qué es la Nochevieja? —Es el último día del año.

2. Use **cuál(-es)** + **ser** when you want to ask *which one(s).*

—¿Cuál es tu asiento? —Es éste.
—¿Cuáles son tus boletos? —Los dos que están sobre la mesa.

ACTIVIDADES

A Escoja la expresión adecuada de acuerdo con la situación.

1. Hay un león enorme en la clase.
   a. ¡Qué lindo!
   b. ¡Qué horrible!
   c. ¡Qué divertido!
2. Sus tíos van a pagarle un viaje a Europa.
   a. ¡Qué bueno!
   b. ¡Qué pena!
   c. ¡Qué miedo!
3. Usted ve el edificio Empire State por primera vez.
   a. ¡Qué edificio tan feo!
   b. ¡Qué edificio tan alto!
   c. ¡Qué edificio más viejo!

4. Usted conoció a una estudiante encantadora.
   a. ¡Qué simpática!
   b. ¡Qué trabajadora!
   c. ¡Qué rara!
5. Su hermano ganó $5.000.000 en la lotería.
   a. ¡Qué dolor!
   b. ¡Qué suerte!
   c. ¡Qué malo!

B **¿Qué es?** o **¿Cuál es?** Haga las preguntas adecuadas. Uno de sus compañeros/as debe contestar su pregunta.

Modelo la definición de la palabra **Carnaval**

Usted **¿Qué es el Carnaval?**
Compañero/a **Es una fiesta muy importante y divertida.**

el nombre del mejor hotel

Usted **¿Cuál es el mejor hotel?**
Compañero/a **Es el Ritz.**

1. el número de teléfono de su compañero/a
2. la definición de la palabra **teléfono**
3. la explicación de **habitación doble**
4. el número de la habitación doble
5. la definición de **postre**
6. el postre más caro

C Complete el siguiente díalogo con su compañero/a.

Compañero/a ¡Hola, ____! ¿Sabes que ganamos el campeonato de fútbol?
Usted ¡Qué ____! ¿Dónde vamos a celebrarlo?
Compañero/a No lo vamos a celebrar hoy. Juan se cayó en el partido y se torció un tobillo.
Usted ¡Qué ____! ¿Y cómo está?
Compañero/a . . .

LECTURA

Antes de leer: the conditional

Since **Lección 7,** you have used the expression **me gustaría. . .** to express what you would like to do. **Gustaría** is a form of the conditional. It is an easy tense to recognize because it is formed by adding the endings **-ía, ías, ía, íamos, íais, ían** to the infinitive.

	hablar	**comer**	**vivir**
yo	habla**ría**	come**ría**	vivi**ría**
tú	habla**rías**	come**rías**	vivi**rías**
él, ella, usted	habla**ría**	come**ría**	vivi**ría**
nosotros/as	habla**ríamos**	come**ríamos**	vivi**ríamos**
vosotros/as	habla**ríais**	come**ríais**	vivi**ríais**
ellos/as, ustedes	habla**rían**	come**rían**	vivi**rían**

Few verbs are irregular in the conditional. They are the same verbs that are irregular in the future and they have the same stem.

INFINITIVE	NEW STEM	CONDITIONAL FORMS
haber:	habr	habría, habrías, habría, habríamos, habríais, habrían
poder:	podr	podría, podrías, podría, podríamos, podríais, podrían
querer:	querr	querría, querrías, querría, querríamos, querríais, querrían
saber:	sabr	sabría, sabrías, sabría, sabríamos, sabríais, sabrían
poner:	pondr	pondría, pondrías, pondría, pondríamos, pondríais, pondrían
tener:	tendr	tendría, tendrías, tendría, tendríamos, tendríais, tendrían
salir:	saldr	saldría, saldrías, saldría, saldríamos, saldríais, saldrían
venir:	vendr	vendría, vendrías, vendría, vendríamos, vendríais, vendrían
decir:	dir	diría, dirías, diría, diríamos, diríais, dirían
hacer:	har	haría, harías, haría, haríamos, haríais, harían

The use of the conditional in Spanish is similar to the use of the construction *would* + verb in English.[1] The only difference is that Spanish may also use the conditional to express probability in the past.

Yo **saldría** temprano.	*I would leave early.*
Serían las diez de la mañana.	*It was probably ten in the morning.*

The conditional and the imperfect subjunctive are used in *if* sentences expressing a condition that is unlikely to happen or contrary to fact in the present.

Si yo consiguiera el dinero, pagaría la cuenta.	*If I were to get the money I would pay the bill.* (It is unlikely that I get the money.)
Si yo tuviera el dinero, pagaría la cuenta.	*If I had the money, I would pay the bill.* (I don't have the money.)

IDENTIFICACIÓN

Identifique el condicional en las siguientes oraciones.

1. Debería comer más frutas y verduras.
2. Iría a México si tuviera dos semanas de vacaciones.
3. Nosotros vendíamos boletos para los conciertos de rock.
4. Andrés vivía y trabajaba cerca de su casa y por eso no tenía que viajar largas distancias.
5. Dijo que escribiría desde Madrid.

COMPRENSIÓN

Un joven indeciso

Lea la siguiente selección sobre Jorge Hermida, un joven que nunca está muy seguro de lo que debe hacer.

A Jorge le encantaban las fiestas y también le gustaba viajar, pero no tenía mucho dinero. Un día estaba caminando por la calle y pasó por un quiosco donde vendían billetes de lotería. Era el sorteo° más importante del año con un premio de cien millones de pesos. A Jorge le gustó uno de los números y pensó que sería una buena idea comprarlo y probar su suerte. *drawing*

Por su mente° pasaron todas las cosas que podría hacer con el dinero del primer premio. ¿Iría a la India o a Egipto? ¿Visitaría la Antártida o Australia? ¿Cuánto tiempo estaría en la América del Sur? ¿Invitaría a sus amigos a una *mind*

---

[1] When *would* implies *used to,* the imperfect is used. Yo salía temprano. *I would (used to) leave early.*

fiesta en su yate o en un hotel? ¿Qué orquesta tocaría en su fiesta? ¿Se compraría una casa en la playa o un apartamento de lujo en la ciudad? ¿Qué auto deportivo compraría? ¿Qué les regalaría a sus padres? ¿Y a su novia? ¿Cuánto dinero daría a obras de caridad°? ¿Viviría parte del año en Europa o en Hawaii? ¿Cuánto tendría que pagar de impuestos°?

charity
taxes

Todo esto le pareció muy complicado y no compró el billete. Era más fácil vivir con poco dinero y sin complicaciones.

Preguntas

1. ¿Es Jorge rico o pobre?
2. ¿Dónde vio Jorge los billetes de lotería?
3. ¿Cuánto dinero podía ganar?
4. ¿Qué lugares pensaba visitar?
5. ¿Qué prefería Jorge, una casa o un apartamento?
6. ¿Compró Jorge el billete? ¿Por qué?
7. ¿Está usted de acuerdo con lo que hizo Jorge? ¿Por qué?
8. ¿Qué haría usted con cien millones de dólares?

Unos regalos para los novios

En este anuncio se ofrecen ciertas ventajas a los novios que celebren su boda (*wedding*) en un hotel. El anuncio menciona a los padrinos de la boda. En los países hispanos el padrino es la persona que acompaña a la novia al altar. Generalmente es el padre de la novia. La madrina de la boda está en el altar con el novio y generalmente es su madre.

Las siguientes palabras le podrán ayudar a entender mejor el anuncio.

traslado	*transportation*
Dpto.	*abbreviation for* departamento

GRATIS

El Hotel El Dorado los invita a probar el menú de su boda. Venga con los padrinos.

Tenemos una amplia selección desde 4500 pesos

Además, si celebran su boda con nosotros tendrán
- Coche de lujo para su traslado al hotel
- Su noche de bodas en una suite
- Desayuno con champán
- Y un fin de semana en su primer aniversario

Todo Totalmente GRATIS

Vengan a Vernos
Departamento de Banquetes
Hotel El Dorado
Avenida de la Constitución 10
Teléfono 236-8800

¿Verdadero o falso?

Diga si las siguientes oraciones son verdaderas o falsas de acuerdo con el anuncio.

1. El hotel invita a comer sólo a los novios.
2. El menú más barato del hotel cuesta 4.500 pesos.
3. Si los novios celebran la boda en el hotel, reciben un auto de regalo.
4. El hotel les ofrece a los novios una habitación muy elegante sin pagar.
5. Los novios pueden pasar una semana en el hotel.

Las corridas de toros

La siguiente selección es sobre las corridas de toros, un espectáculo emocionante y muy popular en algunos países hispanos.

Se cree que hay que buscar el origen de las corridas de toros en la isla de Creta hace unos 6.000 años y que los gladiadores de Julio César lidiaban° toros en el Coliseo de Roma en el siglo I a.C°. Poco a poco este enfrentamiento de hombre y fiera° fue cambiando hasta llegar a la corrida o fiesta brava tal como existe hoy en día en España y en cinco países hispanoamericanos: México, Perú, Ecuador, Colombia y Venezuela. Portugal y Francia también tienen corridas, pero en estos países no se mata° al toro.

lidiaban° *fought*
siglo... *1st century* B.C.
fiera° *beast*
no... *is not killed*

Una corrida de toros en la ciudad de México.

Las corridas empiezan puntualmente a la hora que indica el programa—a las cuatro y media, cinco o seis de la tarde, para que el sol no sea tan fuerte—y duran° unas tres horas. Generalmente participan tres toreros y cada uno lidia dos toros. Éstos son de una raza agresiva y fuerte que se cría° únicamente para las corridas.

last
se... *is bred*

La entrada de los toreros con sus cuadrillas°, el ritmo alegre y vibrante de la música, la emoción de los aficionados y el duelo entre el torero y el toro crean un ambiente° por completo diferente al que existe en una competencia deportiva.

teams
atmosphere

La fiesta brava tiene sus aficionados y detractores. Para los aficionados, el toreo no es un deporte. Es un arte donde el hombre se enfrenta a la fiera demostrando su destreza° y su valor ante la muerte°. Para sus detractores, es un acto bárbaro e inhumano, donde se tortura y se mata a un animal. Según ellos, deberían prohibirse las corridas pues sólo sirven para mostrar los peores instintos del ser humano y no deberían ser un espectáculo de países civilizados.

dexterity / death

¿Verdadero o falso?

Diga si las siguientes oraciones son verdaderas o falsas según la selección anterior.

1. La corrida de toros existe hace muchos años.
2. Los romanos lidiaban toros.
3. Hay corridas en todos los países hispanos.
4. En una corrida generalmente hay seis toros.
5. Puede usarse cualquier toro en una corrida.
6. Las corridas son por la mañana.
7. Los aficionados creen que la corrida es el mejor deporte.
8. Los detractores de la fiesta brava quieren que no haya corridas.

Para completar

Complete las siguientes oraciones según la información que se da en la selección sobre las corridas.

1. Las corridas de toros empezaron en...
2. En las corridas de Portugal y Francia...
3. Los países hispanos donde hay corridas de toros son...
4. Los toros que se usan en las corridas son...
5. Los aficionados creen que la corrida de toros es...
6. Los detractores creen que la corrida de toros es...

Éste es un pequeño articulo periodístico sobre un día muy especial que se celebra en Madrid. Las siguientes palabras le podrán ayudar a entenderlo mejor.

meta = objetivo lucha *fight*

El domingo se celebra la XI fiesta de la bicicleta

La organización de esta fiesta deportiva espera que participen alrededor de trescientos mil ciclistas. Los aficionados al deporte del pedal ocuparán las calles de Madrid durante tres horas y media, en una fiesta que es ya muy popular entre los madrileños. No se trata de obtener meta alguna, sino de luchar, al menos durante un día, contra el ruido y la contaminación, promover el ejercicio físico y afirmar que la ciudad puede ser una ciudad habitable y solidaria.

Durante estas tres horas, los organizadores recomiendan no utilizar los automóviles por las calles por las que pasará el pelotón deportivo, que recorrerá un total de veintiocho kilómetros.

Preguntas

Conteste las siguientes preguntas sobre el artículo.

1. ¿Cuándo va a ser la fiesta?
2. ¿Cuánto tiempo dura?
3. ¿Cuál es el objetivo de esta fiesta?
4. ¿Cuántas personas van a tomar parte?
5. ¿Qué le piden los organizadores al público?
6. ¿Qué le parece esta fiesta a usted? Explique por qué.

SITUACIONES

1. Invite your partner to a party: (a) give date, time, and location, and (b) say that he/she can bring a friend. Your partner should accept and ask some pertinent questions.
2. Invite your partner to go to a concert. Your partner should decline and explain why.
3. Tell your partner what you used to do for Halloween when you were a child and what you liked the most. Then your partner should tell you about the way he/she celebrated Halloween.
4. You are going to have a party. Tell your partner (a) whom you will invite, (b) the food and drinks you will serve, (c) the music you will have, and (d) what you are going to do afterward.
5. A recent immigrant wants to find out what Thanksgiving is. Explain to that person (a) when it is celebrated, (b) why it is celebrated, (c) how people celebrate it, and (d) what the traditional foods are for that occasion.
6. You don't know what **el Día de los Reyes Magos** is. Ask your partner (a) what it is, (b) when it is celebrated, and (c) where.
7. You were invited to a party. Explain to your partner that you don't want to go because (a) your former girl/boyfriend is going to be there, (b) you don't like to dance, and (c) you have a test the following day. Your partner will try to convince you by telling you that (a) many of your friends are going to be there and (b) you are going to have a good time.

El "Cortijo Bacardí"
tiene el honor de invitarle al
concierto de canto que
ofrecerá la soprano

M.ª José González

acompañada del pianista

Manuel del Campo

que tendrá lugar el
próximo viernes 25 de
Septiembre a las 20,30 h.

"Cortijo Bacardí"
Bacardí y Cía., S. A., España
Polígono Industrial Santa Teresa

Málaga, 1987

Confirmar asistencia
al teléfono 33 02 00

VOCABULARIO[2]

las fiestas

la banda	*band*
la bandera	*flag*
el desfile	*parade*
la sorpresa	*surprise*

las personas

el grupo	*group*
la juventud	*youth*

en el mundo moderno

la comodidad	*comfort*
la droga	*drug*
la inconformidad	*dissatisfaction*
la libertad	*liberty, freedom*
el sexo	*sex*
la violencia	*violence*

la música

la melodía	*melody*

en el campo

la finca	*farm*

tiempo

la época	*time, epoch*
hoy en día	*nowadays*

descripciones

horrible	*horrible*
suave	*soft*
terrible	*terrible*

verbos

celebrar	*to celebrate*
disfrazarse	*to wear a costume*
divertirse (ie, i)	*to have a good time*
existir	*to exist, to be*
felicitar	*to congratulate*
había	*there was, there were*
imaginarse	*to imagine*
mover (ue)	*to move*
organizar	*to organize*
recordar (ue)	*to remember, to remind*
respetar	*to respect*
reunirse	*to get together*

palabras útiles

definitivamente	*definitely*
felicidades	*congratulations*
hasta	*even*

expresiones útiles

de todas formas	*anyway*
estar enamorado/a	*to be in love*
por supuesto	*of course*
¡qué barbaridad!	*it's amazing!, good grief!*
¡qué pena!	*what a pity!*
quedar en + inf.	*to agree to + verb*

[2] See pages 364, 365, and 366 for holidays.

In Lección 16 **you will**
a. describe physical conditions and the environment.
b. report facts in the present and past.
c. express disappointment.
d. give opinions.

Los efectos de un terremoto

Lección 16
Problemas ambientales y catástrofes

¿Una ciudad moderna o un infierno?

ACTIVIDADES

A Complete las siguientes oraciones de acuerdo con el primer dibujo.

1. Si la tierra se movió y se cayeron algunos edificios tuvimos un...
2. Llamamos a los bomberos cuando hay...
3. Una organización que ayuda en casos de emergencia es la...
4. Después de un accidente acuestan a los heridos en...
5. El vehículo que generalmente se usa para llevar a los heridos al hospital es la...

B Complete las siguientes oraciones de acuerdo con el segundo dibujo.

1. Muchas personas se enferman y no pueden respirar bien por...
2. Cuando hay muchos autos que casi no se pueden mover decimos que hay un...
3. A veces las personas tienen dolor de oídos por...
4. Es necesario inspeccionar los autos para controlar...
5. Si un auto le da a otro hay un...

C Diga qué cosas debe hacer o no debe hacer usted en caso de un fuego.

usar el ascensor / abrir todas las puertas interiores / tocar una puerta interior antes de abrirla / si la puerta está caliente, tratar de buscar otra salida / abrir una ventana y pedir ayuda / llamar a los bomberos / poner la televisión para ver un buen programa / si entra humo por debajo de la puerta, poner una toalla húmeda / llamar a los amigos para decirles lo que está pasando / si no puede salir, ponerse en una ventana

D Prepare con su compañero/a una lista de cosas que se deben hacer para evitar la contaminación del aire. Comparen su lista con la de otros compañeros.

Modelo **usar menos el auto**

San Juan, igual que casi todas las ciudades importantes, tiene problemas de tráfico.

Cultura

Catástrofes y problemas ambientales en el mundo hispano

Los países hispanos ocupan grandes extensiones de tierra con diferentes climas y características geográficas. En muchos de estos paises existen los mismos problemas ambientales y catástrofes, pero debido a sus diferentes características geográficas, los problemas también varían.

En la América del Sur, la cordillera° de los Andes se extiende a lo largo de la costa oeste y sus montañas dificultan las comunicaciones entre las diferentes regiones. En algunas el desarrollo agrícola resulta imposible debido a la altura. Pero además los Andes son una zona sísmica muy activa y los terremotos han° afectado extensas zonas de la América del Sur. En 1946, un terremoto destruyó Lima, la capital del Perú, y en 1970 otro terremoto y un alud° causaron unos 50.000 muertos° en este país. En Ecuador, unas 6.000 personas murieron en el terremoto de 1949 y en Colombia, en 1985, la erupción del volcán Nevado del Ruiz causó inundaciones y la ciudad de Armero quedó cubierta por el lodo° con la pérdida° de más de 20.000 vidas. Las imágenes de dolor y muerte que presentó la televisión afectaron a todos los que las vieron al mostrar la destrucción que pueden causar estas catástrofes.

En la América Central y México existe una situación similar. Los terremotos han destruido gran parte de la ciudad de Managua tres veces, en 1885, en 1931 y en 1972. En Guatemala, en 1773, un terremoto destruyó la antigua° capital y en 1976 otro terremoto dejó más de 22.000 muertos y 74.000 heridos. El terremoto de 1985 de la ciudad de México causó unos 4.000 muertos y destruyó muchos edificios dejando sin hogar° a numerosas familias.

Una de las muchas casas y edificios que destruyó el terremoto de 1985 en la ciudad de México.

Además de las catástrofes mencionadas anteriormente, hay también serios problemas ambientales que afectan a muchas ciudades hispanas. Según los expertos, la ciudad de México tiene el peor caso de contaminación del aire del mundo. Hoy en día hay un programa vo-

cordillera *mountain range* han *have* alud *landslide* muertos *dead* lodo *mud* pérdida *loss* antigua *former* hogar *home* luntario para que las personas no usen el automóvil un día a la semana, pero se necesitan medidas más estrictas para proteger la salud de la población y la riqueza° artística y arquitectónica de esta ciudad. Un plan que se propone es la prohibición del tráfico por algunas zonas del centro como el Zócalo (la plaza central) y sus alrededores°, donde se encuentran la catedral, muchos edificios coloniales y los últimos descubrimientos del Templo Mayor de los aztecas. Las Naciones Unidas declararon esta área como patrimonio de la humanidad y debe conservarse para las generaciones futuras.

riqueza *wealth* alrededores *surrounding areas*

Dos hombres socorren a una joven que estuvo enterrada en el lodo, en la ciudad de Armero en Colombia, como resultado de la erupción del volcán Nevado del Ruiz.

EN CONTEXTO

Las últimas noticias°

Las... *The latest news*

Bernardo ¿Han oído° las últimas noticias?

Han... *Have you heard*

Margot No, no hemos oído nada.

Bernardo Hubo° un terremoto en San Salvador. Parece que ha sido muy fuerte.

There was

Teresa ¡Qué horror! ¿Hay muchos muertos y heridos?

Bernardo Todavía no se sabe, pero por lo menos doscientos.

Margot ¡Dios mío! Y como siempre los más afectados van a ser los pobres.

Bernardo Hay muchos edificios destruidos. La Cruz Roja ha mandado tiendas de campaña°. Además están pidiendo donaciones en efectivo, pero se pueden mandar mantas, ropa, medicinas...

ha... *has sent tents*

Teresa Dentro de un rato° empieza el noticiero° de la tarde. ¿Por qué no vamos a casa a verlo?

Dentro... *in a while/newscast*

Preguntas

1. ¿Han oído Margot y Teresa las últimas noticias?
2. ¿Quién les da las noticias?
3. ¿Qué noticias les da?
4. ¿Hay muertos y heridos?
5. ¿Quiénes son siempre los más afectados en los terremotos?
6. ¿Qué ha mandado la Cruz Roja?
7. ¿Qué otras cosas piden?
8. ¿Cuándo va a empezar el noticiero de la tarde?

otras catástrofes

el huracán	*hurricane*
la inundación	*flood*
la lluvia ácida	*acid rain*
la sequía	*drought*
el tornado	*tornado*

La cordillera de los Andes, Chile.

ACTIVIDADES

A Asocie las catástrofes y problemas ambientales de la columna de la izquierda con las acciones de la columna de la derecha.

1. un huracán	a. cerrar puertas y ventanas
2. un terremoto	b. ir al sótano (*cellar*)
3. una inundación	c. no gastar mucha agua
4. una sequía	d. buscar lugares altos
5. un tornado	e. ponerse debajo de una mesa o del marco de una puerta

B ¿Qué debemos hacer durante un terremoto? Prepare una lista con su compañero/a y compárela con la de otros/as estudiantes.

C **Entrevista.** Hágale las siguientes preguntas a su compañero/a para saber su opinión sobre los noticieros de la televisión.

1. ¿A qué hora ves el noticiero? 2. ¿En qué canal de la televisión? 3. ¿Ves el noticiero los fines de semana? 4. ¿Crees que los noticieros de la televisión son imparciales y objetivos? 5. ¿Qué harías para mejorar los noticieros?

GRAMÁTICA

The past participle

INFINITIVE	PAST PARTICIPLE
hablar	hablado (*spoken*)
comer	comido (*eaten*)
vivir	vivido (*lived*)

1. All past participles of **-ar** verbs end in **-ado.**
2. Past participles of **-er** and **-ir** verbs end in **-ido,** except the following:

hacer	hecho	abrir	abierto
poner	puesto	escribir	escrito
romper (*to break*)	roto	cubrir	cubierto
ver	visto	decir	dicho
volver	vuelto	morir	muerto

3. Compounds of verbs with irregular past participles normally have the same irregularity.

describir → descrito   posponer → pospuesto

4. If the stem of an **-er** or **-ir** verb ends in **a, e,** or **o,** place a written accent mark over the **i** of **ido** to indicate that no diphthong is formed.

traer → traído   creer → creído   oír → oído

The present perfect

Form the present perfect of the indicative by using the present tense of **haber** (*to have*) as an auxiliary verb with the past participle of the main verb. **Tener** is never used as auxiliary verb in forming the perfect tenses.

	PRESENT TENSE **haber**		PAST PARTICIPLE
yo	he		
tú	has		hablado
él, ella, usted	ha	+	comido
nosotros/as	hemos		vivido
vosotros/as	habéis		
ellos/as, ustedes	han		

1. In general, you can use the present perfect in Spanish in the same instances that you would use the present perfect in English.
2. Normally no word intervenes between the auxiliary verb **haber** and the past participle.

Yo nunca **he estado** aquí.   *I have never been here.*

3. Place object and reflexive pronouns before the auxiliary verb **hacer.**

—¿Has visto a Juan? —No, no **lo** he visto.
—¿**Se** han lavado? —Sí, ya **nos** hemos lavado.

4. The present perfect of **hay** is **ha habido.**

Ha habido mucha contaminación últimamente.   *There has been a lot of smog lately.*

5. Use the present tense of **acabar** + **de** + infinitive, not the present perfect, to state that something *has just* happened.

Acabo de oír las noticias.   *I've just heard the news.*

ACTIVIDADES

A Dígale a su compañero/a las cosas que usted no ha hecho de cada grupo. Después su compañero/a debe decirle a usted las cosas que él/ella no ha hecho.

1. Yo nunca he estado en
   a. un terremoto.
   b. un tornado.
   c. un huracán.
2. Yo nunca he montado en
   a. bicicleta.
   b. avión.
   c. un elefante.
3. Yo nunca he corrido en
   a. las Olimpiadas.
   b. el estadio de la universidad.
   c. un parque.
4. Yo nunca he visto
   a. una jirafa.
   b. un cocodrilo.
   c. una llama.
5. Yo nunca he roto
   a. un plato.
   b. un vaso.
   c. un estéreo.
6. Yo nunca he dicho
   a. una mala palabra.
   b. una mentira.
   c. palabras en chino.

B Usted ha estado muy ocupado/a hoy. Diga que usted ha hecho todo lo que sigue.

Modelo preparar el desayuno
He preparado el desayuno.

1. terminar la tarea
2. escuchar un casete
3. limpiar la casa
4. correr por el parque
5. oír las noticias
6. ir al mercado
7. leer el periódico
8. ver televisión
9. escribirle a una amiga
10. lavarse los dientes dos veces

C Pregúntele a su compañero/a si ha hecho lo siguiente.

Modelo estudiar las lecciones
Usted **¿Has estudiado las lecciones hoy?**
Compañero/a **Sí, ya he estudiado las lecciones** o **Sí, ya las he estudiado** o **No, no las he estudiado todavía.**

1. ir a la biblioteca
2. comer
3. hablar con tu profesor
4. hacer ejercicio
5. comprar los libros nuevos

D Joaquín es un atleta excelente. Dígale a su compañero/a cinco cosas que ha hecho para ser tan buen atleta.

Modelo **Joaquín ha practicado todos los días.**

E Usted y un/a amigo/a van a hacer un viaje, pero no han organizado nada. Su compañero/a le va a hacer las siguientes preguntas. Conteste diciendo que no lo han hecho todavía.

Modelo Compañero/a **¿Han hecho las reservaciones?**
Usted **No las hemos hecho todavía.**

1. ¿Han ido a la agencia de viajes?
2. ¿Han llamado a la línea aérea?
3. ¿Han hecho las maletas?
4. ¿Han comprado los cheques de viajero?
5. ¿Qué han hecho entonces?

F Usted es el jefe/la jefa de una oficina y quiere saber si sus empleados han hecho las siguientes cosas. Su compañero/a va a hacer el papel de su secretario/a.

Modelo terminar el proyecto
Usted **¿Terminaron el proyecto?**
Secretario/a **Sí, ya lo terminaron** o **Todavía no lo han terminado.**

1. traer el papel de cartas
2. programar la computadora
3. hacer las fotocopias
4. llamar a los clientes
5. invitar al Sr. Alonso
6. pedir los programas

G Dígale a su compañero/a todo lo que usted ha hecho esta mañana.

H Ha habido un terremoto y su padre le pide que haga varias cosas. Dígale que Ud. acaba de hacerlas.

Modelo Padre **Hijo/a, llena la bañera de agua.**
Usted **Acabo de llenarla, papá.**

1. Desconecta la electricidad.
2. Apaga el gas.
3. Llama a tus abuelos.
4. Pregúntales a los vecinos si necesitan algo.
5. Pon a los animales en el garaje.
6. Revisa (*check*) la casa.

I Sus amigos salen de diferentes lugares. ¿Qué cree usted que acaban de hacer?

Modelo Juan sale del estadio.
Acaba de ver un partido de fútbol.

1. Maricarmen sale de una discoteca.
2. Pedro sale de un café.
3. Mercedes y Paula salen de la biblioteca.
4. Humberto sale de la cocina.
5. Jorge y Ricardo salen de una tienda.

EN CONTEXTO

Los efectos de un huracán

El huracán va a pasar por la ciudad. Los vecinos están asustados y se están preparando.

A las cinco el huracán había pasado por la ciudad. El supermercado está destruido. Las calles están inundadas. Los cristales de algunas ventanas están rotos.

ACTIVIDADES

A Usted está de vacaciones en casa de unos amigos en Miami. Según las últimas noticias, es probable que un huracán pase esa noche por la ciudad. Para estar preparados, diga qué cosas de la siguiente lista deben o no deben hacer.

Modelo poner al gato en la terraza
No debemos poner al gato en la terraza.

1. comprar comida
2. sacar el auto del garaje
3. tener una linterna (*flashlight*)
4. dejar al perro en el jardín
5. cubrir las ventanas
6. ir al cine
7. cerrar bien las puertas
8. tener agua en la casa
9. comprar pilas (*batteries*)
10. sacar la basura a la acera

B Piense en una experiencia o momento difícil de su vida (accidente, terremoto, etc.). Dígale a otro/a estudiante (a) cuál fue su experiencia, (b) cuándo ocurrió, (c) dónde ocurrió y (d) qué hizo usted.

GRAMÁTICA

The past perfect

Form the past perfect with the imperfect tense of **haber** as an auxiliary verb and the past participle of the main verb.

	IMPERFECT **haber**		PAST PARTICIPLE
yo	había		
tú	habías		hablado
él, ella, usted	había	+	comido
nosotros/as	habíamos		vivido
vosotros/as	habíais		
ellos/as, ustedes	habían		

1. In general, you can use the past perfect in Spanish as you would use the past perfect in English.
2. The past perfect describes an action completed in the past before another event.

La fiesta **había terminado** cuando llegamos.	*The party had ended when we arrived.*
Todos **se habían ido** a las dos.	*Everyone had left at two.*

Past participles used as adjectives

1. When a past participle is used as an adjective, it agrees with the noun it modifies.

un apartamento **alquilado**	*a rented apartment*
una puerta **cerrada**	*a closed door*
los libros **abiertos**	*the open books*
las ventanas **rotas**	*the broken windows*

2. Spanish uses **estar** + the past participle to express a state or condition resulting from a prior action.

ACTION	RESULT
El huracán destruyó el edificio.	El edificio está **destruido.**
El terremoto asustó a la gente.	La gente estaba **asustada.**

3. Use **estar** + past participle to describe a position. In this case English uses an *-ing* verb.

El señor está **parado.** — *The man is standing.*
La gente estaba **sentada.** — *The people were sitting.*

ACTIVIDADES

A Usted llega tarde a una fiesta. Diga qué habían hecho los invitados antes de que usted llegara.

Modelo bailar salsa
Ya habían bailado salsa.

1. escuchar a Julio Iglesias
2. comerse toda la comida
3. irse muchas personas
4. hablar de los exámenes
5. cantar canciones cubanas
6. tomarse todos los refrescos
7. ver un vídeo
8. contar chistes (*tell jokes*)

B Pregúntele a su compañero/a lo que había hecho antes de 1990.

Modelo Usted **¿Habías ido a Europa?**
Compañero/a **Sí, ya había ido en 1989.**

1. vivir en tu propio apartamento
2. estar en un terremoto
3. comprar un auto
4. estudiar una lengua extranjera
5. viajar en avión
6. hacer un viaje largo
7. ganar mucho dinero
8. jugar vóleibol
9. visitar otros estados
10. tomar buenas fotos

C Ayer fue un día muy feliz para la Sra. Jiménez. Cuando ella volvió a su casa después del trabajo encontró que no tenía que hacer nada en la casa. Diga qué habían hecho los diferentes miembros de la familia.

Modelo su esposo / cocinar para toda la familia
Su esposo había cocinado para toda la familia.

1. su madre / lavar la ropa sucia
2. su hija Carmen / limpiar la casa
3. su hijo mayor / poner la mesa
4. su hijo menor / sacar al perro
5. su hija Diana / hacer su postre favorito

D Ayer fue un día terrible para usted. Diga las cosas que habían pasado cuando llegó a su casa.

1. Mi perro...
2. Mi vecino...
3. Mi hermano/a...
4. El cartero...
5. Mi novio/a...

E Usted entra en el cuarto de su mejor amigo/a y observa que está muy desordenado (*messy*). Diga cómo están los objetos de la columna de la izquierda usando **(no) está(n)** y la forma correcta de los participios de la columna de la derecha.

Modelo la puerta del armario   abierto
La puerta del armario está abierta

el espejo del armario	roto
la cama	tendido
los libros de las clases	abierto
la ropa	colgado
el televisor	encendido
las ventanas	cerrado

F Un huracán terrible pasó por la ciudad. Usted llega al día siguiente y ve los efectos del haracán. Descríbale a un/a amigo/a lo que usted vio.

Modelo Inundó las calles.
Las calles estaban inundadas.

1. Rompió las ventanas de las casas.
2. Destruyó muchos edificios.
3. Tumbó (*knocked down*) muchos árboles.
4. Interrumpió las comunicaciones.
5. Asustó a los animales.
6. Dañó (*damaged*) muchos autos y camiones.

G Usted le va a describir una fiesta a su compañero/a. Trate de usar algunos participios en su descripción.

Modelo **Hay tres chicos parados al lado del estéreo.**

EN CONTEXTO

Peligro° de incendio

Danger

Guardia	Lo siento mucho, pero tienen que apagar° el fuego.	*put out*
Miguel	Está bien, pero siempre hemos encendido el fuego aquí.	
Guardia	Sí, pero no llueve hace varios meses y el bosque° está muy seco°. Por eso se prohíbe hacer fuegos aquí. Es muy peligroso porque todo esto se puede quemar° fácilmente.	*forest* / *dry* / *burn*
Hugo	¡Qué pena! ¿Y qué vamos a hacer con toda esta carne?	
Guardia	Se la pueden llevar° a un lugar un poco más arriba°. Allí hay barbacoas y se puede cocinar sin peligro.	Se... *You can take it* / más... *higher up*
Mariana	Pues a guardar° la comida y recoger° los platos.	*put away* / *pick up*
Hugo	Y yo apago el fuego.	
Guardia	Disculpen la molestia°.	Disculpen... *Sorry for the inconvenience*
Miguel	No se preocupe. Hay que evitar los incendios.	

Para completar

Complete las siguientes oraciones con la información que se da en el diálogo.

1. Los jóvenes están...
2. El guardia les dice que deben...
3. Hace varios meses que...
4. El bosque está...
5. Las barbacoas están...
6. Allí se puede cocinar sin...
7. Los muchachos van a guardar...
8. Ellos quieren evitar...

ACTIVIDADES

A Usted y su compañero/a van a hacer una excursión a un bosque. Hagan una lista de las cosas que van a llevar.

B Cuando usted era pequeño/a usted pertenecía a los niños/as exploradores/as (*Boy/Girl Scouts*). Diga las cosas que ustedes hacían.

C Usted está a cargo de una casa muy antigua que está abierta al público. En la casa no se permite fumar, pero uno de los visitantes está fumando. Complete el siguiente diálogo con su compañero/a.

Usted Lo siento, pero ____.
Visitante Perdone, no lo sabía. ¿Dónde ____?
Usted Se puede fumar en ____.
Visitante ¿Dónde está ____?
Usted ...

Unos niños exploradores en la ciudad de Mérida en Yucatán. En esta región de México se pueden visitar muchas de las ciudades que los mayas construyeron antes de la llegada de los españoles.

GRAMÁTICA

Direct and indirect object pronouns

1. When both a direct and an indirect object pronoun are used in the same sentence, the indirect object pronoun precedes the direct object pronoun.

a. Place double object pronouns before conjugated verbs and negative commands.

Ella me da el libro. ⟶ Ella **me lo** da.
No me des el libro. ⟶ No **me lo** des.

b. Place them after and attach to affirmative commands, infinitives, and present participles. Note the written accent over the stressed syllable.

Dame el libro. ⟶ Dá**melo**.
Él quiere darme el libro. ⟶ Él quiere dár**melo**.
Él **me lo** quiere dar.
Está comprándote el libro. ⟶ Está comprándo**telo**.
Te lo está comprando.

2. This combination of direct and indirect object pronouns is often used when the direct object noun has already been mentioned.

—¿**Me** prestas **el libro**? —Sí, **te lo** presto. *"Would you lend me the book?" "Yes, I'll lend it to you."*

—¿Va a dar**te la mesa**? —Sí, va a dár**mela.** *"Is he going to give you the table?" "Yes, he's going to give it to me."*

—¿**Le** pido **un taxi**? —Sí, pída**melo,** por favor. *"Shall I call you a taxi?" "Yes, call it for me, please."*

3. Le or **les** cannot be used with **lo, los, la,** or **las.** Change **le** or **les** to **se.**

Le da **un regalo.** ⟶ **Se lo** da. *He gives it to her.*
Les voy a mandar **una tarjeta.** ⟶ **Se la** voy a mandar. *I'm going to send it to them.*

4. You may use the prepositional phrase **a** + pronoun to clarify or emphasize the indirect object pronoun.

—Alfredo **me lo** dio a **mí.** *"Alfredo gave it to me."*
—No, él **se lo** dio a **ella**. *"No, he gave it to her."*

5. When a direct object pronoun and a reflexive pronoun are together, the reflexive pronoun precedes the direct object pronoun.

Me lavo **las manos.** ⟶ **Me las** lavo.
Juan **se** lava **la cara**. ⟶ **Se la** lava.

ACTIVIDADES

A Unas personas necesitan varias cosas que Agustín tiene. Usted debe decir si Agustín se las presta o no, escogiendo la respuesta adecuada entre las que se dan en la columna de la derecha.

Modelo Juan necesita unos discos.
Sí, se los presta o **No, no se los presta.**

1. Alfredo necesita una chaqueta.
2. Nuria necesita seiscientas pesetas.
3. Sus hermanos necesitan un diccionario.
4. Narciso necesita diez dólares.

a. Sí, se lo presta. No, no se lo presta.
b. Sí, se la presta. No, no se la presta.
c. Sí, se los presta. No, no se los presta.
d. Sí, se las presta. No, no se las presta.

B Ha habido un terremoto muy fuerte en la ciudad de Guatemala. Su compañero/a le pregunta si la Cruz Roja va a mandar ciertas cosas. Conteste usando los pronombres de objeto directo e indirecto.

Modelo Compañero/a ¿La Cruz Roja les va a mandar camillas?
Usted **Sí, se las va a mandar** o **No, no se las va a mandar.**

1. ¿La Cruz Roja les va a mandar mantas?
2. ¿Les va a mandar dinero?
3. ¿Les va a mandar antibióticos?
4. ¿Les va a mandar tiendas de campaña?
5. ¿Les va a mandar ropa?
6. ¿Les va a mandar zapatos?

C Conteste las siguientes preguntas de acuerdo con los dibujos.

Modelo

¿Le explica la lección al director?
No, no se la explica a él.
¿Les explica la lección a los alumnos?
Sí, se la explica a ellos.

1. ¿Le da un regalo a su madre?
   ¿Le da un regalo a su profesor?
   ¿Le da un regalo a su novia?

2. ¿Les escribe una carta a sus padres?
   ¿Le escribe una carta a su mejor amiga?
   ¿Le escribe una carta a su novio?

3. ¿Les sirve la comida a sus amigas?
   ¿Les sirve la comida a los clientes?
   ¿Les sirve la comida a sus hijos?

D **Diálogo.** Usted trabaja de guía de turismo en Buenos Aires. Su jefe/a le va a hacer las siguientes preguntas.

Jefe/a ¿Les mostró la ciudad a los turistas?
Usted Sí, ____.
Jefe/a ¿Les explicó la historia de la ciudad?
Usted ...
Jefe/a ¿Les contestó las preguntas?
Usted ...
Jefe/a ¿Les llevó el equipaje al hotel?
Usted ...

E Usted está en un hotel muy elegante. El botones lo/la ha llevado a su habitación y le hace las siguientes preguntas.

Modelo ¿Le dejo la llave sobre la cómoda?
Sí, déjemela allí, por favor.

1. ¿Le abro la ventana?
2. ¿Le enciendo el aire acondicionado?
3. ¿Le pongo el equipaje aquí?
4. ¿Le traigo el periódico?

F Su amigo/a está enfermo/a y usted va a su apartamento para ayudarlo/a. Complete el siguiente diálogo con su compañero/a.

Usted ¿Te tiendo la cama?
Amigo/a . . .
Usted ¿Te traigo agua?
Amigo/a . . .
Usted ¿Te preparo algo de comer?
Amigo/a . . .

Una ambulancia en una calle de Mérida.

LECTURA

Antes de leer: the passive voice

In the following reading selection, you will encounter the passive voice, which is formed with any tense of the verb **ser** + past participle.

El humo **era producido** por las fábricas. *The smoke was produced by the factories.*

1. Use the preposition **por** when telling who performs the action.

El bosque fue destruido. (*who or what did it is not expressed*)
El bosque fue destruido **por** el fuego. (*the fire did it*)

2. The past participle agrees in gender and number with the subject.

Los árboles fueron **destruidos** por la lluvia ácida.
La casa fue **construida** el año pasado.

3. The passive voice is more common in English than in Spanish. It is found in written Spanish, especially in newspapers and formal writing. However, in conversation, Spanish speakers normally use other constructions.

Vendieron el edificio. *They sold the building.*
Se vendió el edificio. *The building was sold.*

IDENTIFICACIÓN

Identifique la voz pasiva en las siguientes oraciones.

1. Las fábricas producen mucho humo.
2. La contaminación es estudiada por los científicos.
3. Los países fueron afectados seriamente.
4. El muchacho se fue a estudiar.
5. Los atletas son entrenados por expertos.

Murió víctima de un sabotaje

La siguiente selección fue tomada de una noticia sobre un accidente aéreo que apareció en el periódico español *ABC*. Como usted podrá ver, las oraciones que se usan en los periódicos hispanos son generalmente más largas que las que se usan en los periódicos escritos en inglés.

Las siguientes palabras le podrán ayudar a entender mejor el artículo.

dictamen	*opinion*
mediante	*by means of*
descarta	*rejects*
escombros	*debris*

Murió víctima de un sabotaje

Éste es el dictamen de la comisión investigadora que ayer hizo público su informe en el que deja completamente claro que el accidente aéreo fue provocado mediante un acto de sabotaje por una persona o grupo desconocidos.

El informe descarta el error humano, señala que el aparato no fue alcanzado por ningún misil, y en base a los restos de antimonio, sodio y potasio encontrados en cantidades anormales entre los escombros del avión dictamina que la única probabilidad que explique el suceso es un sabotaje.

¿Verdadero o falso?

Diga si las siguientes oraciones son verdaderas o falsas de acuerdo con la selección.

1. La comisión investigadora ya sabe quién atacó al avión.
2. Un error humano fue la causa del accidente.
3. Los restos de sodio y potasio ayudaron a descubrir la causa del accidente.

LA ECOLOGÍA

En los últimos años ha aumentado notablemente el interés en la ecología y muchas personas en diferentes países se preocupan ante la situación alarmante que se observa en algunas partes de este planeta.

Durante muchos años, los seres humanos han vivido sin preocuparse por el medio ambiente° (*environment*). Los ríos, los lagos y el aire que respiramos son contaminados por las industrias. Los derrames de petróleo han causado la muerte de peces° y aves° (*fish / birds*), especialmente en las costas. Además se han cortado árboles y se han dejado zonas extensas sin replantar, lo que ha aumentado la erosión y ha disminuido las lluvias. Como consecuencia, las tierras° (*land*) áridas y los desiertos han aumentado en muchos lugares. Por ejemplo, hoy en día en España, se considera que el 25% de su superficie es desierto, mientras que antes las zonas desérticas sólo ocupaban el 8%.

Los grupos ecologistas piensan que todo esto, unido a la lluvia ácida que ha afectado a diversas zonas, es un problema que tenemos que resolver ahora, pues hemos vivido muchos años sin hacer nada para mejorar° (*improve*) la situación.

La ecología

Preguntas

1. ¿Quiénes se preocupan mucho por el medio ambiente?
2. ¿Qué han hecho muchas industrias?
3. ¿Por qué han muerto muchos peces y aves?
4. ¿Qué pasa cuando se cortan muchos árboles y no se replantan?
5. ¿Ha aumentado la zona de desierto en España?
6. Según los grupos ecologistas, ¿cuándo debemos resolver estos problemas?

OPINIONES

Complete las siguientes oraciones dando su opinión sobre los diferentes temas.

1. Yo creo que es importante tener parques nacionales porque. . .
2. Es necesario mejorar el aire en las ciudades porque. . .
3. Todos debemos cuidar los árboles porque. . .
4. Yo creo que en los aviones (no) se debe prohibir que las personas fumen porque. . .

The present perfect subjunctive

Another tense that you should recognize is the present perfect subjunctive. It is formed with the present subjunctive of the verb **haber** + past participle.

PRESENT SUBJUNCTIVE **haber**		PAST PARTICIPLE
haya		
hayas		hablado
haya	+	comido
hayamos		vivido
hayáis		
hayan		

Use this tense to express a completed action in sentences which require the subjunctive. Its English equivalent is normally *have* + past participle, but it may vary according to the context.

Ojalá que **haya nevado.**	*I hope it has snowed.*
Me alegro que **hayan llegado** temprano.	*I'm glad they arrived early.*
Es posible que **hayas ganado.**	*It's possible you may have won.*

IDENTIFICACIÓN

Identifique el presente perfecto de subjuntivo en las siguientes oraciones.

1. Es necesario que haya más información sobre terremotos.
2. Ojalá que hayan venido a vernos.
3. Han dicho que es un problema serio.
4. Es posible que haya visitado ese lugar.
5. Dudo que haya visto el derrame.

La siguiente selección trata sobre los terremotos y sus efectos físicos y sicológicos.

Los efectos de un terremoto

Las personas que no han experimentado un terremoto piensan básicamente en la destrucción física que éste ocasiona. Los noticieros de la televisión y las fotos que ven en periódicos y revistas les muestran los edificios destruidos, las familias sin hogar°, las personas heridas o muertas. El impacto, como es natural, es muy fuerte, pero pronto olvidan lo que han visto. En cambio°, cualquier persona que haya estado en un terremoto nunca olvidará la experiencia, pues los terremotos, además de la destrucción física, también pueden causar muchos trastornos° sicológicos.

Aunque hoy en día existen edificios diseñados para resistir un temblor°, la destrucción causada por un terremoto puede adquirir proporciones catastróficas. Caminos, carreteras, puentes°, en fin, toda la infraestructura necesaria para las comunicaciones sufre serios daños°.

Probablemente es imposible determinar todos los efectos de un terremoto en las personas. Los niños que hayan experimentado un sismo° pueden sufrir de una variedad de síntomas: no pueden dormir, no quieren ir al baño solos, tienen alguna erupción en la piel o sufren crisis emocionales. En cambio, hay otros niños que no muestran ningún efecto, pero cuando hay otro temblor experimentan síntomas parecidos a los de los primeros. Cuando se pueda saber con anticipación el momento en que va a ocurrir un terremoto se podrán evitar efectos tanto físicos como sicológicos.

sin... *homeless*
En... *On the other hand*
disorders
earthquake
bridges
damages
earthquake

¿Verdadero o falso?

Diga si las siguientes oraciones son verdaderas o falsas, de acuerdo con la selección.

1. Las personas que han estado en un terremoto pueden olvidar esta experiencia fácilmente.
2. Los periódicos, las revistas y la televisión muestran los daños físicos que producen los temblores.
3. Los terremotos pueden afectar sicológicamente a las personas.
4. La destrucción física es más seria que la psicológica.
5. Todos los niños presentan los mismos síntomas después de un terremoto.
6. Hay niños que sólo muestran trastornos sicológicos después de estar en un segundo temblor.

ORENSE, 38 -Suites-

Estimado Cliente:

¡ Bienvenido a ORENSE, 38 -Suites- !

La Dirección de este establecimiento junto con su equipo queremos agradecerle su confianza al elegir nuestro Hotel.

Permítanos Recomendarle:

EN CASO DE INCENDIO

Si descubre un incendio:

1.—Comunique rápidamente a Recepción la situación del fuego.

2.—Mantenga la calma, no grite ni corra.
Si se prende su ropa, tiéndase en el suelo y ruede.
Si hay humo abundante gatee.

3.—Abandone su habitación CERRANDO LA PUERTA.
Sitúese en el cuadro indicativo de situación y localice la escalera más próxima.

4.—No utilice los ascensores.

5.—Si los pasillos están bloqueados ponga ropa húmeda en todas las ranuras de su habitación, puerta, aire acondicionado, etc.

6.—Hágase ver por la ventana si es posible sin abrir ésta.

Si usted fuma, no deje el cigarro encendido al acostarse, puede ocasionar un incendio involuntariamente.

Estamos a su entera disposición en cualquier momento de su estancia en esta, SU CASA, o en esta su CIUDAD. No dude en ponerse en contacto con NOSOTROS en cualquier situación anómala.

La Dirección

SITUACIONES

1. Tell the person sitting next to you (a) that he/she cannot smoke in this area, (b) point out where smoking is permitted, and (c) apologize for the inconvenience.
2. You have been asked to submit a list of things that can be done to improve the environment. Prepare a list with your partner and share it with the class.
3. You are interviewing a famous Spanish writer who lives in the United States. Ask (a) how long ago he/she wrote the first novel, (b) how many he/she has written, (c) how long he/she has been living here, and (d) what his/her favorite book is.
4. You have noticed a fire across the street from your house. You should (a) call the Fire Department, (b) explain what you see, and (c) give them the address. Your partner will answer the phone and ask you some pertinent questions.
5. Some visitors have lit a fire in an area of the forest where fires are prohibited. You will play the part of the forest ranger, and two of your classmates will play the part of the visitors. You should (a) greet the visitors, (b) tell them that fires are prohibited in that area, (c) explain why, (d) ask them to put out the fire, and (e) apologize for the inconvenience and say goodbye. Your classmates should answer accordingly.
6. Tell your partner about an earthquake: (a) when it happened, (b) where you were, and (c) what the condition of the streets, buildings, and people was. Your partner should ask some pertinent questions.

7. You are a client of Banco de Bilbao in Spain and you have been asked to answer a survey regarding the bank's services. Answer the survey according to your experiences at the bank. Then tell your partner (a) what the bank or employees have done to deserve your rating and (b) your suggestions for improvement. You may need the following words to better understand the questionnaire.

atender	*to take care of*
asunto/gestión	*matter, business*
tramitación	*transaction*

Rellene, por favor, el siguiente cuestionario, señalando con una X la casilla correspondiente.

REFIRIENDOSE, CONCRETAMENTE, A LA GESTION O CONSULTA QUE HA REALIZADO HOY EN ESTA OFICINA.

1. ¿Cómo le hemos atendido?
   - Mal ☐ (1)
   - Regular ☐ (2)
   - Bien ☐ (3)
   - Muy bien ☐ (4)

2. ¿Hemos sido rápidos en dar respuesta a su necesidad, problema o consulta?
   - Nada ☐ (1)
   - Poco ☐ (2)
   - Normal ☐ (3)
   - Mucho ☐ (4)

3. ¿Hemos sido amables al atenderle en su problema o necesidad?
   - Nada ☐ (1)
   - Poco ☐ (2)
   - Bastante ☐ (3)
   - Mucho ☐ (4)

4. ¿Ha encontrado facilidades en la tramitación de los asuntos que le han traído a esta oficina?
   - No ☐ (1)
   - A medias ☐ (2)
   - Sí ☐ (3)

5. ¿Ha resuelto las gestiones que le han traído hoy a esta oficina del Banco de Bilbao?
   - No ☐ (1)
   - A medias ☐ (2)
   - Sí, totalmente ☐ (3)

OFICINA DEL BB DONDE HA HECHO LA GESTION

Municipio .... Agencia ....

Fecha .... Hora ....

MUCHAS GRACIAS POR SU COLABORACION. DEPOSITE EL CUESTIONARIO CUMPLIMENTADO EN EL BUZON MAS PROXIMO. NO NECESITA FRANQUEO.

VOCABULARIO[1]

las catástrofes — *disasters*
el derrame de petróleo — *oil spill*
el huracán — *hurricane*
la inundación — *flood*
la lluvia ácida — *acid rain*
la sequía — *drought*
el terremoto — *earthquake*
el tornado — *tornado*

la atención médica — *medical care*
la camilla — *stretcher*
el herido — *injured person*

los incendios — *fires*
el fuego — *fire*
el humo — *smoke*
el peligro — *danger*

la ayuda — *aid*
la Cruz Roja — *Red Cross*
la donación — *donation*
la tienda de campaña — *tent*

la información — *information*
el noticiero — *newscast*

el tráfico
la contaminación del aire/el smog — *smog*
el choque — *accident*
el embotellamiento — *traffic jam*
las emisiones de los coches — *car emissions*

personas
guardia — *guard*
vecino — *neighbor*

descripciones
ambiental — *environmental*
peligroso — *dangerous*
seco — *dry*

verbos
acabar — *to finish*
  acabar + de + inf. — *to have just* + past participle
afectar — *to affect*
apagar — *to put out, to turn off*
destruir — *to destroy*
encender (ie) — *to light, to turn on*
guardar — *to put away*
hubo — *there was, there were*
inundar — *to inundate, to flood*
prepararse — *to get ready*
quemar — *to burn*
recoger — *to put away, to pick up*
romper — *to break, to tear*

expresiones útiles
dentro de un rato — *in a while*
disculpe la molestia — *sorry for the inconvenience*

[1] For irregular past participles see page 396.

In Lección 17 **you will**

a. **talk about and describe social customs.**
b. **describe customary actions.**
c. **project goals and purposes.**
d. **express conjecture.**
e. **talk about and express unexpected occurrences.**

¿Qué ha cambiado y qué no ha cambiado?

Los jóvenes tienen más libertad en muchos aspectos de su vida y esto se refleja en su forma de vestir y en sus relaciones con el otro sexo. Poco a poco se han hecho más independientes de la familia y de los valores tradicionales.

Lección 17
Los cambios de la sociedad

Los adelantos técnicos han afectado a la sociedad y se han creado puestos de trabajo para las personas capacitadas. Más mujeres siguen estudios universitarios y hoy en día tienen más oportunidades en campos como la medicina, la contabilidad, las ciencias y las leyes que antes estaban dominados por los hombres.

No ha cambiado el problema del desempleo en el campo y la ciudad para los que no están preparados. Tampoco ha cambiado la pobreza ni la falta de oportunidades y atención médica para muchas personas.

ACTIVIDADES

A En grupos de cuatro o cinco estudiantes hagan una lista de los cambios que han ocurrido en la sociedad de este país en los últimos años. Comparen su lista con las de otros grupos de la clase.

B Usted ha ganado el Premio Nobel por su contribución en un campo importante (física, medicina, literatura o paz). Diga qué hizo usted para recibir ese premio y por qué es importante lo que usted hizo para la sociedad.

C **¿Qué debe cambiar en nuestra sociedad?** Usted y su compañero/a van a escoger tres cosas que deben cambiar en la sociedad. Después compartan sus ideas con la clase.

Cultura

Cambios en la sociedad hispana

Los últimos veinte años representan una época de muchos cambios en todo el mundo y en particular en los países hispanos. La migración, el alto índice de natalidad° y las modificaciones en la estructura social han afectado a la sociedad hispanoamericana. En España también han ocurrido muchos cambios, pero éstos son diferentes a los de Hispanoamérica.

La estructura social de la mayoría de los países hispanos no es igual a la de los Estados Unidos, pues aunque en ambos existen tres clases sociales (alta, media y baja), su distribución y tamaño son diferentes. En Hispanoamérica la clase más numerosa es la baja, pero el poder y la riqueza están concentrados en la clase alta, que es muy reducida. A pesar de los cambios políticos de Hispanoamérica, esta realidad social ha cambiado muy poco. Sin embargo, en los últimos años se ha notado un ligero aumento en la clase media, lo que le ha ofrecido mayores oportunidades a parte de la población. Si esto continua, se podrá hablar de una verdadera modificación de la estructura social de estos países.

En España la clase media ha aumentado mucho más que en Hispanoamérica. Con la entrada de España en la Comunidad Económica Europea y su total participación en 1992, se espera un mayor crecimiento de esta clase.

En Hispanoamérica, debido a la falta de empleos en el campo, existe una migración interna de las zonas rurales a las urbanas. Esto ha contribuido al creci-

birth rate

miento de muchas ciudades y ha creado numerosos problemas. Con la concentración de gran número de personas en las áreas metropolitanas, las ciudades no han podido darles los servicios necesarios para cubrir sus necesidades. El resultado ha sido el aumento del desempleo en las ciudades, el descenso en la calidad de los servicios y el aumento de las enfermedades, la pobreza y la contaminación. Además de la migración interna existe el problema de la emigración de los que buscan fuera, especialmente en los Estados Unidos, las oportunidades que no han podido encontrar en su país.

Los fenómenos de la migración interna y la emigración también han existido en España en los últimos veinte años, pero sin llegar a alcanzar las proporciones que tienen en Hispanoamérica. En España, las zonas más industrializadas están al norte del país y como consecuencia la migración interna se produce básicamente del sur hacia el norte. Los que emigran van a otros países europeos o a América.

El alto índice de natalidad también ha contribuido a los cambios en Hispanoamérica. En los últimos treinta años la población hispanoamericana ha aumentado más del doble y el número de nacimientos es dos veces el de los Estados Unidos. En España la situación es diferente, pues el aumento de la población es mucho menor. La siguiente tabla muestra el aumento de la población en los Estados Unidos y en algunos países hispanos desde 1970.

	1970	1980	1985	% aumento
Argentina	23.362.204	27.947.446	30.563.833	30,8%
Bolivia	4.930.000	5.600.00	6.429.226	30,4%
Chile	8.884.786	11.100.00	12.121.678	36,4%
Colombia	20.053.000	25.890.000	27.867.326	39%
Ecuador	6.050.000	8.020.000	9.377.980	55%
Guatemala	5.250.000	6.920.000	7.963.356	51,7%
México	48.225.238	66.846.833	77.938.288	61,6%
Venezuela	10.210.000	14.000.000	17.316.741	69,6%
España	33.750.000	37.540.000	38.600.000	14,4%
Estados Unidos	203.302.031	217.000.000	238.741.000	17,4%

EN CONTEXTO

La mujer en la sociedad hispana

Las mujeres trabajadoras españolas ganan por término medio un 22,6% menos que los hombres, y en las jefaturas administrativas y de taller la diferencia supera al 40%. Así lo indica un amplio estudio del Ministerio de Economía y Hacienda que aporta nuevos datos sobre la discriminación femenina[1].

Desgraciadamente la mujer en México ha estado marginada, ocupando siempre un lugar detrás del esposo. Pero este concepto, por fortuna, ha comenzado a cambiar en los tiempos actuales[2].

La situación de las mujeres no es igual en la ciudad y el campo y tampoco es igual en todos los países hispanos. Aunque ha mejorado en los últimos años, especialmente en las ciudades donde hay mujeres que ocupan puestos de importancia, todavía falta mucho para que las mujeres tengan las mismas oportunidades que los hombres.

Hoy en día existen en casi todos los países grupos feministas que trabajan activamente a favor de la mujer. Uno de sus objetivos básicos es la igualdad de salarios. No es justo que la mujer gane menos que el hombre cuando ambos realizan el mismo trabajo. Hasta que no cambie este dualismo sexual en la economía la mujer va a ocupar un puesto inferior en la sociedad.

[1] *El pais,* 4 de abril de 1988.
[2] Niní Trevit, *Visión,* 8 de agosto de 1988.

Una mujer policía ayuda a unos turistas en la ciudad de Sevilla.

Preguntas

Conteste las siguientes preguntas con la información que se da en el artículo sobre la mujer.

1. ¿Qué problema existe en cuanto a salario con las trabajadoras españolas?
2. ¿Qué por ciento de diferencia hay entre los salarios de las mujeres y los hombres en España?
3. En general, ¿qué puesto ocupa la mujer mexicana con respecto al hombre dentro de la sociedad?
4. ¿Cuál es uno de los objetivos principales que quieren conseguir los grupos feministas?
5. El artículo habla del dualismo sexual en la economía. ¿Cree usted que existe ese dualismo en la economía de este país? ¿En qué áreas?

ACTIVIDADES

A Con su compañero/a haga una lista de los cambios que han ocurrido con respecto a la mujer en la sociedad de este país en los últimos años.

B Usted y su compañero/a están a cargo de un programa para buscarle una solución al problema de las personas sin hogar. Infórmenle a la clase qué piensan hacer para mejorar la situación de estas personas.

GRAMÁTICA

Adverbial conjunctions that always require the subjunctive

para que	*so that*	antes (de) que	*before*
con tal (de) que	*provided that*	sin que	*without*
a menos que	*unless*		

1. A dependent clause introduced by these conjunctions always requires the use of the subjunctive.

Van a la ciudad para que sus hijos **puedan** tener una vida mejor.	*They go to the city so their children can have a better life.*
Vamos a salir temprano con tal que **lleguen** a tiempo.	*We're going to leave early provided they arrive on time.*
No vayas a menos que te **paguen.**	*Don't go unless they pay you.*
Voy a terminar antes que **empiece** el programa.	*I'm going to finish before the program begins.*
Sal de la casa sin que te **oigan.**	*Leave the house without them hearing you.*

2. The use of **de** is optional in **antes (de) que** and **con tal (de) que.**

Adverbial conjunctions that use the subjunctive or the indicative

cuando	*when*	en cuanto	*as soon as*
hasta que	*until*	aunque	*although*
después (de) que	*after*	donde	*where, wherever*
mientras	*while, as long as*	según	*according to*
tan pronto (como)	*as soon as*	como	*as*

1. **Cuando, hasta que, después (de) que, mientras, tan pronto (como), en cuanto,** and **aunque** require the subjunctive when the event in the adverbial clause has not yet occurred. Note that the main clause expresses future time.

Ella me va a llamar cuando **venga** a Nueva York.	*She's going to call me when she comes to New York.*
Va a estudiar hasta que **empiece** el programa.	*She's going to study until the program begins.*
Llámalo tan pronto como **llegue** la carta.	*Call him as soon as the letter arrives.*
Voy a salir a comer aunque **sea** tarde.	*I'm going out to eat although it may be late.*

2. They require the indicative when the event in the adverbial clause has taken place, is taking place, or usually takes place.

Ella me llamó cuando **vino** a San Juan.	*She called me when she came to San Juan.*
Ellos hablan mientras ustedes **trabajan.**	*They talk while you work.*
Siempre estudio hasta que **empieza** el programa.	*I always study until the program begins.*

3. The use of **de** in **después (de) que** and **como** in **tan pronto (como)** is optional.

4. **Donde, según,** and **como** require the indicative when they refer to something definite or known, and the subjunctive when they refer to something indefinite or unknown.

Vamos a donde ella **dice.**	*We're going where she says.*
Vamos a donde ella **diga.**	*We're going wherever she says.*

5. **Aunque** also requires the subjunctive when it introduces a condition not regarded as fact.

Lo compro aunque **es** caro.	*I'll buy it although it is expensive.*
Lo compro aunque **sea** caro.	*I'll buy it although it may be expensive.*

ACTIVIDADES

A Usted les va a explicar a sus amigos lo que va a determinar si se muda o no se muda a otra ciudad. Complete la oración **(No) me voy a mudar. . .** usando las expresiones de la columna de la izquierda y la mejor selección de la columna de la derecha.

Modelo a menos que — me suban el sueldo aquí
Me voy a mudar a menos que me suban el sueldo aquí.

a menos que	tenga un buen trabajo
para que	hable con todos los amigos
con tal que	pueda vender la casa
sin que	vayan otros amigos conmigo
antes de que	pueda llevar a mi familia
	me despida de mis padres
	pueda tener una vida mejor
	mi esposo/a esté más cerca del trabajo

B Jorge Rivera no sabe si debe dejar sus estudios universitarios para seguir una carrera profesional en el mundo del deporte. Complete la oración **Jorge (no) va a dejar la universidad. . .** diciendo qué factores van a determinar su decisión. Use frases adverbiales (**para que, sin que,** etc.) en sus oraciones.

Modelo ganen el campeonato
Jorge no va a dejar la universidad antes de que ganen el campeonato.

1. le ofrezcan un buen contrato
2. le paguen muy bien
3. termine el año
4. sus notas mejoren
5. le den un buen seguro médico
6. le ofrezcan la oportunidad de anunciar productos

C Usted y su compañero/a quieren irse a vivir a otro lugar (el campo, otra ciudad, otro país). Deben decir (a) dónde piensan vivir, (b) por qué quieren ir allí y (c) qué tiene que ocurrir para que vayan. Compartan después sus ideas con la clase.

D Usted y su compañero/a deben decir lo que van a hacer después de la clase de hoy. Completen las oraciones de la columna de la izquierda con una frase apropiada de la columna de la derecha o de acuerdo con sus propios planes.

Modelo Voy a estudiar hasta que. . . — tenga tiempo / empiecen las noticias / sea la hora de cenar

Usted: **Voy a estudiar hasta que empiecen las noticias.**
Compañero/a: **(Y yo) voy a estudiar hasta que sea la hora de cenar.**

Voy a trabajar hasta que. . .	vaya a la tienda.
Voy a comer después de que. . .	tenga tiempo.
Voy a jugar básquetbol tan pronto como. . .	termine la tarea.

Una oficina del periódico El Diario en Nueva York, donde las computadoras y el teléfono son elementos indispensables.

Voy a ver mi programa favorito cuando...	lleguen mis amigos.
Voy a dormir aunque...	sea temprano.
Voy a llamar a mi novio/a en cuanto...	sean las 7:00.
	no pueda ver.
	tenga un examen de física.
	me duerma.

E Cuando Esperanza López tiene problemas en una clase siempre habla con el profesor o la profesora bajo ciertas condiciones.

Modelo **Habla con él/ella tan pronto puede.**

1. No habla con el profesor/la profesora hasta que...
2. Va a su oficina cuando...
3. Habla de los exámenes aunque...
4. Cree que es difícil hablar después de que...
5. Le gusta hablar con él/ella tan pronto como...
6. Quiere hablar con él/ella en cuanto...

F Con un/a compañero/a hable de sus planes para después que terminen las clases este año.

Modelo Me voy a casar en cuanto...
Usted **Me voy a casar en cuanto consiga el dinero.**
Me voy a ir a México tan pronto...
Compañero/a **Pues yo me voy a ir a México tan pronto pueda.**

1. Quiero dormir hasta que...
2. No voy a abrir los libros aunque...
3. Tengo que trabajar para que...
4. Me voy de vacaciones cuando...

5. No voy a hacer nada mientras...
6. Voy a ir a la playa todos los días a menos que...
7. Voy a nadar para que...
8. Quiero visitar a mis parientes antes de que...

G Usted y su compañero/a tienen planes para hacer ciertas cosas juntos/as después que se gradúen en la universidad (empezar un negocio, viajar, trabajar, seguir estudios de posgrado). Explíquenles a sus compañeros/as cuáles son sus planes. Traten de usar las expresiones adverbiales que han estudiado.

EN CONTEXTO

Problemas actuales° en una ciudad grande

present

Se le apagaron las luces.

Se les descompuso el teléfono.

Se les acabó el trabajo.

ACTIVIDADES

A Estudie los dibujos anteriores. Use su imaginación y explique por qué tienen problemas esas personas.

B Con su compañero/a haga una lista de los problemas que pueden encontrar las personas que vienen del campo a la ciudad.

C Usted y su compañero/a deben explicar las posibilidades de trabajo en una ciudad grande (a) para una persona que ha terminado sus estudios universitarios y (b) una persona que sólo tiene estudios primarios. Compartan la información con la clase.

GRAMÁTICA

Se for unplanned occurrences

Se me perdió el libro	*I lost the book.*
Se les apagaron las luces.	*Their lights went out.*
A él se le acabó el dinero.	*He ran out of money.*
Se nos olvidó el número.	*We forgot the number.*
A Paz se le rompió la blusa.	*Paz's blouse got torn.*

1. **Se** + indirect object pronoun + verb is used to express unplanned or accidental events. This construction emphasizes the event in order to show that no one is responsible.
2. Use the indirect object pronoun (**me, te, le, nos, os, les**) to indicate whom the unplanned or accidental event affects. Place it between **se** and the verb.
3. The indirect object pronoun may be clarified or emphasized by **a** + noun/pronoun.
4. If the subject of the sentence (what is lost, forgotten, and so on) is plural, the verb must also be plural.

Se me **quedó el dinero** en el hotel.	*I left the money in the hotel.*
Se me **quedaron los boletos** en casa.	*I left the tickets at home.*

ACTIVIDADES

A A las personas de cada grupo les pasó lo mismo. Diga lo que les pasó.

Modelo Se nos acabó el vino. (a Evita)
Se le acabó el vino.
A Pilar se le olvidaron las direcciones. (a ti)
A ti se te olvidaron las direcciones.

1. Se me descompuso el tocadiscos. (a Carlota, a Pedro y a Paco, a Armando y a mí)
2. A Rodolfo se le perdieron las notas. (a Marta y a Carlos, a nosotros, a mí)
3. Se nos acabó el dinero. (a ti, a Leticia, a ellos)

B Hágale las preguntas de la columna de la izquierda a su compañero/a. Él/ella debe contestar completando las oraciones de la columna de la derecha.

Modelo **Usted** ¿Dónde está la cámara de Pedro?
Compañero/a Se me perdió **en la universidad.**

1. ¿Qué pasó anoche?	Se nos apagaron...
2. ¿Por qué llegaste tarde?	Se me descompuso...
3. ¿Por qué no almorzaron?	Se nos olvidó...

4. ¿Qué le pasó a Marta? — Se le cayó...
5. ¿Dónde está tu libro? — Se me quedó...
6. ¿Dónde están los boletos? — Se nos quedaron...

C Explique con las sugerencias a la derecha lo que ha pasado en las siguientes situaciones.

Modelo Carlos no puede comprar el libro. — olvidarse el dinero
Se le olvidó el dinero.

1. Anita está preocupada. — romperse el vestido
2. La profesora no vino hoy. — enfermarse un hijo
3. Ellos llegaron tarde a clase. — acabarse la gasolina
4. No salió en ese vuelo. — olvidarse los boletos
5. Ellas no pudieron entrar en la casa. — perderse las llaves

D Ayer usted tuvo en día terrible. Diga qué pasó usando **se** + pronombre.

Antes de levantarme... Cuando desayunaba... No hice la tarea porque...
No almorcé porque... Cuando iba a la casa en la autopista...

EN CONTEXTO

Letreros°

°signs

En una sociedad hay que respetar las leyes. Muchos ciudadanos recuerdan sus derechos, pero olvidan sus deberes°. Los letreros les recuerdan algunas de sus obligaciones como miembros de la sociedad.

°duties

Preguntas

1. ¿Cree usted que son importantes los letreros? ¿Por qué?
2. Explique por qué se debe obedecer cada uno de los letreros que aparecen en los dibujos anteriores.
3. ¿Cuáles son algunos de los derechos y los deberes de los ciudadanos de esta sociedad?

ACTIVIDADES

A Diga en qué lugares se pueden encontrar letreros como éstos.

1. No correr
2. Prohibido entrar con comida
3. Usar el cinturón de seguridad
4. Favor de apagar la luz
5. Usar cascos (*helmets*) en esta zona
6. Favor de cerrar la puerta
7. No traer vasos de cristal

B Usted y su compañero/a deben preparar unos letreros y decir dónde los pondrían.

GRAMÁTICA

The infinitive as subject of a sentence

(El) Estudiar es importante.	*Studying is important.*
(El) Trotar es buen ejercicio.	*Jogging is good exercise.*
Me interesa saber eso.	*I'm interested in knowing that.*

1. When an infinitive is the subject of a sentence, it corresponds to an English noun ending in *-ing,* or gerund.
2. The article **el** may be used to introduce an infinitive at the beginning of a sentence. It is seldom used in spoken Spanish.

The infinitive as the object of a preposition

Al llegar, / Cuando llegó } llamó a su tío.	*Upon arriving, he called his uncle.*
Vino sin avisarles.	*She came without letting them know.*
Antes de venir, habla con él.	*Before coming, talk to him.*

1. When an infinitive is the object of a preposition, it corresponds to an English noun ending in *-ing* (gerund).
2. **Al** + infinitive is the equivalent of **cuando** + verb.
3. No article is used with other prepositions.

ACTIVIDADES

A Trabaje con un/a compañero/a y escoja una frase con infinitivo para decir lo que es o no es importante (necesario, malo, terrible) para cada uno.

Modelo hacer ejercicio
Usted **Hacer ejercicio es necesario para mí.**
Compañero/a **Hacer ejercicio es terrible para mí.**

1. ir a las fiestas
2. escuchar música
3. no tener trabajo
4. ir de compras
5. tener un auto bonito
6. sacar una F
7. vivir en una ciudad grande
8. llegar tarde a los lugares
9. estar enfermo/a
10. jugar básquetbol
11. bailar salsa
12. tener amigos
13. comer bien
14. dormir bastante

B Hágale las siguientes preguntas a su compañero/a. Él/Ella debe contestar con una frase con infinitivo. Después él/ella le debe hacer las preguntas a usted.

Modelo Usted ¿Qué es difícil para ti?
Compañero/a **Nadar es difícil para mí.**

1. ¿Qué es divertido para ti?
2. ¿Qué es interesante para ti?
3. ¿Qué es fácil para ti?
4. ¿Qué es importante para ti?
5. ¿Qué es difícil para ti?

C Su compañero/a quiere saber qué va a hacer usted en ciertas situaciones. Conteste usando **al** + infinitivo.

Modelo cuando llegues a tu casa
Usted **¿Qué vas a hacer cuando llegues a tu casa?**
Compañero/a **Al llegar a mi casa, me voy a quitar los zapatos.**

1. cuando termines la clase de español
2. cuando salgas de la universidad
3. cuando hables español perfectamente
4. cuando te levantes mañana
5. cuando llegues a viejo/a *(become old)*

D Dígale a su compañero/a todo lo que usted hace en estas situaciones.

Modelo antes de dormir
Antes de dormir, yo hago la tarea y miro televisión.

1. antes de comer
2. después de tomar los exámenes finales
3. después de salir de un concierto
4. antes de ir a un partido de baloncesto
5. después de despertarse
6. antes y después de bañarse

E Usted no sale de su casa sin hacer ciertas cosas. Dígale a su compañero/a cuáles son estas cosas. Después su compañero/a le debe decir a usted qué cosas hace él/ella.

Modelo **No salgo sin llevar la llave.**

LECTURA

Antes de leer: the conditional perfect; the pluperfect subjunctive

In this section, you will learn two new verb tenses: the conditional perfect and the pluperfect subjunctive. You should be able to recognize them when reading.

The conditional of **haber** + past participle is the *conditional perfect* and the past subjunctive of **haber** + past participle is the *pluperfect subjunctive.*

The conditional perfect usually corresponds to English *would have* + past participle.

Sé que le habría gustado esta casa.	*I know she would have liked this house.*

The pluperfect subjunctive corresponds to English *might have, would have,* or *had* + past participle. It is used in structures where the subjunctive is normally required.

Dudaba que hubiera venido más temprano.	*I doubted that he might have come earlier.*
Esperaba que hubieran comido en casa.	*I was hoping that they would have eaten at home.*
Ojalá que hubieran visto ese letrero.	*I wish they had seen that sign.*

The conditional perfect and pluperfect subjunctive are also used in contrary-to-fact *if* sentences.

Si hubieras venido, te habría gustado la comida.	*If you had come, you would have liked the food.*

Unos indocumentados pasan el río Bravo para llegar a El Paso.

The following charts show the forms for the conditional perfect and the pluperfect subjunctive respectively.

CONDITIONAL PERFECT		
yo	habría	
tú	habrías	
él, ella, usted	habría	hablado/comido/vivido
nosostros	habríamos	
vosotros	habríais	
ellos/as, ustedes	habrían	

PLUPERFECT SUBJUNCTIVE		
yo	hubiera	
tú	hubieras	
él, ella, usted	hubiera	hablado/comido/vivido
nosostros	hubiéramos	
vosotros	hubierais	
ellos/as, ustedes	hubieran	

Identificación

Identifique el condicional perfecto o el pluscuamperfecto de subjuntivo en las siguientes oraciones.

1. No creía que hubiera llegado a esa hora.
2. Habría estado muy contento si hubiera sacado una A.
3. Hubiera preferido viajar a Santiago.
4. Lo habría comprado, si hubiera tenido lugar en mi apartamento.
5. Si hubiéramos empezado a las diez, habríamos terminado a las doce.
6. Sentí que no hubieran venido ayer.

En la siguiente selección hay varias oraciones con los tiempos perfectos que acaba de estudiar. Estas oraciones le pueden parecer algo largas o complicadas. No se preocupe por esto y lea la selección tratando de entender la ideas básicas que se presentan.

Eusebio Manrique recuerda su vida

A Eusebio Manrique le parecía mentira que hubieran pasado cuarenta años. Y sin saber ni cómo ni por qué, los diferentes acontecimientos° de su vida pasaron en breves° minutos ante sus ojos como en una película. Recordaba el primer día en la compañía. Él, un chico del campo que hacía unos años había llegado a la ciudad para estudiar y ganarse la vida, sólo había podido conseguir un puesto de mensajero. Sus aspiraciones eran otras, pero la realidad era diferente y decidió aceptarlo ya que «por algo se empieza». ¿Habría hecho algo diferente si pudiera volver a vivir esos momentos de necesidad? ¿Qué otra cosa hubiera podido hacer? No encontró respuesta a estas preguntas y pensó en los primeros años en la compañía. El sueldo era bajo y el trabajo muy duro, pero su voluntad de triunfar era más fuerte. Y así pasaron los años y poco a poco fue ascendiendo y dejó de ser Eusebio el mensajero, a quien mandaban de un lugar a otro, para pasar a ser don Eusebio. ¿Quién hubiera dicho que todo esto iba a ocurrir? Si alguien lo hubiera pensado, él habría dicho que eran sueños. Pero en la vida los sueños a veces se convierten en realidad y hoy, después de cuarenta años, rodeado° de compañeros y amigos, el Presidente de la Compañía Trébol, don Eusebio Manrique, se despedía de todos ellos para disfrutar de un buen descanso después de tantos años de trabajo.

events
en... *a few short*
surrounded

¿Verdadero o falso?

Diga si las siguientes oraciones son verdaderas o falsas de acuerdo con la selección anterior.

1. Eusebio Manrique es un hombre mayor.
2. Él siempre vivió en una ciudad.
3. Ganaba un buen sueldo en su primer puesto.
4. Eusebio trabajó en varias compañías.
5. Eusebio Manrique es un hombre importante hoy en día.

Preguntas

Conteste las siguientes preguntas de acuerdo con la selección.

1. ¿Qué puesto ocupa Eusebio Manrique hoy en día?
2. ¿Cuál fue su primer puesto?
3. ¿Por qué se han reunido los amigos y compañeros de Eusebio?

Los hispanos en los Estados Unidos

La presencia hispana en los Estados Unidos data de la llegada de los españoles a América. Desde entonces y a través de los años, distintos grupos de hispanos han llegado a este país. Con mucho esfuerzo esta minoría compuesta de mexicanos, puertorriqueños, cubanos, colombianos, nicaragüenses y otros han hecho sentir su presencia en los Estados Unidos y han influido en la sociedad del país.

Según el último censo, en 1980 la población hispana representaba un total de más de 14 millones de habitantes. En 1986, según cifras no oficiales, el número de hispanos llegaba ya a 18 millones, y para el año 2000 se cree que sobrepasará los 20 millones. Aunque todos los hispanos tienen muchos rasgos culturales comunes, hay una gran diversidad entre ellos debido a su país de origen, historia, y a la influencia de otras culturas y costumbres.

La presencia hispana es obvia en muchos aspectos de la vida norteamericana, como por ejemplo en la lengua. Se usan palabras españolas o derivadas del español en los nombres de estados (Colorado, California, Montana), y de ciudades (Los Ángeles, San Francisco, Albuquerque, San Antonio), en los términos rancheros (*ranch, lasso, buckaroo*), en los nombres de calles y en muchos otros aspectos de la vida norteamericana.

En la comida la influencia hispana es muy notable y muchas personas disfrutan de la cocina típica de los diferentes países hispanos. Palabras como **tortillas, salsa picante, fritos, chile, pollo** y otras forman parte del vocabulario de muchas personas.

Los nombres de los hispanos que se han destacado en diversos campos artísticos son ya muy conocidos: María Conchita Alonso, Ricardo Montalbán, Bárbara Carrera, Oscar de la Renta, Julio Iglesias, Luis Valdés, Rita Moreno, Fernando Bujones y otros. En el deporte se han distinguido individuos como José Canseco, Fernando Valenzuela, Lee Treviño y Nancy López.

Cada día se ven más hispanos en las universidades, aunque su número debería ser mayor. Se especializan en diversas carreras como medicina, física, matemáticas, derecho, negocios y pedagogía y esperan poder participar en las decisiones de la sociedad.

Se puede notar la importancia de los hispanos por la atención que los medios de comunicación les prestan en los últimos años. Hay cada vez más estaciones de radio y televisión en español. En las ciudades donde hay grandes números de hispanos hay periódicos en español como *La opinión, La voz libre* y *Noticias del mundo* en Los Ángeles, *El Diario/La Prensa* en Nueva York y *El diario de las Américas* en Miami. Tambien se encuentran revistas como *Américas 2001, Geomundo, Buenhogar, Miami mensual, Hispanics* y otras. Algunos periódicos en inglés como el *Miami Herald* tienen secciones en español para los hispanos de su ciudad.

Las compañías grandes y pequeñas se dirigen al público hispano. No es raro ver campañas de publicidad en español para casi cualquier producto y los hogares hispanos reciben cupones en español para toda clase de artículos. Estas compañías ven la importancia del mercado hispano y no quieren perder esta oportunidad.

La influencia que han tenido en la vida norteamericana y el éxito que muchos hispanos han logrado en la educación y los negocios son indicaciones positivas del progreso de los hispanos en los Estados Unidos.

Preguntas

1. ¿Qué grupos de hispanos viven en los Estados Unidos?
2. ¿Son todos los hispanos iguales? Explique.
3. ¿En qué aspectos de la vida norteamericana se nota la influencia hispana?
4. ¿Qué estados y ciudades tienen nombres en español?
5. ¿Qué productos de comida vienen de los hispanos?
6. ¿Quiénes son Ricardo Montalbán y José Canseco?
7. Nombre tres periódicos y dos revistas en español que se publican en este país.
8. ¿Qué hacen algunas compañías ahora para venderle productos al mercado hispano?

Los ángeles de la Guardia Civil marcan el paso en Baeza

La Guardia Civil fue fundada a mediados del siglo XIX en España. Durante esos años ha tenido sus defensores y detractores que la ven como representante del orden y el respeto o como órgano de la represión. Pero tanto unos como otros la han considerado una organización eminentemente masculina donde muchos jóvenes «se hacían hombres». En 1988 esto cambió radicalmente cuando entraron las primeras mujeres a la Guardia Civil. El siguiente artículo tomado de *Blanco y negro* da más detalles sobre este grupo de pioneras que se entrenaron en la ciudad española de Baeza.

Las siguientes palabras le podrán ayudar a entender mejor el artículo.

trato	*treatment*
tocar diana	*play reveille*
pocilga	*pigpen*
aseo	*washing*

España

Los ángeles de la Guardia Civil marcan el paso en Baeza

DOSCIENTOS de los mil setecientos «cetmes» de la Academia de Guardias de la Benemérita de Baeza, en la provincia de Jaén, se sienten diferentes desde que a primeros del pasado mes de septiembre otras tantas mujeres ingresaron en el Centro tras aprobar las pruebas de acceso, que sólo se diferenciaron con las del sector masculino en insignificantes detalles físicos.

Los dos centenares de mujeres que soportan con soltura los 940 kilos del mismo número de «cetmes» (cada uno pesa cuatro kilos setecientos gramos), se han convertido en las pioneras de una renovación en los tradicionales esquemas de la Guardia Civil. Con un ligero toque femenino en el pelo y algo de maquillaje, «aquí como en el resto de los trabajos se pide un poco de discreción—señala el general jefe de Enseñanza de la Benemérita, Arturo Lafuente—, porque no sería lógico que fueran con los pelos a lo *punkie*», las futuras guardias civiles han conseguido, incluso, superar a muchos de sus compañeros.

Y es que entre ellas y ellos no hay diferencias en el trato ni en las obligaciones que impone el duro régimen de la Academia. A las siete de la mañana el corneta toca diana y ellas acuden a la primera formación del día. Lo hacen con la misma rapidez que sus compañeros, pero con la notable diferencia del estado en que dejan la compañía. «No es que la de los hombres sea una pocilga, pero ellas lo tienen todo más ordenado y con un aroma distinto», comenta el director de la Academia, el coronel Pedro Moreno Muñoz.

Nueve casadas

Tras el aseo, disponen de media hora para el desayuno . . . Un café con leche, un «donuts», mortadela, pan y mantequilla, ayudarán a aguantar las dos horas de instrucción que dan paso a las clases teóricas hasta las dos de la tarde.

Después de dos horas de siesta se reanudan las clases y, tras un descanso de sesenta minutos, se encierran para estudiar hasta las nueve de la noche.

Una hora más tarde estarán acostadas y acostados, cada uno en su compañía, para respetar el toque de silencio. Cualquier arresto reduciría la puntuación con la que comienza el curso, un diez, la cifra mágica que les permitiría elegir un destino cercano al de sus familiares.

Este es el caso de Concepción Viyuela, de veintiséis años, casada con un taxista de Madrid y con un hijo de cuatro años. «Sé que será un problema si me destinan fuera de Madrid, porque allí tengo a mi marido y a mi hijo. Por eso voy a hacer todo lo posible para estar entre las primeras de la promoción.»

Además de Concepción, hay otras ocho casadas, una de ellas con un guardia civil, además de cinco separadas y una divorciada. El resto, solteras con y sin compromiso, niegan que exista cualquier tipo de noviazgo en la Academia. «Tampoco hemos tenido problemas con nuestros novios, ya que han entendido muy bien nuestro nuevo papel». No obstante, en otros casos la situación ha sido diferente: una de las mujeres que llegó a Baeza tras aprobar las pruebas abandonó las instalaciones con lágrimas en los ojos después de que su marido viniera a buscarla . . .

Sobre la posibilidad de que Cupido visite las instalaciones de Baeza, el general Lafuente se muestra comprensivo, «ya que entra dentro de las posibilidades de las relaciones humanas y no lo vamos a prohibir, aunque no parece lógico que dos guardias civiles vayan agarrados de la mano por la calle, aunque los dos formen una pareja».

Miguel Berrocal

María del Carmen Zarauza, ex «Miss Asturias», es una de las doscientas mujeres que cada mañana forman en el patio de la Academia de Baeza

«Somos iguales»

Esta el frase que más se escucha entre las guardias civiles cuando se les pregunta por las posibles diferencias de trato con los mandos. Nuria Latorre, de veintiún años, piensa pedir un destino muy especial. «A mí lo que me gustaría es ir destinada a una unidad de desactivación de explosivos o incorporarme a la lucha contra el terrorismo». Para ello piensa pedir destino en el País Vasco, aunque como el resto de sus compañeras y compañeros, tendrá que esperar un año para conseguirlo. «Sé que voy a correr un riesgo. pero me atrae».

¿Verdadero o falso?

Diga si las siguientes oraciones son verdaderas o falsas de acuerdo con la información del artículo.

1. Las mujeres y los hombres reciben el mismo trato.
2. Los guardias civiles se despiertan a las seis.
3. Los dormitorios de las mujeres están tan ordenados como los de los hombres.
4. Los guardias civiles asisten a clase por la mañana y por la tarde.
5. Los guardias civiles se acuestan a las nueve.
6. Cuando empieza el curso todos los guardias civiles tienen diez puntos.
7. Si no siguen las regulaciones pierden puntos.
8. Todas las mujeres que empezaron el curso lo terminaron.
9. No hay mujeres divorciadas entre las guardias civiles.
10. Está prohibido que haya novios o matrimonios entre los guardias civiles.

Opiniones

Usted y su compañero/a van a estar a favor o en contra de que las mujeres formen parte de las Fuerzas Armadas. Deben decir en qué se basan para tener esta opinión.

La calle Olivera en Los Ángeles, California, es parte del centro antiguo de esta ciudad que fue fundada por familias mexicanas y españolas en 1781.

SITUACIONES

1. Your best friend has just moved to town. He/She sounds very unhappy and you want to help. You should (a) determine what the problem is, (b) sympathize with his/her situation, and (c) suggest some solution.
2. You're watching TV with a friend at his/her house. You've been watching the newscast which mentions the following problems: (a) bad telephone service, (b) unemployment, and (c) lack of opportunities for women. Choose one of these areas (or another of your choice) and tell your friend your opinion about this situation. Your friend should ask you two or three questions about it.
3. You are approached by a homeless person on the street. Listen to his/her questions and react accordingly. The homeless person will ask for such things as money, food, shelter, or another type of help.
4. You are a woman and want to interview for a job normally held by men in your country. Tell your partner what the job is. Your partner will tell you that you should not interview for this job. Tell your partner (a) why you want to get it, and (b) your qualifications.
5. You need to make an urgent call and your phone is out of order. You don't know your neighbor, but you go to his/her home and try to convince him/her to let you use the phone.
6. You are going to donate money to four different institutions: a university, a hospital, a museum, and a church. Your partner should ask you how much you want to donate to each. Answer that question and also tell for what purpose the money should be used.

VOCABULARIO[3]

la sociedad

el adelanto	*advance*
el cambio	*change*
el ciudadano	*citizen*
los datos	*data*
el deber	*duty*
la diferencia	*difference*
la discriminación	*discrimination*
el dualismo	*dualism*
la igualdad	*equality*
la ley	*law*
el miembro	*member*
el objetivo	*objective*
la oportunidad	*opportunity*
la pobreza	*poverty*
las relaciones	*relations*
el salario	*salary*
los valores tradicionales	*traditional values*

en el parque

el césped	*lawn*
el letrero	*sign*

descripciones

actual	*present*
capacitado	*prepared, qualified*
feminista	*feminist*
igual	*equal, the same*
independiente	*independent*
inferior	*inferior*
justo	*just*
marginado	*not fully accepted*
sexual	*sexual*
técnico	*technical*

verbos

comenzar	*to begin*
crear	*to create*
descomponer	*to break down*
dominar	*to dominate*
faltar	*to lack, to be necessary*
indicar	*to indicate*
ocupar	*to occupy*
pisar	*to step on*
realizar	*to perform, to accomplish*
reflejar	*to reflect*
tirar	*to throw*

expresiones útiles

a favor de	*in favor of*
en voz baja	*softly, in a soft voice*
poco a poco	*little by little*
por fortuna	*luckily*

---

[3] For a list of adverbial conjunctions, see pages 421 and 422.

Verb Tables

I. REGULAR VERBS

	-ar	-er	-ir
Infinitive (*Infinitivo*)	**hablar**	**comer**	**vivir**
Present participle (*Gerundio*)	hablando	comiendo	viviendo
Past participle (*Participio pasivo*)	hablado	comido	vivido

Simple Tenses

INDICATIVE MOOD (MODO INDICATIVO)

Present (*Presente*)	hablo	como	vivo
	hablas	comes	vives
	habla	come	vive
	hablamos	comemos	vivimos
	habláis	coméis	vivís
	hablan	comen	viven
Imprefect (*Imperfecto*)	hablaba	comía	vivía
	hablabas	comías	vivías
	hablaba	comía	vivía
	hablábamos	comíamos	vivíamos
	hablabais	comíais	vivíais
	hablaban	comían	vivían

Preterit	hablé	comí	viví
(*Pretérito*)	hablaste	comiste	viviste
	habló	comió	vivió
	hablamos	comimos	vivimos
	hablasteis	comisteis	vivisteis
	hablaron	comieron	vivieron
Future	hablaré	comeré	viviré
(*Futuro*)	hablarás	comerás	vivirás
	hablará	comerá	vivirá
	hablaremos	comeremos	viviremos
	hablaréis	comeréis	viviréis
	hablarán	comerán	vivirán
Conditional	hablaría	comería	viviría
(*Condicional*)	hablarías	comerías	vivirías
	hablaría	comería	viviría
	hablaríamos	comeríamos	viviríamos
	hablaríais	comeríais	viviríais
	hablarían	comerían	vivirían

IMPERATIVE MOOD[1] (MODO IMPERATIVO)

Affirmative **tú**	habla	come	vive
Affirmative **vosotros**	hablad	comed	vivid

SUBJUNCTIVE MOOD (MODO SUBJUNTIVO)

Present	hable	coma	viva
(*Presente*)	hables	comas	vivas
	hable	coma	viva
	hablemos	comamos	vivamos
	habléis	comáis	viváis
	hablen	coman	vivan
Past (**-ra**)	hablara	comiera	viviera
(*Imperfecto*)	hablaras	comieras	vivieras
	hablara	comiera	viviera
	habláramos	comiéramos	vivéramos
	hablarais	comierais	vivierais
	hablaran	comieran	vivieran
Past (**-se**)	hablase	comiese	viviese
(*Imperfecto*)	hablases	comieses	vivieses
	hablase	comiese	viviese
	hablásemos	comiésemos	viviésemos
	hablaseis	comieseis	vivieseis
	hablasen	comiesen	viviesen

[1] For the negative **tú** and **vosotros** command forms, and for both affirmative and negative **usted** and **ustedes** command forms, see the corresponding subjunctive verb forms.

Compound Tenses

INDICATIVE MOOD (MODO INDICATIVO)

		-ar	-er	-ir
Present perfect (*Pretérito perfecto*)	he has ha hemos habéis han	hablado	comido	vivido
Past perfect[2] (*Pretérito pluscuamperfecto*)	había habías había habíamos habíais habían	hablado	comido	vivido
Future perfect (*Futuro perfecto*)	habré habrás habrá habremos habréis habrán	hablado	comido	vivido
Conditional perfect (*Condicional perfecto*)	habría habrías habría habríamos habríais habrían	hablado	comido	vivido

[2] The second past perfect, rarely used today, is:

hube hubiste hubo hubimos hubisteis hubieron	hablado	comido	vivido

SUBJUNCTIVE MOOD (MODO SUBJUNTIVO)

Present perfect (*Pretérito perfecto*)	haya hayas haya hayamos hayáis hayan	hablado	comido	vivido
Past perfect (**-ra**) (*Pretérito pluscuamperfecto*)	hubiera hubieras hubiera hubiéramos hubierais hubieran	hablado	comido	vivido
Past perfect (**-se**) (*Pretérito pluscuamperfecto*)	hubiese hubieses hubiese hubiésemos hubieseis hubiesen	hablado	comido	vivido

II. STEM-CHANGING VERBS

A. Stressed **e** changes to **ie** and stressed **o** changes to **ue** throughout the singular and in the third-person plural of the present indicative and in the present subjunctive of some **-ar, -er,** and **-ir** verbs.

1. Stressed e → ie

pensar	perder	sentir			
PRESENT INDICATIVE			PRESENT SUBJUNCTIVE		
pienso	**pierdo**	**siento**	**piense**	**pierda**	**sienta**
piensas	**pierdes**	**sientes**	**pienses**	**pierdas**	**sientas**
piensa	**pierde**	**siente**	**piense**	**pierda**	**sienta**
pensamos	perdemos	sentimos	pensemos	perdamos	sintamos
pensáis	perdéis	sentís	penséis	perdáis	sintáis
piensan	**pierden**	**sienten**	**piensen**	**pierdan**	**sientan**

Other verbs whose stem vowel **e** *changes to* **ie** *are:* atravesar, calentar, cerrar, comenzar, defender, despertar, divertirse, empezar, entender, nevar, preferir, querer, recomendar, sentar, sugerir.

2. Stressed o → ue

contar	volver	morir			
PRESENT INDICATIVE			PRESENT SUBJUNCTIVE		
cuento	**vuelvo**	**muero**	**cuente**	**vuelva**	**muera**
cuentas	**vuelves**	**mueres**	**cuentes**	**vuelvas**	**mueras**
cuenta	**vuelve**	**muere**	**cuente**	**vuelva**	**muera**
contamos	volvemos	morimos	contemos	volvamos	muramos
contáis	volvéis	morís	contéis	volváis	muráis
cuentan	**vuelven**	**mueren**	**cuenten**	**vuelvan**	**mueran**

Other verbs whose stem vowel **o** *changes to* **ue** *are:* acostar, almorzar, contar, costar, doler, dormir, encontrar, llover, poder, probar, recordar, resolver.

Jugar *is the only verb that changes* **u** *to* **ue.**

B. Unstressed **e** changes to **i** and unstressed **o** changes to **u** in the third-person singular and plural of the preterit; in the present participle; in the first and second persons plural of the present subjunctive; and throughout the two versions of the past subjunctive.[3]

1. Unstressed e → i

sentir

PRETERIT	PRESENT SUBJUNCTIVE	PAST SUBJUNCTIVE		
sentí	sienta	**sintiera**		**sintiese**
sentiste	sientas	**sintieras**		**sintieses**
sintió	sienta	**sintiera**	*or*	**sintiese**
sentimos	**sintamos**	**sintiéramos**		**sintiésemos**
sentisteis	**sintáis**	**sintierais**		**sintieseis**
sintieron	sientan	**sintieran**		**sintiesen**

PRESENT PARTICIPLE

sintiendo

Other **-ir** *verbs whose stem vowel* **e** *changes to* **i** *are:* divertirse, preferir.

[3] These verbs belong in the preceding section **A** as well because of their other stem change, stressed **e** to **ie** and stressed **o** to **ue** in the present indicative and present subjunctive.

2. Unstressed o → u

morir

PRETERIT	PRESENT SUBJUNCTIVE	PAST SUBJUNCTIVE		
morí	muera	**muriera**		**muriese**
moriste	mueras	**murieras**		**murieses**
murió	muera	**muriera**	*or*	**muriese**
morimos	**muramos**	**muriéramos**		**muriésemos**
moristeis	**muráis**	**murierais**		**murieseis**
murieron	mueran	**murieran**		**muriesen**

PRESENT PARTICIPLE

muriendo

Another **-ir** *verb whose stem vowel* **o** *changes to* **u** *is* dormir.

C. The change **e** → **i** occurs throughout the singular and in the third-person plural of the present indicative, in the third-person singular and plural of the preterit, in the present participle, and throughout the present and past subjunctive of some **-ir** verbs.

e → i

pedir

PRESENT INDICATIVE	PRETERIT
pido	pedí
pides	pediste
pide	**pidió**
pedimos	pedimos
pedís	pedisteis
piden	**pidieron**

PRESENT SUBJUNCTIVE	PAST SUBJUNCTIVE		
pida	**pidiera**		**pidiese**
pidas	**pidieras**		**pidieses**
pida	**pidiera**	*or*	**pidiese**
pidamos	**pidiéramos**		**pidiésemos**
pidáis	**pidierais**		**pidieseis**
pidan	**pidieran**		**pidiesen**

PRESENT PARTICIPLE

pidiendo

Other **-ir** *verbs whose stem vowel* **e** *changes to* **i** *are:* competir, conseguir, despedir, medir, repetir, seguir, vestir.

III. ORTHOGRAPHIC-CHANGING VERBS

A. Verbs ending in **-car: c → qu** before **e**
The change **c → qu** occurs in the first-person singular preterit and throughout the present subjunctive.

	chocar
Preterit	cho**qu**é, chocaste, chocó, chocamos, chocasteis, chocaron
Present subjunctive	cho**qu**e, cho**qu**es, cho**qu**e, cho**qu**emos, cho**qu**éis, cho**qu**en

B. Verbs ending in **-gar: g → gu** before **e**
The change **g → gu** occurs in the first-person singular preterit and throughout the present subjunctive.

	llegar
Preterit	lle**gu**é, llegaste, llegó, llegamos, llegasteis, llegaron
Present subjunctive	lle**gu**e, lle**gu**es, lle**gu**e, lle**gu**emos, lle**gu**éis, lle**gu**en

C. Verbs ending in **-zar: z → c** before **e**
The change **z → c** occurs in the first-person singular preterit and throughout the present subjunctive.

	comenzar
Preterit	comen**c**é, comenzaste, comenzó, comenzamos, comenzasteis, comenzaron
Present subjunctive	comien**c**e, comien**c**es, comien**c**e, comen**c**emos, comen**c**éis, comien**c**en

D. Verbs ending in **-ger** and **-gir: g → j** before **a** and **o**
The change **g → j** occurs in the first-person singular of the present indicative and throughout the present subjunctive.

	recoger
Present indicative	reco**j**o, recoges, recoge, recogemos, recogéis, recogen
Present subjunctive	reco**j**a, reco**j**as, reco**j**a, reco**j**amos, reco**j**áis, reco**j**an

E. Verbs ending in **-guir: gu → g** before **a** and **o**
The change **gu → g** occurs in the first-person singular of the present indicative and throughout the present subjunctive.

	seguir
Present indicative	si**g**o, sigues, sigue, seguimos, seguís, siguen
Present subjunctive	si**g**a, si**g**as, si**g**a, si**g**amos, si**g**áis, si**g**an

F. Verbs ending in **e** + **er:** unstressed **i** → **y**
The change **i** → **y** occurs in the third-person singular and plural of the preterit, the present participle, and throughout the past subjunctive.

	leer
Preterit	leí, leíste, leyó, leímos, leístes, leyeron
Past subjunctive	leyera, leyeras, leyera, leyéramos, leyerais, leyeran
Present participle	leyendo

G. Verbs ending in a consonant + **cer** or **cir: c** → **z** before **a** and **o**
The change **c** → **z** occurs in the first-person singular of the present indicative and throughout the present subjunctive.

	torcer *to twist, to turn*
Present indicative	tuer**z**o, tuerces, tuerce, torcemos, torcéis, tuercen
Present subjunctive	tuer**z**a, tuer**z**as, tuer**z**a, tor**z**amos, tor**z**áis, tuer**z**an

IV. IRREGULAR VERBS

A. Verbs ending in a vowel + **cer** or **cir: c** → **zc** before **a** and **o**
The letters **zc** occur in the first-person singular of the present indicative and throughout the present subjunctive.

	conocer
Present indicative	cono**zc**o, conoces, conoce, conocemos, conocéis, conocen
Present subjunctive	cono**zc**a, cono**zc**as, cono**zc**a, cono**zc**amos, cono**zc**áis, cono**zc**an

B. Verbs ending in **-uir** (except **-guir**): insert **y** before **a** and **o**[4]
The letter **y** is inserted in all singular forms and in the third-person plural and of the present indicative and throughout the present subjunctive.

	construir
Present indicative	constru**y**o, constru**y**es, constru**y**e, construimos, construís, constru**y**en
Present subjunctive	constru**y**a, constru**y**as, constru**y**a, constru**y**amos, constru**y**áis, constru**y**an

[4] These verbs also have an orthographic change: unstressed **i** changes to **y** in the third-person singular and plural of the preterit (**construyó, construyeron**), throughout the past subjunctive (**construyera, construyeras,** etc.), and in the present participle (**construyendo**).

C. Other irregular verbs[5]

	andar *to walk, to go*
Preterit	anduve, anduviste, anduvo, anduvimos, anduvisteis, anduvieron
Past subjunctive	anduviera, anduvieras, anduviera, anduviéramos, anduvierais, anduvieran

	caer *to fall*
Present indicative	caigo, caes, cae, caemos, caéis, caen
Preterit	caí, caíste, cayó, caímos, caísteis, cayeron
Present subjunctive	caiga, caigas, caiga, caigamos, caigáis, caigan
Past subjunctive	cayera, cayeras, cayera, cayéramos, cayerais, cayeran
Present participle	cayendo

	dar *to give*
Present indicative	doy, das, da, damos, dais, dan
Preterit	di, diste, dio, dimos, disteis, dieron
Present subjunctive	dé, des, dé, demos, deis, den
Past subjunctive	diera, dieras, diera, diéramos, dierais, dieran

	decir *to say, to tell*[6]
Present indicative	digo, dices, dice, decimos, decís, dicen
Preterit	dije, dijiste, dijo, dijimos, dijisteis, dijeron
Present subjunctive	diga, digas, diga, digamos, digáis, digan
Past subjunctive	dijera, dijeras, dijera, dijéramos, dijerais, dijeran
Future	diré, dirás, dirá, diremos, diréis, dirán
Conditional	diría, dirías, diría, diríamos, diríais, dirían
Affirmative **tú** *command*	di
Present participle	diciendo
Past participle	dicho

[5] Only the tenses in which irregularities occur are shown.
[6] Compounds of **decir** (**contradecir, predecir**) have the same irregularities.

	estar *to be*
Present indicative	estoy, estás, está, estamos, estáis, están
Preterit	estuve, estuviste, estuvo, estuvimos, estuvisteis, estuvieron
Present subjunctive	esté, estés, esté, estemos, estéis, estén
Past subjunctive	estuviera, estuvieras, estuviera, estuviéramos, estuvierais, estuvieran
	haber *to have* (auxiliary)
Present indicative	he, has, ha, hemos, habéis, han
Preterit	hube, hubiste, hubo, hubimos, hubisteis, hubieron
Present subjunctive	haya, hayas, haya, hayamos, hayáis, hayan
Past subjunctive	hubiera, hubieras, hubiera, hubiéramos, hubierais, hubieran
Future	habré, habrás, habrás, habremos, habréis, habrán
Conditional	habría, habrías, habría, habríamos, habríais, habrían
	hacer *to do, to make*
Present indicative	hago, haces, hace, hacemos, hacéis, hacen
Preterit	hice, hiciste, hizo, hicimos, hicisteis, hicieron
Present subjunctive	haga, hagas, haga, hagamos, hagáis, hagan
Past subjunctive	hiciera, hicieras, hiciera, hiciéramos, hicierais, hicieran
Future	haré, harás, hará, haremos, haréis, harán
Conditional	haría, harías, haría, haríamos, haríais, harían
Affirmative **tú** *command*	haz
Past participle	hecho
	ir *to go*
Present indicative	voy, vas, va, vamos, vais, van
Imperfect	iba, ibas, iba, íbamos, ibais, iban
Preterit	fui, fuiste, fue, fuimos, fuisteis, fueron
Present subjunctive	vaya, vayas, vaya, vayamos, vayáis, vayan
Past subjunctive	fuera, fueras, fuera, fuéramos, fuerais, fueran
Affirmative **tú** *command*	ve
Present participle	yendo

	oír *to hear*
Present indicative	oigo, oyes, oye, oímos, oís, oyen
Preterit	oí, oíste, oyó, oímos, oísteis, oyeron
Present subjunctive	oiga, oigas, oiga, oigamos, oigáis, oigan
Past subjunctive	oyera, oyeras, oyera, oyéramos, oyerais, oyeran
Affirmative **tú** *command*	oye
Present participle	oyendo

	poder *to be able to, can, may*
Present indicative	puedo, puedes, puede, podemos, podéis, pueden
Preterit	pude, pudiste, pudo, pudimos, pudisteis, pudieron
Present subjunctive	pueda, puedas, pueda, podamos, podáis, puedan
Past subjunctive	pudiera, pudieras, pudiera, pudiéramos, pudierais, pudieran
Future	podré, podrás, podrá, podremos, podréis, podrán
Conditional	podría, podrías, podría, podríamos, podríais, podrían
Present participle	pudiendo

	poner *to put*[7]
Present indicative	pongo, pones, pone, ponemos, ponéis, ponen
Preterit	puse, pusiste, puso, pusimos pusisteis, pusieron
Present subjunctive	ponga, pongas, ponga, pongamos, pongáis, pongan
Past subjunctive	pusiera, pusieras, pusiera, pusiéramos, pusierais, pusieran
Future	pondré, pondrás, pondrá, pondremos, pondréis, pondrán
Conditional	pondría, pondrías, pondría, pondríamos, pondríais, pondrían
Affirmative **tú** *command*	pon
Past participle	puesto

[7] Compounds of **poner** (**componer, disponer, proponer**) have the same irregularities.

	querer *to want*
Present indicative	quiero, quieres, quiere, queremos, queréis, quieren
Preterit	quise, quisiste, quiso, quisimos, quisisteis, quisieron
Present subjunctive	quiera, quieras, quiera, queramos, queráis, quieran
Past subjunctive	quisiera, quisieras, quisiera, quisiéramos, quisierais, quisieran
Future	querré, querrás, querrá, querremos, querréis, querrán
Conditional	querría, querrías, querría, querríamos, querríais, querrían
Affirmative **tú** *command*	quiere

	saber *to know*
Present indicative	sé, sabes, sabe, sabemos, sabéis, saben
Preterit	supe, supiste, supo, supimos, supisteis, supieron
Present subjunctive	sepa, sepas, sepa, sepamos, sepáis, sepan
Past subjunctive	supiera, supieras, supiera, supiéramos, supierais, supieran
Future	sabré, sabrás, sabrá, sabremos, sabréis, sabrán
Conditional	sabría, sabrías, sabría, sabríamos, sabríais, sabrían

	salir *to go (come) out, to leave*
Present indicative	salgo, sales, sale, salimos, salís, salen
Present subjunctive	salga, salgas, salga, salgamos, salgáis, salgan
Future	saldré, saldrás, saldrá, saldremos, saldréis, saldrán
Conditional	saldría, saldrías, saldría, saldríamos, saldríais, saldrían
Affirmative **tú** *command*	sal

	ser *to be*
Present indicative	soy, eres, es, somos, sois, son
Imperfect	era, eras, era, éramos, erais, eran

Preterit	fui, fuiste, fue, fuimos, fuisteis, fueron
Present subjunctive	sea, seas, sea, seamos, seáis, sean
Past subjunctive	fuera, fueras, fuera, fuéramos, fuerais, fueran
Affirmative **tú** *command*	sé

tener *to have*[8]

Present indicative	tengo, tienes, tiene, tenemos, tenéis, tienen
Preterit	tuve, tuviste, tuvo, tuvimos, tuvisteis, tuvieron
Present subjunctive	tenga, tengas, tenga, tengamos, tengáis, tengan
Past subjunctive	tuviera, tuvieras, tuviera, tuviéramos, tuvierais, tuvieran
Future	tendré, tendrás, tendrá, tendremos, tendréis, tendrán
Conditional	tendría, tendrías, tendría, tendríamos, tendríais, tendrían
Affirmative **tú** *command*	ten

traducir *to translate*[9]

Present indicative	traduzco, traduces, traduce, traducimos, traducís, traducen
Preterit	traduje, tradujiste, tradujo, tradujimos, tradujisteis, tradujeron
Present subjunctive	traduzca, traduzcas, traduzca, traduzcamos, traduzcais, traduzcan
Past subjunctive	tradujera, tradujeras, tradujera, tradujéramos, tradujerais, tradujeran

traer *to bring*

Present indicative	traigo, traes, trae, traemos, traéis, traen
Preterit	traje, trajiste, trajo, trajimos, trajisteis, trajeron
Present subjunctive	traiga, traigas, traiga, traigamos, traigáis, traigan
Past subjunctive	trajera, trajeras, trajera, trajéramos, trajerais, trajeran
Present participle	trayendo

[8] Compounds of **tener** (**contener, retener**) have the same irregularities.
[9] Verbs ending in **-ducir,** besides changing **c** → **zc** before **a** and **o,** change **c** → **j** throughout the preterit and the past subjunctive.

	valer *to be worth*
Present indicative	valgo, vales, vale, valemos, valéis, valen
Present subjunctive	valga, valgas, valga, valgamos, valgáis, valgan
Future	valdré, valdrás, valdrá, valdremos, valdréis, valdrán
Conditional	valdría, valdrías, valdría, valdríamos, valdríais, valdrían
Affirmative **tú** *command*	val *or* vale

	venir *to come*[10]
Present indicative	vengo, vienes, viene, venimos, venís, vienen
Preterit	vine, viniste, vino, vinimos, vinisteis, vinieron
Present subjunctive	venga, vengas, venga, vengamos, vengáis, vengan
Past subjunctive	viniera, vinieras, viniera, viniéramos, vinierais, vinieran
Future	vendré, vendrás, vendrá, vendremos, vendréis, vendrán
Conditional	vendría, vendrías, vendría, vendríamos, vendríais, vendrían
Affirmative **tú** *command*	ven
Present particple	viniendo

	ver *to see*
Present indicative	veo, ves, ve, vemos, veis, ven
Imperfect	veía, veías, veía, veíamos, veíais, veían
Present subjunctive	vea, veas, vea, veamos, veáis, vean
Past participle	visto

[10] Compounds of **venir** (**intervenir**) have the same irregularities.

Vocabulary

This vocabulary includes all the active and passive words presented in the **pasos** and **lecciones,** except for proper nouns spelled the same in Spanish and English, diminutives with literal meanings, and certain words encountered only in the pronunciation exercises. The **pasos** are identified as P1, P2, and so forth.

Numbers indicate the lesson in which each word first appears. Italic numbers indicate that the word is passive vocabulary. Words presented in the introduction (dialogs, ads, and so on) of the **pasos** and **lecciones** and those explained in the grammar sections are considered active. All other vocabulary is considered passive. If a word is followed by two numbers, the italic one shows when it appears as passive vocabulary; the other shows when it becomes active.

The following abbreviations are used:

adj	adjective
fam	familiar
fem	feminine
inf	infinitive
masc	masculine
n	noun
part	participle
pl	plural
pron	pronoun
sing	singular
v	verb

SPANISH-ENGLISH VOCABULARY

A

a at, to P4
a.C. B.C. (before Christ) *15*
abajo below *2*
abandonar to abandon *8*
el **abogado,** la **abogada** lawyer 8
el **abrazo** embrace 13
el **abrigo** coat 7
abril April 6
abrir to open *P1,* 3
absoluto/a total *13*
absurdo/a absurd *7*
la **abuela** grandmother 4
el **abuelo** grandfather 4
los **abuelos** grandparents 4

acabar to end, to terminate *8*; to finish 16; **acabar de** + *inf* to have just + *past part* 16
el **accessorio** accessory *7*
el **accidente** accident *8,* 9
la **acción: el Día de Acción de Gracias** Thanksgiving 15
el **aceite** oil *P3,* 10
aceptar to accept *8,* 10
la **acera** sidewalk 3
acercar (qu) to move closely, to approximate *9*
ácido/a acid 16
la **aclaración** clarification *13*
acompañar to accompany 4
acondicionado: el **aire acondicionado** air conditioning 5
el **acontecimiento** event *6*
acostar (ue) to put to bed 5; **acostarse (ue)** to go to bed, to lie down 5
acostumbrar: se acostumbra it's customary *13*
acostumbrado/a accustumed, used to 13
la **actitud** attitude *8*
activamente actively *17*
la **actividad** activity *P1,* 3
activo/a active P2
el **acto** action *15*
el **actor** actor 8
la **actriz** actress 8
actual present *8*
actuar to act, to play *6*
acudir to go *17*
acuerdo: de acuerdo con according to *1*; **estar de acuerdo** to agree 5
acumulado/a accumulated *8*
acústica acoustics *13*
adecuadamente adequately *9*
adecuado/a adequate *1*
adelante forward *13*
el **adelanto** advance *14,* 17
además besides 1
adiós good-bye P1
la **adivinanza** riddle, guessing game *P3*
adivinar to guess *7*
el **administrador,** la **administradora** administrator, manager *8*
administrar to administer, to direct *2*
administrativo/a administrative *8*
la **admiración** admiration *7*
admitir to allow, to admit 10
el/la **adolescente** adolescent, teenager *11*
adónde where (to) 3
adoptar to assume, to follow *9*
adquirir to get, to acquire *16*
la **aduana** customs 12
adverbial adverbial *17*
aéreo/a *adj* air *12*
aeróbico/a aerobic 9
el **aerograma** aerogram *13*
la **aerolínea** airline 12
el **aeropuerto** airport *P4,* 12
afectar to affect 17
afectado/a affected 16
afectivo/a affectionate *13*
afeitar to shave 5
el **aficionado,** la **aficionada** fan 6
el **afiche** poster *14*
afirmar to assert, to declare *15*
afirmativo/a affirmative *13*
afortunado/a fortunate *13*
las **afueras** outskirts 5
agarrado holding; **agarrados de la mano** holding hands *17*
agarrar to grab *6*
la **agencia** agency *2,* 12; la **agencia de viajes** travel agency 12
la **agenda** agenda 3
el **agente,** la **agente** agent 12
agilizar to speed up *14*
agosto August 6
agresivo/a aggressive *P2*
el **agua** *fem* water 4
el **aguacate** avocado *P3,* 10
aguantar to endure *17*
la **ahijada** goddaughter 4
el **ahijado** godson 4
ahora now 3
ahorrar to save *3*
el **aire** air *5*; el **aire libre** open air *9*
el **ajedrez** chess *14*
el **ajo** garlic 10
al (*contraction of **a** + **el***) to the 3; **al lado de** next to P3
el **ala** *fem* wing *12*
alarmante alarming *16*
el **álbum** album *14*
el **alcance** reach *12*
alcanzado/a hit *16*
alcanzar (c) to obtain *13*; to reach *14*
el **alcohol** alcohol *P3*
alcohólico/a alcoholic *11*
alegrarse to be glad 10
alegre happy, glad 2
alejado/a far away *13*
alemán, alemana German 1
la **alergia** allergy *11*
alérgico/a allergic 11
alerta aware *11*
la **alfalfa** alfalfa 10
la **alfombra** carpet, rug 5
el **álgebra** *fem* algebra *P3,* 3
algo something, anything *1*; **algo más** anything else, something else *1,* 3

alguien someone, somebody, anyone 12
algún some *4,* 12; any 12
alguno/a any, some *P3,* 12
algunos/as some, several *1,* 6
la **alimentación** food *8*
alimentar to nourish *10*
el **alimento** food *5*
el **almacén** department store 7
la **almohada** pillow 5
almorzar (ue, c) to have lunch *1,* 4
el **almuerzo** lunch *P4,* 3
aló hello 7
el **alojamiento** lodging *14*
alquilar to rent 5
alrededor around *12*; los **alrededores** surrounding areas *16*
alto/a tall 2; **hacer alto** to stop 12; **más alto** louder *P4,* 13
la **altura** height, elevation 13
el **alud** landslide, avalanche *16*
el **alumno,** la **alumna** student 1
allá there 7; **más allá** beyond *2*
allí there *1,* 2
el **ama:** el **ama de casa** *fem* housewife, homemaker 8
amable kind, nice *2,* 14
amablemente cheerfully, kindly *13*
amarillo/a yellow 2
ambicioso/a ambitious *P2*
ambiental environmental *16*
el **ambiente** atmosphere *8;* background *12*; el **medio ambiente** environment *16*
ambos/as both *15*
la **ambulancia** ambulance *9,* 12
el **ambulatorio** emergency center *11*
americana: la **hora americana** precise time *P4*
el **amigo,** la **amiga** friend P2
la **amistad** friendship *13*
el **amor** love *13*
amplio/a ample *4*
añadir to add *6*
el **análisis** analysis 11
anaranjado/a orange 2
el **anciano,** la **anciana** old, elderly person *4*
ancho/a wide 7
las **andas** platform *15*
la **anestesia** anesthesia *11*
el **ángel** angel *17*
el **anillo** ring 7
el **animal** animal *1,* 4
animar to urge *11*
el **aniversario** anniversary *15*
el **año** year *1,* 3
anoche last night 12
anormal abnormal *16*
anotar to write down *13*
la **ansiedad** anxiety *9*
ante before *17*
anteanoche the night before last 12
anteayer the day before yesterday 12
antenoche the night before last 12
anterior previous *1*
anteriormente previously *16*
antes before *1,* 3; **antes (de) que** before 17
el **antibiótico** antibiotic 11
la **anticipación: con anticipación** beforehand *16*
antiguo/a old 10; former *16*
antihistamínico/a antihistaminic *11*
el **antimonio** antimony *16*
antipático/a unpleasant 2
la **antropología** anthropology 1
antropológico/a anthropological *14*
anunciar to announce 10
el **anuncio** ad *1,* 8
apagar (gu) to turn off *8*
el **aparador** china cabinet 5
el **aparato** airplane *16*
aparecer (zc) to appear *2*
el **apartado** P.O. box 8
el **apartamento** apartment *5*
el **apellido** last name *4*
aplaudir to applaud 6
aportar to supply *10*
apostar (ue) to bet *6*
el **apoyo** support *13*
apreciar to appreciate *2*
aprender to learn *3*
el **aprendizaje** apprenticeship *6*
aprobar (ue) to pass *1*
apropiado/a appropriate *2*
aprovechar to take advantage of *13*
aproximado/a approximate *9*
apuntar to take credit *6*
los **apuntes** notes *14*
aquel, aquella *adj* that (over there) 7; **aquél, aquélla** *pron* that one (over there) 7
aquellos/as *adj* those 7; **aquéllos/as** *pron* those (ones) (over there) 7
aquí here *4*
árabe Arab *12*
el **árbitro** umpire, referee 6
el **árbol** tree *4,* 14
el **área** *fem* area *16*
la **arena** sand 14

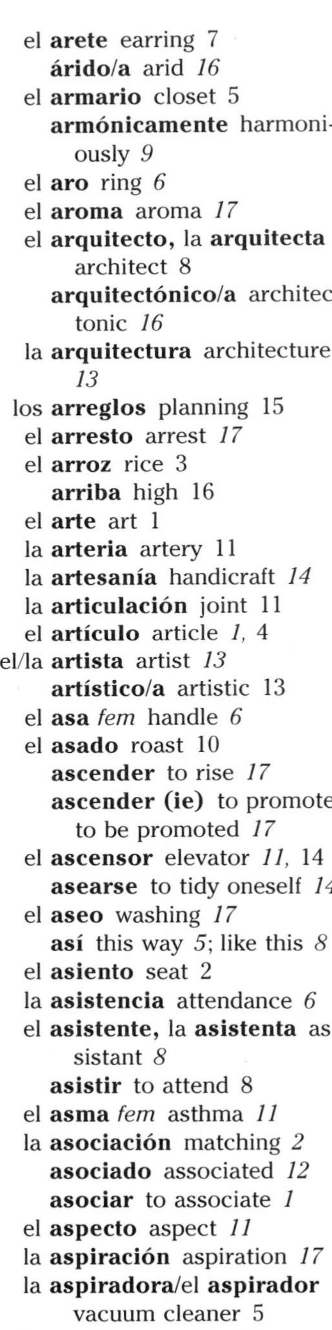

el **arete** earring 7
árido/a arid *16*
el **armario** closet 5
armónicamente harmoniously *9*
el **aro** ring *6*
el **aroma** aroma *17*
el **arquitecto,** la **arquitecta** architect 8
arquitectónico/a architectonic *16*
la **arquitectura** architecture *13*
los **arreglos** planning 15
el **arresto** arrest *17*
el **arroz** rice 3
arriba high 16
el **arte** art 1
la **arteria** artery 11
la **artesanía** handicraft *14*
la **articulación** joint 11
el **artículo** article *1,* 4
el/la **artista** artist *13*
artístico/a artistic 13
el **asa** *fem* handle *6*
el **asado** roast 10
ascender to rise *17*
ascender (ie) to promote, to be promoted *17*
el **ascensor** elevator *11,* 14
asearse to tidy oneself *14*
el **aseo** washing *17*
así this way *5*; like this *8*
el **asiento** seat 2
la **asistencia** attendance *6*
el **asistente,** la **asistenta** assistant *8*
asistir to attend 8
el **asma** *fem* asthma *11*
la **asociación** matching *2*
asociado associated *12*
asociar to associate *1*
el **aspecto** aspect *11*
la **aspiración** aspiration *17*
la **aspiradora**/el **aspirador** vacuum cleaner 5
la **aspirina** aspirin 11
el **asterisco** asterisk *9*
el/la **astronauta** astronaut 8
el **astrónomo** astronomer *6*
el **asunto** matter *13,* 16
asustado/a frightened 16
asustar to frighten 16
atacar (qu) to attack *16*
atareado/a busy *13*
la **atención** attention 11
atender (ie) to take care of *16*
atendido/a staffed *9*
aterrorizar (c) to frighten *8*
el/la **atleta** athlete *16*
el **atletismo** athletics *9*
la **atracción** attraction *14*
atractivo/a attractive *2*
atraer (g) to attract *14*
el **atún** tuna 3
la **audiencia** public *6*
aumentar to increase *11*
el **aumento** increase *17*
aun even *13*
aunque although *11,* 13
ausente absent *P3*
el **auto** car 2
el **autobús** bus *2,* 12
la **autodescripción** self-description 2
automático: el **contestador automático** answering machine *14*
el **automóvil** car *12*
la **autopista** freeway, superhighway *12*
autoritario/a authoritarian *8*
el **avance** improvement 11
el **ave** *fem* bird *16*
la **avenida** avenue *4*
la **aventura** adventure *4*
averiguar to find out *3*
la **aviación** aviation *12*
el **avión** plane 12
avisar to notify *13*
ayer yesterday 12
la **ayuda** help *1*
ayudar to help 5
el **ayuntamiento** city hall 14
la **azafata** stewardess *1*
azteca Aztec *14*
el/la **azúcar** sugar 10
azul blue 2

B

el **bachillerato** high school curriculum *1*
la **bahía** bay *12*
bailar to dance 3
el **bailarín,** la **bailarina** dancer *10*
el **baile** dance *8*
bajar to lower, to bring down 9
bajo/a short, low 2; under *14*
el **baloncesto** basketball 6
el **balonmano** handball *14*
la **bañadera** tub 5
la **banana** banana 3
bañar to bathe 5
el **banco** bank 8
la **bandeja** tray *3,* 17
el **baño** bathroom *4,* 5; el **traje de baño** bathing suit 7
el **banquete** banquet *2*
el **bar** bar 14
barato/a inexpensive, cheap *5,* 7
la **barbacoa** barbecue 5
la **barbaridad: ¿qué barbaridad!** good grief!, it's incredible! 15
bárbaro/a barbarian *15*
el **barbitúrico** barbituric *11*
el **barco** ship 12
barrer to sweep 5
la **barriada** neighborhood *11*
basado/a established, set *11*
basarse to be founded *9*

la **base: en base a** based on *16*
básicamente basically 13
básico/a basic *17*
el **básquetbol** basketball 6
bastante enough P1
la **basura** garbage 5
la **batidora** mixer 5
el **baúl** trunk 12
bautizar (c) to baptize *15*
el **bautizo** christening *15*
el **bebé** baby 4
beber to drink 3
la **bebida** drink, beverage *3,* 10
la **beca** scholarship *9*
el **béisbol** baseball *4,* 6
la **belleza** beauty *3;* el **salón de belleza** beauty parlor *3*
bello/a beautiful *12*
el **beneficio** benefit *14*
el **beso** kiss 13
la **biblioteca** library 1
la **bicicleta** bicycle 6
bien well, fine P1
el **bienestar** well-being *11*
el **bigote** moustache 2
el **billete** ticket *17*
la **billetera** wallet 7
la **biología** biology 1
blanco/a white 2
la **blusa** blouse 7
la **boca** mouth 9
la **boda** wedding *15*
el **boleto** ticket *P4,* 12; el **boleto de ida y vuelta** round-trip ticket 12
el **bolígrafo** ballpoint pen P3
el **bolívar** monetary unit of Venezuela *7*
boliviano/a Bolivian 2
la **bolsa** bag *6*; purse 7
el **bolsillo** pocket 14
el **bombero** fireman 8
bonito/a pretty 2
el **bordado** embroidery *7*
el **borrador** eraser P3
el **bosque** forest 16
la **bota** boot 7
la **botella** bottle 10
el **botón** button *5*; el **botones** bellboy 14
el **boxeo** boxing 6
brava: la **fiesta brava** bullfight *15*
el **brazo** arm 9
brillar to shine *13*
el **brillo** shine *13*
el **bronce** bronze *15*
la **bruja:** el **Día de las Brujas** Halloween *15*
bucear to skin/scuba dive 6
buen good 2; bueno/a good P1
la **bufanda** scarf 7
el **bufete** lawyer's office 8
buscar (qu) to look for 1
la **butaca** armchair 5
el **buzón** mail box 13

C

la **cabeza** head 9
el **cabo: al cabo de** after *9*
cada each, every *P4,* 9
la **cadena** chain *6,* 7
la **cadera** hip 9
caerse to fall 13
café brown 2; café *1,* 3; coffee 3; el **café con leche** strong coffee with hot milk *3*
la **cafetería** cafeteria 1
la **caja** cash register 7
el **cajero,** la **cajera** cashier 8
la **calamidad** calamity *13*
el **calcetín** sock 7
el **calcio** calcium *10*
la **calculadora** calculator 1
el **cálculo** calculus *1*
la **calefacción** heating 5
el **calendario** calendar *P4*
el **calentamiento** warm–up 9
calentar (ie) to warm up 9
la **calidad** quality *5*
caliente hot *2,* 3
el **calor: hace calor** it's hot 6; **tener calor** to be hot 4
la **caloría** calorie 10
caluroso/a hot *7*
callado/a quiet 2
la **calle** street 3
la **cama** bed *2,* 5; **coche cama** sleeper *12*; **guardar cama** to stay in bed 11
la **cámara** camera *12,* 14
la **camarera** waitress 3
el **camarero** waiter 3
el **camarón** shrimp 10
cambiar to change, to exchange *3,* 7
el **cambio** change *1,* 17; **en cambio** on the other hand *16*
la **camilla** stretcher 16
caminar to walk 3
el **camión** truck 12
la **camisa** shirt 5
la **camiseta** T-shirt *3,* 7
el **campamento** camp *14*
la **campaña** campaign *8*; la **tienda de campaña** tent 16
el **campeón,** la **campeona** champion *3*
el **campeonato** championship 6
el **campo** country, countryside *6,* 11; field, area *6,* 11; el **campo de golf** golf course *6*
el **canal** channel *6*
cancelar to cancel 12
el **cáncer** cancer *6*
la **canción** song 3
la **cancha** court *6*

la **canoa** canoe *14*
cansado/a tired 11
cansarse to get tired *11*
el/la **cantante** singer *10*
cantar to sing 3
la **cantidad** amount *8*
capacitado/a prepared, qualified 17
la **capital** capital *P4*
la **cara** face 5
el **carácter** temper *13*
la **característica** characteristic *9*
caracterizar (c) to characterize *13*
el **caramelo** candy *15*
cardiovascular cardiovascular *11*
la **carga** cargo *12*
cargar (gu) to carry *15*
el **cargo: estar a cargo** to be in charge *2*; la **llamada de cargo revertido** collect call 13
la **caridad** charity *15*
el **carnaval** Mardi Gras 15
la **carne** meat 10
la **carnicería** meat market *10*
caro/a expensive 7
la **carrera** career *1*; studies *3*
la **carretera** highway *2,* 12
el **carro** car 12
la **carta** letter *8,* 13
el **cartero** mailman 13
el **cartón** cardboard *15*
la **casa** house *1,* 3; la **casa de socorro** first-aid center *11*
casado/a married 2
casarse to get married *17*
el **casco** helmet *17*
la **caseta** booth *2*
el **casete** cassette 1
casi almost 5
la **casilla** box *16*
el **caso** case *1*
castaño/a brown 2
castellano/a Castilian *P3*
el **castillo** castle *13*
el **catarro** cold 11
la **catástrofe** (natural) disaster 16
catastrófico/a catastrophic *16*
la **catedral** cathedral 14
la **categoría** category *9*
catorce fourteen P4
la **causa** cause *16*
causado/a caused *16*
causar to cause *4*
cazar (c) to hunt, to go hunting *14*
la **cebolla** onion 10
la **cebra** zebra *2*
la **ceja** eyebrow 9
celebrar to celebrate *4,* 15
la **cena** supper 3
cenar to have dinner, supper *3,* 10
el **censo** census *17*
el **centavo** cent *P4*
el **centígrado** centigrade *6*
central central *1*
centrar to focus *13*
el **centro** downtown, center 5; el **centro comercial** shopping center 7
la **cerámica** ceramics *14*
cerca near *1,* 5
cercano/a near, close *17*
el **cerdo** pork 10
el **cereal** cereal 3
el **cerebro** brain *8,* 11
la **ceremonia** ceremony *15*
cero zero *P3,* P4
cerrar (ie) to close *P1,* 8
certificado/a registered *13*
la **cerveza** beer 6
el **césped** lawn 17
la **cesta** basket *6*
el **cesto** basket P3
el **ciclismo** cycling *9*
el/la **ciclista** cyclist *15*
cien one hundred 3
la **ciencia** science 1
el **científico,** la **científica** scientist *13*
ciento one hundred 3
cierto true 11; certain *13*; **por cierto** by the way 5
la **cifra** figure, number *17*
el **cigarrillo** cigarette *11*
cinco five P4
cincuenta fifty P4
el **cine** movies 3
la **cinta** tape 1; ribbon *15*
la **cintura** waist 9
el **cinturón** belt 7; el **cinturón de seguridad** safety belt *11,* 12
el **circuito** tour *6*
circular circular *11*
el **círculo** circle *13*
la **circunstancia** circumstance *13*
la **cirugía** surgery *9*
el **cirujano,** la **cirujana** surgeon *9*
la **cita** date *10*
la **ciudad** city *P4,* 4
ciudadano/a citizen *17*
civil civil *17*; el **estado civil** marital status *3*
la **civilización** civilization *12*
civilizado/a civilized *15*
claramente clearly *13*
claro/a light 2; clear 6
la **clase** class *P1,* P3
clásico/a classic *3*
clasificar (qu) to classify *14*
clave *adj* key *12*
el **cliente,** la **clienta** client *3,* 12
el **clima** climate *6,* 10
la **clínica** clinic, hospital 9
el **closet** closet 5
el **club** club *7*
cobrar: la **llamada a cobrar** collect call 13
la **cocina** kitchen 5

cocinar to cook 5
el **cocinero,** la **cocinera** cook 8
el **cocodrilo** crocodile *16*
el **coche** car 12; el **coche cama** sleeping car *12*
la **cochera** garage *11*
el **código** code *1*; el **código postal** zip code *13*
el **cognado** cognate *P2*
coincidir to coincide *8*
la **cola** line 12; **hacer cola** to stand in line 12
la **colaboración** collaboration *12*
la **colección** collection *13*
el **colegio** school *1*
el **colesterol** cholesterol *11*
colgar (ue) to hang 5; to hang up 13
el **coliseo** coliseum *15*
colocar (qu) to put, to place *3*
colombiano/a Colombian 2
la **colonia** house development, neighborhood *5*
colonial colonial *12*
el **color** color 2; **de color entero** solid color 7
la **columna** column *1*
el **collar** necklace 7
la **coma** comma *13*
la **comadrona** midwife *11*
la **combinación** combination *7*
combinado: el **plato combinado** combination plate 10
combinar to combine *13*; **combinar bien** to go together 7
el **comedor** dining room 5
el **comentario** commentary *7*
comenzar (ie, c) to begin *11,* 17
comer to eat *1,* 3
comercial *adj* business *8*; el **centro comercial** shopping center 7
el **comestible** food *10*
cómico/a funny *4*
la **comida** food *2*; dinner, supper 3
el **comisario** commissioner *14*
la **comisión** commission *16*
como as *3,* 9; since *4*; like *8*
cómo how P1; **cómo no** of course 8
la **cómoda** dresser 5
la **comodidad** comfort *12,* 15
cómodo/a comfortable 2
el **compañero,** la **compañera** classmate *P1,* 2
la **compañía** company *2,* 8
comparar to compare *3*
compartir to share *2*
la **competencia** meet 3
competente competent *P2*
la **competición** competition *6*
competir (i) to compete *14*
completamente completely *16*
completar to complete *1*
completo/a: la **jornada completa** full time *8*; **por completo** completely *15*
la **complicación** complication *13*
complicado/a complex *12*
la **compra** shopping *5,* 7
el **comprador,** la **compradora** buyer *7*
comprar to buy 1
comprender to understand *P3*
la **comprensión** understanding *11*
comprensivo/a comprehensive *17*
el **compromiso** commitment *11*
compulsivo/a compulsive *7*
la **computadora,** el **computador** computer 1
común common *2*
la **comunicación** communication 11
comunicar (qu) to communicate, to link *12*
la **comunidad** community *5*
la **comunión** communion *15*
con with 1; **con permiso** excuse me P1; **con tal (de) que** provided that 17
la **concentración** concentration *17*
concentrado/a concentrated *17*
el **concepto** concept *17*
el **concierto** concert *2*
concretamente specifically *16*
el **concurso** contest *2*
la **condición** condition *6*
el **condominio** condominium *5*
conducir (zc) to drive *11*
la **conducta** behavior *11*
conectar to turn on *6*; to connect *13*
la **conexión** connection 13
la **conferencia** lecture *2*
la **confirmación** confirmation 14
el **conflicto** conflict *4*
conforme agreeable *15*
la **confusión** confusion *13*
congelado/a frozen *15*
conmigo with me 8
la **connotación** connotation *13*
conocer (zc) to know 8

conocido/a known *13*
el **conocimiento** knowledge *8*
la **consecuencia** consequence *16*
conseguir (i) to get, to obtain *3,* 6
el **consejero,** la **consejera** advisor *2*
el **consejo** advice *9*
conservador/a conservative *7*
conservar to conserve, to keep 10
considerar to consider *13*
la **consolación** consolation *10*
la **consonante** consonant *P2*
constituir to make up *14*
la **construcción** construction, building *12*
construido/a built *16*
construir (y) to construct, to build *12*
la **consulta** consultation, visit to the doctor *14*
consultar to consult *1*
el **consultorio** doctor's office 8
consumir to use *12*
el **consumo** consumption *11*
la **contabilidad** accounting 1
el **contacto** contact *3*
la **contaminación** pollution *9,* 11
contaminado/a contaminated *16*
contar (ue) to count *P4,* 4; to tell *13*
contener (g, ie) to contain *10*
contento/a happy, glad 2
el **contestador:** el **contestador automático** answering machine *14*
contestar to answer *P1,* 7
el **contexto** context *2*
contigo with you *fam* 8
la **continuación: a continuación** below *4*
continuar to continue *6*
contra against *6*
contrario/a opposite, contrary 6; **al contrario** on the contrary 9
el **contratiempo** disappointment *13*
contribuir (y) to contribute *9*
controlar to control *13*
convencer (z) to convince *7*
conveniente convenient *13*
el **convento** convent *14*
la **conversación** conversation 4
conversar to talk, to converse *1,* 6
convertir (ie, i) to convert *6*
la **copa** (stemmed) glass 10
el **corazón** heart 11
la **corbata** necktie 7
cordial cordial *4*
la **cordillera** mountain range *16*
el **corneta** bugler *17*
el **coronel** colonel *17*
correcto correct *1*
el **corredor,** la **corredora** sprinter *3,* runner *9*
el **correo** post office 13; el **apartado de correos** P.O. box 8; la **oficina de correos** post office 13
correr to run 3
la **correspondencia** correspondence *13*
corresponder to correspond *14*
correspondiente corresponding *4*
la **corrida (de toros)** bullfight *13*
cortado/a cut *16*
la **cortesía** courtesy *P1*
la **cortina** curtain 5
corto/a short P3
la **cosa** thing *2,* 5
coser to sew *5*
cosmético/a cosmetic *3*
cosmopolita cosmopolitan *12*
la **costa** coast *14*
costar (ue) to cost *P4,* 1
el **costo** cost *4*
la **costumbre** custom *4*
cotidiano/a daily *11*
el **coyote** coyote *P3*
crear to create *8,* 17
la **creatividad** creativity *13*
creativo/a creative *P2*
crecer (zc) to grow *8*
el **crecimiento** growth *10*
el **crédito** credit *7,* 12; la **tarjeta de crédito** credit card 12
creer to believe 3; **creer que sí** to think so 7
criar to breed *15*
la **crisis** crisis *16*
el **cristal** glass 16
el **criterio** judgment *13*
la **crítica** criticism *11*
el **cronómetro** stop watch 3
el **crucero** cruise 12
la **cruz** cross 16; la **Cruz Roja** Red Cross 16
cruzar (c) to cross *6,* 8
el **cuaderno** notebook P3
la **cuadra** city block 8
cuadrado/a square P3
la **cuadrilla** team (in bullfighting) *15*
el **cuadro** chart *2*; picture 5; **de cuadros** plaid, checked 7
cuál which (one) *P4,* 2
la **cualidad** quality *8*
cualquier any 10
cuándo when 2
cuando when 2

cuanto: en cuanto as soon as 17
cuánto/a how much *P4,* 1
cuántos/as how many P4
cuarenta forty P4
el **cuarto** quarter P4; room *2,* 5; fourth 6
cuatro four P4
cuatrocientos four hundred 3
cubano/a Cuban 2
cubierto/a covered *13*
cubrir to cover *3,* 16
la **cuchara** tablespoon 10
la **cucharita** teaspoon 10
el **cuchillo** knife 10
el **cuello** neck 9
la **cuenta** bill *8,* 14; **darse cuenta (de)** to realize 11
el **cuento** story *7*
la **cuerda** cord *15*
el **cuero** leather *6*
el **cuerpo** body *5,* 9
el **cuestionario** questionnaire *16*
el **cuidado: con cuidado** carefully *9*; **tener cuidado** to be careful 4
cuidar to take care of 4
cultivar to grow, to cultivate *13*
la **cultura** culture *P1*
cultural cultural 11
el **cumpleaños** birthday *4,* 7
la **cuñada** sister–in–law 4
el **cuñado** brother–in–law 4
la **cuota: la cuota inicial** down payment *12*
Cupido Cupid *17*
el **cupón** coupon *12*
la **cura** cure *6*
el **curandero,** la **curandera** healer *11*
el **curso** course *1,* school year *3*
curvo/a curved *6*

Ch

el **champán** champagne *15*
la **chaqueta** jacket 7
el **cheque** check 12
chequear to check (luggage) 12
la **chica** girl P2
el **chicle** chewing gum *11*
el **chico** boy P2
el **chile** green pepper *10*
chileno/a Chilean 2
la **chimenea** fireplace 5
chino/a Chinese 1
chismoso/a gossiper *8*
el **chiste** joke *16*
chocar (qu) to collide 12
el **chocolate** chocolate *P3*
el **chofer** driver, chauffeur 12
el **choque** (car) accident 16

D

d.C. A.D. (after Christ) *12*
dañado/a out of order, damaged *13*
dañar to damage *16*
el **daño** damage *16*
la **danza** dance, dancing *9*
dar to give *P4,* 7; to hit 12; **darse cuenta (de)** to realize 11
datar to date *17*
los **datos** data *8,* 17
de of P3; from 2; **de nada** you're welcome P1; **de quién** whose 2
debajo under P3
deber ought to, should *1,* 3; *n masc* duty 17
debido: debido a due to *8,* 13
débil weak 2
decidir to decide *8*
décimo tenth 6
decir (i) to say, *2,* 6; **diga** say *P3*
la **decisión** decision 6
declarar to declare *12*
decorado/a decorated *15*
decorar to decorate *3*
dedicar (qu) to dedicate *8,* 9
el **dedo** finger 9
defender (ie) to defend *13*
el **defensor,** la **defensora** defender *17*
la **definición** definition *15*
definido/a definite *1*
definitivamente definitely 15
dejar to leave 4; dejar + *inf* to let + *verb* 12
delgado/a thin 2
demasiado/a too much *6*
demostrar (ue) to show, to prove *15*
demostrativo/a demonstrative *7*
el/la **dentista** dentist 8
dentro (de) inside *6,* 11; **dentro de un rato** in a while 16
el **departmento** department *2*
depender to depend P4
el **dependiente,** la **dependienta** clerk 1
el **deporte** sport 6
deportivo/a *adj* sport *9,* 11
depositar to deposit *13*
el **depósito** container, box *13*
la **depresión** depression *6*
deprimido/a depressed *9*
la **derecha: a la derecha** to the right *1,* 7
el **derecho** law *4*; right 17; **seguir derecho** to go straight ahead 8
derivado/a derived *17*
el **derrame** spill 16
la **desactivación** defusing *17*
desarrollar to develop *9*
el **desarrollo** development *14*

desayunar to have breakfast *3*
el **desayuno** breakfast 3
descafeinado/a decaffeinated *10*
descansar to rest *8,* 11
el **descanso** rest *8*
descartar to reject *16*
el **descenso** descent, decline *17*
descomponer (g) to break down 17
desconectar to disconnect *16*
desconocido/a unknown *13*
descremado/a nonfat 10
describir to describe *2*
la **descripción** description P3
descrito/a described *16*
el **descubrimiento** discovery *14*
descubrir to discover *6*
el **descuento** discount *12*
descuidado/a careless *11*
desde from *P4*; since *12*
desear to wish, to want 1
desechable disposable *14*
el **desempleo** unemployment *8,* 11
el **deseo** wish *11*
desértico/a *adj* desert *16*
desfavorable unfavorable *13*
desgraciadamente unfortunately *17*
el **desierto** desert *4*
desordenado/a messy *16*
despacio slow *P3*
la **despedida** leave taking, farewell *P1*
despedir (i) to dismiss, to fire 8
despejado/a clear 6
la **despensa** pantry *10*
el **despertador** alarm clock *14*
despertar (ie) to wake up 5
después later, after *3;* then *1,* 3
destacado/a distinguished *17*
destinar assign *17*
el **destino** destination 12
la **destreza** dexterity *15*
la **destrucción** destruction *16*
destruido/a destroyed *13,* 16
destruir (y) to destroy 16
la **desventaja** disadvantage 11
detallado/a detailed *8*
el **detalle** detail *13*
el/la **detective** detective *4*
detener (g, ie) to stop *12*
determinar to determine *11*
el **detractor,** la **detractora** detractor *15*
detrás (de) behind P3
la **deuda** debt *8*
devolver (ue) to return *13*
el **día** day P4; **buenos días** good morning P1; el **día de fiesta** holiday *4*; **todos los días** every day 5
el **diálogo** dialogue *1*
la **diana** reveille *17*
diariamente daily *13*
diario/a daily *5*
el **diario** newspaper *17*
el **dibujo** drawing *1,* 9
el **diccionario** dictionary P3
diciembre December 6
el **dictamen** opinion, judgment *16*
dictaminar to consider *16*
el **dicho** saying *8*
diecinueve nineteen P4
dieciocho eighteen P4
dieciséis sixteen P4
diecisiete seventeen P4
el **diente** tooth 5
la **dieta** diet 3
diez ten P4
la **diferencia** difference *2,* 17
diferente different *1*; *pl* various
difícil difficult *1,* 9
difícilmente with difficulty 13
la **dificultad** difficulty *12*
dificultar to make difficult *12*
difunto/a deceased *15*; el **Día de los Difuntos** All Soul's Day 15
diga hello *13*; **dígame** hello *13*
digerir (ie) to digest *11*
dinámico/a dynamic *6*
el **dinero** money *3,* 4
Dios God 12
diplomático/a diplomatic *13*
la **dirección** address *P4,* 3
directamente directly *12*
el **director,** la **directora** director, manager 8
el **directorio** directory *7*
dirigirse (j) to address *13*
discar (qu) to dial 13
el **disco** record 3
la **discoteca** discotheque *4*
discreto/a discreet *P2*
la **discriminación** discrimination 17
disculpar: disculpe(n) la molestia sorry for the inconvenience 16
la **discusión** argument *13*
discutir to argue 6
diseñado/a designed *16*
el **diseñador,** la **diseñadora** designer *10*
el **diseño** design *7*

disfrazarse (c) to wear a costume 15
disfrutar to enjoy *8,* 12
disminuido/a diminished *16*
disponer (g) to have *17*
disponible available 12
la **disposición** disposal *9;* availability *14*
la **distancia** distance *7,* 13
distinguido/a distinguished *17*
la **distribución** distribution *17*
el **distrito** district *13*; el **distrito postal** zip code *13*
la **diversidad** diversity *17*
la **diversión** entertainment *14*
diversos/as several *13*
divertido/a amusing, funny *15*
divertirse (ie, i) to have a good time *3,* 15
la **división** division *5*
divorciado/a divorced *17*
doblar to fold 5; to turn 8; to bend 9
el **doble** double *4,* 14
doce twelve P4
la **docena** dozen 10
el **doctor,** la **doctora** doctor *P1,* 11
el **dólar** dollar *P4,* 1
doler (ue) to hurt 11
el **dolor** ache, pain 11
doméstico/a *adj* house 5
el **domicilio** address *13*
dominar to dominate 17
el **domingo** Sunday P4
don title of respect *P1,* P2
doña title of respect *P1,* P2
la **donación** donation 16
donde where *1*
dónde where P3
el **donut** doughnut *17*
dormir (ue, u) to sleep 4; **dormirse** to fall asleep 5
el **dormitorio** bedroom *3,* 5
dos two P4
doscientos two hundred 3
el **drama** drama *8*
dramático/a dramatic *5*
la **droga** drug *11,* 15
el **dualismo** dualism 17
la **ducha** shower 5
dudar to doubt 10
el **duelo** duel *15*
el **dueño,** la **dueña** owner *2*
el **dulce** sweet, candy *3*
la **dulcería** pastry shop *10*
durante during *3*
durar to last *15*
duro/a hard *6*

E

e and *13*
el **eco: hacerse eco** to repeat, to reflect *8*
la **ecología** ecology *16*
el/la **ecologista** ecologist *16*
la **economía** economics 1
económico/a economical *2;* economic *17;* la **pretensión económica** desired salary *8*
el **ecuador** equator 13
ecuatorial equatorial *12*
ecuestre equestrian *14*
la **edad** age *7;* la **tercera edad** senior citizenhood *4*
el **edificio** building 1
la **educación** education 11
educado/a raised *8*
el **efectivo: en efectivo** cash *7,* 12
el **efecto** effect 16
eficiente efficient P2
el **ejemplo** example *7*
el **ejercicio** exercise *5,* 9
el the *P1,* P3
él he P2
elaborado/a elaborate *15*
la **electricidad** electricity *16*
el/la **electricista** electrician 8
el **electrodoméstico** electrical appliance 5
el **elefante** elephant *2*
elegante elegant *P2*
elegir (i, j) to choose *3*
elemental elementary *14*
el **elemento** element *1*
eliminar to eliminate, to get rid of *8*
ella she P2
ello it, this *9*
ellos/as they 1
embargo: sin embargo nevertheless *1*
el **embarque** boarding 12
el **embotellamiento** traffic jam 16
la **emergencia** emergency *13*
la **emigración** emigration *17*
eminentemente basically *17*
la **emisión** emission 16
la **emoción** emotion, excitement *15*
emocionado/a excited *6*
emocional emotional *2*
empacar (qu) to pack 12
el **empeño** persistence *13*
empezar (ie, c) to begin, to start *1,* 4
el **empleado,** la **empleada** employee *2,* 6
emplear to employ *2*
el **empleo** employment *2,* 11
la **empresa** corporation *1*
en in *P1,* P3, at 1
enamorado/a: el **Día de los Enamorados** Saint Valentine's Day 15; **estar enamorado (de)** to be in love with *11,* 15

encaminado/a designed *14*
encantado/a delighted P1
encantador/a charming *15*
encantar to delight, to love 7
el **encanto** charm, delight *13*
encapuchado/a hooded *15*
encarar to face *13*
encender (ie) to turn on *13,* 16; to light 16
encerrar (ie) to lock in, to confine *17*
encontrar (ue) to find *5,* 7
el **encuentro** game *6*
la **encuesta** survey *4*
el **encuestado,** la **encuestada** person surveyed *8*
la **enchilada** tortilla filled with meat covered with sauce *2*
la **energía** energy *13*
enero January 6
enfermarse to get sick *12*
la **enfermedad** sickness *8*
el **enfermero,** la **enfermera** nurse 8
enfermo/a sick 11
el **enfrentamiento** confrontation *15*
enfrentar to face, to confront *15*
enfrente (de) in front (of) P3
el **enjuague** rinse *14*
enorme enormous, huge 4
enriquecer (zc) to enrich *13*
la **ensalada** salad 3
enseguida immediately 13
enseñar to teach 1
entender (ie) to understand 8
entero: de color entero solid color 7
entonces then 7
la **entrada** ticket *3,* 6; down payment *5*; entrance *12*; entry *15*
entrar to enter, to come in *2,* 8
entre between P3; among 1; **entre semana** week days *5*
entrecortar to become short *9*
la **entrega** possession *5*; la **entrega especial** special delivery *13*
entrenado/a trained *16*
el **entrenador,** la **entrenadora** trainer, coach 3
el **entrenamiento** training *3*
entrenar to train *10*
la **entrevista** interview *P2,* 8
el **entrevistador,** la **entrevistadora** interviewer *3*
entrevistar to interview *2*
enviar to send 8
la **época** time, epoch 15
el **equilibrio** balance *9*
el **equipaje** luggage 12
el **equipo** team 6
la **equivalencia** equivalency *9*
equivalente equivalent *11*
equivocado/a wrong 4
la **erosión** erosion *16*
el **error** error, mistake *8*
la **erupción** eruption *16*
la **escala: hacer escala** to make a stopover 12
la **escalera** stairs 5; la **escalera mecánica** escalator *11*
el **escaparate** store window 7
la **escena** scene *2*
el **escenario** stage *8*
escoger (j) to choose *2,* 11
escolar *adj* school *14*
el **escombro** debris *16*
escribir to write *P2,* 3; **escribir a máquina** to type *12,* 13
el **escritorio** desk P3
escuchar to listen to 1
la **escuela** school *1,* 6
escurrir to drain *8*
ese, esa *adj* that P2; **ése, ésa** *pron* that one 7
el **esfuerzo** effort *13*
la **esmeralda** emerald *13*
eso that P3
esos/as *adj* those 7; **ésos/as** *pron* those (ones) 7
el **espagueti** spaghetti 3
la **espalda** back 9
español Spanish *P3,* 1; *n* Spaniard 1
especial special *6*
especializado/a specializing 6
especializarse (c) to major *17*
especialmente especially *4*
específico/a specific *1*
espectacular spectacular *6*
el **espectáculo** show *12*; spectacle *15*
el **espectador,** la **espectadora** spectator *6*
el **espejo** mirror 5
la **espera:** la **sala de espera** waiting room 12
esperar to expect *2,* 10; to hope 10
la **espinaca** spinach 10
la **esposa** wife 4
el **esposo** husband 4
el **esquema** pattern *15*
el **esquí** ski 6
el **esquiador,** la **esquiadora** skier *14*

esquiar to ski 6
la **esquina** corner 8
establecer (zc) to establish *8*
la **estación** season 6; station 14; la **estación de gasolina** service station 12
el **estacionamiento** parking 14
estacionar to park 12
el **estadio** stadium *2,* 3
el **estado: estado civil** marital status *3*; **estado** state; el **estado libre asociado** associated commonwealth 12
la **estampilla** stamp 13
la **estancia** stay *4*
estar to be *P1,* 1; **estar a cargo** to be in charge *2*
la **estatura** height 9
este, esta *adj* this 1; **éste, ésta** *pron* this one 7; *n* east *6;* **esta noche** tonight 3
el **estéreo** stereo 3
el **estereotipo** stereotype *2*
el **estilo** style *9*
estimado/a dear *13*
esto this P3
el **estómago** stomach 11
estos/as *adj* these *2,* 7; **éstos/as** *pron* these (ones) 7
estrecho/a narrow, tight 7
la **estrella** star 4
estricto/a strict *16*
la **estructura** structure *17*
el/la **estudiante** student P3
estudiar to study 1
los **estudios** studies 1
la **estufa** stove 5
europeo/a European *7*
el **evento** event *2*
evidente evident 11
evitar to avoid 9
exactamente exactly *15*
el **examen** examination 3
examinar to examine 11
excedido/a: excedido de peso overweight *11*
excelente excellent 1
la **excepción** exception *10*
el **exceso** excess *8*
exclusivo/a exclusive *9*
la **excursión** tour, excursion *3,* 13
la **excusa** excuse *14*
exento/a exempt *13*
existir to exist, to be *4,* 15
el **éxito: tener éxito** to be successful *8*
exitoso/a successful *3*
exótico/a exotic *12*
la **experiencia** experience 8
experimentar to experience *16*
el **experto,** la **experta** expert *8*
explicar (qu) to explain *2*
explorador/a: los **niños exploradores** Boy Scouts; las **niñas exploradoras** Girl Scouts *16*
explosivo/a explosive *17*
expresar to express *1*
la **expresión** expression *1*
el **expreso** express train *12*
la **extensión** extension *16*
extenso/a extended, vast *16*
exterior exterior *2*
externo day (student) *6*
extra extra *8*
extranjero/a foreign *2*; el **extranjero** abroad *13*
extraordinario/a extraordinary *12*
extraterrestre extraterrestrial *8*
extremadamente extremely *13*
el **extremo** end *6*
extravertido/a, extrovertido/a extroverted *P2*

F

la **fábrica** factory *2,* 8, 11
el/la **fabricante** manufacturer *8*
fabuloso/a fabulous, great *13*
fácil easy *5,* 9
la **facilidad: con facilidad** easily *9,* 13; las **facilidades** cooperation *16*
facilitar to facilitate, to make easier *14*
el **factor** factor *13*
facturar to check (luggage) 12
la **facultad** college, school 1
la **falda** skirt 7
falso/a false *P3*
la **falta** lack 11
faltar to be missing *10;* to lack, to be necessary 17
el **fallo** error *13*
la **familia** family 4
el **familiar** relative *4; adj* familiar *13*
famoso/a famous *8,* 10
el **fantasma** phantom *8*
fantástico/a fantastic *P2*
la **farmacia** pharmacy *9*; la **farmacia de turno/guardia** pharmacy that takes turns attending customers during holidays and Sundays *9*
el **favor: a favor de** in favor of 17; **por favor** please P1
favorable favorable *13*
favorito/a favorite *1*
febrero February 6
la **fecha** date 6
la **felicidad** happiness *13*; *pl* congratulations 15

felicitar to congratulate 15
feliz happy 2
el/la **feminista** feminist 17
el **fenómeno** phenomenon *6*
feo/a ugly 2
la **feria** fair *15*
el **ferrocarril** railroad 12
el **fervor** fervor *15*
la **ficción** fiction *4*
la **ficha** token *13*
la **fiebre** fever 11
la **fiera** beast *15*
la **fiesta** party *2,* 3
fijado/a set *11*
fijarse to notice *7*; to set *11*
la **fila** row *6*
la **filmación** filming *12*
la **filosofía** philosophy *8*
el **fin: en fin** in short *16*; el **fin de semana** weekend 3; **tener como fin** to have as a goal *14*
el **final** end *10*
la **finca** farm 15
la **firma** signature *2*
firmar to sign *8,* 14
la **firmeza** resolution *11*
física physics *P4,* 1
físico/a physical *15*
la **flecha** arrow 6
la **flexibilidad** flexibility *9*
la **flor** flower *6*, 14
el **folklore** folklore *12*
folklórico/a folkloric *12*
el **folleto** pamphlet, brochure *13*
la **forma** shape *1*; way 9; **de esta forma** this way *3*; **de todas formas** anyway 15
la **formación** formation *17*
formal formal *7*
formar: formar pareja to be a couple *17*; **formar parte de** to be part of *17*
la **fortaleza** fortress *12*
la **fortuna: por fortuna** luckily 17
la **foto** photo, picture *14*
la **fotografía** photograph, picture *8*
la **fractura** fracture 11
fracturado/a fractured, broken 11
francés/a French 1
la **frase** phrase 11
la **frecuencia: con frecuencia** frequently *2*
frecuentemente frequently *11,* 13
el **fregadero** sink 5
fregar (gu) to wash dishes *5*
frenar to brake 12
la **frente** forehead 9
la **fresa** strawberry 10
fresco/a cool 6; fresh *10*; **hace fresco** it's cool 6
los **frijoles** beans 10
frío/a cold 3; **hace frío** it's cold 6
frito/a fried 3; las **papas fritas** French fries 7
la **fruta** fruit 3
la **frutería** fruit store *10*
el **fuego** fire 16
fuera outside *4,* 5
fuerte strong 2
la **fuerza** strength, force *9*
la **fuga:** la **fuga de cerebros** brain drain *8*
fumar to smoke 11
la **función** show *14*
funcionar to work *8*
fundado/a established, founded *17*
el **fútbol** football, soccer 6
el **futuro** future *1*

G

las **gafas** glasses *8*
la **galería** gallery *13*
la **galletita** cookie *3*
el **gallo:** la **Misa del Gallo** midnight mass on Christmas Eve *15*
el **ganador,** la **ganadora** winner *11*
ganar to win *3,* 6; to earn 8; **ganarse la vida** to earn a living 11
las **ganas: tener ganas de** to feel like 4
los **gandules** peas (in Puerto Rico) *10*
el **garaje** garage 5
la **garganta** throat 11
las **gárgaras: hacer gárgaras** to gargle 11
la **gasolina** gasoline 12
la **gasolinera** service station 12
gastar to spend *3,* 7; to waste *16*
el **gasto** expense *3*
el **gato,** la **gata** cat 4
el **gaucho** Argentine cowboy *6*
la **gelatina** gelatin 10
genealógico/a: el **árbol genealógico** family tree *4*
la **generación** generation *4*
general general *4*
generalmente generally *3,* 13
generoso/a generous *P2*
el **genio** genius 4
la **gente** people *9,* 15
la **geografía** geography 1
geográfico/a geographic *16*
el/la **gerente** manager *2,* 8

la **gestión** matter, business *16*
gigante giant *8*
la **gimnasia** gymnastics *P1*
el **gimnasio** gymnasium 1
el **gladiador** gladiator *15*
el **golf** golf 6
gordo/a fat 2
la **grabadora** tape recorder 1
gracias thank you P1; el **Día de Acción de Gracias** Thanksgiving Day 15
la **graduación** graduation *1*
graduado/a graduate *8*
graduarse to graduate *17*
gráfico/a graphic *9*
la **gramática** grammar *1*
el **gramo** gram 10
gran great 2
grande big P3
la **grasa** fat *11*
gratis gratis, free *15*
la **gripe** flu 11
gris gray 2
el **grupo** group *P4,* 15
el **guante** glove *6,* 7
guapo/a handsome, pretty 2
el **guardabarros** fender 12
guardar to put away 16; **guardar cama** to stay in bed *11*
la **guardería de perros** kennel 4
el/la **guardia** guard 16; la **farmacia de guardia/de turno** pharmacy that takes turns attending customers during holidays and Sundays *11*
la **guayabera** shirt made of light material *7*
la **guerra** war *8*
la **guía** directory *8,* 13; el/la **guía** guide *16*
la **guitarra** guitar 3
gustar to like, to be pleasing to 7
el **gusto: mucho gusto** pleased to meet you P1

H

haber to have 16
había there was, there were 15
la **habilidad** ability *13*
habitable livable *15*
la **habitación** room *4,* 8
el/la **habitante** inhabitant, resident 11
el **hábito** habit *11*
habitualmente habitually *11*
hablador/a talkative 2
hablar to speak 1
hace: hace + *time expression* + *preterit* ago 14
hacer to do, to make *3,* 5; **hacer cola** to stand in line 12; **hacer el papel** to play the part *1;* **hacer escala** to make a stopover 12; **hacer gárgaras** to gargle 11; **hacer la maleta** to pack 12; **hacer una pregunta** to ask a question *1*
hacia towards *15*
hacerse to become *17*
el **hambre** *fem:* **tener hambre** to be hungry 4
la **hamburguesa** hamburger *2,* 3
hasta until P1; up to *8;* even 15
hay there is, there are P4; **hay que** + *inf* it's necessary to + *verb 8,* 11
el **hecho** event *6;* **hecho a mano** hand made *7*
la **heladería** ice-cream shop *10*
el **helado** ice cream 3
el **hemisferio** hemisphere *14*
la **herboristería** health food store *9*
la **herencia** heritage *14*
el **herido** injured person *12,* 16
herir (ie, i) to hurt *13*
la **hermana** sister *2,* 4
el **hermano** brother 4
los **hermanos** brothers, brother and sister *2,* 4
la **herramienta** tool *13*
hervido/a boiled 10
hervir (ie) to boil *8*
la **hierba** grass *2*
el **hierro** iron *10*
la **hija** daughter P4
el **hijo** son 4
hispánico/a Hispanic *15*
hispano/a Hispanic 2
hispanoamericano/a Hispanic American *14*
la **historia** history 1
el **historial** resumé *8*
el **hogar** home *16*
hola hello, hi P1
el **hombre** man *4,* 8
el **hombro** shoulder 9
honrado/a honest *8*
la **hora** time P4
el **horario** schedule *P4*
el **horno** oven 5
el **horóscopo** horoscope *13*
el **horror: ¡qué horror!** how horrible! 16
hospedarse to stay, to lodge *14*
el **hospital** hospital *1,* 8
el **hostal** hostal *3*
la **hostería** inn *14*
el **hotel** hotel *3,* 8

hoy today P4; **hoy en día** nowadays *4,* 15
hubo there was, there were 16
el **hueso** bone 11
el **huésped** guest *1*
el **huevo** egg 3
las **humanidades** humanities 1
humano/a human 11
húmedo/a wet, humid *16*
humillar to humiliate *13*
el **humo** smoke 16
el **huracán** hurricane 16

I

la **ida:** el **boleto de ida y vuelta** round-trip ticket 12
la **idea** idea *1*
ideal ideal *8,* 11
el/la **idealista** idealist *P2*
la **identificación** identification *P2*
identificar (qu) to identify *1*
el **idioma** language *1*
la **iglesia** church 3
ignorar not to know *11*
igual equal, same 17
igualdad equality 17
igualmente likewise P1
ilegal illegal *11*
la **imagen** image *15*
la **imaginación** imagination 4
imaginario/a fictitious *8*
imaginarse to imagine 15
imitar imitate *6*
el **impacto** impact *16*
imparcial impartial *2*
imperfecto/a imperfect *12*
el **impermeable** raincoat 7
impetuoso/a impetuous *13*
la **implantación** introduction *6*
imponer (g) to demand, to order *17*
la **importancia** importance *1,* 17
importante important *P2,* 6
importar to mind, to matter 12; **no importa** it doesn't matter *11*
imprescindible necessary, essential *8*
la **impresión** impression *2*
impresionante impressive *15*
impreso/a printed *13*
el **impuesto** tax *15*
impulsar to move *13*
impulsivo/a impulsive *P2*
la **inauguración** inauguration *8*
inca Inca *14*
el **incendio** fire 16
incluido/a included *14*
incluir to include *12*
la **inconformidad** dissatisfaction 15
incorporarse to join *17*
increíble unbelievable, incredible *13*
incurrir to take on *11*
indeciso/a undecided *15*
indefinido/a indefinite *1*
la **independencia** independence *4,* 15
independiente independent *2,* 17
la **indicación** indication *17*
indicar (qu) to indicate *P4,* 8
el **indicativo** area code 13
el **índice** index, rate 11
indiferente indifferent *13*
el/la **indígena** Indian *7;* indigenous *14*
indiscreto/a indiscrete *P2*
indispensable indispensable *10*
individual individual *4,* 11
el **individuo** individual *17*
la **industria** industry *14*
industrializado/a industrialized *17*
inesperadamente unexpectedly *13*
infantil *adj* children's *14*
la **infección** infection 11
infeliz unhappy *8*
inferior inferior 17
el **infierno** hell 16
infinitesimal infinitesimal *1*
el **infinitivo** infinitive *11*
la **inflación** inflation *8*
la **influencia** influence *11*
influir to affect *9*
influyente important *13*
la **información** information *P4*
informal informal, causal *7*
informar to inform *12*
la **informática** computer science 1
el **informe** report *16*
la **infraestructura** infrastructure *16*
la **ingeniería** engineering *12*
el **ingeniero,** la **ingeniera** engineer 8
ingenioso/a ingenious *10*
ingerir (ie, i) to drink, to eat *11*
inglés, inglesa English 1; la **hora inglesa** precise time *P4*
el **ingrediente** ingredient *10*
inhumano/a inhuman *15*
inicial: la **cuota inicial** down payment *12*
iniciar to begin, to initiate *14*

la **iniciativa** initiative, drive *8*
ininterrumpido/a uninterrupted *1*
inmediato/a immediate *12*
inmenso/a immense *13*
el **inodoro** toilet 5
inolvidable unforgettable *12*
el **inquilino,** la **inquilina** tenant *5*
inspeccionar to inspect *16*
el **inspector,** la **inspectora** inspector 12
inspirar to inspire *7*
la **instalación** installation *9*
el **instinto** instinct *15*
el **instituto** institute, high school *1*
la **instrucción** training *17*; las **instrucciones** directions *8*
integral complete *9*
intelectual intellectual *13*
inteligente intelligent *P2,* 2
intenso/a intense *8*
el **interés** interest *11*
interesante interesting *P2*
interesar to interest 7
interestatal interstate *12*
interior interior *13*; la **ropa interior** underwear *13*
internacional international *8*
interno/a in–house *4;* boarder *6*; internal *17*; la **medicina interna** internal medicine *11*
interrumpir to interrupt *16*
íntimo/a intimate *1*
introvertido/a introverted *P2*
la **inundación** flood 16
inundado/a flooded 16
inundar to inundate 16
invertir (ie, i) to invest *13*
investigador/a *adj* investigating *16*
investigar (gu) to investigate *14*
el **invierno** winter 6
la **invitación** invitation 10
el **invitado,** la **invitada** guest 10
invitar to invite 6
la **inyección** injection 11
ir to go *1,* 3; **irse** to go away, to leave 5
irónico/a ironic *8*
irregular irregular *11*
irritado/a irritated *11*
irse to go away, to leave 5
la **isla** island *12*
italiano/a Italian 1
el **itinerario** itinerary *3*
la **izquierda** left *1,* 8

J

el **jabón** soap 5
el **jai alai** jai alai *6*
el **jamón** ham 3
japonés/japonesa Japanese 1
el **jardín** yard, garden *4,* 5
la **jefatura** headquarters *17*
el **jefe,** la **jefa** boss *2*
la **jirafa** giraffe *16*
la **jornada:** la **jornada completa** full time *8*
joven young 2
el **judo** judo 6
el **juego** game *4*
el **jueves** Thursday P4
el **jugador,** la **jugadora** player 6
jugar (ue) to play (game or sport) 4
el **jugo** juice 3
julio July 6
la **jungla** jungle *8*
junio June 6
la **junta** council *12*
junto next *4*: **juntos** together *4*
jurídico/a legal *8*
justo/a just, fair *8,* 17
la **juventud** youth *6,* 15

K

el **kilo** kilo 9
el **kilogramo** kilogram *9*
el **kilómetro** kilometer *11*

L

la the *P1,* P3; you (*formal, sing*), her, it (*fem*) 5
el **laboratorio** laboratory *P4,* 1
el **lado: al lado (de)** next (to) P3
ladrar to bark *8*
el **ladrón** thief *14*
la **lágrima** tear *17*
la **lámpara** lamp *5*
lanzar (c) to throw *6*: to start *14*
el **lápiz** pencil P3
largo/a long P3; **a lo largo de** along *16*
las the 1; you *formal, fam, pl* them *fem* 4
la **lata** can 10
latino/a Latin *10*
el **lavabo** washbowl 5
la **lavadora** washing machine 5
la **lavandería** laundry 14
el **lavaplatos** dishwasher 5
lavar to wash 5
le (to) you (*formal*) P2; (to) him, her, it 7
leal loyal *8*
la **lección** lesson *1*

la **lectura** reading *1*
la **leche** milk 3
la **lechuga** lettuce 3
leer to read *P2,* 3
lejos far 5
la **lengua** language *1*; tongue 11
lentamente slowly 13
lento/a slow 11
el **león** lion *4*
les (to) you (*formal pl*), them 7
el **letrero** sign 17
levantar to raise 5; **levantarse** to get up *P2,* 5
la **ley** law 17
liberado/a liberated *3*
liberal liberal *P2*
liberar to release *9*
la **libertad** freedom, liberty 15
la **libra** pound 9
libre free *5*: el **aire libre** open air *9*
la **librería** bookstore 1
el **libro** book P3
la **licencia** license 12; la **licencia de manejar** driver's license 12
el **licenciado en derecho** lawyer *8*
el **liceo** high school *1*
el **licor** liquor *11*
la **licuadora** blender 5
lidiar to fight *15*
ligero/a slight *11*
el **límite** limit *11*
el **limón** lemon *2,* 3
limpiar to clean *3,* 5
la **limpieza** cleaning *3*
limpio/a clean *11*
la **línea** line *4*
la **linterna** flashlight *16*
el **líquido** liquid 11
la **lista** roll *P1*; list *1,* 12
listo/a smart 2
la **litera** berth *12*
la **literatura** literature 1
el **litro** liter 10
lo the *3*; you (*formal, sing*), him, it (*masc*) 5; **lo siento** I'm sorry P1
loco/a crazy *8*
el **locutor,** la **locutora** announcer *5*
el **lodo** mud *16*
lógicamente logically 13
lógico/a logical *P2,* 11
lograr to achieve *4*; to provide *14*
la **longevidad** longevity *11*
el **loro** parrot *8*
los the *P4,* 1; you (*formal & fam, pl*), them (*masc*) 5
la **lotería** lottery *4*
la **lucha** fight *15*
luchar to fight *15*
luego so *11*; **hasta luego** so long P1
el **lugar** place *1,* 4
el **lujo** luxury; **de lujo** first class *5*
la **luna** moon *6*
el **lunes** Monday P4
la **luz** light *11,* 12

Ll

la **llama** llama *16*
la **llamada** call *5,* 13
llamar to call 3; **llamarse** to be called, to be named P1
la **llanta** tire 12
la **llave** key 14
la **llegada** arrival 12
llegar (gu) to arrive 3
llenar to fill out *2*
lleno/a full *P3,* 12
llevar to wear 7; to take *10,* 12
llorar to cry 13
llover (ue) to rain 7
la **lluvia** rain *12,* 16

M

la **madre** mother 4
madrileño/a from Madrid *15*
la **madrina** godmother 4
la **madrugada** early morning *15*
maestro/a master *3*
magia magic *12*
mágico/a magical *17*
magnífico/a magnificent, great *12*
magos: los **Reyes Magos** the three Wise Men *15*
el **maíz** corn *P3*
mal not well, sick P1; bad 2
la **maleta** suitcase 12
el **maletero** trunk 12
el **maletín** attaché case 12
malo/a bad 2; la **mala palabra** dirty word *16*
la **mamá** mother P4
mañana tomorrow P1; la **mañana** morning P4
mandar to send 13
el **mandato** command *8*
el **mando** assignment *17*
manejar to drive *5,* 12
la **manera** way, manner *9*
la **manifestación** demonstration *2*
la **mano** hand *P3,* 9
la **manta** blanket 5
el **mantel** tablecloth 10
mantener (ie, g) to maintain *4*
el **mantenimiento** upkeep *9*
la **mantequilla** butter 10
manuscrito/a hand written *8*
la **manzana** apple 3
el **mapa** map 1
maquillarse to put on makeup *5*

la **máquina: escribir a máquina** to type *12,* 13
el **mar** sea 12
maravillarse to marvel *14*
maravilloso/a marvelous 4
la **marca** brand, make *2*
marcado/a: variantes marcadas (multiple choice) answers *11*
marcar (qu) to dial 13; to mark *17*; **marcar el paso** to mark time *17*; **marcar un punto** give a point *13*
el **marco** atmosphere *9*; frame *16*
la **marcha** walking *9*
marginado/a not fully accepted 17
el **marido** husband 4
la **marihuana** marijuana *11*
el **marqués** marquis *14*
el **martes** Tuesday P4
marzo March 6
más more *P2,* P4; **más allá** beyond *2*
masculino/a masculine *17*
masticar (qu) to chew *11*
matar to kill *15*
las **matemáticas** mathematics *P4,* 1
la **materia** subject 1; la **materia económica** business matters *13*
el **material** material *8*
materialista materialistic *P2*
el **matrimonio** married couple 5
máximo/a high, maximum *6*
mayo May 6
la **mayonesa** mayonnaise 10
mayor older *4,* 9; oldest 10; la **persona mayor** adult, older person *4*
la **mayoría** majority *12*
el/la **mayorista** wholesaler *11*
la **mayúscula** capital letter *12*
me myself P1; me 5; (to) me 7
el **mecánico** mechanic *4,* 8
media half P4; *n* stocking 7; la **clase media** middle class *17*
mediados: a mediados de about the middle of *17*
mediano/a medium *9*
la **medianoche** midnight *15*
mediante by means of *16*
la **medicación** medication *11*
la **medicina** medicine *4*; la **medicina familiar** general practice *13*
médico/a medical *4,* 17; *n* doctor 8
la **medida** measure *16*
el **medio** means *8*; el **medio ambiente** environment *16*; el **término medio** average 17
el **mediodía** noon *15*
medir (i) to measure *9*
la **mejilla** cheek 9
mejor better, *2,* 9; best *2,* 10
la **mejora** improvement *13*
mejorar to improve 11
la **melodía** melody 15
melodramático/a melodramatic *11*
la **memoria** memory *8*
mencionar to mention *15*
menor younger *4,* 9; youngest 10
menos to (in telling time) P4; minus *P4*; less, fewer 9; **a menos que** unless 17; **por lo menos** at least 9
el **mensaje** message *13,* 14
el **mensajero,** la **mensajera** messenger *17*
mental mental *13*
la **mente** mind *15*
la **mentira** lie 4
el **menú** menu 3
el **mercado** market *7,* 10
la **merienda** snack in the afternoon *10*
el **mérito** merit *6*
el **mes** month P4
la **mesa** table P3; la **mesa de noche** nightstand *2,* 5
la **meta** goal, objective *15*
el **método** method *13*
el **metro** subway *5,* 12; meter 9
metropolitano/a metropolitan *17*
mexicano/a Mexican 2
mezclar to combine, to mix *12*
mí (to) me 7
mi(s) my P2, 4
el **microondas** microwave 5
el **miedo: tener miedo** to be afraid 4
el **miembro** member *4,* 17
mientras while *4,* 6
el **miércoles** Wednesday P4
la **migración** migration *17*
mil thousand 3
militar military *13*
el **millón** million *5,* 6
millonario/a millionaire 4
mineral *adj* mineral 10
el **minidiálogo** minidialog *P1*
mínimo/a low, minimum *6*
la **minoría** minority *17*
el **minuto** minute 9
mío (-a, -os, -as) (of) mine 14
mirar to look at *1,* 2
el **misil** missile *16*
la **misión** mission *1*

mismo/a same *3*
el **misterio** mystery *4*
misterioso/a mysterious *14*
la **mitad** half *6*
la **mochila** backpack 12
la **moda** fashion 7; **estar de moda** to be fashionable 7
el/la **modelo** model *P4*
moderno/a modern *P2*
la **modificación** modification, change *17*
molestar to bother 14
la **molestia** inconvenience 16
molido/a ground 10
el **momento** moment 6: **en estos momentos** right now, at this moment 6
el **monasterio** monastery *14*
el **monólogo** monolog *15*
la **montaña** mountain *7,* 14
el **montañismo** (mountain) trekking, hiking *9*
montañoso/a mountainous *14*
montar to ride 6
el **monumento** monument *14*
morado/a purple 2
moreno/a brunet(te) 2
morir to die *13*
la **mortadela** mortadella *17*
la **mostaza** mustard 10
el **mostrador** counter 12
mostrar (ue) to show *3,* 7
el **motivo** reason *4*
la **moto(cicleta)** motorcycle *2,* 12
el **motor** motor 12
mover (ue) to move 9
movido/a lively *13*
el **movimiento** movement 9
la **muchacha** girl 3
el **muchacho** boy 3
mucho much, a lot 1; **mucho gusto** nice to meet you P1
muchos/as many *1,* 4
mudarse to move *17*
el **mueble** furniture 5
la **muela: dolor de muelas** toothache *11*
la **muerte** death *15*
muerto/a dead 16: el **Día de los Muertos** All Soul's Day 15
la **mujer** wife 4; woman *4,* 8
la **muleta** crutch 12
la **multa** fine 12
multiplicar (qu) to multiply *6*
multitudinario/a multifaceted *6*
mundial *adj* world *6*
el **mundo** world *1*
la **muñeca** wrist 9
el **músculo** muscle 11
el **museo** museum *7,* 14
la **música** music *9*
musical musical *4*
el **músico** musician *13*
muy very P1

N

nacer (zc) to be born *6*
nacido/a born *13*
el **nacimiento** birth *17*
nacional national *6*
nada nothing 12; **por/de nada** you're welcome P1
nadar to swim 6
nadie no one, nobody *8,* 12
la **naranja** orange 3
la **nariz** nose 9
la **natación** swimming *9*
la **natalidad** birth rate *17*
nativo native *1*
natural natural *7*
la **naturaleza** nature *12*
naturista: el **centro naturista** health food store *9*
la(s) **Navidad(es)** Christmas 15
necesario/a necessary *3,* 11
la **necesidad** need *8*
necesitar to need 1
negar (ie) to deny *17*
negativamente negatively *12*
la **negociación** discussion *13*
el **negocio** business *4,* 8
negro/a black 2
nervioso/a nervous 2
nevar (ie) to snow 6
ni nor 2; **ni . . . ni** neither . . . nor 12
nicaragüense Nicaraguan 17
la **nieta** granddaughter 4
el **nieto** grandson 4
la **nieve** snow 6
ningún no, not any 12
ninguno/a none, not any, *6,* 12
el **niño,** la **niña** child *1,* 4
el **nivel:** el **nivel de vida** standard of living 11
no no P2
la **noche** evening, night P1; **esta noche** tonight 3
la **Nochebuena** Christmas Eve 15
la **Nochevieja** New Year's Eve 15
el **nombre** name P1
la **norma** norm *2*
normal normal *10*
normalmente normally *5,* 13
el **norte** north *4*
norteamericano/a American 1
nos us 5; (to) us 7
nosotros/as we 1
la **nota** grade *1,* 2; note *10*
notable noteworthy, notable 17

notablemente noticeably *16*
notarse to be noticeable *12*
la **noticia** news *3,* 16
el **noticiero** newscast 16
novecientos nine hundred 3
noveno/a ninth 6
noventa ninety P4
la **novia** fiancée, girlfriend 4
el **noviazgo** engagement, courtship *17*
noviembre November 6
el **novio** fiancé, boyfriend 4
el **nubarrón** dark cloud *13*
nublado/a cloudy 6
nuboso/a cloudy 6
la **nuera** daughter–in–law 4
nuestro (-a, -os, -as) our 4
nueve nine P4
nuevo/a new 2
el **número** number P4
numeroso/a numerous 12
nunca never *4,* 12
la **nutrición** nutrition *9*
nutritivo/a nourishing *10*

O

o or *P3,* P4; **o . . . o** either . . . or 12
obedecer (zc) to obey *8*
el **objetivo** objective, goal 11, 17
el **objeto** object *1*
la **obligación** obligation, duty *17*
obligar (gu) to force *8*
la **obra** (construction) site *5*; work *7*; la **obra de teatro** play *14*
el **obrero,** la **obrera** worker 8
observar to observe, to see *6*
la **obsesión** obsession *8*
obstante: no obstante however, nevertheless *17*
obtener (g, ie) to obtain *1,* 11
obvio obvious 11
ocasionalmente occasionally *11*
ocasionar to cause *16*
octavo eighth 6
octubre October 6
la **ocupación** occupation *8*
ocupado/a busy 1
ocupar to cover, to extend over *16*; to occupy, to hold 17; to take over *15*; **ocuparse** to attend to *5*
ocurrir to occur *2*
ochenta eighty P4
ocho eight P4
ochocientos eight hundred 3
oeste *adj* western *4*; *n* west *6*
oficial official *1*
la **oficina** office *2,* 8
el **oficio** occupation 8
ofrecer (zc) to offer *4*
el **oído** (inner) ear 11
oír to hear 13
ojalá I/we hope 11
el **ojo** eye 2
la **ola** wave 14
las **Olimpiadas** Olympic Games *14*
olvidar to forget *8,* 14
once eleven P4
la **opción** option *8*
la **operación** operation *11*
la **operadora** operator 13
la **opinión** opinion *4*
la **oportunidad** opportunity *3,* 17
optimista optimistic *P2*
óptimo/a optimum, best *13*
opuesto/a opposite *2*
la **oración** sentence *1*
la **orden** order 3
ordenado/a tidy *17*
la **oreja** ear 9
la **organización** organization *3*
el **organizador,** la **organizadora** organizer *15*
organizar (c) to organize *3,* 15
el **órgano** body *17*
orgulloso/a proud *14*
el **origen** origin *6*
el **oro** gold *13*
la **orquesta** orchestra *15*
os you (*fam pl*) 5; (to) you 7
oscuro/a dark 2
el **otoño** autumn 6
otro/a other, another 1; **otra vez** again *P4,* 7
el **oxígeno** oxygen *1*

P

paciente patient *P2*
el **padre** father 1
los **padres** parents *2,* 4
el **padrino** godfather 4
la **paella** paella *10*
pagar (gu) to pay for 7
la **página** page *P3*
el **país** country *2,* 10
el **paisaje** landscape *12*
el **pájaro** bird *4*
la **palabra** word *P1*; la **mala palabra** dirty word *16*
el **palacio** palace *14*
el **palo** stick *15*
el **pan** bread 3
la **panadería** bakery *10*
panameño/a Panamanian 2
los **pantalones** slacks 7
la **pantomima** pantomime *6*
el **pañuelo** handkerchief 7

la **papa** potato 3; las **papas fritas** French fries 3
el **papá** father 4
el **papel** paper 1; role *17*; **hacer el papel** to play the part *8*
la **papelería** stationery store *13*
el **paquete** package 13
el **par** pair *11*; **a la par con** equal to *14*
para for 1; to 3; towards, in order to 15; **para que** so that *15,* 17
la **parabólica** satellite dish antenna *4*
el **parabrisas** windshield 12
el **parachoques** bumper 12
la **parada** stop *12*
parado/a standing 16
el **parador** hotel *14*
parar to stop *9,* 12
parcial partial *P2*
parecer (zc) to seem 7
parecido/a similar *16*
la **pared** wall P3
la **pareja** partner *13*; couple *17*
el **parentesco** relationship *4*
el **paréntesis** parenthesis *15*
el **pariente** relative *3,* 4
el **paro** unemployment *8*
el **parque** park *4,* 14
el **párrafo** paragraph *1*
la **parte** part *2,* 9; **¿de parte de quién?** who's calling? 13; **en todas partes** everywhere 10; **por otra parte** on the other hand *6*
la **participación** participation *17*
el/la **participante** participant *6*
participar to participate *12*
particular: en particular particularly *17*
el **partido** game *P4,* 6
partir: a partir de beginning at *6*
pasado/a last 12; **pasado mañana** the day after tomorrow 3
el **pasaje** ticket 12; el **pasaje de ida y vuelta** round-trip ticket 12
el **pasajero,** la **pasajera** passenger 12
el **pasaporte** passport 12
pasar to happen *2,* 12; to spend 4; to come in 8; **pasar la aspiradora** to vacuum 5; **pasar la lista** to call roll *P1*; **pasarlo bien** to have a good time 13; **pasar por** to pick up 7
la **Pascua** Passover 15
el **pasillo** hall 5
pasivo/a passive *P2*
el **paso** step *P1*; **dar paso a** to open way to *17*
el **pastel** pie 3
la **pastelería** pastry shop *10*
la **pastilla** pill 11
la **patata** potato (in Spain) *10*
patinar to skate 6
el **pato** duck, Argentine sport *6*
el **patrimonio** patrimony *16*
el **patrón,** la **patrona** patron *15*
el **pavo** turkey 10
el **payaso** clown *15*
la **paz** peace *6*
el **peaje** toll *12*
el **pecado** sin *8*
la **pedagogía** pedagogy *17*
el **pedal** pedal *15*
el/la **pediatra** pediatrician *11*
pedir (i) to request *3,* 6; to ask for, to order 6
peinar to comb 5
la **pelea** fight *13*
la **película** film 3
el **peligro** danger *11*
peligroso/a dangerous *6,* 16
el **pelo** hair 2
la **pelota** ball *6*
el **pelotari** jai alai player *6*
el **pelotón** crowd *15*
la **peluquería** beauty salon, barber shop 8
el **peluquero,** la **peluquera** hairdresser 8
la **pena: ¡qué pena!** what a pity! 15
pendiente pending *13*
el/la **penitente** penitent *15*
pensar (ie) to think 2, 4; **pensar** + *inf* to plan to + *verb* 4
la **pensión** boardinghouse *1*
peor worse 9; worst 10
pequeño/a small P3
perder (ie) to lose *3,* 4; **perder el tiempo** to waste time 7
la **pérdida** loss *16*
perdón excuse me P1
perezoso/a lazy 2
perfectamente perfectly 13
perfecto/a perfect 7
el **perfil** profile *8*
el **periódico** newspaper *3,* 4
el **período** period *13*
permanecer (zc) to remain, to stay *4*
permanente permanent *4*
permanentemente permanently *9*
permiso: con permiso excuse me P1
permitir to permit, to allow *9,* 10
pero but 1
el **perro,** la **perra** dog *2,* 4

perseguir (i) to pursue *13*
persistente persistent *P2*
la **persona** person P1
el **personaje** person of importance *13*
personal *adj* personal *8*; el **personal** personnel, staff *8*
la **personalidad** personality *8*
pertenecer (zc) to belong *13*
perteneciente part of, belonging *8*
peruano/a Peruvian 2
pesar to weigh 9; **a pesar de** in spite of *12*
la **pescadería** fish market *10*
el **pescado** fish 3
pescar (qu) to fish 6
pesimista pessimistic *P2*
pésimo/a terrible, very bad *13*
peso peso 1; weight *3,* 9
el **pez** (*pl* peces) fish *4*
la **pestaña** eyelash 9
el **petróleo** oil, petroleum *6,* 16
el/la **pianista** pianist *10*
el **piano** piano 3
el **picadillo** ground meat cooked with onions, garlic, and green pepper *10*
picante hot, spicy *17*
el **pie** foot 9
la **piel** skin *11*
la **pierna** leg 9
la **pila** battery *16*
el/la **piloto** pilot 8
la **pimienta** pepper 10
el **pimiento** green pepper 10
pintar to paint *15*
la **pintura** painting *14*
la **piñata** clay pot or cardboard container covered with tissue paper and filled with candy, nuts, and other treats *15*
el **pionero,** la **pionera** pioneer *17*
el **piragüismo** canoeing *14*
la **pirámide** pyramid *12*
pisar to step 17
la **piscina** pool *5,* 6
el **piso** floor 5
el/la **piyama** pajama 5
la **pizarra** blackboard *P2,* P3
la **pizza** pizza 3
el **placer** pleasure *12*
el **plan** plan *3*
la **plancha** iron 5
planchar to iron 5
planear to plan *12*
el **planeta** planet *6*
planificar (qu) plan *3*
el **plano** map *8*
la **planta** plant *2*; floor 5
la **plata** silver *15*
la **plataforma** platform *15*
el **plátano** banana 3, 10
el **plato** dish, plate *3,* 5; el **plato combinado** combination plate 10
la **playa** beach 3
la **plaza** position 8; plaza 8; la **plaza de toros** bullring 14
pleno: a pleno full *12*
el **plomero** plumber 8
plural plural *1*
el **pluriempleo** moonlighting *8*
la **población** population, people *12*
pobre poor 2
la **pobreza** poverty 17
la **pocilga** pigpen *17*
poco: poco a poco little by little 17; **un poco** a little 1
poder (ue) to be able to, can *2,* 4; el **poder** power *17*
el **polen** polen *11*
el **policía** policeman; la **(mujer) policía** policewoman 8
el **político** politician *13*; *adj* political
el **polo** pole *4*
el **pollo** chicken 3
el **ponche** punch *3*
poner (g) to put 5
popular popular 1
por about *1*; for 4; by *11*; by, per, around, through, because of 15; **por cierto** by the way 5; **por ciento** per cent *5*; **por eso** that's why 1; **por favor** please P1; **por lo menos** at least 9; **por qué** why 2
el **porcentaje** percentage *5*
porque because 2
el **portal** porch 5
portátil portable *14*
portugués, portuguesa Portuguese 1
poseer to have *11*
la **posesión** possession *2*
posgrado postgraduate *17*
la **posibilidad** possibility *1*
posible possible *9,* 11
positivamente positively *8*
positivo/a positive *8*
posponer (g) postpone *16*
pospuesto postponed *16*
postal postal *13*; la **tarjeta postal** postcard 13
el **postre** dessert 10
el **potasio** potassium *16*
la **práctica** practice *1*
practicar (qu) to practice 1
el **precio** price 1
precioso/a beautiful 7

precisar to need *8*
precolombino/a pre-Columbian *13*
la **predicción** prediction *13*
preferible preferable *8*
preferido/a favorite *3*
preferir (ie, i) to prefer *3*, 4
el **prefijo** area code 13
la **pregunta** question *P3*, P4
preguntar to ask (a question) *P1*, 8
el **premio** prize *9*
la **prenda (de ropa)** clothes *5*
la **prensa** press *17*
la **preocupación** preoccupation *13*
preocupado/a preoccupied *11*
preocuparse to worry 10
preparar to prepare *3*, 5; **preparar la comida** to cook 5; **prepararse** to get ready 16
el **preparativo** plan, preparation *11*
la **preparatoria** college preparatory *1*
la **presencia** presence *17*
presenciar to watch, to see *6*
la **presentación** introduction *P1*
presentar to introduce P2; to present *2*
presente here, present *P3*; **tener presente** to keep in mind *13*
el **presidente,** la **presidenta** president *9*
la **presión** stress 11
prestar to lend 7; **prestar atención** to pay attention *17*
la **pretensión:** la **pretensión económica** desired salary *8*
el **pretérito** preterit *12*
primario/a elementary *17*; la **primaria** elementary school *1*
la **primavera** spring 6
primer first *P1*, 6
primero/a first 6
primitivo/a primitive *9*
el **primo,** la **prima** cousin 4
principal principal, main *5*
el **príncipe** prince *8*
el **principio** beginning *6*; principle *11*
los **principios** principles *11*
la **prioridad** priority *8*
la **prisa: tener prisa** to be in a hurry 4
privado/a private *12*
la **probabilidad** probability *16*
probable probable 11
probablemente probably *12*
el **probador** fitting room 7
probar (ue) to try 7; **probarse (ue)** to try on 7
el **problema** problem *P4*, 4
la **procedencia** origin *13*
la **procesión** procession *15*
la **producción** production *13*
producido/a produced *16*
producir (zc) to produce *8*
el **producto** product *17*
el **productor,** la **productora** producer *13*
la **profesión** profession 8
profesional professional *6*
el **profesor,** la **profesora** professor P3
el **programa** program *1*
la **programación** programming *1*
el **programador,** la **programadora** programmer 8
programar to program *12*
progresivo/a progressive *9*
el **progreso** progress *14*
la **prohibición** prohibition *16*
prohibir to prohibit, to forbid 10
el **promedio** average *11*
la **promoción** graduating class *17*
promover (ue) to promote *15*
el **pronombre** pronoun *1*
el **pronóstico** forecast *6*
pronto soon 8
la **pronunciación** pronunciation *P1*
la **propina** tip 10
propio same *5*; own *7*
proponer (g) to propose *16*; **proponerse** to set oneself to do to something *13*
la **proporción** proportion *16*
proporcionar to offer *8*
proseguir (i) to continue *9*
la **protección** protection *12*
proteger (j) to protect *12*
la **proteína** protein *10*
la **provincia** province *12*
próximo next 3; near *14*; **próxima entrega** immediate possession *5*
el **proyecto** project *3*
prudente wise *13*
la **prueba** proof *14*
la **psicología** psychology 1
psicológico/a psychological *8*
el **psicólogo,** la **psicóloga** psychologist 8
el/la **psiquiatra** psychiatrist 8
psiquiátrico/a psychiatric *12*
Pts. abbreviation for pesetas
publicado/a published *13*

la **publicidad** advertising *2*
público/a public *2,* 11
el **pueblo** town 11
el **puente** bridge *16*
la **puerta** door P3; gate 12
el **puerto** port 12
puertorriqueño/a Puerto Rican 2
pues well P4; since *2*
el **puesto** position 8
el **pulmón** lung 11
la **pulsera** bracelet 7
el **punto** point *7*; **dos puntos** colon *13*; **en punto** sharp P4
la **puntuación** punctuation *17*
puntual punctual *P2*
puntualmente punctually *13*
el **pupitre** desk P3
el **puré:** el **puré de papas** mashed potatoes 10
puro/a pure 11

Q

qué what P3; **¿qué hay?** hello *13*; **¡qué va!** no way!, of course not 1
que that 2; **lo que** what, that which *1*; **ya que** since *17*
quedar to fit, to have something left 7; to be, to remain 10; **quedar en** + *inf* to agree on + *present participle* 15
quejarse to complain *8*
quemar to burn *8,* 16
querer (ie) to want, to love 4
querido/a dear 13
el **queso** cheese 3
quién who P2
quien who 11
la **química** chemistry 1
quince fifteen P4
la **quinceañera** celebration of a girl's fifteenth birthday, fifteen year-old girl *15*
quinientos five hundred 3
quinto fifth 6
el **quiosco** kiosk *13*
quitar to take away, to remove 5; **quitarse** to take off 5
quizá(s) maybe 7

R

el **radiador** radiator 12
radicalmente radically *17*
el/la **radio** radio *2,* 5
la **radiografía** X-rays 11
rallado/a grated *8*
rápidamente rapidly, fast 13
la **rapidez** speed *17*; **con rapidez** rapidly, fast 13
rápido/a fast *2,* 13
raro/a odd 15; **rara vez** seldom *11*
el **rasgo** characteristic, trait *17*
el **rastrillo** razor (in Mexico and other countries) *14*
el **rato** while *9,* 16; **dentro de un rato** in a while 16
la **raya: de rayas** striped 7
la **raza** race, breed *15*
la **razón: por estas razones** that's why 11; **tener razón** to be right 4
la **reacción** reaction *2*
real real *8*; royal *14*
la **realidad** reality *2*; **en realidad** really *2*
realista realistic *P2*
realizado/a carried out *8*
realizar (c) to do, to perform *8,* 17; to accomplish 17
realmente really 13
reanudar to resume *17*
la **rebaja** sale 7
rebajado/a marked down 7
rebelde rebellious *P2*
la **recepción** reception 14
la **recepcionista** receptionist 8
el **receso** break *P4*
la **receta** recipe *10*; prescription 11
recetar to prescribe 11
recibir to receive *6,* 13
reciente recent *8*
recoger (j) to pick up *13,* 16
recomendar (ie) to recommend *7*
reconocer (zc) to recognize *13*
reconocido/a recognized *13*
reconquistar to win back *13*
recordar (ue) to remember *13,* 15; to remind 17
recorrer to travel *15*
rectangular rectangular P3
rectificar (qu) rectify *8*
los **recuerdos** regards 13
rechazar (c) to turn down, to refuse *13*
la **red** net *6*
el **redactor,** la **redactora** editor *9*
redondo/a round P3
reducido/a small *17*
reducir (zc) to reduce *17*
referir (ie, i) to refer *16*
reflejar to reflect 17
el **refresco** soda 3
el **refrigerador** refrigerator 5
el **refugio** country/mountain resort *4*
regalar to give (a present) *7*
el **regalo** present 7

regatear to bargain, to haggle *7*
el **régimen** system *17*
regio/a royal *14*
la **región** region *12*
el **reglamento** regulation, law *13*
regresar to come back 14
la **regulación** regulation, rule *12*
regular so, so P1
regularmente regularly *11,* 13
el **reino** kingdom *12*
reír(se) (i) to laugh 6
la **relación** relation *1,* 17; relationship 4
relacionado/a related *2,* 13
la **relajación** relaxation *9*
relativamente relatively *4,* 13
religioso/a religious *P2*
el **reloj** clock, watch P3
relleno/a filled *10*; el **chile relleno** green pepper filled with cheese *10*
remodelar to remodel *5*
renovar (ue) to renew *7*
la **renta** rent *12*
reñido/a close (game) 6
repartir to deliver *13*
repasar to review 3
repente: de repente suddenly *13*
repercutir to reflect *11*
repetir (i) to repeat *P1*
replantar to replant *16*
reportar to report *9*
el/la **representante** representative *17*
representar to represent *2*
la **represión** repression *17*
la **república** republic *13*
el **requesón** cottage cheese 10
la **reservación** reservation 12
reservado/a reserved *2*
reservar to make a reservation 12
la **residencia** residence, home *4*
residencial residential *12*
el/la **residente** resident *9*
la **resistencia** resistance *9*
resistir to resist, to withstand *16*
resolver (ue) to solve *13*
respecto: con respecto a with respect to *8*
respetar to respect 15
el **respeto** respect *17*
la **respiración** breathing *9*
respirar to breathe *9*
la **responsabilidad** responsibility *5*
responsable responsible *8*
la **respuesta** answer *1*
el **restaurante** restaurant *3,* 10
el **resto** rest *5*; *pl* traces *16*
el **resultado** result *4*
resultar to be *4*
la **reunión** meeting 8
reunirse to get together *1,* 15
el **revelado** development *14*
revertido/a: la **llamada de cargo revertido** collect call 13
revisar to inspect, to examine 12
la **revista** magazine *3,* 4
el **rey:** los **Reyes Magos** the three Wise Men 15
rico/a rich 2
ridículo/a ridiculous *11*
el **riesgo** danger, risk *11*
la **rifa** raffle *3*
el **rincón** place, corner *12*
el **río** river *12*
la **riqueza** wealth *14*
rítmico/a rhythmic *9*
el **ritmo** rhythm 11
el **robo** theft *14*
el **robot** robot *8*
el **rock** rock *3*
rodeado/a surrounded *17*
rojo/a red 2
el **romance** romance *13*
romántico/a romantic P2
romper to break, to tear 16
el **ron** rum *3*
roncar to snore *8*
la **ropa** clothes 5; la **ropa interior** underwear *13*
la **rosa** rose *2*
rosado/a pink 2
roto/a broken, torn 16
rubio/a blond 2
rudo/a rough *6*
el **ruido** noise 13
las **ruinas** ruins *14*
rural rural 11
ruso/a Russian 1

S

el **sábado** Saturday P4
la **sábana** sheet 5
saber to know *P3,* 8; **sé** I know *P3,* 2
el **sabor** flavor *12*
el **sabotaje** sabotage *16*
sacar (qu) to get *1,* 2; to check out, to take out 3; **sacar fotos** to take pictures *14*
sacudir to dust 5
sagitariano/a Sagittarian *13*
la **sal** salt *8,* 10
la **sala** living room 5; la **sala de espera** waiting room 12
el **salario** salary 17
la **salida** departure *P4,* 12; exit *16*

salir (g) to leave *1*; to go out, to leave 5
el **salón (de clase)** classroom P3
la **salsa** sauce *2,* 10; type of music *13*
saltar to jump 7
el **salto** jumping *9*
la **salud** health *8,* 10
saludable healthy *7*
saludar to greet *2*
el **saludo** greeting P1
salvadoreño/a Salvadoran 2
el **sándwich** sandwich 3
la **sangre** blood 11
la **sanidad: Ministerio de Sanidad** Health Department *11*
sano/a healthy *7,* 10
el **santo,** la **santa** saint *15*
la **satisfacción** satisfaction *8*
satisfacer (g) to satisfy *8*
satisfactorio/a satisfactory *11*
la **sauna** sauna *9*
el **saxofón** saxophone *3*
se yourself P1; himself *3,* 5; herself, itself, yourselves, themselves 5; (to) him, her, you, it 16
sea: o sea that is *15*
la **secadora** drier 5
secar (qu) to dry 5
la **sección** section 12
seco/a dry 16
la **secretaría** department *12*
el **secretario,** la **secretaria** secretary *4,* 8
el **secreto** secret *3*
el **sector** area *8*
la **secundaria** high school *1*
la **sed: tener sed** to be thirsty 4
seguir (i) to follow *P2,* 6; **seguir cursos** to take courses *7*; **seguir derecho** to go straight ahead 8
según according to *P4,* 4
segundo second *P2,* 6
seguramente for sure 7
la **seguridad** security *11*; **cinturón de seguridad** safety belt *11,* 12
seguro/a sure 2; el **seguro** insurance 12
seis six P4
seiscientos six hundred 3
la **selección** selection *13*
selecto/a select *9*
el **sello** stamp 13
la **selva** jungle *12*
el **semáforo** traffic light 12
la **semana** week P4
semanal weekly *5*
el **semestre** semester 1
sencillo/a simple, easy *13*; single 14
sensato/a sensible *11*
sensitivo/a sensitive *10*
sentarse (ie) to sit down *P2,* 5
sentimental sentimental P2
el **sentimiento** feeling *8*
sentir (ie, i) to be sorry 10; **lo siento** I'm sorry P1; **sentirse (ie)** to feel *2,* 11
la **señal** signal *12*; **señal de tráfico** traffic signal *12*
señalar to point to *7*
señor Mr P1
señora Mrs. P1
señorial stately *5*
señorita Miss P1
separado/a separated *17*
se(p)tiembre September 6
séptimo/a seventh 6
la **sequía** drought 16
ser to be P2; el **ser** being *15*
la **serie** series *6*
serio/a serious P2
el **servicio** service *4,* 11
la **servilleta** napkin 10
servir (i) to serve 6; **¿en qué puedo servirle(s)?** may I help you? 7
sesenta sixty P4
la **sesión** session 9
setecientos seven hundred 3
setenta seventy P4
el **sexo** sex 15
sexto sixth 6
sexual sexual 17
sí yes P2
si if *4,* 6
la **sicología** psychology 1
el **sicólogo,** la **sicóloga** psychologist *8*
siempre always 1
la **siesta** nap *4*
siete seven P4
el **siglo** century *15*
el **signatario** person who signs *13*
el **signo** sign *13*
siguiente next *P4,* 9
la **silla** chair P3
el **símbolo** symbol *12*
similar similar *7*
simpático/a nice, charming 2
simplemente simply 13
sin without *7,* 8; **sin embargo** nevertheless *1*; **sin que** without 17
sincero/a sincere *P2*
sino but *8*
el **síntoma** symptom 11
el/la **siquiatra** psychiatrist 8
sísmico/a seismic *16*
el **sismo** earthquake *16*
el **sistema** system *6*
la **situación** situation 16
situado/a situated *8*
el **smog** smog 16
sobre on, above P3; el **sobre** envelope 13

sobrepasar to surpass *17*
la **sobrina** niece 4
el **sobrino** nephew 4
social social 11
la **sociedad** society 17
socorro: casa de socorro first-aid center *11*
el **sodio** sodium *16*
el **sofá** sofa 5
el **sol** sun 6; **hace sol** it's sunny 6
solicitar to ask for *8*
la **solicitud** application *7,* 8
solidario/a solidary *15*
sólo only 2
solo/a alone *4*; **solos/as** by themselves *4*
soltero/a single 2
la **solución** answer *P4*
el **sombrero** hat 7
sonar (ue) to ring *7*
sonreír(se) (i) to smile 6
la **sopa** soup 3
el **sorbete** sherbet 10
sorprenderse to be surprised *13*
la **sorpresa** surprise *13,* 15
el **sorteo** drawing *15*
el **sótano** basement *16*
Sr. abbreviation for **señor** P1
Sra. abbreviation for **señora** P1
Srta. abbreviation for **señorita** P1
su(s) his *P1,* 4; her, your, its, their 4
suave soft 15
subir to increase, to go up *6*; to raise, to go up 9
subrayado/a underlined *4*
subterráneo/a underground *13*
el **suceso** event, happening *16*
sucio/a dirty *16*
la **sucursal** branch *8*
la **sudadera** sweat shirt, jogging suit 7
la **suegra** mother–in–law 4
el **suegro** father–in–law 4
el **sueldo** salary 8
el **sueño: tener sueño** to be sleepy 4
la **suerte: tener suerte** to be lucky 4
el **suéter** sweater 7
suficiente enough 10
sufrir to suffer 11
la **sugerencia** suggestion *7*
sugerir (ie, i) to suggest *11*
la **suite** suite *15*
suizo/a Swiss *14*
la **sujeción** subordination *13*
el **sujeto** subject *3*
la **suma** amount *8*
superar to surpass *17*
superficial superficial *2*
la **superficie** surface, area *16*
el **supermercado** supermarket *7,* 10
el **supervisor,** la **supervisora** supervisor *2*
supuesto: por supuesto of course 15
el **sur** south *8*
surgir (j) to appear *13*
la **sustancia** element, substance *10*
suyo (-a, -os, -as) your, (of) yours, (of) his/her, (of) hers, (of) its, their, (of) theirs 14

T

la **tabla** chart *5*
el **tablero** notice board *13*
tacaño/a stingy *P3*
el **taco** rolled or folded tortilla filled with meat, beans, etc. *2*
tal: con tal (de) que provided that 17; **qué tal** how are you P1; **tal como** as 15; **tal vez** perhaps 10
el **talón** heel 9
la **talla** size 7
el **taller** shop 8
el **tamaño** size *2*
también also, too 2
tampoco neither, not either 8
tan so 1; as 9
tanto as much 9
tantos as many 9
la **taquilla** ticket office 6
tarde late 5; **la tarde** afternoon P1
la **tarea** homework *P2,* 1; la **tarea doméstica** house chore 5
la **tarifa** tariff *14*
la **tarjeta** card *7,* 12
el **taxi** taxi *12*
el/la **taxista** taxi driver *17*
la **taza** cup *3,* 10
te yourself P1; you (*fam sing*) 5; (to) you 7
el **té** tea 3
el **teatro** theater *2,* 14
técnico/a technical 17
la **tecnología** technology *1*
el **techo** roof 5
la **tela** material 7
la **tele** television 5
telefónico/a *adj* telephone *7,* 13
el **teléfono** telephone *P4,* 3
el **telégrafo** telegraph *13*
el **telegrama** telegram 13
la **telenovela** soap opera *11*
la **televisión** television 3
televisivo/a *adj* television, telegenic *6*
el **televisor** television set *2,* 5
el **tema** theme, topic *10*
el **temblor** earthquake *16*
temer to fear 10

la **temperatura** temperature *6,* 13
el **templo** temple *14*
temporal temporary *4*
temprano early 5
la **tendencia** tendency *6*
tender (ie) to hang *5*; **tender la cama** to make the bed 5
el **tenedor** fork 10
tener (g, ie) to have *P3,* 4; **tener presente** to keep in mind *13*; **tener que** + *inf* to have to + *verb* 4
el **tenis** tennis *P4,* 6
la **tensión** pressure, stress 11
teórico/a theoretic, theoretical *17*
tercer third *P3,* 6
tercero third 6
terminado/a finished *13*
terminar to finish, to end *1,* 3
el **término** term *17*; el **término medio** average *17*
el **termómetro** thermometer 11
la **terraza** terrace *4,* 5
el **terremoto** earthquake 16
terrible terrible *P2,* 15
el **terrorismo** terrorism *17*
ti (to, for) you (*fam sing*) 7
la **tía** aunt 4
el **tiempo** weather 6; time 15; **a tiempo** on time 12; **hace buen/mal tiempo** the weather is fine/bad 6; **¿qué tiempo hace?** How's the weather? 6
la **tienda** store 7; la **tienda de campaña** tent 16
la **tierra** land *12*
el **tigre** tiger *2*
tímido/a timid *P2*
la **tintorería** cleaners 14
el **tío** uncle 4
típico/a typical *2,* 10
el **tipo** type *4*; kind *17*
tirar to pull *15*; to throw 17
la **tiza** chalk P3
la **toalla** towel 5
el **tobillo** ankle 9
tocar (qu) to play (an instrument) 3; to knock 8
el **tocino** bacon 10
todavía still 7
todo everything 12; **eso es todo** that's all 10
todos all *2,* 12; **en todas partes** everywhere 10; **todos los días** everyday 6
tomar to drink, to take 3
el **tomate** tomato *P3,* 3
la **tonelada** ton *15*
tonto/a silly, foolish 2
el **toque** sound to signal an activity *17*
torcer (ue, z) to twist 12
el **torero** bullfighter *15*
el **tornado** tornado 16
el **toro** bull *13*; la **corrida de toros** bullfight 13; la **plaza de toros** bullring *13*
la **torta** sandwich (in Mexico) *3*
la **tortilla** thin cornmeal or flour cake *2*; omelette *10*
la **tortura** torture *15*
la **tos** cough 11
toser 11
la **tostada** toast 3
tostado/a: pan tostado toast 3
total total *2*
totalmente totally *15*
trabajador/a hard working 2
trabajar to work 1
el **trabajo** work *1,* 8
el **trabajomaníaco,** la **trabajomaníaca** workaholic *8*
la **tradición** tradition *4,* 15
tradicional traditional *7*
tradicionalmente traditionally 13
traducir (zc) to translate 13
traer to bring 10
el **tráfico** traffic *12*
el **traje** suit 7; el **traje de baño** bathing suit 7
la **tramitación** transaction *16*
tranquilamente calmly 13
el **tranquilizante** tranquilizer *11*
tranquilo/a calm *P2,* 2
la **transacción** transaction *4*
el **tránsito** transit *12*
transmitir to transmit *13*
el **transporte** transportation *12*
el **tranvía** streetcar *11*
tras after *11*
trasladarse to move, to transport *12*
el **traslado** transportation *12*
el **trastorno** disorder *16*
tratar (de) to try to *6*; to treat *14*
el **trato** treatment *17*
través: a través de throughout *14*
trece thirteen P4
treinta thirty P4
el **tren** train 12
tres three P4
trescientos three hundred 3
triste sad 2
triunfar to succeed *17*
el **triunfo** victory *13*
el **trópico** tropics *12*
trotar to jog 3

el **trote** gait *9*
tu(s) your 4
tú you (*fam sing*) P1
tumbar to knock down *16*
el **turismo** tourism *12*
el/la **turista** tourist *4*
turístico/a *adj* tourist *14*
turno session *6*; la **farmacia de turno** pharmacy that takes turns attending customers holidays and Sundays *11*
tuyo (-a, -os, -as) (of) yours 14

U

u or *13*
últimamente lately *16*
último/a last *1*
un/a a, an P3; one P4
únicamente only *15*
la **unidad** unit *17*
unido/a united *4*
la **unión** union *9*
la **universidad** university 1
universitario/a *adj* university *8*
uno one P4
unos some 1
la **urbanización** housing development *4*
urbano/a urban *9,* 11
urgente urgent *12*
urgentemente urgently *8*
usar to use *P4*
usted you (*formal sing*) P1
ustedes you (*formal pl*) 1
útil useful *P1*
utilizar (c) to use *13*

V

va: ¡qué va! of course not, no way 1
las **vacaciones** vacation *3,* 4
vacío/a empty 12
la **vainilla** vanilla 10
la **vajilla** china 10
valiente valiant, brave *P2*
valioso/a useful *13*
valor value *10,* 17; courage *15*
valorar to value *8*
los **vaqueros** jeans 7
variante (multiple choice) answer *11*
variar to vary *7*
la **variedad** variety *12*
varios/as several *3,* 14
vasco/a Basque *6*
el **vaso** glass *3,* 10
vecino/a neighbor *13,* 16
el **vegetal** vegetable 3
vegetariano/a vegetarian *10*
el **vehículo** vehicle 11
veinte twenty P4
veinticinco twenty-five P4
veinticuatro twenty-four P4
veintidós twenty-two P4
veintinueve twenty-nine P4
veintiocho twenty-eight P4
veintiséis twenty-six P4
veintisiete twenty-seven P4
veintitrés twenty-three P4
veintiún/veintiuno twenty-one P4
la **vela** sail, sailboat *14*; candle *15*
la **velocidad** speed *6*
vendado/a bandaged 12
el **vendedor,** la **vendedora** salesperson 8
vender to sell 3
venezolano/a Venezuelan 2
venir (g, ie) to come 4
la **venta** sale 8
la **ventaja** advantage 11
la **ventana** window P3
la **ventanilla** window (car, train, etc.) 12
las **ventas** sales 8
la **ventilación** ventilation *13*
ver to see *2,* 3
el **verano** summer 6
el **verbo** verb *1*
la **verdad** truth 4
verdadero/a true *P3*
verde green 2
la **verdura** vegetable *3,* 10
el **vestido** dress 7
vestir (i) to dress 6; **vestirse** to get dressed 6
la **vez** (*pl* **veces**) time *2,* 9; **alguna vez** sometime 12; **en vez de** instead of 7; **otra vez** again *P4,* 7; **tal vez** perhaps 10; **una vez** once 12; **a veces** sometimes, at times *4,* 12; **algunas veces** sometimes 12
la **vía** lane *12*; (railroad) track *12*
viajar to travel *14*
el **viaje** trip *3,* 4
vibrante vibrant *15*
la **víctima** victim *16*
la **vida** life *6,* 11; living 11
el **vídeo/video** video *4*
viejo/a old 2
el **viento** wind 6; **hace viento** it's windy *6*
el **viernes** Friday P4
vigilar to watch *11*
vigor: en vigor in force *13*
el **vinagre** vinegar 10
el **vino** wine 10
la **violencia** violence *13,* 15
violento/a violent *6*
el **violín** violin *3*
el/la **violinista** violinist *10*
la **visa** visa 12
el **visado** visa 12

la **visita** visit 10
el/la **visitante** visitor *2*
visitar to visit *3,* 4
el **visón** mink *7*
la **vista** view *5*
la **vitalidad** vitality *13*
vivir to live 3
vivo/a *adj* live *6*; alive *13*
el **vocabulario** vocabulary *P1*
la **vocal** vowel *P1*
el **vól(e)ibol** volleyball 6
el **volante** steering wheel 12
volar (ue) to fly *8,* 12
el **volcán** volcano *16*
voluntario/a voluntary *16*
volver (ue) to come 4
vosotros/as you (*fam pl*) 1
la **voz: en voz baja** softly 17
el **vuelo** flight 12
la **vuelta: dar vueltas** to spin around *15*; el **pasaje de ida y vuelta** round trip ticket 12
vuestro/a(s) your (*fam pl*) 4

Y

y and P1
ya already 1; **ya que** since *17*
el **yerno** son-in-law 4
yo I P2
el **yoga** yoga *9*
el **yogur** yogurt 10
el **yudo** judo 6

Z

la **zanahoria** carrot 10
el **zapato** shoe 5; los **zapatos (de) tenis** tennis shoes 7
la **zona** zone *4,* 10

ENGLISH-SPANISH VOCABULARY

A

A.D. (after Christ) d.C.
a un/a
to **abandon** abandonar
ability la habilidad
able: to **be able to** poder (ue)
abnormal anormal
about the middle of a mediados de
above sobre
abroad en el extranjero
absent ausente
absurd absurdo/a
to **accept** aceptar
accessory accesorio/a
accident (*car*) el choque, el accidente
to **accompany** acompañar
to **accomplish** realizar (c)
according to según, de acuerdo con
accounting la contabilidad
accumulated acumulado/a
ache el dolor
to **achieve** lograr
acid ácido/a
acoustics la acústica
to **act** actuar
action el acto
active activo/a
actively activamente
activity la actividad
actor el actor
actress la actriz
ad el anuncio
add añadir
address la dirección; el domicilio; *v* dirigirse
adequate adecuado/a
adequately adecuadamente
to **administer** administrar
administrative administrativo/a
administrator el administrador, la administradora
admiration la admiración
adult la persona mayor
advance el adelanto
advantage la ventaja
adventure la aventura
adverbial adverbial
advertising la publicidad
advice el consejo
advisor el consejero, la consejera
aerobic aeróbico/a
aerogram el aerograma
to **affect** influir (y), afectar
affected afectado/a
affectionate afectivo/a
affirmative afirmativo/a
afraid: to **be afraid** tener miedo
after al cabo de; tras; después
afternoon la tarde
again otra vez
against contra
age la edad
agency la agencia; **travel agency** la agencia de viajes
agenda la agenda
agent el/la agente
ago hace + *time expression* + *preterit*
to **agree** estar de acuerdo; to **agree on** + *pres part* quedar en + *inf*
agreeable conforme
aggressive agresivo/a
ahead: to **go straight ahead** seguir derecho
air el aire; *adj* aéreo/a; **air conditioning** el aire acondicionado; **open air** el (al) aire libre
airline la aerolínea
airplane el avión, el aparato
airport el aeropuerto
alarm clock el despertador
alarming alarmante
album el álbum
alcohol el alcohol
alcoholic alcohólico/a
alfalfa la alfalfa
algebra el álgebra
alive vivo/a
all todo, todos; **that's all** eso es todo
allergic alérgico/a
allergy la alergia
to **allow** admitir; permitir
almost casi
alone solo/a
along a lo largo de
already ya
also también
although aunque
always siempre
ambitious ambicioso/a
ambulance la ambulancia
American norteamericano/a
among entre
amount la cantidad, la suma
ample amplio/a
amusing divertido/a
an un/a
analysis el análisis
and y, e
anesthesia la anestesia
angel el ángel
animal el animal
ankle el tobillo
anniversary el aniversario
to **announce** anunciar
announcer el locutor, la locutora
another otro/a
to **answer** contestar; *n* la contestación, la solución, la respuesta; **answer (multiple choice)** la variante; **answering machine** el contestador automático

anthropological antropológico/a
anthropology la antropología
antibiotic el antibiótico
antihistaminic el antihistamínico
antimony el antimonio
anxiety la ansiedad
any alguno/a; algún; cualquier
anyone alguien
anything algo; **anything else?** ¿algo más?
apartment el apartamento
to **appear** aparecer (zc); surgir (j)
to **applaud** aplaudir
apple la manzana
application la solicitud
to **appreciate** apreciar
apprenticeship el aprendizaje
appropriate apropiado/a
approximate aproximado/a
April abril
Arab árabe
architect el arquitecto, la arquitecta
architectonic arquitectónico/a
architecture la arquitectura
area el sector, el área *fem;* **area code** el indicativo, el prefijo; **surrounding areas** los alrededores
Argentine cowboy el gaucho
to **argue** discutir
argument la discusión
arid árido/a
arm el brazo
armchair la butaca
aroma el aroma
around alrededor
arrest el arresto
arrival la llegada
to **arrive** llegar (gu)
arrow la flecha
art el arte
artery la arteria
article el artículo
artist el/la artista
artistic artístico/a
as como; tal como; **as much as** tanto como; **as many as** tantos/as como; **as soon as** en cuanto
to **ask (a question)** preguntar; hacer (g) una pregunta; to **ask for** pedir (i), solicitar
aspect el aspecto
aspiration la aspiración
aspirin la aspirina
to **assert** afirmar
to **assign** destinar
assignment el mando
assistant el asistente, la asistenta
to **associate** asociar
associated commonwealth el estado libre asociado
to **assume** adoptar
asterisk el asterisco
asthma el asma
astronaut el/la astronauta
astronomer el astrónomo, la astrónoma
at a; en; **at least** por lo menos
athlete el/la atleta
athletics el atletismo
atmosphere el ambiente; el marco
attaché case el maletín
to **attack** atacar (qu)
to **attend** asistir; to **attend to** ocuparse de
attendance la asistencia
attention la atención; to **pay attention** prestar atención
attitude la actitud
to **attract** atraer
attraction la atracción
attractive atractivo/a
August agosto
aunt la tía
authoritarian autoritario/a
autumn el otoño
availiability la disposición
available disponible
avenue la avenida
average el promedio, el término medio
aviation la aviación
avocado el aguacate
to **avoid** evitar
aware alerta
Aztec azteca

B

B.C. (before Christ) a.C.
baby el bebé
back la espalda
background el marco; el ambiente
backpack la mochila
bacon el tocino
bad mal, malo/a; **very bad** pésimo
bag la bolsa
bakery la panadería
balance el equilibrio
ball la pelota
ballpoint pen el bolígrafo
banana la banana, el plátano
bandaged vendado/a
bank el banco
banquet el banquete
to **baptize** bautizar (c)
bar el bar
barbarian bárbaro/a
barbecue la barbacoa
barber shop la peluquería
barbituric barbitúrico
to **bargain** regatear
to **bark** ladrar
baseball el béisbol
based on en base a
basement el sótano
basic básico/a

basically básicamente; eminentemente
basket el cesto; la cesta
basketball el baloncesto, el básquetbol
Basque vasco/a
to **bathe** bañar(se); **bathing suit** el traje de baño
bathroom el baño
battery la pila
bay la bahía
to **be** estar; ser; resultar; to **be a couple** formar pareja; to **be able to, can** poder (ue); to **be afraid** tener miedo; to **be born** nacer; to **be called,** to **be named** llamarse; to **be careful** tener cuidado; to **be founded on** basarse en; to **be glad** alegrarse; to **be hot** tener calor; to **be hungry** tener hambre; to **be in a hurry** tener prisa; to **be in charge** estar a cargo; to **be in love** estar enamorado/a (de); to **be lucky** tener suerte; to **be missing** faltar; to **be necessary** hacer falta; to **be noticeable** notarse; to **be part of** formar parte de; to **be right** tener razón; to **be sleepy** tener sueño; to **be sorry** sentir (ie, i); to **be successful** tener éxito; to **be surprised** sorprenderse; to **be thirsty** tener sed; to **be used to** estar acostumbrado/a
beach la playa
beans los frijoles
beast la fiera
beautiful precioso/a; bello/a
beauty la belleza; **beauty parlor (beauty salon)** el salón de belleza, la peluquería
because porque
to **become** hacerse; to **become short** entrecortar
bed la cama; to **go to bed** acostarse; to **put to bed** acostar; to **stay in bed** guardar cama
bedroom el dormitorio
beer la cerveza
before antes; antes (de) que; ante
beforehand con anticipación
to **begin** empezar (ie, c), comenzar (ie, c), iniciar
beginning el principio; **beginning at** a partir de
behavior la conducta
behind detrás (de)
being el ser
to **believe** creer
bellboy el botones
to **belong** pertenecer (zc); **belonging to** perteneciente a
below abajo; a continuación
belt el cinturón; **safety belt** el cinturón de seguridad
to **bend** doblar
benefit el beneficio
berth la litera
besides además
best mejor; óptimo
to **bet** apostar (ue)
better mejor
between entre
beyond más allá (de)
bicycle la bicicleta
big grande
bill la cuenta
biology la biología
bird el pájaro, el ave
birth el nacimiento
birthday el cumpleaños
birthrate la natalidad
black negro/a
blackboard la pizarra
blanket la manta
blender la licuadora
blond rubio/a
blood la sangre
blouse la blusa
blue azul
boarder el interno, la interna
boarding el embarque; **boardinghouse** la pensión; **boarding pass** tarjeta de embarque 12
body el cuerpo; el órgano
to **boil** hervir (ie, i)
boiled hervido/a
bolívar (monetary unit of Venezuela) bolívar
Bolivian boliviano/a
bone el hueso
book el libro
bookstore la librería
boot la bota
booth la caseta
born: to **be born** nacer
boss el jefe, la jefa
both ambos/as
to **bother** molestar
bottle la botella
box la casilla
boxing el boxeo
boy el chico, el muchacho; **Boy Scouts** niños exploradores
boyfriend el novio
bracelet la pulsera
brain el cerebro; **brain drain** la fuga de cerebros
to **brake** frenar
branch la sucursal
brand la marca
brave valiente
bread el pan
break el receso; *v* romper; to **break down** descomponer(se) (g)
breakfast el desayuno
to **breathe** respirar
breathing la respiración
to **breed** criar
bridge el puente
to **bring** traer (g)
brochure el folleto
broken roto/a; fracturado/a

bronze el bronce
brother el hermano; **brother–in–law** el cuñado; **brothers, brother and sister** los hermanos
brown café, castaño/a
brunette moreno/a
bugler el corneta
to **build** construir (y)
building el edificio, la construcción
built construido/a
bull el toro
bullfight la corrida (de toros), la fiesta brava
bullfighter el torero
bullring la plaza de toros
bumper el parachoques
to **burn** quemar
bus el autobús
business *adj* comercial; *n* el negocio; **business matters** la materia económica
busy ocupado/a, atareado/a
but pero; sino
butter la mantequilla
button el botón
buy comprar
buyer el comprador, la compradora

C

café el café
cafeteria la cafetería
calamity la calamidad
calcium el calcio
calculator la calculadora
calculus el cálculo
calendar el calendario
to **call** llamar; to **call roll** pasar (la) lista; *n* la llamada; **collect call** la llamada a cobrar, la llamada de cargo revertido; to **be called** llamarse; **who's calling?** ¿de parte de quién?
calm tranquilo/a
calmly tranquilamente
calorie la caloría
camera la cámara
camp el campamento
campaign la campaña
can la lata; *v* poder (ue)
cancel cancelar
cancer el cáncer
candle la vela
candy el caramelo, el dulce
canoe la canoa
canoeing el piragüismo
capital la capital; **capital letter** la mayúscula
car el auto, el automóvil, el coche, el carro; **sleeping car** coche cama
card la tarjeta
cardboard el cartón
cardiovascular cardiovascular
career la carrera
careful: to **be careful** tener cuidado
carefully con cuidado
careless descuidado/a
cargo la carga
carpet la alfombra
carried out realizado/a
carrot la zanahoria
to **carry** cargar (gu)
case el caso; **attaché case** el maletín
cash en efectivo; **cash register** la caja
cashier el cajero, la cajera
cassette el casete
Castilian castellano/a
castle el castillo
casual informal
cat el gato, la gata
catastrophic catastrófico/a
category la categoría
cathedral la catedral
to **cause** causar, ocasionar; *n* la causa
caused causado/a
to **celebrate** celebrar
census el censo
cent el centavo
center: shopping center el centro comercial
centigrade centígrado
central central
century el siglo
ceramics la cerámica
cereal el cereal
ceremony la ceremonia
certain cierto/a
chain la cadena
chair la silla
chalk la tiza
champagne el champán
champion el campeón, la campeona
championship el campeonato
change cambiar; *n* el cambio
channel el canal
characteristic el rasgo, la característica
to **characterize** caracterizar (c)
charge: to **be in charge** estar a cargo
charity la caridad
charm el encanto
charming encentador/a; simpático/a
chart la tabla, el cuadro
cheap barato/a
to **check (luggage)** chequear, facturar; *n* el cheque; to **check out** sacar (qu)
checked de cuadros
cheek la mejilla
cheerfully amablemente
cheese el queso
chemistry la química
chess el ajedrez
to **chew** masticar (qu); **chewing gum** el chicle
chicken el pollo
child el niño, la niña
children *adj* infantil; *n* los niños, las niñas
Chilean chileno/a

china la vajilla; **china cabinet** el aparador
Chinese chino/a
chocolate el chocolate
cholesterol el colesterol
to **choose** escoger (j), elegir (j)
chore: house chore la tarea doméstica
christening el bautizo
Christmas la(s) Navidad(es); **Christmas Eve** la Nochebuena
church la iglesia
cigarette el cigarrillo
circle el círculo
circular circular
circumstance la circunstancia
citizen el ciudadano, la ciudadana
city la ciudad; **city block** la cuadra; **city hall** el ayuntamiento
civil civil
civilization la civilización
civilized civilizado/a
clarification la aclaración
class la clase; **first class** de lujo
classic clásico/a
to **classify** clasificar (qu)
classmate el compañero, la compañera
classroom el salón (de) clase
to **clean** limpiar; *adj* limpio/a
cleaners la tintorería
cleaning la limpieza
clear despejado/a; claro/a
clearly claramente
clerk el dependiente, la dependienta
client el cliente, la clienta
climate el clima
clinic el hospital, la clínica
clock el reloj
to **close** cerrar (ie); *adj* (game) reñido/a
closet el armario, el closet
clothes la ropa, la prenda (de ropa)
cloud (dark) el nubarrón
cloudy nublado/a, nuboso/a
clown el payaso
club el club
coach el entrenador, la entrenadora
coast la costa
coat el abrigo
code el código; **zip code** código postal
coffee el café
cognate el cognado
to **coincide** coincidir
cold el frío; el catarro; **it's cold (weather)** hace frío
coliseum el coliseo
collaboration la colaboración
collect call llamada a cobrar, llamada de cargo revertido
collection la colección
college la facultad; **college preparatory** la preparatoria
to **collide** chocar (qu)
Colombian colombiano/a
colon dos puntos
colonel el coronel
colonial colonial
color el color; **solid color** color entero
column la columna
to **comb** peinar
combination la combinación; **combination plate** el plato combinado
to **combine** combinar
to **come** venir (g, ie); to **come back** volver (ue), regresar; to **come in** entrar, pasar
comfort la comodidad
comfortable cómodo/a
comma la coma
command el mandato
commentary el comentario
commission la comisión
commissioner el comisario
commitment el compromiso
common común
to **communicate** comunicar (qu)
communication la comunicación
communion la comunión
community la comunidad
company la compañía
to **compare** comparar
to **compete** competir (i)
competent competente
competition la competencia, la competición
to **complain** quejarse
to **complete** completar; *adj* integral
completely completamente, por completo
complex complicado/a
complication la complicación
comprehensive comprensivo/a
compulsive compulsivo/a
computer la computadora, el computador; **computer science** la informática
concentrated concentrado/a
concentration la concentración
concept el concepto
concert el concierto
condition la condición
condominium el condominio
confirmation la confirmación
conflict el conflicto
confrontation el enfrentamiento
confusion la confusión
congratulations felicidades
to **congratulate** felicitar
to **connect** conectar
connection la conexión
connotation la connotación

consequence la consecuencia
conservative conservador/a
to **consider** considerar
consolation la consolación
consonant la consonante
construction la construcción
to **consult** consultar
consultation la consulta
consumption el consumo
contact el contacto
to **contain** contener (g, ie)
contaminated contaminado/a
contest el concurso
context el contexto
to **continue** continuar, proseguir
contrary contrario/a; **on the contrary** al contrario
to **contribute** contribuir (y)
to **control** controlar
convenient conveniente
convent el convento
conversation la conversación
to **convert** convertir (ie, i)
to **convince** convencer (z)
to **cook** cocinar, preparar la comida; *n* el cocinero, la cocinera
cookie la galletita
cool fresco/a; **it's cool (weather)** hace fresco
cord la cuerda
cordial cordial
corn el maíz
corner la esquina; el rincón
corporation la empresa
correct correcto/a
to **correspond** corresponder
correspondence la correspondencia
corresponding correspondiente
cosmetic el cosmético
cosmopolitan cosmopolita
cost el costo; *v* costar (ue)
cottage cheese el requesón
to **cough** toser; *n* la tos
council la junta
to **count** contar (ue)
counter el mostrador
country el país; el campo
couple la pareja; to **be a couple** formar pareja
courage el valor
course el curso; **of course** por supuesto; **of course not** ¡qué va!; to **take courses** seguir cursos
court la cancha
courtesy la cortesía
cousin el primo, la prima
to **cover** cubrir
covered cubierto/a
coyote el coyote
crazy loco/a
to **create** crear
creative creativo/a
creativity la creatividad
credit crédito; **credit card** la tarjeta de crédito
crisis la crisis
criticism la crítica
crocodile el cocodrilo
to **cross** cruzar (c); *n* la cruz; **Red Cross** la Cruz Roja
crowd el pelotón
cruise el crucero
crutch la muleta
to **cry** llorar
Cuban cubano/a
to **cultivate** cultivar
cultural cultural
culture la cultura
cup la taza
Cupid Cupido
cure la cura
curtain la cortina
curved curvo/a
custom la costumbre
customary: it's customary se acostumbra
customs la aduana
cut cortado/a
cycling el ciclismo
cyclist el/la ciclista

D

daily diario/a; cotidiano/a; *adv* diariamente
to **damage** dañar; *n* el daño
damaged dañado
to **dance** bailar; *n* el baile, la danza
dancer el bailarín, la bailarina
danger el peligro
dangerous peligroso/a
dark oscuro/a
data los datos
date la fecha; la cita; *v* datar
daughter la hija; **daughter–in–law** la nuera
day el día; **All Souls' Day** el Día de los Muertos/Difuntos; **day student** el externo; **everyday** todos los días; **holiday** día de fiesta; the **day after tomorrow** pasado mañana; the **day before yesterday** anteayer; **weekdays** entre semana
dead muerto/a
dear estimado/a; querido/a
death la muerte
debris el escombro
debt la deuda
decaffeinated descafeinado
deceased difunto/a
December diciembre
to **decide** decidir
decision la decisión
to **declare** declarar; afirmar
to **decorate** decorar
decorated decorado/a
to **dedicate** dedicar (qu)
to **defend** defender (ie)
defender el defensor
definite definido/a
definitely definitivamente

definition la definición
defusing la desactivación
to **delight** encantar
delighted encantado/a
to **deliver** repartir
delivery: special delivery entrega especial
to **demand** imponer (g)
demonstration la manifestación
demonstrative demostrativo
dentist el/la dentista
to **deny** negar (ie)
department el departamento; la secretaría; **department store** el almacén
departure la salida
to **depend** depender
to **deposit** depositar
depressed deprimido/a
depression la depresión
derived derivado/a
descent el descenso
to **describe** describir
described descrito/a
description la descripción
desert el desierto; *adj* desértico/a
design el diseño
designed encaminado/a; diseñado/a
designer el diseñador, la diseñadora
desired salary pretensión económica
desk el escritorio, el pupitre
dessert el postre
destination el destino
to **destroy** destruir
destroyed destruido/a
destruction la destrucción
detail el detalle
detailed detallado/a
detective el detective
to **determine** determinar
detractor el detractor
to **develop** desarrollar
development el desarrollo; el revelado
dexterity la destreza
to **dial** marcar (qu), discar (qu)
dialogue el diálogo
dictionary el diccionario
to **die** morir (ue, u)
diet la dieta
difference la diferencia
different diferente
difficult difícil
difficulty la dificultad; **with difficulty** difícilmente
to **digest** digerir (ie, i)
diminished disminuido/a
dining room el comedor
dinner la comida, la cena
diplomatic diplomático/a
to **direct** administrar
directions las instrucciones
directly directamente
director el director, la directora
directory el directorio, la guía
dirty sucio/a; **dirty word** mala palabra
disadvantage la desventaja
disappointment el contratiempo
disaster la catástrofe
to **disconnect** desconectar
discoteque la discoteca
discount el descuento
to **discover** descubrir
discovery el descubrimiento
discreet discreto/a
discrimination la discriminación
discussion la negociación
dish el plato
dishwater el lavaplatos
disorder el trastorno
disposable desechable
disposal la disposición
dissatisfaction la inconformidad
distance la distancia
distinguished distinguido/a, destacado/a
distribution la distribución
district el distrito; **zip code** el distrito postal
diversity la diversidad
division la división
divorced divorciado/a
to **do** hacer (g); realizar (c)
doctor el doctor, la doctora; **doctor's office** el consultorio
dog el perro, la perra
dollar el dólar
to **dominate** dominar
donation la donación
door la puerta
double doble
to **doubt** dudar
doughnut el donut
down payment la cuota inicial, la entrada
downtown el centro
dozen la docena
to **drain** escurrir
drama el drama
dramatic dramático/a
drawing el dibujo; el sorteo
to **dress** vestir (i); to **get dressed** vestirse; *n* el vestido
dresser la cómoda
to **drink** beber, tomar; *n* la bebida
to **drive** manejar, conducir (zc)
driver el chofer
drought la sequía
drug la droga
dry seco/a; *v* secar (qu)
dryer la secadora
dualism el dualismo
duck (Argentine sport) el pato
due to debido a
duel el duelo
during durante

to **dust** sacudir
duty el deber
dynamic dinámico/a

E

each cada
ear la oreja; **(inner) ear** el oído
early temprano/a; **early morning** la madrugada
to **earn** ganar; to **earn a living** ganarse la vida
earring el arete
earthquake el terremoto, el temblor, el sismo
easily con facilidad
easy fácil, sencillo
to **eat** comer, ingerir (ie, i)
ecologist el/la ecologista
ecology la ecología
economical económico/a
economics la economía
editor el redactor, la redactora
education la educación
effect el efecto
efficient eficiente
effort el esfuerzo
egg el huevo
eight ocho; **eight hundred** ochocientos
eighteen dieciocho
eighth octavo
eighty ochenta
either: not either tampoco 8
elaborate elaborado/a
electrical appliance el electrodoméstico
electrician el/la electricista
electricity la electricidad
elegant elegante
element el elemento; la sustancia
elementary elemental; primario/a; **elementary school** la primaria
elephant el elefante
elevation la altura
elevator el ascensor
eleven once
eliminate eliminar
embrace el abrazo
embroidery el bordado
emerald la esmeralda
emergency la emergencia; **emergency center** el ambulatorio
emigration la emigración
emission la emisión
emotional emocional
emotion la emoción
to **employ** emplear
employee el empleado, la empleada
employment el empleo
empty vacío/a
to **end** acabar, terminar; *n* el extremo; el final
to **endure** aguantar
energy la energía
engagement el noviazgo
engineer el ingeniero, la ingeniera
engineering la ingeniería
English inglés, inglesa
to **enjoy** disfrutar (de)
enormous enorme
enough batante, suficiente
to **enrich** enriquecer (zc)
to **enter** entrar
entertainment la diversión
entrance la entrada
environment el medio ambiente
environmental ambiental
equal igual; **equal to** a la par con
equality la igualdad
equator el ecuador
equatorial ecuatorial
equestrian ecuestre
equivalency la equivalencia
equivalent equivalente
eraser el borrador
erosion la erosión
error el error; el fallo
eruption la erupción
escalator la escalera mecánica
especially especialmente
essential imprescindible
to **establish** establecer (zc)
established basado/a; fundado/a
European europeo/a
even aun; hasta
evening la noche
event el evento, el acontecimiento, el suceso, el hecho
every cada; **every day** todos los días
everything todo
everywhere en todas partes
evident evidente
exactly exactamente
examination el examen
to **examine** examinar; revisar
example el ejemplo
to **exceed** sobrepasar
excellent excelente
exception la excepción
excess el exceso
to **exchange** cambiar
excited emocionado/a
excitement la emoción
exclusive exclusivo/a
excuse la excusa; **excuse me** con permiso, perdón
exempt exento/a
exercise el ejercicio
to **exist** existir
exit la salida
exotic exótico/a
to **expect** esperar
expense el gasto
expensive caro/a
experience la experiencia; *v* experimentar
expert el experto, la experta
to **explain** explicar (qu)
explosive el explosivo

to **express** expresar; **express train** el expreso
expression la expresión
extended extenso/a
extension la extensión
exterior el exterior
extra extra
extraordinary extraordinario/a
extraterrestial extraterrestre
extremely extremadamente
extroverted extrovertido, extravertido/a
eye el ojo
eyebrow la ceja
eyelashes las pestañas

F

fabulous fabuloso/a
face la cara; *v* encarar, enfrentar
to **facilitate** facilitar
factor el factor
factory la fábrica
fair la feria; *adj* justo/a
to **fall** caer(se)
false falso/a
familiar familiar
family la familia
famous famoso/a
fan el aficionado, la aficionada
fantastic fantástico/a
far lejos (de); **far away** alejado/a
farewell la despedida
farm la finca
fashion la moda; to **be fashionable** estar de moda
fast rápidamente, con rapidez
fat gordo/a; *n* la grasa
father el padre, el papá; **father–in–law** el suegro
favor: in favor of a favor de
favorable favorable; **favorable conditions** la facilidad
favorite favorito/a, preferido/a
to **fear** temer
February febrero
to **feel like** tener ganas de
feeling el sentimiento
feminist el/la feminista
fender el guardabarros
fervor el fervor
fever la fiebre
fewer menos
fiancé el novio
fiancée la novia
fiction la ficción
fictitious imaginario/a
field el campo
fifteen quince; **fifteen year-old girl** la quinceañera
fifth quinto
fifty cincuenta
fight la pelea, la lucha; *v* lidiar, luchar
figure la cifra
to **fill out** llenar
filled relleno/a
film la película
filming la filmación
to **find** encontrar (ue); to **find out** averiguar
fine la multa; *adv* bien
finger el dedo
to **finish** terminar, acabar
finished terminado/a, acabado/a
fire el fuego, el incendio; *v* despedir (i)
fireman el bombero
fireplace la chimenea
first primer, primero/a; **first–aid center** la casa de socorro; **first class** de lujo
to **fish** pescar (qu); *n* el pescado; el pez (los peces); **fish market** la pescadería
to **fit** quedar; **fitting room** el probador
five cinco; **five hundred** quinientos
flashlight la linterna
flavor el sabor
flexibility la flexibilidad
flight el vuelo
flood la inundación
flooded inundado/a
floor el piso; la planta
flower la flor
flu la gripe
to **fly** volar (ue)
to **focus** centrar
to **fold** doblar
folklore el folklore
folkloric folklórico/a
to **follow** seguir (i)
food la comida, el alimento; la alimentación; el comestible
foolish tonto/a
foot el pie
football el fútbol
for para
to **forbid** prohibir
to **force** obligar (gu); *n* la fuerza
forecast el pronóstico
forehead la frente
foreign extranjero/a
forest el bosque
to **forget** olvidar
fork el tenedor
formal formal
formation la formación
former antiguo/a
fortress la fortaleza
fortunate afortunado/a
forty cuarenta
forward adelante
founded: to **be founded on** basarse en
four cuatro; **four hundred** cuatrocientos
fourteen catorce
fourth cuarto/a
fracture la fractura
fractured fracturado/a
free libre; gratis
freedom la libertad

freeway la autopista
French francés, francesa
frequently con frecuencia, frecuentemente
fresh fresco/a
Friday el viernes
fried frito/a; **French fries** las papas fritas
friend el amigo, la amiga
friendship la amistad
frighten aterrorizar (c); asustar
frightened asustado/a
from de; desde
frozen congelado/a
fruit la fruta; **fruit store** la frutería
full lleno/a; **full–time** jornada completa
funny cómico/a; divertido
furniture los muebles
future el futuro

G

gait el trote
gallery la galería
game el partido, el juego; el encuentro
garage el garaje, la cochera
garbage la basura
garden el jardin
to **gargle** hacer gárgaras
garlic el ajo
gasoline la gasolina
gate la puerta
gelatin la gelatina
general general; **general practice** la medicina familiar
generally generalmente
generation la generación
generous generoso/a
genius el genio
geographic geográfico/a
geography la geografía
German alemán/a
to **get** conseguir (i); adquirir (ie, i); sacar (qu); to **get married** casarse; to **get ready** prepararse; to **get sick** enfermarse; to **get tired** cansarse; to **get together** reunirse; to **get up** levantarse
giant el gigante
giraffe la jirafa
girl la chica, la muchacha; **Girl Scouts** niñas exploradoras
girlfriend la novia
give dar; to **give a present** regalar
glad contento/a; to **be glad** alegrarse
gladiator el gladiador
glass el cristal; el vaso; **stemmed glass** la copa
glasses la gafas
glove el guante
to **go** ir; acudir; to **go away** irse; to **go straight ahead** seguir derecho; to **go to bed** acostarse; to **go together** combinar bien; to **go up** subir; aumentar
goal la meta, el objetivo; to **have as a goal** tener como fin
God Dios
goddaughter la ahijada
godfather el padrino
godmother la madrina
godson el ahijado
gold el oro
golf el golf; **golf course** el campo de golf
good bueno/a; buen; **good–bye** adiós; **good grief!** ¡qué barbaridad!
gossiper el chismoso, la chismosa
grab agarrar
grade la nota
graduate el graduado, la graduada; *v* graduar(se);
graduating class la promoción
graduation la graduación
gram el gramo
grammar la gramática
granddauther la nieta
grandfather el abuelo
granddaughter la nieta
grandparents los abuelos
grandson el nieto
graphic gráfico/a
grass la hierba
grated rallado/a
gratis gratis
gray gris
great gran; fabuloso
green verde; **green pepper** el pimiento, el chile
to **greet** saludar
greeting el saludo
ground molido/a
group el grupo
to **grow** crecer (zc); cultivar
growth el crecimiento
guard el/la guardia
to **guess** adivinar
guest el invitado, la invitada; el huésped
guide el/la guía
guitar la guitarra
gymnasium el gimnasio
gymnastics la gimnasia

H

habit el hábito
habitually habitualmente
hair el pelo
hairdresser el peluquero, la peluquera
half medio/a; *n* la mitad
hall el pasillo
Halloween el Día de las Brujas
ham el jamón
hamburger la hamburguesa
hand la mano; **on the other**

hand en cambio, por otra parte
handball el balonmano
handicraft la artesanía
handkerchief el pañuelo
handle el asa *fem*
handmade hecho a mano
handsome guapo/a
handwritten manuscrito/a
to **hang** colgar (ue); tender (ie); to **hang up** colgar
to **happen** pasar
happiness la felicidad
happy alegre, contento/a, feliz
hard duro/a; **hard working** trabajador/a
harmoniously armónicamente
hat el sombrero
to **have** haber; poseer; disponer de (g); tener (g, ie); to **have a good time** divertirse (ie, i), pasarlo bien; to **have as a goal** tener como fin; to **have breakfast** desayunar; to **have dinner, supper** cenar; to **have lunch** almorzar (ue); to **have to** + *verb* tener que + *inf*
he él
head la cabeza
headquarters la jefatura
healer el curandero, la curandera
health la salud; la sanidad, **health food store** la herboristería, el centro naturista
healthy saludable; sano/a
to **hear** oír
heart el corazón
heating la calefacción
heel el talón
height la estatura; la altura
hell el infierno
hello hola; aló, diga, dígame, ¿qué hay?
helmet el casco
to **help** ayudar; *n* la ayuda
hemisphere el hemisferio
her ella; *adj* su(s); suyo/a
here aquí; presente
heritage la herencia
high arriba; alto/a; **high school** la escuela secundaria, el liceo; **high school curriculum** el bachillerato
highway la carretera
hiking (*mountain*) el montañismo
hip la cadera
his su(s); suyo/a
Hispanic hispano/a, hispánico/a; **Hispanic American** hispanoamericano/a
history la historia
hit alcanzado/a; *v* dar
holding agarrado/a; **holding hands** agarrados de la mano
home el hogar
homework la tarea
honest honrado/a
hooded encapuchado/a
to **hope** esperar; **I/we hope** ojalá (que)
horoscope el horóscopo
hospital el hospital
hostal el hostal
hot *adj* caluroso/a; caliente; picante; to **be hot** tener calor
hotel el hotel; el parador
house la casa; *adj* doméstico/a; **house chore** la tarea doméstica
housewife el ama de casa *fem*
housing development la colonia; la urbanización
how cómo; **how are you?** ¿qué tal?; **how horrible!** ¡qué horror!; **how many** cuántos/as; **how much** cuánto/a
however no obstante
huge enorme
human humano/a
humanities las humanidades
humid húmedo/a
to **humiliate** humillar
hungry: to **be hungry** tener hambre
to **hunt** cazar
hurricane el huracán
hurry: to **be in a hurry** tener prisa
to **hurt** doler (ue); herir (ie, i)
husband el esposo, el marido

I

I yo
ice cream el helado; **ice–cream shop** la heladería
idea la idea
ideal ideal
idealist el/la idealista
identification la identificación
to **identify** identificar (qu)
if si
illegal ilegal
image la imagen
imagination la imaginación
to **imagine** imaginarse
to **imitate** imitar
immediate inmediato/a; **immediate possession** próxima entrega
immediately enseguida
immense inmenso/a
impact el impacto
impartial imparcial
imperfect imperfecto/a
impetuous impetuoso/a
importance la importancia
important importante; influyente
impression la impresión
impressive impresionante
to **improve** mejorar

improvement el avance; la mejora
impulsive impulsivo/a
in en; **in force** en vigor; **in front (of)** enfrente (de); **in–house** *adj* interno/a
inauguration la inauguración
Inca inca
to **include** incluir (y)
included incluido/a
inconvenience la molestia
to **increase** subir; aumentar; *n* el aumento
incredible increíble
indefinite indefinido/a
independence la independencia
independent independiente
index el índice
Indian *n* el/la indígena
to **indicate** indicar (qu)
indication la indicación
indifferent indiferente
indiscrete indiscreto/a
indispensable indispensable
individual *adj* individual; *n* el individuo
industrialized industrializado/a
industry la industria
inexpensive barato/a
infection la infección
inferior inferior
infinitesimal infinitesimal
infinitive el infinitivo
inflation la inflación
influence la influencia
to **inform** informar
informal informal
information la información
infrastructure la infraestructura
ingenious ingenioso/a
ingredient el ingrediente
inhabitable livable
inhabitant el/la habitante
inhuman inhumano/a
initiative la iniciativa
injection la inyección
injured person el herido
inn la hostería
inside dentro (de); en
to **inspect** revisar; inspeccionar
inspector el inspector, la inspectora
to **inspire** inspirar
installation la instalación
instead of en vez de
instinct el instinto
institute el instituto
insurance el seguro
intellectual intelectual
intelligent inteligente
intense intenso/a
to **interest** interesar; *n* el interés
interesting interesante
interior interior
internal interno/a; **internal medicine** la medicina interna
international internacional
to **interrupt** interrumpir
interstate interestatal
to **interview** entrevistar; *n* la entrevista
interviewer el entrevistador, la entrevistadora
intimate íntimo/a
to **introduce** presentar
introduction la presentación; la implantación
introverted introvertido/a
to **inundate** inundar
to **invest** invertir (ie, i)
to **investigate** investigar (gu)
investigating *adj* investigador/a
invitation la invitación
to **invite** invitar
to **iron** planchar; *n* la plancha; *n* el hierro
ironic irónico/a
irregular irregular
irritated irritado/a
island la isla
it ello
Italian italiano/a
itinerary el itinerario
its su(s); suyo/a

J

jacket la chaqueta
jai alai jai alai; **jai alai player** el pelotari
January enero
Japanese japonés, japonesa
jeans los vaqueros
to **jog** trotar
to **join** incorporarse
joint la articulación
joke el chiste
judgment el criterio; el dictamen
judo el judo
juice el jugo
July julio
to **jump** saltar
jumping el salto
June junio
jungle la jungla; la selva
just justo/a

K

to **keep** conservar; to **keep in mind** tener presente
kennel la guardería de perros
key *adj* clave; *n* la llave
to **kill** matar
kilo el kilo
kilogram el kilogramo
kilometer el kilómetro
kind amable; *n* el tipo
kindly amablemente
kingdom el reino
kiosk el quiosco
kiss el beso
kitchen la cocina
knife el cuchillo
to **knock** tocar (qu); to **knock down** tumbar

to **know** conocer (zc); saber; **I know** sé
knowledge el conocimiento
known conocido/a

L

laboratory el laboratorio
lack la falta; *v* faltar
lamp la lámpara
land la tierra
landscape el paisaje
landslide el alud
lane la vía
language el idioma, la lengua
to **last** durar; *adj* último/a; pasado/a; **last night** anoche
late tarde
lately últimamente
later después
Latin latino/a
to **laugh** reír(se) (i)
laundry la lavandería
law el derecho, la ley
lawn el césped
lawyer el abogado, la abogada; el licenciado en derecho; **lawyer's office** el bufete
lazy perezoso/a
to **learn** aprender
least: at least por lo menos
leather el cuero
to **leave** irse; salir; dejar; **leave taking** la despedida
lecture la conferencia
left izquierdo/a
leg la pierna
legal jurídico/a
lemon el limón
to **lend** prestar
less menos
lesson la lección
to **let** + *verb* dejar + *inf*
letter la carta
lettuce la lechuga
liberal liberal
liberated liberado/a
liberty la libertad
library la biblioteca
license la licencia; **driver's license** licencia de manejar
lie la mentira; to **lie down** acostarse (ue)
life la vida
light claro/a; *n* la luz; *v* encender (ie)
like como
to **like** gustar
likewise igualmente
limit el límite
line la cola; la línea; to **stand in line** hacer cola
lion el león
liquid el líquido
liquor el licor
list la lista
to **listen** escuchar
liter el litro
literature la literatura
little poco; un poco; **a little bit** un poquito/a; **little by little** poco a poco
to **live** vivir; *adj* vivo/a
lively movido/a
living: to earn a living ganarse la vida; **living room** la sala
llama la llama
to **lock in** encerrar (ie)
to **lodge** hospedarse
lodging el alojamiento
logical lógico/a
logically lógicamente
long largo/a
longevity la longevidad
to **look (at)** mirar; to **look for** buscar (qu)
to **lose** perder (ie)
loss la pérdida
lottery la lotería
louder más alto
love el amor; to **be in love** estar enamorado/a (de)
low bajo/a
to **lower** bajar
loyal leal
luckily por fortuna
lucky: to be lucky tener suerte
luggage el equipaje
lunch el almuerzo
lung el pulmón
luxury lujo

M

machine: answering machine el contestador automático
magazine la revista
magic la magia
magical mágico/a
magnificent magnífico/a
mail box el buzón; el depósito
mailman el cartero
main principal
to **maintain** mantener (g, ie)
to **major** especializarse (c)
majority la mayoría
to **make** hacer; to **make a reservation** reservar; to **make a stopover** hacer escala; to **make difficult** dificultar; to **make up** constituir
man el hombre
manager el/la gerente
manufacturer el/la fabricante
many muchos/as
map el mapa; el plano
March marzo
Mardi Gras el carnaval
marijuana la marihuana
marital status el estado civil
to **mark** marcar (qu); **marked down** rebajado/a; to **mark time** marcar el paso
market el mercado
marquis el marqués

married casado/a; **married couple** el matrimonio
to **marvel** maravillarse
marvelous maravilloso/a
masculine masculino/a
mashed potatoes el puré de papas
master el maestro
matching la asociación
material la tela; el material
materialistic materialista
mathematics las matemáticas
matter la gestión; el asunto; *v* importar; **business matters** la materia económica; **it doesn't matter** no importa
maximum máximo/a
May mayo
maybe quizá(s)
mayonnaise la mayonesa
me mí; me
means medios; **by means of** mediante
to **measure** medir (i); *n* la medida
meat la carne; **ground meat** la carne molida; **meat market** la carnicería
mechanic mecánico/a
medical médico/a
medication la medicación
medicine la medicina
medium mediano/a
meet la competencia; *v* conocer (zc); **nice (pleased) to meet you** mucho gusto
meeting la reunión
melodramatic melodramático/a
melody la melodía
member el miembro
memory la memoria
mental mental
to **mention** mencionar
menu el menú
merit el mérito
message el mensaje
messenger el mensajero, la mensajera
messy desordenado/a
meter el metro
method el método
metropolitan metropolitano/a
Mexican mexicano/a
microwave el microondas
middle class la clase media
midnight la medianoche; **midnight mass** la Misa del Gallo
midwife la comadrona
migration la migración
military militar
milk la leche
million el millón
millionaire millonario/a
mind la mente
mine mío(-a, -os, -as)
mineral mineral
minidialog el minidiálogo
minimum mínimo/a
mink el visón
minority la minoría
minus menos
minute el minuto
mirror el espejo
Miss señorita, Srta.
missile el misil
missing: to **be missing** faltar
mission la misión
to **mix** mezclar
mixer la batidora
model el/la modelo
modern moderno/a
modification la modificación
moment el momento, el momentito; **at this moment** en estos momentos
monastery el monasterio
Monday el lunes
money el dinero
monologue el monólogo
month el mes
monument el monumento
moon la luna
moonlighting el pluriempleo
more más
morning la mañana; **early morning** la madrugada
mortadella la mortadela
mother la mamá, la madre; **mother–in–law** la suegra
motor el motor
motorcycle la moto(cicleta)
mountain la montaña; **mountain range** la cordillera
mountainous montañoso/a
moustache el bigote
mouth la boca
to **move** mover(se) (ue); trasladarse; impulsar; mudarse; to **move close** acercarse (qu)
movement el movimiento
movies el cine
Mr. señor, Sr.
Mrs. señora, Sra.
much mucho/a
mud el lodo
multifaceted multitudinario/a
multiply multiplicar (qu)
muscle el músculo
museum el museo
music la música
musical musical
musician el músico
mustard la mostaza
my mi(s)
myself me
mysterious misterioso/a
mystery el misterio

N

name el nombre; to **be named** llamarse
nap la siesta
napkin la servilleta
narrow estrecho/a

national nacional
native nativo/a
natural natural
nature la naturaleza
near cerca; *adj* cercano/a
necessary necesario/a; **it's necessary to** + *verb* hay que + *inf*; to **be necessary** hacer falta
neck el cuello
necklace el collar
necktie la corbata
to **need** necesitar, precisar; *n* la necesidad
negatively negativamente
neighbor el vecino, la vecina
neighborhood la barriada; la colonia; la urbanización
neither tampoco
nephew el sobrino
nervous nervioso/a
net la red
never nunca
nevertheless sin embargo
new nuevo/a
news la(s) noticia(s)
newscast el noticiero
newspaper el periódico, el diario
next próximo/a; *n* el siguiente; **next to** al lado de, junto a
Nicaraguan nicaragüense
nice simpático/a; amable; **nice to meet you** mucho gusto
niece la sobrina
night la noche; the **night before last** antenoche, anteanoche
nightstand la mesa de noche
nine nueve; **nine hundred** novecientos
nineteen diecinueve
ninety noventa
ninth noveno/a
no no; **no one** nadie
nobody nadie
noise el ruido
none ninguno/a
nonfat descremado/a
noon el mediodía
nor ni; **neither . . . nor** ni . . . ni
norm la norma
normal normal
normally normalmente
north el norte
nose la nariz
not no; **not to know** ignorar; **not fully accepted** marginado/a
notably notablemente
note la nota; **notes** los apuntes
notebook el cuaderno
noteworthy notable
nothing nada
to **notice** fijarse; **notice board** el tablero
noticeable: to **be noticeable** notarse
to **notify** avisar
to **nourish** alimentar
nourishing nutritivo/a
November noviembre
now ahora; **right now** en estos momentos
nowadays hoy en día
number el número
numerous numeroso/a
nurse el enfermero, la enfermera
nutrition la nutrición

O

to **obey** obedecer (zc)
object el objeto
obligation la obligación
to **observe** observar
obsession la obsesión
to **obtain** obtener (g, ie); alcanzar (c); conseguir (i)
obvious obvio/a
occasionally ocasionalmente
occupation el oficio; la ocupación
to **occupy** ocupar
to **occur** ocurrir
October octubre
odd raro/a
of de; **of course** por supuesto; **of course not** ¡qué va!
to **offer** ofrecer (zc); proporcionar
office la oficina
official oficial
oil el aceite; el petróleo
old viejo/a; antiguo/a; **old person** el anciano, la anciana
older mayor
Olympic Games las Olimpiadas
omelette la tortilla
on sobre; en
once una vez
one uno/a, un; **one hundred** ciento, cien
onion la cebolla
only sólo, únicamente
to **open** abrir; to **open the way to** dar paso a
operation la operación
operator la operadora
opinion la opinión
opportunity la oportunidad
opposite opuesto/a
optimistic optimista
optimum óptimo/a
option la opción
or o, u; **either . . . or** o . . . o
orange anaranjado/a; *n* la naranja
orchestra la orquesta
order la orden; *v* pedir (i); **in order to** para
organization la organización
organize organizar (c)

organizer el organizador, la organizadora
origin el origen, la procedencia
other otro/a; **on the other hand** en cambio, por otra parte
ought to deber
our nuestro/a
out of order dañado/a
outside fuera
outskirts las afueras
oven el horno
overweight excedido de peso
own propio/a
owner el dueño, la dueña
oxygen el oxígeno

P

P. O. Box el apartado (de correos)
to **pack** empacar (qu), hacer la maleta
package el paquete
paella la paella
page la página
pain el dolor
to **paint** pintar
painting la pintura
pair el par
pajama el/la piyama
palace el palacio
pamphlet el folleto
Panamanian panameño/a
pantomime la pantomima
pantry la despensa
paper el papel
paragraph el párrafo
parenthesis el paréntesis
parents los padres
to **park** estacionar; *n* el parque
parking el estacionamiento
parrot el loro
part la parte; to **be part of** formar parte de; to **play the part** hacer el papel
partial parcial
participant el participante, la participante
to **participate** participar
participation la participación
particularly en particular
partner la pareja
party la fiesta
to **pass** aprobar (ue)
passenger el pasajero, la pasajera
passive pasivo/a
Passover la Pascua
passport el pasaporte
pastry shop la dulcería, la pastelería
patient paciente
patrimony el patrimonio
patron el patrón, la patrona
pattern el esquema
to **pay (for)** pagar (gu); to **pay attention** prestar atención
peace la paz
peas (*Puerto Rico*) los gandules
pedagogy la pedagogía
pedal el pedal
pediatrician el/la pediatra
pen: ballpoint pen el bolígrafo
pencil el lápiz
pending pendiente
penitent el/la penitente
people la gente
pepper la pimienta; **green pepper** el chile, el pimiento
percentage el porcentaje
perfect perfecto/a
perfectly perfectamente
perhaps tal vez, quizá(s)
period el período
permanent permanente
permanently permanentemente
to **permit** permitir
persistence el empeño
persistent persistente
person la persona; **person from Madrid** madrileño/a; **person of importance** el personaje; **person surveyed** el encuestado, la encuestada; **person who signs** el signatario
personal personal
personality la personalidad
personnel el personal
Peruvian peruano/a
peso el peso
pessimistic pesimista
phantom el fantasma
pharmacy farmacia
phenomenon el fenómeno
philosophy la filosofía
photo la foto
photograph la fotografía
phrase la frase
physical físico/a
physics la física
pianist el/la pianista
piano el piano
to **pick up** recoger (j); pasar por
picture el cuadro
pie el pastel
pigpen la pocilga
pill la pastilla
pillow la almohada
pilot el/la piloto
pink rosado/a
pioneer el pionero, la pionera
pizza la pizza
place el lugar
plaid de cuadros
plan el plan; *v* planificar (qu); planear; to **plan to** + *verb* pensar + *inf*
plane el avión
planet el planeta
planning los arreglos
plant la planta

plate el plato; **combination plate** el plato combinado
platform las andas; la plataforma
to **play** (*game or sport*) jugar (ue); (*an instrument*) tocar (qu); *n* la obra de teatro; to **play the part** hacer el papel
player el jugador, la jugadora
please por favor; **pleased to meet you** mucho gusto
pleasure el placer
plumber el plomero
plural plural
pocket el bolsillo
point el punto; to **give a point** marcar un punto; to **point to** señalar
pole el polo
policeman el policía
policewoman la mujer policía
political político/a
politician el político
pollen el polen
pollution la contaminación
pool la piscina
poor pobre
popular popular
population la población
porch el portal
pork el cerdo
port el puerto
portable portátil
Portuguese portugués/portuguesa
position el puesto, la plaza
positive positivo/a
positively positivamente
possession la posesión; **immediate possession** próxima entrega
possibility la posibilidad
possible posible
postcard la tarjeta postal
post office el correo, la oficina de correos
postal postal
poster el afiche
postgraduate posgrado
postpone posponer
postponed pospuesto/a
potassium el potasio
potato la papa; (*Spain*) la patata
pound la libra
poverty la pobreza
to **practice** practicar (qu); *n* la práctica; **general practice** la medicina familiar
pre-Columbian precolombino/a
precise time hora americana, hora inglesa
prediction la predicción
to **prefer** preferir (ie, i)
preferable preferible
preparation el preparativo
to **prepare** preparar
prepared capacitado/a
to **prescribe** recetar
prescription la receta
presence la presencia
present actual; *n* el regalo; *v* presentar
president el presidente, la presidenta
press la prensa
pressure la presión, la tensión
preterit el pretérito
pretty bonito/a
previous anterior
previously anteriormente
price el precio
primitive primitivo/a
prince el príncipe
principal principal
principle el principio
printed impreso/a
priority la prioridad
private privado/a
prize el premio
probability la probabilidad
probable probable
probably probablemente
problem el problema
procession la procesión
to **produce** producir (zc)
produced producido/a
producer el productor, la productora
product el producto
production la producción
profession la profesión
professional profesional
professor el profesor, la profesora
profile el perfil
to **program** programar; *n* el programa
programmer el programador, la programadora
programming la programación
progress el progreso
progressive progresivo/a
to **prohibit** prohibir
prohibition la prohibición
project el proyecto
to **promote** ascender (ie); promover (ue)
pronoun el pronombre
pronunciation la pronunciación
proof la prueba
proportion la proporción
to **propose** proponer (g)
to **protect** proteger (j)
protection la protección
protein la proteína
proud orgulloso/a
to **provide** lograr; **provided that** con tal (de) que
province la provincia
psychiatrist el/la (p)siquiatra
psychologist el (p)sicólogo, la (p)sicóloga
psychology la (p)sicología
peseta (*monetary unit of Spain*) la peseta

public público/a; *n* la audiencia
published publicado/a
Puerto Rican puertorriqueño/a
to **pull** tirar
punch el ponche
punctual puntual
punctually puntualmente
punctuation la puntuación
pure puro/a
purple morado/a
purse la bolsa
to **pursue** perseguir (i)
to **put** poner (g), colocar (qu); to **put away** guardar; to **put on makeup** maquillarse; to **put to bed** acostar (ue)
pyramid la pirámide

Q

qualified capacitado/a
quality la calidad; la cualidad
quarter el cuarto
question la pregunta
questionnaire el cuestionario
quiet callado/a

R

race la raza
radiator el radiador
radically radicalmente
radio el radio
raffle la rifa
railroad el ferrocarril
rain la lluvia; *v* llover (ue)
raincoat el impermeable
to **raise** levantar
raised educado/a
rapid rápido/a
rapidly rápidamente, con rapidez
razor (*Mexico and other countries*) el rastrillo
reach el alcance; *v* alcanzar (c)
reaction la reacción
to **read** leer
reading la lectura
ready listo/a; **to get ready** prepararse
real real
realistic realista
reality la realidad
to **realize** darse cuenta (de)
really realmente, en realidad
reason el motivo
rebellious rebelde
to **receive** recibir
recent reciente
reception la recepción
receptionist el/la recepcionista
recipe la receta
to **recognize** reconocer (zc)
recognized reconocido/a
to **recommend** recomendar (ie)
record el disco
rectangular rectangular
to **rectify** rectificar (qu)
red rojo/a
to **reduce** reducir (zc)
to **refer** referir (ie, i)
referee el árbitro
to **reflect** repercutir; reflejar
refrigerator el refrigerador
to **refuse** rechazar (c)
regards los recuerdos
region la región
registered certificado/a
regularly regularmente
regulation la regulación; el reglamento
to **reject** descartar
related relacionado/a
relation la relación
relationship el parentesco; la relación
relative el pariente, la parienta; el familiar
relatively relativamente
relaxation la relajación
release liberar
religious religioso/a
to **remain** permanecer (zc), quedar(se)
to **remember** recordar (ue)
to **remind** recordar (ue)
to **remodel** remodelar
to **remove** quitar
to **renew** renovar (ue)
to **rent** alquilar; *n* el alquiler, la renta
to **repeat** repetir (i); hacerse eco
to **replant** replantar
to **report** reportar; *n* el informe
to **represent** representar
representative el/la representante
repression la represión
republic la república
to **request** pedir (i)
reservation la reservación
reserved reservado/a
residence la residencia
resident el/la residente
residential residencial
to **resist** resistir
resistance la resistencia
resolution la firmeza
resort (*country/mountain*) el refugio
to **respect** respetar; *n* el respeto; **with respect to** con respecto a
responsibility la responsabilidad
responsible responsable
rest el descanso; el resto; *v* descansar
restaurant el restaurante
result el resultado
resumé el curriculum, el historial
to **resume** reanudar
to **return** devolver (ue)
reveille la diana

to **review** repasar
rhythm el ritmo
rhythmic rítmico/a
ribbon la cinta
rice el arroz
rich rico/a
riddle la adivinanza
to **ride** montar
ridiculous ridículo/a
right derecho/a; *n* el derecho; **right now** en estos momentos; to **be right** tener razón; **to the right** a la derecha
ring el aro; el anillo; *v* sonar (ue)
rinse el enjuague
rising ascendiendo
risk el riesgo
river el río
roast asado/a
robot el robot
rock el rock
role el papel
roll la lista; to **call roll** pasar (la) lista
romance el romance
romantic romántico/a
roof el techo
room la habitación, el cuarto, el dormitorio; **dining room** el comedor; **living room** la sala; **waiting room** la sala de espera
rose la rosa
rough rudo/a
round redondo/a; **round–trip ticket** el boleto/pasaje de ida y vuelta
row la fila
royal regio/a, real
rug la alfombra
ruins las ruinas
rule la regulación
rum el ron
to **run** correr
runner el corredor, la corredora
rural rural
Russian ruso/a

S

sabotage el sabotaje
sad triste
Sagittarian sagitariano/a
sail la vela
saint el santo, la santa
salad la ensalada
salary el sueldo, el salario; **desired salary** la pretensión económica
sale la rebaja; la venta
salesman el vendedor
saleswoman la vendedora
salt la sal
Salvadoran salvadoreño/a
same mismo/a; igual
sand la arena
sandwich el sándwich; (*Mexico*) la torta
satellite dish antenna la parabólica
satisfaction la satisfacción
satisfactory satisfactorio/a
satisfy satisfacer (g)
Saturday el sábado
sauce la salsa
sauna la sauna
to **save** ahorrar
saxophone el saxofón
to **say** decir (g, i)
saying el dicho
scarf la bufanda
scene la escena
schedule el horario
scholarship la beca
school el colegio; la escuela; la facultad; *adj* escolar; **school year** el año escolar
science la ciencia
scientist el científico, la científica
Scout: Boy Scouts niños exploradores; **Girl Scouts** niñas exploradoras
sea el mar
season la estación
seat el asiento
second segundo/a
secret el secreto
secretary el secretario, la secretaria
section la sección
security la seguridad
to **see** ver
to **seem** parecer (zc)
seismic sísmico/a
seldom rara vez
select selecto/a
selection la selección
self–description la autodescripción
to **sell** vender
semester el semestre
to **send** enviar, mandar
senior citizenhood la tercera edad
sensible sensato/a
sensitive sensitivo/a
sentence la oración
sentimental sentimental
separated separado/a
September septiembre
series la serie
serious serio/a
to **serve** servir (i)
service el servicio; **service station** la gasolinera, la estación de gasolina
session la sesión
set fijado/a; *v* fijar; to **set oneself to do something** proponerse
seven siete; **seven hundred** setecientos
seventeen diecisiete
seventh séptimo
seventy setenta
several varios/as; diversos/as
to **sew** coser
sex el sexo
sexual sexual
shape la forma

to **share** compartir
sharp en punto
to **shave** afeitar(se)
she ella
sheet la sábana
sherbet el sorbete
shine el brillo; *v* brillar
ship el barco
shirt la camisa; la guayabera
shoe el zapato; **tennis shoes** zapatos (de) tenis
shop el taller
shopping la compra; **shopping center** el centro comercial
short corto/a; bajo/a; **in short** en fin
should deber
shoulder el hombro
to **show** mostrar(se) (ue); demostrar; *n* la función, el espectáculo
shower la ducha
shrimp el camarón
sick enfermo/a; mal
sickness la enfermedad
sidewalk la acera
to **sign** firmar; *n* el signo; el letrero
signal la señal; **traffic signal** señal de tráfico
signature la firma
silly tonto/a
silver la plata
similar similar, parecido/a
simple sencillo/a
simply simplemente
sin el pecado
since ya que; como; desde; pues
sincere sincero/a
to **sing** cantar
singer el/la cantante
single soltero/a; sencillo
sink el fregadero
sister la hermana; **sister–in–law** la cuñada
to **sit down** sentarse (ie)
site (*construction*) la obra
situated situado/a
situation la situación
six seis; **six hundred** seiscientos
sixteen dieciséis
sixth sexto
sixty sesenta
size la talla; el tamaño
to **skate** patinar
to **ski** esquiar; *n* el esquí
skier el esquiador, la esquiadora
skin la piel
to **skin/scuba dive** bucear
skirt la falda
slacks los pantalones
to **sleep** dormir (ue, u); to **fall asleep** dormirse (ue)
sleeper (car) coche cama
sleepy: to **be sleepy** tener sueño
slight ligero/a
slow *adv* despacio; *adj* lento/a
slowly lentamente, despacio
small pequeño/a; reducido/a
smart listo/a
to **smile** sonreír(se) (i)
smog el smog, la contaminación del aire
to **smoke** fumar; *n* el humo
snack la merienda
to **snore** roncar (qu)
snow la nieve; *v* nevar (ie)
so tan; luego; **so long** hasta luego; **so–so** regular; **so that** para que
soap el jabón; **soap opera** la telenovela
soccer el fútbol
social social
society la sociedad
sock el calcetín
soda el refresco
sodium el sodio
sofa el sofá
soft suave
softly en voz baja
solid color de color entero
solidary solidario/a
to **solve** resolver (ue)
some alguno/as; algún; unos
somebody alguien
someone alguien
something algo; **something else** algo más
sometime alguna vez
sometimes a veces
son el hijo; **son–in–law** el yerno
song la canción
soon pronto
sorry: sorry for the inconvenience disculpe(n) la molestia; to **be sorry** sentir (ie, i)
sound (*to signal an activity*) el toque
soup la sopa
south el sur
spaghetti el espagueti
Spaniard el español, la española
Spanish el español
to **speak** hablar
special especial; **special delivery** entrega especial
specializing especializado/a
specific específico/a
specifically concretamente
spectacle el espectáculo
spectacular espectacular
spectator el espectador, la espectadora
speed la rapidez, la velocidad; to **speed up** agilizar (c)
to **spend** gastar; pasar
spill el derrame
to **spin around** dar vueltas
spinach la espinaca
spite: in spite of a pesar de
sport el deporte; *adj* deportivo/a
spring la primavera
square cuadrado/a
stadium el estadio

staff el personal
staffed atendido/a
stage el escenario
stairs la escalera
stamp la estampilla, el sello
standard of living el nivel de vida
standing parado/a
star la estrella
to **start** empezar (ie, c); comenzar (ie, c)
stately señorial
station la estación; **service station** la estación de gasolina, la gasolinera
stationery store la papelería
status: marital status el estado civil
stay la estancia; *v* quedar(se), permanecer
steering wheel el volante
to **step** pisar; *n* el paso
stereo el estéreo
stereotype el estereotipo
stewardess la azafata
stick el palo
still todavía
stingy tacaño/a
stocking la media
stomach el estómago
to **stop** detener(se) (g, ie), parar(se); hacer alto; *n* la parada
stopover: to **make a stopover** hacer escala
stopwatch el cronómetro
store la tienda; **store window** el escaparate
story el cuento
stove la estufa
straight: to **go straight ahead** seguir derecho
strawberry la fresa
street la calle
streetcar el tranvía
strength la fuerza
stress la presión, la tensión
stretcher la camilla
strict estricto/a
striped de rayas
strong fuerte
structure la estructura
student el/la estudiante; el alumno, la alumna
studies los estudios
to **study** estudiar
style el estilo
subject la materia; el sujeto
subordination la sujeción
subway el metro
to **succeed** triunfar
successful exitoso/a; to **be successful** tener éxito
suddenly de repente
to **suffer** sufrir
sugar el/la azúcar
to **suggest** sugerir (ie, i)
suggestion la sugerencia
suit el traje; **bathing suit** el traje de baño
suitcase la maleta
suite la suite
summer el verano
sun el sol; **it's sunny** hace sol
Sunday el domingo
superficial superficial
supermarket el supermercado
supervisor el supervisor, la supervisora
supper la cena, la comida
to **supply** aportar
support el apoyo
sure seguro/a
surface la superficie
surgeon el cirujano
surgery la cirugía
to **surpass** superar, sobrepasar
surprise la sorpresa; to **be surprised** sorprenderse
surrounded rodeado/a
surrounding areas los alrededores
survey la encuesta
sweater el suéter
sweatshirt la sudadera
sweep barrer
sweet dulce
to **swim** nadar
swimming la natación
Swiss suizo/a
symbol el símbolo
symptom el síntoma
system el sistema; el régimen

T

T-shirt la camiseta
table la mesa
tablecloth el mantel
tablespoon la cuchara
to **take** llevar; tomar; to **take advantage of** aprovechar; to **take away** quitar; to **take care of** cuidar, atender (ie); to **take courses** seguir cursos; to **take credit** apuntar; to **take off** quitarse; to **take on** incurrir; to **take out** sacar; to **take pictures** sacar fotos
to **talk** conversar
talkative hablador/a
tall alto/a
tape la cinta
tape recorder la grabadora
tariff la tarifa
tax el impuesto
taxi el taxi; **taxi driver** el/la taxista
tea el té
to **teach** enseñar
teacher el maestro, la maestra
team el equipo; (*in bullfighting*) la cuadrilla
tear la lágrima; *v* romper, romperse
teaspoon la cucharita
technical técnico/a
technology la tecnología
teenager el/la adolescente

telegram el telegrama
telegraph el telégrafo
telephone el teléfono; *adj* telefónico/a
television la televisión, la tele; **television set** el televisor
telegenic *adj* televisivo/a
to **tell** contar (ue)
temper el carácter
temperature la temperatura
temple el templo
temporary temporal
ten diez
tenant el inquilino, la inquilina
tendency la tendencia
tennis el tenis
tent la tienda de campaña
tenth décimo
term el término
terrace la terraza
terrible terrible
terrorism el terrorismo
thank you gracias
Thanksgiving Day Día de Acción de Gracias
that aquel, aquello/a; esa, ese, eso; que; **that is** o sea; **that one** aquél, aquélla; ésa, ése; **that which** lo que
the el, la, los, las; lo
theater el teatro
theft el robo
their su(s); suyo/a
them ellos; les; los
theme el tema
themselves se
then entonces; después
theoretical teórico/a
there allí, allá; **there is, there are** hay; **there was, there were** hubo; había
thermometer el termómetro
these estos, estas
they ellos, ellas
thief el ladrón
thin delgado/a
thing la cosa
to **think** pensar (ie); to **think so** pensar que sí
third tercero/a; tercer
thirsty: to **be thirsty** tener sed
thirteen trece
thirty treinta
this esto; este, esta; **this way** así
those aquellos/a; esos/as, aquéllos/as; ésos/as
thousand mil
three tres; **three hundred** trescientos
throat la garganta
throughout a través de
to **throw** lanzar (c), tirar
Thursday el jueves
ticket el boleto, el billete, el pasaje; la entrada; **round–trip ticket** boleto (pasaje) de ida y vuelta; **ticket office** la taquilla
tidy ordenado/a; to **tidy oneself** asearse
tiger el tigre
tight estrecho
time la hora; la época; la vez; el tiempo; **full–time** jornada completa; to **have a good time** pasarlo bien; **on time** a tiempo; **precise time** hora americana/inglesa; to **waste time** perder (el) tiempo
timid tímido/a
tip la propina
tire la llanta
tired cansado/a
to a; para
toast el pan tostado, la tostada
today hoy
together juntos/as; to **go together** combinar bien
toilet el inodoro
token la ficha
toll el peaje
tomato el tomate
tomorrow mañana; **the day after tomorrow** pasado mañana
ton la tonelada
tongue la lengua
tonight esta noche
too también; **too much** demasiado
tool la herramienta
tooth el diente
toothache el dolor de muelas
topic el tema
torn roto/a
tornado el tornado
tortilla la tortilla
torture la tortura
total absoluto/a; total
totally totalmente
tour la excursión; el circuito
tourism el turismo
tourist el/la turista; *adj* turístico/a
toward(s) hacia, para
towel la toalla
town el pueblo
track (*railroad*) la vía
tradition la tradición
traditional tradicional
traditionally tradicionalmente
traffic el tráfico; **traffic jam** el embotellamiento; **traffic light** el semáforo
train el tren; *v* entrenar
trained entrenado/a
trainer el entrenador, la entrenadora
training el entrenamiento; la instrucción
trait el rasgo
tranquilizer el tranquilizante
transaction la transacción; la tramitación

transit el tránsito
to **translate** traducir (zc)
to **transmit** transmitir
transportation el traslado, el transporte
to **travel** recorrer, viajar
tray la bandeja
to **treat** tratar
treatment el trato
tree el árbol; **family tree** el árbol genealógico
trip el viaje
tropics el trópico
truck el camión
true verdadero/a; cierto/a
trunk el baúl, el maletero
truth la verdad
to **try** probar (ue); to **try on** probarse (ue); to **try to** tratar (de)
tub la bañadera
Tuesday el martes
tuna el atún
turkey el pavo
to **turn** dar vueltas; doblar; to **turn down** rechazar (c); to **turn off** apagar (gu); to **turn on** conectar, encender (ie)
twelve doce
twenty veinte; **twenty–eight** veintiocho; **twenty–five** veinticinco; **twenty–four** veinticuatro; **twenty–nine** veintinueve; **twenty–one** veintiuno, veintiún; **twenty–seven** veintisiete; **twenty–six** veintiséis; **twenty–three** veintitrés; **twenty–two** veintidós
to **twist** torcer (ue, z)
two dos; **two hundred** doscientos
type el tipo; *v* escribir a máquina
typical típico/a

U

ugly feo/a
umpire el árbitro
unbelievable increíble
uncle el tío
undecided indeciso/a
under debajo, bajo
underground subterráneo/a
underlined subrayado/a
understand comprender, entender (ie)
understanding la comprensión
underwear la ropa interior
unemployment el desempleo, el paro
unexpectedly inesperadamente
unfavorable desfavorable
unforgettable inolvidable
unfortunately desgraciadamente
unhappy infeliz
uninterrupted ininterrumpido/a
union la unión
unit la unidad
united unido/a
university la universidad; *adj* universitario/a
unknown desconocido/a
unless a menos que
unpleasant antipático/a
until hasta; (*when telling time*) menos
upkeep el mantenimiento
urban urbano/a
to **urge** animar
urgent urgente
urgently urgentemente
us nos; nosotros/as
to **use** usar, consumir, utilizar (c); to **be used to** estar acostumbrado/a
useful útil

V

vacation las vacaciones
to **vacuum** pasar la aspiradora; **vacuum cleaner** la aspiradora/el aspirador
Valentine's Day el Día de los Enamorados
valuable valioso/a
value el valor; *v* valorar
vanilla la vainilla
variety la variedad
various diferentes
to **vary** variar
vast extenso/a
vegetable la verdura, el vegetal
vegetarian vegetariano/a
vehicle el vehículo
Venezuelan venezolano/a
ventilation la ventilación
verb el verbo
very muy
vibrant vibrante
victim la víctima
victory el triunfo
video el vídeo/video
view la vista
vinegar el vinagre
violence la violencia
violent violento/a
violin el violín
violinist el violinista, la violinista
visa el visado, la visa
to **visit** visitar; *n* la visita
visitor el/la visitante
vitality la vitalidad
vocabulary el vocabulario
volcano el volcán
volleyball el vól(e)ibol
voluntary voluntario/a
vowel la vocal

W

waist la cintura
waiter el camarero

waiting room la sala de espera
waitress la camarera
to **wake up** despertar(se) (ie)
to **walk** caminar
walking la marcha
wall la pared
wallet la billetera
to **want** querer (ie); desear
war la guerra
warm up el calentamiento; *v* calentar (ie)
to **wash** lavar; to **wash dishes** fregar (ie, gu)
washbowl el lavabo
washing el aseo; **washing machine** la lavadora
to **waste** gastar; to **waste time** perder (el) tiempo
to **watch** presenciar; vigilar
water el agua *fem*
wave la ola
way la manera, la forma; **anyway** de todas formas; **by the way** por cierto; to **open the way to** dar paso a; **this way** de esta forma
we nosotros/as
weak débil
wealth la riqueza
to **wear** llevar; to **wear a costume** disfrazarse (c)
weather el tiempo; **how's the weather?** ¿qué tiempo hace?; **the weather is fine/bad** hace buen/mal tiempo
wedding la boda
Wednesday el miércoles
week la semana
weekdays entre semana
weekend el fin de semana
weekly semanal
to **weigh** pesar
weight el peso
welcome: you're welcome de nada
well bien; pues; **well–being** el bienestar
west oeste
wet húmedo/a
what qué; lo que; **what a pity!** ¡qué pena!
when cuándo; cuando
where dónde; donde; **where to** adónde
which cuál(es); **which one(s)** cuál(es)
while mientras; *n* el rato; **in a while** dentro de un rato
white blanco/a
who quién(es); **who's calling?** ¿de parte de quién?
wholesaler el mayorista
whose de quién
wide ancho/a
wife la esposa, la mujer
to **win** ganar; to **win back** reconquistar
wind el viento; **it's windy** hace viento
window la ventana; (*car, train, etc.*) la ventanilla
windshield el parabrisas
wine el vino
winner el ganador, la ganadora
winter el invierno
wise prudente; **the Three Wise Men** los Reyes Magos
to **wish** desear; *n* el deseo
with con; **with difficulty** difícilmente; **with me** conmigo; **with you** *fam* contigo
without sin; sin que
woman la mujer
word la palabra; **dirty word** la mala palabra
work el trabajo, la obra; *v* trabajar, funcionar
workaholic el trabajomaníaco, la trabajomaníaca
worker el obrero, la obrera
world el mundo; *adj* mundial
worried preocupado/a
to **worry** preocuparse; *n* la preocupación
worse peor
worst peor
wrist la muñeca
to **write** escribir; to **write down** anotar
wrong equivocado/a

X

X-ray la radiografía

Y

yard el jardín
year el año; **New Year's Eve** la Nochevieja; **school year** el curso
yellow amarillo/a
yes sí
yesterday ayer; **the day before yesterday** anteayer
yoga el yoga
yogurt el yogur
you tú; usted, Ud.; vosotros/as; ustedes, Uds.; te; os; lo, la, los, las; le, les, ti
young joven
younger menor
your tu; su; vuestro/a
yours tuyo/a; suyo/a; vuestro/a
yourself te; se; os
youth la juventud

Z

zebra la cebra
zero el cero
zone la zona

Index

Illustration Acknowledgments

Black and White Photographs

Primer paso: 5, David Kupferschmid; 6, Robert Frerck/Odyssey Productions; 9, Beryl Goldberg. **Segundo paso:** 13, David Kupferschmid; 16, Stuart Cohen/Comstock; 18, Peter Menzel. **Tercer paso:** 19, Robert Frerck/Odyssey Productions; 21, David Kupferschmid; 25, Stuart Cohen/Comstock. **Cuarto paso:** 30, Peter Menzel; 32, left, Beryl Goldberg; 32, right, Peter Menzel. **Lección 1:** 38, Beryl Goldberg; 41, 45, Peter Menzel; 47, Stuart Cohen/Comstock. **Lección 2:** 62, Peter Menzel; 63, The Bettmann Archive; 70, Stuart Cohen/Comstock; 71, Tony Savino; 77, Alan Carey/The Image Works. **Lección 3:** 85, Stuart Cohen/Comstock; 88, Peter Menzel; 90, Larry Mangino/The Image Works; 94, Peter Menzel; 97, Robert Frerck/Odyssey Productions; 98, Peter Menzel; 99, Stuart Cohen/Comstock. **Lección 4:** 104, 106, Stuart Cohen/Comstock; 108, Alan Carey/The Image Works; 110, Beryl Goldberg; 113, Stuart Cohen/Comstock; 117, Beryl Goldberg; 118, Peter Menzel. **Lección 5:** 125, Beryl Goldberg; 126, Peter Menzel; 127, Robert Frerck/Odyssey Productions; 137, 139, Stuart Cohen/Comstock. **Lección 6:** 146, Mark Antman/The Image Works; 148, 150, 151, Stuart Cohen/Comstock; 153, Carl Frank/Photo Researchers; 166, Mark Antman/The Image Works. **Lección 7:** 172, Stuart Cohen/Comstock; 173, David Kupferschmid; 175, Peter Menzel; 178, 183, Stuart Cohen/Comstock; 186, Mark Antman/The Image Works; 191, Hazel Hankin. **Lección 8:** 194, Robert Frerck/Odyssey Productions; 195, David Kupferschmid; 197, Peter Menzel; 198, Hazel Hankin; 202, 206, David Kupferschmid; 210, Larry Mangino/The Image Works. **Lección 9:** 219, Stuart Cohen/Comstock; 221, Mark Antman/The Image Works; 223, Hazel Hankin; 231, David Kupferschmid; 232, Stuart Cohen/Comstock. **Lección 10:** 241, 242, 244, Peter Menzel; 247, Mark Antman/The Image Works, 249; Peter Menzel; 251, Robert Frerck/Odyssey Productions; 252, Peter Menzel; 255, Beryl Goldberg. **Lección 11:** 262, Peter Menzel; 263, Beryl Goldberg; 264, Peter Menzel; 272, Mark Antman/The Image Works; 281, Robert Frerck/Odyssey Productions. **Lección 12:** 284, Victor Englebert/Photo Researchers; 286, Arlene Collins/Monkmeyer; 287, 291, Peter Menzel; 305, left, Ulrike Welsch/Photo Researchers, right, Peter Menzel. **Lección 13:** 315, Peter Menzel; 316, David Kupferschmid; 323, Robert Frerck/Odyssey Productions; 326, 333, Peter Menzel. **Lección 14:** 342, top, Stuart Cohen/Comstock, bottom, Alan Carey/The Image Works; 344, Larry Mangino/The Image Works; 345, Beryl Goldberg; 353, Peter Menzel. **Lección 15:** 366, Peter Menzel; 367, 368, Robert Frerck/Odyssey Productions; 369, Peter Menzel; 379, Jonathan Snow/The Image Works; 385, David Kupferschmid. **Lección 16:** 392, 393, Peter Menzel; 394, AP/Wide World Photos; 395, 404, 408, Peter Menzel. **Lección 17:** 420, Peter Menzel; 424, Beryl Goldberg; 430, Mike Douglas/The Image Works; 436, Howard Dratch/The Image Works.

Color Photographs

Plate 1: (top) Peter Menzel
(bottom) Robert Frerck/Odyssey Productions

Plate 2: (top) Beryl Goldberg
(bottom) Peter Menzel

Plate 3: (left, top) Luis Villota/Stock Market
(right, top) Luis Villota/Stock Market
(bottom) Robert Frerck/Woodfin Camp & Assoc.

Plate 4: (top) Peter Menzel
(center) Beryl Goldberg
(bottom) Beryl Goldberg

Plate 5: (top) Hazel Hankin
(bottom) Mangino/Image Works

Plate 6: (top) Robert Frerck/Woodfin Camp & Assoc.
(left, bottom) Robert Frerck/Odyssey Productions
(right, bottom) Owen Franken

Plate 7: (top) Steve Vidler/Leo de Wys, Inc.
(bottom) Richard Steedman/Stock Market

Plate 8: (top) Peter Menzel
(bottom) Howard Dratch/The Image Works

Realia

Lección 1: 44, ad, Idiomas Serrano, Madrid, Spain; 53, ad, courtesy of Linguacenter, S.A., Caracas, Venezuela. **Lección 2:** 76, courtesy of Instituto Mexicano de televisión. **Lección 3:** 96, chart with illustration, *Revista Coqueta,* Bogotá, Colombia; 101, ad, Pulco. **Lección 4:** 119, ad, Regersa, Urbanización Parque Rozas, Las Rozas. **Lección 5:** 140, 3 ads, VYCSA, Madrid, Spain; 141, extract of article "Solo ante el peligro" with art, courtesy Ediciones Conica, S.A., *Revista Telva,* Madrid, Spain. **Lección 6:** 155, 3 ads, Sport Club; 164, 2 charts, *Cambio;* 165, extract of article on basketball, *Blanco y negro,* courtesy Luis María Anson, ABC, Prensa Española. **Lección 7:** 187 (left), Blusa's, Madrid, Spain, (center) Donjota, Madrid, Spain, (right), Felix Saenz. **Lección 9:** 219, 233, extracted text of and charts from *Salud y nutrición* by Virginia Diez del Moral, courtesy Editorial Tiempo Libre S.A.; 234, ad, courtesy Pardiñas 50, S.A., Madrid, Spain; 235, ad, from Spanish newspaper, ABC. **Lección 10:** 257, Comunidad Autónoma de Canarias, Gabinete de Prensa, Spain; 259, Restaurante Cueva del Tesoro. **Lección 11:** 276, extracted TV guide, *Tiempo;* 277, *Blanco y negro,* courtesy Luis María Anson, ABC, Prensa Española; 278, ad, Gabinete de Prensa, Madrid, Spain; 279, cartoon, courtesy Mr. Kiraz. **Lección 12:** 285, boarding pass, Iberia Airlines of Spain; 295, ad, Latitud 4, Cunard Lines, Spain; 296, ad, Eastern airlines; 302, ad, courtesy Turismo Las Hamacas, S.A.; 307, ad, courtesy Iberia Airlines of Spain; 308, ad, courtesy, Al-Andalus Expreso, RENFE; 311, ad, Sedeco, Servicio del Conductor, S.A., Málaga, Spain. **Lección 13:** 334, ad, *Blanco y negro,* courtesy Luis María Anson, ABC, Prensa Española; 335, ad, courtesy *Vanidades* Continental; 338, ad, Telefónica. **Lección 14:** 343, ad, Conserjería de Cultura y Bienestar Social, Junta de Castilla y León; 349, ad, Grebol electrónica, Caracas, Venezuela; 354, ad, Ros Fotocolor, Madrid, Spain; 357, ad, La silla, Madrid, Spain; 360, ad, Red Nacional de Ferrocarriles Españoles; 361, ad, Hotel Crown Plaza, Mexico; 362, ad, Gran Rex Hotel, Miramar. **Lección 15:** 381, lottery ticket, ONCE; 384, ad, Hotel El Dorado; 387, ad, Plaza de Toros de Málaga; 388, ad, Bacardi y Cia, S.A., España. **Lección 16:** 410, article, "Murió víctima de un sabotaje," *Blanco y negro,* Luis María Anson, ABC, Prensa Espanola; 413, extracted ad, Orense, Madrid, Spain. **Lección 17:** 434–435, extracted article "Los Ángeles de la Guardia Civil marcan el paso en Baeza," *Blanco y negro,* courtesy Luis María Anson, ABC, Prensa Española.

MAR DEL CARIBE
Barranquilla
Cartagena
Maracaibo
Caracas
Mérida
Medellín
Río Orinoco
GUYANA
SURINAM
GUAYANA FRANCESA
Bogotá
VENEZUELA
Cali
COLOMBIA
ECUADOR
Quito
ECUADOR
Guayaquil
Manaus
Río Amazonas
Belém
Iquitos
PERÚ
Lima
ANDES
Cuzco
OCÉANO
BOLIVIA
Brasilia
Arequipa
La Paz
BRASIL
Arica
Sucre
Iquique
ATLÁNTICO
PARAGUAY
São Paulo
Río de Janeiro
TRÓPICO DE CAPRICORNIO
Asunción
Antofagasta
Santos
PACÍFICO
Tucumán
CHILE
Córdoba
OCÉANO
Mendoza
URUGUAY
Valparaíso
Rosario
Montevideo
Santiago
Buenos Aires
La Plata
Río de la Plata
ARGENTINA
Concepción
Bahía Blanca
Puerto Montt
Bariloche
América del Sur
0
600
1200
Kilómetros
ANDES
Estrecho de Magallanes
Islas Malvinas
Punta Arenas
TIERRA DEL FUEGO
Cabo de Hornos